Windows Server 2003
Network Administration

Other Microsoft Windows resources from O'Reilly

Related titles

Windows Server Cookbook™

Securing Windows Server
  2003

Windows Server Hacks™

Windows Server 2003 in a
  Nutshell

Active Directory Cookbook™

Active Directory

Exchange Server Cookbook™

DNS on Windows Server
  2003

Windows Books Resource Center

windows.oreilly.com is a complete catalog of O'Reilly's Windows and Office books, including sample chapters and code examples.

oreillynet.com is the essential portal for developers interested in open and emerging technologies, including new platforms, programming languages, and operating systems.

Conferences

O'Reilly brings diverse innovators together to nurture the ideas that spark revolutionary industries. We specialize in documenting the latest tools and systems, translating the innovator's knowledge into useful skills for those in the trenches. Visit *conferences.oreilly.com* for our upcoming events.

Safari Bookshelf (*safari.oreilly.com*) is the premier online reference library for programmers and IT professionals. Conduct searches across more than 1,000 books. Subscribers can zero in on answers to time-critical questions in a matter of seconds. Read the books on your Bookshelf from cover to cover or simply flip to the page you need. Try it today for free.

Windows Server 2003
Network Administration

Craig Hunt and Roberta Bragg

O'REILLY®

Beijing · Cambridge · Farnham · Köln · Paris · Sebastopol · Taipei · Tokyo

Windows Server 2003 Network Administration
by Craig Hunt and Roberta Bragg

Copyright © 2005 O'Reilly Media, Inc. All rights reserved.
Printed in the United States of America.

Published by O'Reilly Media, Inc., 1005 Gravenstein Highway North, Sebastopol, CA 95472.

O'Reilly books may be purchased for educational, business, or sales promotional use. Online editions are also available for most titles (*safari.oreilly.com*). For more information, contact our corporate/institutional sales department: (800) 998-9938 or *corporate@oreilly.com*.

Editors:	Robbie Allen and John Osborn
Production Editor:	Matt Hutchinson
Production Services:	GEX, Inc.
Cover Designer:	Ellie Volckhausen
Interior Designer:	David Futato

Printing History:

September 2005:	First Edition.

 This book uses RepKover™, a durable and flexible lay-flat binding.

ISBN: 0-596-00800-7
[M]

To Winslow, who keeps me on the ball,
or at least chasing it.

—Craig Hunt

To the many Microsoft employees and MVPs, as
well as readers who have often helped me or
asked for my help. We are a community in all
senses of the word. Without your input, support,
and challenges, my job would be much less
interesting.

—Roberta Bragg

Table of Contents

Preface

Windows computers are rarely used without an active network connection, and they often play major roles in supporting the network by providing routing, firewall protection, name resolution, IP address allocation, and remote access. Given the ubiquity of networking, every system administrator must master network administration. This book will help you master networking on Windows Server 2003 systems.

Windows Server 2003 supports a rich networking environment. Windows servers provide implementations of a full array of TCP/IP network services. Well-known protocols and services such as DNS and DHCP are included, as well as less widely deployed protocols such as OSPF and IPSec. Additionally, Windows servers provide the best support for proprietary Microsoft networking services and protocols, such as CIFS. One of the advantages of using Windows servers is that they do an excellent job of integrating Microsoft network services into an Internet built on standard Internet protocols. This book covers the standard TCP/IP protocols, the Microsoft protocols, and the tools and techniques used to integrate them.

Windows Server 2003 Network Administration is the combined effort of Craig Hunt and Roberta Bragg. Craig is an expert on networking and is the author of nine books, including *TCP/IP Network Administration*. Roberta is a Microsoft Windows networking MVP and an expert on information security. She is also the author of all or part of 10 books, including *Designing Security for Windows Server 2003 Network* and *Hardening Windows*. The combination of Windows and networking expertise provides the perfect blend for a book about Windows network administration. This book covers the issues that are most important to the Windows system administrator who is building or managing a network.

Windows Server 2003 Network Administration provides practical, detailed network information for the Windows system administrator. It is a book about building and maintaining your own network based on Windows servers. It is a tutorial covering the why and how of networking, as well as a reference providing the details about specific network programs as they are implemented on Windows servers. This book strives to find the correct balance of theory and practice, so that you understand what needs to be done and why it is done.

Who Should Read This Book

Windows Server 2003 Network Administration is intended for everyone who has to configure a network service on a Windows server. This obviously includes the network managers and the system administrators who are responsible for setting up and running computers and networks, but the audience also includes anyone who needs to understand how a computer communicates with and provides services to other systems. Large and mid-size organizations have dedicated system administrators, but many small organizations depend on someone who is not really a full-time system administrator to install and configure their network services. You may not think of yourself as a system administrator, but if you have to configure network services, you're involved in system administration tasks. Regardless of your job description, if you're responsible for configuring or managing network services, this book is for you.

However, this is not a book for beginners. If you have been given system administration tasks, it is probably because you already have skill with computers. In this book, we assume that you have a good understanding of computers and their operation, and that you're generally familiar with Windows system administration. Over the years, there has been a rash of books for "dummies" and "idiots." If you really think of yourself as an "idiot" when it comes to Windows servers, this book is not for you. Likewise, if you are a network administration genius, this book is probably not suitable for your needs. However, if you fall anywhere in between the two extremes, this book has something to offer you.

What's in This Book

Windows Server 2003 Network Administration has three distinct parts: fundamental concepts, tutorial, and reference. The first three chapters are a basic discussion of the network protocols and services. This discussion provides the fundamental concepts necessary to understand the rest of the book. The remaining chapters provide a how-to tutorial for planning, installing, and configuring various important network services. The book concludes with three appendixes that are technical references for various configuration options.

This book contains the following chapters:

- Chapter 1, *Overview of TCP/IP*, describes TCP/IP, which is the protocol suite upon which modern networks are built. The chapter gives the history of TCP/IP, a description of the structure of the protocol architecture, and a basic explanation of how the protocols function.

- Chapter 2, *Delivering the Data*, describes addressing and how data passes through a network to reach the proper destination.

- Chapter 3, *Network Services*, discusses the relationship between clients and server systems, as well as the various services that are central to the function of a modern network.

- Chapter 4, *Basic TCP/IP Configuration*, covers the basic "client" configuration required by all systems running TCP/IP. Planning for and choosing the necessary configuration values is also covered.

- Chapter 5, *Managing DHCP Services*, describes how to install, configure, and maintain a Windows DHCP server.

- Chapter 6, *Creating a DNS Server*, describes how to install, configure, and manage a Microsoft DNS server.

- Chapter 7, *Using AD to Support Network Administration*, concentrates on the symbiotic relationship between TCP/IP and Active Directory. Active Directory-integrated DNS zones, integration with DHCP and AD, and integration with WINS and AD are covered.

- Chapter 8, *Controlling Remote Communications with Microsoft Routing and Remote Access Service*, describes how to install and configure the RRAS software that permits a Windows server to run a variety of TCP/IP routing protocols and to provide the security protocols needed to create encrypted connections. In addition to providing routing and encryption support, RRAS is used to allow remote dial-up Internet access. RRAS also provides NAT services.

- Chapter 9, *Protecting Hosts with Windows Host Firewalls*, discusses the different implementations of the native Windows firewall. Internet Connection Sharing, Internet Connection Firewall, Windows protocol filters, IPSec policies, and firewall management via Group Policy are all discussed.

- Chapter 10, *Centralizing Authentication and Authorization with Internet Authentication Server*, describes the installation and configuration of an IAS to provide centralized authentication, audit, and authorization services for RADIUS clients. The RADIUS protocol, as well as wireless security, secure communications between IAS and RRAS, and Network Access Quarantine are discussed.

- Chapter 11, *Protecting Network Communications with Internet Protocol Security*, provides the background necessary to understand, install, and configure IPSec. In addition to discussing IPSec protocol basics, this chapter covers the details of IPSec policies. Using NAT-T to allow an IPSec VPN to traverse NAT servers is also covered.

- Chapter 12, *Configuring Internet and Intranet Web Services with IIS*, describes how to install, configure, and manage the Internet Information Server software. The IIS software provides web services, an FTP server, an SMTP email server, and more. SSL security is also covered.

- Chapter 13, *Network Security Administration*, describes how to design proper security into your network and how to understand the overall security framework within which the network resides. Topics include Group Policy, Security Templates, and more.

- Chapter 14, *Troubleshooting TCP/IP*, tells you what to do when something goes wrong. It describes the techniques and tools used to monitor the network and troubleshoot it when problems develop.

There are also three appendixes included with this book:

- Appendix A, *DHCP Options*, describes all of the DHCP options configurable through the Windows DHCP management console. (DHCP options are the TCP/IP configuration values exchanged by a DHCP server and a client.)

- Appendix B, *DHCP Audit Log Identifiers*, is a reference that lists all of the numeric identifiers used by the DHCP server to identify log entries.

- Appendix C, *DNS Resource Records*, is a reference for the records used to build a DNS database. All of the resource records available through the Windows DNS management console are covered. Additionally, the syntax of the rarely used DNS boot file is covered.

Conventions Used in This Book

The following typographical conventions are used in this book:

Constant width

Indicates commands, command-line elements, computer output, and code examples

Constant width italic

Indicates placeholders (for which you substitute an actual name) in examples and in registry keys

Constant width bold

Indicates user input

Italic

Introduces new terms and URLs, file extensions, filenames, directory or folder names, and UNC pathnames

Indicates a tip, suggestion, or general note. For example, we'll tell you if you need to use a particular version or if an operation requires certain privileges.

Indicates a warning or caution. For example, we'll tell you if Active Directory does not behave as you'd expect or if a particular operation has a negative impact on performance.

Using Code Examples

This book is here to help you get your job done. In general, you may use the code in this book in your programs and documentation. You do not need to contact us for permission unless you're reproducing a significant portion of the code. For example, writing a program that uses several chunks of code from this book does not require permission. Selling or distributing a CD-ROM of examples from O'Reilly books *does* require permission. Answering a question by citing this book and quoting example code does not require permission. Incorporating a significant amount of example code from this book into your product's documentation *does* require permission.

We appreciate, but do not require, attribution. An attribution usually includes the title, author, publisher, and ISBN. For example: "*Windows Server 2003 Network Administration,* by Craig Hunt and Roberta Bragg. Copyright 2005 O'Reilly Media, Inc., 0-596-00800-7."

If you feel your use of code examples falls outside fair use or the permission given above, feel free to contact us at *permissions@oreilly.com*.

We'd Like to Hear from You

Please address comments and questions concerning this book to the publisher:

O'Reilly Media, Inc.
1005 Gravenstein Highway North
Sebastopol, CA 95472
(800) 998-9938 (in the United States or Canada)
(707) 829-0515 (international or local)
(707) 829-0104 (fax)

We have a web page for this book, where we list errata, examples, and any additional information. You can access this page at:

http://www.oreilly.com/catalog/windowsvrnet

To comment or ask technical questions about this book, send email to:

bookquestions@oreilly.com

For more information about our books, conferences, Resource Centers, and the O'Reilly Network, see our web site at:

http://www.oreilly.com

Safari Enabled

 When you see a Safari® Enabled icon on the cover of your favorite technology book, that means the book is available online through the O'Reilly Network Safari Bookshelf.

Safari offers a solution that's better than e-books. It's a virtual library that lets you easily search thousands of top tech books, cut and paste code samples, download chapters, and find quick answers when you need the most accurate, current information. Try it for free at *http://safari.oreilly.com*.

Acknowledgments

Craig and Roberta would like to thank Mike Loukides for the spark that started this project, and Robbie Allen for his persistence and professionalism in keeping this book moving forward despite the inevitable setbacks.

Jeff Shawgo, Laura Hunter, and Paul Robichaux deserve special thanks. They provided a detailed technical review of all of the chapters. Their comments improved the technical accuracy and the readability of the text. Rodney Fournier and David Shaw also provided helpful feedback for parts of the book.

Kevin Shafer also deserves special thanks for jumping in to help us organize text in some of the most complex chapters. His organizational skills brought order and structure to some very challenging technical topics.

We would also like to thank the excellent production team at O'Reilly.

Last, but not least, Craig needs to thank Kathy, a loving spouse with the patience of Job.

## CHAPTER 1

Overview of TCP/IP

When you place your computer on a network, it interacts with many other systems. The way you do network administration tasks has effects, good and bad, not only on your system but also on other systems on the network. A sound understanding of basic network administration benefits everyone.

Networking computers dramatically enhances their ability to communicate—and most computers are used more for communication than computation. Many computers are busy crunching the numbers for business and science, but the number of such systems pales in comparison to the millions of systems busy moving email to a remote colleague or retrieving information from a remote repository. When you think of the hundreds of millions of desktop systems that are used primarily for preparing documents to communicate ideas from one person to another, it is easy to see why most computers can be viewed as communications devices.

The positive impact of computer communications increases with the number and type of computers participating in the network. One of the great benefits of TCP/IP is that it provides interoperable communications between all types of hardware and all kinds of operating systems.

The name "TCP/IP" refers to an entire suite of data communications protocols. The suite gets its name from two of its protocols: the Transmission Control Protocol (TCP) and the Internet Protocol (IP). The TCP/IP protocol suite is sometimes just called IP. Both names are acceptable. TCP/IP is the traditional name for this protocol suite and it is the name used in this book.

Protocols are the rules of data communications. The software that network administrators deal with implements those protocols. This book is a practical, step-by-step guide to configuring and managing TCP/IP networking software on Windows server systems. TCP/IP is the leading communications software for local area networks and enterprise intranets, and it is the foundation of the worldwide Internet. TCP/IP is the most important networking software available to a network administrator.

The first part of this book discusses the basics of TCP/IP and how it moves data across a network. The second part explains how to configure and run TCP/IP on a Windows server. Let's start with a little history.

TCP/IP and the Internet

In 1969, the Advanced Research Projects Agency (ARPA) funded a research and development project to create an experimental packet-switching network. This network, called the *ARPANET*, was built to study techniques for providing robust, reliable, vendor-independent data communications. Many techniques of modern data communications were developed in the ARPANET.

The experimental network ARPANET was so successful, many of the organizations attached to it began to use it for daily data communications. In 1975, the ARPANET was converted from an experimental network to an operational network, and the responsibility for administering it was given to the Defense Communications Agency (DCA), which has since changed its name to Defense Informations Systems Agency (DISA). However, development of the ARPANET did not stop just because it was being used as an operational network; the basic TCP/IP protocols were developed after the network ARPANET was operational.

The TCP/IP protocols were adopted as Military Standards (MIL STD) in 1983, and all hosts connected to the network were required to convert to the new protocols. To ease this conversion, DARPA* funded Bolt, Beranek, and Newman (BBN) to implement TCP/IP in Berkeley (BSD) Unix. This provided a reference implementation that could be used by anyone who wanted to implement TCP/IP.

About the time that TCP/IP was adopted as a standard, the term *Internet* came into common usage. In 1983, the old ARPANET was divided into MILNET, the unclassified part of the Defense Data Network (DDN), and a new, smaller ARPANET. "Internet" was used to refer to the entire network: MILNET plus ARPANET.

In 1985, the National Science Foundation (NSF) created NSFNet and connected it to the then-existing Internet. The original NSFNet linked together the five NSF supercomputer centers. It was smaller than the ARPANET and no faster—56 Kbps. Nonetheless, the creation of the NSFNet was significant because NSF brought with it a new vision of the use of the Internet. NSF wanted to extend the network to every scientist and engineer in the United States. To accomplish this, in 1987 NSF created a new, faster backbone and a three-tiered network topology that included the backbone, regional networks, and local networks. In 1990, the ARPANET formally

---

* During the 1980s, ARPA, which is part of the U.S. Department of Defense, was called Defense Advanced Research Projects Agency (DARPA). Whether it is known as ARPA or DARPA, the agency and its mission of funding advanced research has remained the same.

passed out of existence, while the NSFNet ceased its role as a primary Internet backbone network in 1995.

Today, the Internet encompasses hundreds of thousands of networks worldwide. It is no longer dependent on a core (or backbone) network or on governmental support. Today's Internet is built by commercial providers. National network providers, called tier-one providers, and regional network providers create the infrastructure. Internet Service Providers (ISPs) provide local access and user services. This network of networks is linked together in the United States at several major interconnection points called Network Access Points (NAPs).

The Internet has grown far beyond its original scope. The networks and agencies that built the Internet no longer play an essential role. The Internet has evolved from a simple backbone network, through a three-tiered hierarchical structure, to a huge network of interconnected, distributed hubs, growing exponentially during the 1980's and 1990's. Through all of this incredible change, one thing has remained constant: the Internet is built on the TCP/IP protocol suite.

Because TCP/IP is required for Internet connection, the growth of the Internet spurred interest in TCP/IP. As more organizations became familiar with TCP/IP, they saw its power could be applied in other network applications. The Internet protocols are often used for local area networking, even when the local network is not connected to the Internet. TCP/IP is also widely used to build enterprise networks. TCP/IP is the foundation of all of these varied networks.

TCP/IP Features

The popularity of the TCP/IP protocols did not grow rapidly just because the protocols were there, or because connecting to the Internet mandated their use. They met an important need (worldwide data communications) at the right time, and they had several important features that allowed them to meet this need:

- Open protocol standards, freely available and developed independently from any specific computer hardware or operating system. Because it is so widely supported, TCP/IP is ideal for uniting different hardware and software, even if you don't communicate over the Internet.

- Independence from specific physical network hardware. This allows TCP/IP to integrate many different kinds of networks. TCP/IP can be run over an Ethernet, a DSL connection, a wireless connection, an optical network, and virtually any other kind of physical transmission medium.

- A common addressing scheme that allows any TCP/IP device to uniquely address any other device in the entire network, even if the network is as large as the worldwide Internet.

- Standardized high-level protocols for consistent, widely available user services.

Protocol Standards

Protocols are formal rules of behavior. In international relations, protocols minimize the problems caused by cultural differences when various nations work together. By agreeing to a common set of rules that are widely known and independent of any nation's customs, diplomatic protocols minimize misunderstandings; everyone knows how to act and how to interpret the actions of others. Similarly, a set of rules is necessary to govern computer communications.

In data communications, these sets of rules are also called *protocols*. In homogeneous networks, a single computer vendor specifies a set of communications rules designed to use the strengths of the vendor's operating system and hardware architecture. But homogeneous networks are like the culture of a single country—only the natives are truly at home. TCP/IP creates a heterogeneous network with open protocols independent of operating systems and architectural differences. TCP/IP protocols are available to everyone and developed and changed by consensus—not by the fiat of one manufacturer. Everyone is free to develop products that meet these open protocol specifications.

The open nature of TCP/IP protocols requires an open standards development process and publicly available standards documents. The Internet Engineering Task Force (IETF) develops Internet standards in open, public meetings. The protocols developed in this process are published as *Requests for Comments* (RFCs). RFCs are available online at *http://www.rfc-editor.org*. To find out how Internet standards are created, read *The Internet Standards Process*, RFC 2026.

As the title "Request for Comments" implies, the style and content of these documents are much less rigid than most standards documents. RFCs contain a wide range of interesting and useful information, and are not limited to the formal specification of data communications protocols. There are three basic types of RFCs: standards (STD), best current practices (BCP), and informational (FYI).

RFCs that define official protocol standards are STDs and are given an STD number in addition to an RFC number. Creating an official Internet standard is a rigorous process. *Standards track* RFCs pass through three *maturity levels* before becoming standards:

Proposed standard
    This specification is important enough and has received enough Internet community support to be considered for a standard. The specification is stable and well understood, but it is not yet a standard and may be withdrawn from consideration to be a standard.

Draft standard
    This is a protocol specification for which at least two independent, interoperable implementations exist. A draft standard is a final specification undergoing widespread testing. It will only change if the testing forces a change.

Internet standard

A specification is declared a standard only after extensive testing and only if the protocol defined in the specification is considered to be of significant benefit to the Internet community.

There are two categories of standards. A *Technical Specification* (TS) defines a protocol. An *Applicability Statement* (AS) defines when the protocol is to be used. There are three *requirement levels* that define the applicability of a standard:

Required

This standard protocol is a required part of every TCP/IP implementation. It must be included for the TCP/IP stack to be compliant.

Recommended

This standard protocol should be included in every TCP/IP implementation, although it is not required for minimal compliance.

Elective

This standard is optional. It is up to the software vendor to implement or not.

Two other requirements levels (*limited use* and *not recommended*) apply to RFCs not part of the standards track. A "limited use" protocol is applied only in special circumstances, such as during an experiment. A protocol is "not recommended" when it has limited functionality or is outdated. There are three types of *non-standards track* RFCs:

Experimental

An experimental protocol is limited to use in research and development.

Historic

An historic protocol is outdated and no longer recommended for use.

Informational

An informational RFC provides information of general interest to the Internet community; it does not define an Internet standard protocol.

A subset of the informational RFCs is called the FYI (For Your Information) notes. An FYI document is given an FYI number in addition to an RFC number. FYI documents provide introductory and background material about the Internet and TCP/IP networks. While RFC 2026, *The Internet Standards Process*, defines most of the document types described above and explains how those documents are used in the standards process, FYI documents are not mentioned in the RFC because they are not included in the Internet standards process. Nevertheless, there are several interesting FYI documents available. To find out more about FYI documents, read RFC 1150, *FYI on FYI: An Introduction to the FYI Notes*.

Another group of RFCs that go beyond documenting protocols is the Best Current Practices (BCP) RFCs. BCPs formally document techniques and procedures. Some of these document the way that the IETF conducts itself. RFC 2026 is an example of this type of BCP. Others provide guidelines for the operation of a network or service; RFC 1918,

Address Allocation for Private Internets, is an example of this type of BCP. BCPs that provide operational guidelines are often of great interest to network administrators.

There are now almost 4,000 RFCs. As a network system administrator, you may read several. With so many to choose from, it is as important to know which ones to read, as it is to know how to understand them. Use the RFC categories and the requirements levels to help you determine which RFCs are applicable to your situation. (A good starting point is to focus on RFCs with STD numbers.) Stick with the most current version of an RFC. (The RFC index found at *http://www.rfc-editor.org/rfc-index.html* will tell you if an RFC has been made obsolete by a newer RFC.) To understand what you read, you need to understand the language of data communications. RFCs contain protocol implementation specifications defined in terminology that is unique to data communications.

A Data Communications Model

To discuss computer networking, terms with special meanings to network professionals need to be used. Even other computer professionals may not be familiar with all the terms in the networking alphabet soup. As is always the case, English and computer-speak are not equivalent (or even necessarily compatible) languages. Although descriptions and examples should make the meaning of the networking jargon more apparent, sometimes terms are ambiguous, so a common frame of reference is necessary.

An architectural model developed by the International Standards Organization (ISO) is frequently used to describe the structure and function of data communications protocols. This architectural model, which is called the *Open Systems Interconnect* (OSI) *Reference Model*, provides a common reference for discussing communications. The terms defined by this model are well understood and widely used—so widely used, in fact, that it is difficult to discuss data communications without using OSI's terminology.

The OSI Reference Model contains seven *layers* that define the functions of data communications protocols. Each layer of the OSI model represents a function performed when data is transferred between cooperating applications across an intervening network. Figure 1-1 identifies each layer by name and provides a short functional description for it. Looking at this figure, the protocols are like a pile of building blocks stacked one upon another. Because of this appearance, the structure is often called a *stack* or *protocol stack*.

A layer does not define a single protocol—it defines a data communications function that may be performed by any number of protocols. Therefore, each layer may contain multiple protocols, each providing a service suitable to the function of that layer. For example, a file transfer protocol (ftp) and an electronic mail protocol both provide user services, and both are part of the Application Layer.

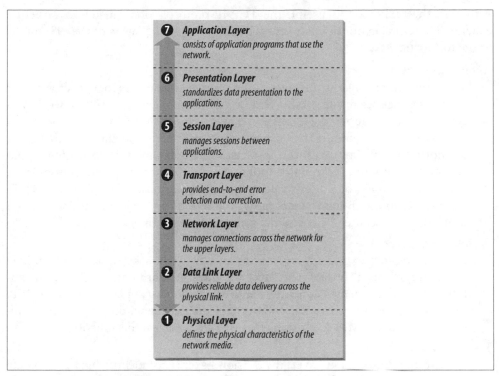

Figure 1-1. The OSI Reference Model

Every protocol communicates with its peer. A *peer* is an implementation of the same protocol in the equivalent layer on a remote system; i.e., the local file transfer protocol is the peer of a remote file transfer protocol. Peer-level communications must be standardized for successful communication. In the abstract, each protocol is concerned only with communicating to its peers; it does not care about the layer above or below its peers.

However, there must also be agreement on how to pass data between the layers on a single computer, because every layer is involved in sending data from a local application to an equivalent remote application. The upper layers rely on the lower layers to transfer the data over the underlying network. Data is passed down the stack from one layer to the next, until it is transmitted over the network by the Physical Layer protocols. At the remote end, the data is passed up the stack to the receiving application. The individual layers do not need to know how the layers above and below them function; they only need to know how to pass data to them.

Isolating network communications functions in different layers minimizes the impact of technological change on the entire protocol suite. New applications can be added without changing the physical network, and new network hardware can be installed without rewriting the application software.

Although the OSI model is useful, the TCP/IP protocols don't match its structure exactly. Therefore, in our discussions of TCP/IP, we use the layers of the OSI model in the following way:

Application Layer

The Application Layer is the level of the protocol hierarchy where user-accessed network processes reside. In this text, a TCP/IP application is any network process that occurs above the Transport Layer. This includes all of the processes that users directly interact with as well as other processes at this level that users are not necessarily aware of. In most cases, the user's interaction with an application layer protocol is through a tool that hides most of the protocol from view. An example would be a user's interactions with the Post Office Protocol (POP) through Outlook. But in some cases, the Windows ftp command is a good example; the user literally enters the protocol commands.

Presentation Layer

In order for cooperating applications to exchange data, they must agree on how data is represented. In OSI, this layer provides standard data presentation routines. This function is frequently handled within the applications in TCP/IP, though TCP/IP protocols such as External Data Representation (XDR) and Multipurpose Internet Mail Extensions (MIME) also perform this function.

Session Layer

As with the Presentation Layer, the Session Layer is not identifiable as a separate layer in the TCP/IP protocol hierarchy. The OSI Session Layer manages the sessions (connections) between cooperating applications. In TCP/IP application protocols, the term "session" is used to refer to the connection between cooperating applications, but the functions defined for the OSI Session Layer largely occurs in the TCP/IP Transport Layer. In the Transport Layer the term "session" is not used; instead the terms "socket" and "port" are used to describe the path over which cooperating applications communicate. (Much more on sockets and ports later in this chapter.)

Transport Layer

Much of our discussion of TCP/IP is directed to the protocols that occur in the Transport Layer. The Transport Layer in the OSI reference model guarantees that the receiver gets the data exactly as it was sent. In TCP/IP, this function is performed by the *Transmission Control Protocol* (TCP). However, TCP/IP offers a second Transport Layer service, *User Datagram Protocol* (UDP), that does not perform the end-to-end reliability checks.

Network Layer

The Network Layer manages connections across the network and isolates the upper layer protocols from the details of the underlying network. The Internet Protocol (IP), which isolates the upper layers from the underlying network and handles the addressing and delivery of data, is usually described as TCP/IP's Network Layer.

Data Link Layer

The reliable delivery of data across the underlying physical network is handled by the Data Link Layer. Data Link Layer protocols are rarely defined specifically for the TCP/IP protocol suite. Most RFCs that relate to the Data Link Layer discuss how IP can make use of existing data link protocols.

Physical Layer

The Physical Layer defines the characteristics of the hardware needed to carry the data transmission signal. Features such as voltage levels, and the number and location of interface pins, are defined in this layer. Examples of standards at the Physical Layer are interface connectors such as RS232C and V.35, and standards for local area network wiring such as IEEE 802.3. TCP/IP does not define physical standards; it makes use of existing standards.

The terminology of the OSI reference model helps describe TCP/IP, but to fully understand it, an architectural model must be used that more closely matches the structure of TCP/IP. The next section introduces the protocol model to describe TCP/IP.

TCP/IP Protocol Architecture

While description of TCP/IP with a layered model is not universally agreed upon, it is generally viewed as being composed of fewer layers than the seven used in the OSI model. Most descriptions of TCP/IP define three to five functional levels in the protocol architecture. The four-level model illustrated in Figure 1-2 is based on the three layers (Application, Host-to-Host, and Network Access) shown in the DOD Protocol Model in the *DDN Protocol Handbook—Volume 1*, with the addition of a separate Internet layer. This model provides a reasonable pictorial representation of the layers in the TCP/IP protocol hierarchy.

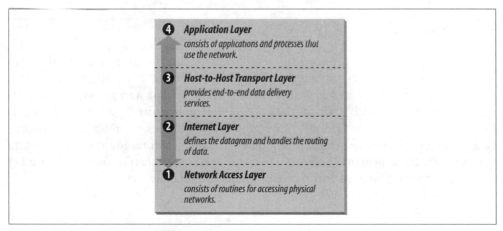

Figure 1-2. Layers in the TCP/IP protocol architecture

As in the OSI model, data is passed down the stack when it is being sent to the network and up the stack when it is being received from the network. The four-layered structure of TCP/IP is seen in the way data is handled as it passes down the protocol stack from the Application Layer to the underlying physical network. Each layer in the stack adds control information to ensure proper delivery. This control information is called a *header* because it is placed in front of the data to be transmitted. Each layer treats all of the information it receives from the layer above as data and places its own header in front of that information. The addition of delivery information at every layer is called *encapsulation*. (See Figure 1-3 for an illustration of this.) When data is received, the opposite happens. Each layer strips off its header before passing the data on to the layer above. As information flows back up the stack, information received from a lower layer is interpreted as both a header and data.

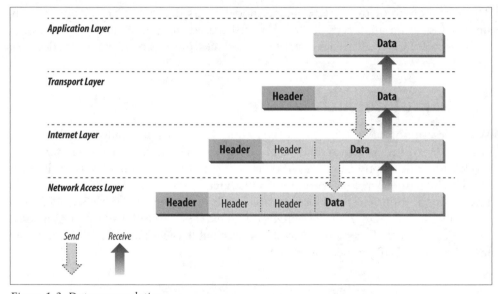

Figure 1-3. Data encapsulation

Figure 1-4 shows the terms used by different layers of TCP/IP to refer to the data being transmitted. Applications using TCP refer to data as a *stream*, while applications using the User Datagram Protocol (UDP) refer to data as a *message*. TCP calls data a *segment*, and UDP calls its data a *packet*. The Internet layer views all data as blocks called *datagrams*. TCP/IP uses many different types of underlying networks (e.g., frame relay or token-ring), which may have a different terminology for the data it transmits. Most networks refer to transmitted data as *packets* or *frames*. Figure 1-4 shows a network that transmits pieces of data it calls frames.

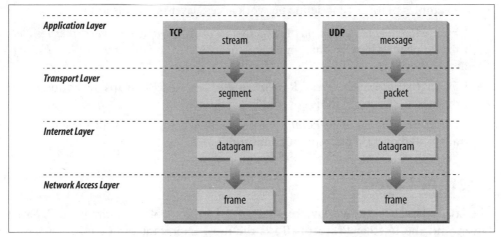

Figure 1-4. How each layer refers to data

Following is a closer look at the function of each layer, working up from the Network Access Layer to the Application Layer.

Network Access Layer

The *Network Access Layer* is the lowest layer of the TCP/IP protocol hierarchy. The protocols in this layer provide the means for the system to deliver data to the other devices on a directly attached network. This layer defines how to use the network to transmit an IP datagram. Unlike higher-level protocols, Network Access Layer protocols must know the details of the underlying network (its packet structure, addressing, etc.) to format the data being transmitted to comply with the network constraints. The TCP/IP Network Access Layer can encompass the functions of all three lower layers of the OSI reference Model (Network, Data Link, and Physical).

The design of TCP/IP hides the function of the lower layers, and the better known protocols (IP, TCP, UDP, etc.) are all higher-level protocols. As new hardware technologies appear, new Network Access protocols are developed so that TCP/IP networks can use the new hardware.

Functions performed at this level include encapsulation of IP datagrams into the frames transmitted by the network and mapping of IP addresses to the physical addresses used by the network. One of TCP/IP's strengths is its universal addressing scheme. The IP address must be converted into an address that is appropriate for the physical network over which the datagram is transmitted.

Some examples of RFCs that define network access layer protocols follow:

- RFC 894, *A Standard for the Transmission of IP Datagrams over Ethernet Networks*, specifies how IP datagrams are encapsulated for transmission over Ethernet networks.
- RFC 826, *Ethernet Address Resolution Protocol (ARP)*, maps IP addresses to Ethernet addresses. (ARP is covered in Chapter 2.)
- RFC 1661, *The Point-to-Point Protocol (PPP)*, specifies how IP datagrams are transmitted over point-to-point connections.

Internet Layer

The layer above the Network Access Layer in the protocol hierarchy is the *Internet Layer*, and the Internet Protocol (IP) is the most important protocol in that layer. The release of IP used in the current Internet is IP Version 4 (IPv4), which is defined in RFC 791. It is called Version 4 because it is identified by the value 4 in the version field of the IP datagram header, which is shown in Figure 1-5. However, IPv4 is the first version of IP deployed in the Internet and it is still in use today.* There are later versions of IP. IP Version 5 (IPv5) is an experimental Stream Transport (ST) protocol used for real-time data delivery. IPv5 never came into operational use. IPv6 is an IP standard that provides greatly expanded addressing capacity. Because IPv6 uses a completely different address structure, it is not interoperable with IPv4. While IPv6 is a standard version of IP that is delivered with Windows Server 2003, it is not yet widely used in operational, commercial networks. Our focus is on practical, operational networks, so, while IPv6 is discussed in Chapter 2, we do not cover IPv6 in great detail. In this chapter, and throughout the main body of the text, we refer to IPv4 whenever we say IP. IPv4 is the protocol you will configure on your system when you want to exchange data with remote systems, and it is the focus of this text.

The Internet Protocol is the heart of TCP/IP. IP provides the basic packet delivery service on which TCP/IP networks are built. All protocols, in the layers above and below IP, use the Internet Protocol to deliver data. All TCP/IP data flows through IP, incoming and outgoing, regardless of its final destination.

Internet Protocol

The Internet Protocol is the building block of the Internet. Its functions include the following:

- Defining the datagram, which is the basic unit of transmission in the Internet
- Defining the Internet addressing scheme

---

* Experimental versions of IP using version numbers 0 to 3 were proposed in 1977 and 1978, but were superceded by IPv4 in August 1979.

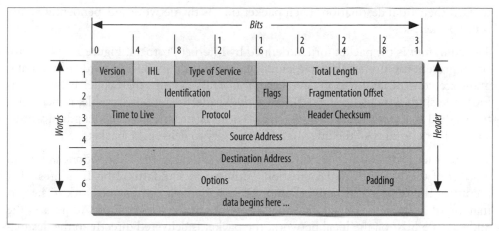

Figure 1-5. IP datagram format

- Moving data between the Network Access Layer and the Transport Layer
- Routing datagrams to remote hosts
- Performing fragmentation and reassembly of datagrams

Before describing these functions in more detail, let's look at some of IP's characteristics. First, IP is a *connectionless protocol*. This means that IP does not exchange control information (called a "handshake") to establish an end-to-end connection before transmitting data. In contrast, a *connection-oriented protocol* exchanges control information with the remote system to verify that it is ready to receive data before any data is sent. When the handshaking is successful, the systems are said to have established a *connection*. Internet Protocol relies on protocols in other layers to establish the connection if they require connection-oriented service.

IP also relies on protocols in the other layers to provide error detection and error recovery. The Internet Protocol is sometimes called an *unreliable protocol* because it contains no error detection and recovery code. This is not to say that the protocol cannot be relied on—quite the contrary. IP can be relied upon to accurately deliver data to the connected network, but it doesn't check whether that data was correctly received. Protocols in other layers of the TCP/IP architecture provide this checking when it is required.

The datagram

The TCP/IP protocols were built to transmit data over the ARPANET, which was a *packet switching network*. A *packet* is a block of data that carries the information necessary to deliver it—in a manner similar to a postal letter, which has an address written on its envelope. A packet-switching network uses the addressing information in the packets to switch packets from one physical network to another, moving them toward their final destination. Each packet travels the network independently of any other packet.

The *datagram* is the packet format defined by Internet Protocol. Figure 1-5 is a pictorial representation of an IP datagram. The first five or six 32-bit words of the datagram are control information called the *header*. By default, the header is five words long; the sixth word is optional. Because the header's length is variable, it includes a field called *Internet Header Length* (IHL) that indicates the header's length in words. The header contains all the information necessary to deliver the packet.

The Internet Protocol delivers the datagram by checking the *Destination Address* in word 5 of the header. The Destination Address is a standard 32-bit IP address that identifies the destination network and the specific host on that network. (The format of IP addresses is explained in Chapter 2.) If the Destination Address is the address of a host on the local network, the packet is delivered directly to the destination. If the Destination Address is not on the local network, the packet is passed to a gateway for delivery. *Gateways* are devices that switch packets between the different physical networks. Deciding which gateway to use is called *routing*. IP makes the routing decision for each individual packet.

Routing datagrams

Internet gateways are commonly (and perhaps more accurately) referred to as *IP routers* because they use Internet Protocol to route packets between networks. In traditional TCP/IP jargon, there are only two types of network devices—*gateways* and *hosts*. Gateways forward packets between networks, and hosts don't. However, if a host is connected to more than one network (called a *multi-homed host*), it can forward packets between the networks. When a multi-homed host forwards packets, it acts just like any other gateway and is considered a gateway. Current data communications terminology makes a distinction between gateways and routers,* but we'll use the terms *gateway* and *router* interchangeably.

Figure 1-6 shows the use of gateways to forward packets. The hosts (or *end systems*) process packets through all four protocol layers, while the gateways (or *intermediate systems*) process the packets only up to the Internet Layer where the routing decisions are made.

Systems can only deliver packets to other devices attached to the same physical network. Packets from *A1* destined for host *C1* are forwarded through gateways *G1* and *G2*. Host *A1* first delivers the packet to gateway *G1*, with which it shares network *A*. Gateway *G1* delivers the packet to *G2* over network *B*. Gateway *G2* then delivers the packet directly to host *C1* because they are both attached to network *C*. Host *A1* has

---

* In current terminology, a gateway moves data between different protocols and a router moves data between different networks. So a system that moves mail between TCP/IP and X.400 is a gateway, but a traditional IP gateway is a router.

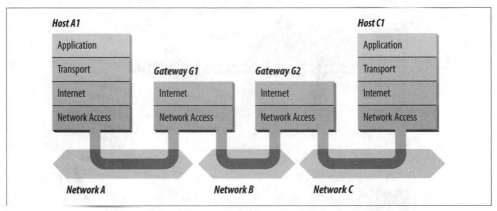

Figure 1-6. Routing through gateways

no knowledge of any gateways beyond gateway *G1*. It sends packets destined for both networks *C* and *B* to that local gateway and then relies on that gateway to properly forward the packets along the path to their destinations. Likewise, host *C1* sends its packets to *G2* in order to reach a host on network *A*, as well as any host on network *B*.

Figure 1-7 shows another view of routing. This figure emphasizes that the underlying physical networks a datagram travels through may be different and even incompatible. Host *A1* on the fiber optic network routes the datagram through gateway *G1* to reach host *C1* on the Ethernet. Gateway *G1* forwards the data through the frame relay network to gateway *G2* for delivery to *C1*. The datagram traverses three physically different networks, but eventually arrives intact at *C1*.

Fragmenting datagrams

As a datagram is routed through different networks, it may be necessary for the IP module in a gateway to divide the datagram into smaller pieces. A datagram received from one network may be too large to be transmitted in a single packet on a different network. This condition occurs only when a gateway interconnects dissimilar physical networks.

Each type of network has a *maximum transmission unit* (MTU), which is the largest packet that it can transfer. If the datagram received from one network is longer than the other network's MTU, it is necessary to divide the datagram into smaller *fragments* for transmission. This process is called *fragmentation*. Think of a train delivering a load of steel. Each railway car can carry more steel than the trucks that will take it along the highway, so each railway car is unloaded onto many different trucks. In the same way that a railroad is physically different from a highway, an Ethernet is physically different from an X.25 network. IP must break an Ethernet's relatively large packets into smaller packets before it can transmit them over an X.25 network.

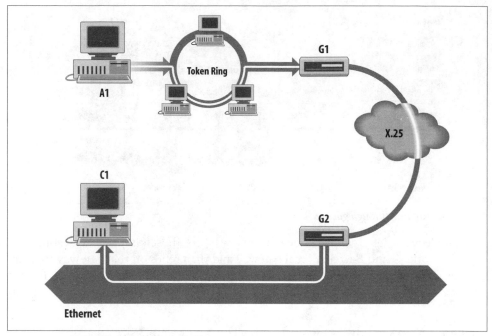

Figure 1-7. Networks, gateways, and hosts

The format of each fragment is the same as the format of any normal datagram. Word 2 in the header, as shown in Figure 1-5, contains information that identifies each datagram fragment and provides information about how to reassemble the fragments back into the original datagram. The Identification field identifies what datagram the fragment belongs to, and the Fragmentation Offset field tells what piece of the datagram this fragment is. The Flags field has a "More Fragments" bit that tells IP if it has assembled all of the datagram fragments.

Passing datagrams to the Transport Layer

When IP receives a datagram that is addressed to the local host, it must pass the data portion of the datagram to the correct Transport Layer protocol. This is done by using the *protocol number* from word 3 of the datagram header. Each Transport Layer protocol has a unique protocol number that identifies it to IP. Protocol numbers are discussed in Chapter 2.

You can see from this short overview that IP performs many important functions. Don't expect to fully understand datagrams, gateways, routing, IP addresses, and all the other things that IP does from this short description. Each chapter adds more details about these topics.

Internet Control Message Protocol

An integral part of IP is the *Internet Control Message Protocol* (ICMP) defined in RFC 792. This protocol is part of the Internet Layer and uses the IP datagram delivery facility to send its messages. ICMP sends messages that perform the following control, error reporting, and informational functions for TCP/IP:

Flow control

When datagrams arrive too fast for processing, the destination host or an intermediate gateway sends an ICMP Source Quench Message back to the sender. This tells the source to stop sending datagrams temporarily so that the destination host can catch up.

Detecting unreachable destinations

When a destination is unreachable, the system detecting the problem sends a Destination Unreachable Message to the datagram's source. If the unreachable destination is a network or host, the message is sent by an intermediate gateway. But if the destination is an unreachable port, the destination host sends the message (more on ports in Chapter 2). The tracert command takes advantage of the Destination Unreachable Message to create its list of gateways along the route. Exactly how it does this is explained in Chapter 14.

Redirecting routes

A gateway sends the ICMP Redirect Message to tell a host to use another gateway, presumably because the other gateway is a better choice. This message can be used only when the source host is on the same network as both gateways. To better understand this, refer to Figure 1-7. If a host on the frame relay network sent a datagram to *G1*, it would be possible for *G1* to redirect that host to *G2* because the host, *G1*, and *G2* are all attached to the same network. On the other hand, if a host on the fiber optic network sent a datagram to *G1*, the host could not be redirected to use *G2*. This is because *G2* is not attached to the fiber optic network.

Checking remote hosts

A host can send the ICMP Echo Message to see if a remote system's Internet Protocol is up and operational. When a system receives an echo message, it replies and sends the data from the packet back to the source host. The ping command uses this message.

IP Security

IP Security (IPSec) provides security services for IP datagrams. IPSec is not a single protocol. It is a security framework made up of several protocols. IPSec can provide both authentication services and data encryption. An overview of IPSec is found in RFC 2401, *Security Architecture for the Internet Protocol*.

IPSec requires each host to be authenticated, called *endpoint authentication*, before it sends the data. Windows Server 2003 supports host authentication using shared secret keys, public key certificates or Kerberos. (Active Directory can provide Kerberos authentication.) IPSec provides data authentication by using a hash-based message authentication code (HMAC). The HMAC verifies the source of the data and the data integrity. Windows Server 2003 supports HMAC MD5 (Message Digest 5), as described in RFC 2403, and HMAC SHA1 (Secure Hash Algorithm 1), as described in RFC 2404. IPSec can also provide encryption to ensure that the transmitted data is kept secret. Windows supports both the Data Encryption Standard (DES) and Triple DES (3DES) for data encryption.

IPSec uses two header formats to provide authentication and encryption security services. The *Authentication Header* (AH), which is described in RFC 2402, provides source and data authentication for all headers and data. The *Encapsulating Security Payload* (ESP) header and trailer, which is described in RFC 2406, provides encryption services and authentication of the ESP header and the encrypted portion of the datagram.

In addition to two header formats, IPSec runs in two different modes. *Tunnel mode* is used by secure routers passing data across an unsecured network, such as the Internet, and *transport mode* is used by end systems for end-to-end security. Tunnel mode provides protection for the complete original IP datagram. Transport mode provides protection for the upper layer data carried by the original datagram. Figure 1-8 shows an IPSec tunnel mode packet that contains both AH and ESP headers.

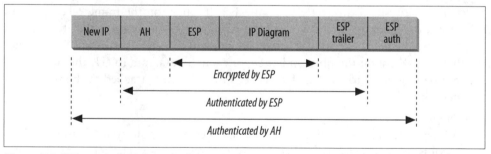

Figure 1-8. IPSec tunnel mode packet

In tunnel mode, IPSec creates a new IP header to route the packet to a specific remote secure router. The destination address used for this header is the address specified on the Tunnel Setting tab when the IPSec properties are configured. (IPSec configuration is covered in Chapter 11.) In transport mode, the IP header from the original datagram begins the IPSec packet and the AH and ESP headers come between the original IP header and the data from the original datagram. In tunnel mode, the entire original datagram (headers and all) is the payload data field of the IPSec packet, and the new IP, AH and ESP headers are placed before the entire original datagram.

The AH contains half-a-dozen fields. However, it is the Sequence Number and the Authentication Data fields that provide the source authentication, data integrity checks and replay protection. The Authentication Data field contains an *Integrity Check Value* (ICV), which is either an HMAC MD5 or HMAC SHA1 value. The ICV provides a data integrity check of the entire IPSec packet, including the AH header itself. Only those fields in the IP header that by their nature change during transmission, are exempted from the ICV such as the Time-To-Live (TTL) field. Because the Sequence Number is included in the ICV, any attempt by an attacker to modify the Sequence Number is detected, thus providing protection against replay attacks. Finally, the ICV provides source authentication because only a source with the correct secret key can produce a valid HMAC MD5 or HMAC SHA1 value.

When the ESP protocol is used in tunnel mode, as it is in Figure 1-8, the complete, original IP header is encrypted and encapsulated in an ESP header and an ESP trailer. (In transport mode, the payload data field would only contain the data field from the original IP datagram.) The ESP header contains a Sequence Number used by the ESP protocol and information relating to the *Security Association* (SA) used for this encrypted communication. The trailer contains any padding required by the encryption method. The payload data and the ESP trailer are encrypted. The ESP header and everything before it (the new IP header and the AH in Figure 1-8) are sent as clear text.

The IPSec packet shown in Figure 1-8 concludes with ESP authentication data. This field contains an ICV calculation that authenticates the ESP header, trailer, and payload data. The reason that AH is frequently used with ESP is that AH authenticates the entire packet from the new IP header through and including the ESP authentication data field, which provides more complete coverage than the ESP authentication data.

Figure 1-8 shows IPSec running in tunnel mode to protect complete IP datagrams. IPSec can also be run in transport mode to protect the data received from the Transport Layer protocol. The Transport Layer is our next topic.

Transport Layer

The protocol layer just above the Internet Layer is the *Transport Layer*. The two most important protocols in the Transport Layer are *Transmission Control Protocol* (TCP) and *User Datagram Protocol* (UDP). TCP provides reliable, connection-oriented data delivery service with end-to-end error detection and correction. UDP provides low-overhead, connectionless datagram delivery service. Both protocols deliver data between the Application Layer and the Internet Layer. Applications programmers can choose whichever service is more appropriate for their specific applications.

User Datagram Protocol

The User Datagram Protocol gives application programs direct access to a datagram delivery service, like the delivery service that IP provides. This allows applications to exchange messages over the network with a minimum of protocol overhead.

UDP is an unreliable, connectionless datagram protocol. As noted previously, "unreliable" means that there are no techniques in the protocol for verifying that the data reached the other end of the network correctly. UDP uses 16-bit *Source Port* and *Destination Port* numbers in word 1 of the message header, to deliver data to the correct applications process. Figure 1-9 shows the UDP message format.

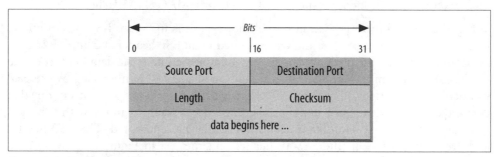

Figure 1-9. UDP message format

Applications programmers choose UDP as a data transport service for a number of good reasons. If the amount of data being transmitted is small, the overhead of creating connections and ensuring reliable delivery may be greater than the work of retransmitting the entire data set. In this case, UDP is the most efficient choice for a Transport Layer protocol. Applications that fit a *query-response* model are also excellent candidates for using UDP. The response can be used as a positive acknowledgment to the query. If a response isn't received within a certain time period, the application just sends another query. Still other applications provide their own techniques for reliable data delivery and don't require service from the transport layer protocol. Imposing another layer of acknowledgment on any of these types of applications is inefficient.

Transmission Control Protocol

Applications that require the transport protocol to provide reliable data delivery use TCP because it verifies that data is delivered across the network accurately and in the proper sequence. TCP is a *reliable*, *connection-oriented*, *byte-stream* protocol. Let's look at each of the terms—reliable, connection-oriented, and byte-stream—in more detail.

TCP provides reliability with a mechanism called *Positive Acknowledgment with Retransmission* (PAR). Simply stated, a system using PAR sends the data again, unless it hears from the remote system that the data has arrived. The unit of data exchanged between cooperating TCP modules is called a *segment* (see Figure 1-10). Each segment contains a checksum that the recipient uses to verify that the data is undamaged. If the data segment is received undamaged, the receiver sends a *positive acknowledgment* back to the sender. If the data segment is damaged, the receiver discards it. After an appropriate time-out period, the sending TCP module retransmits any segment for which no positive acknowledgment has been received.

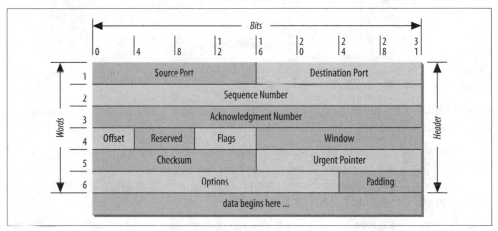

Figure 1-10. TCP segment format

TCP is connection-oriented. It establishes a logical, end-to-end connection between the two communicating hosts. Control information, called a *handshake*, is exchanged between the two endpoints to establish a dialogue before data is transmitted. TCP indicates the control function of a segment by setting the appropriate bit in the Flags field in word 4 of the *segment header*.

The type of handshake used by TCP is called a *three-way handshake* because three segments are exchanged. Figure 1-11 shows the simplest form of the three-way handshake. Host *A* begins the connection by sending host *B* a segment with the "Synchronize Sequence Numbers" (SYN) bit set. This segment tells host *B* that *A* wishes to set up a connection, and it tells *B* what Sequence Number host *A* will use as a starting number for its segments. (Sequence Numbers are used to keep data in the proper order.) Host *B* responds to *A* with a segment that has the "Acknowledgment" (ACK) and SYN bits set. *B*'s segment acknowledges the receipt of *A*'s segment, and informs *A* what Sequence Number host *B* will start with. Finally, host *A* sends a segment that acknowledges receipt of *B*'s segment, and transfers the first actual data.

After this exchange, host *A*'s TCP has positive evidence that the remote TCP is alive and ready to receive data. As soon as the connection is established, data can be transferred. When the cooperating modules have concluded the data transfers, they will exchange a three-way handshake with segments containing the "No more data from

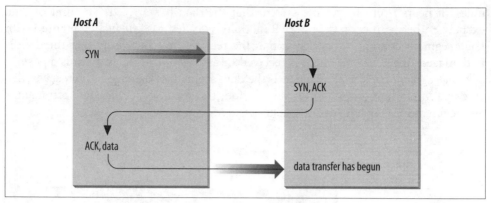

Figure 1-11. Three-way handshake

sender" bit (called the *FIN* bit) to close the connection. The end-to-end exchange of control data provides the logical connection between the two systems.

TCP views the data it sends as a continuous stream of bytes, not as independent packets. Therefore, TCP takes care to maintain the sequence in which bytes are sent and received. The Sequence Number and Acknowledgment Number fields in the TCP segment header keep track of the bytes.

The TCP standard does not require that each system start numbering bytes with any specific number; each system chooses the number it will use as a starting point. To keep track of the data stream correctly, each end of the connection must know the other end's initial number. The two ends of the connection synchronize byte-numbering systems by exchanging SYN segments during the handshake. The Sequence Number field in the SYN segment contains the *Initial Sequence Number* (ISN), which is the starting point for the byte-numbering system. For security reasons, the ISN is a random number.

Each byte of data is numbered sequentially from the ISN, so the first real byte of data sent has a Sequence Number of ISN+1. The Sequence Number in the header of a data segment identifies the sequential position in the data stream of the first data byte in the segment. For example, if the first byte in the data stream is Sequence Number 1 (ISN=0) and 4,000 bytes of data have already been transferred, then the first byte of data in the current segment is byte 4001, and the Sequence Number would be 4001.

The Acknowledgment Segment (ACK) performs two functions: *positive acknowledgment* and *flow control*. The acknowledgment tells the sender how much data has been received and how much more the receiver can accept. The Acknowledgment Number is the Sequence Number of the next byte the receiver expects to receive. The standard does not require an individual acknowledgment for every packet. The Acknowledgment Number is a positive acknowledgment of all bytes up to that number. For example, if the first byte sent was numbered 1 and 2000 bytes have been successfully received, the Acknowledgment Number would be 2001.

The Window field contains the number of bytes the remote end is able to accept. If the receiver is capable of accepting 6,000 more bytes, the Window is 6000. The Window indicates to the sender that it can continue sending segments as long as the total number of bytes it sends is smaller than the Window of bytes the receiver can accept. The receiver controls the flow of bytes from the sender by changing the size of the Window. A zero Window tells the sender to cease transmission until it receives a nonzero Window value.

Figure 1-12 shows a TCP data stream that starts with an Initial Sequence Number of 0. The receiving system has received and acknowledged 2,000 bytes, so the current Acknowledgment Number is 2001. The receiver also has enough buffer space for another 6,000 bytes, so it has advertised a Window of 6000. The sender is currently sending a segment of 1,000 bytes starting with Sequence Number 4001. The sender has received no acknowledgment for the bytes from 2001 on, but continues sending data as long as it is within the Window. If the sender fills the Window and receives no acknowledgment of the data previously sent, it will, after an appropriate time-out, send the data again starting from the first unacknowledged byte. In Figure 1-12, retransmission would start from byte 2001 if no further acknowledgments are received. This procedure ensures that data is received reliably at the far end of the network.

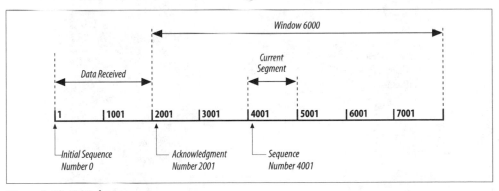

Figure 1-12. TCP data stream

TCP is also responsible for delivering data received from IP to the correct application. The application that the data is bound for is identified by a 16-bit number called the *port number*. The Source Port and Destination Port are contained in the first word of the segment header. Correctly passing data to and from the Application Layer is an important part of what the Transport Layer services do.

Transport Layer Security

IPSec provides security in the IP layer. Security can also be provided in the Transport Layer. *Transport Layer Security* (TLS) is an evolutionary outgrowth of the *Secure Sockets Layer* (SSL) protocol developed by Netscape for web security. TLS is an Internet standard based on SSL Version 3 (SSLv3). These protocols are very similar though not directly interoperable.

TLS is documented in RFC 2246, *The TLS Protocol Version 1.0*. TLS is composed of two sub-protocols: the *Handshake Protocol* negotiates connection parameters, and the *Record Protocol* moves the bulk of the data. Figure 1-13 shows a sample packet flow for a TLS handshake.

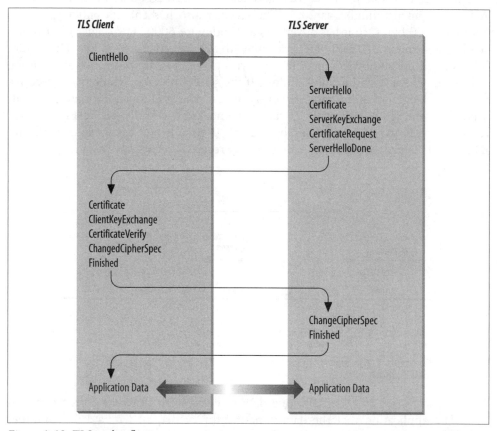

Figure 1-13. TLS packet flow

The client initiates the connection with a ClientHello message. The ClientHello lists the authentication methods, encryption methods and versions of TLS supported by the client. If the server accepts the connection request, it responds with a Server-Hello message that defines the session identifier for the connection and selects security parameters for the session from the list of supported authentication and encryption methods advertised by the client.

At this point in Figure 1-13, the server sends a Certificate message that contains the server's public key certificate. This message is optional, but is used when authentication is required for the handshake. If the Certificate message is not used, i.e., if the handshake will not be authenticated, a ServerKeyExchange message can be used in its place to provide key exchange information to the client. In fact, the optional ServerKeyExchange message can be used along with and following the Certificate message if an encryption technique is selected that requires more key exchange material than is provided by the Certificate.

SSL was originally developed to promote web-based commerce. As you might imagine with a protocol developed for electronic commerce, the server commonly sends the Certificate in order to authenticate itself. Before you send money to a remote web site, you want to make sure it is what it claims to be. For this reason, server authentication is common in SSL, which is the parent of TLS. It is much less common, however, for the client to be required to authenticate itself in an e-commerce environment. (The only thing most e-commerce sites want from a client is a valid credit card!) TLS is, however, intended for use in a wide variety of applications. Therefore, it is possible for the server to ask the client to authenticate itself. The server does this by sending the optional CertificateRequest message.

The sequence of messages from the server terminates with a ServerHelloDone message. As the paragraphs above make clear, there are several optional messages that the server can send after the ServerHello. The ServerHelloDone message lets the client know the server is finished sending.

The client responds to the ServerHelloDone message with a series of packets. If the server sent a CertificateRequest message, the client responds by sending a Certificate message. If the client does not have a valid certificate, it sends an empty message. When the server receives an empty Certificate message, it may terminate the session. Often, however, the session continues and it is up to the application to decide how to treat an unauthenticated client.

The client then sends the ClientKeyExchange message, which contains key exchange data. This message is not optional. It is always sent.

If the client sent a Certificate message that contained a valid public key certificate, the client may also send a CertificateVerify message that contains a digest of all handshake messages sent and received by the client starting from the ClientHello and going on through to the ClientKeyExchange. The server can use the client's public key certificate to verify the digest and thus ensure that the client and server have both seen exactly the same messages.

Next, the client sends a ChangeCipherSpec message to switch to the encryption technique negotiated by the handshake. The messages that follow and the bulk data transmission are all encrypted using the negotiated technique. Finally, the client sends a Finished message. The server responds with its own ChangeCipherSpec and Finished messages and the encrypted data stream starts to flow.

TLS is generally invoked by applications, such as a web program or a mail delivery program, when they need a secure connection. The Application Layer is discussed next.

Application Layer

At the top of the TCP/IP protocol architecture is the *Application Layer*. This layer includes all processes that use the Transport Layer protocols to deliver data. There are many applications protocols. Most of these protocols provide user services, and new services are always being added to this layer.

Some widely known and implemented applications protocols follow:

Telnet
  The Network Terminal Protocol provides remote login over the network.

FTP
  The File Transfer Protocol is used for interactive file transfer.

SMTP
  The Simple Mail Transfer Protocol delivers electronic mail.

HTTP
  The Hypertext Transfer Protocol delivers web pages over the network.

While HTTP, FTP, SMTP, and Telnet are widely implemented TCP/IP applications that provide services directly to end users, you will work with other applications that primarily provide services from one host to another. Examples of these types of TCP/IP applications follow:

Domain Name System (DNS)
  Also called *name service*, this application maps IP addresses to the names assigned to network devices. DNS is discussed in detail in Chapter 6.

Dynamic Host Configuration Protocol (DHCP)
  This protocol is used to automatically configure networked computers. DHCP is covered in Chapter 5.

Some protocols, such as Telnet and FTP, can only be used if the user has some knowledge of the network. Other protocols, like DHCP, run without the user even knowing they exist. As network administrator, you are aware of all these applications and all the protocols in the other TCP/IP layers. And you're responsible for configuring them for your Windows Server.

Summary

This chapter discussed the structure of TCP/IP, the protocol suite upon which the Internet is built. TCP/IP is a hierarchy of four layers: Applications, Transport, Internet, and Network Access. This chapter examined the function of each of these layers. The next chapter looks at how the IP datagram moves through a network when data is delivered between hosts.

CHAPTER 2
Delivering the Data

Chapter 1 touched on the basic architecture and design of the TCP/IP protocols. From that discussion, we know that TCP/IP is a hierarchy of four layers. This chapter explores in finer detail how data moves between the protocol layers and the systems on the network. We examine the structure of Internet addresses, including how addresses route data to its final destination and how address structure is locally redefined to create subnets. We also look at the protocol and port numbers used to deliver data to the correct applications. These additional details move us from an overview of TCP/IP to the specific implementation details that affect your system's configuration.

Addressing, Routing, and Multiplexing

To deliver data between two Internet hosts, it is necessary to move the data across the network to the correct host, and within that host to the correct application or process. TCP/IP uses three schemes to accomplish these tasks:

Addressing
> IP addresses, which uniquely identify every host on the network, deliver data to the correct host.

Routing
> Gateways deliver data to the correct network.

Multiplexing
> Protocol and port numbers deliver data to the correct software module within the host.

Each of these functions—addressing between hosts, routing between networks, and multiplexing between layers—is necessary to send data between two cooperating applications across the Internet. Let's examine each of these functions in detail.

The IP Address

An IPv4 address is a 32-bit value that uniquely identifies every device attached to a TCP/IP Internet. Some of the bits identify a specific network within the Internet, and are referred to as *network bits*, or the *network number*. Other bits identify the device on the network and are called *host bits*, or the *host number*. We'll talk much more about the structure of the IP address in the next section.

IP addresses are usually written as four decimal numbers separated by dots (periods) in a format called *dotted decimal notation.*[*] Each decimal number represents a byte (8 bits) of the 32-bit address, and each of the four numbers is in the range of 0 through 255 (the decimal values possible in a single byte).

IP addresses are often called host addresses. Although this is common usage, it is slightly misleading. IP addresses are assigned to network interfaces, not to computer systems. A gateway has a different address for each network to which it is connected. The gateway is known to other devices by the address associated with the network that it shares with those devices.

Systems can be addressed in three different ways. Individual systems are directly addressed by a host address, which is called a *unicast address*. A unicast packet is addressed to one individual host. Groups of systems can be addressed using a *multicast address*, e.g., 224.0.0.2. Routers along the path from the source to destination recognize the special address and route copies of the packet to each member of the multicast group.[†] All systems on a network are addressed using the *broadcast address*, e.g., 172.16.255.255. The broadcast address depends on the broadcast capabilities of the underlying physical network.

The broadcast address is a good example of the fact that not all network addresses or host addresses can be assigned to a network device. Some host addresses are reserved for special uses. On all networks, host numbers 0 and 255 are reserved. An IP address with all host bits set to 1 is a broadcast address. The broadcast address for network 172.16 is 172.16.255.255. A datagram sent to this address is delivered to every individual host on network 172.16. An IP address with all host bits set to 0 identifies the network itself. For example, 10.0.0.0 refers to network 10, and 172.16.0.0 refers to network 172.16. Addresses in this form are used in routing tables to refer to entire networks.

Network addresses with a first byte value greater than 223 cannot be assigned to a physical network because those addresses are reserved for special use. There are two other network addresses that are used only for special purposes. Network 0.0.0.0

---

[*] Addresses are occasionally written in other formats, e.g., as hexadecimal numbers. Whatever the notation, the structure and meaning of the address are the same.

[†] This is only partially true. Multicasting is not supported by every router. Sometimes it is necessary to tunnel through routers and networks by encapsulating the multicast packet inside a unicast packet.

designates the *default route* and network 127.0.0.0 is the *loopback address*. The default route is used to simplify the routing information that IP must handle, as explained in the section "The Routing Table" later in this chapter. The loopback address simplifies network applications by allowing the local host to be addressed in the same manner as a remote host. These special network addresses play an important part when configuring a host, but these addresses are not assigned to devices on real networks. Despite these few exceptions, most addresses are assigned to physical devices and are used by IP to deliver data to those devices.

The Internet Protocol moves data between hosts in the form of datagrams. Each datagram is delivered to the address contained in the Destination Address (word 5) of the datagram's header. The Destination Address is a standard 32-bit IP address, which contains sufficient information to uniquely identify a network and a specific host on that network.

Address Structure

An IP address contains a *network part* and a *host part*, but the format of these parts is not the same in every IP address. The number of address bits used to identify the network and the number used to identify the host vary according to the prefix length of the address. The prefix length is determined by the address bit mask.

An *address bit mask* works in this way: if a bit in the mask is on, that equivalent bit in the address is interpreted as a network bit; if a bit in the mask is off, the bit belongs to the host part of the address. For example, if address 172.22.12.4 is given the network mask 255.255.255.0, which has 24 bits on and 8 bits off, the first 24 bits are the network number and the last 8 bits are the host address. Combining the address and the mask tells us that this is the address of host 4 on network 172.22.12.

Specifying both the address and the mask in dotted decimal notation is cumbersome when writing out addresses. A shorthand notation is available for writing an address with its associated address mask. Instead of writing network 172.31.26.32 with a mask of 255.255.255.224, we can write 172.31.26.32/27. The format of this notation is *address/prefix-length*, where *prefix-length* is the number of bits in the network portion of the address. Without this notation, the address 172.31.26.32 could easily be interpreted as a host address.

Organizations can obtain public IP addresses by purchasing a block of addresses from their Internet service provider (ISP). In this case, the ISP normally assigns a single organization a continuous block of addresses that is appropriate for the needs of the organization. For example, a moderately large business might purchase 192.168.16.0/20 while a small business might buy 192.168.32.0/24. Because the prefix shows the length of the network portion of the address, the number of host address bits that are available to an organization (the host portion of the address) is determined by subtracting the prefix from the total number of 32 bits in an address. Thus, a prefix of 20 leaves 12 bits that are available to be locally assigned to network devices such as servers. This is called a "12-bit block" of addresses. A prefix of 24 creates an "8-bit block." Of the two sample address blocks, the first is a 12-bit block that encompasses 4,096 addresses from 192.168.16.0 to 192.168.31.255, and the second is an 8-bit block that includes the 256 addresses from 192.168.32.0 to 192.168.32.255.

Each of these address blocks appears to the outside world to be a single "network" address. Thus, external routers have one route to the block 192.168.16.0/20 and one route to the block 192.168.32.0/24, regardless of the size of the address block. Internally, however, the organization may have several separate physical networks within the address block. The flexibility of address masks means that service providers can assign arbitrary length blocks of addresses to their customers, and the customers can subdivide those address blocks using different length masks.

Subnets

To locally modify the structure of an IP address, use host address bits as additional network address bits. Essentially, the dividing line between network address bits and host address bits can be moved to create additional networks, by reducing the maximum number of hosts that can belong to each network. These newly designated network bits define an address block within the larger address block, which is called a *subnet*.

Organizations usually decide to subnet in order to overcome topological or organizational problems. Subnetting allows decentralized management of host addressing. With the standard addressing scheme, a central administrator is responsible for managing host addresses for the entire network. By subnetting, the administrator can delegate address assignment to smaller organizations within the overall organization—which may be a political expedient rather than a technical requirement. If you don't want to deal with the data processing department, assign them their own subnet and let them manage it themselves.

Subnetting can also be used to overcome hardware differences and distance limitations. IP routers can link dissimilar physical networks together, but only if each physical network has its own unique network address. Subnetting divides a single address block into many subnet addresses, so that each physical network can have its own unique address.

A subnet is defined by changing the bit mask of the IP address. A *subnet mask* functions in the same way as a normal address mask: an "on" bit is interpreted as a network bit; an "off" bit belongs to the host part of the address. The difference is that a subnet mask is only used locally. In the outside world, the address is still interpreted using the address mask known to the outside world.

Assume you have a small real estate business that has been assigned the address block 192.168.32.0/24. The bit mask associated with that address block is 255.255.255.0

and the block contains 256 addresses. Further, assume that your business has 10 offices each with a half-dozen computers and you want to allocate some addresses to each office and have some for future expansion. You can subdivide the 256-address block with a subnet mask that extends the network portion of the address by a few additional bits.

To subdivide 192.168.32.0/24 into 16 subnets, use the mask 255.255.255.240, i.e., 192.168.32.0/28. The first three bytes contain the original network address block; the fourth byte is divided between the subnet address and the address of the host on that subnet. Applying this mask defines the four high-order bits* of the fourth byte as the subnet part of the address, and the remaining four bits—the last four bits of the fourth byte—as the host portion of the address. This creates 16 subnets, each containing 14 host addresses, which is better suited to the network topology of your small real estate business. Table 2-1 shows the subnets and host addresses produced by applying this subnet mask to network address 192.168.32.0/24.

Table 2-1. Effect of a subnet mask

Network number	Host address range	Broadcast address
192.168.32.0	192.168.32.1–192.168.32.14	192.168.32.15
192.168.32.16	192.168.32.17–192.168.32.30	192.168.32.31
192.168.32.32	192.168.32.33–192.168.32.46	192.168.32.47
192.168.32.48	192.168.32.49–192.168.32.62	192.168.32.63
192.168.32.64	192.168.32.65–192.168.32.78	192.168.32.79
192.168.32.80	192.168.32.81–192.168.32.94	192.168.32.95
192.168.32.96	192.168.32.97–192.168.32.110	192.168.32.111
192.168.32.112	192.168.32.113–192.168.32.126	192.168.32.127
192.168.32.128	192.168.32.129–192.168.32.142	192.168.32.143
192.168.32.144	192.168.32.145–192.168.32.158	192.168.32.159
192.168.32.160	192.168.32.161–192.168.32.174	192.168.32.175
192.168.32.176	192.168.32.177–192.168.32.190	192.168.32.191
192.168.32.192	192.168.32.193–192.168.32.206	192.168.32.207
192.168.32.208	192.168.32.209–192.168.32.222	192.168.32.223
192.168.32.224	192.168.32.225–192.168.32.238	192.168.32.239
192.168.32.240	192.168.32.241–192.168.32.254	192.168.32.255

In Table 2-1, the first row describes a subnet with a subnet number that is all zeros (the first four bits of the fourth byte are all set to 0). The last row in the table describes a subnet with a subnet number that is all ones (the first four bits of the

---

* The high-order bits are the leftmost bits, i.e., those bits on the left hand side of the number when it is written in binary format.

fourth byte are all set to 1). Originally, the RFCs implied that you should not use subnet numbers of all zeros or all ones. However, RFC 1812, *Requirements for IP Version 4 Routers*, makes it clear that subnets of all zeros and all ones are legal and should be supported by all routers.

You don't have to manually calculate a table like Table 2-1 to know what subnets and host addresses are produced by a subnet mask. The calculations have already been done for you. RFC 1878, *Variable Length Subnet Table For IPv4*, lists all possible subnet masks and the valid addresses they produce.

RFC 1878 describes all 32 prefix values. But little documentation is needed because the prefix is easy to understand and remember. Writing 10.104.0.19 as 10.104.0.19/8 shows that this address has 8 bits for the network number and therefore 24 bits for the host number. Unfortunately, things are not always this neat. Sometimes the address is not given an explicit address mask and you need to know how to determine the natural mask that an address is assigned by default.

The Natural Mask

Originally, the IP address space was divided into a few fixed-length structures called *address classes*. The three main address classes were *class A*, *class B*, and *class C*. IP software determined the class, and therefore the structure, of an address by examining its first few bits. Address classes are no longer used. However, the same rules that used to determine the address class are now used to create the default address mask, which is called the *natural mask*. These rules are as follows:

- If the first bit of an IP address is 0, the default mask is 8 bits long (prefix 8). This is the same as the old *class A network* address format. The first 8 bits identify the network, and the last 24 bits identify the host.

- If the first 2 bits of the address are 1 0, the default mask is 16 bits long (prefix 16), which is the same structure as the old *class B network* address format. The first 16 bits identify the network, and the last 16 bits identify the host.

- If the first 3 bits of the address are 1 1 0, the default mask is 24 bits long (prefix 24). This mask is the same as the old *class C network* address format. In this format, the first 24 bits are the network address, and the last 8 bits identify the host.

- If the first four bits of the address are 1 1 1 0, it is a multicast address. These addresses were sometimes called *class D addresses*, but they don't really refer to specific networks. Multicast addresses are used to address groups of computers all at one time. Multicast addresses identify a group of computers that share a common application, such as a videoconference, as opposed to a group of computers that share a common network. All bits in a multicast address are significant for routing, so the default mask is 32 bits long (prefix 32). Figure 2-1 shows examples of class A, class B and class C addresses. A sample multicast address is 224.0.0.9.

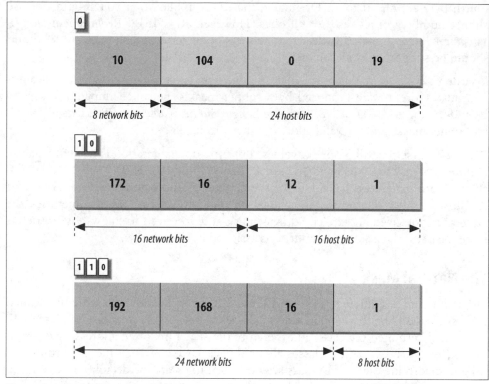

Figure 2-1. Default IP address formats

When an IP address is written in dotted decimal format, it is sometimes easier to think of the address as four 8-bit bytes instead of as a 32-bit value. We can look at the address as composed of full bytes of network address and full bytes of host address when using the natural mask, because the three default masks all create prefix lengths that are multiples of eight. A simple way to determine the default mask is to look at the first byte of the address. If the value of the first byte is:

Less than 128

> The default address mask is 8 bits long; the first byte is the network number, and the next three bytes are the host address.

128 to 191

> The default address mask is 16 bits long; the first two bytes identify the network, and the last two bytes identify the host.

192 to 223

> The default address mask is 24 bits; the first three bytes are the network address, and the last byte is the host number.

224 to 239

The entire address identifies a specific multicast group; therefore the default mask is 32 bits.

Greater than 239

The address is reserved. We can ignore reserved addresses.

Figure 2-1 illustrates the two techniques for determining the default address structure. The first address is 10.104.0.19. The first bit of this address is 0; therefore, the first 8 bits define the network, and the last 24 bits define the host. Explained in a byte-oriented manner, the first byte is less than 128, so the address is interpreted as host 104.0.19 on network 10. One byte specifies the network and three bytes specify the host.

The second address in Figure 2-1 is 172.16.12.1. The two high-order bits are 1 0, meaning that 16 bits define the network and 16 bits define the host. Viewed in a byte-oriented way, the first byte falls between 128 and 191, so the address refers to host 12.1 on network 172.16. Two bytes identify the network and two identify the host.

Finally, in the address 192.168.16.1, the three high-order bits are 1 1 0, indicating that 24 bits represent the network and 8 bits represent the host. The first byte of this address is in the range from 192 to 223, so this is the address of host 1 on network 192.168.16—three network bytes and one host byte.

Evaluating addresses according to the old class rules discussed above limits the length of network numbers to 8, 16, or 24 bits—1, 2, or 3 bytes. The IP address, however, is not really byte-oriented. It is 32 contiguous bits. The address *bit mask* provides a flexible way to define the network and host portions of an address. IP uses the network portion of the address to route the datagram between networks. The full address, including the host information, is used to identify an individual host. Because of the dual role of IP addresses, the flexibility of address masks not only makes more addresses available for use, it also has a positive impact on routing.

CIDR Blocks and Route Aggregation

The IP address, which provides universal addressing across all of the networks of the Internet, is one of the great strengths of the TCP/IP protocol suite. However, the original class structure of the IP address had weaknesses. The TCP/IP designers did not envision the enormous scale of today's network. When TCP/IP was being designed, networking was limited to large organizations that could afford substantial computer systems. The idea of a powerful PC system on every desktop did not exist. At that time, a 32-bit address seemed so large that it was divided into classes to reduce the processing load on routers, even though dividing the address into classes sharply reduced the number of host addresses actually available for use. For example, assigning a single class B address instead of six class C addresses to a large network reduced the load on the router because the router needed to keep only one route for that entire organization. However, an organization that was assigned the class B address probably did not have 65,536 computers, so most of the host addresses available to that organization were never used.

The class-structured address design was critically strained by the rapid growth of the Internet. At one point, it appeared that all class B addresses might be rapidly exhausted. The rapid depletion of the class B addresses showed that three primary address classes were not enough: class A was much too large and class C was much too small. Even a class B address was too large for many networks but was used because it was better than the alternatives.

The obvious solution to the class B address crisis was to force organizations to use multiple class C addresses. There were millions of these addresses available and they were in no immediate danger of depletion. As is often the case, the obvious solution is not as simple as it may seem. In the core of the Internet, each class C address might require its own entry within the routing table. Assigning thousands or millions of class C addresses could cause the routing table to grow so rapidly for major network providers that their routers would soon be overwhelmed. The solution not only required the new way of looking at addresses that address masks provide but also required a new way of assigning addresses.

Originally, network addresses were assigned in more or less sequential order as they were requested. This worked fine when the network was small and centralized. However, it did not take network topology into account. Thus, only random chance would determine if the same intermediate routers would be used to reach network 195.4.12.0 and network 195.4.13.0, which makes it difficult to reduce the size of the routing table. Addresses can only be aggregated if they are contiguous numbers and are reachable through the same route. For example, if addresses are contiguous for one service provider, a single route can be created for that aggregation because that service provider will have a limited number of connections to the Internet. But if one network address is in France and the next contiguous address is in Australia, creating a consolidated route for these addresses is not possible.

Today, large, contiguous blocks of addresses are assigned to large network service providers in a manner that better reflects the topology of the network. The service providers then allocate chunks of these address blocks to the organizations to which they provide network services. Because the assignment of addresses reflects the topology of the network, it permits route aggregation. Under this scheme, we know that network 195.4.12.0 and network 195.4.13.0 are reachable through the same intermediate routers. In fact, both of these addresses are in the range of the addresses assigned to Europe (194.0.0.0 to 195.255.255.255).

Assigning addresses that reflect the topology of the network enables route aggregation but does not implement it. As long as network 195.4.12.0 and network 195.4.13.0 are interpreted as separate class C addresses, they require separate entries in the routing table. For this reason, address masks are included in routing table entries to ensure that destination addresses are interpreted correctly.

The use of an address mask instead of the old address classes to determine the destination network is called *Classless Inter-Domain Routing* (CIDR).* Supporting CIDR required modifications to the routers and routing protocols. The protocols need to distribute, along with the destination addresses, address masks that define how the addresses are interpreted. Routers and hosts need to know how to interpret these addresses as "classless" addresses and how to apply the bit mask that accompanies the address. All new operating systems and routing protocols support address masks.

CIDR was intended as an interim solution, though it has proved much more durable than its designers imagined. CIDR has provided address and routing relief for many years and is capable of providing it for many more years to come. Another innovation that has slowed the depletion of IP addresses is the standardization of private network numbers.

Private Network Numbers

Every interface on a TCP/IP network must have a unique IP address. If a host is directly connected to the Internet, its IP address must be unique within the entire Internet. If a host is connected to a private network, such as an enterprise network, its IP address only needs to be unique within that private network. RFC 1918, *Address Allocation for Private Internets*, lists network numbers that are reserved for private use.† The private network numbers are:

- Network 10.0.0.0 (10/8 prefix) is a 24-bit block of addresses.
- Networks 172.16.0.0 to 172.31.0.0 (172.16/12 prefix) are a 20-bit block of addresses.
- Networks 192.168.0.0 to 192.168.255.0 (192.168/16 prefix) are a 16-bit block of addresses.

The disadvantage to using a network address from RFC 1918 is that you may have to change your address in the future if you directly connect your full network to the Internet and wish to make all of the systems on the network accessible from the Internet. There are some advantages to choosing a private network address:

- It's easy. You do not have to apply for an official address or get anyone's approval.
- It's friendly. You save address space for those who need to connect to the Internet.
- It's free. RFC 1918 addresses cost nothing—public addresses cost money.

---

* CIDR is pronounced "cider."

† The addresses used in this book are treated as if they were public network addresses, but they are really private network numbers.

If you do choose an address from RFC 1918, the hosts on your network can still have access to systems on the Internet. But it will take some effort. You'll need *network address translation* (NAT) or a proxy server. NAT is available as a separate piece of hardware or as a piece of software in some routers and firewalls. It works by converting the source address of datagrams leaving your network from your private address to your official address. Address translation has several advantages:

- It conserves IP addresses. Most network connections are between systems on the same enterprise network. Only a small percentage of systems need to connect to the Internet at any one time. Therefore, far fewer official IP addresses are needed than the total number of systems on an enterprise network. NAT makes it possible to use a large address space from RFC 1918 for configuring the enterprise network while using only a small official address space for Internet connections.

- It has some security advantages because it reduces address spoofing, a security attack in which a remote system pretends to be a local system. The addresses in RFC 1918 cannot be routed over the Internet. Therefore, even if a datagram is routed off of your network toward the remote system, the fact that the datagram contains an RFC 1918 destination address means that the routers in the Internet will discard the datagram.

- It eliminates the need to renumber your hosts when you connect to the Internet.

Network address translation also has disadvantages:

- NAT may add cost for new hardware or optional software. However, these costs tend to be very low.

- Address translation adds overhead to the processing of every datagram. When the address is changed, the checksum must be recalculated. Furthermore, some upper-layer protocols carry a copy of the IP address that also must be converted.

- Routers never modify the addresses in a datagram header, but NAT does. This might introduce some instability. Additionally, protocols and applications that embed addresses in their data may not function correctly with NAT.

- NAT may impact end-to-end encryption and authentication. Authentication and encryption schemes that include the IP address within the calculation are affected because the NAT box changes the IP addresses. (See the description of IPSec in Chapter 1 for an example of a protocol that includes the IP address in authentication and encryption.)

Windows Server 2003 handles the NAT security problem by supporting *NAT-Traversal* (NAT-T). NAT-T resolves the potential IPSec encryption and authentication security problems caused by NAT. A system that supports NAT-T indicates its NAT-T capability during the IPSec connection negotiation. It also sends two messages, one containing a hash of the destination IP address and port, and the other containing a hash of the source IP address and port. The receiving system can then compare the hashed addresses to the ones it sees in the IP header. If the header addresses have been changed by an intervening NAT box, the fact is easily detected. When an intervening NAT box is detected, the IPSec end-systems continue by encapsulating the IPSec messages inside of UDP packets. The NAT box does its address translation on the UDP header leaving the IPSec messages unmolested. The data gets through, and the authentication and encryption are preserved.

Combining NAT with a private network address gives every host on the private network access to the outside world, but it does not allow outside users access into your network. For that level of direct access, you need to obtain an official IP address as described in Chapter 4.

CIDR and private network numbers have extended the usefulness of IPv4 addresses. However, the long-term solution for address depletion is to replace the current addressing scheme with a new one. In the TCP/IP protocol suite, addressing is defined by the IP protocol. Therefore, to define a new address structure, the Internet Engineering Task Force (IETF) created a new version of IP called IPv6.

IPv6

IPv6 provides an enormous 128-bit address to solve the address depletion problem. A 128-bit address can uniquely identify 3.4×10^{38} devices. Of course, not all 128 bits are used to specify a device address. Like the IPv4 address, the IPv6 address has a structure that defines the network and the device on the network. Figure 2-2 is an example of the basic IPv6 address structure currently being assigned by the *Internet Assigned Number Authority* (IANA) as shown in RFC 3587, *IPv6 Global Unicast Address Format*.

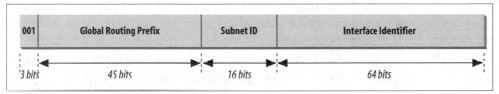

Figure 2-2. Sample IPv6 unicast address format

The first three bits of the address shown in Figure 2-2 indicate the address type. A variable-length binary prefix determines the IPv6 address type. RFC 3513, *Internet Protocol Version 6 (IPv6) Addressing Architecture*, assigns the prefixes shown in Table 2-2.

Table 2-2. IPv6 address types

Assignment	Variable-length binary prefix
Special use	0000 0000
NSAP allocation	0000 001
IANA allocation	001

Table 2-2. IPv6 address types (continued)

Assignment	Variable-length binary prefix
Link-local unicast addresses	1111 1110 10
Site-local unicast addresses	1111 1110 11
Multicast addresses	1111 1111

The currently defined special-use addresses include the following:

Unspecified address
> This is an address where all 128 bits are 0. The unspecified address is used to explicitly indicate that an address has not been assigned. For example, a client might use an unassigned address as the source address before being assigned an address by a configuration server.

Loopback address
> This is an address where the first 127 bits are set to zeros followed by one bit set to 1. It serves the same purpose as the IPv4 loopback address.

IPv4-compatible IPv6 address format
> This address contains 96 bits of zeros followed by a 32-bit IPv4 address. This type of address is used to tunnel IPv6 packets over IPv4 networks.

IPv4-mapped IPv6 address format
> This address has 80 bits of zeros, 16 bits of ones, and then a 32-bit IPv4 address. This is used to represent an IPv4 address as an IPv6 address.

Network Service Access Point (NSAP) addresses are used at the NSAPs that connect the global Internet. IANA addresses are the public IPv6 addresses an ISP would obtain for its network, in the same way an ISP uses public IPv4 addresses. (Chapter 4 provides more information about official address registries and how public addresses are obtained.) The addresses used to move packets across a global IPv6 Internet are of this type.

Link-local addresses and *site-local addresses* are analogous to IPv4 private network numbers. Site-local addresses are for private use within an enterprise. These addresses are not to be routed across a global Internet. Link-local addresses have an even smaller scope. Link-local addresses are private addresses limited to a single physical link. They cannot be routed even within the enterprise.

Finally, IPv6 also provides multicast addresses. These are used in exactly the same way as IPv4 multicast addresses. However, IPv6 has a related address called an anycast address. Like a multicast address, an anycast address identifies members of a group, but the anycast address references only one member of the group—the member that is closest to the source system. Despite the logical relationship of anycast addresses to multicast addresses, these two addresses are not syntactically related. Anycast addresses do not come from the multicast address space. Instead, anycast addresses are taken from the unicast address space.

The first three bits in the address format shown in Figure 2-2 indicate that this is a global unicast address from the address space currently assigned by IANA. This three-bit field is followed by the *Global Routing Prefix*. The Global Routing Prefix is the portion of the IPv6 address that is synonymous with the network portion of an IPv4 address. It is the portion of the address that is assigned to the enterprise by the address registry, and it is the portion evaluated by intermediate routers to move packets to the enterprise site.

The *Subnet ID* is a 16-bit field used to create subnets within the larger network. It is used just like subnets in IPv4, but unlike IPv4, it does not require taking bits away from the host-specific portion of the address. The IPv6 global unicast address structure shown in Figure 2-2 sets aside 16 bits specifically for subnetting.

The 64-bit *Interface Identifier* is the part of the IPv6 address analogous to the host portion of an IPv4 address. The Interface Identifier is assigned in a number of ways:

- By using the MAC address of the interface
- By DHCP
- By PPP
- By using a randomized value

DHCP and PPP are address assignment techniques used in IPv4. The pseudo-random value is a technique used to emulate the device-independent addressing used in IPv4. Using the MAC address is perhaps the most interesting of the address assignment methods because the availability of this type of address assignment means that the network interface can be self-configured. Here's how. Ethernet interfaces, and many other types of network interfaces, have a unique physical layer address, called a *Media Access Control* (MAC) address, encoded in the device hardware. The IPv6 software can retrieve the address from the hardware and use it to create the Interface Identifier. The Interface Identifier uses a modified EUI-64 format. If the device uses a MAC address that complies with the EUI-64 format, the IPv6 software can use that address as an Interface Identifier with very little modification. In the far more common case where the device uses an IEEE 802.3 Ethernet-style 48-bit MAC address, the IPv6 software simply extends the MAC address to 64 bits by inserting the hexadecimal value FFFE between the *company identifier* and the *vendor-supplied identifier* of the 802.3 MAC address to create an EUI-64 compliant MAC address. It then modifies this address to create an Interface Identifier. In either case, the conversion is easily done in the IPv6 software without any external configuration servers or any special configuration input from the network administrator.

IPv6 addresses are written using a colon-hexadecimal syntax. The addresses are written as eight 16-bit values separated by colons. Leading zeros within a 16-bit value do not have to be written out, and a long string of zero values can be indicated by the use of a double-colon. An example will make this notation clear.

The multicast address used to address all routers can be written out as:

    FF01:0000:0000:0000:0000:0000:0000:0002

or the leading zeros could be dropped and the address could be written as:

    FF01:0:0:0:0:0:0:2

or the double colon syntax could be used in place of the contiguous run of zeros:

    FF01::2

The prefix length notation defined by CIDR can also be used with IPv6 addresses to identify a route, subnet or address range. For example, FF::/8 would match every address that begins with FF, which is every multicast address.

As you might imagine, the large address means that the IPv6 header is substantially larger than an IPv4 header. However, it is less complex and more easily processed. Figure 2-3 shows the IPv6 header format.

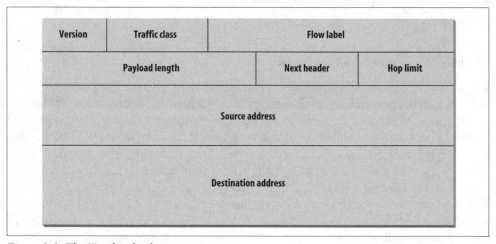

Figure 2-3. The IPv6 header format

The Version field specifies the version of IP. In an IPv4 header, this field contains the value 4 and in an IPv6 header, it contains 6.

Traffic class and Flow label are used to implement quality of service. Traffic class provides for *differentiated service* by identifying the type of data being carried in the datagram payload. For example, voice traffic might be given different handling than email traffic. The Flow label allows the source to request special handling for a sequence of packets, which is called a *flow*. This might be used to maintain sequence and timing within a flow of real-time data. Built-in support for Quality of Service (QoS) is one of the advantages of IPv6.

Payload length specifies the length of the packet that follows the IPv6 header. Next header identifies the type of header that follows the IPv6 header. (This is similar to the Protocol field in an IPv4 header.) The Hop limit field is similar to the Time-to-Live field of an IPv4 header. It is decremented by each router that handles the packet and is used to ensure that the packet is not caught in a routing loop. Last are the Source address and the Destination address.

Compare this header to the IPv4 header shown in Figure 1-5. This IPv6 header has fewer fields to process and the header is always a fixed length.

The address structure and the header format are not the only things that have changed with IPv6. A new ICMP, called ICMPv6, was also created. And beyond that, network protocols in the layers above the Internet Layer also had to change. Changing something as fundamental as IP causes changes throughout the protocol stack. Switching from IPv4 to IPv6 is a major change that affects all layers of the network software.

The lack of demand for IPv6

IPv6 is an improvement on the IP protocol based on 20 years of operational experience. The original motivation for the new protocol was the threat of address depletion, which IPv6 solves with a very large 128-bit address space. The large address space also makes it possible to use a hierarchical address structure to reduce the burden on routers while still maintaining more than enough addresses for future network growth. But large addresses are only one of the benefits of the new protocol. Other benefits of IPv6 are:

- Improved security built into the protocol
- Simplified, fixed-length, word-aligned headers to speed header processing and reduce overhead
- Improved techniques for handling header options
- Improved quality of service (QoS) support
- Support for automatic configuration

IPv6 has several good features, but it is still not widely used. In part, this is because of enhancements to IPv4, improvements in hardware performance, and changes in the way that networks are configured have lessened the demand for the new features of IPv6.

A critical shortage of addresses has not yet materialized for three reasons:

- CIDR makes the assignment of addresses more flexible, which in turn makes more addresses available and permits aggregation to reduce the burden on routers.
- Private addresses and NAT have greatly reduced the demand for official addresses. Many organizations prefer to use private addresses for all systems on

their internal networks because private addresses reduce the administrative burden and improve security.

- Permanent, fixed address assignment is less common than dynamic address assignment. The majority of systems use dynamic addresses temporarily assigned by a configuration protocol such as DHCP.

The creation of the IPSec standards for IPv4 lessened the need for the security enhancements of IPv6. In fact, many of the security tools and features available for IPv4 systems are not being fully utilized, indicating that the demand for tools to secure the link may have been overestimated.

IPv6 eliminates hop-by-hop segmentation, has a more efficient header design, and enhanced option processing. These things make it more efficient to process IPv6 packets than to handle IPv4 packets. However, for the vast majority of systems, this increased efficiency is unneeded because processing IP datagrams is a very minor task. Most systems exist at the edge of the network and handle relatively few communications packets. Processor speed and memory have increased enormously while hardware prices have fallen. Most managers would rather buy more hardware using the proven IPv4 protocol than undertake implementing the new IPv6 protocol just to save a few machine cycles. Only those systems located near the core of the network would truly benefit from this efficiency, and although important, those systems are relatively few in number.

All of these things have worked together to lessen the demand for IPv6. The lack of demand has limited the number of organizations that have adopted IPv6 as their primary communications protocol, and a large user community is the one thing that a protocol needs to be truly successful. We use communications protocols to communicate with other people. If there are not enough people using the protocol, we don't feel the need to use it. IPv6 is still in the early-adopter phase. Most organizations do not use IPv6 at all, and many of those that do, use it only for experimental purposes. Between organizations, most IPv6 communications are encapsulated inside IPv4 datagrams and sent over the Internet inside IPv4 tunnels. It will be some time yet before it is the primary protocol of operational networks.

If you run an operational network, you should not be overly concerned with IPv6. The current generation of TCP/IP (IPv4), with the enhancements that CIDR and other extensions provide, should be more than adequate for your current network needs. On your network and on the Internet, you will most likely use IPv4 and 32-bit IP addresses. IPv4 is the version of IP on which this book focuses.

Internet Routing Architecture

Chapter 1 described the evolution of the Internet architecture over the years. Along with these architectural changes have come changes in the way that routing information is disseminated within the network.

In the original Internet structure, there was a hierarchy of gateways. This hierarchy reflected the fact that the Internet was built upon the existing ARPAnet. When the Internet was created, the ARPAnet was the backbone of the network: a central delivery medium to carry long-distance traffic. This central system was called the *core*, and the centrally managed gateways that interconnected it were called the *core gateways*.

In that hierarchical structure, routing information for all of the networks on the Internet was passed into the core gateways. The core gateways processed the information and then exchanged it among themselves using the *Gateway to Gateway Protocol* (GGP). The processed routing information was then passed back out to the external gateways. The core gateways maintained accurate routing information for the entire Internet.

Using the hierarchical core router model to distribute routing information has a major weakness: every route must be processed by the core. This places a tremendous processing burden on the core, and as the Internet grew larger, the burden increased. In network-speak, we say that this routing model does not "scale well." For this reason, a new model emerged.

Even in the days of a single Internet core, groups of independent networks called *autonomous systems* (AS) existed outside of the core. The term "autonomous system" has a formal meaning in TCP/IP routing. An autonomous system is not merely an independent network. It is a collection of networks and gateways with its own internal mechanism for collecting routing information and passing it to other independent network systems. The routing information passed to the other network systems is called *reachability information*. Reachability information simply says which networks can be reached through that autonomous system. In the days of a single Internet core, autonomous systems passed reachability information into the core for processing. The *Exterior Gateway Protocol* (EGP) was the protocol used to pass reachability information between autonomous systems and into the core.

The new routing model is based on co-equal collections of autonomous systems called *routing domains*. Routing domains exchange routing information with other domains using *Border Gateway Protocol* (BGP). Each routing domain processes the information it receives from other domains. Unlike the hierarchical model, this model does not depend on a single core system to choose the "best" routes. Each routing domain does this processing for itself; therefore, this model is more expandable.

The problem with this model is this: how are "best" routes determined in a global network if there is no central routing authority, like the core, that is trusted to determine the "best" routes? In the days of the NSFNET, the *policy-routing database* (PRDB) was used to determine whether the reachability information advertised by an autonomous system was valid. But now, even the NSFNET does not play a central role.

To fill this void, NSF created the *Routing Arbiter* (RA) servers when it created the *Network Access Points* (NAPs) that provide interconnection points for the various service provider networks. A routing arbiter is located at each NAP. The server provides access to the *Routing Arbiter Database* (RADB), which replaced the PRDB. ISPs can query servers to validate the reachability information advertised by an autonomous system.

The RADB is only part of the *Internet Routing Registry* (IRR). As befits a distributed routing architecture, there are multiple organizations that validate and register routing information. The Europeans were the pioneers in this. The Reseaux IP Européens (RIPE) Network Control Center (NCC) provides the routing registry for European IP networks. Big network carriers provide registries for their customers. All of the registries share a common format based on the RIPE-181 standard.

Many ISPs do not use the route servers. Instead, they depend on formal and informal bilateral agreements. In essence, two ISPs get together and decide what reachability information each will accept from the other. They create, in effect, private routing policies. Small ISPs have criticized the routing policies of the tier-one providers claiming that they limit competition. In response, tier-one providers have made the policies public to clarify the basis for the current architecture.

Creating an effective routing architecture continues to be a major challenge for the Internet, and the routing architecture will certainly evolve over time. No matter how it is derived, eventually the routing information winds up in your local gateway, where it is used by IP to make routing decisions.

The Routing Table

Gateways route data between networks, but all network devices, hosts as well as gateways, must make routing decisions. For most hosts, the routing decisions are simple:

- If the destination host is on the local network, the data is delivered to the destination host.
- If the destination host is on a remote network, the data is forwarded to a local gateway.

IP routing decisions are simply table look-ups. Packets are routed toward their destination as directed by the *routing table*.* The routing table maps destinations to the router and network interface that IP must use to reach that destination. Examining the routing table on a Windows Server 2003 system shows this.

---

* This table is also called the *forwarding table*.

Use the route command with the print option to display the routing table. Here is a simple routing table from a small system:

```
C:\>route print

IPv4 Route Table
===========================================================================
Interface List
0x1 ........................ MS TCP Loopback interface
0x10003 ...00 50 ba 3f c2 5e ...... D-Link DFE-530TX+ PCI Adapter
===========================================================================
===========================================================================
Active Routes:
Network Destination        Netmask          Gateway       Interface  Metric
        0.0.0.0          0.0.0.0      172.16.12.1    172.16.12.20      30
      127.0.0.0        255.0.0.0      127.0.0.1        127.0.0.1        1
    172.16.12.0    255.255.255.0    172.16.12.20    172.16.12.20      30
   172.16.12.20  255.255.255.255    127.0.0.1        127.0.0.1       30
  172.16.12.255  255.255.255.255   172.16.12.20    172.16.12.20      30
      224.0.0.0        240.0.0.0   172.16.12.20    172.16.12.20      30
255.255.255.255  255.255.255.255   172.16.12.20    172.16.12.20       1
Default Gateway:       172.16.12.1
===========================================================================
Persistent Routes:
  None
```

The route print command displays the routing table in three sections:

Interface List
Lists the network interfaces used by TCP/IP. In the example, only the loopback interface and a single Ethernet interface are used.

Active Routes
Contains the bulk of the routing table. Active routes are routes that can be updated based on changing network conditions.

Persistent Routes
Lists static routes that have been manually defined by the system administrator and marked as persistent. These routes are not updated to reflect the current status of the network. Persistent routes are not usually required. However, Chapter 4 shows how manually defined routes are created and the effect they have on the routing table.

The routes listed in the Active Routes section are displayed with the following fields:

Network Destination
The value against which the destination IP address is matched.

Netmask
The address mask used to match an IP address to the value shown in the Network Destination field.

Gateway
> The router used to reach the specified destination.

Interface
> The name of the network interface used by the route.

Metric
> The "cost" of the route. The metric is used to sort duplicate routes if any appear in the table. Beyond this, a dynamic routing protocol is required to make any use of the metric.

Each entry in the routing table starts with a destination value. The *destination value* is the key against which the IP address is matched to determine if this is the correct route to use to reach the IP address. The destination value is usually called the "destination network," although it does not need to be a network address. The destination value can be a host address; it can be a multicast address; it can be an address block that covers an aggregation of many networks; it can be a special value for the default route or loopback address. In all cases, however, the Destination Network field contains the value against which the destination address from the IP packet is matched to determine if IP should use this route.

The Netmask field is the bit mask IP applies to the destination address from the packet to see if the address matches the destination value in the table. If a bit is "on" in the bit mask, the corresponding bit in the destination address is significant for matching the address. Thus, the address 172.16.12.183 would match the second entry in the sample table because ANDing the address with 255.55.255.0 yields 172.16.12.0.*

When an address matches an entry in the table, the Gateway field tells IP how to reach the specified destination. If the Gateway field contains the IP address of a router, the router is used. If the Gateway field contains the address of one of the system's network interfaces, the destination network is a directly connected network and the "gateway" is one of the computer's network interfaces.

The Interface field displays the address of the network interface used for each route. In the example, it is either the Ethernet interface that was assigned the address 172.16.12.20 or the loopback interface, which is always given the address 127.0.0.1. The destination, mask, gateway, and interface define the route.

The remaining field displays supporting information about the route. The Metric field displays a numeric cost associated with the route. The Metric value is only used when a routing protocol is run on the system. For the Windows server administrator, the heart of the routing table is the route, which is composed of the destination, the mask, the gateway, and the interface.

---

* ANDing refers to one way that binary values are manipulated. It means that if a bit is "on" in the first value AND in the second value, the resulting value also has a bit "on" in that location.

The first route displayed in the Active Routes section of this routing table is the *default route*, and the gateway specified in this entry is the *default gateway*. The default route uses one of the reserved network numbers mentioned earlier: 0.0.0.0. The default gateway is used whenever there is no specific route in the table for a destination network address. For example, this routing table has no entry for network 192.168.10.0. If IP receives a datagram addressed to this network, it will send the datagram to the default gateway 172.16.12.1. (The default gateway is also identified with the Default Gateway tag at the end of the Active Routes section.)

The second route displayed is the *loopback route* for the local host. This is the loopback address, mentioned earlier as a reserved network number, which is used to simplify software and reduce network load. Because every system uses the loopback route to send datagrams to itself, an entry for the loopback interface is in every host's routing table. The loopback network is 127.0.0.0. The host address 127.0.0.1 associated with the loopback interface is often assigned the hostname *localhost*.

The third route displayed is the route to the local network (172.16.12.0). The gateway to this network is the Ethernet interface of the Windows system. The last three routes also use the Ethernet interface as their gateway. These three routes are

- A route for the network broadcast address 172.16.12.255
- A route for multicast addresses
- A route for the limited broadcast address 255.255.255.255

Finally, the fourth route is a route to the local host. This Windows system was assigned the address 172.16.12.20. A datagram sent to this address goes through the loopback interface because of the gateway for the fourth route is 127.0.0.1. Without this route, datagrams from the local host addressed to 172.16.12.20 would be sent out over the Ethernet.

All of the gateways that appear in the routing table are on networks directly connected to the local system. In the sample shown above, this means that regardless of the destination address, the gateway addresses all begin with 172.16.12, which is the address of the local Ethernet, or 127.0.0, which is the address of the loopback network. These are the only networks to which *this sample host* is directly attached, and therefore the only networks to which *it* can directly deliver data. The gateways that *this* host uses to reach the rest of the Internet must be on *its* subnet.

In Figure 2-4, the IP layer of two hosts and a gateway on our imaginary network is replaced by a small piece of a routing table, showing destination networks and the gateways used to reach those destinations. Assume that the address mask used for network 172.16.0.0 is 255.255.255.0. When the source host (172.16.12.2) sends data to the destination host (172.16.1.2), it applies the address mask to determine that it should look for the destination network address 172.16.1.0 in the routing table. The routing table in the source host shows that data bound for 172.16.1.0 is sent to gateway 172.16.12.3. The source host forwards the packet to the gateway.

The gateway does the same steps and looks up the destination address in its routing table. Gateway 172.16.12.3 then makes direct delivery through its 172.16.1.5 interface. Examining the routing tables in Figure 2-4 shows that all systems list only gateways on networks to which they are directly connected. This is illustrated by the fact that 172.16.12.1 is the default gateway for both 172.16.12.2 and 172.16.12.3, but because 172.16.1.2 cannot reach network 172.16.12.0 directly, it has a different default route.

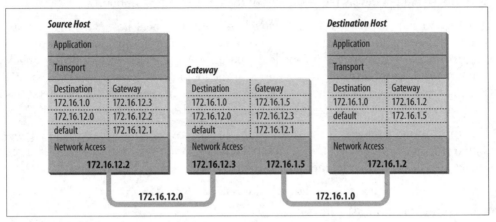

Figure 2-4. Table-based routing

A routing table does not contain end-to-end routes. A route points only to the next gateway, called the *next hop*, along the path to the destination network.* The host relies on the local gateway to deliver the data, and the gateway relies on other gateways. As a datagram moves from one gateway to another, it should eventually reach one that is directly connected to its destination network. It is this last gateway that finally delivers the data to the destination host.

IP uses the network portion of the address to route the datagram between networks. The full address, including the host information, is used to make final delivery when the datagram reaches the destination network.

Address Resolution

The IP address and the routing table direct a datagram to a specific physical network, but when data travels across a network, it must obey the physical layer protocols used by that network. The physical networks that underlay the TCP/IP network do not understand IP addressing. Physical networks have their own addressing

---

* Some routing protocols, such as Open Shortest Path First (OSPF) and BGP, obtain end-to-end routing information. Nevertheless, the packet is still passed to the next-hop router.

schemes. One task of the network access protocols is to map IP addresses to physical network addresses.

A good example of this network access layer function is the translation of IP addresses to Ethernet addresses. The protocol that performs this function is *Address Resolution Protocol* (ARP), which is defined in RFC 826.

The ARP software maintains a table of translations between IP addresses and Ethernet addresses. This table is built dynamically. When ARP receives a request to translate an IP address, it checks for the address in its table. If the address is found, it returns the Ethernet address to the requesting software. If the address is not found in the table, ARP broadcasts a packet to every host on the Ethernet. The packet contains the IP address for which an Ethernet address is sought. If a receiving host identifies the IP address as its own, it responds by sending its Ethernet address back to the requesting host. The response is then cached in the ARP table.

The arp command displays or modifies the contents of the ARP table. To display the entire ARP table, use the arp -a command. Display individual entries by specifying the individual host after the -a argument on the arp command line. For example, to check the ARP table entry for IP address 192.168.0.2 enter:

```
C:\>arp -a 192.168.0.2

Interface: 192.168.0.20 --- 0x10003
  Internet Address      Physical Address      Type
  192.168.0.2           00-e0-4c-9b-99-19     dynamic
```

Check all entries in the table by using with the -a option with no host address. arp -a produces the following output:

```
C:\> arp -a

Interface: 192.168.0.20 --- 0x10003
  Internet Address      Physical Address      Type
  192.168.0.2           00-e0-4c-9b-99-19     dynamic
  192.168.0.3           00-00-c0-9a-72-ca     dynamic
  192.168.0.12          00 10 a4 8b 8b 97     static
```

This table tells you that when this host forwards datagrams addressed to 192.168.0.2, it puts those datagrams into Ethernet frames and sends them to Ethernet address 00-00-c0-9a-72-ca.

Two of the entries in the sample table were added dynamically as a result of ARP queries by the local host. These entries are of the type *dynamic*. The other entry is a static entry added manually by the Windows administrator. We know this because it is of the type *static*.

ARP tables normally don't require any static entries because they are built automatically by the ARP protocol, which is very stable. However, if things go wrong, the

ARP table can be manually adjusted, as indicated by the static entry in the sample table. See Chapter 14 for an example of when a static ARP table entry might be useful.

Protocols, Ports, and Sockets

Once data has been routed through the network and delivered to a specific host, it must be delivered to the correct user or process. As the data moves up or down the TCP/IP layers, a mechanism is needed to deliver it to the correct protocols in each layer. The system must be able to combine data from many applications into a few transport protocols, and then from the transport protocols into the Internet Protocol. Combining many sources of data into a single data stream is called *multiplexing*.

Data arriving from the network must be *demultiplexed*: divided for delivery to multiple processes. To accomplish this task, IP uses *protocol numbers* to identify transport protocols, and the transport protocols use *port numbers* to identify applications.

Some protocol and port numbers are reserved to identify *well-known services*. Well-known services are standard network protocols, such as FTP and Telnet, which are commonly used throughout the network. The IANA assigns protocol numbers and port numbers to well-known services. Officially, *assigned numbers* are documented at the web site *http://www.iana.org*. Windows Server 2003 systems document protocol and port numbers in two simple text files.

Protocol Numbers

The protocol number is a single byte in the third word of the datagram header. The value identifies the protocol in the layer above IP to which the data should be passed.

On a Windows system, the protocol numbers are documented in the *protocol* file.[*] This file is a simple table containing the protocol name and the protocol number associated with that name. The format of the table is a single entry per line, consisting of the official protocol name, separated by whitespace from the protocol number. The protocol number is separated by whitespace from the alias for the protocol name. Comments in the table begin with a #. An example of a protocol file is shown below:

```
C:\>type %SystemRoot%\system32\drivers\etc\protocol
# Copyright (c) 1993-1999 Microsoft Corp.
#
# This file contains the Internet protocols as defined by RFC 1700
# (Assigned Numbers).
#
```

---

[*] This file and some other TCP/IP configuration files are found in the *%SystemRoot%\system32\drivers\etc* directory. *%SystemRoot%* is an environment variable that contains the name of the top-level directory where the operating system files are stored.

```
# Format:
#
# <protocol name>   <assigned number>   [aliases...]   [#<comment>]

   ip        0    IP        # Internet protocol
   icmp      1    ICMP      # Internet control message protocol
   ggp       3    GGP       # Gateway-gateway protocol
   tcp       6    TCP       # Transmission control protocol
   egp       8    EGP       # Exterior gateway protocol
   pup      12    PUP       # PARC universal packet protocol
   udp      17    UDP       # User datagram protocol
   hmp      20    HMP       # Host monitoring protocol
   xns-idp  22    XNS-IDP   # Xerox NS IDP
   rdp      27    RDP       # "reliable datagram" protocol
   rvd      66    RVD       # MIT remote virtual disk
```

The listing above is the contents of the *protocol* file from a sample Windows Server 2003 system. This list of numbers is by no means complete. If you refer to the Protocol Numbers section of the IANA web site, you'll see many more protocol numbers. However, even the limited list shown here contains some protocols that this system doesn't use, but the additional entries do no harm. The protocols table is only used to map protocol numbers to names for programs that reference protocols by name or for programs that wish to display names for protocol number. The protocol numbers are included in the TCP/IP software through header files.

What exactly do the numbers in this table mean? When a datagram arrives and its destination address matches the local IP address, the IP layer knows that the datagram has to be delivered to one of the transport protocols above it. To decide which protocol should receive the datagram, IP looks at the datagram's protocol number. Using this table, you can see that if the datagram's protocol number is 6, IP delivers the datagram to TCP. If the protocol number is 17, IP delivers the datagram to UDP. TCP and UDP are the two transport layer services we are concerned with, but all of the protocols listed in the table use IP datagram delivery service directly. Some, such as ICMP, EGP, and GGP, have already been mentioned. Others haven't, but you don't need to be concerned with the minor protocols in order to configure and manage a TCP/IP network.

Port Numbers

After IP passes incoming data to the transport protocol, the transport protocol passes the data to the correct application process. Application processes (also called *network services*) are identified by port numbers, which are 16-bit values. The source port number, which identifies the process that sent the data, and the destination port number, which identifies the process that is to receive the data, are contained in the first header word of each TCP segment and UDP packet.

Port numbers below 1024 are reserved for well-known services (like FTP and Telnet) and are assigned by the IANA. Well-known port numbers (those below 1024) are considered "privileged ports," which should not be bound to a user process. Ports numbered from 1024 to 49151 are "registered ports." IANA tries to maintain a registry of services that use these ports, but it does not officially assign port numbers in this range. The port numbers from 49152 to 65535 are the "private ports." Private port numbers are available for any use.

Port numbers are not unique between transport layer protocols; the numbers are only unique within a specific transport protocol. In other words, TCP and UDP can, and do, both assign the same port numbers. It is the combination of protocol and port numbers that uniquely identifies the specific process to which the data should be delivered.

On Windows Server 2003 systems, port numbers are listed in the *services* file in the *%SystemRoot%\system32\drivers\etc* directory. There are many more network applications than there are transport layer protocols, as the size of the services table shows. A partial listing of the Windows *services* file follows:

```
# Copyright (c) 1993-1999 Microsoft Corp.
#
# This file contains port numbers for well-known services defined by IANA
#
# Format:
#
# <service name>  <port number>/<protocol>  [aliases...]   [#<comment>]
#

echo            7/tcp
echo            7/udp
discard         9/tcp    sink null
discard         9/udp    sink null
systat          11/tcp   users               #Active users
systat          11/tcp   users               #Active users
daytime         13/tcp
daytime         13/udp
qotd            17/tcp   quote               #Quote of the day
qotd            17/udp   quote               #Quote of the day
chargen         19/tcp   ttytst source       #Character generator
chargen         19/udp   ttytst source       #Character generator
ftp-data        20/tcp                       #FTP, data
ftp             21/tcp                       #FTP. control
telnet          23/tcp
smtp            25/tcp   mail             #Simple Mail Transfer Protocol
time            37/tcp   timserver
time            37/udp   timserver
rlp             39/udp   resource         #Resource Location Protocol
nameserver      42/tcp   name                #Hostname Server
nameserver      42/udp   name                #Hostname Server
nicname         43/tcp   whois
domain          53/tcp                       #Domain Name Server
domain          53/udp                       #Domain Name Server
```

The format of this file is very similar to the *protocol* file. Each single-line entry starts with the official name of the service separated by whitespace from the port number/protocol pairing associated with that service. The port numbers are paired with transport protocol names because different transport protocols may use the same port number. An optional list of aliases for the official service name may be provided after the port number/protocol pair.

This file, combined with the *protocol* file, provides all of the information necessary to deliver data to the correct application. A datagram arrives at its destination based on the destination address in the fifth word of the datagram header. Using the protocol number in the third word of the datagram header, IP delivers the data from the datagram to the proper transport layer protocol. The first word of the data delivered to the transport protocol contains the destination port number that tells the transport protocol to pass the data up to a specific application. Figure 2-5 shows this delivery process.

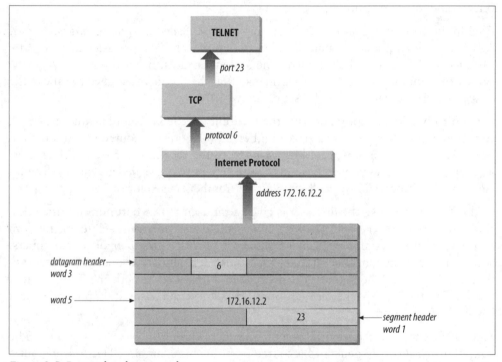

Figure 2-5. Protocol and port numbers

Despite its size, the *services* file does not contain the port number of every important network service. You won't find the port number of every *Remote Procedure Call* (RPC) service in the services file. Sun Microsystems developed a different technique for reserving ports for RPC services that doesn't involve getting a well-known port number assignment from IANA. RPC services generally use registered port numbers, which do not need to be officially assigned. When an RPC service starts, it registers its port number with the *portmapper*, which is is a program that keeps track of the port numbers being used by RPC services. When a client wants to use an RPC service, it queries the portmapper running on the server to discover the port assigned to the service. The client can find portmapper because it is assigned well-known port 111. Portmapper makes it possible to install widely used services without formally obtaining a well-known port. Windows Server 2003 fully supports the portmapper and RPC services.

Sockets

Well-known ports are standardized port numbers that enable remote computers to know which port to connect to for a particular network service. This simplifies the connection process because both the sender and receiver know in advance that data bound for a specific process will use a specific port. For example, all systems that offer Telnet do so on port 23.

Equally important is a second type of port number called a *dynamic allocated port*. As the name implies, dynamically allocated ports are not preassigned. They are assigned to processes when needed. The system ensures that it does not assign the same port number to two processes and also that the numbers assigned are above the range of well-known port numbers, i.e., above 1024.

Dynamically allocated ports provide the flexibility needed to support multiple users. If a Telnet user were assigned port number 23 for both the source and destination ports, what port numbers would be assigned to the second concurrent Telnet user? To uniquely identify every connection, the source port is assigned a dynamically allocated port number, and the well-known port number is used for the destination port.

In the Telnet example, the first user is given a random source port number and a destination port number of 23 (Telnet). The second user is given a different random source port number and the same destination port. It is the *pair* of port numbers, source and destination, that uniquely identifies each network connection. The destination host knows the source port because it is provided in both the TCP segment header and the UDP packet header. Both hosts know the destination port because it is a well-known port.

Figure 2-6 shows the exchange of port numbers during the TCP handshake. The source host randomly generates a source port, in this example 3044. It sends out a segment with a source port of 3044 and a destination port of 23. The destination host receives the segment, and responds back using 23 as its source port and 3044 as its destination port.

The combination of an IP address and a port number is called a *socket*. A socket uniquely identifies a single network process within the entire Internet. Sometimes the terms "socket" and "port number" are used interchangeably. In fact, well-known

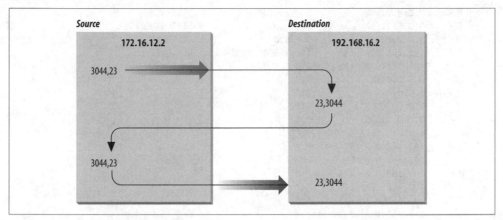

Source 172.16.12.2 Destination 192.168.16.2

3044,23 → 23,3044

3044,23 → 23,3044

Figure 2-6. Passing port numbers

services are frequently referred to as "well-known sockets." In the context of this discussion, a "socket" is the *combination* of an IP address and a port number. A pair of sockets, one socket for the receiving host and one for the sending host, define the connection for connection-oriented protocols such as TCP.

Let's build on the example of dynamically assigned ports and well-known ports. Assume a user on host 172.16.12.2 uses Telnet to connect to host 192.168.16.2. Host 172.16.12.2 is the source host. The user is dynamically assigned a unique port number—3382. The connection is made to the Telnet service on the remote host that is, according to the standard, assigned well-known port 23. The socket for the source side of the connection is 172.16.12.2:3382 (IP address 172.16.12.2 plus port number 3382). For the destination side of the connection, the socket is 192.168.16.2:23 (address 192.168.16.2 plus port 23). The port of the destination socket is known by both systems because it is a well-known port. The port of the source socket is known by both systems, because the source host informed the destination host of the source socket when the connection request was made. The socket pair is therefore known by both the source and destination computers. The combination of the two sockets uniquely identifies this connection; no other connection in the Internet has this socket pair.

Use the `netstat` command to see the active sockets on your Windows Server 2003 system. The -a command-line argument directs the `netstat` command to show the active sockets and the -n argument shows the sockets as numeric IP addresses and ports. Here is an example:

```
D:\>netstat -na

Active Connections

  Proto  Local Address          Foreign Address        State
  TCP    0.0.0.0:135            0.0.0.0:0              LISTENING
  TCP    0.0.0.0:445            0.0.0.0:0              LISTENING
```

```
TCP     0.0.0.0:1025        0.0.0.0:0               LISTENING
TCP     0.0.0.0:1026        0.0.0.0:0               LISTENING
TCP     0.0.0.0:1029        0.0.0.0:0               LISTENING
TCP     192.168.0.20:135    192.168.0.12:32802     ESTABLISHED
TCP     192.168.0.20:139    0.0.0.0:0               LISTENING
UDP     0.0.0.0:445         *:*
UDP     0.0.0.0:500         *:*
UDP     0.0.0.0:1027        *:*
UDP     0.0.0.0:4500        *:*
UDP     127.0.0.1:123       *:*
UDP     192.168.0.20:67     *:*
UDP     192.168.0.20:68     *:*
UDP     192.168.0.20:123    *:*
UDP     192.168.0.20:137    *:*
UDP     192.168.0.20:138    *:*
UDP     192.168.0.20:2535   *:*
```

This sample server has active TCP sockets and UDP sockets, as shown by the values in the Proto field of the netstat output. The Local Address column shows the sockets on which the server is actively listening for inbound traffic or on which it is actively communicating with a remote host. When the IP address in the Local Address field is 0.0.0.0, it means the server is listening on every address assigned to the local system's network interfaces. Note that even if the IP address of the Local Address is 0.0.0.0, a specific port number is always used. The port number maps to the specific application protocol that services the socket. When a specific IP address is displayed in the Local Address, it means the local system will only accept traffic for the socket on the network interface that is assigned that specific address.

In the Foreign Address column, 0.0.0.0:0 means that input from any port or any address is accepted, while a specific address or port means that only traffic originating at that specific host or port will be accepted. Notice that UDP uses *:* instead of 0.0.0.0:0 in this column when UDP will accept input from any port on any host. The different format is used to clearly indicate that UDP is not a connection-oriented protocol and that no connection to the remote address will be made. For the same reason, UDP does not maintain any connection state and therefore the State column is unused for the UDP section of the output. TCP does maintain state. The output shows that most of the sockets are listening for connections and that one connection is currently established. Notice that the connection is between port 135 on the local host and port 32802 on a remote host. Further, notice that 135 is still listening for connections. The well-known port, 135 in this case, is free to listen for more connections even though a connection already exists that uses that well-known port, because it is the pair of socket that define a connection, not the well-known port.

This netstat example illustrates how sockets are used on your system and how you can view them in action. There is much more about the netstat command in Chapter 14.

Summary

This chapter showed how data moves through the global Internet from one specific process on the source computer to a single cooperating process on the other side of the world. TCP/IP uses globally unique addresses to identify any computer on the Internet. It uses protocol numbers and port numbers to uniquely identify a single process running on that computer.

Routing directs the datagrams destined for a remote process through the maze of the global network. Routing uses part of the IP address to identify the destination network. Every system maintains a routing table that describes how to reach remote networks. The routing table usually contains a default route that is used if the table does not contain a specific route to the remote network. A route only identifies the next computer along the path to the destination. TCP/IP uses hop-by-hop routing to move datagrams one step closer to the destination until the datagram finally reaches the destination network.

At the destination network, final delivery is made by using the full IP address (including the host part) and converting that address to a physical layer address. An example of the type of protocol used to convert IP addresses to physical layer addresses is Address Resolution Protocol (ARP). It converts IP addresses to Ethernet addresses for final delivery.

The first two chapters described the structure of the TCP/IP protocol stack and the way in which it moves data across a network. In the next chapter, we move up the protocol stack to look at the type of services the network provides to simplify configuration and use.

CHAPTER 3
Network Services

Some network services provide essential computer-to-computer functions. These differ from application services in that they are not directly accessed by end users. Instead, these services are used by networked computers to simplify the installation, configuration, and operation of the network.

The functions performed by the services covered in this chapter are varied. They include:

- Name service for converting IP addresses to hostnames and hostnames to addresses

- Configuration servers that simplify the installation of networked hosts by handling part, or all, of the TCP/IP configuration

- Electronic mail services for moving mail through the network from the sender to the recipient

- File servers that allow client computers to transparently share files, and print servers that allow printers to be shared

- Directory services that provide a shared repository for information about network objects, such as users, computers, files printers, and other servers

The protocols discussed in this chapter are a combination of:

- Standard TCP/IP protocols, such as Domain Name System (DNS), Internet Message Access Protocol (IMAP), and Dynamic Host Configuration Protocol (DHCP)

- Microsoft network services, such as Windows Internet Name Service (WINS), Common Internet File System (CIFS), and Active Directory

We begin with a discussion of name service. It is an essential service that you will certainly use on your network.

Names and Addresses

RFC 791, *Internet Protocol*, defines names, addresses, and routes as follows:

> A name indicates what we seek. An address indicates where it is. A route indicates how to get there.

Names, addresses, and routes all require the network administrator's attention. Routes and addresses are covered in the previous chapter. This section discusses names and how they are disseminated throughout the network. Every network interface attached to a TCP/IP network is identified by a unique 32-bit IP address. A name (called a *hostname*) can be assigned to any device that has an IP address. Names are assigned to devices because, compared to numeric Internet addresses, names are easier to remember and type correctly. Applications use IP addresses, but names are easier for humans to use.

In most cases, hostnames and numeric addresses can be used interchangeably. A user can ping the PC at IP address 172.16.12.2 by entering:

```
C:\>ping 172.16.12.2
```

or by entering the equivalent command using the hostname associated with that address:

```
C:\>ping pooh.example.com
```

Whether a command is entered with an address or a hostname, the network connection always takes place based on the IP address. The system converts the hostname to an address before the network connection is made. The network administrator is ultimately responsible for names and addresses and the database used to store them.

There are two common methods used to organize computer system names:

Flat namespace
> Uses a simple one-part name to identify each host. Using a flat namespace, each hostname must be unique within the network. For example, once the name *pooh* has been assigned to a host, no other host on that network should be assigned that name.

Hierarchical namespace
> Subdivides the network into multiple named parts called domains. Each hostname must be unique within a domain, but may be duplicated in other domains on the same network. For example, a host named *pooh.example.com* and another host named *pooh.oreilly.com* may exist within the same network—in this case, the Internet.

Originally, both NetBIOS and TCP/IP used a flat namespace. This worked well in the early days of networking, when few networks existed and those that did were seldom

interconnected. In today's environment, however, using a flat namespace is inadequate, for the following reasons:

Limited name availability
    A good computer name is short, easily remembered, and meaningful. In a flat
    namespace, all the good computer names are taken quickly, and you find your-
    self assigning essentially random names to your hosts.

Centralized administration requirements
    In a flat namespace, a centralized naming authority is needed to ensure unique
    hostnames. The central authority assigns every hostname, which can be a slow
    tedious process.

Clearly, something better than a flat namespace is needed. That something is a hierarchical namespace. Just as the Windows directory structure allows you to have
duplicate filenames in different directories, a hierarchical naming structure allows
you to have duplicate computer names in different domains.

Using a hierarchical namespace also minimizes the need for a central administrative
authority. In a hierarchical namespace, administration devolves to the local level. If,
for example, you're the administrator responsible for the domain example.com, you
can name your hosts anything you'd like.

A central naming authority is still needed, but the degree to which it is involved in
the naming process is determined by the extent to which the networks in question
are interconnected. Internet names are centralized at the top level. You cannot, for
example, just decide on your own that your Internet domain will be widget.com or
gadget.org. Official domain registrars are responsible for guaranteeing the unique-
ness of domain names assigned at the top level. On the other hand, private networks
running Microsoft Networking use whatever Windows domain name they please. In
fact, it's a safe bet that quite a few Windows domains are named simply DOMAIN.
This generally causes no naming problems because the like-named domains do not
communicate across the Internet using Microsoft networking protocols. However, it
is best to use a unique hierarchical name for the Windows domain and to base that
name on your DNS domain name, if you have one.

Because both TCP/IP and NetBIOS started with a flat namespace, the original
method of name resolution was to simply look up the hostname in a flat file called a
host table. The file that contains TCP/IP hostnames is *HOSTS,* and the file that contains NetBIOS hostnames is *LMHOSTS*. Now, however, both TCP/IP and NetBIOS
support name servers. The database system used to translate TCP/IP hostnames to
addresses is called *Domain Name System* (DNS). The name server system used for
NetBIOS names is *Windows Internet Name Service* (WINS). We discuss all of these
files and database systems in this chapter. Let's begin by examining host tables first.

The HOSTS File

The *HOSTS* file is a simple text file that associates IP addresses with hostnames. On Windows Server 2003 systems, the file is *%SystemRoot%\System32\Drivers\etc\hosts*. Each table entry in the *HOSTS* file contains an IP address separated by whitespace from a list of hostnames associated with that address. Comments begin with #.

The host table on the workstation *pooh* might contain the following entries:

```
#
# Table of IP addresses and hostnames
#
172.16.12.2      pooh.example.com pooh
127.0.0.1        localhost
172.16.12.1      thoth.example.com thoth www
172.16.12.4      wotan.example.com wotan
172.16.12.3      kerby.example.com kerby
172.16.1.2       kiwi.example.com kiwi
172.16.6.10      thor.sales.example.com thor.sales thor
```

The first entry in the sample table is for *pooh* itself. The IP address 172.16.12.2 is associated with the hostname *pooh.example.com* and the alternate hostname (or alias) *pooh*. The hostname and all of its aliases resolve to the same IP address, in this case 172.16.12.2.

Aliases provide for name changes, alternate spellings, and shorter hostnames. They also allow for generic hostnames. Look at the entry for 172.16.12.1. One of the aliases associated with that address is *www*, which is the generic name most users expect to find when searching for information via the Web. Other commonly used generic hostnames are *ns* for name servers, *mailhost* for mail servers, and *news* for network news servers.

The second entry in the sample file assigns the address 127.0.0.1 to the hostname *localhost*. As we have discussed, the network address 127.0.0.0 is reserved for the loopback network. The host address 127.0.0.1 is a special address used to designate the loopback address of the local host—hence the hostname *localhost*. This special addressing convention allows the host to address itself the same way it addresses a remote host. The loopback address simplifies software by allowing common code to be used for communicating with local or remote processes. This addressing convention also reduces network traffic because the *localhost* address is associated with a loopback device that loops data back to the host before it is written out to the network.

Although the host table system has been superseded by DNS, it is still used in some situations. Some systems have a small host table containing name and address information about the important hosts on the local network as a backup for those times when DNS is not running. Windows Server 2003 systems come with a sample *HOSTS* file containing a single entry for *localhost*.

The old host table system is inadequate for the global Internet for two reasons: inability to scale and lack of an automated update process. We have already addressed the problems with scaling a flat namespace. A flat space simply lacks sufficient unique names and requires too much central administration. There is no way that a flat filesystem could provide adequate service for the enormous number of hosts in today's Internet.

Another problem with the host table system is that it lacks a technique for automatically distributing information about newly registered hosts. Newly registered hosts can be referenced by name as soon as a site receives the new version of the host table. However, there is no way to guarantee that the host table is distributed to a site. The lack of guaranteed uniform distribution is a major weakness of the host table system. Today, of course, the host table has been superseded by DNS for all but the smallest applications.

All hosts connected to the Internet necessarily use DNS because translating names into addresses isn't simply a local issue. The command ping pooh.example.com is expected to work correctly on every host that's connected to the network. If *pooh. example.com* is connected to the Internet, hosts all over the world should be able to translate the name *pooh.example.com* into the proper address. Therefore, some facility must exist for disseminating the hostname information to all hosts on the network. The host table lacks this facility.

TCP/IP hostnames are not the only computer names used by Windows systems. Traditional Microsoft networking is based on NetBIOS, and Windows systems still use a NetBIOS computer name when they need to use a legacy service. These NetBIOS names must be converted to IP addresses when NetBIOS connections are made over a TCP/IP network. The flat file *LMHOSTS* is one method for NetBIOS to IP address resolution.

LMHOSTS

The *LMHOSTS* file looks similar to a *HOSTS* file and functions in a similar way. The difference is that the *LMHOSTS* file maps NetBIOS names to IP addresses, and the *HOSTS* file maps TCP/IP hostnames to IP addresses. A sample *LMHOSTS* file shows how similar these two files look:

```
172.16.6.16    anubis
172.16.6.10    thor
172.16.6.7     theodore
```

Each entry in an *LMHOSTS* file contains an IP address that is separated by whitespace from the NetBIOS name associated with that address. An entry must not exceed a single line and comments begin with the pound sign (#). The *LMHOSTS* file is stored in the *%SystemRoot%\system32\drivers\etc* directory.

The *LMHOSTS* file does have some features that are not supported by the *HOSTS* file. These special commands begin with pound signs (#) so that old Microsoft operating systems that do not understand these commands will treat them as comments, allowing the same file to be used on both new and old Windows systems. The commands are:

#PRE

> Causes the entry to be preloaded into the cache and permanently retained there. Normally entries are cached only when they are used for name resolution and are only retained in the cache for a few minutes. Use #PRE to speed up address resolution for frequently used hostnames.

#DOM:*domain*

> Identifies a Windows server that can validate network logon requests. The *domain* variable is the name of the domain for which this system provides service.

#INCLUDE *file*

> Specifies a remote file that should be incorporated in the local *LMHOSTS* file. This allows a centrally maintained *LMHOSTS* file to be automatically loaded. To provide redundant sources for *LMHOSTS*, enclose a group of #INCLUDE commands inside a pair of #BEGIN_ALTERNATE and #END_ALTERNATE statements. The system tries the various sources in order and stops as soon as it successfully downloads one copy of the *LMHOSTS* file.

The following *LMHOSTS* file contains examples of all of these commands. The first line of the file assigns the IP address 172.16.6.16 to the NetBIOS host *anubis*, which is the domain controller (DC) for the domain *ACCOUNTS*. The #PRE command is combined with #DOM to preload the address of the domain controller. The second line simply assigns the IP address 172.16.6.10 to the NetBIOS name *thor*. Next the file assigns the address 172.16.6.7 to *theodore* and loads that address into the cache with the #PRE command. The #BEGIN_ALTERNATE and #END_ALTERNATE commands enclose the network paths to additional sources of address information. The two #INCLUDE statements define the alternate sources of *LMHOSTS* information. Notice that the address of *theodore*, the system specified in the second #INCLUDE statement, is defined in this file. If a source of *LMHOSTS* information is not in the local broadcast area, the address of that source must be included in the file.

```
172.16.6.16     anubis      #PRE #DOM:ACCOUNTS
172.16.6.10     thor
172.16.6.7      theodore    #PRE
#BEGIN_ALTERNATE
#INCLUDE \\mandy\admin\lmhosts
#INCLUDE \\theodore\admin\lmhosts
#END_ALTERNATE
```

The cache is preloaded during the system boot. Additional information is added to the cache every time the system references the *LMHOSTS* file, but only the entry used to resolve an address is added. When new #PRE entries are added to the

LMHOSTS file they are not cached unless the system reboots or the existing cache is flushed and forced to reload with the `nbtstat -R` command. The `nbtstat -c` command shows the entries that are currently cached.

Like the *HOSTS* file, the *LMHOSTS* file has limited utility. It is worth understanding the structure of these files, both to understand how these network services have evolved and to troubleshoot older systems. However, even for a small network, the flat file has been superseded by a server-based system called Windows Internet Name Service (WINS). We cover WINS later in the chapter. First, let's discuss the Domain Name System (DNS)—the distributed database that converts TCP/IP hostnames to IP addresses.

Domain Name System

The DNS overcomes both major weaknesses of the host table:

- DNS scales well. It doesn't rely on a single large table; it is a distributed database system that doesn't bog down as the database grows. DNS currently provides information on tens of millions of hosts, while fewer than 10,000 were ever listed in the host table.
- DNS guarantees that new host information will be disseminated to the rest of the network as it is needed.

DNS information is disseminated automatically, and only to those who are interested. Here's how it works. If a DNS server receives a request for information about a host for which it has no information, it passes on the request to an *authoritative server*. An authoritative server is any server responsible for maintaining accurate information about the domain being queried. When the authoritative server answers, the local server saves (*caches*) the answer for future use. The next time the local server receives a request for this information, it answers the request itself. The ability to control host information from an authoritative source and to automatically disseminate accurate information makes DNS superior to the host table, even for networks not connected to the Internet.

The Domain Hierarchy

DNS is a distributed hierarchical system for resolving hostnames into IP addresses. Under DNS, there is no central database with all of the Internet host information. The information is distributed among thousands of name servers organized into a hierarchy similar to the hierarchy of the filesystem. DNS has a *root domain* at the top of the domain hierarchy that is served by a group of name servers called the *root servers*.

Directly under the root domain are the *top-level domains*. There are two basic types of top-level domains—geographic and organizational. Geographic domains have been set aside for each country in the world and are identified by a two-letter country code. Thus, this type of domain is called a *country code top-level domain* (ccTLD). For example, the ccTLD for the United Kingdom is *.uk*, for Japan it is *.jp*, and for the United States it is *.us*. When *.us* is used as the top-level domain, the second-level domain is usually a state's two-letter postal abbreviation (e.g., *.wy.us* for Wyoming). U.S. geographic domains are usually used by state governments and K–12 schools but are not widely used for other hosts.

Within the United States, the most popular top-level domains are organizational— that is, membership in a domain is based on the type of organization (commercial, military, etc.) to which the system belongs.[*] These domains are called *generic top-level domains* or *general-purpose top-level domains* (gTLDs). The official generic top-level domains are:

com
> Commercial organizations

edu
> Educational institutions

gov
> Government agencies

mil
> Military organizations

net
> Network support organizations, such as network operation centers

int
> International governmental or quasi-governmental organizations

org
> Organizations that don't fit in any of the above, such as non-profit organizations

aero
> Organizations involved in the air-transport industry

biz
> Businesses

coop
> Cooperatives

museum
> Museums

pro
> Professionals, such as doctors and lawyers

---

[*] There is no relationship between the organizational and geographic domains in the United States. Each system belongs to either an organizational domain *or* a geographical domain, not both.

info
> Sites providing information

name
> Individuals

There are currently 14 gTLDs. The first seven domains in the list (*com*, *edu*, *gov*, *mil*, *net*, *int*, and *org*) have been part of the domain system since the beginning. The last seven domains in the list (*aero*, *biz*, *coop*, *museum*, *pro*, *info*, and *name*) were added in 2000 to increase the number of top-level domains. One motivation for creating the new gTLDs is the huge size of the *com* domain. It is so large that it is difficult to maintain an efficient *com* database. Whether or not these new gTLDs will be effective in drawing registrations away from the *com* domain remains to be seen.

Figure 3-1 illustrates the domain hierarchy by using six of the original organizational top-level domains. At the top is the root. Directly below the root domain are the top-level domains. The root servers only have complete information about the top-level domains. No servers, not even the root servers, have complete information about all domains, but the root servers have pointers to the servers for the second-level domains.* So while the root servers may not know the answer to a query, they know whom to ask.

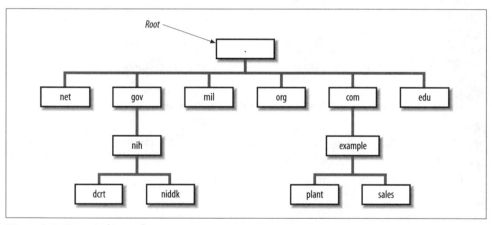

Figure 3-1. Domain hierarchy

Creating Domains and Subdomains

Several domain name registrars have been authorized by the *Internet Corporation for Assigned Names and Numbers* (ICANN), which is a non-profit organization that was formed to take over the responsibility for allocating domain names and IP addresses,

---

* Figure 3-1 shows two second-level domains: *nih* under *gov* and *example* under *com*.

which was previously handled by the U.S. government. ICANN has authorized these registrars to allocate domains. To obtain a domain, apply to a registrar for authority to create a domain under one of the top-level domains. Once the authority to create a domain is granted, you can create additional domains, called *subdomains*, under your domain. Let's look at how this works for an imaginary network.

Our company is a commercial profit-making (we hope) enterprise. It clearly falls into the *com* domain. We apply to the registrar for authority to create a domain named *example* within the *com* domain. If you plan to provide your own name service, which we do, the request for the new domain contains the hostnames and addresses of at least two servers that will provide name service for the new domain. When the registrar approves the request, it adds pointers in the *com* domain to our domain's name servers. Now when queries are received by the root servers for the *example.com* domain, the queries are referred to the new name servers.

The registrar's approval grants us complete authority over our new domain. Any registered domain has authority to divide its domain into subdomains. Our imaginary company can create separate domains for the sales organization (*sales.example.com*) and for the production facility (*plant.example.com*). This is done without consulting the registrar or any other "higher" authority. The decision to add additional subdomains is completely up to the local domain administrator.

A new subdomain becomes accessible when pointers to the servers for the new domain are placed in the domain above it (see Figure 3-1). Remote servers cannot locate the *example.com* domain until a pointer to its server is placed in the *com* domain. Likewise, the subdomains *sales* and *plant* cannot be accessed until pointers to them are placed in *example.com*. The DNS database record that points to the name servers for a domain is the name server record. This record contains the name of the domain and the name of the host that is a server for that domain. Chapter 6 discusses the actual DNS database and how it is configured on a Windows Server 2003 system. For now, let's just think of these records as pointers.

Figure 3-2 illustrates how the NS records are used as pointers. A local server has a request to resolve *mandy.sales.example.com* into an IP address. The server has no information on *example.com* in its cache, so it queries a root server (*a.root-servers.net* in our example) for the address. The root server replies with an NS record that points to *komodo.example.com* as the source of information on *example.com*. The local server queries *komodo*, which in turn points to *jamis.sales.example.com* as the server for *sales.example.com*. The local server then queries *jamis.sales.example.com*, and finally receives the desired IP address. The local server caches the A (address) record and each of the NS records. The next time it has a query for *mandy.sales.example.com*, it will answer the query itself. And the next time the server has a query for other information in the *example.com* domain, it will go directly to *komodo* without involving a root server.

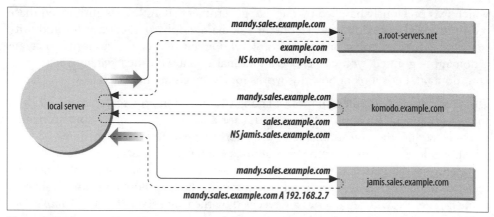

Figure 3-2. Nonrecursive query

Each remote server in Figure 3-2 performs a *nonrecursive query*. In a nonrecursive query, the remote server tells the source of the query whom to ask next. The source of the query must follow the pointers itself. In a *recursive query*, the server follows the pointers and returns the final answer to the source of the query. In the figure, the local server is performing a recursive query. The root servers generally perform only nonrecursive searches.

Domain Names

Domain names reflect the domain hierarchy. Domain names are written from most specific (a hostname) to least specific (a top-level domain), with each part of the domain name separated by a dot. The root domain is identified by a single dot, i.e., the root name is a null name written simply as ".".

A *fully qualified domain name* (FQDN) starts with a specific host and ends with a top-level domain. *pooh.example.com.* is the FQDN of PC *pooh*, in the *example* domain, of the *com* top-level domain.

Domain names are not always written as fully qualified domain names. Sometimes domain names are written relative to a *default domain* in the same way that filenames are written relative to the current (default) working directory. DNS adds the default domain to the user input when constructing the query for the name server. For example, if the default domain is *example.com*, a user can omit the *example.com* extension for any hostnames in that domain. *thoth.example.com* could be addressed simply as *thoth*. DNS adds the default domain *example.com*.

On Windows Server 2003 systems the extension is added to a hostname request unless it ends with a dot, in other words, is qualified out to the root. For example, assume that there is a host named *thor* in the subdomain *sales* of the *example.com* domain. Further, assume that the default domain of the local host has been set to *example.com*. *thor.sales* does not end with a dot, so *example.com* is added to it giving the domain name *thor.sales.example.com*. The sample that follows is from a system running Windows Server 2003.

```
C:\>ping thor.sales

Pinging thor.sales.example.com [172.16.6.10] with 32 bytes of data:

Reply from 172.16.6.10: bytes=32 time=3ms TTL=64
Reply from 172.16.6.10: bytes=32 time<1ms TTL=64
Reply from 172.16.6.10: bytes=32 time<1ms TTL=64
Reply from 172.16.6.10: bytes=32 time<1ms TTL=64

Ping statistics for 172.16.6.10:
    Packets: Sent = 4, Received = 4, Lost = 0 (0% loss),
Approximate round trip times in milli-seconds:
    Minimum = 0ms, Maximum = 3ms, Average - 0ms
```

How the default domain is used and how queries are constructed varies depending on the operating system. It can even vary by release level. For this reason, you should exercise caution when embedding a hostname in a program. Only a fully qualified domain name or an IP address is immune from changes in the name server software.

DNS Resolver and Server

DNS software is conceptually divided into two components—a resolver and a name server. The *resolver* is the software that forms the query; it asks the questions. The name server is the process that responds to the query; it answers the questions.

All computers resolve hostnames, but not all computers act as a name server. A computer that does not run a local name server process and relies on other systems for all name service answers is called a *resolver-only* system. Resolver-only configurations are common on single-user systems. Most PCs run resolver-only configurations.

Name servers are classified differently depending on how they are configured. There are three main categories of name servers:

Primary
> The *primary server*, or *master server*, is the server from which all data about a domain is derived. The primary server loads the domain's information directly from a local disk file. Primary servers are *authoritative*, meaning they have complete information about their domain and their responses are always accurate. Traditionally, there is only one primary server for a domain.

Secondary
> Secondary servers transfer the entire domain database from the primary server. A particular domain's database file is called a *zone file*; copying this file to a secondary server is called a *zone file transfer*. A secondary server, also called a *slave server*, assures that it has current information about a domain by periodically

transferring the domain's zone file. Secondary servers are also authoritative for their domain.

Caching-only

Caching-only servers get the answers to all name service queries from other name servers. Once a caching server has received an answer to a query, it caches the information and uses it in the future to answer queries itself. Most name servers cache answers and use them in this way. What makes the caching-only server unique is that this is the only technique it uses to build its domain database. Caching servers are *nonauthoritative*, meaning that their information is secondhand and incomplete, though usually accurate.

The relationship between the different types of servers is an advantage that DNS has over the host table for most networks, even very small networks. Under DNS, the primary server provides central control of the hostname information, while the secondary servers provide redundant servers and database replication. Caching-only servers reduce load on the authoritative servers, and maintain only the information actually requested by their users. An automatically distributed, centrally controlled database is an advantage for a network of any size.

Windows Server 2003 takes this a step further by offering *Active Directory Integrated DNS*, which uses the replication features of Active Directory to replicate the DNS database. The replication features of Active Directory make it possible to have multiple master servers for each domain. Traditional DNS replication is from a single primary server to multiple secondary servers. Active Directory allows replication from any domain controller to any domain controller. If those domain controllers are also DNS servers running Active Directory–integrated DNS, any changes made to the DNS database on any server can be replicated to all other servers.

Chapter 6 discusses the configuration of all types of traditional DNS servers. Chapter 7 covers Active Directory Integrated DNS.

Windows Internet Name Service

Historically, Microsoft Networking meant small, peer networks running NetBIOS. NetBIOS and the associated *NetBIOS Extended User Interface protocol* (NetBEUI) were designed with small networks in mind. It was never intended to function in a large-scale network environment, let alone in a TCP/IP internetworking environment. The NetBIOS and NetBEUI protocols are only suitable for LAN applications. They cannot be used by themselves for a WAN or an enterprise network because they are nonroutable protocols and they depend on an underlying broadcast medium. What do these two limitations mean?

Nonroutable

The protocol cannot be passed through routers. Packets can only be passed on a single physical network. The protocol has no associated routing protocol and no independent address structure. It depends completely on the underlying physical network address, which limits it to a single physical network.

Broadcast-dependent

The protocol depends on an underlying network that supports physical layer broadcasts. It cannot be used over serial lines, point-to-point networks, or Internets built from dissimilar physical networks.

Originally, Windows systems depended on broadcasting to register its NetBIOS name. When a system first joins the network, it broadcasts a *name registration request* packet. The packet contains the proposed NetBIOS name that identifies the system. If another computer on the network already uses this name, it responds to the broadcast with a *negative name registration response* packet. If the new node does not receive any negative responses to its broadcast, it uses the name as its identifier.

The name is literally used as the node's "address." The source and destination fields of a NetBIOS frame contain the names of the source and destination computers. Therefore, if a computer named *kerby* sends a frame to a system named *thoth*, the source address is kerby, and the destination address is thoth.

This naming scheme has some advantages. For one, it is intuitive. Most people prefer to identify things by names instead of by numbers, and NetBIOS names can be descriptive, for example, *hpprinter*. Each system is automatically self-registering. The scheme requires no central name authority or name server. However, this scheme does not scale well. Each name must be broadcast to every node on the network, which is difficult in a large network, and each name must be unique throughout the network. With no central name authority and no hierarchical name structure, it is difficult to maintain unique names on large networks. This is clearly an inadequate scheme for a large enterprise network. When Microsoft decided to extend their networking to encompass the enterprise, they implemented NetBIOS-over-TCP/IP (NetBT) as defined in the Internet standards:

RFC 1001 - Protocol standard for a NetBIOS service on a TCP/UDP transport: Concepts and methods

This RFC provides an overview of NetBIOS over TCP/IP protocols, focusing on underlying concepts rather than on implementation details.

RFC 1002 - Protocol standard for a NetBIOS service on a TCP/UDP transport: Detailed specifications

This RFC defines the detailed implementation issues for NetBIOS over TCP/IP, including packet definitions, protocols, and so forth.

There are, of course, complications. Encapsulating NetBIOS inside IP datagrams reduces the performance and increases the complexity of the protocol. Both protocols require some level of configuration. Additionally, computers using NetBT must have some method for mapping NetBIOS computer names, which are the addresses of a NetBIOS network, to the IP addresses of a TCP/IP network. Windows can resolve NetBIOS computer names to IP addresses using IP broadcast, the *LMHOSTS* file, or the WINS NetBIOS name server (NBNS). NetBIOS network nodes are classified by the name resolution method they use. The node types are:

B-node

Stands for broadcast-node and depends entirely on IP broadcasts to resolve names. A b-node client broadcasts IP packets that contain a message that says something like, "Is there a computer on this network with the following NetBIOS name? If so, please send me your IP address." If a host hears its own NetBIOS name in such a broadcast, it returns its IP address to the source IP address of the broadcast packet.

P-node

Stands for point-to-point-node or peer-to-peer-node, and uses point-to-point communication with a name server to resolve names. A p-node directly queries the WINS NBNS when it needs the IP address associated with a NetBIOS name. The biggest problem with using p-node is that it introduces a single point of failure. If the server fails, no clients that depend on it can communicate until the problem has been resolved.

M-node

Stands for mixed-node. An m-node client first uses an IP broadcast to resolve the name, and then, if necessary, it asks the WINS server to resolve the address. The m-node attempts to solve the problems associated with b-node and p-node by combining these two earlier methods. The biggest problem with m-node is that it uses the least preferred address resolution method (broadcasting) first.

H-node

Stands for hybrid-node. An h-node client first attempts to resolve the address using the name server. If the name server is unavailable, or if the name in question is not registered in that name server's database, the client then uses IP broadcast to resolve the name.

Windows supports all of these modes. However, h-node is generally preferred and is the method that's used by default when a WINS server is installed and the clients are WINS-enabled. Our discussions assume that h-node is being used.

WINS Name Registration and Name Resolution

The two sides of the naming coin are called *name registration* and *name resolution*. NetBIOS name registration provides each computer with a unique computer name. A computer normally registers its name when it boots. NetBIOS name resolution maps a computer name to a numeric IP address.

Registering, renewing, and releasing NetBIOS names

A WINS client registers its NetBIOS computer name with the WINS server in the following manner:

1. The WINS client sends the WINS server a *name registration request* UDP packet that includes the NetBIOS name by which the client wishes to be known.

2. The WINS server that receives the name registration request packet examines its database. If the requested name is not already in use, a database entry that includes the NetBIOS computer name, the associated IP address, and a unique incremental version number is created. The WINS server then sends a *positive name registration response* packet to the client to notify the client that the NetBIOS name has been registered successfully.

3. If the requested NetBIOS name is already registered to a different IP address, the WINS server sends a challenge to the IP address associated with the current entry to determine if a host will actually respond. If a host does respond, the WINS server sends a *negative name registration response* packet to the client that submitted the name registration request packet to inform it that the NetBIOS name it wants to use is already in use by another host. The client must then begin the registration process over again using a different name.

Once a client has successfully registered a name, the client has two responsibilities. First, when it receives an IP broadcast name query packet addressed to its NetBIOS name, it must respond with a *positive name query response* packet that includes its IP address. Simply put, it must provide name resolution for b-node clients. Second, the client must generate a negative name registration response packet whenever it receives an IP broadcast name registration request that contains its own NetBIOS computer name to prevent any other client on the local subnet from registering a duplicate NetBIOS computer name.

Periodically WINS client computers must renew their name registrations with the WINS server. When a WINS client initially registers its name with the WINS server, the success message the server returns to the client contains a *renewal interval* that tells the client how long it has before it must renew the registration. When half of the renewal interval has expired, the client renews its name for another period equal to the original renewal interval. By default, the renewal interval is set to 144 hours, which means that WINS clients renew their names every three days by default. The renewal interval is one of the four configurable timers described later in this section.

When a computer discontinues using a NetBIOS name, it notifies the server to make that name available for use by other clients. In response to a client's name release packet, the WINS server takes several possible actions:

- When a WINS client is shut down normally, it informs the WINS server that it will no longer be participating on the network. The server marks the database entry for that client as *released*.

- If the original WINS client subsequently reconnects to the network while the database entry is marked as released, the WINS server issues no challenge, honors the client's request for its original NetBIOS computer name, and updates the WINS database to reflect the fact that the client is now connected.

- If, while the database entry is marked released, a client with an IP address different from that of the original client requests the released name, the WINS server immediately grants the request. It need not issue a challenge because the released status of the database entry indicates that the original client has relinquished its claim on the name. This situation commonly occurs when a computer reconnects using a different IP address assigned by DHCP.

- If the released entry remains unused for a specified period (see the WINS timers list that follows), the server marks the entry *extinct*, assigns a new incremental version number, and broadcasts this changed information to the other WINS servers on the network.

These actions take place when a client shuts down gracefully and releases its Net-BIOS name. If a WINS client is not shut down properly, for example, when the power fails or someone simply powers down the computer, the WINS server is not aware that the client is no longer participating on the network, and accordingly leaves its associated database entry marked as *active*. Subsequent attempts to register the NetBIOS name cause the WINS server to issue a challenge to the registered owner of the name because the server believes that the name is already in use. The challenge fails and the WINS server is free to reassign that name to the requesting client because the original client is no longer active.

WINS defines four configurable timers that directly relate to the renewal and release of NetBIOS names. These timers are as follows:

Renewal interval
> Specifies how frequently a WINS client must reregister its name with the WINS server

Extinction interval
> Specifies the amount of time the WINS server will wait before marking a released name extinct

Extinction timeout
> Specifies the amount of time an entry marked extinct will be kept in the WINS database before it is deleted

Verify interval
> Specifies how often the WINS server must revalidate active names that originated on a remote WINS server and were replicated to the local WINS server

Resolving a NetBIOS name

An h-node WINS client attempts to resolve a NetBIOS name to an IP address in the following manner:

1. If the WINS client cannot resolve the name from its local cache, it sends a *name query request* directly to the WINS server. The name query request is a UDP packet that contains the NetBIOS name of the computer to be resolved. In response to a name query request, the WINS server returns the IP address that the WINS database maps to the NetBIOS name provided by the client. The client then uses that IP address to establish a session directly with the target computer.

2. If the WINS query fails, the client sends an IP broadcast packet containing a name query request. If the target computer is on the same subnet, it returns its IP address to the querying computer and a direct session is established.

3. If the IP broadcast name query request fails to return an IP address, the client examines its local *LMHOSTS* file and, if the local *LMHOSTS* contains an #INCLUDE statement pointing to a remote *LMHOSTS* file on a server, it examines the remote *LMHOSTS* file as well.

NetBIOS is closely associated with Windows file and printer sharing. The Windows file and printer sharing protocols are described next.

SMB and CIFS

NetBIOS networks have been traditionally used for file and printer sharing. The Windows file and printer sharing protocol is *Server Message Block* (SMB) protocol. For Microsoft Windows NT 4.0, Microsoft extended and updated SMB and rechristened it the *Common Internet File System* (CIFS). The added features provided by CIFS include the following:

- CIFS supports all of the file and printer sharing capabilities of SMB, and it extends them to support *Andrew File System* (AFS)–style referrals.[*] CIFS calls this support the *Distributed File System* (DFS).

- CIFS also frees file and printer sharing from dependence on NetBIOS. Traditionally, SMB relies on NetBIOS running over some transport protocol—TCP or

---

[*] AFS was developed at Carnegie Mellon University. It was commercialized under the name Transarc.

NetBEUI, for example. CIFS removes the dependence on NetBIOS by enhancing SMB so that it can run directly over TCP. This is called *Self Host* and uses TCP port 445. When SMB uses NetBIOS over TCP, the connection takes place on port 139.

There are several steps involved in sharing a file or printer using CIFS. First, the client resolves the server name to an IP address using either the NetBIOS name resolution process when NetBIOS is used, or using DNS when NetBIOS is not used. NetBIOS name resolution and DNS name resolution are both described earlier in this chapter. Using the IP address returned by name resolution, the client establishes a TCP connection to the server on port 139 when NetBIOS is used or on port 445 when Self Host is used.

The client opens the session with an SMB SESSION REQUEST packet and begins negotiating session parameters by sending a NEGOTIATE packet. The NEGOTIATE packet lists all of the SMB dialects supported by the client. Windows Server 2003 supports the following dialects:

PC NETWORK PROGRAM 1.0
This is the SMB core protocol. It is the original SMB protocol.

LANMAN1.0
This is the LAN Manager LANMAN 1.0 protocol. It is the first full version of the LAN Manager protocol.

Windows for Workgroups 3.1a
This is the version of SMB used by Windows for Workgroups Version 1.

NT LM 0.12
This is the version of SMB created for Windows NT.

There are seven other intermediate SMB dialects. However, the range of dialects supported by Windows Server 2003 allows it to provide some support for all versions of Windows.

The server responds to the client's NEGOTIATE packet by sending its own NEGOTIATE REPLY packet. That packet selects the newest dialect that both the client and the server support, and it defines various session parameters.

The client responds with a SESSION SETUP ANDX message that accepts the session parameters and provides authentication information. If everything is acceptable to the server, it responds with its own SESSION SETUP ANDX message that assigns a *User ID* (UID) to the client. The client will use that UID to access files and printers for the remainder of the session.

Using its new UID, the client issues a TREE CONNECT packet that specifies the pathname of the share the client wishes to access. In reply, the server sends a TREE CONNECT RESPONSE, which assigns a *Tree Identifier* (TID) for the requested share. The TID identifies the share and the permissions associated with the share.

Using the UID and TID, the client can open, read, write, and close files within the share. If the share is a printer, the client can print something by writing to the printer.

File and printer sharing are basic services found on all local area networks. Another service that you are sure to use is electronic mail.

Mail Services

Electronic mail is an important network service because it is used for interpersonal communications. Some applications are newer and fancier. Other applications consume more network bandwidth. Others are more important for the continued operation of the network. But email is the application people use to communicate with each other. It isn't fancy, but it's vital.

TCP/IP provides a reliable, flexible email system built on a few basic protocols. These are: *Simple Mail Transfer Protocol* (SMTP), *Post Office Protocol* (POP), *Internet Message Access Protocol* (IMAP), and *Multipurpose Internet Mail Extensions* (MIME). There are other TCP/IP mail protocols. However, these are the basic mail protocols. Our coverage concentrates on the four protocols you are most likely to use in building your network: SMTP, POP, IMAP and MIME. We start with SMTP, the foundation of all TCP/IP email systems.

Simple Mail Transfer Protocol

SMTP is the TCP/IP mail delivery protocol. It moves mail across the Internet and across your local network. SMTP was originally defined in RFC 821, *A Simple Mail Transfer Protocol*. It runs over the reliable, connection-oriented service provided by Transmission Control Protocol (TCP), and it uses well-known port number 25. Table 3-1 lists some of the simple, human-readable commands used by SMTP.

Table 3-1. SMTP commands

Command	Syntax	Function
Hello	HELO <sending-host>	Identify sending SMTP
From	MAIL FROM:<from-address>	Sender address
Recipient	RCPT TO:<to-address>	Recipient address
Data	DATA	Begin a message
Reset	RSET	Abort a message
Verify	VRFY<string>	Verify a username
Expand	EXPN<string>	Expand a mailing list
Help	HELP[string]	Request online help
Quit	QUIT	End the SMTP session

SMTP is such a simple protocol you can literally do it yourself. Telnet to port 25 on a remote host and type mail directly into the Telnet window using the SMTP commands. This technique is sometimes used to test a remote system's SMTP server, but we use it here to illustrate how mail is delivered between systems.

To Telnet to a specific port, add the port number to the `telnet` command when it is entered at the Windows command prompt. You can use either the numeric value for the port or the name associated with the numeric value in the *services* file. An example of entering the port number at the command prompt is

```
C:\>telnet mail.example.com 25
```

Once the connection is made, SMTP commands can be entered directly in the Telnet window. The sample lines below show the commands, and the responses to those commands, that could be input through the Telnet window:

```
220 Ready at Tue, 28 Jun 2004 17:21:26 EST
HELO pooh.example.com
250 Hello pooh.example.com, pleased to meet you
MAIL FROM:<daniel@pooh.example.com>
250 <daniel@pooh.example.com>... Sender ok
RCPT TO:<tyler@thoth.example.com>
250 <tyler@thoth.example.com>... Recipient ok
DATA
354 Enter mail, end with "." on a line by itself
Hi Tyler!
.
250 Mail accepted
QUIT
221 Delivering mail
```

In the example, mail is manually input from Daniel on *pooh.example.com* to Tyler on *thoth.example.com*. The user input is shown in bold type. All of the other lines are output from the system. The example shows how simple it is. A TCP connection is opened. The sending system identifies itself. The *From* address and the *To* address are provided. The message transmission begins with the DATA command and ends with a line that contains only a period (.). The session terminates with a QUIT command. Very simple, and very few commands are used.

SMTP provides direct end-to-end mail delivery. Direct delivery allows SMTP to deliver mail without relying on intermediate hosts. If the delivery fails, the local system knows it right away. It can inform the user who sent the mail or queue the mail for later delivery without reliance on remote systems. The disadvantage of direct delivery is that it requires both systems to be fully capable of handling mail. Some systems cannot handle mail, particularly small desktop systems or mobile systems such as laptops. These systems are often shut down at the end of the day and are frequently offline. Mail directed from a remote host fails with a "cannot connect" error when the local system is turned off or offline. To handle these cases, features in the DNS system are used to route the message to a mail server in lieu of direct delivery.

The mail is then moved from the server to the client system when the client is back online. The TCP/IP protocols used for this task are POP and IMAP.

Post Office Protocol

There are two versions of POP: POP2 and POP3. POP2 is defined in RFC 937 and POP3 is defined in RFC 1939. POP2 uses port 109 and POP3 uses port 110. These are incompatible protocols that use different commands, but they perform the same basic functions. The POP protocols verify the user's logon name and password and then move the user's mail from the server to the user's local mail reader. POP2 is rarely used anymore. POP3 is the more recent protocol, and it is the one provided by Windows software: both as a client implementation in the *Outlook* mailer and as a server implementation as part of the mail server role available through the Windows Server 2003 *Configure Your Server* wizard.

A sample POP3 session clearly illustrates how a POP protocol works. POP3 is a simple request/response protocol, and just as with SMTP, you can type POP3 commands directly into its well-known port (110) and observe their effect. First Telnet to the POP3 port on a mail server:

```
C:\>telnet mail.example.com 110
```

Next, enter the POP commands directly in the Telnet window. Here's an example with the user input shown in bold type:

```
+OK POP3 Server Process ready
USER hunt
+OK User name (hunt) ok. Password, please.
PASS Watts?Watt?
+OK 3 messages in folder NEWMAIL
STAT
+OK 3 459
RETR 1
+OK 146 octets
 The full text of message 1
 .
DELE 1
+OK message # 1 deleted
RETR 2
+OK 155 octets
 The full text of message 2
 .
DELE 2
+OK message # 2 deleted
RETR 3
+OK 158 octets
 The full text of message 3
 .
DELE 3
+OK message # 3 deleted
QUIT
+OK POP3 Server exiting (0 NEWMAIL messages left)
```

The USER command provides the username, and the PASS command provides the password for the account of the mailbox that is being retrieved. (This is the same username and password used to log onto the mail server.) In response to the logon, the server displays the number of messages in the mailbox, three in our example. The STAT command causes the server to display the number of messages and the total number of bytes contained in those messages. RETR 1 retrieves the full text of message number 1. DELE 1 deletes message 1 from the server. We retrieve and delete messages until there are no more messages to be retrieved and the client ends the session with the QUIT command. Simple! Table 3-2 lists the full set of POP3 commands.

Table 3-2. POP3 commands

Command	Syntax	Function
User	USER *username*	The user's account name
Password	PASS *password*	The user's password
Statistics	STAT	Display the number of unread messages/bytes
Retrieve	RETR *n*	Retrieve message number *n*
Delete	DELE *n*	Delete message number *n*
Last	L*	Display the number of the last message accessed
List	LIST [*n*]	Display the size of message *n* or of all messages
Reset	RSET	Undelete all messages; reset message number to 1
Top	TOP *n l*	Print the headers and *l* lines of message *n*
No operation	NOOP	Do nothing
Quit	QUIT	End the POP3 session

The retrieve (RETR) and delete (DELE) commands use message numbers that allow messages to be processed in any order. Additionally, there is no direct link between retrieving a message and deleting it. It is possible to delete a message that has never been read or to retain a message even after it has been read. However, POP clients do not normally take advantage of these possibilities. On an average POP server the entire contents of the mailbox is moved to the client and either deleted from the server or retained as if never read. Deletion of individual messages on the client is not reflected on the server because all of the messages are treated as a single unit that is either deleted or retained after the initial transfer of data to the client. Email clients that want to remotely maintain a mailbox on the server are more likely to use IMAP.

Internet Message Access Protocol

IMAP is an alternative to POP. It provides the same basic service as POP and adds features to support mailbox synchronization, which is the ability to read individual mail messages on a client or directly on the server while keeping the mailboxes on both systems completely up-to-date. IMAP provides the ability to manipulate individual messages on the client or the server and to have those changes reflected in the mailboxes of both systems.

IMAP uses TCP for reliable, sequenced data delivery. The IMAP port is TCP port 143. Port 220 is used by IMAP 3. IMAP 4 and IMAP 2 use port number 143. IMAP 4 is the only version of IMAP in widespread use, and it is the version supported by Microsoft clients.

Like the POP protocol, IMAP is also a request/response protocol with a small set of commands. The IMAP command set is more complex than the one used by POP because IMAP does more. Yet there are still fewer than 25 IMAP commands. Table 3-3 lists the basic set of IMAP commands as defined in RFC 3501, *Internet Message Access Protocol - Version 4rev1*.

Table 3-3. IMAP4 commands

Command	Use
CAPABILITY	Lists the features supported by the server
NOOP	Literally "No Operation"
LOGOUT	Closes the connection
AUTHENTICATE	Requests an alternate authentication method
LOGIN	Provides the username and password for plain text authentication
SELECT	Opens a mailbox
EXAMINE	Opens a mailbox as read-only
CREATE	Creates a new mailbox
DELETE	Removes a mailbox
RENAME	Changes the name of a mailbox
SUBSCRIBE	Adds a mailbox to the list of active mailboxes
UNSUBSCRIBE	Deletes a mailbox name from the list of active mailboxes
LIST	Displays the requested mailbox names from the set of all mailbox names
LSUB	Displays the requested mailbox names from the set of active mailboxes
STATUS	Requests the status of a mailbox
APPEND	Adds a message to the end of the specified mailbox
CHECK	Forces a checkpoint of the current mailbox
CLOSE	Closes the mailbox and removes all messages marked for deletion
EXPUNGE	Removes from the current mailbox all messages that are marked for deletion
SEARCH	Displays all messages in the mailbox that match the specified search criterion
FETCH	Retrieves a message from the mailbox.
STORE	Modifies a message in the mailbox.
COPY	Copies the specified messages to the end of the specified mailbox.
UID	Locates a message based on the message's unique identifier

This command set clearly illustrates the "mailbox" orientation of IMAP. The protocol is designed to remotely maintain mailboxes that are stored on the server. Despite the increased complexity of the protocol, it is still possible to run a simple test of your IMAP server using `telnet` and a small number of the IMAP commands. First Telnet to the IMAP port on your server:

```
C:\> telnet mail.example.com 143
```

Next, enter the IMAP commands directly into the Telnet window. Here is an example with the user input shown in bold:

```
* OK mail.example.com IMAP4 server ready
a0001 LOGIN craig Wats?Watt?
a0001 OK LOGIN completed
a0002 SELECT inbox
* 3 EXISTS
* 0 RECENT
* OK [UIDVALIDITY 965125671] UID validity status
* OK [UIDNEXT 5] Predicted next UID
* FLAGS (\Answered \Flagged \Deleted \Draft \Seen)
* OK [PERMANENTFLAGS (\* \Answered \Flagged \Deleted \Draft \Seen)] Permanent flags
* OK [UNSEEN 1]
a0002 OK [READ-WRITE] SELECT completed
a0003 FETCH 1 BODY[TEXT]
* 1 FETCH (BODY[TEXT] {1440}
... an email message that is 1440 bytes long ...
* 1 FETCH (FLAGS (\Seen))
a0003 OK FETCH completed
a0004 STORE 1 +FLAGS \DELETED
* 1 FETCH (FLAGS (\Seen \Deleted))
a0004 OK STORE completed
a0005 CLOSE
a0005 OK CLOSE completed
a0006 LOGOUT
* BYE mail.example.com IMAP4 server terminating connection
a0006 OK LOGOUT completed
```

The IMAP command `LOGIN` provides the username and password used to authenticate this user. Notice that the command is preceded by the string A0001. This is a "tag," which is a unique identifier generated by the client for each command. Every command must start with a tag. When you manually type in commands for a test, you are the source of the tags.

IMAP is a mailbox-oriented protocol. The `SELECT` command selects the mailbox that will be used. In the example, the user selects a mailbox named "inbox." The IMAP server displays the status of the mailbox, which contains three messages. Associated with each message are a number of flags. The flags are used to manage the messages in the mailbox by marking them as *Seen*, *Unseen*, *Deleted*, and so on.

The FETCH command downloads a message from the mailbox. In the example, the user downloads the text of the message, which is what you normally see when reading a message. It is possible, however, to download only the headers or flags.

After the message has been downloaded, the user deletes it. This is done by writing the *Deleted* flag with the STORE command. The DELETE command is not used to delete messages; it deletes entire mailboxes. Individual messages are marked for deletion by setting the *Deleted* flag. Messages with the *Deleted* flag set are not deleted until either the EXPUNGE command is issued or the mailbox is explicitly closed with the CLOSE command, as is done in the example. The session is then terminated with the LOGOUT command.

Clearly, the IMAP protocol is more complex than POP. It is just about at the limits of what can be reasonably typed in manually. Of course, you don't really enter these commands manually. The client and the server exchange them automatically. They are only shown here to give you a sense of the IMAP protocol. About the only IMAP test you would ever do manually is to test if the IMAP server is up and running. To do that, you don't even need to log in. If the server answers the telnet you know it is up and running. All you then need to do is send the LOGOUT command to gracefully close the connection.

SMTP is used by every system to send mail. POP and IMAP are used by clients to retrieve mail from servers that collect and store the mail for clients. Microsoft clients can use IMAP when dealing with a non-Microsoft mail server that requires IMAP for downloading mail. However, basic Microsoft software does not use the IMAP features that allow the user to synchronize a local mailbox with a mailbox on the server. Additionally, Microsoft servers do not support the server side of IMAP. POP is still the most widely used software for downloading email.

Multipurpose Internet Mail Extensions

The last email protocol on our quick tour is Multipurpose Internet Mail Extensions (MIME). As its name implies, MIME is an extension of the original TCP/IP mail system, not a replacement for it. MIME is more concerned with what the mail system delivers than it is with the mechanics of delivery. It doesn't attempt to replace SMTP or TCP; it extends the definition of what constitutes mail.

The structure of the mail message carried by SMTP is defined in RFC 822, *Standard for the Format of ARPA Internet Text Messages*. RFC 822 defines a set of mail headers that are so widely accepted that they are used by many mail systems that do not use SMTP. This is a great benefit to email because it provides a common ground for mail translation and delivery through gateways to different mail networks. MIME extends RFC 822 into two areas not covered by the original RFC:

Support for various data types
> The mail system defined by RFC 821 and RFC 822 only transfers 7-bit ASCII data. This is suitable for carrying text data composed of US ASCII characters, but it does not support several languages that have richer character sets and it does not support binary data transfer.

Support for complex message bodies
> RFC 822 does not provide a detailed description of the body of an electronic message. It concentrates on the mail headers.

MIME addresses these two weaknesses by defining encoding techniques for carrying various forms of data, and by defining a structure for the message body that allows multiple objects to be carried in a single message. RFC 2045, *Multipurpose Internet Mail Extensions (MIME) Part One: Format of Internet Message Bodies*, defines two headers that give structure to the mail message body and allow it to carry various forms of data. These are the *Content-Type* header and the *Content-Transfer-Encoding* header.

As the name implies, the Content-Type header defines the type of data being carried in the message. The header has a Subtype field that refines the definition. Many subtypes have been registered. There are eight content types:

text
> Text data. Sample subtypes are *plain*, *richtext*, *enriched*, and *html*.

application
> Binary data. Sample subtypes are *octet-stream*, which indicates the data is a stream of 8-bit binary bytes, *PostScript*, which is Adobe PostScript data, and *msword*, which is Microsoft Word data. More than 90 application subtypes have been registered for different applications.

image
> Still graphic images. Sample image subtypes are *jpeg*, *gif*, and *tiff*.

video
> Moving graphic images. Sample video subtypes are *mpeg* and *quicktime*.

audio
> Audio data. Sample subtypes are *basic*, which means the sounds are encoded using pulse code modulation (PCM), and MP4A-LATM.

model
> Modeling data. Sample subtypes are *vrml* and *mesh*.

multipart
> Data composed of multiple independent sections. A multipart message body is made up of several independent parts. RFCs 2045 and 2046 define four initial subtypes. The primary subtype is *mixed*, which means that each part of the message

can be data of any content type. Other subtypes are *alternative*, meaning that the same data is repeated in each section in different formats; *parallel*, meaning that the data in the various parts is to be viewed simultaneously; and *digest*, meaning that each section is data of the type *message*. Several subtypes have since been added, including support for voice messages (*voice-message*) and *encrypted* messages.

message

Data that is an encapsulated mail message. RFCs 2045 and 2046 define three initial subtypes. The primary subtype, *rfc822*, indicates that the data is a complete RFC 822 mail message. The other subtypes, *partial* and *External-body*, are both designed to handle large messages. *partial* allows large encapsulated messages to be split among multiple MIME messages. *External-body* points to an external source for the contents of a large message body, so that only the pointer, not the message itself, is contained in the MIME message. Some other additional subtypes have been defined. Two examples are *news* for carrying network news, and *http* for HTTP traffic formatted to comply with MIME content typing.

The Content-Transfer-Encoding header identifies the type of encoding used on the data. Traditional SMTP systems only forward 7-bit ASCII data with a line length of less than 1000 bytes. To ensure that the data from a MIME system is forwarded through gateways that may only support 7-bit ASCII, the data can be encoded. Six types of encoding are defined. Some types are used to identify the encoding inherent in the data. Only two types are actual encoding techniques. The six encoding types are listed below:

7bit

US ASCII data. No encoding is performed on 7-bit ASCII data.

8bit

Octet data. No encoding is performed. The data is binary, but the lines of data are short enough for SMTP transport; in other words, the lines are less than 1000 bytes long.

binary

Binary data. No encoding is performed. The data is binary, and the lines may be longer than 1000 bytes. There is no difference between *binary* and *8bit* data except the line length restriction; both types of data are unencoded byte (octet) streams. MIME does not handle unencoded bitstream data.

quoted-printable

Encoded text data. This encoding technique handles data that is largely composed of printable ASCII text. The ASCII text is sent unencoded, while bytes with a value greater than 127 or less than 33 are sent encoded as strings made up of the equals sign followed by the hexadecimal value of the byte. For example: the ASCII form feed character, which has the hexadecimal value of 0C, is sent as =0C. Naturally there's more to it than this—for example, the literal equals sign has to be sent as =3D, and the newline at the end of each line is not encoded. But this is the general idea of how *quoted-printable* data is sent.

base64

Encoded binary data. This encoding technique can be used on any byte-stream data. Three octets of data are encoded as four 6-bit characters, which increases the size of the file by one-third. The 6-bit characters are a subset of US ASCII, chosen because they can be handled by any type of mail system. The maximum line length for *base64* data is 76 characters. Figure 3-3 illustrates this three-to-four encoding technique.

x-token

Specially encoded data. It is possible for software developers to define their own private encoding techniques. If they do so, the name of the encoding technique must begin with "X-". Doing this is strongly discouraged because it limits interoperability between mail systems.

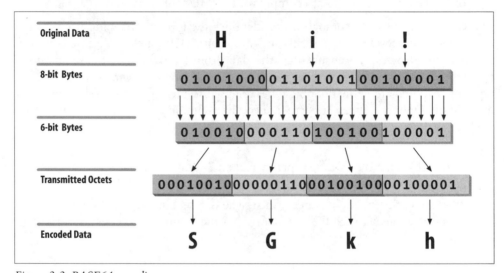

Figure 3-3. BASE64 encoding

The number of supported data types and encoding techniques grows as new data formats appear and are used in message transmissions. New RFCs constantly define new data types and encoding. Read the latest RFCs to keep up with MIME developments.

MIME defines data types that SMTP was not designed to carry. To handle these and other future requirements, RFC 1869, *SMTP Service Extensions*, defines a technique for making SMTP *extensible*. The RFC does not define new services for SMTP; in fact, the only service extensions mentioned in the RFC are defined in other RFCs. What this RFC does define is a simple mechanism for systems to negotiate which SMTP extensions are supported. The RFC defines a new hello command (EHLO) and the legal responses to that command. One response is for the receiving system to return a list of the SMTP extensions it supports, which allows the sending system to know what extended services can be used, and to avoid those that are not implemented on the remote system. SMTP implementations that support the EHLO command are called Extended SMTP (ESMTP).

Several ESMTP service extensions have been defined for MIME mailers. Table 3-4 lists some of these. The table lists the EHLO keyword associated with each extension and its purpose.

Table 3-4. SMTP service extensions

Keyword	Service extension
8BITMIME	Accept 8-bit binary data
CHUNKING	Accept messages cut into chunks
CHECKPOINT	Checkpoint/restart mail transactions
PIPELINING	Accept multiple commands in a single send
SIZE	Display maximum acceptable message size
DSN	Provide delivery status notifications
ETRN	Accept remote queue processing requests
ENHANCEDSTATUSCODES	Provide enhanced error codes

It is easy to check which extensions are supported by your server by using the EHLO command. Telnet to port 25 of your mail server. Enter EHLO in response to the server's greeting. The server will display the list of optional SMTP commands it supports. The specific SMTP extensions implemented on each operating system are different. The purpose of EHLO is to identify these differences at the beginning of the SMTP mail exchange.

ESMTP and MIME are important because they provide a standard way to transfer non-ASCII data through email. Users share lots of application-specific data that are not 7-bit ASCII. Most users depend on email as a file transfer mechanism.

Dynamic Host Configuration Protocol

The powerful features that add to the utility and flexibility of TCP/IP also add to its complexity. TCP/IP is not as easy to configure as some other networking systems, such as NetWare, which can take its address information directly from the hardware interface. TCP/IP is designed to be independent of any specific underlying network hardware, so configuration information that can be built into the hardware in some network systems cannot be built in for TCP/IP. This independence requires that hardware, addressing, and routing information be provided by a person who is knowledgeable about the network environment. Such knowledgeable people are in short supply.

Dynamic Host Configuration Protocol (DHCP) servers make it possible for the network administrator to control TCP/IP configuration from a central point. DHCP makes it possible for one highly skilled technical person to design the configuration for many systems. It also relieves the end user of most of the burden of configuration and improves the quality of the information used to configure systems.

The configuration parameters provided by a DHCP server can include everything defined in RFC 1123, *Requirements for Internet Hosts*. DHCP provides a client with the complete set of TCP/IP configuration values, which are called *options*.

You don't usually need to define all of the configuration options. Don't get us wrong. The parameters are needed for a complete TCP/IP configuration. It's just that you don't need to define values for them. Default values are provided in most TCP/IP implementations, and the defaults only need to be changed in special circumstances. Chapter 6 discusses how you can see the defaults Microsoft sets for the various DHCP options and how you can change those defaults.

The extensive configuration parameters of DHCP cover all facets of the client's TCP/IP configuration, but for most network administrators, automatic allocation of IP addresses is the most interesting feature of DHCP. A DHCP server dynamically assigns IP addresses to DHCP clients for a limited period of time, called a *lease*. The client can return the address to the server at any time, but it must request an extension from the server to retain the address longer than the time permitted. The server automatically reclaims the address after the lease expires if the client has not requested an extension.

Dynamic IP address allocation is useful in a large distributed network where many systems are being added and removed. Unused addresses are returned to the pool of addresses without relying on users or system administrators to take action to return them. Addresses are used only when and where they're needed. Dynamic allocation is particularly well suited to mobile systems that move from subnet to subnet and must be constantly reassigned addresses appropriate for their current network location.

How DHCP Works

A DHCP client broadcasts a UDP packet called a *DHCPDISCOVER* message that contains, at a minimum, a transaction identifier and the client's DHCP identifier, which is normally the client's physical network address. The client sends the broadcast using the address 255.255.255.255, which is a special address called the *limited broadcast address*. The limited broadcast address is used because, unlike the normal broadcast address, it doesn't require the system to know the network number of the network to which it is connected. The client waits for a response from a DHCP server. If a response is not received within a specified time interval, the client retransmits the request.

The server responds to the client's message with a DHCPOFFER packet. DHCP uses two different well-known port numbers. UDP port number 67 is used for the server and UDP port number 68 is used for the client. This is very unusual. Most software uses a well-known port on the server side and a randomly generated port on the client side.* The random port number ensures that each pair of source/destination ports identifies a unique path for exchanging information. A DHCP client, however, is still in the process of booting. It probably does not know its IP address. Even if the client generates a source port for the DHCPDISCOVER packet, a server response that is addressed to that port and the client's IP address won't be read by a client that doesn't recognize the address. Therefore, DHCP sends the response to a specific port on all hosts. A broadcast sent to UDP port 68 is read by all hosts, even by a system that doesn't know its specific address. The system then determines if it is the intended recipient by checking the transaction identifier and the physical network address embedded in the response.

The server fills in the DHCPOFFER packet with the configuration data it has for the client. The network administrator controls the TCP/IP configuration data provided to the client by using the DHCP server configuration. Chapter 5 provides a tutorial on setting up a DHCP server.

As the name implies, the DHCPOFFER packet is an *offer* of configuration data. That offer has a limited lifetime—typically 120 seconds. The client must respond to the offer before the limited lifetime expires. This is done because more than one server may hear the DHCPDISCOVER packet from the client and may respond with a DHCPOFFER. If the servers did not require a response from the client, multiple servers might commit resources to a single client, thus wasting resources that could be used by other clients. If a client receives multiple DHCPOFFER packets, it responds to only one and ignores the others.

The client responds to the DHCPOFFER with a DHCPREQUEST message. The DHCPREQUEST message asks the server to assign the client the configuration information that was offered. The server checks the information in the DHCPREQUEST to make sure that the client got everything right and to ensure that all of the offered data is still available. If everything is correct, the server sends the client a DHCPACK message letting the client know that it is now configured to use all of the information from the original DHCPOFFER packet. If another client is now using the IP address in the DHCPREQUEST packet, or the configuration values in the DHCPRE-QUEST packet are otherwise invalid, the DHCP server returns a DHCPNACK packet to notify the client of that fact. When the client receives a DHCPNACK packet, it restarts the DHCP negotiation process by broadcasting another DHCPDIS-COVER packet. Figure 3-4 shows the normal packet flow when DHCP is used to configure a client.

---

* How and why random source port numbers are used is discussed in Chapter 1.

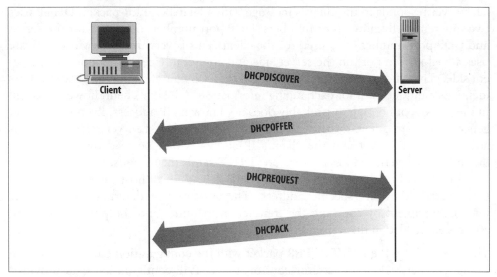

Figure 3-4. DHCP client/server protocol

DHCP simplifies network configuration. Dynamic address assignment is particularly useful. However, dynamic address allocation may not be practical for every system. Name servers, email servers, logon hosts, and other shared systems are always online, and they are not mobile. These systems are accessed by name, so a shared system's domain name must resolve to the correct address. For these reasons, shared systems are usually allocated permanent, fixed addresses. This happens through traditional system administration or through address reservations handled by DHCP. Using DHCP for some systems doesn't mean it must be used for all systems. The Windows DHCP server makes it easy to set aside some addresses for permanent assignment to shared systems while making all of the other addresses available for dynamic assignment to DHCP clients. The Windows DHCP server is covered in detail in Chapter 5.

Dynamic DNS

Dynamic address assignment also has major repercussions for DNS. DNS is required to map hostnames to IP addresses. It cannot perform this job if IP addresses change and DNS is not informed of the changes. To make dynamic address assignment work for all types of systems, *Dynamic DNS* permits a DNS server to be dynamically updated by the DHCP server or client.

Dynamic DNS (DDNS) is defined in RFC 2136, *Dynamic Updates in the Domain Name System (DNS Update)*. DNS uses a five-field format for DNS queries and responses. DDNS replaces three of the five fields in the basic DNS message with three fields that carry the DNS update. A basic DNS message contains the following:

Header

The header section provides administrative data about the message, such as an OPCODE that indicates the type of operation requested and a QR field that indicates whether this is a query or a response.

Question

The question section is the query sent by the client to the server.

Answer

The answer section contains the response sent by the server in answer to the client's query.

Authority

The authority section contains pointers to the authoritative servers for the zone being queried.

Additional

In a response, the additional section contains additional DNS records that help in interpreting or utilizing the answer.

The DDNS message changes the basic format in the following ways:

Header

The header serves the same purpose. The OPCODE for an update is 5. The QR is set to 0 (i.e. query) when the client sends an update to the server, and it is set to 1 (i.e. response) when the server responds to an update. In a response, the RCODE field of the header indicates whether or not the update was successful.

Zone

The zone section replaces the query section of the basic DNS message. The zone section identifies the zone that the client intends to modify.

Prerequisites

The prerequisites section replaces the answer section of the basic message. The prerequisites section defines the conditions, imposed by the client, which must be met before the zone is modified. The DDNS protocol defines five types of prerequisites:

Name exists

Do not perform the update unless at least one database record already exists in the zone for the specified name. Only the name field is significant for the prerequisite, not the record type.

Name does not exist

Do not perform the update if a database record already exists in the zone for the specified name. Again, only the name, not the record type, is significant for this check.

RRset exists with the same name and type

> Do not perform the update unless the database already contains a record of the specified type for the specified name.

RRset exists with the same name, type, and data

> Do not perform the update unless the database already contains a record of the specified type for the specified name containing the specified data.

RRset does not exist

> Do not perform the update if any database records of the specified type already exist in the zone for the specified name.

Update

> The update section replaces the authority section of a basic DNS message. The update section contains the modifications that the client wishes to make. The client can add records to the zone or delete records from the zone. To change a specific record, the client first deletes the old record and then adds a new one.

Additional

> The additional section contains additional resource records that might be helpful in processing the update. For example, if the update is an NS record to delegate a subdomain, the additional section might contain the glue records for the server of that subdomain. In DNS, the server creates the additional section. In DDNS, the client creates this section.

The idea of allowing the client to modify the DNS database may alarm many DNS administrators for whom the zone file is sacrosanct. Clearly, this requires careful configuration of the server and strong authentication of the clients. How Dynamic DNS is configured is covered in Chapter 6.

Microsoft provides a level of integration that goes beyond that provided by basic Dynamic DNS. Microsoft integrates DHCP on both the client and the server with Microsoft DNS, WINS, and Active Directory. To get the maximum benefits from this tight integration, you must run Microsoft operating systems on all of your servers and clients. On many networks that's not a hardship because Microsoft systems dominate those networks, and other non-Microsoft DHCP devices can still participate, although with a somewhat reduced level of integration. Many of the benefits of tightly integrated network services come when Active Directory is used.

Active Directory Basics

Understanding Active Directory is critical. An improperly implemented Active Directory infrastructure can hamper network operations because network resources depend on Active Directory for authentication and authorization. A vulnerable Active Directory infrastructure also makes network resources more vulnerable to attack and compromise. A properly implemented and secured Active Directory infrastructure can provide centralized management and security controls for thousands of computers and millions of users.

The Active Directory is a hierarchical structure. Every object, with the exception of the root, resides within some other object. Active Directory has both a logical and a physical structure. The following terms are used to describe the logical structure:

Container

> The container class defines an object that can contain other objects. The Computers and Users objects are examples of containers.

Domain

> A domain is a logical collection of computers that includes at least one domain controller. The domain creates an autonomous administrative boundary.

Domain controller

> A domain controller stores a copy of the Active Directory database for its domain and specialized software that provides domain services and centralized management capabilities.

Domain naming

> Windows 2000 and Windows Server 2003 domains are named using DNS formatted names consisting of a name and extension. Domains that cannot be accessed via the Internet do not have to use registered DNS domain names; however, care should be taken to use an unregistered or unregisterable DNS name to avoid confusion. Acceptable internal DNS names should use extensions that are not currently utilized on the Internet. If the organization has a registered DNS name it may chose to use this name as the name of a tree root domain in its Active Directory forest, but it does not have to.

Tree

> A tree is a hierarchical collection of domain controllers in the same DNS domain namespace.

Forest

> A Windows forest is composed of one or more Windows domains arranged in one or more trees. Because domains are part of a forest, they can be administered by privileged users who hold forest-wide authority. The forest is created when the first DC in the first domain of the forest is created. This first domain is called the forest root domain. It is also the first domain in the first forest tree.

A forest can contain multiple trees. Figure 3-5 illustrates a multiple-tree forest. Each tree consists of parent and child domains that use the same domain namespace. The two domain names are *nomoore.local* and *nada.local*. The name of each tree is the same as the name of the root domain for that tree; therefore one tree is *nomoore.local* and one is *nada.local*. In this illustration, the *nomoore.local* domain is the forest root domain as well as the parent domain of the *nomoore.local* tree. Therefore, the name of the forest is *nomoore.local*. The *nada.local* domain is the tree root domain of the *nada.local* tree of the *nomoore.local* forest. In a Windows forest composed of a single domain, the name of the forest, the name of the tree, and the name of the domain would be the same.

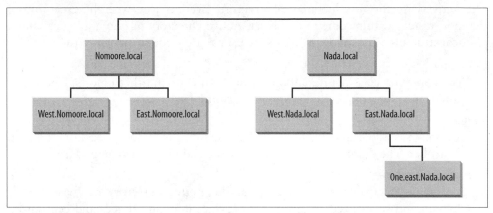

Figure 3-5. A multiple-tree forest

The preceding figure uses unregisterable domain names. You might choose to do this when you do not intend to make domain resources directly available over the Internet. However, the same structure could be built using two registered DNS domain names. Don't be confused by the use of DNS domain names to name Active Directory domains. DNS domains and Active Directory domains are not required to be equivalent. DNS domain names assist in the location of computers on the network by providing a mapping between recognizable names composed of characters, and IP addresses. Active Directory domain names logically identify a collection of Windows computers that can be centrally managed. DNS services manage a database of computer names in a hierarchical structure and provide name resolution services. Active Directory is a database of network infrastructure information for related Windows domains. Active Directory domains use DNS formatted names and DNS services for domain name resolution. A DNS database may store information that can be used to locate Active Directory service locations. Active Directory is dependent on DNS, but Windows DNS services are not dependent on Active Directory, unless they are implemented as Active Directory integrated zones as described in Chapter 7. When implemented as Active Directory integrated zones, DNS zone information is only stored in the Active Directory database: thus if Active Directory is not working properly, DNS services may not be accessible.

Active Directory domains may contain *Organizational Units* (OUs). OUs are containers that subdivide domains; each OU can contain objects such as users, groups and other OUs. Each domain has a single default OU, the domain controllers OU, which by default contains every DC in the domain. OUs cannot contain objects from other forests. OUs are often used to separate users and groups for administrative needs, for example creating OUs to contain objects that belong to different organizational divisions, departments or other functional units. They can also be used to manage computers that perform different roles, such as DNS servers, database servers, Domain Controllers, desktop computers and the like. The administration of objects within an OU can be delegated to groups or individual users. Group Policy objects, collections of security and other administrative elements, can be assigned to specific OUs and used to distribute things such as software and security configuration to computers and users whose accounts exist within the OU. (More information on Group Policy can be found later in this chapter.) User and computer objects can be included in either OUs or other ordinary subdomain Containers, however, users and or computers contained in OUs can be managed via Group Policy and those in ordinary subdomain containers cannot.

While domains and OUs represent logical entities that exist within the forest, *sites* are used to represent the physical structure of the forest. A site is defined as a region of uniformly good network access and is specified by recording in Active Directory the specific subnets used in that region and is usually, therefore, represented by a physical location. Even so, if separate physical locations are connected by a high-speed network, multiple physical locations may be combined into one site. Each site is defined in Active Directory by identifying one or more IP subnets. A site can contain one or more DCs from a single domain and/or one or more DCs from multiple domains. Figure 3-6 is a logical diagram representing a part of the physical site design for the *nomoore.local* forest. Note that the Boston site has domain controllers from both the *nomoore.local* domain and the *east.nomoore.local* domain, while the Seattle site has domain controllers only from the *west.nomoore.local* domain.

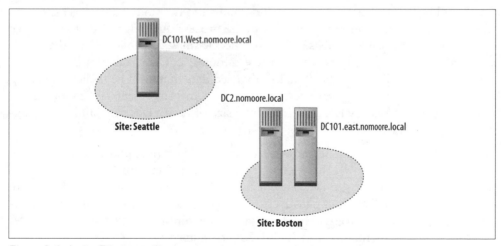

Figure 3-6. Active Directory sites

A new site does not have to be created for each specific physical location. DCs physically located in different cities can belong to the same site. However, high-speed communications are necessary because both authentication and replication use site definitions. For example, during the authentication process, a Windows domain member will determine its site and then attempt to find DCs in that site to use for authentication. This means that a user logging onto the *east.nomoore.local* domain from its location at the Boston site will use the DC located in the Boston site rather than attempt to authenticate across a WAN connection to another DC in the *east.nomoore.local* domain. If all DCs, no matter what their physical location, are located in the same site, authentication processes might traverse the WAN and take longer than usual due to network latency. Replication is also improved because some replication will not have to traverse the WAN.

Active Directory Replication Basics

Replication is the manner in which changes to Active Directory data are updated on DCs and *global catalog* (GC) *servers*. GC servers contain a forest-wide Active Directory database while DCs only contain local domain data. Replication between DCs in the same domain and GCs in the same forest that are located in the same site occurs by default, but it is configurable. Replication between sites requires a *site link*, a defined connection between two sites (more information is in Chapter 7). Replication occurs when a Windows Server becomes a DC and periodically thereafter. When replication is scheduled, it can be scheduled over site links as often as every 15 minutes to as little as once a week. Actual replication frequency depends on the schedule (which represents when the link is available) and the replication period (how frequently replication can occur). During the process, data is not replicated directly between all DCs, but from one DC to another in a predetermined replication topology that efficiently ensures all domains receive modified data. This means that there is a certain amount of latency in the process. A change made to an Active Directory object in the database of a specific DC may be replicated to that DC's assigned replication partners within a few minutes, but may take much longer to fully replicate to all DCs in the domain. Changed data that must be replicated among global catalog servers may take longer because it may represent replication across many more sites. Latency is a function of the size of Active Directory and the configuration of the Active Directory replication topology.

When a change is made in Active Directory the new information does not replicate directly from the DC on which the change was made to every other DC. Instead, replication occurs between the DC on which the change was made and one or more other DCs. These DCs then replicate changes to other DCs and so on until the information is updated appropriately throughout the forest. These *replication routes* (which DCs pass information to which DCs) are defined in the Active Directory *replication topology*. While the Active Directory replication topology can be manually configured, this is not required, nor is it beneficial except in very large environments. The Knowledge Consistency Checker (KCC), a process running on all DCs, creates the replication topology. The KCC runs by default every 15 minutes and creates a topology based on the current connection routes (network connections available between DCs). It ensures that all DCs have at least one connection to another

DC and that the combination of these connections represents a topology in which every DC eventually receives Active Directory changes.

The replication topology is divided into several topologies to account for the complete and appropriate replication of the different types of Active Directory data. For example, all DCs must be able to receive changes to the Schema and Configuration data (more on these data types in the next section), but only DCs within a specific domain should replicate domain-specific data. Likewise, only some DCs within a domain may be authorized to replicate application-specific data. Replication of both domain and forest data between sites must also be considered in the topology creation. Site, domain, and network information in the forest-wide configuration container is used to develop the replication topology. The data being replicated comes from the Active Directory database.

Active Directory Database Basics

When a Windows server becomes a DC, a default Active Directory database (included in the default *ntds.dit* file from the Windows server installation files) is installed. During the process, data is added to the database. If the DC is the first DC in a new domain in an existing forest, the new domain and computer information are added to the forest data and forest data is replicated to the new domain's DC database. If the DC is joining an existing Windows domain, its computer information is added to the domain Active Directory and the data in the domain's Active Directory database is replicated to the new DC.

The Active Directory Schema provides the data definitions for the objects that can exist in the Active Directory database. It is modeled on the International Standards Organization (ISO) directory services X.500 standard. The Schema consists of *object classes* that are defined by a list of *attributes*. Two examples of object classes are *user* and *server*. Attributes are items such as *type* and *common name*. Attributes are defined independently of classes. Hence, both the user class and the server class can contain an attribute that defines their common name or their password, and both classes may contain attributes that are not contained by the other. For example, a *first name* attribute makes sense for a user object but not for a server object. Attributes are classified further according to their use. For example, the user class attributes are *base*, a type that exists for all attributes.

The Schema is extensible, and is often extended by directory-based applications such as Microsoft Exchange. The Windows Server 2003 Schema extends the Windows 2000 Schema with additional classes such as the `inetOrgPerson` class. Classes and attributes added to the Schema cannot be removed. Schema objects are contained in the *Schema* partition of the Active Directory database. The database consists of several partitions or distinct parts, each of which includes a different type of data. Some data is present on all DCs while others are not. Table 3-5 lists the Active Directory database partitions.

Table 3-5. Active Directory database partitions

Partition	Definition	Location
Schema	A copy of the base Active Directory Schema and any extensions added after installation.	Replicated to all DCs in the forest.
Domain	Data specific to the domain such as information on user and computer accounts.	Replicated to all DCs in a domain.
Configuration	Contains the Active Directory topology information including a list of all domains, trees, sites, and the location of domains and global catalog servers.	Replicated to all DCs in the forest.
Application Directory partitions	Partitions that replicate only to specific DCs within the domain. These partitions can hold any type of data except security principles. Security principles are objects such as users and computers that can be assigned permissions on domain resources.	Only Windows Server 2003 DCs can hold Application Directory partitions. There can be multiple application partitions and each is replicated only to the DCs specified by its configuration.

As Table 3-5 makes clear, the Active Directory database is replicated among domain controllers. However, DCs do more than just store the Active Directory database.

Domain Controllers

DCs within a domain are often discussed as if they are exactly alike. They are said to contain replicas of the Active Directory, allow local modification of directory data, and support replication with other DCs. Replication is even defined using a multiple-master model (information can be modified at all DCs and then replicated to all other DCs). However, there are exceptions to this description.

The first DC in the root forest domain is also made a GC server. The GC server performs additional functions. The Active Directory database on a GC server includes domain data from every domain in the forest. The non-GC DC only stores its own domain's data. (All DCs store forest-wide data, such as schema.)

Some Active Directory data can only be managed by specific DCs in the forest that have been assigned *flexible single master operations* (FSMO) roles. These DCs are called *operations masters*. The operations master roles are:

Schema master
>   Controls the management of schema objects. Extensions to the schema must be made at the schema master and are then replicated to all other DCs in the forest. Only a single schema master can exist in the forest. The default location is the first DC created in the root forest domain.

Domain-naming master
>   Controls addition or removal of domains in the forest. The domain naming master is consulted when a new domain is created to avoid naming conflicts. In a

Windows 2000 domain, the domain naming master must be a global catalog server. In a Windows Server 2003, this is not a requirement. Only a single domain naming master can exist in the forest. The default location is the first DC created in the root forest domain.

RID master

Allocates a series of *relative IDs* (RIDs) to each DC in a domain. A RID is assigned to each new user, group, and computer object in a domain as part of the objects *security identifier* (SID). The SID also contains data that represents the domain. This combination of domain information and RID creates a unique SID for each user, group, and computer in the domain. Each domain has one RID master. The default location is the first DC created in the domain.

PDC emulator master

Plays the role of the Windows NT Primary Domain Controller (PDC) when Window NT 4.0 computers are domain members. The PDC emulator is also responsible for synchronization of time with all DCs in the domain and receives replicated password changes preferentially to other DCs in the domain. Each domain has only one PDC emulator master. The default location is the first DC created in the domain.

Infrastructure master

Updates references from its domain's objects to objects in other domains. It compares its information to that in the global catalog. Since the global catalog receives information from all domains, the global catalog information will always be correct. The infrastructure master updates its information to all DCs in its domain. Each domain has one infrastructure master. The default location is the first DC created for the domain.

DCs store, update, and replicate the Active Directory database, and respond to database queries. They also use the database to perform important authentication and authorization tasks.

Authentication, Authorization, and Trusts

Each domain has its own set of user and computer accounts. When a user needs to authenticate or prove its identity on the network, it must locate a domain controller in its own domain. However, access to forest-wide resources, authorization to open, read, write, delete or otherwise manipulate the resource, can be allowed or denied based on the user account or of the Windows groups the user has memberships in. This is possible because in an Active Directory forest every domain trusts every other domain. When a domain trusts another domain it means that accounts in one domain can be assigned access to resources in another domain. Without a trust relationship, accounts from one domain in the forest can only be assigned access to resources that exist on computers that are members of that domain. For example, if Jane has a user account in domain A, and needs access to some files on a server in domain B, and there is no trust relationship between domain A and domain B, Jane must also have an account in domain B to obtain access to the files. When the right kind of trust relationship exists between the domains, Jane can be provided access to the files, and she will not have to use a different account. Trusts in Windows 2000 and Windows Server 2003 domains are:

Kerberos style
> Kerberos is a standard authentication protocol described in RFC 1510 and implemented in Windows 2000 and Windows Server 2003. It is the preferred network authentication technique for users and computers in an Active Directory domain.

Transitive
> When a trust exists between domain A and domain B and a trust exists between domain B and domain C, domain A also trusts domain C.

Two-way
> If a trust exists between domain A and domain B, a trust also exists between domain B and domain A. This means that users in domain A can be assigned access to resources in domain B and users in domain B can be assigned access to resources in domain A. Contrast this to a one-way trust, which may either allow users in domain B, known as the trusted domain, to access resources in domain A, the trusting domain, or vice versa, but not both.

Authentication is the process by which users and systems prove that they are who they claim to be. *Authorization* is the level of privileges granted to an authenticated user or system. *Trust* is the authentication and authorization relationship established between domains.

Users can be authorized special privileges through membership in a security group. These groups can have special administrative roles. Administration of Active Directory including the administration of domains, users, and computers is the responsibility of various administrative roles. These administrative roles, which, because of the central part that Active Directory plays in the administration of various network services, are mentioned in various places in this book, are as follows:

Enterprise Admins
> Forest-level administrators. Members of the *Enterprise Admins* group can administer any domain in the forest. The *Enterprise Admins* group exists only in the root domain in the forest. However, it can contain user members from any domain in the forest. By default, the *Administrator* account belonging to the forest's root domain is its only member.

Schema Admins
> Manage the Active Directory Schema including adding new Schema classes and attributes and changing default ACLs on Schema objects. The *Schema Admins* group exists only in the root domain of the forests. By default, the *Administrator* account is its only member. Extreme care should be taken to limit membership

in this group as the impact of Schema changes is far-reaching in the forest. Many security experts advise removing the *Administrator* account and only adding an account to this group when Schema management is required and approved. This can eliminate possible accidental and some malicious Schema modifications.

Domain Admins

Manage all aspects of a specific domain. A unique *Domain Admins* group is present in each domain.

DnsAdmins

Administer DNS services. A unique domain local *DnsAdmins* group is created in each domain in which DNS is integrated in Active Directory. By default it has no members. (Members of *Domain Admins* and *Enterprise Admins* groups can administer DNS by default.)

Group Policy Creator Owners

Administer Group Policy for the domain. A unique Global group is created for each domain. The *Administrator* account is the only default member.

Account Operators

Members can administer domain user and group accounts. A unique group exists for each domain.

Backup Operators

Members can back up files even if they have no other access permissions to the files. A unique built-in local group exists in each domain with no default members.

Incoming Forest Trust Builders

Members can configure their domain's side of an incoming forest trust or one-way, incoming forest trusts. A unique built-in local group exists in the root domain of the forest with no default members.

Network Configuration Operators

Members have administrative privileges to configure TCP/IP settings for domain controllers in the domain. A unique built-in local group exists in each domain with no default members.

Performance Log Users

Members have remote access to performance logs on domain controllers. A unique built-in local group exists in each domain with no default members.

Performance Monitor Users

Members have remote access to monitor domain controllers using the Performance Monitor tool. A unique built-in local group exists in each domain with no default members.

Printer Operators

Members can manage domain printers. A unique built-in local group exists in each domain with no default members.

Remote Desktop Users
> Member can remotely log on to domain controllers. A unique built-in local group exists in each domain with no default members.

Server Operators
> Members can manage domain controllers. A unique built-in local group exists in each domain with no default members.

Windows Authorization Access Group
> Members have access to the `tokenGroupsGlobalAndUniversal` attribute on user objects. This attribute is a dynamically created list of global and universal group memberships for users. Access to this information is necessary for some applications to function, and access is not broadly granted in Windows Server 2003. Access to this information can be provided by adding an applications service account to this group. A unique built-in local group exists in each domain. Enterprise Domain Controllers group (this group includes all domain controller accounts) is the default member.

While other Windows administrative roles exist, they have only local computer authority and therefore are not included in the previous list. Don't imagine that this is a complete list of the available groups. Also don't confuse groups with group policies. Group policies are our next topic.

Group Policy Basics

Group Policy is used to deliver software installation and configuration settings to selected users and computers with accounts in an Active Directory domain. It is part of a group of management technologies, commonly known as IntelliMirror, available in an Active Directory domain including Windows installer, Folder Redirection, Offline Folders, and Roaming User Profiles. Group Policy consists of a Group Policy engine and client-side extensions. The engine is responsible for interactions between the server-side elements of Group Policy and the local application of the Group Policy downloaded from Active Directory. Server side elements include:

- *Group Policy Objects* (GPOs), which store the configuration settings. There are two default GPOs, the Default Domain Controllers Policy and the Default Domain Policy.

- *Resultant Set of Policy* (RSoP), a tool that can be used to review the effect of proposed or actual Group Policy settings for specific computers and clients. When the tool is used, the resultant review is stored and can be examined later.

- Administrative tools.

Group Policy provides configuration information for many Windows services and processes. It can deliver an almost infinite number of settings, and provide a mechanism for software installation. When a GPO is configured and linked to an appropriate

Active Directory object (site, domain, or OU), it can be used to configure thousands of systems automatically.

Group Policy works by transferring and applying configuration settings in a GPO to a local computer. The basic concept is simple: GPOs are linked to site, domain, or OU objects and applied to the accounts that exist within those objects. The actual Group Policy process is complex due to the many possible settings, to the number of GPOs established and the constraints that can be applied to them. The basic process follows these steps from GPO creation to application:

1. A GPO is created, edited, and linked to a site, domain, or OU object.

2. If a computer account resides within the object and has not been filtered by computer group membership or WMI filter, nor constrained by GPO constraints, and the computer portion of the GPO is enabled, the configuration settings are downloaded and applied at computer boot. (More on constraints and filters in a moment.)

3. If a user account resides within the object and has not been filtered by user group membership, nor constrained by GPO constraints, and the user portion of the GPO is enabled, the configuration settings are downloaded and applied during logon.

4. Changes to GPO settings are periodically refreshed, that is a change will be applied and will not wait for user logoff/logon or computer shutdown and start. (However, some settings, though applied, will not take effect until a computer is restarted.)

5. Security Settings configuration is periodically applied (every 13 hours) whether or not there are changes.

6. GPOs linked to objects that contain the object in which the user or computer account resides are also applied in a similar fashion. The GPOs that may impact a user or computer are applied in a top-down hierarchical fashion. First, any Group Policy Settings on the local computer are applied, next those on the site object, followed by those linked to domain, OU, and any nested OU objects until the account container is reached. If a conflict exists between the Security Setting or Administrative Template setting during the application of multiple GPOs, the setting in the GPO closest to the account wins. Where no conflict exists, all settings are cumulatively applied.

Constraints and filters are mentioned in the preceding list. These GPO features are:

Enabled/Disabled
   The computer and/or user section of the GPO must be enabled in order for that section to be applied. If the section is disabled, then it will not be applied.

Security Filter
   A user or computer account must have the Read and Apply Group Policy permission on the GPO. By default, the Authenticated Users group (all computers

and users that have successfully authenticated to the domain) has these permissions. However, a Group Policy administrator can configure permissions so that only certain groups of computers or users can apply the GPO.

WMI Filter

A Windows Management Instrumentation (WMI) filter can be used to prevent a GPO from being applied to computers that have specific features detectible through WMI. WMI supports monitoring and management of system resources such as CPU, memory, disk space, and devices installed on the computer. When a WMI filter is implemented for a GPO, it can detect whether a computer has a specific feature and prevent GPO application based on that information.

Block Inheritance

When a domain or OU object has the Block Inheritance property, GPOs at a higher level in the GPO hierarchy are not inherited (not applied).

Enforced (also known as Override)

The GPO is applied regardless of any use of the Block Inheritance feature.

Loopback

A policy that reapplies the user portion of the computers GPO settings to a computer after the application of user based policy. This means that there is a consistent user policy in place on the computer. This is useful for kiosk and other publicly available computers where the privileges of the user logged on should have no bearing on the application of Group Policy restrictions.

Group Policy settings are not stored in one location. Local GPO information is stored on the client computer in the *Windows\system32\Group Policy* folder. Active Directory-based GPOs are stored partially in Active Directory and partially in the domain controller filesystem. GPO properties are recorded in Active Directory and therefore are replicated when Group Policy is replicated. GPO settings, such as those set in Administrative template *.adm* files and the Security Settings *.inf* files are stored in the filesystem of the domain controller in the *%systemroot%\SYSVOL\sysvol\ <domainname>\Policies* folder. This means that they are not replicated with Group Policy but are replicated using the File Replication Service (FRS).

FRS is a multimaster file replication service that can be used to replicate files between two or more Windows Server 2003 or Windows 2000 server systems. By default, all folders and files in the *SYSVOL\sysvol* folder are replicated using FRS but other folders can be configured for FRS replication. *SYSVOL\sysvol* replication approximates Active Directory replication, that is, it typically uses the same connections created for Active Directory replication and the same schedule but there is no guarantee that both Active Directory and filesystem parts of a GPO will always be synchronized on all DCs. This disassociation is temporary, but can be the source of Group Policy application problems. Fortunately, administrative template and security settings data is always stored only in the filesystem and is not the source of these problems. Software installation, on the other hand, stores data in both places.

(*gpotool.exe* and *repadmin.exe* can be used to identify when GPO versions are out of synch.)

Active Directory is both important and complex. This chapter provides an introduction to the nomenclature used to discuss Active Directory and Chapter 7 provides information on getting started with Active Directory. However, a subject as complex as this one can fill a book. Two such books from O'Reilly are *Active Directory*, by Robbie Allen and Alistair G. Lowe-Norris, and *Active Directory Cookbook*, by Robbie Allen. Additionally, Microsoft has published several documents and books on Active Directory planning, including extensive information in the six-book set, *Microsoft Windows Server 2003 Deployment Kit*. Also information is available online at *http://www.microsoft.com*.

Summary

TCP/IP provides some network services that simplify network installation, configuration, and use. This chapter has discussed the protocols and technologies used to implement various network services.

This chapter concludes our introduction to the architecture, protocols, and services of a TCP/IP network. In the next chapter, we begin to look at how to install and configure TCP/IP on a Windows Server 2003 system.

## CHAPTER 4

Basic TCP/IP Configuration

This chapter covers the configuration of the basic components of Windows Server TCP/IP networking. Installing and configuring other aspects of Windows Server networking—the Remote Access Service, Active Directory, Domain Name Service, Dynamic Host Configuration Protocol, and so on—are covered in later chapters. You use the procedures described in this chapter when you install Windows Server 2003, but you can return to them later to make changes to your network configuration.

Typically, the majority of the computers on a network obtain the network configuration from a DHCP server. In Chapter 5 we look at how to install and configure a DHCP server so that you can provide the TCP/IP configuration for the bulk of systems on the network. However, it is important for a network administrator to know how to set and change the configuration values directly, both because it is a basic skill that every network administrator must have and because there are always some number of systems that require direct configuration.

Not only is the *how* of basic configuration covered, this chapter also covers the *what* and *why*. What configuration values are required and why specific values are selected are discussed.

Network Device Configuration

During the initial Windows Server 2003 installation, the Network Settings window appears. It presents two choices:

1. Use the "Typical settings" selection to obtain the configuration via DHCP. Most clients use this setting. As a network administrator, it is your job to ensure that the clients obtain the correct configuration from DHCP, as described in Chapter 5.

2. Use the "Custom settings" selection to manually define the configuration for the system. Custom configuration is the focus of this chapter.

Selecting "Custom settings" opens the "Networking components" window. (This window is almost identical to the one shown in Figure 4-3.) Highlight a component and select Properties to configure that component. For example, highlighting Internet Protocol (TCP/IP) and selecting Properties allows you to set the host's IP address, to define the IP addresses of the DNS servers, and more. (The window opened by highlighting Internet Protocol (TCP/IP) and selecting Properties during the initial installation is the same as the window shown in Figure 4-5.)

Of course, initial installation is not the only time you might want to define or modify the configuration for a network interface. To configure the interface for a running system, open the Network Connections applet in the Control Panel. You can use the New Connections Wizard to add a new interface configuration. To modify the configuration of an existing interface, select that interface from the Network Connections menu.

> By default, the first Ethernet interface is called Local Area Connection. The second Ethernet interface is named Local Area Connection 2, the third is named Local Area Connection 3, and so on. If your system has interface names of this type, you can rename the interfaces to something more meaningful in exactly the same way that you would rename a file. Simply right-click on the interface in the Network Connections menu, select Rename from the right-click menu, and enter a new, more descriptive name.

Selecting a network interface from the Network Connections menu opens the Adapter Status window, which contains two tabs: General and Support. Selecting the Support tab shows the current interface configuration and states whether it was manually entered or provided by DHCP. Figure 4-1 shows the Support tab.

Figure 4-1. The Support tab of the Adapter Status window

The system shown in Figure 4-1 was manually configured. Clicking the Repair button on a manually configured computer causes the system to flush various network caches and to reregister with DNS and WINS, if that is appropriate. If this system had been configured using DHCP, clicking Repair would do the same things done for a manually configured system and, in addition, would cause the system to renew its address lease.

Clicking the Details button on the Support tab shows a few more details of the configuration. Figure 4-2 shows the Network Connection Details window opened by the Details button.

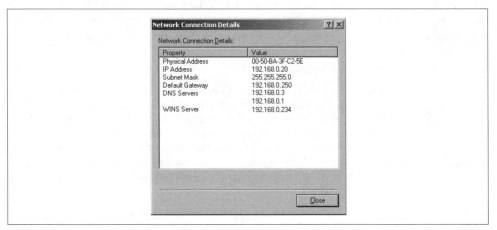

Figure 4-2. Network Connection Details

The General tab of the Adapter Status window tells you whether or not the interface is running, how long it has been running, its rated speed, and the number of packets sent and received by the interface. This tab has two buttons:

- Use the Disable button to down the interface. This can be useful during troubleshooting. Normally, of course, the interface is left up and running. To reenable the interface after it has been disabled, simply select the interface from the Network Connections menu and it will automatically be reenabled. Disabling and reenabling the interface resets the connection time and the number of packets sent and received.

- Use the Properties button to reconfigure the interface.

The Properties button opens the Adapter Properties window, which has three tabs:

Advanced
    This tab allows you to select the *Internet Connection Firewall* (ICF). When you select the checkbox, the Settings button becomes active, which allows you to select the level of security logging the system will use, the types of services that

will be offered to remote users, and the types of ICMP packets to which the system will respond. The ICF is covered in Chapter 9.

Authentication

This tab allows you to select and configure IEEE 802.1X authentication. One of the configuration parameters is the type of *Extensible Authentication Protocol* (EAP) that will be used. Configuring authentication, including EAP, is covered in Chapter 8.

General

This tab allows you to configure the network adapter device driver and the network protocols used by this interface. This is the focus of this chapter.

Figure 4-3 shows the General tab of the Adapter Properties window.

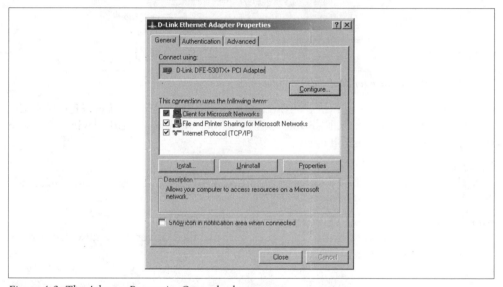

Figure 4-3. The Adapter Properties General tab

Clicking the Configure button opens a window that allows you to configure the network adapter hardware.

Adapter Configuration

The level of hardware configuration offered depends upon the capabilities of the hardware and the associated device driver. The tabs displayed will vary from device to device. Figure 4-4 shows an example for a specific D-Link Ethernet card.

The properties window shown in Figure 4-4 displays five tabs. The Advanced tab lists configuration properties specific to this device. Another Ethernet card would have different settings on the Advanced tab, if it offered an Advanced tab at all. The Driver tab displays information specific to the driver for this device. The information

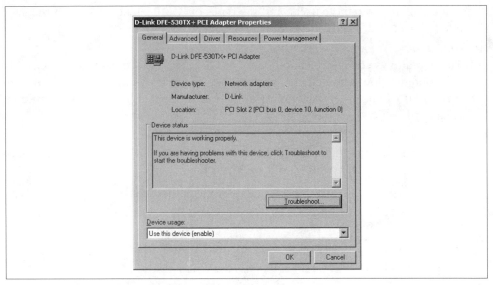

Figure 4-4. Ethernet adapter configuration window

displayed on the Driver tab varies from manufacturer to manufacturer. However, the essential buttons on this tab should be the same for any network device. The key Driver tab buttons are as follows:

Update Driver
> This button starts the Hardware Update Wizard. Use it to install a new driver for this device.

Rollback Driver
> Use this button to return to the previously installed driver if the new driver does not function properly.

Uninstall
> Use this button only if you intended to completely remove the driver for this device. Do not use this to simply disable the device. As noted earlier, and as we'll see again, there are simpler ways to temporarily disable a device.

Windows Server 2003 ships drivers for numerous network adapter cards bundled with the operating system. The drivers are of high quality, but things change. Bugs are discovered and drivers are improved. Because of these changes you may find yourself clicking the Update Driver button. Before you do, make sure you have the latest driver available for your adapter:

1. Check the adapter card manufacturer's web site for the latest released version of a production driver. Make sure you don't unintentionally get a beta or unsupported version of the driver. These are commonly posted, but they should only be installed on a production server after a very thorough evaluation.

2. If you don't find a suitable driver on the manufacturer's web site, check the Microsoft web site for the latest version of the Microsoft driver for your adapter.

Microsoft drivers are nearly always stable and fast, although they may not implement some special features supported by the manufacturer's driver, in particular management functions.

3. If you use Windows Update, it can automatically notify you when a new driver is available for your network adapter.

The General, Resources, and Power Management tabs shown in Figure 4-4 are more generic than the Driver tab. The Power Management tab is there for devices that support *Advanced Power Management* (APM). APM allows for two-way power control:

- The PC can shut off the device to conserve power when the device is not in use. This is generally not an important feature for Ethernet cards because they consume very little power.

- The device can bring the PC out of standby mode. This is a more interesting feature for a network device. When the user leaves work and places the PC in a low-power standby mode, this feature allows the PC to continue collecting data from the network. Of course, this feature only saves power if the PC is normally left running at full power in order to collect data from the network.

The Resources tab lists the hardware resources used by the network device and notifies you if any hardware conflicts exist. PC adapter cards require up to four distinct hardware configuration parameters. The parameters are the Interrupt Request number (IRQ), Direct Memory Access (DMA) Direct Request number (DRQ),* I/O Port Address (or I/O Range), and Adapter Memory Address.

Of the four configuration values, IRQ assignment traditionally caused the most trouble because there were a limited number of interrupts and interrupts could not be shared. Interrupts on the original PC bus were edge triggered, which means that the transition of the signal on the IRQ line caused the system to detect an interrupt. (Specifically, IBM defined the signal as a transition from low to high.) An IRQ could not be reliably shared because when more than one card attempted to use a single IRQ line the interrupt could be lost.

The *Peripheral Component Interconnect* (PCI) bus has, by and large, eliminated this problem. The PCI bus is an intelligent bus that supports automatic adapter configuration through Plug and Play (PnP). With PnP, the adapter, the bus and the operating system cooperate to find and assign unused hardware values, thus eliminating conflicts. The NTDETECT.COM software collects the hardware information for the Windows Server 2003 system.

If a conflict is found, the Resources tab lists the device that conflicts with the network adapter. One possible cause of a conflict is an adapter that allows manual configuration

---

* The DRQ parameter is rarely used.

that has been incorrectly configured. The problem is not necessarily in the network card. It could be caused by misconfiguration of the conflicting adapter.

The General tab identifies the device, displays the current device status, and allows you to select the "Device usage," which can be either enable or disabled—yet another way to disable the interface. (Disabling the device via the "Device usage" drop-down box has exactly the same effect as disabling the interface through the Disable button described in the previous section of this chapter.) If the device status is not "This device is working properly," you can click on the Troubleshoot button, which opens the Help and Support Center window. This is the same Help and Support Center that is available from the Start menu. The difference is that when you enter the Help and Support Center using the Troubleshoot button shown in Figure 4-4, the Help and Support Center has already been primed with the problem: "I'm having a problem with my hardware device." While not as generic as the Help and Support Center window invoked from the Start menu, it is still not specific to network troubleshooting or even troubleshooting network hardware. See Chapter 14 for network-oriented troubleshooting advice.

Network adapters do not need any manual configuration for most systems. Most of the time, Windows Server 2003 correctly identifies the adapter and installs a properly configured driver for the adapter. The Configure button is useful but rarely needed.

Installing and Removing Network Components

Refer back to Figure 4-3. The window in the middle of the properties dialog shown in Figure 4-3 lists the network components used for the network connection. Three network components are listed:

Client for Microsoft Networks
    This is the client side of the NetBIOS protocol discussed in Chapter 3.

File and Printer Sharing for Microsoft Networks
    This includes the server side of NetBIOS and both the Server Message Block (SMB) protocol and the Common Internet File System (CIFS) protocol. All three of these are described in Chapter 3.

Internet Protocol (TCP/IP)
    This is the Transmission Control Protocol/Internet Protocol suite described in Chapters 1 and 2. This is the protocol we will be manually configuring in this chapter.

Directly under the list of network components are three buttons: Install, Uninstall, and Properties. Click the Install button to install a network component. The Install button opens the Select Network Component Type window. Three component types are offered:

Client

A client component is the client side of some network service. The Client for Microsoft Networks component described above is one example. Another one offered by default on a Windows Server 2003 system is the Client Service for NetWare.

Service

A service component is the server side of a network service. For example, the File and Printer Sharing for Microsoft Networks component is a service component. Highlighting Service in the Select Network Component Type window and clicking Add, opens the Select Network Service window. By default, it lists only three components: Network Load Balancing, QoS Packet Scheduler, and Service Advertising Protocol. All three of these components are enhancements to the basic TCP/IP protocol, and none of the three pops to mind when one thinks of a network service. Most network administrators think of services such as DHCP or DNS when they think of TCP/IP services. Services such as DHCP and DNS are installed through the Manage Your Server window, not through the Select Network Service window. (DHCP and DNS installation and configuration are covered in subsequent chapters.)

Protocol

A protocol component is a network communications protocol. For example, the Internet Protocol (TCP/IP) component described earlier is a protocol component. Of course, the client and service components also contain protocol elements, so the distinction is somewhat arbitrary. In general, protocol components are lower layer protocols upon which client/service protocols are built—but not always. By default, the Select Network Protocol window offers the following five protocol component selections:

AppleTalk Protocol

This is the AppleTalk protocol used by Apple computers.

Microsoft TCP/IP version 6

This is the IPv6 protocol described in Chapter 2.

Network Monitor Driver

This is packet capture software required by the Netmon application.

NWLink IPX/SPX/NetBIOS Compatible Transport Protocol

This is the Microsoft implementation of the Novell IPX/SPX protocols that are used by NetWare.

Reliable Multicast Protocol

This is a reliable transport protocol for multicast messages that can be used only by Microsoft Message Queuing (MSMQ).

If you install a component that you don't need, it is easily removed. The Uninstall button removes an unneeded network component. To remove a component, simply highlight the component name in the list box and click Uninstall. You will be asked to verify the removal. Click Yes and the network component is removed. Any network component can be removed in this manner except for TCP/IP, which is always required.

The Properties button is used to configure a protocol. Protocol configuration is the principal topic of this chapter.

General TCP/IP Configuration

TCP/IP is configured automatically by a DHCP server or manually through the Internet Protocol (TCP/IP) Properties dialog. The Internet Protocol (TCP/IP) Properties dialog is accessed by highlighting the Internet Protocol (TCP/IP) network component on the General tab of the adapter properties window, which is shown in Figure 4-3, and by then clicking the Properties button. The remainder of this chapter is about the Internet Protocol (TCP/IP) Properties window and how it is used to configure TCP/IP.

Figure 4-5 shows the General tab of the Internet Protocol (TCP/IP) Properties dialog. This tab is used to manually define the basic configuration or to select automatic configuration from the DHCP server. DHCP is a key component of a manageable, reliable, and efficient network. Therefore you should configure as many systems as possible by selecting the "Obtain an IP address automatically" option button. This is, in fact, the default configuration created by the Windows Server 2003 installation unless the "Custom settings" option in selected during the installation.

Despite the label on this option button, it does much more than just obtain the IP address automatically. The DHCP server provides the complete TCP/IP configuration. Nothing remains to be done because everything can be provided by the DHCP server when the DHCP server is properly configured. Of course, as the administrator of the network it is your responsibility to set up the DHCP server as described in Chapter 5. But your work relieves end users of configuration responsibilities and reduces the number of user configuration errors that you have to fix. The configuration steps described in the next section are not needed for the majority of systems on a network that uses DHCP.

Manually Defining the IP Address

Unfortunately, not every Windows system can use a DHCP server for its configuration. Some systems don't have access to a DHCP server. Also a DHCP server itself cannot be configured by DHCP, and the administrators of other servers often choose not to configure their systems via DHCP. To configure a system without using DHCP, select the "Use the following IP address" option button, and complete the

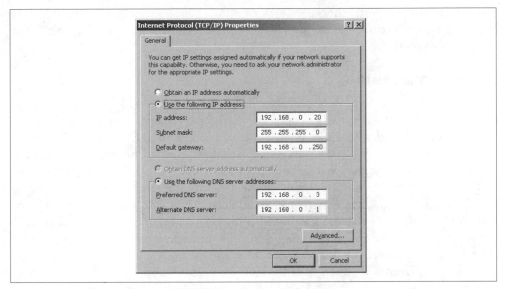

Figure 4-5. The Internet Protocol (TCP/IP) Properties window

configuration manually. Below are the manual configuration fields on the IP address portion of the General tab:

IP Address
Enter a valid IP address for this computer, using dotted decimal format. This is a single address from your address range. The section "Selecting an IP address block" provides advice on defining an address range for your network if you are creating a completely new network.

Subnet Mask
Enter the appropriate subnet mask, again using dotted decimal format. By default, this field will use the natural mask for the address entered above. If you subnet, you should place your subnet mask here. If you do not subnet, use the prefix-length assigned with the address block to determine the mask. Chapter 2 covers subnets and address masks.

Default Gateway:
Enter the IP address for the default router in dotted decimal format. Chapter 2 provides background on routing and the use of default gateways, and there is more on routing and gateways later in this chapter.

Of course, before manually entering data into any of these fields you must know exactly what you are going to enter. The network administrator is responsible for making and communicating decisions about overall network configuration. If you're adding a system to an existing network, you can simply provide the correct values to the person configuring the system from the range of values valid for your network. If you are creating a new network, you will have to make some basic decisions. One of these decisions is how to choose a network number for your new network, which is the topic of the next section. If you already have IP addresses for your network, you can skip this section.

Selecting an IP address block

First, you must decide how many hosts on a new network will be *fully* accessible from the Internet. Many new networks attach to the Internet indirectly so that access into the new network from other Internet networks is limited. An example of an indirectly attached network is a TCP/IP network that attaches to the outside world via a firewall or network address translation (NAT) device. Users on the new network can access remote Internet hosts but remote users cannot directly access all of the hosts on the indirectly connected network. Because the hosts on this network are not accessible to users in the outside world, they do not require public IP addresses. (Only the subset of systems exposed to the outside world requires public IP addresses.) Therefore, the network administrator of this network can select a network address from RFC 1918, *Address Allocation for Private Internets*. The private network numbers are 10.0.0.0, 172.16.0.0 to 172.31.0.0, and 192.168.0.0 to 192.168.255.0. The pros and cons of using a network address from RFC 1918 are covered in Chapter 2, where private network numbers are discussed in detail. But, in general, if you can use a private network number, you should.

Some organizations choose to give every device on the network an address that will make that device fully accessible from the Internet. A network that wants to be fully accessible from all sites on the Internet must obtain a public network address to allow outside users direct access into the systems on your network. An official address is needed for every system on the network that is *directly* accessible to remote Internet hosts. Every network that communicates with the Internet, even those that use NAT, has at least one public address, although that address may be assigned to the NAT box. To make many or all of the systems on your network accessible, you need a block of addresses. The first step toward obtaining a block of addresses is to determine how many addresses you need.

Determining your "organizational type" helps you assess your address needs and how you should satisfy those needs. RFC 2901, *Guide to Administrative Procedures of the Internet Infrastructure*, describes four different organizational types:

Internet end-user
> A small- to medium-sized organization focused on connecting itself to the Internet. This could be as small as a single user connecting to the Internet with a dynamic address assigned by the ISP's DHCP server, or as large as a network of thousands of hosts using NAT on the enterprise network and official addresses on a limited number of publicly accessible systems. What categorizes this organizational type is that

it wants to use the Internet while limiting the number of systems it makes available to remote users. "Internet end-user" organizations obtain official addresses from their ISP. From the point of view of the Internet, all Internet end-user organizations appear small because they use only a limited number of official addresses.

High-volume end-user

A medium- to large-sized organization that distributes official addresses to systems throughout its network. This type of organization tends to have a distributed management under which divisions within the overall organization are allowed to make systems remotely accessible. High-volume end-user organizations usually satisfy their address requirements through their ISP or a Local Internet Registry. If the organization needs more than 8,000 addresses, it may go directly to a Regional Internet Registry. While in reality a high-volume end-user organization may not be any larger than an Internet end-user organization, it appears to be larger from the point of view of the Internet because it exposes more systems to the Internet.

Internet Service Provider

An organization that provides Internet connection services to other organizations and provides those organizations with official addresses. Even an ISP connects to the Internet in some way. If it connects through another ISP, that ISP is its *upstream provider*. The upstream provider assigns addresses to the ISP. If it connects directly to a network access point (NAP), the ISP requests addresses from the Local Internet Registry or the Regional Internet Registry.

Local Internet Registry

An organization that provides addresses to ISPs. In effect a Local Internet Registry is an organization that provides addresses to other organizations that provide addresses. A Local Internet Registry must obtain its addresses from a Regional Internet Registry.

RFC 2901 lists four organizational types in order to be thorough. Most organizations are either Internet end users or high-volume end users. In all likelihood, your organization is one of these, and you will obtain all of your addresses from your ISP.

Your ISP has been delegated authority over a group of network addresses and should be able to assign you a network number. If your local ISP cannot meet your needs, perhaps the ISP's upstream provider can. Ask your local ISP whom it receives service from and ask that organization for an address. If all else fails, you may be forced to go directly to an Internet registry. If you are forced to take your request to a registry, you will need to take certain steps before you make the application.

You need to prepare a detailed network topology. The topology must include a diagram that shows the physical layout of your network and highlights its connections to the Internet. You should include network engineering plans that, in addition to diagramming the topology, describe:

- Your routing plans, including the protocols you will use and any constraints that forced your routing decisions.
- Your subnetting plans, including the mask you will use, and the number of networks and hosts you will have connected during the next year. RFC 2050, *Internet Registry IP Allocation Guidelines*, suggests the following details in your subnet plan:
  - A table listing all subnets
  - The mask for each subnet
  - The estimated number of hosts
  - A descriptive remark explaining the purpose of each subnet

The biggest challenge is accurately predicting future requirements for addresses. If you have previously been assigned an address block, you may be required to provide a history of how that address block was used. Even if it is not requested by the Internet registry, a history can be a helpful tool for your own planning. Additionally, you will be asked to prepare a network deployment plan. This plan typically shows the number of hosts you currently have that need official addresses and the number you expect to have in six months, one year and two years.

One factor used to determine how much address space is needed is the *expected utilization rate*. The expected utilization rate is the number of hosts assigned official addresses divided by the total number of hosts possible for the network. The deployment plans must show the number of hosts that will be assigned addresses over a two-year period. The total number of possible hosts can be estimated from the total number of employees in your organization and the number of systems that have been traditionally deployed per employee. Clearly you need to have a global knowledge of your organization and its needs before applying for an official address assignment.

In addition to providing documentation that justifies the address request, obtaining an official address requires a formal commitment of resources. Most address applications require at least two contacts: an administrative contact and a technical contact. The administrative contact should have the authority to deal with administrative issues ranging from policy violations to billing disputes. The technical contact must be a skilled technical person who can deal with technical problems and answer technical questions. Internet registries require that these contacts live in the same country as the organization that they represent. You must provide the names, addresses, telephone numbers, and email addresses of these people. Don't kid yourself. These are not honorary positions. These people have targets on their backs when things go wrong.

In addition to human resources, you need to commit computer resources. You should have systems set up, running, and ready to accept the new addresses before you apply for official addresses.

When all of the background work is done, you're ready to present your case to an Internet registry. A three-level bureaucracy controls the allocation of IP addresses:

IANA
> The Internet Assigned Numbers Authority (IANA) allocates large blocks of addresses to regional Internet registries.

Regional Internet Registry
> Regional Internet Registries (IRs) have been given authority by the IANA to allocate addresses within a large region of the world. There are three IRs:
>
> APNIC
> > The Asian Pacific Network Information Center (APNIC) has address allocation authority for Asia and the Pacific region.
>
> ARIN
> > The American Registry for Internet Numbers (ARIN) has address allocation authority for the Americas.
>
> RIPE
> > Reseaux IP Européens (RIPE) has address allocation authority for Europe.

Local Internet Registry
> Local IRs are given authority, either by IANA or by a regional IR, to allocate addresses within a specific area. An example might be a national registry or a registry created by a consortium of ISPs.

No matter how much address space you need, you should start at the bottom of the hierarchy and work your way up. Always start with your local ISP. If they cannot handle your needs, ask them if there is a local IR that can help you. As a last resort, take your request to the regional IR that serves your part of the world.

The most important thing to remember is that most organizations *never* have to go through this process. Most organizations do *not* want to expose the bulk of their computers to the Internet. For security reasons, they use private address numbers for most systems and only have a limited number of official IP addresses. That limited number of addresses can usually be provided by a local ISP.

One final note, when you obtain a block of official IP address, you may also need to apply for an *in-addr.arpa* domain This special domain is sometimes called a *reverse lookup domain*. Chapter 6 contains more information about how the *in-addr.arpa* domain is set up and used, but basically the reverse lookup domain maps numeric IP addresses into domain names. This is the reverse of the normal domain name lookup process, which converts domain names to addresses. If your ISP provides your name service or your ISP assigned you an address from a block of its own addresses, you probably do not need to apply for an *in-addr.arpa* domain. Check with your ISP *before* applying. If, however, you obtain a block of addresses from a Regional IR, you probably will need to register your own *in-addr.arpa* domain. If you do need to get a reverse lookup domain, register it with the same organization from which you obtained your address assignment.

Again, the most important thing to note about reverse address registration is that most organizations don't have to do this. If you obtain your address from your ISP, you probably do not have to take care of this paperwork yourself. These services are one of the reasons you pay your ISP.

Basic DNS Configuration

Refer to Figure 4-5. The lower half of the General tab of the Internet Protocol (TCP/IP) Properties window defines the IP addresses of two DNS servers. If the "Obtain an IP address automatically" checkbox is selected, you will be offered the opportunity to select the Obtain DNS server address automatically checkbox. This means that if you obtain the host's IP address from the DHCP server, you have the option of either obtaining the DNS server address from DHCP or entering the DNS server address manually. However, if you enter the host IP address manually, you must also enter the DNS server address manually.

Two DNS server addresses can be entered in this window:

Preferred DNS server
> The preferred DNS server is simply the server to which this system should first direct DNS queries. It is not necessarily the same system as the primary (or master) DNS server for your domain. In fact, it probably is not. (See Chapter 3 for information on DNS server types.) Most often, this is the address of the DNS server that is topographically the closest to the system being configured, which is frequently a server located on the same local network as the host.

Alternate DNS server
> The alternate DNS server is a backup server. This server is only queried when the preferred DNS server fails to respond to a query. The alternate server provides reliability for those times when the preferred server is offline. Frequently, an authoritative server, such as the primary or a secondary server for the local domain, is specified here because, given the importance of the authoritative servers, it is highly unlikely that the authoritative servers will be offline when the local DNS server is down. Another factor to consider when picking an alternate server is reachability. In general, it is a good idea to pick preferred and alternate DNS servers that are reached through different network paths so that the servers are less vulnerable to a network outage.

The General tab creates a minimal configuration. There are, of course, more TCP/IP configuration options than the few shown on the General tab. We will examine these additional configuration options in the following sections.

Adding More Configuration Details

Note the Advanced button near the bottom of the General tab shown in Figure 4-5. Click the Advanced button to display the Advanced TCP/IP Settings window. The IP Settings tab of this window is shown in Figure 4-6.

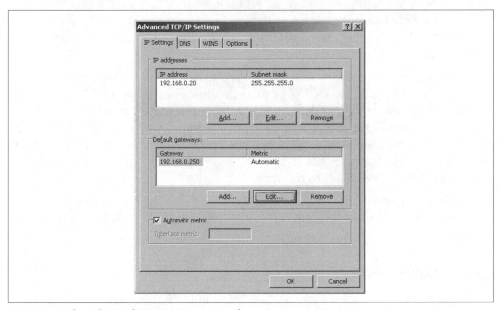

Figure 4-6. The Advanced TCP/IP Settings window

The default Advanced TCP/IP Settings window contains four tabs:

IP Settings
> This tab defines additional IP addresses with their associated subnet masks, and it defines additional routers.

DNS
> This tab defines additional DNS server addresses and the value used to fully qualify unqualified domain names when constructing DNS queries.

WINS
> This tab defines the WINS server addresses and options for NetBIOS name resolution.

Options
> By default, the only option this tab provides access to is "TCP/IP filtering."

The Advanced TCP/IP Setting window has two buttons at the bottom: OK and Cancel. These buttons are global to all tabs in the window. Do not click on OK until you have completed all tabs. Clicking on OK exits the TCP/IP configuration process, perhaps before you have finished. Similarly, clicking Cancel discards the changes, not just to the page currently displayed but to all pages.

Adding IP Addresses

Windows Server 2003 allows you to assign multiple IP addresses to a single physical network adapter. This is useful, for example, if you want to run multiple subnets on the same physical network. We'll see a use for this in the discussion of superscopes in Chapter 5.

Add IP addresses to a network adapter by clicking Add in the "IP addresses" pane to display the TCP/IP Address dialog box. In the dialog, enter the IP address and its associated netmask. Windows defaults the subnet mask to the natural mask of the IP address you entered. If the IP address is part of a block with a specifically assigned prefix-length or is a member of a subnet, the correct value must be entered manually. Always verify that the subnet mask is correct to avoid connectivity problems that can be extremely difficult to resolve.

Highlight an address in the "IP addresses" pane and click Edit to modify an existing IP address and subnet mask. Remove an IP address by highlighting it and clicking Remove.

Adding Gateways

Windows Server 2003 allows you to define multiple default gateways through the Add button in the "Default gateways" pane of the IP Settings tab. (Refer back to the IP Settings tab in Figure 4-6.) Clicking the Add button displays the TCP/IP Gateway Address dialog box. In the dialog, enter the IP address of the gateway and select the routing metric that you want to assign to this route. You can either check the "Automatic metric" checkbox to allow Windows to assign the metric, or you can uncheck that box and manually enter a numeric value for Metric. The automatic metric is determined by the characteristics of the network interface. Therefore when multiple routers are added through the "Default gateways" pane of the same IP Settings tab, they are all given the same automatic metric because they are all associated with the same interface. The following route print command shows an example of this:

```
D:\>route print
IPv4 Route Table
===========================================================================
Interface List
0x1 ......................... MS TCP Loopback interface
0x10003 ...00 50 ba 3f c2 5e ...... D-Link DFE-530TX+ PCI Adapter
===========================================================================
===========================================================================
Active Routes:
Network Destination        Netmask          Gateway       Interface  Metric
          0.0.0.0          0.0.0.0    192.168.0.250    192.168.0.20      20
```

```
          0.0.0.0           0.0.0.0     192.168.0.1    192.168.0.20     20
        127.0.0.0         255.0.0.0       127.0.0.1       127.0.0.1      1
      192.168.0.0     255.255.255.0    192.168.0.20    192.168.0.20     20
     192.168.0.20   255.255.255.255       127.0.0.1       127.0.0.1     20
    192.168.0.255   255.255.255.255    192.168.0.20    192.168.0.20     20
        224.0.0.0         240.0.0.0    192.168.0.20    192.168.0.20     20
  255.255.255.255   255.255.255.255    192.168.0.20    192.168.0.20      1
Default Gateway:       192.168.0.250
===========================================================================
Persistent Routes:
  None
```

The details of the routing table are explained in Chapter 2. In this case, we are only interested in the first two active routes. They both are default gateways as indicated by the fact that they both have destinations and netmasks of 0.0.0.0. Both of these gateways were entered into the configuration through configuration windows associated with the D-Link Ethernet interface on this sample system. (The interface is assigned the IP address 192.168.0.20.) The first gateway—the one assigned address 192.168.0.250—was defined in the "Default gateway" box of the General tab of the Internet Protocol (TCP/IP) Properties window for this interface, as shown in Figure 4-5. The second gateway was defined through the Add button of the "Default gateways" pane of the IP Settings tab shown in Figure 4-6. When it was defined, the "Automatic metric" checkbox was used. Both routes are associated with the same interface, and both have the same metric. Given the routing table shown above, the system will attempt to use default gateway 192.168.0.250 first because it is listed first in the table and has the same metric as the other default gateway.

 This discussion is only about default gateways. If a specific route to a destination is included in the routing table, it is always preferred over the default route for packets addressed to that specific destination.

Both of the default gateways in the table shown above are reached through the same interface (192.168.0.20), therefore, they are automatically assigned the same metric. To use a different metric, manually enter the metric in the Metric box of the TCP/IP Gateway Address dialog when adding a default gateway. In the routing table shown below, a metric of 5 was manually entered for the 192.168.0.1 default router:

```
D:\>route print

IPv4 Route Table
===========================================================================
Interface List
0x1 ........................... MS TCP Loopback interface
0x10003 ...00 50 ba 3f c2 5e ...... D-Link DFE-530TX+ PCI Adapter
===========================================================================
===========================================================================
Active Routes:
Network Destination        Netmask          Gateway       Interface  Metric
          0.0.0.0           0.0.0.0    192.168.0.250    192.168.0.20     20
```

```
      0.0.0.0            0.0.0.0       192.168.0.1     192.168.0.20    5
    127.0.0.0          255.0.0.0         127.0.0.1       127.0.0.1     1
  192.168.0.0      255.255.255.0     192.168.0.20     192.168.0.20   20
 192.168.0.20    255.255.255.255       127.0.0.1       127.0.0.1     20
192.168.0.255    255.255.255.255    192.168.0.20     192.168.0.20   20
    224.0.0.0          240.0.0.0     192.168.0.20     192.168.0.20   20
255.255.255.255  255.255.255.255    192.168.0.20     192.168.0.20    1
Default Gateway:      192.168.0.250
==========================================================================
Persistent Routes:
  None
```

The metric defines the order of precedence among routers that can reach the same destination. The lower the metric, the lower the cost, and thus the more preferred the route. Given the routing table shown above, the system will attempt to use default gateway 192.168.0.1 first because it has the lowest metric, even though it is not the first default gateway listed in the table.

When multiple gateways are defined for a single destination, only one gateway is active at any one time. Windows Server 2003 uses the gateway with the lowest metric. If multiple gateways have the same metric, Windows uses the first gateway listed. Only if the preferred gateway is down or otherwise not accessible does it attempt to use additional gateways.

Specifying multiple default gateways has limited utility because it requires that more than one router be directly attached to the same local network as the host, and that more than one of those routers be capable of reaching all destinations. In many cases where there is more than one router on the network some of the routers only reach other internal networks and therefore are not suitable to be default routers.

Don't try to use the "Default gateways" pane to build complex static routes. It is simply not flexible enough because it can only be used to define default gateways. If static routes are required, use the route command, which is available through the Windows Server 2003 command interface. It lets you manually configure the routes in the routing table. The command syntax is:

```
route [-f] [-p] [command [destination] [mask netmask] [gateway] [metric metric] [if
interface]
```

The options are used as follows:

-f

Flush all of the routes from the routing tables. If used with one of the commands, the table is flushed before the command is executed.

-p

Create a permanent route that is reinstalled in the routing table every time the system boots.

command

The *command* field specifies the action that the route command should take. There are four command keywords:

add
> Add a route.

delete
> Delete a route.

change
> Modify an existing route.

print
> Display the routing table.

destination
> This is the IP address of the network or host that is reached through this route.

mask *netmask*
> The *netmask* is applied to the address provided in the destination field to determine the true destination of the route. If a bit in the *netmask* is set to 1, the corresponding bit in the destination field is a significant bit in the destination address. For example, a destination of 172.16.12.1 with a *netmask* of 255.255.0.0 defines the route to network 172.16.0.0, but the same destination with a mask of 255.255.255.255 defines the route to the host 172.16.12.1. If no value is specified for the *netmask*, it defaults to 255.255.255.255.

gateway
> This is the IP address of the gateway for this route.

Assume we are configuring a system that has the IP address 192.168.0.20 and that is located on subnet 192.168.0.0. In the following example we add a route to the host 172.16.12.3 and a route to the subnet 172.16.8. In each case, the address mask determines if the route is interpreted as a network route or a host route. After entering the new routes, we display the routing table with the route print command to examine our handiwork:

```
C:\>route -p add 172.16.12.3 mask 255.255.255.255 192.168.0.1
C:\>route -p add 172.16.8.0 mask 255.255.255.0 192.168.0.1 metric 5
C:\>route print
IPv4 Route Table
===========================================================================
Interface List
0x1 ........................ MS TCP Loopback interface
0x10003 ...00 50 ba 3f c2 5e ...... D-Link DFE-530TX+ PCI Adapter
===========================================================================
===========================================================================
Active Routes:
Network Destination        Netmask          Gateway       Interface  Metric
          0.0.0.0          0.0.0.0    192.168.0.250    192.168.0.20      20
        127.0.0.0        255.0.0.0        127.0.0.1        127.0.0.1       1
```

```
          172.16.8.0      255.255.255.0       192.168.0.8      192.168.0.20       1
         172.16.12.3    255.255.255.255       192.168.0.5      192.168.0.20       1
        192.168.0.0      255.255.255.0      192.168.0.20      192.168.0.20      20
       192.168.0.20    255.255.255.255         127.0.0.1         127.0.0.1      20
      192.168.0.255    255.255.255.255      192.168.0.20      192.168.0.20      20
           224.0.0.0        240.0.0.0      192.168.0.20      192.168.0.20      20
     255.255.255.255    255.255.255.255      192.168.0.20      192.168.0.20       1
     Default Gateway:       192.168.0.250
==========================================================================
Persistent Routes:
   Network Address             Netmask   Gateway Address   Metric
        172.16.12.3    255.255.255.255       192.168.0.1       1
         172.16.8.0      255.255.255.0       192.168.0.1       5
```

As the display shows, there are several more routes than the two we just entered. All of the other routes are part of the basic routing table, which is described in Chapter 2.

The routes we are interested in are both listed in the Persistent Routes section of the route print display. Routes added by the route add command will not survive a boot without the -p option. Use the -p option when you want to add permanent static routes to the routing table. The -p option is not used when the routes are installed for some temporary purpose, such as troubleshooting.

Note that the default metric used with the route command is 1. This is not the same default metric used by the "Automatic metric" checkbox in the TCP/IP Gateway Address dialog. The default metric can be overridden on the route command-line using the metric argument, as in the example above.

The sample system used in this example has only one network interface adapter. All of the routes added by the route add command are associated with that interface. When more than one network interface is available, Windows selects the default interface for a route based on the gateway address used for the route. For example, if the gateway address shows that the gateway is on network 192.168.0.0, Windows will use the network interface attached to network 192.168.0.0. To manually specify the interface a route should use, add the if argument to the route command-line. The interface should be specified by its interface number—not by its IP address. The interface number is the first field displayed for each interface in the Interface List section of the routing table. On our sample system, the interface number associated with the D-Link Ethernet card is 0x10003. The following route add command associates the route to network 172.16.81.0 with the D-Link interface on our sample system:

```
D:\>route -p add 172.16.81.0 mask 255.255.255.0 192.168.0.8 if 0x10003
```

Use the route command only when your system requires complex static routes. Most workstations use a single default route, allowing that default router to redirect packets as necessary. Let's return to the Advanced TCP/IP Settings window to finish entering configuration data.

The DNS Tab

An important part of a TCP/IP network is the DNS. The client portion of DNS, which is called the *resolver*, must be configured on every system. To customize the resolver configuration, select the DNS tab, which is shown in Figure 4-7.

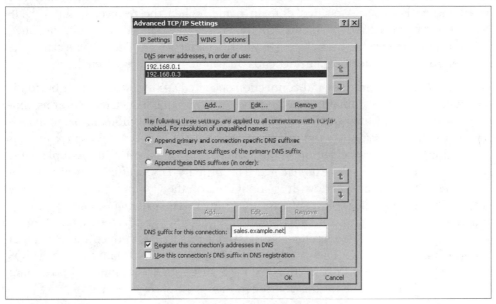

Figure 4-7. The DNS tab of the Advanced TCP/IP Settings window

The "DNS server addresses, in order of use" pane, by default, contains the server addresses entered on the General tab of the Internet Protocol (TCP/IP) Properties window, as shown in Figure 4-5. Use the Add button to enter the IP address of any additional DNS servers that you wish to use. Additional DNS servers provide added redundancy, but they rapidly reach a point of diminishing returns. Each server is queried in turn, but only after the server above it in the list fails to respond to the query. Each server is queried multiple times and each query is given a reasonable timeout. These timeouts add up if too many servers are placed in this list, which unnecessarily makes the user wait for the inevitable error message. If the servers are properly chosen, they are not all going to be down at the same time. It is far more likely that multiple servers are unreachable at the same time because of a network problem or a local problem. Adding more servers to the list, cannot fix a network problem. Two well-chosen servers are adequate, and three are probably the most you want. If you cannot contact any of three different well-chosen servers, the problem is not with the remote servers; it is with the network or your local system. Use the Add, Edit, and Remove buttons as needed to configure the list of servers.

Use the up and down arrow buttons to arrange the servers in the order that you want them searched. When Windows needs to resolve an IP address, it starts with the first server on the list. If that server is unavailable, it then tries the second server. If that server fails to respond, Windows continues to try servers in the order they are listed until it either is able to resolve the address or runs out of servers to try.

Two option buttons and a checkbox in the middle of the DNS tab are used to configure how Windows qualifies unqualified hostnames. An unqualified hostname is a hostname without an associated domain name. When the resolver builds a DNS query for an unqualified hostname, the hostname is extended to a fully qualified domain name before the query is passed to the name server. The domain name the resolver appends to the hostname depends on which options are selected.

When the "Append primary and connection specific DNS suffixes" option button is selected, the primary domain name and the domain name associated with this connection are used to fully qualify unqualified hostnames. The domain name associated with the connection is the domain name entered in the "DNS suffix for this connection" box near the bottom of the DNS tab. In Figure 4-7, the sample value entered in this box is *sales.example.net*. The primary DNS suffix, however, is not configured through this window. It is configured on the Computer Name tab of the System Properties dialog. To configure the primary DNS domain name, go to the Start menu, open the Control Panel menu and select System. In the System Properties window, select the Computer Name tab. Click Change to open the Computer Name Changes window. Then click More to open the DNS Suffix and NetBIOS Computer Name dialog. In the "Primary DNS suffix for this computer" box, enter the primary domain name for this computer. Figure 4-8 shows this dialog.

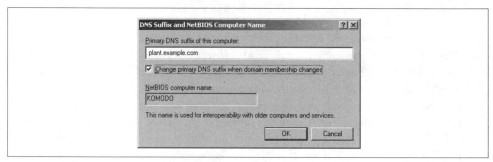

Figure 4-8. The DNS Suffix and NetBIOS Computer Name dialog

Given the values in Figures 4-7 and 4-8, the primary DNS suffix for this system is *plant.example.com*, and the DNS suffix for this connection is *sales.example.net*. The "Append parent suffixes of the primary suffix" checkbox impacts how these domain names are used. If the checkbox had been selected with the settings shown in Figures 4-7 and 4-8, a request for the IP address of *mandy* generates a query for *mandy.plant.example.com*, then one for *mandy.example.com* (assuming the first query was not successful), and finally one for *mandy.sales.example.net* (assuming the second query was not successful). The system does not, however, search *example.net*, which is the parent domain of *sales.example.net*. If the "Append parent suffixes of the primary suffix" checkbox is not selected, a query for *mandy* would generate a query for *mandy.plant.example.com* and then one for *mandy.sales.example.net*. No parent domains would be searched.

Defining your own domain search list is the alternative to using the primary and connection DNS suffixes. To define your own search list, click the "Append these DNS suffixes (in order)" option button. This enables the Add, Edit, and Remove buttons. Click the Add button to add a DNS suffix to the search list. Use the up and down arrows to define the search sequence. Domains are searched in order from the top to the bottom of the list. Figure 4-9 shows an example domain search list.

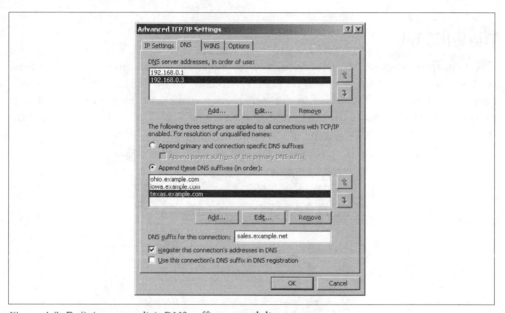

Figure 4-9. Defining an explicit DNS suffixes search list

With the configuration shown in Figure 4-9, a query for *mandy* would generate queries for *mandy.ohio.example.com*, *mandy.iowa.example.com*, and *mandy.texas.example.com*, in exactly that order. No other domains would be searched. Even the domain provided in the "DNS suffix for this connection" box in Figure 4-9 is not searched when an explicit search list is defined. When a search list is provided, it must include all of the domains that you want searched.

> A query is also issued for the name exactly as it is typed in by the user, regardless of what is defined on the DNS tab. The DNS suffixes are only used to extend hostnames so that it is possible for a user to enter the names in a shorter form. They do not interfere with the normal processing of a query.

The two checkboxes at the bottom of the DNS tab configure dynamic DNS. Selecting the "Register this connection's address in DNS" checkbox causes the system to attempt to register its IP address with DNS using the hostname and domain defined for this system via the Computer Name tab of the System Properties window. The "Use this connection's DNS suffix in DNS registration" checkbox is active only if the first checkbox is selected. This checkbox causes the system to also register its address using the hostname from the Computer Name tab and the domain name from the "DNS suffix for this connection" box. Of course, these client-side settings are only useful if you have a server running dynamic DNS. Chapter 3 provides more information about dynamic DNS, and Chapter 6 provides information about the server side of dynamic DNS.

The WINS Tab

The Windows Internet Name Service (WINS) maps NetBIOS names to IP addresses, as described in Chapter 3. The WINS client needs to know the address of the WINS server in order to use the server to register its own name and resolve other NetBIOS names. The WINS client can be configured through DHCP or manually configured through the WINS tab shown in Figure 4-10.

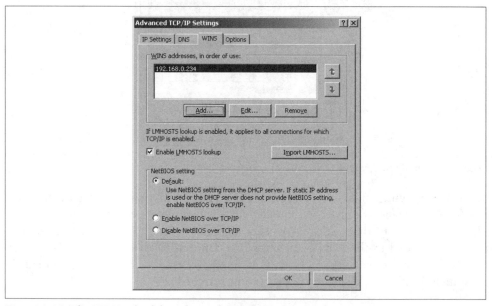

Figure 4-10. The WINS tab of the Advanced TCP/IP Settings window

The basic configuration of the WINS client is very straightforward. Use the Add button in the "WINS addresses, in order of use" pane to enter the IP addresses of the WINS servers this client should use. Use the up and down arrows to define the order in which the servers are used for registration and resolution. If no servers are specified in this pane, the client will use broadcasting for registration and resolution. Chapter 3 describes how WINS registration and resolution functions.

Chapter 3 also describes how the *LMHOSTS* file is created and used. Mark the Enable *LMHOSTS* Lookup checkbox to use the *LMHOSTS* file for NetBIOS name resolution. The *LMHOSTS* file is located in the *%SystemRoot%\System32\Drivers\Etc* folder. Use any text editor to create an *LMHOSTS* file based on the sample file *Lmhosts.SAM*, also located in this folder. You can import an existing *LMHOSTS* file by clicking the Import *LMHOSTS* button and browsing for the file. The function of the Import *LMHOSTS* button is the same as that of the #INCLUDE command that can be placed inside the *LMHOSTS* file. See Chapter 3 for a detailed description of this file.

The three option buttons in the "NetBIOS setting" pane of the WINS tab control whether or not NetBIOS over TCP/IP (NetBT) is enabled, and how it is enabled. The functions of two of these buttons are obvious: "Enable NetBIOS over TCP/IP" manually enables NetBT, and "Disable NetBIOS over TCP/IP" manually disables it. Use these buttons to manually control NetBT without regard to the DHCP configuration. The Default button takes the NetBT setting from DHCP. If DHCP does not provide a NetBT setting or DHCP is not used, the Default option enables NetBT by default. Given the mix of NetBIOS network components and the TCP/IP network component shown in Figure 4-3 for this sample system, we need NetBT. Therefore, we would use either the Default option or the "Enable NetBIOS over TCP/IP" option for this sample configuration.

The Options Tab

By default, the Options tab of the Advanced TCP/IP Settings window lists only "TCP/IP filtering" in the "Optional settings" pane. To filter incoming traffic based on ports and protocols, highlight "TCP/IP filtering" and then click Properties to display the TCP/IP Filtering dialog shown in Figure 4-11. Through this dialog Windows Server 2003 allows you to control which TCP ports, UDP ports, and IP Protocols are available to network users.

By default, Windows Server 2003 sets Permit All for all three categories. This means that any network user can access any TCP/IP service available on the server. Of course, this default could change with the next service pack.

In Chapter 2 we saw that each port number represents a network service and that each protocol number identifies a protocol that communicates directly with IP. You can control access to a network service or protocol by controlling access to its TCP port, UDP port, or IP protocol. To restrict one of these elements, click the Permit Only option button for that pane, and use the Add and Remove buttons to list only those ports or protocols that users will be permitted to access. Marking the Permit Only option button for a pane and leaving the associated list blank prohibits users from accessing any resources in that category.

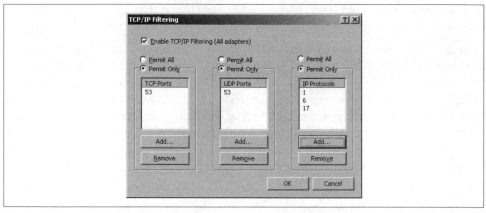

Figure 4-11. The TCP/IP Filtering dialog

The port filtering defined in the TCP/IP Filtering dialog only affects inbound traffic. Figure 4-11 shows a possible configuration for a dedicated DNS server, which is configured to permit only TCP and UDP port 53 (DNS), and only IP protocols, 1 (ICMP), 6 (TCP), and 17 (UDP). With these settings DNS would function normally but other inbound connections would be blocked. For example, this would prevent email from coming into the SMTP port but it would not prevent the administrator of this system from sending email out to some remote server's SMTP port. Outbound traffic is not affected by these filters.

> The port filtering ability offered by the TCP/IP Filtering dialog is very similar to the *inetd.conf* port filtering on Unix systems. It is useful in some security situations, though not all. If you need more capability— for example, the ability to filter port ranges or the ability to deny outbound traffic for a particular port—consider installing Microsoft Routing and RAS. The expanded protocol filtering provided by RRAS is covered in Chapter 8. In addition, the Internet Connection Firewall covered in Chapter 9 provides enhanced protocol filtering.

The "Enable TCP/IP Filtering (All adapters)" checkbox, near the top of the TCP/IP Filtering dialog, should be checked. If it is not checked, the filtering configuration you build with this dialog will not be used. The only time the "Enable TCP/IP Filtering (All adapters)" checkbox should be unchecked is during network troubleshooting, and then only for certain problems. If you have a specific network application that is failing, it is possible that you made a mistake when building your TCP/IP filters. Using this checkbox you can temporarily disable the filters and retest the application. If it still fails, the problem is not in the TCP/IP filters. If the application runs with the filter disabled, the problem *might* be the filter. In that case, you should carefully examine the filter to see if you made a mistake entering port numbers or protocol numbers.

Summary

Basic TCP/IP configuration takes place during the initial Windows Server 2003 installation. At any time, however, you can reconfigure the system through the Network Connections applet in the Control Panel. The configuration is entered on a adapter-by-adapter basis.

An alternative to manually defining the TCP/IP configuration is to use DHCP to automatically provide all of the require configuration information. In Chapter 5 we learn how to set up a DHCP server.

CHAPTER 5
Managing DHCP Services

A Dynamic Host Configuration Protocol (DHCP) server automatically configures TCP/IP clients running DHCP client software. Centralize the management of IP addresses, netmasks, and other TCP/IP configuration information on a DHCP server to reduce the amount of administration needed to manage your network.

DHCP extends an older protocol called Bootstrap Protocol (BOOTP), which provided similar, although more limited functionality. BOOTP was the first comprehensive configuration protocol to provide all of the information commonly used to configure TCP/IP from the client's IP address to what print server the client should use. BOOTP was simple and effective, so effective in fact that it became the basis for DHCP. DHCP operates over the same UDP ports, 67 and 68, as BOOTP. The DHCP protocol exchanges are covered in Chapter 3.

DHCP adds several configuration options to BOOTP along with the ability to temporarily allocate, or *lease*, IP addresses. DHCP provides:

Complete TCP/IP configurations
> A DHCP server provides a complete set of TCP/IP configuration parameters—even rarely used parameters are provided. This allows a network administrator to handle the TCP/IP configuration of clients from a central server.

Dynamic address assignments
> A DHCP server can provide permanent addresses automatically and temporary addresses dynamically. The network administrator can tailor the type of address to the needs of the network and the client system.

BOOTP was originally defined in RFC 951, *Bootstrap Protocol*, dated September 1, 1985. DHCP was originally defined in RFC 1541, *Dynamic Host Configuration Protocol*, dated October 27, 1993. Clearly, the Internet community has long recognized the need for centralized configuration control. Although Microsoft did not define DHCP, Microsoft was instrumental in popularizing it and was one of the first companies to use DHCP to its maximum potential. Additionally, Microsoft has integrated DHCP with Active Directory, Microsoft's DNS server and client, and

Microsoft WINS to ensure that names and IP addresses are kept fully synchronized in all services.

Basic Microsoft DHCP Concepts

Chapter 3 describes how the DHCP protocol works, which provides an important basis for planning a server installation. There are some other basic DHCP concepts that you should also understand in order to properly configure and manage a Microsoft DHCP server.

DHCP Options

The configuration parameters and control information passed in DHCP messages are called DHCP options. DHCP options are defined in several RFCs—there are currently more than 30. However, the bulk of the standard DHCP options are defined in RFC 2131, *DHCP Options and BOOTP Vendor Extensions*.

Most of the options you will work with are DHCP standard options. However, the DHCP protocol makes allowances for vendor-specific options, which are options defined by a hardware or software vendor to provide additional configuration data that is specific to their product. The collection of options associated with a vendor is called a *vendor class*. The options defined in a vendor class are only sent to clients that provide the appropriate Vendor Class Identifier in the DHCP request. Microsoft defines vendor class options for clients running Microsoft operating systems. The standard DHCP options and the Microsoft vendor class options are all described in Appendix A.

Options flow both ways. Most options are provided by the server to the client to configure the client. However, the client can provide options to the server in the DHCP request packet. There are two reasons that clients do this:

- A client may send an option value to the server to request that value from the server. In effect, the client is saying it would like to use a specified value for a particular configuration option. For example, a client may send the server the value it would like to use for the Host Name option.

- Some options are supposed to be set by the client. Examples of this type of option are Client Identifier, Vendor Class Identifier, and User Class. In general, these are options that provide additional information about the client to help the server better configure the client.

This chapter looks primarily at the options provided by the server and how the administrator sets and manages those options. Use the DHCP Microsoft Management Console (MMC) to select the DHCP options that your server will provide and to configure the values it will provide for those options.

In the DHCP message, options are defined as tagged data fields. Each option begins with a one-byte tag called the *code*, which identifies the option. The tag is followed by a length field that defines the length of the option's data field. All configuration options use this variable length format. The DHCP console clearly shows the tag value of each option when displaying the option name. For example, the default DNS domain name is provided in the option identified by the tag value 15. The DHCP console lists this option as 015 DNS Domain Name, clearly providing both the tag value and a descriptive name for the option. The DHCP console is covered later in this chapter.

Options can be defined globally for every network serviced by the server. These are called *server options*. Server options can be overridden for a specific physical network by defining *scope options* (more on scopes in the next section). Finally, server and scope options can be overridden for individual clients by defining *user class options*. User class options are only sent to clients that provide the correct User Class identifier in the DHCP request packet, scope options are provided to every client on a specific network, and server options are provided to every client serviced by the server. This hierarchy provides enough flexibility to handle any configuration.

DHCP Scopes

A DHCP *scope* identifies a specific physical network and defines the DHCP options associated with that network. An administrator defines a scope with the New Scope Wizard by providing the wizard the following information:

Name
> The name of the scope used in the DHCP console. This should be a short, descriptive name that helps you quickly identify the network associated with the scope.

Description
> A more detailed description of the purpose of the DHCP scope. This also appears in the DHCP console and is used to help identify the scope.

IP Address Range
> The range of addresses assigned to the network covered by the scope.

Subnet Mask
> The subnet mask associated with the IP address range.

Excluded Address Range
> Individual or groups of IP addresses within the IP Address Range that are not available for assignment to DHCP clients.

Lease Duration
> The period of time the DHCP server grants to a client to use the IP address.

A server should have at least one scope, but it can have multiple scopes. Different scopes are normally associated with different physical networks. Use a *superscope* to associate multiple scopes with a single physical network. A superscope is an administrative structure that allows multiple scopes to be treated as a single administrative entity. Superscopes are covered in more detail later in this chapter.

In addition to scopes and superscopes, the DHCP console can be used to define a *multicast scope*. Perhaps the most surprising thing about this is that a multicast scope is not strictly speaking a DHCP construct. In reality, the Multicast Address Dynamic Client Assignment Protocol (MADCAP) uses the multicast scope for dynamic multicast address allocation. A multicast scope has no DHCP options associated with it. But it does have an address range, and it does use protocol messages similar to DHCP messages. For these reasons, Microsoft put MADCAP configuration inside the DHCP console.

Planning for DHCP

The characteristics of the DHCP protocol need to be taken into consideration when planning your DHCP server architecture. There are three protocol characteristics to consider:

- DHCP is a broadcast protocol.
- DHCP is an unauthenticated protocol.
- DHCP makes no allowance for backup servers in the protocol.

A DHCP client that does not know its IP address, the network it is on, or the address of the DHCP server cannot send a unicast packet to the server or even a standard IP broadcast. It is forced to send a *limited broadcast* to locate a server. (A limited broadcast is address 255.255.255.255, which is an address that routers are not allowed to forward off of the local network.) Your DHCP server plan needs to take this into consideration when placing servers.

The simplest way to address this protocol limitation is to place a DHCP server on each physical subnet. This has some advantages:

- A server on each subnet generally provides the best performance. The server load is light because the number of clients handled by each server is limited to the number of clients on a single subnet. Additionally, the clients are not separated from the server by any low speed links, and no intervening routers or relays need to handle the DHCP packets flowing between the server and the client.

- This design is often the simplest, particularly if there are a limited number of subnets. This design does not require the addition of routers or relays configured to forward DHCP packets. This design does not require complex DHCP server configurations because each server is configured to handle only one network. And despite the distributed nature of the servers, the DHCP configurations can still be centrally managed through a single DHCP console.

- While this design is just as vulnerable to denial-of-service attacks as is a single-server design, the damage from such an attack is limited to a single subnet. A denial-of-service attack against a central server can affect the entire enterprise.

Of course, there are also disadvantages to placing a server on each network:

- Placing a DHCP server on each subnet may require additional computer hardware. The computer does not need to be a dedicated DHCP server; DHCP can be added to an existing server. However, some server system must exist on each subnet to act as a DHCP server. If no server is available, one must be purchased, configured, and installed on the subnet.

- One server per subnet may not be enough. DHCP is a critical service that requires redundancy. A failover plan must be developed for each subnet server, which may be more complicated than creating redundancy for a single server and may also require more hardware.

- A single DHCP console can centrally manage the DHCP configuration but other remote management issues will still exist. The hardware and software on which the DHCP server is hosted may require some level of local management. If DHCP is hosted on an existing server that has a local administrator, this may not be an issue. But it should be considered when planning the DHCP server placement.

The alternative to placing a server on every network is to create a central server to serve all networks. The problem with this approach is that, as defined in the RFCs, a limited broadcast is not forwarded through a router. However, routers that implement the DHCP/BOOTP relay agent defined by RFC1542 make an exception for DHCP. RFC1542-compliant routers intercept DHCP broadcast requests from clients on the local subnet and forward those packets to a DHCP server on a remote subnet. When the DHCP server responds, the router forwards the response to the local client. Even if your routers don't pass DHCP broadcast packets, you can install the Microsoft DHCP relay agent on each subnet. The DHCP relay agent that comes with the Routing and Remote Access Service forwards DHCP packets just like an RFC1542-compliant router.

The advantages to using a central server are:

- A central server is often easier to manage than a group of distributed servers and requires less staff for administration and operation. The central computer facility usually has better climate control, more reliable power, and more controlled access than distributed computer facilities.

- Implementing redundancy for a central system is generally easier than it is to implement for distributed systems.

- Less server hardware is needed to implement a central server than is needed to implement distributed servers. This advantage, however, may be offset if DHCP relay agents are required for the subnets.

The disadvantages of using a central server are:

- A central DHCP server can be a single point of failure for a critical service. Redundancy addresses system failures, but it does not fully address the security issues surrounding denial-of-service attacks.

- The performance of a central server can be noticeably less than that of a distributed server. This is not necessarily the server's fault. DHCP is an I/O intensive service that places its major burden on disk storage and system memory. With fast disks and abundant RAM, one server should be able to handle a large network easily. However, packets traveling from remote subnets depend on more than just the server. Packets may need to be handled by multiple routers or relay and they may transit slow network links, such as WAN connections. The network topology must be taken into account when deciding where to place DHCP servers.

For many networks the best solution is a hybrid architecture that combines a centralized server with some distributed servers. By combining both types of servers you can draw on the advantages of both and minimize the impact of the disadvantages of both. For example, a central server could be placed on the main campus to serve the bulk of the networks there. Distributed servers could then be placed at any remote campuses and on a few of the larger subnets of the main campus. The central server could then act as the backup server for the distributed servers, and some of the distributed servers on the main campus could act as the backup servers for the central server.

Redundancy Issues

DHCP is a critical network service. Clients configured to use DHCP cannot properly initialize TCP/IP when denied access to a DHCP server. Different types of clients react to the lack of a server in different ways. Windows 2000 and Windows XP clients use Automatic Private IP Addressing (APIPA) when no DHCP server is available. The clients assign themselves addresses from the private network number 169.254.0.0/16 when they cannot obtain an address from a DHCP server. The APIPA address allows the client's network configuration process to continue, but it is not a perfect solution. The APIPA address is only an address; it is not a complete configuration. Additionally, it is unlikely to be the address used on your network. Therefore, clients using APIPA addresses will not be able to fully participate in the network. Finally, because the client believes the APIPA is a valid address lease, it will not renew its address as quickly when the DHCP server comes back online as it would if it were actively searching for an address. (When using an APIPA address the client only attempts to renew its address every five minutes.) For these reasons some network administrators disable the default APIPA address.

To disable the use of default APIPA addressing on Windows 2000 clients, add a DWORD named IPAutoconfigurationEnabled with a value of 0 to the client's registry. Follow these steps to create the necessary DWORD:

1. On each client for which APIPA addressing is to be disabled, run regedit.

2. Go to *HKEY_LOCAL_MACHINE\SYSTEM\CurrentControlSet\Services\Tcpip\Parameters\ Interfaces\<adapter>*, where *<adapter>* is a hexadecimal value assigned to the adapter. If the client has more than one network interface you may need to highlight each interface in turn and examine the configuration data associated with the interface to locate the exact interface you want to work on.

3. Right-click on the *<adapter>* and select New → DWORD Value.

4. Enter IPAutoconfigurationEnabled as the name of the new DWORD value. The default value for a new DWORD is 0, so you probably will not need to modify the value assigned to the DWORD.

Figure 5-1 shows a highlighted adapter and the menus necessary to create a new DWORD. Figure 5-1 also shows the IPAutoconfigurationEnabled DWORD after it has been added to the adapter. You can see it as the last entry in the left pane of this registry window.

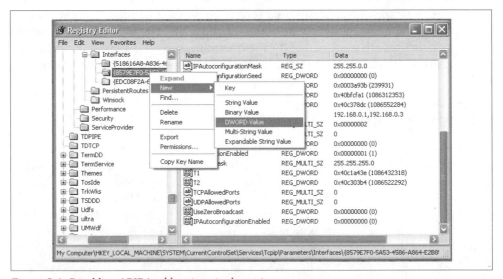

Figure 5-1. Disabling APIPA addressing via the registry

Windows XP provides more choices than simply relying on APIPA addressing. Windows XP allows you to specify an alternative configuration for the client to use when no DHCP server is available. When "Obtain an IP address automatically" is selected on the General tab of the Internet Protocol (TCP/IP) Properties window, DHCP is enabled and the Alternate Configuration tab is added to the Properties window. Select the Alternate Configuration tab to open the window shown in Figure 5-2.

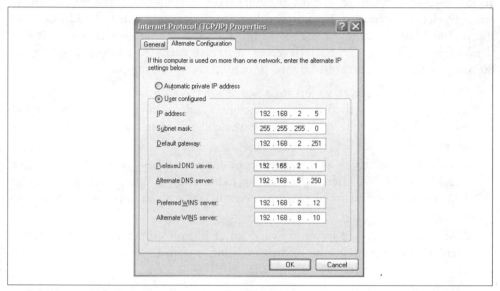

Figure 5-2. Defining an alternate client configuration

As Figure 5-2 shows, the Alternate Configuration tab can be used to select APIPA addressing, or it can be used to define an alternative configuration. The default is to use APIPA, which is selected using the "Automatic private IP address" button. Of course, the only thing APIPA provides is an IP address. Selecting the "User configured" button allows you to define a full basic configuration, including an IP address, the address mask, the default gateway, the addresses of two DNS servers and the IP addresses of two WINS servers. This is certainly a more complete configuration, but it is a static configuration that must be manually defined on each client. For this reason, alternative configurations are primarily used on a small subset of systems that move between two distinct networks environments. An example of such a system is a laptop that is given a DHCP address when it connects to one network and a static address when it connects to another network.

Both APIPA addressing and alternative client configurations have major limitations as techniques for increasing the robustness of the DHCP service. The best way to provide a robust service is at the server, not at the client. Unfortunately the DHCP protocol does not make allowances for redundancy as does, for example, DNS, which automatically queries a backup server when the primary server fails to respond. The DHCP protocol makes no allowances for two servers to share responsibility for the same group of addresses. You must plan your own failover strategy and plan for the allocation of redundant servers.

Microsoft recommends an 80/20 failover strategy. The 80/20 failover strategy places 80% of the addresses under the control of the primary DHCP server and 20% of the addresses under the control of the backup server. To implement the 80/20 failover strategy, define a scope on each server that covers the same range of addresses. On the primary server, exclude the 20% of the addresses that are under the control of the backup server. On the backup server, define an excluded address range for the 80% of the addresses controlled by the primary server. For example:

- On the primary server we create a scope for the address range 192.168.3.1 to 192.168.3.254. We then define an excluded address range of 192.168.3.200 to 192.168.3.254 so that the primary server will not assign any addresses in this range.

- On the backup server we create a scope for the address range 192.168.3.1 to 192.168.3.254. We then define an excluded address range of 192.168.3.1 to 192.168.3.200 so that the backup server will not assign any addresses in this range.

- Addresses from either server are valid for clients on subnet 192.168.3.0/24. Yet there is no overlap in the addresses being assigned, so the servers will not directly interfere with each other.

The 80/20 strategy assumes that there is a primary and a backup server. However, there is no way for the client to know that one server is the primary and one is the backup. The client will simply respond to the first server that provides a valid DHCP offer. This certainly provides redundancy, but it also means that if the backup server is usually faster in responding, the 20% of addresses that it controls will be exhausted first. When its addresses are exhausted there is essentially no redundancy. For this reason, the 80/20 strategy works best when the primary server generally responds first, as would be the case when the primary server is local and the backup server is remote.

The 50/50 failover strategy is an alternative approach that works well when there is no obvious primary server—for example, when two servers of essentially the same capacity are both directly attached to the subnet they are serving. To implement this strategy, each server takes half of the addresses in the scope and excludes half of the addresses. If the number of clients on the subnet substantially exceeds 50% of the addresses in the scope, limiting each server to half of the available addresses may cause problems if one server is down for an extended time or goes down during a time of peak activity.

The limitations of the 50/50 failover strategy can be addressed by the 100/100 failover strategy; however, the 100/100 strategy requires an abundance of addresses. Like the 50/50 strategy, this approach assumes that the servers are equivalent and that there is no clear primary server. But unlike the 50/50 strategy, the 100/100 failover strategy does not halve the number of addresses, it doubles them. For all practical purposes this approach can be used only by organizations that use private network numbers and benefit from proper address allocation planning. As an example, assume we have a subnet of 150 clients, which could easily be served by the address allocation 192.168.2.0/24. Assigning that subnet the address block 192.168.2.0/23 provides twice the number of addresses actually needed, but that is just the number of addresses needed for the 100/100 failover strategy. We implement the 100/100 plan as follows:

- On server A we create a scope for the address range 192.168.2.1 to 192.168.3.254 with an address mask prefix length of 23. We then define an excluded address range of 192.168.3.1 to 192.168.3.254. With this configuration server A will assign addresses in the 192.168.2.0/24 address block, but it will not assign any addresses in the 192.168.3.0/24 range.

- On server B we create a scope for the address range 192.168.2.1 to 192.168.3.254 with an address mask prefix length of 23. We then define an excluded address range of 192.168.2.1 to 192.168.2.254. Server B will assign addresses in the 192.168.3.0/24 address block, but it will not assign any addresses in the 192.168.2.0/24 range.

- Addresses from either server are valid for clients on subnet 192.168.3.0/24. Yet there is no overlap in the addresses being assigned, so the servers will not directly interfere with each other.

All of the failover strategies described above assume that there is a substantial number of unused addresses that can be allocated to the backup server. While this is generally the case with networks that use private network numbers, it is not always the case with older networks that still use public network addresses internally. If addresses are a scarce resource on your network, you may not be able to allocate enough addresses to implement any of these failover strategies. An alternative is to create a hot-standby server. To create a hot standby, provide the standby server with exactly the same configuration as the primary server. But, do not activate the scope on the standby server. During an outage of the primary server, the standby server is put into service by manually activating the scope. The need for manual intervention and the possibility of human error when activating and deactivating the scope make this the least desirable way to provide redundancy. Sometimes, however, it may be the only choice.

A hardware solution to DHCP redundancy is available to those who use hardware clusters for their servers. DHCP is a *cluster-aware application*. If you have a cluster of systems running Windows Server 2003 Enterprise Edition, you can assign cluster resources to the DHCP Server service so that any server in the cluster can handle DHCP requests. The service must be assigned a name resource, an IP address resource, and a disk resource. The virtual IP address assigned to the service should be a statically assigned, excluded address from the scope covered by the DHCP service. The disk resource is a shared device where all DHCP files should reside.

Installing the DHCP Server

As the "General TCP/IP Configuration" section of Chapter 4 made clear, the DHCP client software is installed on all Windows systems by default. The DHCP server software, however, is only installed if the system administrator takes the necessary steps to install it. There is a very good reason for this. Every system needs to receive an IP address assignment, but only a limited number of servers are needed to assign those addresses. Additionally, systems that inadvertently run DHCP server software cause problems for clients by interfering with communication between the clients and the real DHCP server. This section covers the steps needed to install the DHCP server role on a Windows 2003 Server system.

The DHCP server software can be installed by using the traditional Add or Remove Programs tool, or alternatively, through the newer Manage Your Server window, as can many essential network services. Run the Manage Your Server tool by selecting it from the Administrative Tools menu of the All Programs menu in the Start menu. Add the DHCP server role by clicking the "Add or remove a role" link found near the top of the Manage Your Server window. This opens the Configure Your Server Wizard shown in Figure 5-3. (After the DHCP server has been installed and configured, it is listed on the Manage Your Server window as one of the roles configured for the server. If it is already listed there, there is no need to reinstall it. You can skip this section and jump to the section "Using the DHCP Console.")

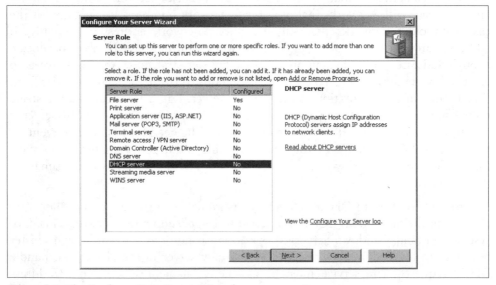

Figure 5-3. The Configure Your Server Wizard

Highlight DHCP Server in the Server Role list box and click Next. This, of course, assumes that DHCP server is listed in this window and that the Configured field of the DHCP server listing says No:

- If the Configured field says Yes, the DHCP software is already installed and configured. Click Back to return to the Manage Your Server window and click the "Manage this DHCP server" link to go to the DHCP console, which is covered later in this chapter.

- If DHCP Server is not listed in the Server Role list box, click the Add or Remove Programs link to run the Add or Remove Programs Wizard and use that wizard to add the required DHCP software. However, unless someone previously removed the software, it should not be necessary to add it in now because the DHCP server software is included as a basic part of a Windows Server 2003 installation.

After highlighting "DHCP server" and clicking Next, a Summary of Selections is displayed. The summary will include two items:

- Install the DHCP server
- Configure a new DHCP scope

Click Next to undertake these two tasks.

Installing the DHCP server software requires no real input since you are only copying the necessary files and Registry settings to your server's hard drive. However, the New Scope Wizard that is launched when you click Next requires input from a knowledgeable system administrator who understands DHCP scopes.

Configuring a DHCP Scope

The Configure Your Server window launches the New Scope Wizard during the initial installation and configuration of the DHCP server. Once the DHCP server is installed, the New Scope Wizard can be launched from the Action menu of the DHCP console, which is covered later in this chapter.

Click Next when the welcome window of the New Scope Wizard appears. This takes you to the Scope Name window. This window contains two boxes: Name and Description. Enter the scope name in the Name box. The name can be up to 128 characters long, but should be a short, technically descriptive name. For example, if the scope provides values for subnet 172.16.2.0 on network 172.16.0.0, a reasonable scope name might be "Subnet-172.16.2". Use the Description field to provide a more complete description of the scope. For example, "DHCP settings for the sales group at the Clopper Road office" might be a reasonable description value. When appropriate values are entered, click Next to move to the IP Address Range window.

Use the "Start IP address" and "End IP address" boxes on the IP Address Range window to define the range of addresses associated with the scope. This is the full pool of addresses from which the server can dynamically assign addresses to clients in this scope, although as we will see in a moment some addresses within the range can be excluded from dynamic assignment. Normally, the address range maps to a specific subnet served by the server. Figure 5-4 shows the IP Address Range window after an address range has been defined.

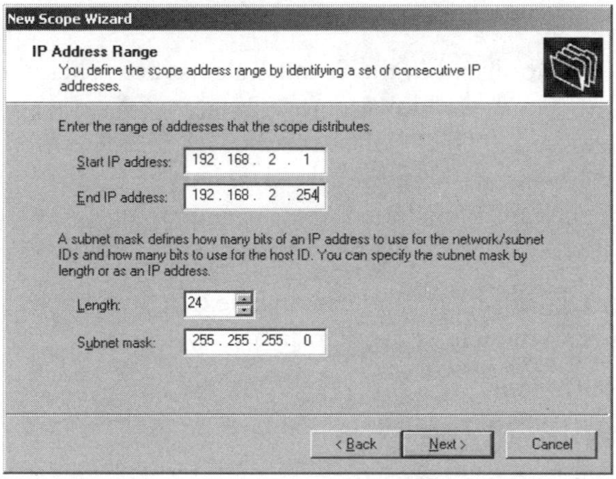

Figure 5-4. New scope IP address range

The subnet mask associated with the address range is specified at the bottom of the window using either the Length box or the Subnet mask box. By default, Windows automatically fills in the Length and Subnet mask boxes using the natural mask associated with the IP address entered in the "Start IP address" box. (See Chapter 2 for information on addresses and masks.) If this default value is not correct for your network, enter the mask as a prefix-length in the Length box or as an address mask using dotted decimal notation in the Subnet mask box. When the address and mask values are correct, click Next to go to the Add Exclusions window, shown in Figure 5-5.

To exclude addresses from dynamic address assignment, enter the range of addresses to be excluded in the "Start IP address" and "End IP address" boxes and then click Add. Once a range of addresses has been defined, it is listed in the "Excluded address range" list box. To return excluded addresses to the pool of addresses that can be dynamically assigned, highlight the address range in the "Excluded address range" list box and click the Remove button. Figure 5-5 shows one range of excluded addresses that has already been defined (192.168.2.1 to 192.168.2.31) and one range that is about to be defined (192.168.2.200 to 192.168.2.254). Some common reasons for excluding addresses from the dynamic address pool are to hold addresses in reserve for future expansion, to set aside addresses that will be used by the backup DHCP server, and to use some addresses for static assignment. After you have defined all excluded addresses, click Next to go to the Lease Duration window.

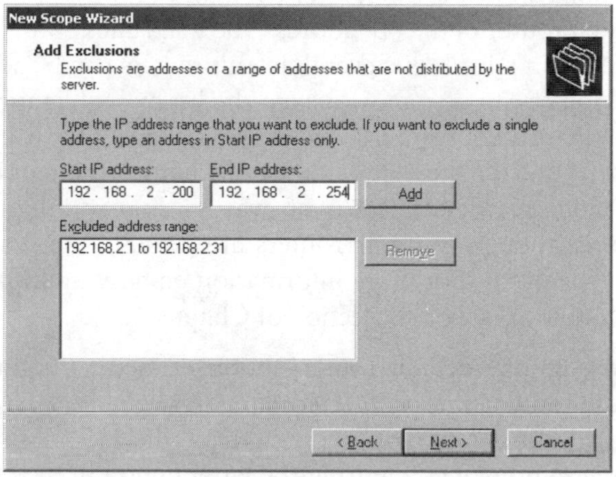

Figure 5-5. Excluding addresses from a DHCP scope

Use the Days, Hours, and Minutes boxes on the Lease Duration window to define the length of time an address in this scope will be leased. Windows sets this to eight days by default. Eight days or more is a fine value for the average office environment where most clients are desktop systems that simply stay attached to the network. On the other hand, if clients come and go rapidly, as they do in, for example, a dial-up environment, a short duration of one day or less may be more appropriate. The type of address being assigned is another factor that influences the length of the lease. If the server is assigning official, public addresses, the number of addresses available to the organization is probably limited and each address costs you money. In that case, a short lease duration can be helpful to ensure that all addresses are being effectively used. If, however, the server is assigning private network addresses, the addresses cost the organization nothing and are abundant. In this case, there is no need to recover addresses rapidly and a long lease duration is fine. Set a duration that is appropriate for your environment and your address space and then click Next.

The Configure DHCP Options window is next. Select Yes to configure the options for this scope or No to skip this part of the configuration. Scope options override server options. Server options apply to all scopes serviced by the server, but scope options apply to only one scope. Both scope and server options can be defined later using the DHCP console, which is covered in the "Using the DHCP Console" section. However, it is usually a good idea to say Yes at this point and define a few scope options now. There are two reasons for this. First, scopes often require unique option values. A good example is the default router option, which varies from subnet to subnet. The second reason is that this is the initial installation of DHCP. At this point there are no server options defined. Create at least a minimal set of configuration settings with the initial configuration. They can always be changed later.

The first scope option window is the Router (Default Gateway) window. Enter the IP address of the default router in the "IP address" box and click Add. The newly added router address appears in a list box. Several default routers can be added in this manner. An unneeded router can be removed from the list by highlighting it and clicking Remove. Reorder the routers in the list with the Up and Down buttons. Order is important because (1) all of these routers are default routers, and (2) they are all given the same routing metric. (There is no way to set a routing metric using this window.) Thus, even though multiple routers are defined, the first router listed is generally the only one used. (For more information on how multiple default routers are used, see the "Adding Gateways" section of Chapter 4.)

Most scopes have only one default router option defined. If additional routes are needed, other static routers can be entered later through the DHCP console using either the 030 Static Route Option or, my preference, the 249 Classless Static Routes option. There is an example of configuring the latter option in the "Using the DHCP Console" section later in this chapter.

After defining a default router, click Next to go to the Domain Name and DNS Servers window. Figure 5-6 shows this window.

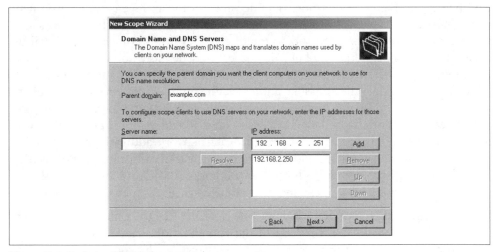

Figure 5-6. Defining DNS information for a new scope

Specify the name of the DNS domain to which the DHCP clients belong in the "Parent domain" box. The clients will use this domain name to create a default domain search list for name resolution. It is this domain and the parents of this domain that will be appended to unqualified domain names when the clients issue DNS queries. (The way in which the default domain name is used to build DNS queries is described in Chapter 4 in the section "The DNS Tab.")

Enter the IP address of each DNS server in the "IP address" box. A DNS server may be identified by name as an alternative to entering the DNS server's IP address.

When a name is entered, the Resolve button becomes active. Click the Resolve button to retrieve the IP address associated with the DNS server's hostname, which then appears in the "IP address" box. When the address is defined, click Add to add the address to the server list. Use the Up and Down buttons to define the order in which the servers are queried. Again, order is important. Set the order to match the DNS server architecture you have defined for your organization. Don't enter too many servers in this list. As explained in Chapter 4, defining more than three DNS servers is usually counterproductive.

Unlike the default router, which is usually a scope option, the DNS server information is often a server option because (1) every client needs to know the address of a DNS server, and (2) the same DNS server may be used by multiple scopes. If you use the same DNS servers across all scopes, define the 006 DNS Servers option as a server option, using the DHCP console. If you have only one scope or if you place DNS servers on individual subnets, define the DNS server information as a scope option. If this is the initial installation, define the DNS server information as a scope option. You can always change it later when another scope is added, but defining it now ensures that this important value is there for the clients without any additional configuration steps being taken—additional steps that could be overlooked.

Enter the correct DNS domain name and the correct DNS server addresses and then click Next. This takes you to the WINS Servers window. This window looks much like the bottom half of the window shown in Figure 5-6. Enter the address of a WINS server in the "IP address" box and then click Add to add it to the list of servers. Alternatively, you can enter the name of the server in the "Server name" box and click Resolve to obtain the IP address of the WINS server. When resolved, the address appears in the IP address box. Clicking Add then adds the server to the WINS server list. When the server list is complete and accurate, click Next.

Finally you'll see the Activate Scope window. Choose Yes to make the scope immediately active or No to create the scope but leave it inactive. As soon as a scope is active, the server will respond to client requests. For many clients, the only information needed is an IP address, a default router, a domain name, and the address of a DNS server. That basic information has been defined. If the scope definition is complete enough for your clients, choose Yes. If the scope is not yet ready to go, choose No and use the DHCP console to complete the configuration.

Using the DHCP Console

The DHCP console is the Microsoft Management Console (MMC) used to manage and configure the DHCP service. Launch the DHCP console by clicking the "Manage this DHCP server" link in the Manage Your Server window or by selecting DHCP from the Administrative Tools menu in the Start menu. The DHCP console is shown in Figure 5-7 as it appears after the initial server installation described in the section "Installing the DHCP Server" earlier in this chapter.

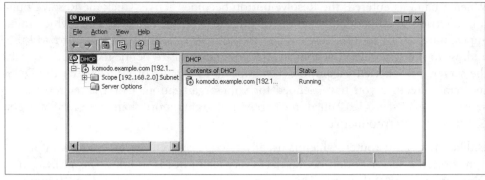

Figure 5-7. The DHCP console

The DHCP console window is divided into two panes. On the left is a navigation pane that lists the various DHCP servers, scopes, and options controlled by this console. The lefthand pane is called the *console tree* because the display is in the form of a hierarchical tree. The righthand pane shows detailed information about the object that is selected in the console tree, and is called the *details pane*. Selecting an object in the console tree changes the context of the console—it changes the type of object being managed and therefore the type of management operations needed. This is reflected by the fact that the contents of the Action menu changes depending on the type of object selected in the navigation window.

Figure 5-7 lists only one server in the navigation window, which is the local server just installed in the previous section of this chapter. The DHCP console can manage multiple servers, and it is often useful to do so. DHCP servers are frequently located near their clients to reduce the amount of broadcast traffic crossing the network and to improve responsiveness. Despite the distributed placement of the servers, many organizations still want those servers centrally managed, which can be done with a single DHCP console.

Adding a Server

To add a DHCP server to the console, highlight DHCP in the console tree (lefthand pane) of the DHCP console window. Open the Action menu and select "Add server" to open the Add Server window. The Add Server window offers two ways to select a server. The lower half of the window contains a list box that lists the authorized DHCP servers found in the Active Directory. (How and why a DHCP server needs to be authorized is covered in the section "Authorizing" later in this chapter.) To add an authorized server, highlight it in the list box and select the "This authorized server" button. Alternatively, you can specify the name of the server you want to add using the box at the top of the Add Server window and selecting the "This server" button. To search the network for a server, click the Browse button, which opens the Select Computer window shown in Figure 5-8.

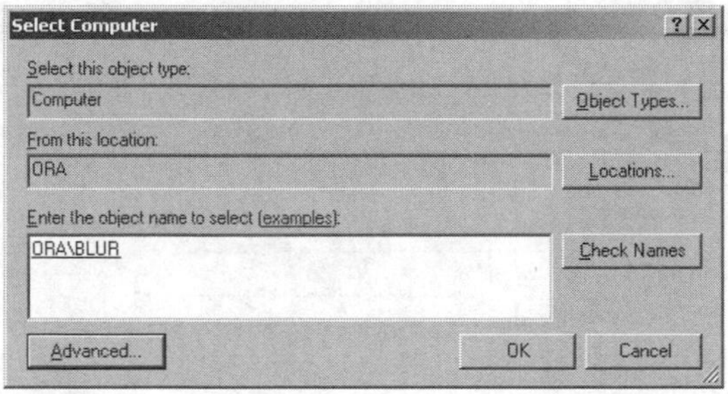

Figure 5-8. Browsing for a server

Use the Select Computer window to specify the network object type, location, and name. In this particular case, the object type is always Computer. Clicking the Object Types button presents a window with only one object type choice—Computers. The Location box can contain the name of any Windows domain available on the network. Click the Locations button to view the Windows domains known to this system. In the Locations window, highlight the domain you want to search and click OK. Finally, enter the name of the DHCP server that you wish to add in the list box at the bottom of the window and click Check Names. The local system will query the domain controller and insert the proper form of the object name in the list box. For example, in Figure 5-8, the computer name BLUR was typed into the list box. When Check Names was pressed, the system changed the name to ORA\BLUR. If this is the name of the DHCP server you want to add, click OK. This name will be transferred to the This server box of the Add Server window. In that window, click OK to add the server to the list of servers managed by the DHCP console.

The Select Computer window is not what I am likely to think of when I want to browse for a value. As Figure 5-8 shows, you must enter everything about the server (name, location, type). I generally use browsing to find a value when I'm not sure exactly what the value is. The Advanced button on the Select Computer window provides this more traditional browsing service. Figure 5-9 shows the window that opens when you click the Advanced button.

The window shown in Figure 5-9 is essentially an expansion of the Select Computer window in Figure 5-8. The key feature of this expanded window is the Find Now button. Click Find Now to find all computers in the specified domain. The computers found by the search are listed in the box at the bottom of the window, which provides a selection more like the traditional browse mechanism used in most Windows functions. Simply highlight the name of the DHCP server in the list and click OK to add a server to the DHCP console.

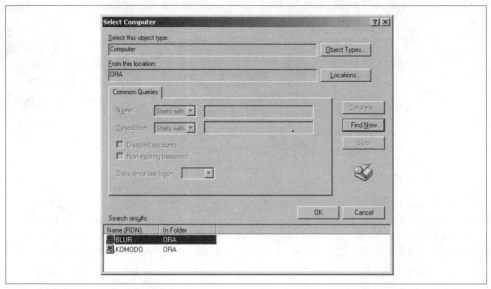

Figure 5-9. Advanced DHCP server search

Adding a Scope or a Superscope

To add a scope to a server, highlight the server in the console tree, open the Action menu and select New Scope. This launches the same New Scope Wizard that was described in the section "Configuring a DHCP Scope" earlier in this chapter. Each server has at least one scope, but can have multiple scopes.

A scope covers a single address range associated with a single physical network. In the examples shown so far, we have defined the Subnet 2 scope with the address range 192.168.2.0/24 for a single subnet. Traditionally, each scope is associated with a different physical network. Thus, simply adding a new scope to our sample system would not provide additional addresses for the physical network covered by the Subnet 2 scope. To do that, you need a superscope.

Superscopes increase the configuration flexibility of DHCP servers by combining multiple scopes into a single administrative entity. Using a superscope, the Subnet 2 scope and a new scope could work together to provide sufficient addresses for a large physical network. A superscope is easier and more flexible way to increase the addresses available to a network than creating a larger address block, because the address ranges of the various scopes in a superscope do not need to be contiguous. Changing the address block assigned to the Subnet 2 scope to 192.168.2.0/23 doubles the number of addresses available to the network, but this approach only works if the contiguous block of addresses from 192.168.2.0 to 192.168.3.255 is available. Superscopes don't have this limitation.

As an example, assume that the sales department has grown substantially and now needs more addresses than can be provided by the Subnet 2 scope. The first step is to use the New Scope Wizard to create an additional scope. Let's assume that we name the scope Subnet 5 and give it the address range 192.168.5.1 to 192.168.5.254 with some addresses excluded. When the wizard prompts us for the basic options for scope Subnet 5, we use the same DNS domain name, the same DNS server addresses, and the same WINS server addresses that we used for the Subnet 2 scope. We must, however, provide a new value for the default gateway option because the address of the default gateway must have the same network number as the address of the client using that gateway. In our example, this means that clients covered by Scope 2 must use a default gateway with an address that falls in the 192.168.2.0/24 address space, and clients covered by scope Subnet 5 must use a default gateway with an address in the 192.168.5.0/24 address space. This is despite the fact that all of these clients are on the same physical network and use the same physical router. Of course, this also means that the router must be configured to directly attach to both the logical network 192.168.2.0/24 and the logical network 192.168.5.0/24. This can be done by either installing two physical network interfaces in the router or by assigning two different addresses to a single network interface of the router. (The router configuration you choose depends on the hardware and software capabilities of the router.) Once the new scope is created and the router is properly configured, we create the superscope.

To create a superscope from these scopes, highlight the server in the DHCP console tree and select New Superscope from the Action menu to start the New Superscope Wizard. Click Next at the welcome screen. The wizard prompts for the name of the superscope. Enter a short, descriptive name and click Next. The window shown in Figure 5-10 appears.

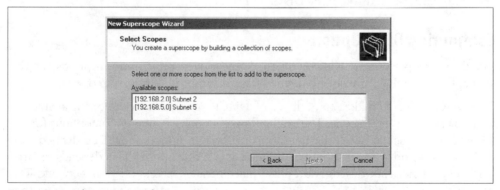

Figure 5-10. Selecting scopes for a superscope

The "Available scopes" box lists all of the scopes available on this server. Highlight the scopes to be included in the superscope and click Next. Not necessarily every scope listed in the "Available scopes" box will be included in a superscope. A DHCP server can service several networks, some of which require only a single scope and others of which require superscopes. Therefore, the server may have a mixture of scopes and superscopes.

The New Superscope Wizard concludes with a summary window that identifies the new superscope and lists the scopes included in the superscope. Figure 5-11 shows the summary page for the sample superscope we just created.

Figure 5-11. A newly created superscope

Click Finish and the newly created superscope will appear in the DHCP console tree. The hierarchy in the console tree is servers, scopes, and superscopes directly under the server, and scopes under the superscopes. Each object in this hierarchy is managed and configured through the DHCP console.

Configuring DHCP Options

The New Scope Wizard allows you to define three configuration options for the scope. Use the DHCP console to define server options or additional scope options.

The DHCP console makes the full set of DHCP configuration options available for both the server and the scope. The availability of identical configuration options for the server and the scope raises the question of when an option should be defined as a server option and when it should be defined as a scope option. This depends in large part on your network design and on the placement of servers on your network. The basic rule of thumb is to define a server option for every configuration value that applies to most of your networks and to define scope options for only those configuration values that are unique to the network covered by the scope. Scope options override server options, so even if a server option is defined for the bulk of your networks, it can be overridden by a scope value when necessary for an individual network.

The sample scopes Subnet 2 and Subnet 5 created in the previous section used the same values for DNS domain name, domain server addresses, and WINS server addresses. Only the default router address was unique for each scope. In that case, the DNS domain name, DNS server addresses, and WINS server addresses all could have been defined as server options.

To add a server option, select the Server Option object in the DHCP console tree, open the Action menu and select Configure Options to open the Server Options window. The window lists all of the standard DHCP configuration options. Scroll down the list of options and check the option you want to configure. Only the options you check will be sent to the client. There are many options, but only a small number are usually configured.

When you check an option, the lower portion of the Server Options window (i.e., the "Data entry" portion of the window), changes as necessary so that the appropriate values can be entered for the selected option. Figure 5-12 shows the Server Options window as it appears when the 006 DNS Servers option has been selected.

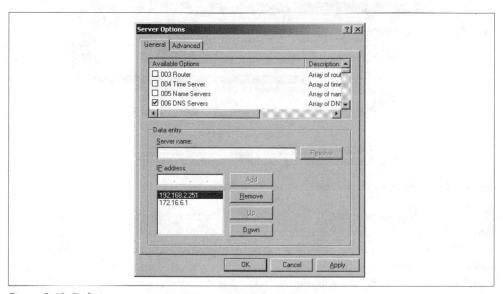

Figure 5-12. Defining a server option

The data entry area of the window provides the same boxes and buttons for this option as we saw and used when we ran the New Scope Wizard. In Figure 5-12 two server addresses have already been entered. Click Apply to add the option to the configuration and to continue configuring more options. Click OK to close the Server Options window.

Notice that directly above the 006 DNS Servers option is an option named 005 Name Servers. It is possible to confuse Name Servers and DNS Servers, but they are two different things. (The 005 Name Servers option refers to an obsolete type of name server.) There are many different options and the purpose of some of them may not be clear from the option name and the short description shown in the option list. For a more complete explanation of the options see Appendix A.

When an option is defined as a server option, there is no need to define that option as a scope option if the scope option will contain the same value as the server option. Redundantly defining a value does no direct harm, but it does increase the possibility of an administrative error if someone updates the server value and fails to update the duplicate scope value. For this reason, administrators usually delete scope options that exactly duplicate server options and only keep unique scope options. To delete a scope option, first expand the listing of scope objects by clicking on the + next to the scope name in the console tree. Next, highlight Scope Options under the expanded scope. This displays in the righthand pane all of the scope options that have been configured. In the righthand pane, highlight the option that you want to delete and select Delete from the Action menu. Figure 5-13 provides an example.

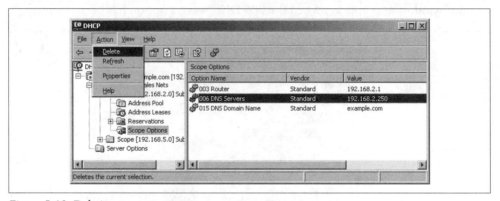

Figure 5-13. Deleting a scope option

The Action drop-down menu in Figure 5-13 partially obscures the console tree. However, this is the server we have configured with two scopes, Subnet 2 and Subnet 5. The Subnet 2 scope, which is partially obscured, has been expanded and the subordinate objects (Address Pool, Address Leases, Reservations, and Scope Options) can be clearly seen. In Figure 5-13, it is the scope options of scope Subnet 2 that are shown in the righthand pane and it is these options that are being acted upon. Scope Subnet 5 has not yet been expanded. Deleting the 006 DNS Servers option in the Subnet 2 scope has no effect on Subnet 5. The same steps detailed above would need to be repeated for Subnet 5 to delete all of the duplicate DNS Servers options.

In addition to deleting scope options, the DHCP console can be used to add scope options. The New Scope Wizard can define no more than four scope options: 003

Routers, 006 DNS Servers, 015 DNS Domain Name, and 044 WINS/NBNS Servers. All other scope options must be defined with the DHCP console. To add a scope option, click on the + next to the scope name in the console tree to expand the listing of scope objects, highlight Scope Options under the expanded scope and select Configure Options from the Action·menu. Figure 5-14 shows an option being added to the Subnet 2 scope.

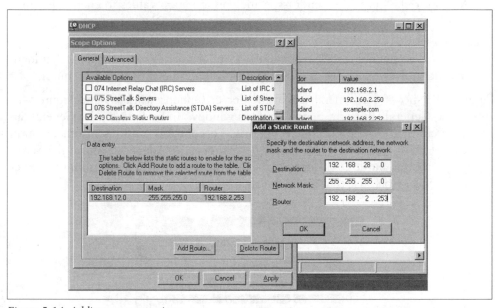

Figure 5-14. Adding a scope option

Options dealing with routing are good examples of DHCP options that are often scope options. As described earlier in this chapter and in Chapter 4, defining multiple default routes, as can be done with the 003 Routers option, has definite limitations. In most cases, one default router is all that is needed, and if additional routes are needed those routes are static routes to specific destinations—not default routes. Figure 5-14 illustrates how static routes are defined as scope options. In the Scope Options window, option 249 Classless Static Routes is selected. Clicking Add Route opens the Add a Static Route dialog box, where the destination, mask, and router are defined. Click OK in the Add a Static Route dialog box to add the route to the list of static routes in the Scope Options window, then click Apply to add those routes to the configuration.

Classless Static Routes is just an example of one of the options that can be defined as a scope option. Every option listed in the Available Options box is a valid scope option.

Using Option Classes

All of the server and scope options described so far in this chapter are standard DHCP options. However, other option classes can be defined. Option classes fall into two basic categories:

Vendor classes
> A vendor class provides vendor-specific configuration values to clients that provide the correct Vendor Class Identifier option in the DHCP request.

User classes
> A user class defines DHCP configuration options for a group of clients that identify themselves with a specific User Class option value in the DHCP request.

Figure 5-12 shows the General tab of the Server Options window, and Figure 5-14 shows the General tab of the Scope Options window. In both cases, the General tab can only configure standard DHCP options. To configure options in other option classes, select the Advanced tab. Figure 5-15 shows the Advanced tab of the Scope Options window, but it could just as easily show the Advanced tab from the Server Options window because they are identical.

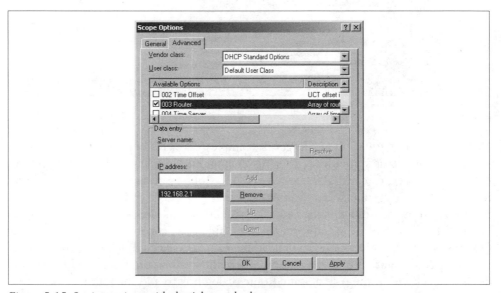

Figure 5-15. Setting options with the Advanced tab

The Advanced tab adds a "Vendor class" drop-down box and a "User class" drop-down box, which are used to select the vendor class and the user class of the options being configured. In Figure 5-15, the vendor class is DHCP Standard Options, and the user class is Default User Class. Select these two values to set exactly the same standard DHCP options as those set through the General tab. Of course, there are other vendor and user class values available.

Working with user classes

By default, the "User class" drop-down list contains three values:

Default BOOTP Class
> Select this class to define unique option values for BOOTP clients. DHCP servers can support both DHCP clients and BOOTP clients. However, BOOTP clients do not have all of the capabilities of DHCP clients. For example, they do not understand address leases and therefore do not attempt to renew leases. Happily, most clients support DHCP, and only some old or specialized systems are limited to BOOTP. But it is possible that you have such systems on your network and that those systems require additional or different option values. The server will provide the options defined in the Default BOOTP Class in its response to a BOOTP request.

Default Routing and Remote Access Class
> Use this class to define options for remote clients that enter the network through a Routing and Remote Access Service (RRAS) server. For example, you might select this class and define a short lease time with the 051 Lease option so that dial-up clients that attach to the network through a RRAS server are given a shorter lease time than clients attached directly to the local network.

Default User Class
> This class defines options for all clients. A value defined in this class can be overridden by values defined in other classes. For example, if the Default User Class defines a lease time, a domain name, and DNS server addresses, and the Default Routing and Remote Access Class defines a lease time, a dial-up client gets the lease time from the Default Routing and Remote Access Class and all other values from the Default User Class.

You can add your own classes to these three predefined classes. To do so, highlight the server in the console tree and then select Define User Classes from the Action menu to open the Define User Classes dialog box. In that box, click the Add button to open the New Class dialog box shown in Figure 5-16.

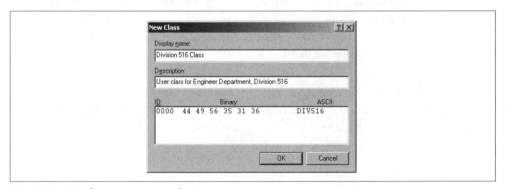

Figure 5-16. Defining a new user class

Enter a short, descriptive name for the new class in the Display Name box. In the Description box enter additional details that explain the purpose of this new class. Both of these fields are displayed by the DHCP console when this class is selected, and they are intended solely to help the administrator determine what class is being worked on. These values have no impact on the DHCP protocol.

In the area at the bottom of the dialog box, enter the User Class identifier you will be using for this user class. Enter the identifier in ASCII text under the ASCII heading or in hexadecimal under the Binary heading. This is an arbitrary value that can be any-thing you wish, but to prevent conflicts with vendor class identifiers, avoid using hardware or software product names. In Figure 5-16, we use DIV516 as the User Class identifier. When the value you have chosen is entered, click OK in the New Classes dialog and then click Close in the Define User Classes dialog. The new class will now appear in the "User class" drop-down list of the Advanced tab.

No special client configuration is required to use the predefined user classes because the DHCP server can determine that a request comes from a BOOTP client or through a RRAS server. However, when you define your own user class, it is not used unless clients are configured to request it. A client does this by placing the correct User Class identifier in the DHCP request. The client must be configured with the correct identifier using the ipconfig command. For example, the following command defines DIV516 as the user class identifier on a Windows XP client:

```
C:\>ipconfig /setclassid "Local Area Connection" DIV516
Windows XP IP Configuration
        DHCP ClassId successfully modified for adapter "Local Area Connection"
```

Creating user classes allows you to define unique DHCP option values for subsets of clients within a single scope. Vendors also define classes, but for the somewhat different purpose of providing additional options beyond the standard set of DHCP options.

Working with vendor classes

Refer back to the Advanced tab shown in Figure 5-15. In addition to selecting a user class, the Advanced tab allows you to select a vendor class. The "Vendor class" drop-down box found on the Advanced tab provides four vendor class values. These ven-dor class values are available by default:

DHCP Standard Options
> This value is available through the "Vendor class" drop-down box, but it is not really a vendor class. DHCP Standard Options is provided in the vendor drop-down box so that the same window can be used to configure standard options and vendor-specific option. Vendor-specific options do not provide a complete configuration. Vendor-specific options are always combined with some number of standard DHCP options. Select this value to configure the standard DHCP

options that are provided to every client regardless of the Vendor Class Identifier option in the client's DHCP request.

Microsoft Options

Select this value to configure Microsoft-specific options for Microsoft clients. These options apply to Windows 98, Windows 2000, Windows XP, and Windows Server 2003 clients. The available options are a concatenation of the options defined for the following two vendor classes.

Microsoft Windows 2000 Options

Select this value to configure options specific to Windows 2000, Windows XP, and Windows Server 2003 clients. When Microsoft Windows 2000 Options is selected, the Available Options list box contains only three options: the Microsoft Disable NetBIOS Option, the Microsoft Release DHCP Lease on Shutdown Option, and the Microsoft Default Router Metric Option. (These options are explained in Appendix A with the other DHCP options.)

Microsoft Windows 98 Options

Select this value to configure options specific to Windows 98 clients. By default, there are no configurable Windows 98–specific options. Therefore, when Microsoft Windows 98 Options is selected, the Available Options list box is empty. You can, however, add options to an existing option class, as we will see later.

Vendor classes extend the options available to configure a client. They do not replace or override the standard DHCP options; they simply create additional options that can be used to convey vendor-specific configuration data.

You cannot invent a vendor class. The hardware or software vendor defines the Vendor Class Identifier. If you want your DHCP server to provide vendor-specific configuration data to non-Microsoft clients, you must obtain the correct vendor class identifier from the vendor, and you must then manually add that new vendor class to the DHCP server configuration. Here's how.

In the DHCP console tree, highlight the server to which the vendor class is to be added. (Vendor classes are not scope or superscope values; they apply to an entire server and therefore a server must be selected.) Select Define Vendor Classes from the Action menu to open the DHCP Vendor Classes window shown in Figure 5-17.

The DHCP Vendor Classes window lists the vendor classes that have been defined for this system. To delete an existing vendor class, highlight it and click the Remove button. To modify an existing class, highlight it and click the Edit button. Windows Server 2003 systems come preconfigured with the three Microsoft vendor classes described above. The Edit and Remove buttons are not active when a preconfigured Microsoft vendor class is highlighted because those classes cannot be modified or deleted. The Add button, however, is always active. Click Add to add a new vendor class. The Add button opens the New Class dialog box, shown earlier in Figure 5-16.

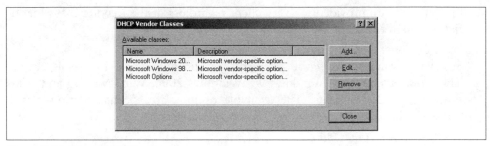

Figure 5-17. The DHCP Vendor Classes window

The first two fields in the New Class dialog box are "Display name" and Description. The "Display name" should be a short, descriptive name for the vendor class. Description is a short description of the purpose of the class. These two fields can be anything that you want because they are only used inside the various tools of the DHCP console and have no effect on the DHCP protocol. However, the freedom to choose a value you like does not extend to the third field in the dialog box. The third field defines the exact value of the Vendor Class Identifier option the server expects to receive in the client's DHCP request. This value must be defined exactly as specified by the vendor. The New Class dialog box accepts the Vendor Class Identifier in either hexadecimal or in ASCII. Enter a hexadecimal value under the Binary heading or enter an ASCII value under the ASCII heading. See Figure 5-16 for an example of this dialog box.

Of course, defining a class does not define the options included in that class. Options can be added to any class using the instructions found in the next section. However, the options for a vendor class should be those options required by the vendor. In the same way that the value for the Vendor Class Identifier must come from the vendor, the special options and the values required for those options must also come from the vendor.

Defining new options and setting defaults

To define new options for any class or to change the default value for an existing option, begin by highlighting the server in the console tree. From the Action menu, select Set Predefined Options to open the Predefined Options and Values dialog shown in Figure 5-18.

Use the "Option class" drop-down list to select the option class you will be working on. This list contains the DHCP Standard Options class, the three Microsoft option classes, and any vendor and user option classes that you have defined. The "Option name" drop-down list lists every option that has been defined for this class. In Figure 5-18, option 002 Time Offset, which is an option in the DHCP Standard Options class, is selected. The Description field and the Value box change according to the option selected.

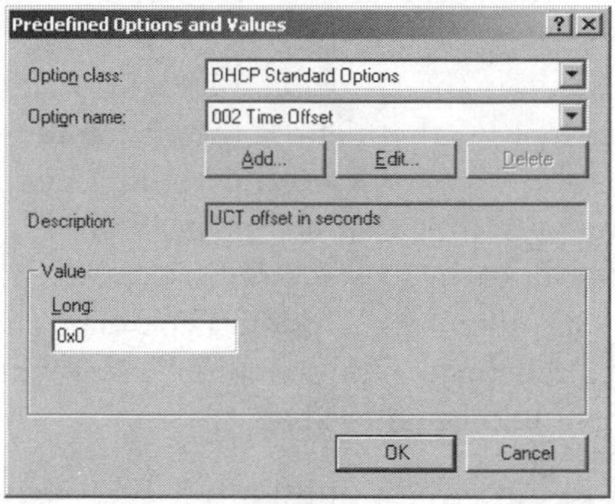

Figure 5-18. Creating new options and setting defaults

To define a different default value for the option, simply enter the new value in the correct format in the Value box. In the figure, the value is a Long and the value is entered as a hexadecimal number. Some other options, such as 006 DNS Servers, are displayed as an array of values. When that is the case, an Edit Array button is displayed, which must be clicked before you can enter the new default values. The defaults defined here are the defaults you see in the Server Option and Scope Option windows when configuring an option. Defining a default value does not mean that the option is used or sent to the client. The option must still be configured through a Scope Option or Server Option window. The Value box of the Predefined Options and Values window only sets a default value for the option.

Also use the Predefined Options and Values window to add a new option to an option class. To add an option, select the desired option class from the Option class drop-down list and then click the Add button. This opens the Option Type box shown in Figure 5-19.

Figure 5-19. Defining a new option

The Class field in the Option Type window indicates the option class selected in the Predefined Options and Values window. In this case, the field contains Global, which is the value used when the DHCP Standard Options class is selected. The Name and Description fields are only used in the DHCP console displays. They have no impact on the DHCP protocols and can be anything you wish. Of course, these fields should be assigned short, descriptive values that clearly identify the option to the administrator. The Code is the tag value officially assigned to this option. The correct Code specified in the RFC that defines the option must be used. In this example, the code assigned to the Location Coordinate Information (LCI) option in RFC 3825 is used, and it is the only code that can be used for this option. The Data Type field defines the type of data carried by the option. Select the correct type from the Data Type drop-down list. When the Option Type dialog is completed, click OK. This returns you to the Predefined Options and Values window where the default value for the new option should be entered.

No matter what is done on the server, options are not used unless the client has the software to make use of them. There are already more options available to the server in the DHCP Standard Options class than can be used or understood by a Windows client. Do not add more options to the server unless you're sure you need them and you know how to use them. The LCI Option example shown in Figure 5-19 provides location coordinates to the client. These coordinates are intended for use by VOIP telephone devices. Effective use of this option requires software on the server that can map circuit identifiers to latitude, longitude, and altitude coordinates, and software in the VOIP device that can interpret and store this information. Adding a new option is a very, very small part of using that option.

Creating a Reservation

Superscopes, scopes, vendor classes, and user classes all deal with collections of addresses and options that are defined to service groups of clients. *Reservations* are created to service a single client by reserving a single address for the client and by defining specific options for the client. Reservations are subordinate to scopes because the address used by the reservation must be taken from the address range of any existing scope. Click on the + next to a scope in the console tree to expand that scope and reveal the Reservations object that it contains. To create a reservation, highlight the Reservations object in the console tree and select New Reservation from the Action menu to open the New Reservation dialog box shown in Figure 5-20.

Reservation name and Description are values used within the DHCP console to help the system administrator identify each reservation. These values can be anything you wish, but they should be short and descriptive. The "IP address" value must be a valid, available IP address from the scope in which this reservation is located. To avoid address conflicts, the IP address should not be an address in use by any other client. For this reason, the addresses used for reservations are often taken from an excluded address range that falls within the address range of the scope. Excluded addresses can be assigned through reservations even though the DHCP server does not automatically assign them. The "MAC address" field is the physical network address of the client for whom the reservation is being created. Generally, this is the

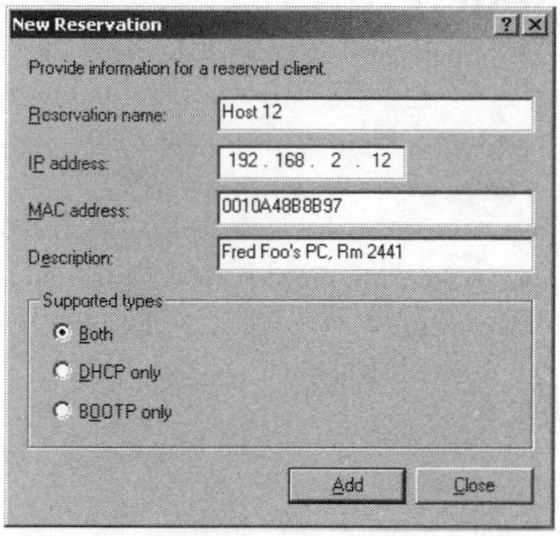

![Figure 5-20: New Reservation dialog box]

Figure 5-20. Defining a new reservation

Ethernet address of the client. Note that the colons often used to separate the bytes when writing an Ethernet address are not used when entering an Ethernet address in the "MAC address" box.

The "Supported types" box allows you to define the type of client for which the reservation is being created. Traditionally, BOOTP clients required reservations because they did not understand address leases. However, you can create reservations for DHCP clients as well as BOOTP clients. Select Both if you want the DHCP server to ignore the protocol being used and to base the reservation simply on the MAC address. Use BOOTP only if the reservation is being created for a BOOTP client and you want that client to transition to an address lease when it is upgraded to DHCP. (Of course, the reservation for that client will need to be manually removed after the client upgrades.)

To remove a reservation, highlight the reservation in the console tree and select Delete from the Action menu.

To configure DHCP options for a reservation, highlight the reservation in the console tree and select Configure Options from the Action menu. This opens the Reservation Options window, which is identical to the Server Options and Scope Options windows shown earlier and is used in exactly the same way. The client identified by the reservation will be sent all of the reservation options, any scope options that were not overridden by reservation options, and any server options that were not overridden by scope or reservation options. The righthand pane of the DHCP console shows the full list of options provided to the client when the reservation is highlighted in the console tree.

DHCP Server Administration

DHCP installation and option configuration are the largest DHCP administrative tasks. There are, however, several other administrative tasks—some are involved in initial configuration, and some are on-going maintenance tasks. Windows Server 2003 provides a security group named DHCP Administrators for the users who handle these ongoing administrative tasks. Add individual users or groups of users to the DHCP Administrators group to give them the necessary permissions to administer DHCP without giving them full administrator privileges. Several of the administrative tasks required by a DHCP server are covered in this section.

Authorizing

As was mentioned in the section "Planning for DHCP," DHCP is an unauthenticated protocol, which means that a DHCP client cannot tell the difference between a legitimate DHCP server and one that was accidentally enabled by someone experimenting with their system. Windows 2000 and Windows Server 2003 address this shortcoming by listing the legitimate DHCP servers in Active Directory. When a DHCP server is added to the list, it is said to be *authorized*.

To authorize a server, highlight DHCP in the console tree and select "Manage authorized servers" from the Action menu, which opens the Manage Authorized Servers window. This window lists all of the authorized servers by DNS name and IP address. To add a server to the list of authorized servers, you must have Enterprise Administrator privileges for the domain. If you do, click the Authorize button and enter either the server's domain name or its IP address when prompted. (For this application, there is a 64-character limit on the server's fully qualified domain name (FQDN). If the server's FQDN is more than 64 characters long, use its IP address to identify it.) Click OK. You'll be asked to confirm the authorization. Click OK again. The server is now added to the list of authorized servers.*

Clients do not query the domain controller for a list of authorized servers. Instead, servers use the list to verify their own authorization. When a Windows Server 2003 DHCP server starts, it queries the domain controller for the list of authorized servers. If its own IP address is in that list, it provides DHCP service to the clients. Once authorized, the DHCP server rechecks its authorization status with the domain controller every hour. If the DHCP server does not find itself in the authorized servers list, it does not answer client requests. It does, however, check back with the domain controller every 10 minutes to see if it has been authorized. This authorization scheme works only with DHCP servers running on Windows 2000 or Windows

---

* If a member of Enterprise Admins group installs the DHCP server, it is automatically authorized.

Server 2003. Other operating systems, e.g., Windows NT 4.0 and Unix systems, do not support this Active Directory authorization scheme.

Authorized servers must be either members of the domain or domain controllers. However, standalone Windows 2000/2003 DHCP servers understand this authorization scheme and react properly if they encounter an authorized server on the local subnet to which they are connected.

Activating

The final question asked by the New Scope Wizard during the initial DHCP installation is whether or not the scope should be activated. A scope must be activated before the server will answer DHCP requests from clients covered by that scope. However, as soon as the scope is activated the server starts answering requests. Therefore, if the scope is activated before the options for the scope are fully configured, it is possible that some clients will receive an incomplete configuration. For this reason, you may decide not to activate the scope during the initial configuration, and you may therefore need to activate the scope later from the DHCP console.

To activate a scope from the console, highlight the scope in the console tree. Select Activate from the Action menu. The scope is now active and the server will immediately begin serving clients in the scope.

A scope can also be deactivated to prevent the server from answering DHCP requests from clients on the scope's subnet. To deactivate a scope, highlight the scope in the console tree and select Deactivate from the Action menu. When asked to verify the deactivation, click Yes.

Deactivating a scope should be avoided unless the scope is going out of service permanently. Deactivating a scope is not a graceful process. Clients do not know that the scope has been deactivated A client will still attempt to renew its lease through the server even after the scope is deactivated. The server will respond to the client with a DHCP negative acknowledgement (DHCP NAK) indicating that the requested address is invalid, which is not the desired result if the scope is only temporarily being taken offline and will soon be reactivated. Use the exclusion range to temporarily prevent a server from allocating addresses in a specific scope.

Detecting Conflicts

IP addresses cannot be shared between networked devices. Each device must have a unique address. A DHCP server ensures that it always assigns a unique address. But it is possible that another improperly configured DHCP server will assign overlapping addresses or that a client is statically configured with the wrong address, thus causing an address conflicts. Microsoft offers two different ways to detect address conflicts: one is from the client side, the other is from the server side.

Windows 2000, Windows XP, and Windows Server 2003 clients automatically detect address conflicts. When one of these clients receives a DHCP offer, it broadcasts an ARP request for the address found in the offer. If another host on the network responds to the ARP, the client knows the address is already in use and sends a DHCP decline back to the server. This procedure is automatic and requires no configuration. It is also, from the server's perspective, the most efficient method for detecting address conflicts. Unfortunately, not every client can detect address conflicts on its own. Older Windows systems and older Unix systems do not detect address conflicts. If your server supports Windows 95, Windows 98, Windows ME, or Windows NT clients, you should enable address conflict detection on the server.

To enable address conflict detection on the server, highlight the server in the DHCP console tree and select Properties from the Action menu. In the properties window, select the Advanced tab. The Advanced tab of the DHCP server properties window is shown in Figure 5-21.

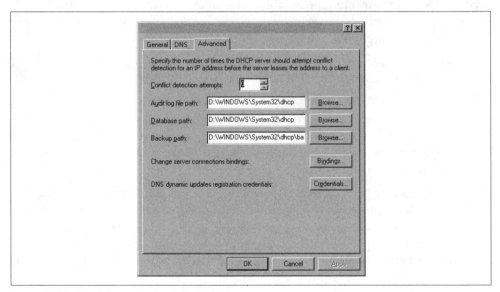

Figure 5-21. The Advanced tab of the DHCP server properties window

Enable server-side address conflict detection using the "Conflict detection attempts" box, which you will see near the top of the Advanced tab. By default this box is set to 0, meaning that no attempt will be made by the server to detect address conflicts. Set the value in this box to 1 or 2 to enable address conflict detection. The number in the box defines the number of times the server will issue a ping of the address in question before it assigns the address to a client. One ping is usually sufficient. Anything above two pings can have a negative impact on server performance. If possible, rely on client-side address conflict detection. Don't enable conflict detection on the server unless it is required to support older client operating systems.

Selecting the Interface

By default, the DHCP service binds to every network interface that has been assigned a static IP address. If the server has multiple interfaces that have been assigned static addresses, the DHCP service binds to all of them. When we say that the "service binds to the interface," we mean that the DHCP service listens for and responds to DHCP requests using that interface. The DHCP service does not bind to an interface that has been assigned a dynamic address, because a DHCP server must have a static address. If multiple static addresses are assigned to a single interface, the DHCP service only binds to the first static address assigned to that interface. This paragraph describes the default behavior of the DHCP service. The administrator can control the DHCP server bindings using the DHCP console.

To manage server bindings, highlight the server in the DHCP console tree and select Properties from the Action menu. In the properties window select the Advanced tab, and then click Bindings to open the Bindings window. (The Advanced tab of the DHCP server properties window is shown in Figure 5-21.)

The Bindings window lists all of the available interfaces with a checkbox next to each interface. To bind an interface to the DHCP service, click the checkbox next to the interface until a check appears in the box. To remove an interface from the DHCP service, click the checkbox next to the interface until the check disappears from the box. When the interfaces you want to use for DHCP are checked, and the ones that you don't want to use do not have a check next to them, click OK.

Even if you have only one interface, it is useful to open the Bindings window after the initial DHCP installation to ensure that the interface appears in the list and is bound to DHCP. If the interface does not appear in the list, it probably was not configured with a static IP address. The interface must be reconfigured to use a static address and should then be manually bound to DHCP through the Bindings window.

Backup and Restore

The Windows DHCP server provides two techniques for backing up the DHCP database. The database is automatically backed up, a method that Microsoft calls *synchronous backup*, every 60 minutes. Additionally, the database can be manually backed up using the DHCP console, which Microsoft calls *asynchronous backup*. Both methods provide a complete backup of the DHCP database, scopes, reservations, leases, options, configuration settings, and related registry keys.

The synchronous backup method requires very little configuration. The path where the backup file is written is defined by the "Backup path" box of the Advanced tab of the DHCP server properties window, which is shown in Figure 5-21. By default, that path is *%SystemRoot%\system32\dhcp\backup*. Unless you have a reason to change the path, no action is required to define the path. The same goes for the backup interval. By default, the synchronous backup runs automatically every 60 minutes. The interval is defined in the *HKEY_LOCAL_MACHINE\SYSTEM\CurrentControlSet\Services\DHCPServer\Parameters\BackupInterval* registry key, which can be changed to select another backup interval. However, 60 minutes is adequate for most installations.

To manually backup the DHCP database, highlight the server in the console tree and select Backup from the Action menu. A Browse For Folder window then appears displaying a list of available file folders—one of which is highlighted. The highlighted folder is the one defined by the Backup path box of the Advanced tab of the DHCP server properties window, which is discussed in the previous paragraph. If the highlighted folder is the one you want to use, click OK. You should know, however, that if you place a manual backup in the folder used for synchronous backups, the manual backup will be overwritten the next time a synchronous backup is created. To use a different folder, simply highlight the folder in which you want to place the database backup file before clicking OK. If you want to create a new folder for the backup file, highlight the directory in which you want to create the new folder and click "Make a new folder." When the symbol for the new folder appears, type in the name of the new folder and click OK. Regardless of what folder you pick for the task, as soon as you click OK, the backup file is created.

After a backup has been created, it should be moved off of the server for safe storage. The backup folder can be copied to removable storage or to an external file server, or it can be backed up as part of the normal system backup.

Use the DHCP console to restore a DHCP database backup file. To do so, highlight the server in the console tree and select Restore from the Action menu. When the Browse For Folder window appears, highlight the folder containing the backup file and click OK. You will be told that the restored database does not take effect until the DHCP service is restarted, and you will be asked if it should be restarted now. Click Yes to restart the service immediately. If you click No, you must restart the service later by highlighting the server in the console tree, selecting All Tasks from the Action menu and then selecting Restart from the All Tasks menu.

Integrating with DNS

DHCP dynamically assigns IP addresses to clients. Until the assignment is made, there is no way of knowing which host will be given what address. Yet, the DNS server is required to map hostnames to IP addresses, which it cannot do if it does not know which host has been given what address. Clearly, there needs to be a tight link between DHCP and DNS so that the DNS server can learn of the addresses assigned by the DHCP server. Dynamic DNS (DDNS) provides the link.

Microsoft provides dynamic updates to the DNS service through two different channels—some updates are provided by the DHCP client, and some are provided by the DHCP server:

- Windows 2000, Windows XP, and Windows Server 2003 DHCP clients are able to use DDNS to register their hostnames and IP addresses with the DNS server. A client running one of these operating systems, creates an A (address) record in the DNS database using the IP address received from the DHCP server and, by default, the FQDN defined for the client on the Computer Name tab of the System Properties window. The A record is the DNS database record that maps a domain name to an IP address. (The section "The DNS Tab" in Chapter 4 describes the DDNS configuration of the DHCP client.)

- The DHCP server uses DDNS to create a pointer (PTR) record in the DNS database. The PTR record does the reverse of the A record; the PTR record maps an IP address to a hostname. To create the PTR record, the server uses the IP address that it assigned to the client and the hostname that the client provided in the DHCP request.

The preceding paragraph describes how things work with a Windows Server 2003 DHCP server and Windows 2000, Windows XP, and Windows 2003 clients. The client controls this default behavior using the DHCP Client FQDN option, which is option 81. Some clients, for example clients running older Windows operating systems, do not send DHCP option 81. Others may use option 81 to direct different behavior. Use the DHCP console to configure how your server handles these situations.

To configure the DDNS interaction of the DHCP server with the DHCP client and the DNS server, highlight the DHCP server in the console tree and select Properties from the Action menu. In the Properties window, select the DNS tab. The DNS tab of the DHCP server properties window is shown in Figure 5-22.

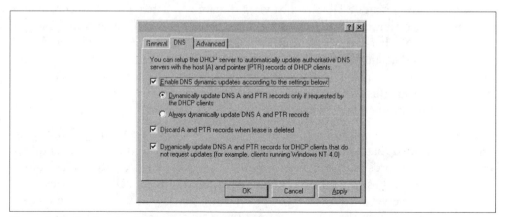

Figure 5-22. Configuring DHCP Dynamic DNS properties

To support DDNS, the "Enable DNS dynamic updates according to the settings below" checkbox must be checked. When this setting is selected, the DHCP server sends a PTR record update for each address the server leases. When it is not checked, DDNS is disabled on the DHCP server and none of the other selections on this tab are available.

Selecting "Dynamically update DNS A and PTR records only if requested by the DHCP clients" causes the server to perform DDNS updates as directed by the client in DHCP option 81. This is the default behavior described earlier in this section, and is generally the preferred setting for clients that send DHCP option 81. The alternative for handling DHCP option 81 is to select "Always dynamically update DNS A and PTR records." When this setting is selected, the server ignores the option 81 received from the client and creates both A and PTR records. This setting places the DHCP server in sole charge of DDNS updates.

The "Discard A and PTR records when lease is deleted" checkbox causes the DHCP server to send an update to the DNS server telling it to discard the unneeded A and PTR records when the address is no longer leased to the DHCP client. Even if this setting is not selected, the DHCP server issues an update to discard the PTR record when it is not longer needed. This setting simply causes the server to handle the A record in addition to the PTR record. This setting should be used when the DHCP server is responsible for creating both the A and PTR records.

The "Dynamically update DNS A and PTR records for DHCP clients that do not request updates" checkbox tells the server to handle DDNS updates for clients that do not provide DHCP option 81 in the DHCP request. This setting causes the server to send an A record update in addition to the normal PTR record update. Use this setting if you want the server to provide updates for older systems that cannot provide their own DDNS updates.

The system that creates a DNS record via a dynamic update owns the record and is the only system that can change or delete the record. This can cause complications. For example, if a backup server replaces the server that created a DNS record, it is not able to update that record. To handle this, DHCP servers can be added to the security group DnsUpdateProxy. Every member of that security group has ownership rights over the DNS records created by any member of the group. (See Chapter 7 for information on security groups and dedicated user accounts.)

The records created by the DnsUpdateProxy group can be secured by a username and password, so that authentication is required before the records can be modified. To secure the records in this manner, create a user account solely for the use of the DHCP servers, and use the user credentials associated with the account to secure the records. Every server within the DnsUpdateProxy group will use the same credentials—all derived from the same account. To enter the credentials associated with this dedicated account, click the Credentials button on the Advanced tab of the DHCP server properties sheet, an example of which is shown in Figure 5-21. In the

"DNS dynamic update credentials" dialog box, enter the username, the domain, and the password of the dedicated user account that is to be used to secure DNS records generated by the DHCP server. Click OK and then Apply. It should be noted that not all zones require secured updates and that credentials are only needed if required by the DNS server.

Logging

The Windows DHCP server maintains a log of server activity called the *audit log*. The audit log file is stored in the directory defined in the "Audit log file path" box of the Advanced tab of the DHCP server properties window, which is shown in Figure 5-21. By default, the path is *%SystemRoot%\system32\dhcp*.

The log files are created every day at midnight and named for the days of the week using the format *DhcpSrvLog-<day>.log*, where *<day>* is a three-character abbreviation for the day of the week. When a new daily log file is written, it overwrites the file of the same name that was created the previous week. This scheme creates a weekly audit history. The following dir command shows the log files on our sample server:

```
D:\>dir %SystemRoot%\system32\dhcp\DhcpSrvLog-*.*
 Volume in drive D has no label.
 Volume Serial Number is 7842-58E3

 Directory of D:\WINDOWS\system32\dhcp

10/15/2004  10:22 PM               1,934 DhcpSrvLog-Fri.log
10/18/2004  12:31 PM               1,369 DhcpSrvLog-Mon.log
10/16/2004  10:50 PM               2,642 DhcpSrvLog-Sat.log
10/14/2004  11:01 PM               2,996 DhcpSrvLog-Thu.log
10/12/2004  10:10 PM               3,350 DhcpSrvLog-Tue.log
10/13/2004  08:45 PM               2,996 DhcpSrvLog-Wed.log
               6 File(s)          15,287 bytes
               0 Dir(s)   4,347,084,800 bytes free
```

The log files are text files that can be examined with any tool that reads ASCII text—Notepad, for example. All entries in the log file have the same format:

```
ID,date,time,description,IPaddress,hostname,MACaddress
```

The fields in each entry are:

ID
> A two-character numeric code that identifies the event being logged. For example, an event might be an address lease renewal, which is given an ID of 11. There are more than 30 possible IDs—too many to be described inline in this chapter. For a complete listing of the possible IDs, see Appendix B.

date
> The date the event was logged.

time
> The time the event was logged.

description
> A text description of the event.

IPaddress
> The IP address affected by the event. If the event does not affect an address then this field is blank.

hostname
> The DNS domain name of the client affected by the event. If the event does not affect a host then this field is blank.

MACaddress
> The physical network address of the client affected by the event. Most often, this is an Ethernet address. If the event does not affect a client then this field is blank.

Commas separate the fields in an audit log entry. Even empty fields are enclosed in commas. The last three fields described above are empty in some entries. Here are a few examples:

```
00,10/12/04,10:42:17,Started,,,,
55,10/12/04,10:42:22,Authorized(servicing),,,,
24,10/12/04,11:42:19,Database Cleanup Begin,,,,
```

Use the DHCP console to enable logging. First, highlight the server in the console tree and then select Properties from the Action menu. Select the General tab of the DHCP server properties window. Check the "Enable DHCP audit logging" checkbox to log all events. Removing the check from the checkbox turns logging off. However, it is generally a good idea to use the audit log. It does not add much processing overhead, and it can be very useful for tracking down information about addresses leases and for monitoring the server's workload.

Creating a MADCAP Server

Scopes and superscopes both provide clients with a basic IP configuration. A multicast scope is different. It does provide clients with an address, but it is not a unicast address, and it does not provide the client with any other element of an IP configuration. In fact, a client must be configured with a unicast IP address separately before it can make any use of a multicast address.

Multicast addresses are described in Chapter 2, but a short summary of their purpose might be useful here. A *multicast address* addresses a group of systems, in a manner similar to the way that a broadcast address addresses a group of system. But where a broadcast address reaches every host on a specific network, a multicast address targets every host involved in a session of a specific application. A simple example is Routing Information Protocol Version 2 (RIPv2), which listens to the multicast address 224.0.0.9. Every RIPv2 router on the local network receives a routing update sent to that multicast address. In the case of RIPv2, the multicast address is hard-coded into the protocol because that address is reserved for the specific use of that protocol. It is a static multicast address.

While RIPv2 is a simple example, there are more interesting examples. Most organizations are interested in multicasting to distribute streaming audio and video for conferencing, training, entertainment, and similar applications. In these cases, the multicast address is associated with the audio or video stream, and every system in the multicast group joins the group specifically to receive the audio or video stream from the multicast server. The multicast group is dynamic in that individual hosts join or exit the group at will. The multicast server associates the multicast address with a specific application. MADCAP allows the multicast server to dynamically obtain a multicast addresses it can use for its multicast applications, which provides the same flexibility for multicast address assignment that DHCP provides for unicast address assignment.

There are two types of multicast addresses suitable for creating the multicast scope needed for your MADCAP server:

Globally scoped multicast addresses
> The address range 233.0.0.0/8 is set aside for globally scoped multicast addresses, also referred to as GLOP. This type of multicast address is analogous to a public unicast address. Like other public addresses, a globally scoped multicast address requires formal approval. To create a globally scoped multicast address you must obtain an official Autonomous System Number (ASN) from a regional address registry (discussed in Chapter 2). After the ASN is obtained, convert the ASN into the second and third bytes of the multicast address by writing the ASN as a binary number padded on the left with zeros. RFC 3180 shows the example of ASN 5662, which produces the binary number 0001011000011110 that in turn produces the dotted decimal byte values 22.30. Putting this together, the GLOP for ASN 5662 is 233.22.30.0/24. Note that a globally scoped multicast address is limited to 256 available addresses. A globally scoped multicast address is required only if you offer multicast services to users in the outside world, and it can only be used effectively if you have border routers that can advertise multicast routes to the outside world using a protocol such as Distance Vector Multicast Routing Protocol (DVMRP). Note that Windows Server 2003 does not fully support any multicast routing protocols. Windows Server 2003 only supports Internet Group Management Protocol (IGMP) as a forwarder; it does not support the IGMP messages for multicast routing updates.

Administratively scoped multicast addresses
> This type of multicast address is analogous to the private network addresses available for unicast address assignment. Because administratively scoped multicast addresses are not forwarded through multicast-capable border routers, they

are limited to your private network. Therefore, no outside approval is required to use administratively scoped multicast addresses. The full range of addresses reserved for administratively scoped multicast addresses is 239.0.0.0/8. Within this range, 239.192.0.0/14 is the range designated as the *organization local scope*, and it is the address block recommended for private multicast scopes.

Once you have picked an administratively scoped multicast address or obtained approval for a globally scoped multicast address, you can use the DHCP console to create a multicast scope. To do so, highlight the server in the console tree and select New Multicast Scope from the Action menu. This opens the New Multicast Scope Wizard. Click Next after reading the welcome screen. You are then prompted for a multicast scope name and description. These serve the same purpose as the scope name and description discussed earlier. They simply identify the multicast scope in the DHCP console window and are only used to make it easy for the system administrator to identify the various scopes, superscopes and multicast scopes managed through the console. Enter a short descriptive name and text description and then click Next. The IP Address window shown in Figure 5-23 appears.

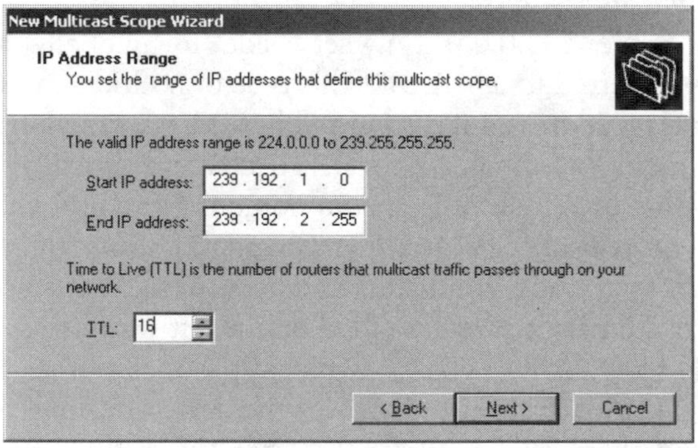

Figure 5-23. Defining a multicast scope address range

In the Start IP address and End IP address boxes enter the range of addresses covered by this multicast scope. In the example, we define 239.192.1.0 to 239.192.2.255, which is an administrative scope taken from the block of addresses defined for an organization local scope. In this case, we use just a small number of the available addresses, which is often all that is required.

The TTL field at the bottom of this window defines an important parameter. Time-to-Live (TTL) sets administrative boundaries for multicasting. Every time a router handles an IP datagram it decrements the TTL field in the datagram header, and when the TTL reaches 0, the datagram is discarded. Multicast routers handle multicast packets in a slightly different manner. They examine the TTL value in the header and if it exceeds some threshold value then they decrement the TTL and route the packet out to the Internet in the same way that a unicast datagram is processed. When the TTL value falls below the threshold, the router does not route the packet off the local network. The threshold value is configured on the router by the person who administers the router. The value configured here for the MADCAP server should take the router threshold value into consideration to ensure that the local multicast packets stay local. In this case, there is probably no reason to be overly concerned about the TTL value because the multicast addresses used here are taken from the organization local scope, and are therefore addresses that multicast routers do not forward. However, it does no harm to set both the address range and the TTL value in a manner that ensures these packets are not forwarded to the Internet. When the values are configured properly, click Next.

The next window is the Add Exclusion window in which address exclusion ranges are defined. This window looks and functions exactly like the window shown in Figure 5-5. You can use it to exclude some of the multicast addresses from automatic assignment. However, I generally don't. I have had some problems with the wizard when I define the exclusion ranges here. (I'm not sure why. Probably just fat fingers.) I generally skip this step and add the exclusion range later. How to do this is covered next.

Click Next to go to the Lease Duration window. Use the Days, Hours, and Minutes boxes in this window to set the lease duration. How long you set the lease depends on how the multicast address will be used and how much demand you have compared to the supply of multicast addresses. If you use administratively scoped addresses, you have a very large pool of addresses you can draw upon. If you use globally scoped addresses you will have a small set of addresses. By default, Microsoft sets the lease to 30 days. A lease of that length is appropriate if you have low demand for addresses or an abundance of addresses. Otherwise a shorter lease, such as the seven-day lease used for unicast addresses, is more appropriate. Set the value suitable for your environment and click Next.

You are now asked whether or not the server should activate the multicast scope. If the configuration is to your liking, select Yes. Otherwise, choose No. If, like me, you choose No because you haven't yet defined the exclusion range, you will need to activate the multicast scope later after you finish the configuration. Click Next and then Finish, and the multicast scope will be added to the server.

The new multicast scope is managed through the DHCP console. The multicast scope appears in the console window with two subordinate items: the Address Pool and the Address Leases. To define an exclusion range, highlight Address Pool in the console tree and select New Exclusion Range from the Action menu. Enter the "Start IP address" and "End IP address" in the dialog box that appears, and then click Add. Do this for each exclusion range that you desire. When the configuration is to your liking, highlight the multicast scope in the console tree and select Activate from the Action menu to activate the scope, if it has not been previously activated.

The multicast scope configuration can also be changed using the DHCP console. To do so, highlight the multicast scope in the console tree and select Properties from the Action menu to open the properties sheet shown in Figure 5-24.

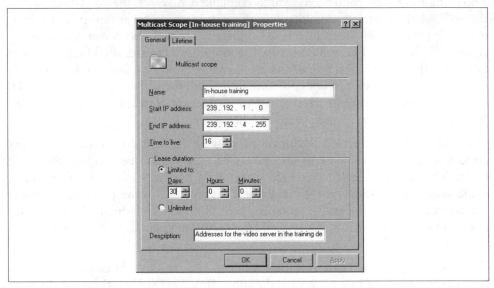

Figure 5-24. Multicast scope properties

Nearly everything that was defined using the New Multicast Scope Wizard, except the exclusion range, can be defined using this window. Type in a new value, click Apply, and then OK to effect an immediate change to the scope configuration. In this example, notice that the "End IP address" is different from the "End IP address" shown in Figure 5-23. In effect, the setting in this window doubles the number of addresses in the address range of this scope when compared to the setting in Figure 5-23.

After making a change to the scope range, such as the one shown in Figure 5-24, it is extremely important to manually check the address pool for the multicast scope. I have noticed that sometimes the act of adding to the scope range also adds an unintended exclusion range. Look at Figure 5-25.

The details of the Address Pool are listed on the righthand side of the screen. Notice the address exclusion range listed first. It excludes the addresses from 239.192.4.0 to 239.192.4.255. The system administrator did *not* enter this exclusion range. It simply appeared when the address range was updated. Looking at the last entry in the detailed list shows that the address range was indeed updated to 239.192.1.0– 239.192.4.255, which is what the administrator intended. The extra exclusion range is just an unwanted side effect. To delete the unwanted exclusion range, highlight it in the righthand pane and select Delete from the Action menu. You can then add the

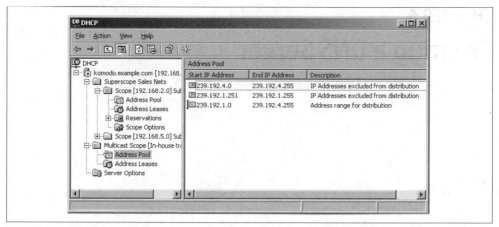

Figure 5-25. Checking the address pool values

exclusion range you actually want following the instructions provided earlier in this section.

MADCAP server support is a relatively new feature of the Microsoft DHCP service. The few minor bugs I have encountered when working with multicast scopes are easily worked around and will no doubt be fixed in upcoming revisions of the software.

Summary

A DHCP centralizes network configuration, which greatly reduces the burden on the network administrator. DHCP can provide all TCP/IP configuration parameters, which eliminates the need for the administrator to go to the desktop system just to adjust the TCP/IP configuration. Additionally, DHCP can dynamically assign IP addresses from a pool of addresses, which frees the administrator from the burden of assigning an address every time a new system is added to the network. The Microsoft DHCP server is tightly integrated with Active Directory, WINS and the Microsoft DNS server. In the next chapter we look at how to configure a Microsoft DNS server to map the name entered by the user into the address required by the network.

CHAPTER 6

Creating a DNS Server

Strictly speaking, name resolution service is not needed for computers to communicate. It is, as the name implies, a service—specifically, a service intended to make the network more user-friendly. Computers are perfectly happy with IP addresses, but people prefer names. Domain Name System (DNS) is the Internet standard service for mapping the names preferred by users into the IP addresses required by network protocols.

DNS is a client/server software system. The client side of DNS is called the *resolver*. It generates the queries for domain name information that are sent to the server. The DNS server software, which is called the name server, answers the resolver's queries. Both sides of DNS require configuration.

This book covers three basic DNS configuration tasks: configuring the resolver, configuring the name server, and constructing the name server database files, called the *zone files*. All Windows systems, clients and servers, run the resolver, so it is part of the basic system configuration covered in Chapter 4. This chapter covers installing and configuring the DNS server and the zone files.

See the sections "Basic DNS Configuration" and "The DNS Tab" in Chapter 4 for a description of how the DNS client (the resolver) is configured.

Domains Versus Zones

Chapter 3 introduced the use of the terminology zone file when speaking of the DNS database file. The distinction between a DNS domain and a DNS zone can be confusing. A *domain* is a logical grouping that encompasses the domain itself, all subdomains of that domain, and all hosts within that domain and its subdomains. A *zone*, on the other hand, is a collection of domain information over which a name server has authority. The zone is an administrative grouping that may encompass parts of domains, entire domains, and groups of domains.

Rather than being a purely logical grouping, a zone has physical reality, as reflected in the existence of a zone file, which contains database records for a zone. A DNS server may manage one or several zone files. The zone may encompass the complete domain, or only a portion of it, as shown in Figure 6-1.

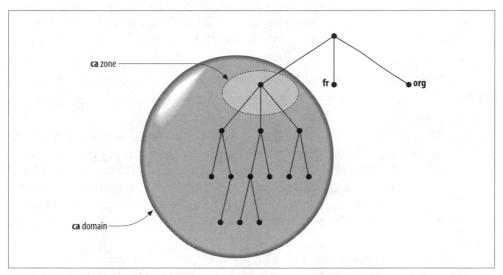

Figure 6-1. A DNS zone

The term *zone* is often used interchangeably with the word *domain*, but in this book we use zone to refer to the information in the domain database file, while the term domain is used in more general contexts. In this book, a domain is a part of the DNS hierarchy identified by a domain name. A zone is a collection of domain information contained in a domain database file. The file that contains the domain information is called a zone file.

RFC 1033, the *Domain Administrators Operations Guide*, defines the basic set of standard records used to construct zone files. Many RFCs propose new DNS records—some that are useful and some that are not widely implemented. We cover all of the resource records supported by the DNS Microsoft Management Console (MMC) in Appendix C. In this chapter, we stick to the basic resource records and to those that you are most likely to use. These basic records construct the zone files used in this chapter.

The Microsoft DNS Server

DNS server software has been available since the late 1980s. Microsoft did not make a DNS server available until Windows NT Server 3.51. That original server offered limited functionality and was not well integrated with the other TCP/IP services provided by Windows NT. Most administrators would not use that product in a production environment. However, those days are long gone. The DNS server included with Windows Server 2003 is a solid product that provides definite advantages for Microsoft environments.

The Microsoft DNS server is fully compliant with Internet standards, and interoperates well with other DNS servers. The Microsoft DNS server is fully compatible with the popular Berkeley Internet Name Domain (BIND) implementation of DNS. Applications running on any platform can use the Microsoft DNS server for name resolution.

The Microsoft DNS server uses the same zone file structure and resource records types used by other DNS servers. It does, however, have some advantages for a Windows networking environment:

Improved integration

> The Microsoft DNS server is integrated with Active Directory, Microsoft WINS, and the Microsoft DHCP server. Using all three of these services on the network allows WINS clients and clients assigned a dynamic IP address by the DHCP Server to participate fully in DNS. Integrating DNS into Active Directory allows DNS to take advantage of Active Directory replication services and provides enhanced Dynamic DNS security.

Improved management

> Traditional implementations of DNS are managed by creating and maintaining ASCII text configuration files. Microsoft DNS server usually is maintained using the graphical DNS console. Many administrators find the DNS console an easier and faster way to configure and manage DNS.

Planning a DNS Server Installation

A Microsoft DNS server is either added to an existing DNS architecture or it is used to create a new DNS environment. The venerable age and vital importance of DNS guarantee that all large, networked organizations already have an established DNS architecture. In most network environments, a Windows Server 2003 DNS server is either used to replace an outdated server or to extend the current DNS service.

Microsoft simplifies the transition from an old BIND 4 DNS server by ensuring that the Microsoft DNS server is able to read and process the old BIND 4 configuration files—both the zone files and the BIND 4 boot file. To use existing zone files, select "Use this existing file" and enter the name of the zone file on the Zone File page of the New Zone Wizard. (This wizard is covered in detail later.) Instead of using the BIND 4 boot file directly, we recommend replicating the configuration with the DNS console, which is the preferred tool for configuring a Microsoft DNS server and more intuitive to use than the boot file. However, if you decide to use a BIND 4 boot file, see the discussion of the boot file syntax in Appendix C.

A DNS service can be extended by adding an additional server to take some of the load off existing servers or by adding additional servers to support a new zone. (The various server types are discussed in Chapter 3.) A caching-only server or a slave server can be used to lighten the load of other servers. For example, a caching-only server can be placed on a subnet, and all of the clients on that subnet can be configured to send DNS queries to that server.

Adding a new zone in a large DNS environment is similar to creating a new domain for a small organization that has never had DNS service. In either case, you need to create a primary (master) server and at least one secondary (slave) server. The master server should be located in the facility that has the best, most reliable network connectivity, and that is conveniently located for the domain administrator. If you plan to integrate DNS and WINS, the master DNS server should be located on the same LAN segment as the WINS server. If you plan to use Active Directory Integrated DNS, the master DNS server must be a domain controller. Chapter 7 covers Active Directory, including integrating DNS with AD.

When adding a new zone that will contain public addresses, you should have at least one slave server with a separate path to the Internet. On a large enterprise network you may have a redundant Internet connection that the slave server could use, but most small networks will need to ask their ISP to host the slave server.

A special type of slave server is sometimes used in distributed networks that have low speed or costly wide area network connections between the remote locations. These special slave servers, sometimes called *stealth servers*, only provide service to their local networks because they are not advertised as official slave servers by the master server. On pay-per-use networks, such as some ISDN networks, network costs are controlled by setting a high refresh rate to limit the number of times the slave server loads data from the master.

One final type of server that you may consider installing is a forwarder. The server acting as a forwarder requires no special configuration—it is simply configured as a master, slave, or caching-only server as appropriate for your environment. However, other servers on the network are configured to forward queries to the forwarder. The purpose of this is to create a rich cache on the forwarder or to take advantage of the superior network connectivity of the forwarder. For example, you may have an authoritative server that is multihomed, with a public address directly connecting one side of the server to the Internet and a private address connecting the other side of the server to the enterprise LAN. When this server is used as a forwarder, other servers on the LAN can forward queries to the multihomed server and those queries are resolved without involving NAT or any other proxy. How a server is configured to use a forwarder is covered later in this chapter.

In addition to planning for servers, you may need to plan for the allocation of subdomains within your domain. Subdomains are created for the same reasons that subnets are created:

For organizational reasons
> A piece of an organization may be assigned a subdomain because it wants or needs local control over naming. An example of an organizational domain name might be *sales.example.com*.

For topological reasons
> A remote location of an enterprise may be assigned a subdomain that encompasses the systems at that location. This type of domain reduces the number of queries sent over a WAN because on most networks the majority of queries are for local systems. An example of this type of subdomain is *denver.example.com*.

To distribute control
> Sometimes an organization is so large the only efficient way to handle naming is to break the namespace up into smaller, more manageable pieces. The domains that are created for this reason can be either organizational or topological.

Most subdomains are organizational because organizational considerations are generally viewed as more important than network considerations. However, topological subdomains are more useful for improving performance and reducing the load in a WAN.

Once you have decided what servers are needed and where they should be placed, you can begin the installation.

Installing the DNS Server

The DNS client software is installed on all Windows systems by default. The server software, however, must be installed by the system administrator. This section covers the steps needed to install the DNS server role on a Windows Server 2003 system.

The DNS server software is installed through the Manage Your Server window, in essentially the same manner as the DHCP server role described in Chapter 5. Run the Manage Your Server tool from the Administrative Tools menu of the All Programs menu in the Start menu. After the DNS server has been installed, it is listed on the Manage Your Server window as one of the roles configured for the server. If it is already listed there, there is no need to reinstall it. If it is not listed there, add the DNS server role by clicking the "Add or remove a role" link found near the top of the Manage Your Server window. This opens the Configure Your Server Wizard. (If you want to see what this wizard looks like, refer to Figure 5-3.)

In the window displayed by the wizard, highlight "DNS server" in the Server Role list box and click Next. (If "DNS server" is not listed in the Server Role list box, click the Add or Remove Programs link to run the Add or Remove Programs Wizard and use that wizard to add the required DNS software.) When you click Next, the Summary of Selections window appears displaying two items:

- Install the DNS server
- Run the Configure a DNS Server Wizard

Click Next to undertake these two tasks.

Windows copies several files to install the DNS server software. If Windows cannot find the necessary files, you will be prompted to provide the Windows Server 2003 CD-ROM or DVD that you used to initially install the operating system. After the files are copied, the Configure a DNS Server Wizard is launched.

Initial Configuration

The Configure a DNS Server Wizard adds a server to the DNS console (more on the DNS console later), and it creates basic zone files and a *hints file*. The hints file contains the names and addresses needed by the Windows server to locate the DNS root servers. The zone files created by this wizard are essentially empty shells that can be populated with resources records automatically by using Dynamic DNS (DDNS) and manually by using the DNS console.

When the Configure a DNS Server Wizard starts, it presents a welcome screen with a link to useful documentation about DNS. Click *DNS Checklists* to view the documentation and Next to start working with the wizard. The wizard then asks you to select one of the following three configuration actions:

Create a forward lookup zone
> This selection is intended for organizations that use the Microsoft DNS server to map hostnames to IP addresses while relying on external servers to map IP addresses to hostnames. An example is an organization that has a registered domain name for which it provides DNS name lookup service, and that also uses only public IP addresses provided by an ISP for which the ISP provides reverse lookup service. Microsoft recommends this selection for small networks. Many small networks, however, use private addresses internally and must therefore provide the reverse mapping for the private address. Actually, this selection is specifically for networks that use addresses from some other organization's addresses space, such as the previous example that describes a network that uses addresses purchased from the local ISP's address space. This selection is not used if you use addresses for which you have full responsibility, such as private addresses or a block of public addresses for which you have registered an *in-addr.arpa* domain.

Create forward and reverse lookup zones
> This selection creates a standard DNS server that can map hostnames to IP addresses and IP addresses to hostnames. Use this selection if you use private

addresses or a block of public addresses for which you have registered an *in-addr.arpa* domain. Use this selection even if you have a mixture of addresses—some managed locally and some managed remotely by the ISP. The *in-addr.arpa* domain delegations in the root servers will ensure that the correct server gets the reverse lookup query. Making this selection when some of your addresses are managed remotely will have no negative effects. During the initial installation this is the configuration action you are most likely to select.

Configure root hints only

Use this selection to create a caching-only configuration. Despite the fact that the parenthetical comment on this selection says "recommended for advanced users only," this is actually the simplest server configuration. Simply make this selection, click Next and then click Finish to create a caching-only configuration. The "advanced user" comment probably springs from the fact that many users do not understand the purpose and uses of a caching-only server, and those confused users do not really intend to create a nonauthoritative server.

The following discussion assumes that you choose to create a forward and a reverse zone because that provides the most complete example.

You are now asked if the wizard should create the forward lookup zone file. Choose Yes and click Next. You'll now notice that the New Zone Wizard is running. This wizard begins by asking you to select the zone type. In effect, the wizard is asking you to define the relationship of this server to this zone. Are you creating the master server for the zone, a slave server or a stub server? There are three choices:

Primary zone

Select this choice if the server will be the master server for this zone. The zone file you create will be the ultimate source of authoritative information for this zone. If you are the domain administrator who will be manually entering resource records into this zone file and on this server, then you are creating a primary zone.

Secondary zone

Use this selection if the server will be a slave server used to back up the master server. If you make this selection, you will not be manually entering any of the resource records into this zone file. Instead you will be asked to provide the IP address of the master server of this zone so that the zone file can be transferred from the master server. To increase the robustness of the zone transfer system you will be able to enter more than one source's IP address in the Master DNS Servers window displayed by the wizard. When Active Directory Integrated DNS is used, there really can be more than one master server. When standard DNS is used, only one of the servers listed in the window is truly the master server—the others are the additional slave servers that can also be used as sources for the zone file when the master server is unresponsive.

Stub zone

Select "Stub zone" if you are creating this zone specifically to simplify the management of subdomain delegation information. The stub server learns the delegation information from the servers that are authoritative for the zone. Therefore, the wizard will display the Master DNS Servers window, and you should enter the IP address of the master server of the delegated zone in that window. Stub zones are primarily used by sites that manage large numbers of subdomain delegations. To learn more about stub zones, see the section "Understanding Stub Zones" later in this chapter.

There is one additional selection that may or may not be available in the Zone Type window depending on your server configuration: "Store the zone in Active Directory." This selection is only available if the DNS server system is also a domain controller. If it is, you can select any of the available zone types and then store the zone in the Active Directory to gain the redundancy and replication services inherent in Active Directory.

Select the zone type and click Next. The wizard now asks for the zone name. This is just the domain name of the piece of the domain name system whose resource records will be stored in this zone file. On the sample system used in this chapter, the zone name is *example.com*. Later we will delegate a subdomain named *eng.example.com*, and when we create its zone file we will select the zone name *eng.example.com* because that is the name of the highest level domain that will be included in that zone. Enter the appropriate name for the zone you will be serving and click Next.

You are now asked to define a filename for the zone file. By default, the New Zone Wizard creates a name for the forward lookup zone file using the zone name just provided and the extension *.dns*. Thus, if the zone name was *example.com*, the default zone filename would be *example.com.dns*. You can override the default and enter any filename you wish. However, the default name chosen by the wizard is a good one. The name clearly identifies the domain being served and is in a format understood by all Windows DNS system administrators. When the name is acceptable to you, click Next.

At this point in the configuration you specify whether or not the system accepts dynamic updates. The wizard offers three choices:

Allow only secure dynamic updates

This option is only available for Active Directory Integrated DNS. As mentioned earlier, you can create an Active Directory Integrated DNS zone file only if the DNS service is running on a domain controller. This is a powerful reason for using Active Directory Integrated DNS. Dynamic updates can be misused to corrupt a zone file. Allowing unsecured dynamic updates threatens the security and stability of the server.

Allow both nonsecure and secure dynamic updates

> If you do not use Active Directory Integrated DNS and you want to allow DDNS updates, you must accept both secured and unsecured updates. This is not an inherent requirement of DDNS. This is a design decision by Microsoft. This selection exposes your server to the possibility of a malicious attack through DDNS.

Do not allow dynamic updates

> This is the best choice to make during the initial configuration. As soon as dynamic updates are allowed, DHCP and other services can start updating the zone file. It is generally best to make sure that DNS is configured and running the way that you want before you enable dynamic updates. Once you have had a chance to check the configuration, you can enable updates using the DNS console, as we will see later in this chapter.

Select the dynamic update setting you want and click Next. You will exit the New Zone Wizard and return to the Configure a DNS Server Wizard where you're asked if you want to create the reverse lookup zone. Choose Yes and click Next to jump back to the New Zone Wizard where you are asked essentially the same questions for the reverse zone that you were previously asked for the forward zone. The Zone Type window and the Dynamic Updates window are exactly the same. The Zone File window varies only in the default zone filename provided—although the filename extension, *.dns*, is the same. The only real difference between running the wizard for a reverse lookup zone is that instead of a Zone Name window, there is a Reverse Lookup Zone Name window, which is shown in Figure 6-2.

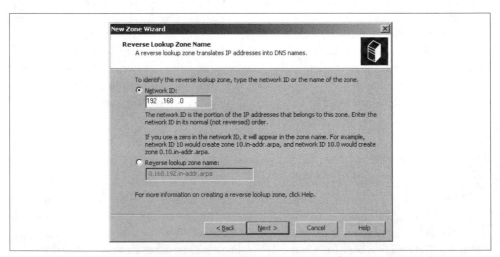

Figure 6-2. Defining a zone name for a reverse lookup zone

Instead of a zone name, this window asks for a Network ID, which is the portion of the IP address that is fixed relative to the reverse lookup query. In Figure 6-2, the fixed part of the IP address relative to the query is 192.168.0, meaning that only addresses that start with those three bytes are looked up in this zone. The Network ID field of this window can accept only full byte values and only for, at most, the first three bytes of the IP address. If your reverse lookup zone does not match these restrictions, you can select "Reverse lookup zone name" and enter the name of the zone as a text string.

After all values have been entered for the forward and reverse zones, the Configure a DNS Server Wizard asks for the IP address of the forwarders. If you use forwarders, select Yes and enter the IP addresses of up to two forwarders. If you do not use forwarders, select No. If you're not sure, answer No. Forwarders can be added easily later using the DNS console. (Forwarders are explained in the section "Planning a DNS Server Installation," and a more detailed explanation of how a system is configured to use forwarders is covered in the section "Forwarders.") When the Forwarders window is configured as appropriate for your server, click Next. Then click Finish to complete the initial configuration.

DNS Server now appears on the Manage Your Server Roles page of the Manager Your Server window. Click the "Manage this DNS server" link on the Manage Your Server window to open the DNS console, which is shown in Figure 6-3.

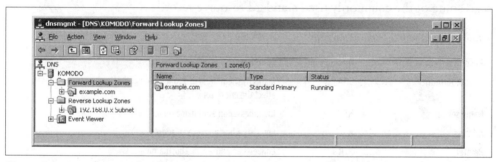

Figure 6-3. A newly created zone in the DNS console

The management console is divided into two panes. The details pane (the right-hand pane) shows the details of the item that is highlighted in the lefthand pane. The lefthand pane contains the *console tree*. The console tree shows the hierarchy of managed items including the service (DNS), the servers providing that service, the forward and reverse domains serviced by each server, and the DNS event log for the server. In Figure 6-3, there is only one server (KOMODO), and that server provides information on one forward domain (*example.com*) and one reverse zone (*0.168.192.in-addr.arpa*, which is shown in the console tree as the domain for *192.168.0.x* Subnet). The console can manage multiple servers, and each server can service many zones. To manage a server or zone, highlight the item that you wish to manage and then select the management task you want to perform from the Action menu. The Action menu is context-sensitive. The selections in the menu change according to the object highlighted in the console tree. The DNS console is used repeatedly in this chapter.

The DNS Files

In this chapter, DNS is installed as an independent service. When the DNS server is installed on a system that is already functioning as an Active Directory domain controller, DNS can be integrated into AD. In that case, the zone data is stored in the AD database and not in the separate zone files described in this section. See Chapter 7 for more information on integrating DNS into AD.

The initial DNS server installation, described earlier in this chapter, automatically creates the *cache.dns* file needed to locate the Internet root name servers and skeleton zone files for the zones that you told the wizard to create. These files are located in the *%SystemRoot%\system32\dns* directory, and are built from standard resource records.

Zone files all have the same basic format and use the same type of database records, which are called standard resource records or RRs. These are defined in RFC 1033, the *Domain Administrators Operations Guide*, and other RFCs. Table 6-1 summarizes some of the commonly used standard resource records.

Table 6-1. Standard resource records

Resource record name	Record type	Function
Start of Authority	SOA	Marks the beginning of a zone's data and defines parameters that affect the entire zone
Name server	NS	Identifies a domain's name server
Address	A	Converts a hostname to an address
Pointer	PTR	Converts an address to a hostname
Mail Exchanger	MX	Identifies where to deliver mail for a given domain name
Canonical Name	CNAME	Defines an alias hostname

The records in Table 6-1 are the ones placed in the zone file by the New Zone Wizard and the ones listed directly in the Action menu of the DNS console. All of these records and all of the other resource records available through the Resource Record Type dialog box are covered in detail in Appendix C. The limited set of records listed in Table 6-1 are, however, enough to allow you to understand the basic structure and content of the DNS zone files.

 The DNS console, the Action menu, and the Resource Record Type dialog box are all covered later in this chapter.

The resource record syntax is described in Appendix C, but a little understanding of the structure of these records is necessary to read the zone files created in this chapter. The format of DNS resource records is [*name*] [*ttl*] IN *type data*.

name

> Is the name of the domain object the resource record references. It can be an individual host or an entire domain. The string in the *name* field is relative to the current domain unless it ends with a dot. If the name field is blank, the record applies to the domain object that was named last. For example, if the A record for jamis is followed by an MX record with a blank *name* field, both the A record and the MX record apply to jamis.

ttl

> Defines the length of time, in seconds, that the information in this resource record should be kept in a remote system's cache. Often this field is left blank and the default time-to-live (TTL), set for the entire zone in the SOA record, is used.*

IN

> Identifies the record as an Internet DNS resource record. There are other classes of records, but they are not used on a Microsoft DNS server.

type

> Identifies the kind of resource record. Table 6-1 lists some record types under the heading Record Type. The available record types are listed in the Resource Record Type dialog, which lists many more record types than Table 6-1. The table lists only the most basic RRs.

data

> Defines information specific to this type of resource record. For example, in an A record this is the field that contains the actual IP address, while in an NS record this field contains the name of a server.

In the following sections, we look at the three DNS database files created by the initial installation. As you look at the files, remember that all of the records in these files are standard resource records that follow the format described above.

The cache.dns File

The *cache.dns* file is the cache initialization file. This file is also called the *hints file* or the *root hints file*. It contains the names and addresses of the root servers and is used to help the local server locate a root server during startup. Once a root server is found, an authoritative list of root servers is downloaded from that server. The initialization file is not referred to again until the local server is forced to restart. The

---

* See the section on SOA properties later in this chapter.

information in the *cache.dns* file is not referred to often, but it is critical for starting a DNS server.

The *cache.dns* file contains NS records that name the root servers and A records that provide the addresses of the root servers. The *cache.dns* file that is created automatically when the DNS software is installed on a Windows server is shown below:

```
C:\WINDOWS\system32\dns>type cache.dns
;
;   Root Name Server Hints File:
;
;       These entries enable the DNS server to locate the root name servers
;       (the DNS servers authoritative for the root zone).
;       For historical reasons this is known often referred to as the
;       "Cache File"
;
@                       NS      i.root-servers.net.
i.root-servers.net      A       192.36.148.17
@                       NS      e.root-servers.net.
e.root-servers.net      A       192.203.230.10
@                       NS      d.root-servers.net.
d.root-servers.net      A       128.8.10.90
@                       NS      a.root-servers.net.
a.root-servers.net      A       198.41.0.4
@                       NS      h.root-servers.net.
h.root-servers.net      A       128.63.2.53
@                       NS      c.root-servers.net.
c.root-servers.net      A       192.33.4.12
@                       NS      g.root-servers.net.
g.root-servers.net      A       192.112.36.4
@                       NS      f.root-servers.net.
f.root-servers.net      A       192.5.5.241
@                       NS      b.root-servers.net.
b.root-servers.net      A       192.228.79.201
@                       NS      j.root-servers.net.
j.root-servers.net      A       192.58.128.30
@                       NS      k.root-servers.net.
k.root-servers.net      A       193.0.14.129
@                       NS      l.root-servers.net.
l.root-servers.net      A       198.32.64.12
@                       NS      m.root-servers.net.
m.root-servers.net      A       202.12.27.33
```

The file begins with a few comment lines that identify it as the root hints file. In all DNS database files, lines beginning with a semicolon are comment lines.

This file contains only name server and address records. Each NS record identifies a name server for the root domain. The name field of each NS record could identify the root domain by name—the name of the root domain is dot (.). Instead the name field in the Microsoft version of this file uses a different naming convention. The @ in the name field refers to the zone that is currently being loaded. Therefore if the server is loading the root zone, the @ tells the server to use the records for the root zone. In another file being loaded for a different zone, the @ would tell the server that the records belong to that zone. (We will see this again later.) The associated A record gives the address of each root server.

Note that the *cache.dns* file designates several root name servers, all of which can be used interchangeably. All of these servers contain the same information, which is replicated between them continually. There are multiple root name servers for two reasons:

Redundancy
> The entire DNS resolution process is based on the fact that a root name server is available any time one is needed. If only one root name server existed and it failed, the Internet would be out of business until the root name server was again available. Multiple, widely dispersed root name servers remove this single point of failure, and they also guard against network communication failures that temporarily render one or another of the root name servers inaccessible.

Load sharing
> Because the root name servers are at the top of the DNS tree, they are accessed frequently by other, subordinate DNS servers. The enormous size of the Internet places a large burden on the root name servers, which process thousands of queries per second. The use of multiple root name servers allows the burden to be spread across many servers.

The addresses of the root name servers are subject to change. This does not happen frequently, but it is possible. The list of root name servers can be easily updated using the DNS console. To do so, open the Root Hints tab of the DNS server properties sheet by highlighting the server name in the console tree of the DNS console and then double-clicking on Root Hints in the righthand pane of the console window. (The Root Hints tab is shown in Figure 6-4.) Next click on the Copy from Server button, enter the IP address of a name server in the Server to Copy From dialog and click OK. Your server will download the list of root servers from the server you specified and use that list to replace its own list of root servers. Clearly the remote server you specify should be one that you are sure has a good list of root servers. Generally, the IP address of a nearby root server is used in the Server to Copy From dialog to ensure that you get a truly up-to-date root server list.

It is also possible to manually update the root server list using the Add, Remove, and Edit button on the Root Hints tab. To do so, you need an accurate list of the current root servers. You can download the current names and addresses of the root name servers in the file *domain/named.root* from *rs.internic.net* via anonymous FTP.[*] Download, open, and manually check the *named.root* file for any changes. If there

---

[*] The *named.root* file is not in exactly the same format as the *cache.dns* file, yet the *named.root* file is compatible with Windows Server 2003 system and could be downloaded directly into the local system's *cache.dns* file without editing. Generally, however, this is not done.

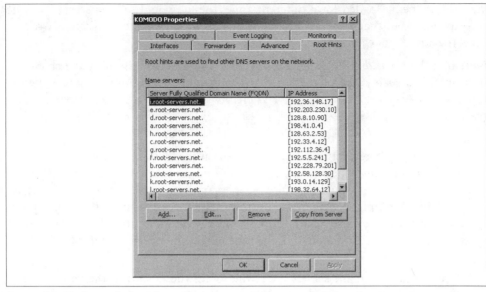

Figure 6-4. Updating the list of root servers

are any address changes, the changes can be made directly to the local root hints file using the Root Hints tab. Manually update the IP address of a server by highlighting the server in the "Name servers" scroll list, clicking Edit, and then removing the old address and adding the new one in the Edit Record dialog. If a new server has been added to the list of root servers, click the Add button and enter the name and address of the new server in the New Resource Record dialog. In the highly unlikely event that the list of root name servers has gotten smaller, highlight the unneeded server in the scroll box and click Remove. Using whichever method you prefer, update the root server hints every few months to keep accurate root server information in your cache.

The list of root servers provided by Microsoft and shown here assumes that your network has access to the Internet and therefore needs to communicate with the global root servers. If your system is not connected to the Internet, it won't be able to communicate with these root servers, and therefore initializing the cache with these servers would be useless. In this case, initialize your cache with entries that point to name servers on your local network that will act as "root" servers. Those local servers must be configured to answer queries for the "root" domain. However, the root domain on these local root servers would only contain NS records pointing to the domain servers on your local network. For example: assume that *example.com* is not connected to the Internet and that *komodo* and *jamis* are going to act as root servers for this isolated domain. Both servers are configured as primary for the root domain. They load the root from a zone file that contains NS records and A records, stating that they are authoritative for the root and delegating the *example.com* and *0.168.192.in-addr.arpa* domains to the local name servers that service those domains. Details of this type of configuration are provided in *DNS and BIND* (O'Reilly).

Other than the special case noted in the previous paragraph, configuring the cache initialization file requires very little effort from the system administrator. Most of the work in configuring DNS goes into creating the zone files.

The Forward Lookup Zone File

The forward lookup zone file contains most of the domain information. This file converts hostnames to IP addresses, so A records predominate; but it also contains MX, CNAME, and other records. With standard DNS, the zone file is only created on the master server. All other servers get this information from the master server.

The skeleton zone file created during the initial installation is shown here:

```
C:\WINDOWS\system32\dns>type example.com.dns
;
;  Database file example.com.dns for example.com zone.
;     Zone version:  1
;

@               IN  SOA komodo.example.com.  hostmaster.example.com. (
                        1               ; serial number
                        900             ; refresh
                        600             ; retry
                        86400           ; expire
                        3600           ) ; default TTL

;
;  Zone NS records
;

@               NS      komodo.example.com.

;
;  Zone records
;
```

All zone files begin with an SOA record. The @ in the name field of the SOA record references the current domain. In this case, it is the domain name defined in the Zone Name box when a new zone is created with the New Zone Wizard. The @ is used in the name field on every zone's SOA record; it always references the correct domain defined for that particular zone file in the New Zone Wizard.

The SOA record has perhaps the most complicated data field of any resource record. It contains so many subfields that it spans several lines. (Parentheses are required whenever a resource record continues across multiple lines.) The subfields in the SOA data field are as follows:

Origin
> This is the hostname of the primary master server for this domain. Active Directory Integrated DNS allows for multiple master servers. In the case of multiple master servers, this is the name of the master server on which this zone was originally created.

Contact
> This field contains the email address of the technical contact for this domain. Notice that the @ normally found in an email address is replaced with a dot (.) when the address is entered in the contact field.

Serial number
> This is the version number of the file. It is incremented every time the zone is updated to alert slave servers that they need to do a zone file transfer to update their versions of the zone file.

Refresh
> This value tells a slave server how often it should check to see if the zone file has been updated. Refresh is the interval, in seconds, that the slave server should wait between checking whether or not a zone refresh is necessary.

Retry
> The retry field defines the number of seconds a slave server should wait before trying again when the master server fails to respond to a zone refresh request.

Expire
> This defines how long the slave should retain data when the master server fails to respond to all requests to refresh the zone. In other words, this defines how long the slave should wait before deciding that the zone no longer exists and that all of the data in the zone is invalid.

Default TTL
> Microsoft uses this field for two purposes. The first purpose is to tell remote servers how long they should cache negative information. This purpose is defined in the RFCs. The second purpose is to use this value as a default TTL if no explicit TTL is provided for an individual resource record.

Customizing SOA parameters

All of the values in the SOA record shown earlier in the zone file listing are default values generated by the New Zone Wizard that created this zone. Those values can be overridden using the DNS console. To do so, highlight the zone in the DNS console tree and double-click on the SOA record in the righthand pane of the DNS console window. This opens the Start of Authority (SOA) tab of the zone properties sheet, shown in Figure 6-5.

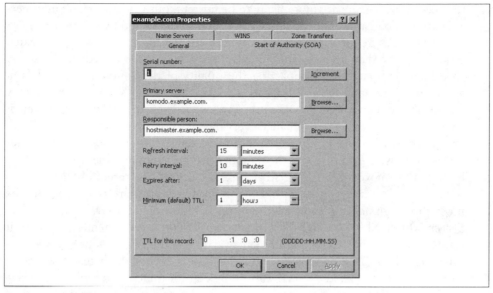

Figure 6-5. Setting SOA parameters

Use the Start of Authority (SOA) tab to change the SOA settings that define parameters for the entire zone file. The name of the master server, displayed in the "Primary server" box, should not need to be edited. The New Zone Wizard uses the name of the local server when the wizard is directed to create a primary zone. This value is usually correct.

The email address of the domain contact is displayed in the "Responsible person" box. The default responsible person email address is the *hostmaster* account on the master server. The contact address must be a real email address. If the server doesn't have an active *hostmaster* account where a real person reads email, you must either change the value in the "Responsible person" box to point to a real user account or you must create a *hostmaster* account and make sure someone monitors it. A real, live contact for every domain is not an option, it is a responsibility.

Most of the values displayed on the Start of Authority (SOA) tab control the timing of zone transfers. Use the Start of Authority (SOA) tab to set the following values that affect zone transfers:

Serial Number
> The serial number is initially set to 1 and is automatically incremented by 1 each time a change is made to DNS zone data. To manually increment the serial number, click the Increment button. (This might be done, for example, to force a zone refresh.) This simple serial number format works well; do not change it.

Refresh interval
> This value, 15 minutes by default, tells the secondary DNS servers how frequently to check the primary server for changes. Setting a low value means that

the secondary servers are more likely to be current, but may also result in unnecessary workload and unneeded network traffic. If the data on your primary DNS server changes frequently, set a low value to ensure that new data is propagated quickly. If the data changes infrequently, set a high value to reduce the server workload without greatly impacting the quality of the zone data. The default value of 15 minutes is an extremely low refresh value suitable for a highly changeable environment. Don't set it any lower. Even in a DHCP/DDNS environment, IP addresses don't change every day, let alone every 15 minutes. Leases are generally for a week or longer and most systems retain the same address after a lease renewal. Additionally, the systems that have changeable leases, such as laptops that move around a network, are not usually the target of DNS queries because remote connections into a highly mobile laptop are rare. Probably the most thorough and authoritative book on Windows DNS is *DNS on Windows Server 2003* (O'Reilly). *DNS on Windows Server 2003* recommends a three-hour refresh interval. In stable environments, a refresh interval of four (21,600 seconds) to eight (10,800 seconds) times a day is often adequate. However, it should be noted that the short, 15-minute refresh interval only places a heavy burden on the slave server if the server provides backup for a large number of big, changeable domains that all use the short interval.

Retry interval

The retry value, 10 minutes by default, specifies how long the secondary server should wait before again trying to contact the primary when the primary server fails to respond to a zone refresh request. The length of the retry interval should be less than the length of the refresh interval. Given the default 15-minute refresh interval, a 10-minute retry interval is reasonable. However, 10 minutes is a low retry value that can cause problems for a secondary server if that server backs up a large number of zones and all of those zones use a short interval. If you decide to use the three-hour refresh interval recommended by *DNS on Windows Server 2003*, you should use the one-hour retry interval that is also recommended in that text.

Expires after

The short default values for the refresh and retry intervals are not a problem for most sites. Those values only have a negative impact on secondary servers that back up a large number of zones. The 24-hour default for "Expires after" could be a problem for any site. "Expires after" specifies how long a slave server responds to queries after the primary server has gone offline. The assumption is that the zone data on the secondary DNS server becomes more and more dated, the longer the secondary server goes without getting an update from the primary server. After the amount of time defined for "Expires after" has passed, the secondary DNS server assumes that its data is invalid and stops responding to queries for the expired zone. The value provided as a default is much too short. If the primary server crashes on Friday night, the secondary server will shut down the domain on Saturday night. By the time the system administrator discovers the problem on Monday, email and other services would have been interrupted for a day and a half for no other reason than a poorly chosen default value. Use a much longer expire value—a week or even a month would be more reasonable.

In addition to the four values described, the Zone Transfers tab and the Name Servers tab of the zone properties sheet are also used to configure zone updates. How those tabs are used to configure zone transfers is covered later when we discuss the DNS console.

The last two values on the Start of Authority (SOA) tab both relate to the TTL. The "Minimum (default) TTL" value, one hour by default, defines the default TTL subfield of the SOA record's data field. Microsoft uses this subfield for both the negative cache TTL and as a default TTL for resource records in this zone that don't have explicit TTL values. Because this field is used for two different purposes, it is difficult to optimize the value for either purpose. The default value of one hour is a short default TTL but a relatively long negative cache TTL. It is, however, a reasonable compromise value for its dual purpose.

The other TTL value shown in Figure 6-5 is the explicit TTL value for the SOA record itself. The value is defined in the "TTL for this record" box. It too defaults to one hour. However, this field does not have a dual purpose, and can therefore be given an optimized value. One day would be a better value for this field.

Defining a list of name servers

This long discussion of the complex SOA record may have overshadowed the fact that the SOA record is not the only resource record in the skeleton zone file created by the New Zone Wizard. The other record is a name server (NS) record. Again, the @ in the name field means that the NS record applies to the entire zone. The NS records that follow the SOA record usually define all of the authoritative name servers for this zone—both the master and the official slave servers. However, the New Zone Wizard inserts only one NS record in the skeleton zone file—the one that defines the master server. Define the other authoritative name servers through the DNS console.

Highlight the name of the zone in the DNS console tree. Double-click on the Name Server (NS) record in the righthand pane of the DNS console. This opens the Name Servers tab of the zone properties sheet, an example of which is shown in Figure 6-6.

Figure 6-6 shows the tab after two servers (*jamis.example.com* and *ns1.foobar.org*) have been added to the list of authoritative servers. (*komodo.example.com* was the master server added to the list of servers by the New Zone Wizard.) Name servers are added to the list by clicking the Add button and entering the hostname and IP address of the server in the New Resource Record dialog box that appears. Names servers can be removed from the list by highlighting them and clicking the Remove

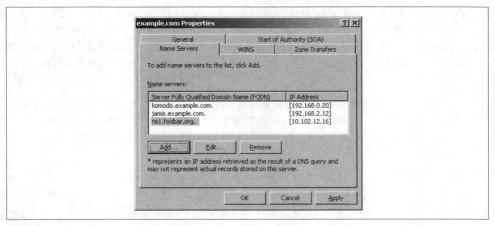

Figure 6-6. The Name Servers tab

button. Modify individual NS records by highlighting the name server in the list and clicking Edit. When you do so, the same New Resource Record dialog box appears that was used to add the server to the list. Use that dialog to enter the corrected values. Once the name server list is to your liking, click Apply and then OK to update the cached zone information. To update the zone files with the new information, highlight the server name in the console tree and select Update Server Data Files from the DNS console's Action menu. An updated forward lookup zone file is shown below:

```
C:\WINDOWS\system32\dns>type example.com.dns
;
;  Database file example.com.dns for example.com zone.
;      Zone version:  6
;

@               86400   IN  SOA komodo.example.com.  patrick.example.com. (
                        6               ; serial number
                        10800           ; refresh
                        3600            ; retry
                        2592000         ; expire
                        3600            ) ; default TTL

;
;  Zone NS records
;

@                       NS      komodo.example.com.
@                       NS      jamis.example.com.
@                       NS      ns1.foobar.org.
ns1.foobar.org.         A       10.102.12.16

;
;  Zone records
;
```

```
jamis               A       192.168.2.12
komodo              A       192.168.0.20
```

This is the zone file after the updates to the SOA record and to the name server list described previously. Notice that the SOA record now has an explicit value in the TTL field (86,400 seconds, which is one day). Also, the contact field has been changed to show the actual email address of the administrator of this zone. Further, notice that the refresh, retry, and expire values have been changed as discussed earlier. Perhaps the most interesting change to the SOA records is the change in the serial number. The serial number is incremented automatically every time the cached zone data is updated. (In this case, we updated the SOA record, added two NS records and three A records for a total of six changed records.) So even though this is only the second version of the zone file written to disk, the serial number is 6 because we made several intermediate changes to the cache before writing the updated zone to a file.

The name servers are listed immediately after the SOA, and before any other records in the zone. This is the same list of servers we created in Figure 6-6. The three NS records are followed by three address (A) records that provide the addresses of the servers. The two servers that exist inside this zone (*komodo* and *jamis*) must, of course, have addresses inside this zone. The external server (*ns1.foobar.org*) also has an address declared inside this file, but that is merely a Microsoft convention. The correct address for this server could easily be obtained from the server for the *foobar.org* domain, and, in fact, it would be more accurate if it were obtained from an authoritative source when needed instead of storing a potentially stale address in the local zone file. However, the New Resource Record dialog mentioned in the discussion of Figure 6-6 requires both an IP address and a server hostname when adding a server to the name server list, and it uses the two values to create both an NS record and an A record. If you're concerned that this external address might become stale, you can manually remove this A record from the zone file. Make sure, however, that you never remove the addresses of the local servers from the zone file. Remember, this zone file is the ultimate source of information about everything in the local zone, including the servers.

The skeleton zone file is now ready to receive data. A records can be dynamically added via DDNS. Others resource records, such as mail exchange (MX) records and host alias (CNAME) records must be added manually. We'll see how the DNS console is used to add those records later in this chapter. But before we do, let's look at the reverse zone file that was created by the New Zone Wizard during the initial DNS installation.

The Reverse Lookup File

The *0.168.192.in-addr.arpa.dns* file in our example is the zone file for the reverse domain *0.168.192.in-addr.arpa*. Using standard DNS, the person responsible for the domain creates this file on the primary server, and every other host that needs this information gets it from that server. The skeleton reverse zone file created by the New Zone Wizard is listed below:

```
C:\WINDOWS\system32\dns>type 0.168.192.in-addr.arpa.dns
;
;  Database file 0.168.192.in-addr.arpa.dns for 0.168.192.in-addr.arpa zone.
;      Zone version:  1
;

@               IN  SOA komodo.example.com.  hostmaster.example.com. (
                         1                 ; serial number
                         900               ; refresh
                         600               ; retry
                         86400             ; expire
                         3600        )  ; default TTL


;
;  Zone NS records
;

@                      NS       komodo.example.com.


;
;  Zone records
;
```

Like the forward lookup zone file, the reverse zone file begins with an SOA record that defines parameters for the entire zone. Again, the New Zone Wizard uses default values that may not be exactly what you want. Use the DNS console to customize these values to your liking, as follows. Highlight the reverse zone in the console tree and double-click the SOA record in the righthand pane of the DNS console window to open the Start of Authority (SOA) tab of the reverse zone properties sheet. This tab is identical to the one shown in Figure 6-5 and is used in exactly the same way to set the zone parameters that you want.

The listing above also shows that the New Zone Wizard added an NS record identifying the master server. The complete list of name servers for the reverse zone is usually the same list of name servers used for the forward lookup zone, which is composed of the master server and the official slave servers. To create a complete server list, highlight the reverse zone in the console tree and double-click the NS record in the righthand pane of the DNS console window to open the Name Servers tab of the reverse zone properties sheet. This tab is identical to the one shown in Figure 6-6 and is used in exactly the same way to define a full list of name servers. However, the IP addresses that you define for the name servers do not appear in the reverse zone file. Address records and most other types of resource records appear only in the forward lookup zone file. The reverse zone file is almost entirely composed of PTR records.

PTR records dominate the reverse lookup file because they are used to translate addresses to hostnames. A Microsoft DHCP server can add PTR records directly to the reverse zone file using DDNS. PTR records can also be added to the reverse zone manually using the DNS console.

The DNS Console

The DNS console was introduced in the discussion of Figure 6-3 and has already been used to refine the skeleton zone files created by the initial DNS installation. Yet, the DNS console can do much more. In fact, a single DNS console can be used to manage multiple Microsoft DNS servers from a central location. Simply highlight DNS in the console tree and select Connect to DNS Server from the Action menu. In the Connect to DNS Server dialog, select "The following computer" and enter the hostname or IP address of the remote server in the box. Click OK, and the console will connect to the remote Microsoft DNS server and provide you with remote management capability. In this section we manage zone files on the local server, but these same management functions could be used on a remote server by adding that server to the console as described in the preceding sentences.

Defining Records for a Forward Lookup Zone

Most zone file maintenance happens in the forward lookup zone file. This file holds a much wider variety of resource records than does the reverse lookup zone file.

The bulk of the resource records in the forward lookup zone file are A records that map hostnames to IP addresses. A records can be added automatically to the zone file via DDNS, but they are also added manually using the DNS console. To do so, highlight the specific forward zone to which you want to add the A record and select New Host (A) from the Action menu. The New Host dialog, shown in Figure 6-7, appears.

Enter the hostname of the system being added to the zone file, and the IP address associated with that host. If you also control the reverse zone in which the IP address of the host is located, check the "Create associated pointer (PTR) record" checkbox. Adding a PTR record when you add an A record, and vice versa, helps to keep the zones "balanced," so that the IP address returned for a given hostname in a forward lookup returns the same hostname when that IP address is used in a reverse lookup.

A records are the only resource records in the forward lookup zone file that can be added by a DHCP server using DDNS. Even if you use DDNS, you must add some other records manually. One of the most important of these is the MX record that directs email delivery for your domain to the correct mail server.

To add an MX record to the zone, highlight the specific forward zone to which the record is to be added and select New Mail Exchanger (MX) from the Action menu.

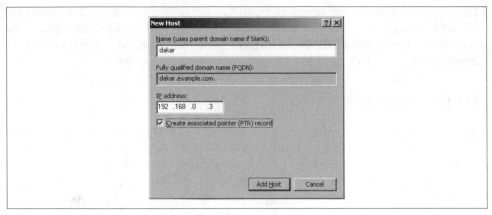

Figure 6-7. Adding an A record

The Mail Exchanger (MX) tab of the New Resource Record dialog, shown in Figure 6-8, appears.

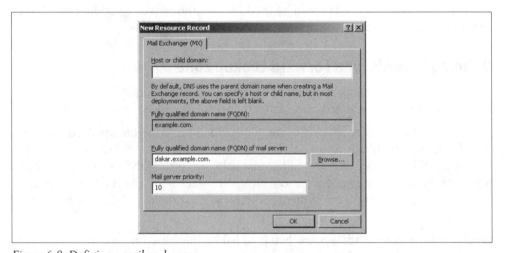

Figure 6-8. Defining a mail exchanger

The "Host or child domain" box at the top of the tab should be left blank if you are defining a mail exchanger for your own domain, which is usually the case. Leaving this box blank causes the DNS console to create an MX record with an @ in the name field. As we know from earlier discussions, an @ in the name field means that the record pertains to the current domain. The "Host or child domain" box is only used if you are defining an MX server for another domain that is served from the same zone. (More later on adding a domain to the current zone.)

The "Mail server priority" box and the "Fully qualified domain name (FQDN) of the mail server" box define the data field of the MX record. The FQDN of the server should be defined all the way to the root, i.e., the FQDN should end with the name of a top-level domain followed by a dot. The priority defines whether this is the primary mail exchanger for the domain or a backup mail exchanger. For increased reliability, there should be more than one mail exchange server. The one given the lowest priority number is the primary server. Backup servers are given higher priority numbers, with each server given a unique number. A remote mail client first tries to deliver mail to the mail exchanger with the lowest priority number. If that server fails to respond to the mail connection request, the client tries each backup server in turn starting with the next lowest priority number and working up until a server accepts the email. It is then the responsibility of the backup server to forward the mail to the primary server when the primary server comes back online. Assume that *dakar* is the primary server with a priority of 10. We could then add *stumpy.example.com* as a backup server with a priority of 20.

The CNAME record is another commonly used resource record. It defines an alias hostname for an existing host. The most common reason to do this is to define a well-known hostname, such as *www*, *smtp*, *pop*, and others, that users and application software expect to find. Figure 6-9 shows how the alias *http://www.example.com* could be defined for the real host *dakar.example.com*.

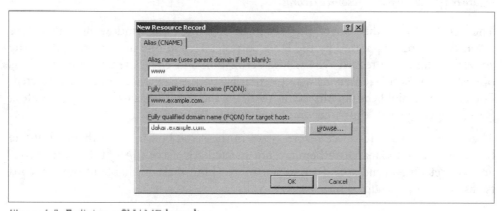

Figure 6-9. Defining a CNAME host alias

The "Alias name" box defines the value that will be used in the name field of the CNAME record. The value entered in this box is usually entered as a hostname relative to the current domain name. The "Fully qualified domain name" box shows you how the value entered in the Alias name box is interpreted by the system. The "Fully qualified domain name (FQDN) for target" box defines the value that will appear in the data field of the CNAME record. This is the FQDN of the real host that is being given an alias. The value entered in this box must be fully qualified; it cannot be a relative hostname. Additionally, this must be a real hostname, i.e., a hostname defined on an A record. This box cannot contain another alias.

While A, MX, and CNAME records are the most common resource records defined for the forward lookup zone, there are many other resource records that can be defined using the DNS console. To see a full list of those other records, highlight the specific forward zone to which you want to add a record and select Other New Records from the Action menu. The Resource Record Type window, shown in Figure 6-10, appears.

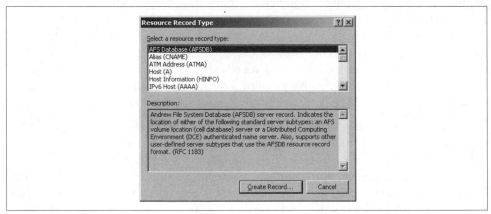

Figure 6-10. All supported resource records

The scroll box at the top of the Resource Record Type window lists all of the resource records supported by the DNS console. To add one of these records to the zone, highlight the record type in the scroll box and click Create a Record. This opens a New Resource Record window that is specific to the type of record selected. For example, highlighting Alias (CNAME) in the scroll box and clicking Create a Record opens exactly the same window shown in Figure 6-9.

There are too many resource record types in the scroll box to cover them all in line here. (And frankly, many of them are not particularly useful.) All of them, however, are covered in Appendix C. To find out more about these available resource record types, see the appendix.

Working with Subdomains

There are two ways to manage the subdomains of your domain. One way is to add the subdomain directly to your zone. A zone can include more than one domain, so it is perfectly legitimate to simply add the new domain to your current zone. The other way to manage a subdomain is to delegate that domain to a new zone. Before discussing how a domain is delegated, let's look at how a subdomain can be added to your existing zone.

Imagine that the marketing department wants its own domain name, *sales.example.com*, but they have no resources to run their own domain name service. Further, assume that you decide to add the *sales.example.com* domain directly to the *example.com* zone. You can do that in the following manner using the DNS console.

Highlight *example.com* in the console tree. Select New Domain from the Action menu. Enter the name of the subdomain, *sales* in our example, in the New DNS Domain dialog and click OK. Note that we entered only the first part of the domain name. This value is interpreted as relative to the current domain, which is *example.com* for our zone. Therefore, only that portion of the domain name that occurs before *example.com* is entered in the New DNS Domain dialog.

After clicking OK a new folder named *sales* appears in the DNS console tree as a subordinate entry to *example.com*. To add a resource record to *sales.example.com*, highlight *sales* in the console tree and select the entry for the desired record from the Action menu. Resource records are added to this domain exactly as they were added to the *example.com* domain in the previous section. All resource records for both the *example.com* domain and the *sales.example.com* domain appear in the *example.com.dns* file because they are all part of the same zone. The following listing shows an example of this:

```
C:\WINDOWS\system32\dns>type example.com.dns
;
;  Database file example.com.dns for example.com zone.
;      Zone version:  12
;

@               86400    IN  SOA komodo.example.com.  patrick.example.com. (
                         12               ; serial number
                         10800            ; refresh
                         3600             ; retry
                         2592000          ; expire
                         3600          )  ; default TTL

;
;  Zone NS records
;

@                        NS       komodo.example.com.
@                        NS       jamis.example.com.
@                        NS       ns1.foobar.org.
ns1.foobar.org.          A        10.102.12.16

;
;  Zone records
;

@                        MX       10      dakar.example.com.
dakar                    A        192.168.0.3
jamis                    A        192.168.2.12
komodo                   A        192.168.0.20
dollars.sales            A        192.168.3.8
euros.sales              A        192.168.3.15
www                      CNAME    dakar.example.com.
```

The A records for *dollars.sales.example.com* and *euros.sales.example.com* were both added to this zone file by highlighting *sales* in the console tree and selecting New Host (A) from the Action menu. This file illustrates how two domains can exist within a single zone.

Running multiple domains from one zone works, but it is not as robust or as scalable as delegating domains to other zones. Delegating domains allows you to use multiple database files, and more importantly, multiple servers. Domain delegation is easily accomplished using the DNS console.

Delegating a domain

Imagine that, unlike the marketing department, the engineering department has all the resources needed to run its own name server and that it wants to do so. Furthermore, imagine that you have agreed to delegate the engineering department the domain name *eng.example.com*. Delegate this domain as follows.

Highlight the zone in which the delegation will be made (*example.com* in our example). Select New Delegation from the Action menu to launch the New Delegation Wizard. Click Next in the wizard's welcome window to go to the Delegated Domain Name window where you type in the subdomain's name in the "Delegated domain" box. Again, this name is relative to the current domain. Thus in our example, we enter *eng* for the domain name *eng.example.com*. Click Next to go to the Name Servers window.

In the Name Servers window, define the master server for the *eng.example.com* domain and at least one slave server for that domain. Figure 6-11 shows the wizard after two servers have been defined for the *eng.example.com* domain.

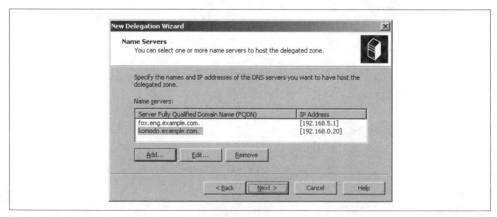

Figure 6-11. Selecting servers for a delegated zone

Servers are added to the "Name server" list box using the Add button, deleted with the Remove button and changed with the Edit button. In this example, *fox.eng.example.com* is the master server of the *eng.example.com* domain, and *komodo.example.com* is the master server of the *example.com* domain. In this case, however, it is acting as the slave server for the *eng.example.com* domain. It is very common for the master server of the parent domain (the master server for the *example.com* domain in our example) to act as a slave server for its subdomains. Click Next and Finish to create the domain delegation.

The delegation adds the following records to the *example.com.dns* zone file:

```
;
;  Delegated sub-zone:  eng.example.com.
;
eng                     NS      fox.eng.example.com.
fox.eng                 A       192.168.5.1
eng                     NS      komodo.example.com.
;  End delegation
```

The two NS records identify the servers for the new domain. The A record is a *glue record*. It defines the address for *fox.eng.example.com* in the *example.com* domain so that when remote sites contact the *example.com* domain for information about the *eng.example.com* domain they are provided with the address of the master server of that domain.

Of course, this delegation assumes that *komodo.example.com* is ready to be a slave server for the *eng.example.com* domain. To make it ready for that task, highlight Forward Lookup Zones in the DNS console tree and select New Zone from the Action menu. Select Secondary zone when asked for a zone type. Enter *eng.example.com* when asked for the zone name. And enter the IP address of *fox.eng.example.com* when asked for the master DNS server. This creates the slave zone files into which *komodo*, acting as a slave server, will copy the *eng.example.com* zone transfer data.

Managing a Reverse Lookup Zone

Use the DNS console to maintain a reverse lookup zone in much the same way as you would maintain a forward lookup zone. The biggest difference is that the reverse zone is composed almost entirely of PTR records. A DHCP server using DDNS can do most of this maintenance for you because the DHCP server generates a PTR record each time it leases an address. (You must, of course, enable dynamic updates on the DNS server. How that is done is covered in the section "Other Zone Management Features.") Even when DHCP with DDNS is used, some reverse mappings, such as those associated with servers that are given fixed addresses, need to be added manually. To manually add a PTR record to a reverse zone, highlight the zone in the console tree and select New Pointer (PTR) from the Action menu to open the New Resource Record window shown in Figure 6-12.

Figure 6-12 adds the reverse mapping for the server *komodo.example.com* to the *0.168.192.in-addr.arpa* zone. Because the first three bytes of the IP address are fixed for this specific zone, the "Host IP number" box accepts only the last byte of the address. In another reverse zone, the number of fixed and variable bytes

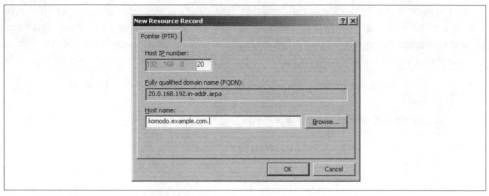

Figure 6-12. Manually adding a PTR record

could be different. Enter the address and hostname values and click OK to update the cached zone. To update the zone file, select Update Server Data File from the Action menu. The following listing shows the reverse lookup file after two PTR records have been added:

```
C:\WINDOWS\system32\dns>type 0.168.192.in-addr.arpa.dns
;
;  Database file 0.168.192.in-addr.arpa.dns for 0.168.192.in-addr.arpa zone.
;     Zone version:  6
;

@              86400    IN  SOA komodo.example.com.  patrick.example.com. (
                            6              ; serial number
                            10800          ; refresh
                            3600           ; retry
                            2592000        ; expire
                            3600          ) ; default TTL


;
;  Zone NS records
;

@                        NS      komodo.example.com.
@                        NS      jamis.example.com.
jamis.example.com.       A       192.168.2.12


;
;  Zone records
;

20                       PTR     komodo.example.com.
3                        PTR     dakar.example.com.
```

The two PTR records we manually added to this file appear at the bottom of the listing. Notice that there is an A record in the reverse zone file! This is exactly like the A record we saw for the external server in the name server list of the forward lookup file.

It is a Microsoft implementation-specific characteristic. Clearly, no remote system will query the *0.168.192.in-addr.arpa* zone for the address of *jamis.example.com*—that query would go to the *example.com* zone. (Just ignore this oddity and view it as a comment.) It is also worth noting that there is no PTR record for *jamis.example.com* in this zone. That is because this zone is *0.168.192.in-addr.arpa*, and the PTR for jamis would be found in the *2.168.192.in-addr.arpa* zone.

Delegating a reverse zone

Like forward zones, reverse zones can also contain delegations for subdomains. The delegation is done in exactly the same way as a forward zone file delegation. Highlight the zone in the console tree and select New Delegation from the Action menu to launch the New Delegation Wizard. The only difference between delegating a forward and a reverse zone is the structure of the domain name—a reverse domain name is numeric. Figure 6-13 shows the Delegated Domain Name window for a reverse domain delegation.

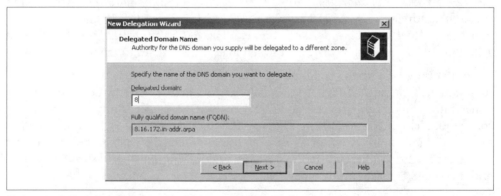

Figure 6-13. Defining the name for a delegated reverse lookup zone

Notice that this example does not delegate a subdomain within the *0.168.192.in-addr.arpa* domain used in previous examples. The reason is simple: we cannot delegate a subdomain within that domain using this technique because there are no bytes left in the address to use for the delegation. The basic delegation technique delegates reverse zones on full byte boundaries. The 192.168.0/24 address uses the first three bytes to define the domain name and the fourth byte to define the host within the domain. There are no bytes left for delegation. If you plan to do subdomain delegation for reverse zones, you should use a large private address, such as the one shown on Figure 6-13. The private address 172.16/16 provides a full byte to define the host in the zone and a full byte for reverse zone delegation, which allows you to create up to 256 reverse zones.

If you have a large public address space, it is just as easy to delegate as a large private address space. If, however, you are stuck using a small public address space, you might not be able to simply obtain a larger space that is easy to delegate. In that case, it is easiest not to delegate any reverse subdomains. Simply keep a single reverse zone on your central DNS server. All DHCP server updates can be directed to that server, as can all DNS queries. Because the PTR records are created automatically through DDNS, there is very little maintenance cost involved in keeping all reverse lookup data in a single file. Particularly given the fact that small zones are the only ones that are hard to delegate. However, if you absolutely must delegate subdomains in a small reverse domain it can be done.

Assume that we are forced to subdivide the *0.168.192.in-addr.arpa* domain into two equal parts. To do this we delegate one zone named *0-127.0.168.192.in-addr.arpa* and one zone named *128-255.0.168.192.in-addr.arpa* using the New Delegation Wizard. We then fully populate the *0.168.192.in-addr.arpa* zone with CNAME records—one for each possible address. (CNAME records are added to a reverse zone by highlighting the zone in the console tree and selecting Alias (CNAME) from the Action menu.) The CNAME records for addresses 0 to 127 point to the *1.0-127.0.168.192.in-addr.arpa* to *127.0-127.0.168.192.in-addr.arpa* names and those for addresses 128 to 255 point to the *128.128-255.0.168.192.in-addr.arpa* to *255.128-255.0.168.192.in-addr.arpa* names. The *0-127.0.168.192.in-addr.arpa* and *128-255.0.168.192.in-addr.arpa* zones then map the addresses to the real hostnames.

Do not subdivide a single, small reverse zone. As noted above, it is simply easier to maintain it as a single zone. Additionally, if you need to subdivide many reverse zones into many smaller reverse zones, Microsoft DNS server is not the correct tool for the job. The BIND 9 software available for Unix systems is much better suited to exotic configurations. It is not as easy to use as Microsoft DNS server, but exotic configurations are inherently not easy to maintain. Bottom line: do things simply, and if you can't, make sure you have the correct tool for the job.

Understanding Stub Zones

Forward lookup zones and reverse lookup zones are the zone types that spring to mind when you think about DNS. After all, these are the zones used to map hostnames to IP addresses and from IP addresses back to hostnames. Stub zones are different; they are primarily used to simplify DNS administration.

A stub zone stores resource records just like the other zone types. However, the RRs are limited to the SOA record, the NS records and the A glue records necessary to clearly define the parameters of the zone and the authoritative servers for the zone. When a server is configured as a secondary server for a zone, it transfers all of the data for the zone from the master server. When a server is configured as a stub server, it transfers from the master server only those records needed to identify the authoritative servers for the zone. The listing that follows shows the zone file created for a stub zone on a Microsoft DNS server:

```
C:\WINDOWS\system32\dns>type example.net.dns
;
;  Database file example.net.dns for example.net zone.
;     Zone version:  2004021201
;

@                  IN   SOA ox.example.net.  admin.ox.example.net. (
                        2004021201  ; serial number
                        21600       ; refresh
                        1800        ; retry
                        604800      ; expire
                        900        ) ; default TTL

;
;  Zone NS records
;

@                  NS      ox.example.net.
@                  NS      gw.example.net.

;
;  Zone records
;

gw                 A       192.168.0.1
ox                 A       192.168.0.3
```

This zone file contains only the SOA record, and the NS records and the A records associated with the authoritative servers for this zone, despite the fact that the real *example.net* zone contains many more records. Compared to secondary zones, stub zones reduce the amount of data transferred and stub servers assume less of a workload for the zone than secondary server do for the zones they support. These characteristics make stub zones useful for large or geographically dispersed organizations.

Stub zones are particularly useful on servers that delegate a large number of domains. As the sections on domain delegation made clear, a domain is delegated by adding information to the parent domain that identifies the authoritative servers for the subdomain. The information is manually added to the parent domain, and when that information changes, it must be manually updated unless a stub zone is used. A stub zone on the parent server automatically loads any changes to the list of authoritative servers for the subdomain from the subdomain's master server without any manual updates. The only thing that must remain constant is the master server for the subdomain. In environments that service a very large number of subdomains, stub domains simplify subdomain maintenance without placing the full burden of a secondary zone on the parent server.

Stub zones also simplify the query process by preloading the DNS server cache with information about the authoritative servers for a domain. The discussion of Figure 3-2 explained that a server must first query the root and the parents of a desired domain to obtain the information needed to find the authoritative servers for the domain. Those queries are unnecessary when the information can be obtained from a local stub zone. Certainly, this is a fairly minor benefit, but nonetheless it is a benefit of stub zones.

As mentioned earlier in this chapter, stub zones are created through the New Zone Wizard in the same way that primary and secondary zones are created. After selecting stub zone as the zone type, you are asked if it is a forward or reverse zone, what domain name the zone is associated with, what the zone filename is, and the IP address of the master server for the stub zone—exactly as if you were creating a secondary zone. Once the stub zone is created, it can be managed through the DNS console just like any other zone. However, the management functions available to a stub zone are limited to updating the master server address or reloading the zone data.

Other Zone Management Features

Zone file management is the main use for the DNS console. The zone properties window, which we first saw in Figure 6-5, provides several more ways to customize the management of zone file. For one thing, the DNS console can be used to provide additional controls for zone file transfer beyond those provided on the SOA record.

Managing zone transfers

The serial number, refresh, and retry values on the SOA record control how often slave servers attempt a zone refresh. These values do not control which remote servers are allowed to do a zone transfer, and the SOA values do not enable the master server to *push* an update down to the slaves. (The SOA parameters are only used to tell slave servers when to *pull* down a zone update.) Use the Zone Transfers tab, shown in Figure 6-14, to control access to zone transfers and to enable the master server to push zone transfers.

Use the "Allow zone transfers" checkbox to enable zone transfers. If this box is not checked, slave servers are not able to keep their copies of the zone synchronized with the master server. The only time that it is practical to disable zone file transfers is when Active Directory Integrated DNS is used and all servers, the master and all of the slaves, are domain controllers that keep the zone synchronized through replication. It is best to always leave this box checked.

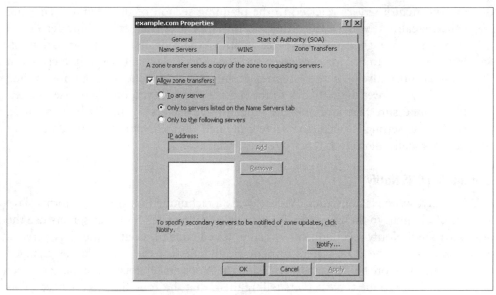

Figure 6-14. The Zone Transfers tab

When zone transfers are enabled, you have three choices of which servers should be allowed to receive a zone transfer:

To any server

This setting permits any host anywhere in the Internet to transfer the zone. Most sites do not use this setting because of security concerns. Some security people block zone transfers to the world at large to prevent malicious people from discovering all of the hostnames in the zone. Other security people block zone transfers to reduce the risk of denial-of-service attacks. Certainly zone transfers place a burden on the master server, and repeated zone transfers could be used as a denial-of-service tool. But DNS is vulnerable to denial-of-service attacks even when zone transfers are carefully controlled. Don't fool yourself into thinking one checkbox is sufficient security.

Only to servers listed on the Name Servers tab

This is the default, and it is the most common setting. Recall that we used the *Name Servers* tab to define the master server and the official slave servers. This setting limits zone transfers to the official slave servers, which is exactly what most sites want to do.

Only to the following servers

When this setting is selected, all of the servers permitted to receive zone file transfers must be defined in the box on this window. Enter the address of an approved name server in the "IP address" box and click Add to add it to the list box. To delete a server, highlight it in the list box and click Remove. This setting is used to create secondary servers that are not official slave servers. Unofficial slave servers are the *stealth servers* referred to the planning section of this chapter. They are called stealth servers because they do not appear in the list of name servers. A stealth server might be used to place a copy of the zone at a remote office that has limited access to the master server and the official slaves. The stealth server can then authoritatively answer queries about the local zone without forwarding those queries over the network to the master server. If you decide to use this setting, make sure that you add the official slave servers to the list box, because, when this setting is used, the servers defined on the Name Servers tab are not automatically allowed to receive zone transfers.

Configuring DNS Notify

DNS Notify, which is defined in RFC 1996, is a technique that quickly informs slave servers of changes to the zone file. By default, Windows DNS master servers use the standard DNS Notify mechanism to push updated zone files out to the slave servers. Slave servers use the SOA timers to periodically check if the zone file has changed and should therefore be downloaded. Using the Notify mechanism, the master server sends a message to the slave servers telling them that the zone file has changed. This short-circuits the refresh timers causing the slaves to immediately transfer the zone.

Click the Notify button on the Zone Transfers tab, shown near the bottom of Figure 6-14, to open the Notify window. Use the Notify window, shown in Figure 6-15, to control the configuration of the Notify mechanism.

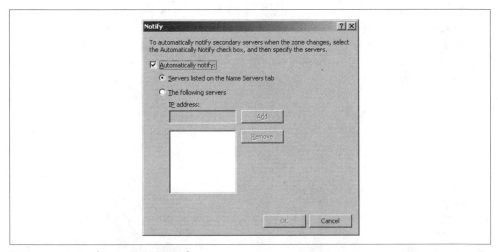

Figure 6-15. Configuring DNS Notify

Use the "Automatically notify" checkbox to enable or disable the DNS Notify mechanism. By default, this box is checked, and therefore DNS Notify is enabled. Leave it enabled. Disabling DNS Notify provides no advantages. By default, "Servers listed on the Name Servers" tab is selected. This is a reasonable default selection because it means that the master server will send Notify messages to all of the official slave servers every time the zone is updated. This keeps the slave servers tightly synchronized with the master. The other selection, "The following servers," sends Notify messages to all of the servers listed in the list box on this page. Use this selection if you defined stealth servers on the Zone Transfers tab and you want to send Notify messages to those servers. If you select "The following servers," take care to define all of the servers, including the official slave servers that should receive Notify messages.

Integrating a zone and WINS

A Microsoft DNS server can forward a name query to a WINS server for name resolution. This is not done by default, but the DNS server can be configured to do this using the DNS console. To do so, highlight the zone for which queries are to be forwarded to a WINS server and select Properties from the Action menu. In the zone properties sheet select the WINS tab, which is shown in Figure 6-16.

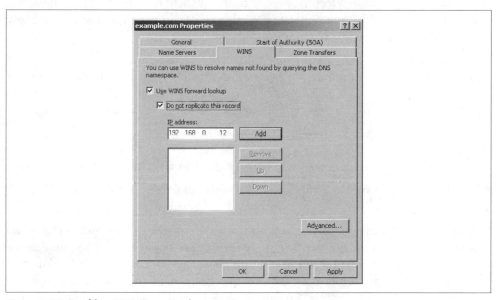

Figure 6-16. Enabling WINS queries from DNS

To forward name queries to a WINS server, check the "Use WINS forward lookup" checkbox, then enter the IP address of a WINS server in the "IP address" box and click Add to add it to the list of WINS servers. Check the "Do not replicate this record" checkbox to prevent the DNS server from adding the WINS data to the zone and transferring the WINS data on to the slave servers. (Always use the "Do not replicate this record" setting in mixed Unix and Windows environments; transferring WINS data to Unix servers can cause zone file transfer problems.) Use the Advanced button to define how long the DNS server should cache data learned from the WINS server and how long the DNS servers should wait for the WINS server to respond to a query. By default, WINS data is cached for 15 minutes, and a DNS server waits for a WINS query response for up to two seconds. In general, these are adequate settings.

Although still needed by some applications, WINS is an outdated solution and its use should be minimized when possible. If you do use WINS, avoid having DNS rely on WINS queries. It is better to enter information for all clients directly into the DNS zone than it is to rely on WINS for some of that information because a complete set of information eases the transition to new technologies. The preferred way to integrate DNS with a Microsoft domain is through Active Directory, as described in Chapter 7.

Server Properties

In addition to the zone properties discussed so far in this section, the management console can be used to define server properties. To do so, highlight the server name in the console tree and select Properties from the Action menu to open the server properties window. This window has several tabs, one of which, the Root Hints tab, was discussed earlier in this chapter.

The Interfaces tab is only useful on multihomed DNS servers. By default, a DNS server answers queries on every interface. For security or address management reasons, you might want to answer queries on selected interfaces. Use the Interfaces tab to limit DNS service to selected network interfaces.

Advanced tab

The Advanced tab, which is shown in Figure 6-17, defines a variety of server settings.

The Advanced tab provides a checklist of six server options:

Disable recursion
> By default, Microsoft servers perform recursive queries. This means the server attempts to find the answer to a query even if the answer cannot be found in the server's cache or zone files. If this option is selected, recursion is disabled. In that circumstance, the server only answers questions that can be answered from the server's cache or zone file. For all other queries, the server sends the client a referral, which is a list of servers that can give the client more information. It is then the client's job to ask those other servers for the answer. Recursion is sometimes disabled on servers that are dedicated to handling queries that come from external sources, and on very large servers, such as the root servers, that do not have the resources to recursively process every query. Recursion is not disabled on servers that handle queries for internal clients.

BIND secondaries
> Use this selection to ensure compatibility with old BIND servers. This setting is useful only if the Microsoft server is the master server and some of its slave servers are Unix systems running a release of BIND prior to BIND 4.9.4. Using this

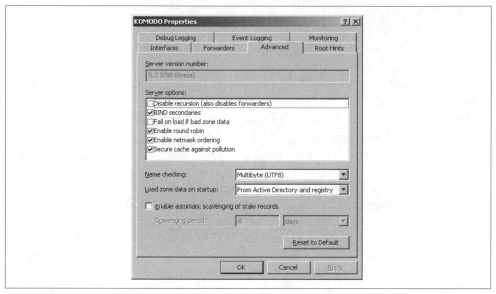

Figure 6-17. Advanced DNS server properties

selection slows down zone file transfers, so don't use it unless you absolutely must. The preferred solution is for the Unix systems to upgrade to a more recent version of BIND for enhanced performance and security. Note that Microsoft states that the default for this option is to have the checkbox cleared, thus providing the best performance. However, the settings shown in Figure 6-17 were produced by selecting the Reset to Default button of the Advanced tab, and in this case the system reset "BIND secondaries" to enabled. For this reason, review the Advanced tab settings on your server and make sure that all values are set the way that you want them set; do not rely entirely on documentation.

Fail on load if bad zone data

By default, the server logs an error for any bad data found in the zone file and then proceeds to load the zone file. Selecting this option causes the server to log the error and abort loading the zone file. The hostnames in the zone file are checked using the method you select from the "Name checking" drop-down list. The drop-down list offers four name-checking methods:

Strict RFC (ANSI)

Names must comply fully with the requirements of RFC 1123.

Non RFC (ANSI)

Names must use the American National Standards Institute (ANSI) characters set, but do not need to strictly adhere to RFC 1123. The character set used is American Standard Code for Information Interchange (ASCII).

Multibyte (UTF8)
> Names can be written in other character sets besides ASCII. Multibyte character sets must be represented n Unicode Transformation Format (UTF-8).

All names
> Any hostname is acceptable—essentially no hostname checks are performed.

Enable round robin
> Round robin causes the server to rotate a list of resource records each time the list is used in response to a query. Round robin is a simple load-sharing technique. Here's how it works. Assume that four systems share duties as web servers, and that four A records exist for the hostname *www* each pointing to a different IP address. Without round robin, each client would receive the same list of addresses for *www* and each client would use the first address in the list causing every client to connect to one server. With round robin, the DNS server rotates the address list before sending it to the client, so that the first address in the list is different for each client causing the clients to connect to different servers. While this example uses A records, round robin applies to all types of resource records as long as multiple records of the same type are included in the response. Microsoft DNS server uses round robin by default.

Enable netmask ordering
> Netmask ordering causes the server to reorder A records so that the first address offered to a client is the address that appears to be topologically closest to the client. Therefore, if the client is on subnet 192.168.0 and one of the addresses in the response is also on subnet 192.168.0, then that address will be placed first in the response to the client. Microsoft DNS servers perform netmask ordering by default.

Secure cache against pollution
> This option prevents the server from caching information that is unrelated to the original query. This helps prevent the cache from being either maliciously or accidentally corrupted by remote servers.

The Advanced tab contains two other settings. One setting is the "Load zone data on startup" drop-down list, which defines the source that the DNS server uses for zone data when the cache is created at startup. The drop-down list offers three choices:

From registry
> Loads the zone from the local registry.

From file
> Loads the zone from the local zone files.

From Active Directory and registry
> Loads the zone from the local registry and from the Active Directory server. This is the default setting.

Scavenging

The other setting on the Advanced tab is "Enable automatic scavenging of stale records," which causes the server to periodically check the cache for outdated resource records and to remove them from the cache. The frequency of the periodic checks is defined in the "Scavenging period" box. When "Enable automatic scavenging of stale records" is checked, the "Scavenging period" defaults to seven days, which is a reasonable period for most systems. The "Scavenging period" defines how soon scavenging starts after an event, such as reloading a primary zone.

Scavenging is only done to primary zones on the master server for the zone, and only when the zone permits dynamic updates, because scavenging is only used to remove outdated records that were dynamically added to the zone. Despite this narrow focus, scavenging is important because client systems do not always remove the records that they dynamically add to the zone. For example, when a laptop is not properly shut down before it is removed from the network, it will not delete the address record it added to the zone. Stale records can cause name resolution problems and, in sufficient numbers, can cause poor server performance. These problems can be exacerbated when AD integrated DNS is used because multiple systems can acts as zone masters with AD integrated DNS and each one of these systems may allow dynamic updates.

The "Enable automatic scavenging of stale records" setting on the Advanced tab of the server properties window enables scavenging on the server. Scavenging should also be enabled on individual zones. This can be done using the "Scavenge stale resource records" checkbox shown in Figure 6-18. To launch the dialog shown in Figure 6-18, highlight the zone you want to scavenge in the console tree and select Properties from the Action menu. Then in the General tab of the zone properties window, click the Aging button to open the dialog.

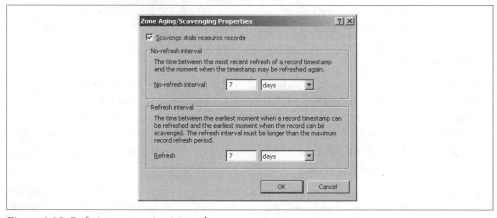

Figure 6-18. Defining scavenging intervals

Microsoft DNS does not use the resource record TTL for scavenging. Instead each dynamically added RR is given a timestamp when it is added to the zone, and the client that added the record to the zone periodically renews that timestamp. If the timestamp is not renewed within a specified time interval, the server removes the record from the zone. You specify the time interval using the two values shown in Figure 6-18.

The No-refresh and Refresh intervals are used to determine when a record should be deleted. In Figure 6-18, both intervals are 7 days for a total of 14 days. This means that, when a record is found that has not had its timestamp updated within the last 14 days, that record is deleted.

The No-refresh interval is the period of time in which the client is not allowed to renew the resource record's timestamp. It begins when the record is added or updated. Given the no-refresh value in Figure 6-18, the client would be prevented from updating the timestamp for seven days following a successful update. The no-refresh interval controls the amount of Active Directory replication traffic by limiting the number of unnecessary changes to the zone. Of course, if AD integrated DNS is not being used, there is no AD replication traffic caused by changes to the zone, and therefore the no-refresh interval is not as important.

The refresh interval begins when the no-refresh interval ends. The refresh interval is the period of time in which the client is permitted to renew the resource record's timestamp. By default, a Windows XP or Windows Server 2003 client attempts to renew the timestamp every 24 hours, which means that the update should easily be accomplished within the 7 days allowed for the refresh interval in Figure 6-18.

 Highlight the server in the console tree and select Set Aging/Scavenging for All Zones from the Action menu to launch a similar dialog for the server. That dialog sets default refresh and no-refresh intervals for all zones on the server. However, scavenging must still be enabled for the individual zones as well as for the server.

Forwarders

A system configured to use forwarders adds the forwarders to the process it uses to resolve a DNS query. Normally, a DNS server first attempts to resolve a query using information in its cache. If it can't answer the query from its cache, it then locates the authoritative servers for the information and directly queries them, as described in Chapter 3. When forwarders are configured for the server, the two-step query process becomes a three-step process:

1. The server looks for the answer in its own cache, and if it finds the requested information the server answers the query itself. This means that the server will never use the forwarder for any queries against zones for which the server is authoritative because the server will always have information about those zones in the local cache.

2. If the server was not able to answer the query from its cache, the server sends the query to the forwarder for processing. Normally, when a server queries another server the query is *nonrecursive* (or *iterative*). During a *nonrecursive query*, the server iteratively collects all of the information required to answer the query and passes the final answer back to the resolver. When forwarders are used, the server acts as if it were a resolver and sends a *recursive query* to the forwarder. A recursive query indicates that the issuer will not actively search for the answer to the query and is relying on the system that receives the query to locate the answer. It is then the forwarder's job to iteratively resolve the query and send the final answer back to the server. By default, the server will wait five seconds for an answer from the forwarder. If no answer is received within the allotted time period, the server will send a recursive query to the next forwarder in the list of forwarders, and again wait the timeout period.

3. If the server has queried all of the forwarders in the forwarders list and not obtained an answer, the server will locate the authoritative servers for the requested information and query them directly, as shown in Figure 3-2. Configuring forwarders adds a step to the basic name resolution process; it does not completely replace it.

Using forwarders can enhance DNS performance by funneling queries to the servers that have the best Internet connectivity and by mining the rich cache those servers develop. Because forwarders handle a large number of queries, they rapidly build up a rich cache. In many organizations the quality of network connectivity varies among server systems because of bandwidth differences, firewalls, and NAT. Of course, the performance advantages of forwarders can be overwhelmed if too many queries are sent to a forwarder. Large organizations need to use multiple forwarders and need to carefully balance the workload among those forwarders. Forwarders require careful planning and monitoring to be used effectively.

Figure 6-19 shows the Forwarders tab used to create the forwarder configuration.

The "DNS domain" box defines the domain for which queries will be forwarded. By default, this is set to "All other domains," which defines the list of forwarders used for all domains that are not explicitly listed in the "DNS domains" box. Notice that when the "All other domains" entry is highlighted, the Remove button of the "DNS domain" box is inactive. The "All other domains" entry cannot be deleted. However, an additional domain can be added by clicking the New button and entering the domain name.

Add specific domains to the DNS domains box to enable conditional forwarding. The *example.org* domain list in Figure 6-19 is an example of conditional forwarding. Conditional forwarding allows you to define a different set of forwarders for each domain. Conditional forwarding is used to route queries directly to a selected server

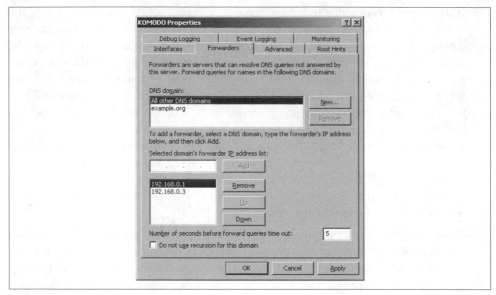

Figure 6-19. The Forwarders tab

without querying the root or any parent servers. Note that conditional forwarding is not used to build a rich cache or to route queries to a system with superior Internet connectivity; those things relate to the forwarders defined for the "All other domains" entry. A common example of when conditional forwarding might be used is the merger of two companies with independent domain names. Using conditional forwarding, queries can be sent directly to the servers for these internal domains without iteratively querying the parents of these servers. Of course, the problem with conditional forwarding is that it is manually entered and manually maintained. DNS is a dynamic system that automatically maintains database synchronization. Hard-coded forwarding undermines the adaptive nature of DNS, and therefore should only be used when needed.

The order of forwarders in the list of forwarders is important. Each forwarder is queried in turn from top to bottom of the list. Network topology and geography are not taken into account. Don't confuse the way DNS handles the root servers list with the way it handles the forwarders list. DNS automatically optimizes the list of root servers using round trip time (RTT). Nothing like that happens with forwarders. They are manually entered and manually maintained. You are responsible for optimizing the list as you see fit.

Each server in the forwarders list is given five seconds to respond to the query. This can be changed using the "Number of seconds before forward queries time out" box shown in Figure 6-19.

The "Do not use recursion for this domain" checkbox essentially eliminates step 3 from the process the local server uses to resolve queries. The server still begins by checking its local cache. If the cache does not contain the answer, the server will then query the list of forwarders. But if this box is checked, the server will not attempt to find the answer on its own, if the forwarders do not respond. The server will not attempt to iteratively locate the authoritative servers for this domain, and it will not attempt to query those servers. The query process stops with the forwarders.

There is one final topic to cover before leaving the subject of forwarders. Microsoft reports that conditional forwarders and stub zones are sometimes confused. Both features reference the servers for specific domains, but these features are unrelated. Stub zones are used by parent servers to automatically update the list of authoritative servers for subordinate zones. The stub zone keeps the NS records for the subdomain updated. Conditional forwarding bypasses NS records, and there is nothing automatic about it—it is manually entered and manually maintained. Stub zones are used to identify authoritative servers. A forwarder does not need to be an authoritative server for the specified zone, and frequently is not. Stub zones tightly integrate parent servers with subdomains. Conditional forwarding allows parents to be bypassed to simplify certain queries. One thing that both features have in common is that both are used only in special circumstances.

So far we have discussed the Root Hints, Interfaces, Forwarders, and Advanced tabs of the server properties window shown in Figure 6-17. The three other server properties tabs all relate to DNS system monitoring. They are covered in the next section.

Logging and monitoring

The Event Logging, Debug Logging and Monitoring tabs all provide ways to monitor and troubleshoot the servers. Event logging is enabled by default, and by default all events are logged. Use the Event Logging tab to disable logging by selecting "No events" or to reduce the amount of event logging by selecting either "Errors only" or "Errors and warnings." Reduce event logging to "Errors and warnings" if you find the log grows too large too fast or is simply too "busy" to effectively monitor. Don't disable logging; you need to know when errors occur. Periodically clear the log by highlighting Event Viewer in the console tree and DNS Events in the righthand pane, and then selecting Clear All Events from the Action menu.

Use the Debug Logging tab to capture DNS packets. Check the "Log packets for debugging" checkbox to enable packet capture. Then specify the packets to be captured using the "Packet direction" and "Packet contents" settings. You can also limit the capture to packets going to or coming from a specific address. Use debug logging only when necessary and only for as long as necessary. The packet capture log can become enormous very rapidly. Microsoft attempts to control this growth by setting a maximum size for the debug log file, configurable by you, and by limiting the amount of data captured from each packet (you can override this using the Details checkbox to capture every byte of the packet). Nonetheless, the log can easily become so large that its size inhibits effective analysis.

The Monitoring tab allows you to perform a simple query against the server and a recursive query through the server. The tests can be run immediately or scheduled for periodic runs. The results of the tests are displayed in a box on the tab. It is worth running these tests when the server is first configured; however, nslookup is a much more thorough test tool.

Using nslookup

A debugging tool provided with Windows Server 2003 is nslookup. It allows anyone to directly query a name server and retrieve any of the information known to the DNS system. It is helpful for determining whether the server is properly configured, running correctly, and for querying for information provided by remote servers.

To start nslookup from the DNS console, highlight the server in the console tree and select Launch nslookup from the Action menu. (nslookup can also be run from the Windows command prompt.) Figure 6-20 shows the nslookup window.

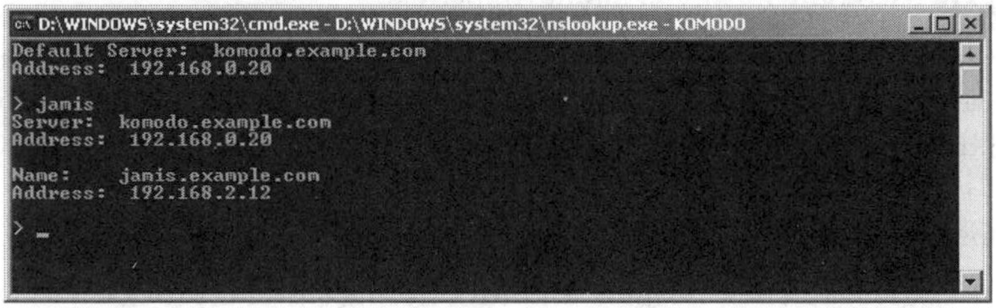

Figure 6-20. The nslookup test tool

The greater-than symbol (>) is the nslookup command prompt. Terminate an nslookup session by entering the exit command at the prompt or by closing the nslookup window.

In Figure 6-20, the hostname *jamis* is entered at the prompt. By default, entering a hostname at the nslookup command prompt generates a query for the IP address of the host. Also notice that when no domain is specified with the hostname, the default domain name configured on the local system is used. Because *jamis* is in the zone controlled by this server, this response proves the server is running properly, and the test allows us to verify the data entered for this host.

By default, nslookup queries for A records. Use the set type command to change the query to another resource record type, or to the special query type ANY. ANY is used to retrieve all available resource records for the specified host.

The following test checks MX records for *example.net* and *pooh.example.net*. Note that once the query type is set to MX, it stays MX. It doesn't revert to the default A query type. Another set type command is required to reset the query type:

```
> set type=MX
> example.net
Server:  komodo.example.com
Address: 192.168.0.20

example.net preference = 10, mail exchanger = thoth.example.net
example.net preference = 20, mail exchanger = kerby.example.net
thoth.example.net internet address = 172.16.12.1
kerby.example.net internet address = 172.16.12.3

> pooh.example.net
Server:  komodo.example.com
Address: 192.168.0.20

pooh.example.net preference = 5, mail exchanger = kerby.example.net
pooh.example.net internet address = 172.16.12.2
```

The query shown above is a recursive query for information in an external domain—a domain not served by the local server *komodo.example.com*. Sometimes a response for information about an external domain will be marked as nonauthoritative. Here is an example:

```
> set type=A
> www.nist.gov
Server:  komodo.example.com
Address:  192.168.0.20

Name:    potomac.nist.gov
Address:  129.6.13.23
Aliases:  www.nist.gov

> www.nist.gov
Server:  komodo.example.com
Address:  192.168.0.20

Non-authoritative answer:
Name:    potomac.nist.gov
Address:  129.6.13.23
Aliases:  www.nist.gov
```

In the previous example, nslookup is asked for the address of *www.nist.gov* and displays the name and address of the server used to resolve the query. In this case, the server is the local server *komodo.example.com*. The first time *komodo* is asked this question it goes to the authoritative servers for the *nist.gov* domain to obtain the answer, which it then displays. The same question is asked again. This time *komodo* answers the query directly from its own cache. Notice the "Non-authoritative" message in the second response, which tells us that the local server retrieved this answer from its cache and did not directly query the remote server. It is useful to know exactly where the answer came from when debugging a DNS problem. When you need to do so, nslookup allows you to go directly to the remote authoritative server for an answer.

Use the server command to control the server used to resolve queries. This is particularly useful for going directly to an authoritative server to check some information. The following example does just that:

```
> set type=NS
> zoo.edu
Server:  komodo.example.com
Address: 192.168.0.20

Non-authoritative answer:
zoo.edu nameserver = NOC.ZOO.EDU
zoo.edu nameserver = NS.ZOO.EDU
zoo.edu nameserver = NAMESERVER.AGENCY.GOV

NOC.ZOO.EDU internet address = 172.28.2.200
NS.ZOO.EDU internet address = 172.28.2.240
NAMESERVER.AGENCY.GOV internet address = 172.21.18.31
> server NOC.ZOO.EDU
Default Server: NOC.ZOO.EDU
Address: 172.28.2.200

> set domain=zoo.edu
> set type=any
> tiger
Server: NOC.ZOO.EDU
Address: 172.28.2.200

tiger.zoo.edu inet address = 172.28.172.8
tiger.zoo.edu preference = 10, mail exchanger = tiger.ZOO.EDU
```

This example contains several interesting commands:

1. We set type=NS and get the NS records for the *zoo.edu* domain.

2. From the information returned by the NS query, we select a server and use the server command to direct nslookup to use that server.

3. Using the set domain command, we set the default domain to *zoo.edu*, the default domain name that nslookup uses to expand the hostnames in its queries, in the same way that the resolver uses the default domain name.

4. We reset the query type to ANY. If the query type is not reset, nslookup would still query for NS records.

5. We query for information about the host *tiger.zoo.edu*. Because the default domain is set to *zoo.edu*, we simply enter **tiger** at the prompt.

The following example shows how to download an entire domain from an authoritative server and examine it on your local system. The ls command requests a zone transfer and displays the contents of the zone it receives.

```
> server minerals.example.biz
Default Server: minerals.example.biz
Address: 172.30.20.1

> ls example.biz > temp.txt
[minerals.example.biz]
########
Received 406 records.
> view temp.txt
 acmite 172.30.20.28
 adamite 172.30.20.29
 adelite 172.30.20.11
 agate 172.30.20.30
 alabaster 172.30.20.31
 albite 172.30.20.32
 allanite 172.30.20.20
 altaite 172.30.20.33
 alum 172.30.20.35
 aluminum 172.30.20.8
 amaranth 172.30.20.85
 amethyst 172.30.20.36
 andorite 172.30.20.37
 apatite 172.30.20.38
 beryl 172.30.20.23
—More— ^C
> exit
```

 For security reasons, most names servers do not respond to the ls command. See the discussion of the zone properties Zone Transfers tab for information on how to limit access to zone transfers.

If the zone file is more than a few lines long, redirect the output to a file, and use the view command to examine the contents of the file. (View sorts a file and displays it using the more command.) In the example that above, the ls command retrieves the *example.biz* zone and stores the information in *temp.txt*. Then view is used to examine *temp.txt*.

The examples in this section show that nslookup allows you to:

* Query for any specific type of standard resource record
* Directly query the authoritative servers for a domain
* Get the entire contents of a domain into a file so you can view it

Use the help command to see the other features of nslookup. Turn on debugging (with set debug) and examine the additional information this provides. As you play with this tool, you'll find many helpful features.

Summary

DNS is an important client/server service that is used on every system connected to the Internet.

The DNS client issues name queries. It is called the resolver. The resolver is configured during the basic TCP/IP configuration. All systems run the resolver.

The DNS server answers name queries and is called the name server. The name server is configured by the DNS console, which defines the servers, the zones, and the database information contained in the zones.

DNS servers can be primary (master), secondary (slave), and caching-only servers. The original domain database source files are found on the master server. The domain database file is called a zone file. The zone file is constructed from standard resources records (RR) that are defined in RFCs. The RRs share a common structure and are used to define all DNS database information. All other servers derive the database information from the primary server. Slave servers make complete copies of the zone information. Caching-only servers cache data one answer at a time.

The Microsoft DNS server is tightly integrated with the Windows network environment. Microsoft DNS works closely with DHCP, WINS and Active Directory. In fact, DNS can be integrated directly into Active Directory to obtain the security advantages and database replication features offered by Active Directory. Active Directory is the subject of the next chapter.

## CHAPTER 7

Using AD to Support Network Administration

Every Windows network administrator must have a basic knowledge and understanding of Active Directory (AD) because AD is both a consumer and a supporter of network services. You have learned in the last few chapters how to configure, manage, and create TCP/IP, DHCP, and DNS services. In a Windows AD environment, it's fair to say that if DNS and TCP/IP networking are not correctly configured and working, then AD itself will not work; and if AD is not working, a large number of other networking services will not work either. If a Windows 2000 or Windows Server 2003 domain exists on the network, TCP/IP services and AD are so intertwined that an administrator must thoroughly understand both in order to properly administer the network.

Chapter 3 introduced some basic AD terms and information. Every prospective AD administrator should spend further time with Windows documentation, both in the product help files and in Microsoft online technical information.

To fully appreciate the significance of AD in a Windows network, an administrator should understand the important role this component plays. AD supports centralized management of the following network-related services and administrative tasks:

- Authentication
- Computer configuration, including network configuration
- Management of user accounts and user rights
- Remote access management
- Security policy management
- Authorization of DHCP servers
- Secure dynamic name registration when DNS is integrated with AD
- Certificates and public-key infrastructure

This chapter covers the configuration and implementation of AD to ensure that it is functioning properly. Here you will build on the knowledge you gained in Chapters 4–6, where you became familiar with key network services. You will learn how to successfully initialize the AD environment and configure the network when moving from current workgroups to domain environments. This chapter provides insights on configuring TCP/IP, DNS, and DHCP to properly work with AD. Later in the chapter, you will discover how to use Group Policy to manage network protocols (such as TCP/IP, SNMP, WINS, and others).

 Think of DNS as the backbone of AD. Then think of AD itself as the genetic code that allows and enforces the proper operation of DNS and all TCP/IP services in a Windows network.

Before tackling the details surrounding proper AD implementation, you should be sure that, as a network administrator, you have thoroughly planned and designed your AD solution. Once you have a clear idea of how AD will service your network, you can begin setting things up. If you have a network environment that includes existing workgroups, one of the first items of business will be to move those workgroups into a domain environment.

Moving from Workgroups to Domain Environments

To understand how to administer a network in an AD environment, you should be familiar with the steps taken to initialize and configure the network environment. To accomplish this, you must first set up your servers and ensure that the proper services have been installed. You will be working with the dcpromo tool to "promote" a Windows 2003 server to a domain controller (DC). Once you have properly set up a domain environment with an appropriate number of DCs, you will be reviewing and working with DNS registration and configuring sites.

 While the basic information provided here enables you to set up a minimal test network, this discussion is not meant to be an AD planning-and-design primer, nor a substitute for spending time developing the AD solution that meets the needs of your organizations.

To begin working with AD, first ensure that you have DNS services available on the network or plan to install them during dcpromo. Next, install the Windows Server 2003 server software on a computer whose hard drive has been cleaned of any previous software or data. (Do not install Microsoft IIS or other optional components.) You must then configure DNS for each Windows server that will be used as a DC. If the server will become a new DC in an existing domain, join the server to the domain.

With these preliminaries out of the way, you are now ready to begin using the dcpromo tool.

Using dcpromo

Any Windows 2000 server or Windows Server 2003 server (except the Windows Server 2003 web server edition) can be used as a domain controller. This process is known as *promotion* and uses the dcpromo tool. (DCs can be returned to server status as well, which is known as *demotion*.) Before you can use the dcpromo tool to promote a server, the following conditions must be met:

Administrative privileges are required. Anyone running the dcpromo tool of the first DC in the root of the first domain of a new forest must be a member of the local Administrators group of the server being promoted. (A *forest* consists of one or more AD domains sharing the same schema, configuration, and global search capabilities. The hierarchical structure of one or more domains in a forest consists of *trees*.) To create new domains, or add new trees to an existing forest, the administrator using the dcpromo tool must be a member of the Enterprise Admins group, or have been delegated the right to create the domain.

DNS services must provide DNS service (SRV) record support. A DNS SRV record is used to map a service such as LDAP or Kerberos to a computer name. (See RFC 2782, *A DNS RR for Specifying the Location of Services*.) Windows 2000 and Windows Server 2003 DNS support SRV records, as do DNS BIND server's Version 4.97 and later. If non-Microsoft DNS is used, you should use BIND Version 8.2.1 or later because these also support dynamic updates and incremental zone transfers. If DNS services are not available, the dcpromo process can implement Microsoft DNS services on the server being promoted.

TCP/IP should be correctly configured and operational on the server. TCP/IP configuration should include the address of the DNS server that will store the domain controller SRV records. During the dcpromo process, these records will be dynamically stored on the DNS server if the DNS server supports dynamic updates. If DNS services will be installed on the local server during the dcpromo process, the TCP/IP configuration should point to the local server for DNS services.

Know the new DC's location in the AD hierarchy. The DC can either create a new domain in the forest, or join an existing domain. A new DC can also create a new forest, create a new forest tree, or become an additional domain in an existing tree.

Know the domain name. If the new domain is the root domain of a new forest or a new forest tree, then it might be the registered Internet domain for the organization, or it may not be. If the new domain is a child domain, you must know the parent domain name. The selection of the domain name in either case is not arbitrary, and should not be made up during implementation.

Be at the correct functional level. If the functional level of the domain is Windows Server 2003, a Windows 2000 server cannot become a DC in that domain.

Refer to Chapter 6 for more information on installing and configuring DNS. Before running the dcpromo tool, you should check the DNS configuration on the server. The DNS properties page of the TCP/IP configuration shown in Figure 7-1 should point to the DNS server that will be used by AD. If DNS will be installed on the DC, you may do so during the dcpromo process.

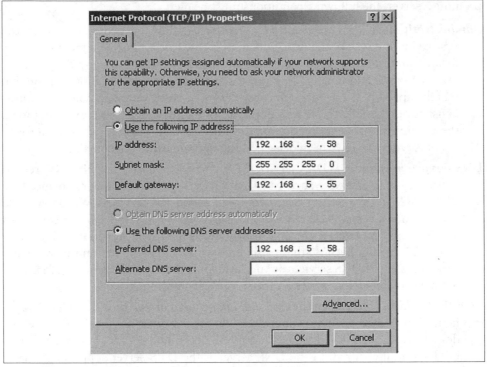

Figure 7-1. The DC's DNS domain DNS server location for the domain should be recorded as the server's preferred (primary) DNS server

You can initialize the dcpromo process by running the dcpromo command or selecting the Domain Controller role from the Manage Your Server wizard. In our discussion, we will use the command-line initialized wizard to show how to create a forest in the first DC in the root forest domain, how to create a new tree, how to add a child domain to an existing domain, and how to create an additional DC for an existing domain.

Creating a forest

To create a forest and the first DC in the root forest domain, begin by clicking Start and then Run. Enter **dcpromo** and then click OK. From the ensuing screen, read the information on Operating System Compatibility. By default, the DC will be configured assuming that all member computers will be Windows XP, Windows 2000, or

Windows Server 2003 computers. (If they are not, you may need to select pre-Windows compatibility mode, which we'll discuss later.) Click Next to continue.

Now select Domain Controller for a New Domain and then click Next. Click "Domain in a new forest" and then click Next. From here you will begin entering some important information. Enter the full DNS name for the new domain and then click Next. Verify the NetBIOS name and then click Next. Enter the location to install the database and log folders (or accept the default) and then click Next. Enter the location the location for the sysvol folder (or accept the default) and then click Next.

If DNS is available on the network and the DNS settings for this server are correct, the Installation Wizard should note that. If no DNS is found and DNS is available, you have a problem. Check that the IP address of the DNS server and that the appropriate gateway addresses are correctly entered in the network configuration for this server. Additional steps include those for troubleshooting TCP/IP, as described in Chapter 14.

Do not elect to install DNS on the domain controller if DNS is supposed to be available on the network. If, however, DNS will reside on the DC, then select "Install and configure the DNS server on this computer" and "Set this computer to use this DNS server as its preferred DNS server," and then click Next.

If all member computers are not Windows XP, Windows 2000, or Windows Server 2003 computers, select "Permissions compatible with pre-Windows 2000 server operating systems"; otherwise, select "Permissions compatible only with Windows 2000 or Windows Server 2003 operating systems."

Enter and confirm a password for the Directory Services Restore Mode Administrator account for this computer and then click Next. This is the local Administrator account and will be used if a directory restore is necessary. Ensure that this password is recorded in a safe place with your disaster recovery information.

Finally, review the summary and then click Next to begin the installation. When installation is complete, you must restart the computer

When the dcpromo tool is run to create a new forest, it creates the forest, the first forest tree, and the first DC in the root forest domain. To create additional trees, a new domain must be created. The domain must be created as the first domain in a new tree of an existing forest. Each DC must be created on a different Windows Server 2003 server.

For example, say that your organization, Nomoore, Inc., is located in Boston. A possible design would be to create the *Nomoore.local* forest by promoting a server to be the first DC of the root forest *domain.nomoore.local*. Because growth is possible, you create a subdomain, *Boston.nomoore.local*, to contain and manage the resources and people located in Boston. If you have a new location (say in New York), a new subdomain can easily be created.

This design is common and is often called an "empty root" forest. It consists of creating a forest root domain that merely establishes the forest and houses the forest-wide administrative groups and administrators. Subdomains are created to facilitate administration at different locations or for different divisions. New trees are created to denote distinct entities within the organization or, when registered DNS names will be used, to allow for centralized administration of domains with different root names. In this example, if your organization purchases another company and wants to maintain the new company's autonomy, a new tree of the forest (*nada.local*) can be added. Note that separate trees of the forest can all be administered by forest administrators (such as members of the Enterprise Admins group). Figure 7-2 illustrates the final result.

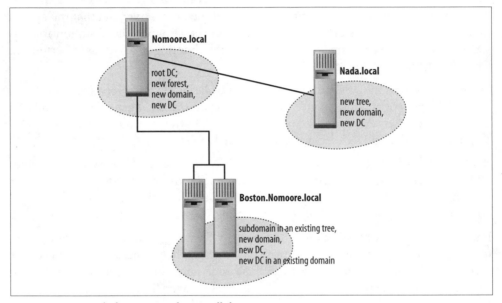

Figure 7-2. A simple forest created using all dcpromo options

Creating a new tree

To create the new tree, start the dcpromo process as described earlier. While the process is similar, the following differences exist. First, you must use a username, password, and domain name that already exists in the forest, and the user must be a member of the Enterprise Admins group. Next, during dcpromo, you will click to select "Domain tree in an existing forest." Finally, if DNS is available on the network and the DNS settings for this server are correct, the Installation Wizard should note that. If no DNS is found and DNS is available, you should troubleshoot why this problem is occurring, as described earlier in this chapter in the discussion of the dcpromo tool.

Adding a child domain

A single domain may suit the purposes of many organizations. In this model, all users and all resources reside in the single domain. There are, however, many reasons why this may not be suitable. For example, legal, administrative, political, technical, and even geographical reasons may lead AD designers to create multiple domain forests. Separate domains provide opportunities to decentralize administration to provide separate control over people and resources as required for any of these reasons, while maintaining overall supervision and consistency. Child domains (or subdomains) are created using the dcpromo tool as described shortly. Child domains are named by prepending a name to the parent domain name. The example above, *boston.nomoore.local*, is an example of naming a child domain.

To add a child domain to an existing domain, use the dcpromo process as described earlier. However, this time you will select "Domain controller for a new domain" and then select "Child domain in an existing domain tree." You will need to enter the username, password, and user domain of the user account to use for this operation and verify the parent domain.

Creating an additional DC

A domain should have at least two DCs to provide redundancy in the case of failure. Additional DCs may be added for load balancing, or to serve different locations.

Creating an additional DC for an existing domain is similar to creating a forest and the first DC in the root forest domain. However, after you launch dcpromo, in the first screen to appear after the information on Operating System Compatibility, select "Additional Domain Controller for an existing domain" and then click Next.

As described earlier, verify the NetBIOS name and then click Next. Enter the location to install the database and log folders (or accept the default) and then click Next. Enter the location the location for the sysvol folder (or accept the default) and then click Next.

If DNS is available on the network and the DNS settings for this server are correct, the Installation Wizard should note that. If no DNS is found and DNS is available, you should troubleshoot why this problem is occurring in the same manner as described in the earlier discussion on the dcpromo process.

Do not elect to install DNS on the domain controller if DNS is supposed to be available on the network. If, however, DNS will reside on the DC, then select "Install and configure the DNS server on this computer" and "Set this computer to use this DNS server as its preferred DNS server," and then click Next.

If all member computers are not Windows XP, Windows 2000, or Windows Server 2003 computers, select "Permissions compatible with pre-Windows 2000 server operating systems" or "Permissions compatible only with Windows 2000 or Windows Server 2003 operating systems."

Enter and confirm a password for the Directory restore mode Administrator account for this computer and then click Next. This is the local Administrator account and will be used if a directory restore is necessary. Ensure that this password is recorded in a safe place along with your disaster recovery information.

Finally, review the summary and then click Next to begin the installation. When installation is complete, you must restart the computer.

Confirming DNS Registration of DC Information

After you create a domain in a forest, the new domain's domain service (SRV) records will be automatically populated on the DNS server. These records must be available in DNS and they must correct. These records are used when computers that are joined to a domain in the forest must communicate with other computers joined to a domain in the forest.

For example, client computers must locate the Kerberos service (a service that runs on every DC) of a domain controller during boot so that they can authenticate to the domain and download Group Policy. User logon must also locate this service. DCs also use DNS to locate other DCs to find replication peers. SRV records added in DNS for domain controllers are stored in the containers shown in Figure 7-3.

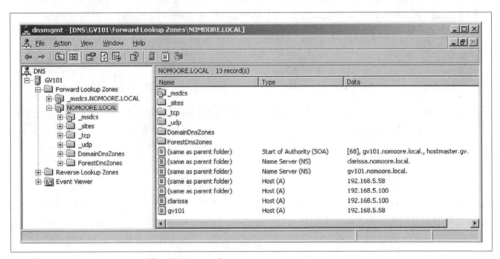

Figure 7-3. DNS containers for SRV records

The pane on the left of this window shows the following subdomains used to store SRV records:

_msdcs

    This is a Microsoft-specific subdomain that stores SRV records for domain controllers with roles in AD. These roles include domain controllers (*dc*), global catalog servers (*gc*), and primary domain controller emulators (*pdc*). Domain controllers include a copy of the domain, infrastructure, and schema partitions of the AD. Global catalog servers include the forest-wide AD data account database for the domain. The forest-wide AD database is a partial attribute database for all objects in the forest. The primary domain controller emulator performs NT 4.0 primary domain controller services for NT 4.0 backup domain controllers joined in the AD domain, as well as special password and time synchronization services for the domain. Domain controllers and global catalog servers are also divided into sites.

_sites

This contains records for domain controllers based on site. Clients can use this record to locate domain controllers and global catalog servers that are in their site, so that they can avoid using services across the WAN.

_tcp

This contains domain controllers in the AD domain.

If clients need to find a DC in a specific site, they will look here. The TCP protocol will be used to request the information, hence the name *tcp*.

_udp

Kerberos clients can use UDP port 88 to request tickets and port 464 for password changes. Since the UDP protocol is used, the section is named *udp*.

DomainDnsZones

Zone information that should be replicated to all DCs in the domain that have the DNS service installed.

ForestDnsZones

Zone information that should be replicated to all DCs in the forest that have the DNS service installed.

As shown in Figure 7-3, when the domain is selected, the right side (or detail pane) of the management console mirrors the list in the left pane and includes the DNS host records as described in Chapter 6.

You have three options to choose from in order to verify that the proper records have been installed for a DC:

- Visually inspect the records in the DNS Manager console.
- View the records in the *netlogon.dns* file located in the *%systemroot%\System32\Config* folder; the first records will be the LDAP SRV record in the form *ldap.tcp.<domainname>*.
- Use nslookup to query for SRV service location records.

To use the third option, nslookup, you must have a reverse lookup zone for the domain. To use this option, begin by opening a command prompt. Type **nslookup** and then press Enter. Type **set type=all** and then press Enter. Type **ldap.tcp.dc._msdcs.*domainname*** and then press Enter. Repeat this process for as many SRV records as you want to confirm. Figure 7-4 shows some sample results.

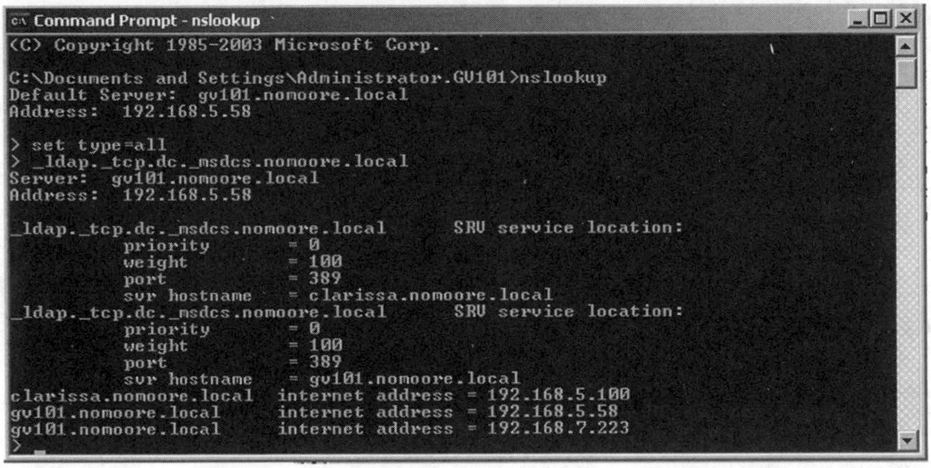

```
Command Prompt - nslookup                                         _ |□| x|
(C) Copyright 1985-2003 Microsoft Corp.

C:\Documents and Settings\Administrator.GV101>nslookup
Default Server:  gv101.nomoore.local
Address:  192.168.5.58

> set type=all
> _ldap._tcp.dc._msdcs.nomoore.local
Server:  gv101.nomoore.local
Address:  192.168.5.58

_ldap._tcp.dc._msdcs.nomoore.local        SRV service location:
          priority      = 0
          weight        = 100
          port          = 389
          svr hostname  = clarissa.nomoore.local
_ldap._tcp.dc._msdcs.nomoore.local        SRV service location:
          priority      = 0
          weight        = 100
          port          = 389
          svr hostname  = gv101.nomoore.local
clarissa.nomoore.local    internet address = 192.168.5.100
gv101.nomoore.local       internet address = 192.168.5.58
gv101.nomoore.local       internet address = 192.168.7.223
>
```

Figure 7-4. Use nslookup to verify SRV records

Once you have run nslookup, the resulting screen shows you the SRV record if it exists. Note in Figure 7-4 that the correct name for the ldap SRV record for the *nomoore.local* domain was entered (see the second ">") and that two actual DNS records (one for DC *clarissa* and one for DC *gy101*) are returned. If these are the only two DCs in the *nomoore.local* domain, then you have verified that they have been correctly registered in DNS. However, if you have three DCs in the *nomoore.local* domain, then one of them is not registered.

When you have successfully verified that the DC information has been registered accurately with DNS, you are ready to begin configuring sites.

Configuring Sites

Sites represent collections of forest member computers that have high speed network connectivity between them. This typically means that the computers are located at the same geographical location, but this does not have to be so. The key requirement is that all members of the site have high-speed network connectivity between them. Sites can contain DCs, servers, and desktop computers. These systems may be all from the same domain or from multiple domains in the same forest. Systems from different forests cannot be in the same AD site. (They may, of course, be in the same physical location.), For example, a site may consist of six servers in Boston, two DCs and 300 desktops in New York, and 100 desktops in Jersey City if all of the computers are members of the same forest. If, however, 50 of the desktops in Jersey City and 10 of the New York desktops are members in a different forest they cannot be members of the same site with the other desktops and the two DCs.

Creating and configuring sites entails using the AD Sites and Services administration tool to add a site, and then moving DCs and computers to the new site. When you create and configure sites, your network realizes several important benefits, including the following:

- Authentication may improve because it does not have to take place across the WAN.
- Replication is more frequent within sites, as opposed to between them. This means less replication traffic on the WAN.
- Services and the location of DCs is site-sensitive and, therefore, should be more efficient.
- Multiple sites can make the most efficient use of bandwidth for replication, improve granular replication control, and reduce authentication latency. *Granular replication control* is the ability that sites provide to control replication at a lower level. For example, when all computers are in one site, replication occurs across all DCs under the control of AD. When multiple sites are created, replication between sites can be scheduled and administered by administrators. *Authentication latency* is the delay caused when users must authenticate across a wide area network. User Joe, for example, may be sitting at his desktop in New York, but his credentials may have to travel across the network to Los Angeles, even though a DC may be present in New York. If a New York site is created and both the DC and Joe's desktop are placed in the site, the local DC will most likely be used because the authentication process attempts to locate a DC in the same site as the logon user's computer. Thus, the process has been speeded up.
- Clients are dynamically assigned to sites by their IP address and subnet mask during logon.
- DC site membership is determined by the location of the associated server object in AD.

If these benefits will improve your network functionality, determine the sites that should be created and which computers will be in which sites, and then create and configure the sites. Sites can also be modified to keep up with changes in your network.

Creating, configuring, and modifying sites

To create a site, begin by opening Start → Administrative Tools → AD Sites and Services. Right-click the Sites node and then click New Site. Enter the name for the new site. Select a site link object as shown in Figure 7-5 and then click OK. (A site-link object defines the protocol and scheduling required for linking two sites. Use the Default Site Link Object unless you have defined a site link object specifically for this connection.) When prompted, click OK to complete the creation of the site.

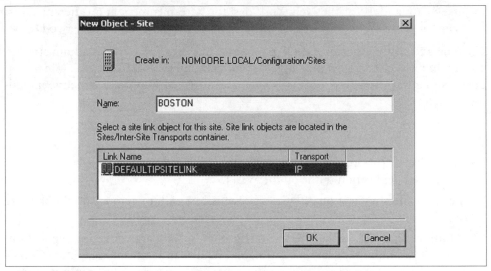

Figure 7-5. A new site must designate a site link

To add additional sites, begin by creating new site as just explained. Ensure that the site is connected to at least one other site via a site link, as shown in Figure 7-5.

After creating the sites, you must configure them.

To configure site links, begin by opening AD Sites and Services. Expand the Inter-Site Transports node. Right-click the site link and select Properties, which results in the screen shown in Figure 7-6.

Enter a site link cost in the Cost field. The Cost field is used if multiple network paths (and hence multiple site links) exist. Multiple network paths are often configured for redundancy. The Cost field is assigned a number based on the speed and perhaps the actual monetary cost of the link. If the speed is slow, or the monetary cost high, a high number is assigned. Cost field numbers are relative (that is, a slow network link such as dial-up might be assigned the number 500, but a high-speed connection such as a T-1 line might be assigned the number 100). A low-cost site link will be used in preference to a high-cost link. For example, if two site links (dial-up and T-1) exist and are assigned a cost as described previously, the T-1 link will be used if it is available or if both links are available. Click the Change Schedule button to enter a *site link schedule*, which represents the times at which the site link is available for replication. In the Replicate every field enter a *site link replication frequency*, which is the frequency at which replication should occur. Finally, click OK.

Sites must be defined in AD by identifying the TCP/IP subnets at their location(s). To do so, you add the subnet information to the subnet node and associate (or identify) the site where the subnet is located. This information is used by AD in many ways. For example, when user Joe attempts to log on, the authentication process uses his TCP/IP information to determine which subnet (and, therefore, which site)

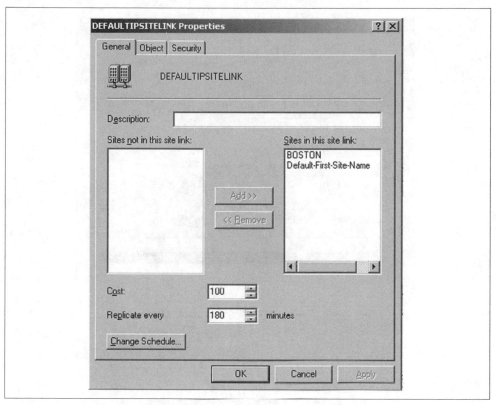

Figure 7-6. Configure a site links properties to make replication more efficient

he is located in. The site information is then used to locate a DC in the same site if one exists.

To create a subnet and associate a subnet with a site, begin by opening AD Sites and Services and then expand the Sites → Subnets node. Right-click the Subnet node and select "New subnet." Enter the new subnet address and subnet mask. Select the site object for the subnet as shown in Figure 7-7, and then click OK.

If DCs are physically located in the area served by a site but were created before the AD site was created, use the AD Sites and Services console to move the DC to the new AD site. If DCs are moved to from one site to another, use the AD Sites and Services console to move the DC to the new site.

To move DCs to the site, begin by opening AD Sites and Services. Right-click on the DC to move and select Move. Select the site as shown in Figure 7-8 and click OK.

The site-licensing server for a site is used to help an organization comply with the license agreements for Windows Server 2003. Noncompliance can result in heavy fines. The site-licensing server collects license information using the License Logging service. Each server uses this service to replicate its information to a centralized database on the

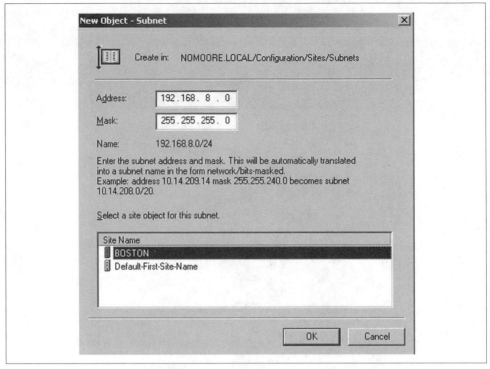

Figure 7-7. Sites are defined by subnets

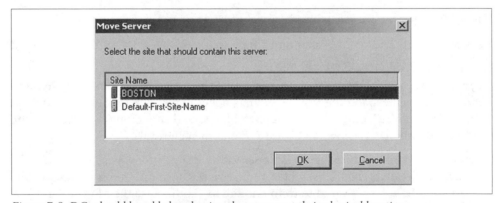

Figure 7-8. DCs should be added to the sites that represent their physical location

site license server. Licensing information is essential for proving compliance with your Microsoft licensing agreement. Since a site administrator can use the Licensing console to view the licensing history for the site, using this tool makes this job easier. The site licensing server is usually the first domain controlled created for the site.

To create a site licensing server in a site, begin by selecting the site. Double-click the Licensing Site Settings object in the detail pane to open its properties. Click the Change button. Use the object picker to select the computer. Click OK.

A *bridgehead server* for a site is the server used for AD replication between sites. Each replication transport can have its own bridgehead server. Creating bridgehead servers establishes more control over replication. In addition, because the DC used for replication between sites is designated, you can ensure that it is adequately provisioned for this extra activity.

To create a bridgehead server, begin by opening AD Sites and Services. Expand the site container. Right-click the server that will be a bridgehead server and click Properties. Select the General tab, then select the transport for which the server will be a bridgehead server. Click Add, as shown in Figure 7-9 to move the transport. The server is now a bridgehead server for that transport in its site.

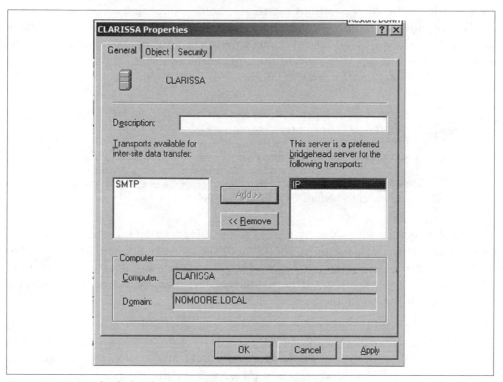

Figure 7-9. Create bridgehead servers to better manage replication

Now that you have correctly configured your sites, you are ready to correctly position the operations masters within the domain.

Moving Operations Master Roles

Chapter 3 describes the operations masters and the roles they play within the forest. As discussed, both forest and domain operation master roles are assigned to the first DC in the forest root domain. The first DC in each new domain in the forest is assigned its own domain operations master roles.

You may need to move operations master roles to another DC. For example, the Infrastructure Master role should not be on a DC that is also a global catalog (GC) server (unless only one DC exists, or all DCs are GCs). If you do not separate these roles, domain information in forest-wide GCs may not be properly updated. As you recall, GCs store forest-wide information that is necessary for proper AD operation. If GCs are not updating properly, authentication, then directory-wide searching and other functions will not work correctly (or at all). You may also want to move roles when upgrading servers or recovering a failed DC that held one of the operations master roles. When the operations master role holder is still alive on the network, the process of moving operations master roles is referred to as a *role transfer* (the role is removed from one DC and placed on another). When it is not, the process is called *seizing the operations master role*. In this process, since the DC the role is on is not available, the role cannot be removed. Instead, the role is added to the new DC.

 Never seize the operations master role when the current operations master is still alive on the network—even if it is currently shut down. If you restart a former operations master after seizing its role, it will still believe it owns that role. When a role is transferred, the old master is informed and at the same time the new master is given the role. Only seize roles when a former operations master is totally removed (for example, because of hardware failure).

To transfer the operations master roles, you must meet group member requirements and use the appropriate administration tool or the correct command line. Be sure to follow the instructions specific to each role; they are not all the same. The instructions for each role are provided here, followed by instructions on how to change roles using the command line.

To transfer the schema master operations role, you must be a member of the Schema Admins group. Begin by opening the AD Schema console. If the console has not been installed, install it by typing **regsvr32 schmmgmt.dll** at a command line and then pressing Enter. (Click OK when a pop up advises the dll has been registered.) To transfer the role, right-click on AD Schema node in the AD Schema console and then click Change Domain Controller.

In most cases of transferring an operations master role, you will want to keep the selection Any DC (the process will select a DC), as shown in Figure 7-10. However, you may run into situations where you want to specifically name a DC (for example, when DCs for the domain are located at different physical locations and you want a local DC to have the role). In those cases, click Specify Name and then enter the name of the DC to switch the role to. When you have finished, click OK.

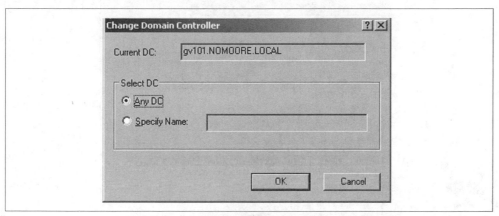

Figure 7-10. To transfer an operations role you must connect to the DC you wish to transfer the role to

You should now be back at the console screen. To verify your changes, right-click AD Schema and then click Operations Master. The "Current schema master" and proposed schema master DC is identified, as shown in Figure 7-11. If this is correct, click Change.

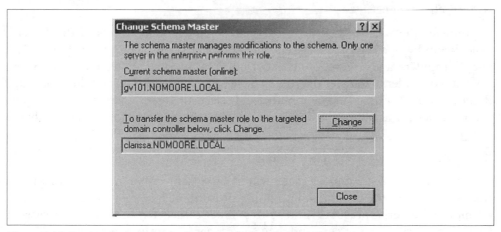

Figure 7-11. Review the transfer arrangements before clicking Change

To transfer the domain-naming master role, open the AD Domains and Trusts console. Right-click the Active Director Domains and Trusts and select Connect to Domain Controller. Enter the name of the domain controller to transfer the role to, or select an available DC, as shown in Figure 7-12 and then click OK.

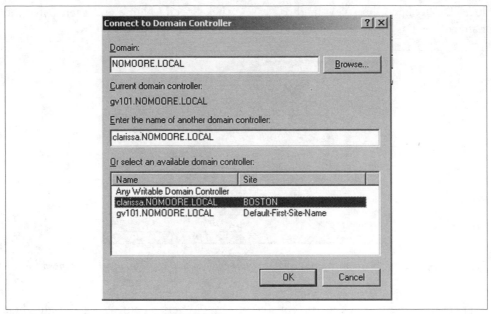

Figure 7-12. Select the DC to transfer the role to and connect

Right-click on AD Users and Computers and select All Tasks then select Operations Masters. The current and proposed domain naming master DC is identified. If this is correct, click Change.

To transfer the relative identifier (RID), PDC emulator, or Infrastructure Master Role, begin by opening the AD Users and Computers console. Right-click AD Users and Computers and select Connect to Domain Controller. Enter the name of the domain controller to transfer the role to or select an available DC and then click OK. Right-click on AD Users and Computers and select All Tasks. Then select Operations Masters. Select the tab for the operations master role you wish to transfer, as shown in Figure 7-13.

If the information is correct, click Change.

If you prefer to make your changes manually, all operations master roles can be transferred using the command-line utility ntdsutil. Begin by opening a command prompt and entering **ntdsutil**. Enter **roles**. Enter **connection** and then enter **connect to server** *<server>*. Enter **quit** and then enter **transfer** *<server>* **master**.

You should never seize an operations master role if the current operations master is available. However, if you must seize an operations master role because the current role holder crashed, begin by opening a command prompt and entering **ntdsutil**. Enter **roles**, and then enter **connection**. Enter **connect to server** *<server>*. Then enter **quit** and enter **seize** *<server>* **master**.

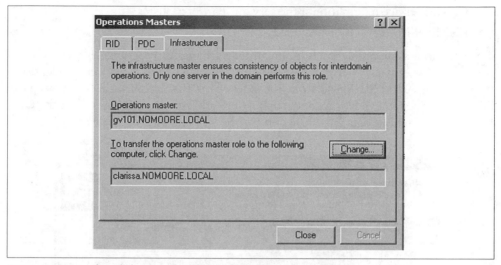

Figure 7-13. Use the tab for the role that should be changed

Now that you have successfully set and configured domains, sites, and subnets, and (if necessary) moved operations master roles, it is time to look at backing up AD. Backing up AD is important because you may need to recover AD after hardware or software failure.

Back Up AD

To back up AD, you must perform a system state backup. A *system state backup* backs up the AD and other important components of the system (such as the registry). You should not substitute a backup of the AD database file (*ntds.dit*) for a system state backup because many of the items in the system state backup are interrelated. Windows native backup software (Ntbackup) and some third-party backup software can perform a system state backup.

A system state backup always backs up the following:

- Registry
- COM+ class Registration database
- Boot files and system files
- System files that are under Windows File Protection

A system state backup backs up the following items if the associated service is installed on the computer:

- Certificate services database if the server is a certification authority (CA)
- AD database if the server is a domain controllers
- SYSVOL directory if the server is a DC

- Cluster service information if the server is part of a cluster
- IIS Metadirectory if IIS is installed.

To perform a system state backup, begin by selecting All Programs → Accessories → System Tools → Backup. If you have not already switched to Advanced Mode, do so by selecting Advanced Mode from the Backup or Restore Wizard Welcome page. Select the Schedule Jobs tab and click "Add job"; then click Next. Select "Only backup System State data," as shown in Figure 7-14 and then click Next.

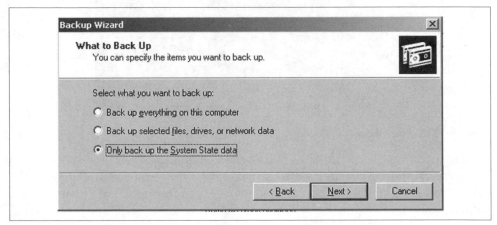

Figure 7-14. The system state data should be periodically backed up

Select the backup type information. For a tape drive, select the Tape type; for a disk the File type. Select "Verify data after backup." This step reads the backup data to verify that its integrity. If required and available, select "Use hardware compression, if available" and click Next. If you are replacing an existing backup, click "Allow only the owner and the Administrator access to the backup data and to any backups appended to this medium" and click Next. To run the backup right away, click Now. Otherwise, enter a job name and then click the Set Schedule button to schedule the backup. Use the Settings tab as shown in Figure 7-15 to complete the schedule.

After the schedule is set, click OK and, if prompted, enter the account name and password of an account authorized to perform a backup. Click OK, followed by Next and then Finish.

Now that you have created and configured a new AD infrastructure and backed up AD, it's time to reflect on the interrelationship between AD and TCP/IP. Your correct understanding of this relationship is crucial. Without it you are doomed to fail in your efforts to efficiently and correctly administer AD domains and the AD infrastructure. Earlier chapters in this book introduce key TCP/IP concepts and protocols, as well as basic AD concepts. Thus far, this chapter has provided basic AD creation and configuration instructions. Now it's time to show how TCP/IP and AD work together.

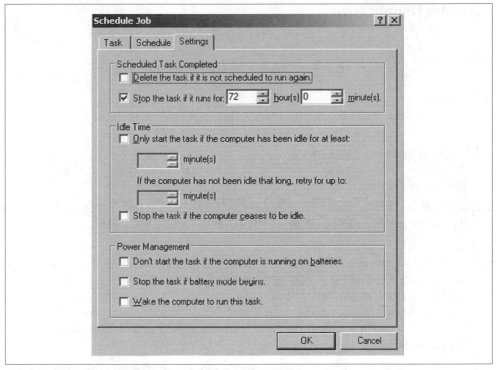

Figure 7-15. Configure the details of the scheduled job

TCP/IP for AD Transport, Access, and Support

An AD forest relies on TCP/IP for communications between member computers, between domain controllers, and between member computers and domain controllers. DNS provides name resolution and assists in the location of domain services through the use of SRV records. All of the benefits of AD (such as the centralized authentication database, computer management through Group Policy, and the centralization of multiple services) will not be available if DNS is incorrectly configured. Other TCP/IP-based protocols (such as the Windows Time Service, DHCP, and SMTP) are also important components.

This section discusses how TCP/IP relates to AD transport, access, and support. Here we will examine dependencies between AD and DNS, how to configure DNS for AD, how to use Windows Server 2003 AD application partitions to manage DNS Zone information, how AD uses DNS, how to configure the Windows Time Service, how to integrate DHCP with AD, and how NetBIOS and WINS are used in an AD domain. This is a long section, but critically important to AD administration. The most important subsection (the one that discusses dependencies between AD and DNS) is covered first because AD malfunction is often the result of DNS problems.

AD / DNS Dependencies

The interdependency between AD and DNS involves the following AD components:

Domain controller locator
> This is implemented in the NetLogon service and enables clients to locate a DC.

AD domain names in DNS
> Each domain has a DNS domain name. Every Windows Server 2003 server has a DNS name.

DNS delegation resource records
> These reside in the parent zone of the zone that is delegated (that is, the zone that supports the AD domain).

DNS forwards
> These are used by AD clients in one domain to locate a DC in another domain.

AD DNS objects
> Domains are represented as objects in AD and as nodes in DNS. DNS domain names and AD domain names appear to be the same. However, they represent two different namespaces. While DNS resolves domain names and computer names to resource records and eventually to IP addresses, AD resolves domain object names to object records. An AD object name and a DNS host record can, however, represent the same computer.

To troubleshoot problems with logon, replication, Group Policy, and other domain activities, you should be familiar with how DNS and its SRV records are used.

For domain resources to be located on the network, they must be registered with appropriate name services. DNS registration must occur either dynamically or manually. If the Windows domain is configured for dynamic updates, it follows the standard described in RFC 2136, *Dynamic Updates in the Domain Name System (DNS UPDATE)*.

When a Windows Server 2003 DC starts, several processes interact with a DNS and/or WINS name server(s), including DNS name registration, DNS host record creation, and LDAP lookup. First, the DC registers its name with any name services configured for the network. For example, let's say that the domain controller *regalinn* is in the domain *chicago.local*, where both DNS and Windows Internet Name Service (WINS) services are configured. This DC registers its DNS name *regalinn.chicago.local* with DNS and its NetBIOS name, *regalinn* with WINS. If other, third-party name services are configured for the network and the DC is properly configured, the DC can also register its name in the appropriate format with that name service. When a workstation or server starts, in order to find its DC, it must use the name services (DNS, WINS) provided to locate the DC on the network. Once it finds the DC, the information is cached for later use.

Domain name registration in WINS (the creation of a *domain_name*[1C] record) occurs by broadcast, or by directing a NetBIOS name registration request to the NetBIOS name server. Windows clients that are not DNS-enabled can use WINS to find Windows Server 2003, Windows 2000, and Windows NT 4.0 domain controllers.

In addition to name registration, the NetLogon service on the DC dynamically creates the host or A record (server name and IP address) and SRV records in DNS. SRV records identify the services that the DC provides (such as LDAP, Kerberos, TCP, and, if the DC is a GC, that record as well).

Finally, the *_msdcs.dnsdomainname* is used to find an LDAP server that is running TCP and is performing a specific server role (such as domain controller or Kerberos server). Finding these servers is important to domain and forest operations such as authentication, resource location, replication, and so on.

Configuring DNS to properly interact with AD is important because if it is not, these functions (as well as others that are based on them) cannot occur. It is possible to correctly configure DNS so that it functions as a name server on your network and still not have it correctly configured so that AD can work correctly. Your DNS administrator must understand AD's requirements and correctly configure DNS for AD.

How AD Uses DNS

As shown in Table 7-1, there are multiple listings of SRV records for each service offered by AD DCs. Each SRV record can be found in multiple containers. This provides multiple options for locating specific DCs in the forest. This section explains the ways these records are used, including the following:

- How DCs are located
- How site information is used during logon
- How DNS is used for AD replication

Table 7-1. SRV records used in AD

SRV record	Description
_kerberos	Indicates the location of a Key Distribution Center (KDC)
_kpasswd	Indicates the location where password changes are recorded
_ldap	Indicates the location of an LDAP server
_gc	Indicates the location of a global catalog (GC) server

How DCs are located

When member computers boot, when users log on, or when replication initiates, a DC must be located. Let's look at how the process works when locating a DC using DNS. (A similar process is used by legacy Windows clients to locate a DC via WINS.)

On the client, a remote procedure call (RPC) is made to the local NetLogon service. The NetLogon service implements the Locator API (DsGetDcName). The client collects information needed to select a DC and provides it to the NetLogon service using DsGetDcName. (For example, the user's credentials entered during logon specify the domain in which his or her account resides.) The NetLogon service queries DNS by using the DNS-compatible LocatorDsGetDcNme to obtain the SRV records and A records from DNS.

The NetLogon service queries the discovered DCs using an LDAP UDP search. The search attempts to find a DC in the site closest to the client. In an AD domain, the site information in DNS is used to aid in this discovery. Site information is included in many places in DNS so that a search for the different roles that a DC may play all can be located in the closest site.

Available DCs respond. NetLogon services returns information to the client from the first DC to respond. The NetLogon service caches the discovered DC information for use in future requests.

How site information is used during logon

During logon, NetLogon attempts to find a DC in the site closest to the client. While site information for DCs is included in the DNS SRV records, site information of clients is stored in the client's registry in the *HKEY_LOCAL_MACHINE\SYSTEM\Current-ControlSet\Services\Netlogon\Parameters\DynamicSiteName* value. This information is used to aid in the selection of a DC in the site closest to it. When the computer is located in the site that is recorded in the registry, the NetLogon query quickly locates a DC from this site (or one that is close to it). However, the NetLogon service on the DC uses the client's IP address to determine its site and returns this information to the client. If the two sites (the client registry site and the DC calculated site) do not match, then additional DC queries and even additional DNS queries may result.

When site information doesn't match, it is usually because the computer has been moved into another site. (A laptop, for example, may be moved from location to location. Its registry-based site information may then easily be out of date.) This is why the site information in the DynamicSiteName value in the registry is not used alone. During NetLogon startup, the NetLogon service on each DC enumerates the site object in the AD Configuration container and NetLogon is also notified of any changes to Site objects. This information is used by NetLogon to create (in the DC's memory) a subnet-to-site mapping table.

The client receives DC IP address information from DNS and queries each DC in turn to find out which ones are available. AD on the DC intercepts the query and passes it to NetLogon on the DC. NetLogon on the DC takes the client IP address (included in the query) and looks it up in its subnet-to-site mapping table. The DC then returns information to the client, including the name of the site of the client, the site name of the DC, and an indication of whether it (the DC) is located in the site closest to the client.

The client uses this information to determine whether to try to find a better DC:

- If the DC is located in the site closest to the client, then this DC is used.
- If no DC is in the site closest to the client, but the client has already tried to find a DC in the site the DC says the client is in, the client uses the current DC.
- If the DC is not in the site closest to the client and the client has not looked for a DC in that site, the client updates its site information and sends a new DNS query. If this one is not successful, then the original DC is used.

You can override the DyanmicSiteName value, but you should do so by modifying the SiteName entry at the same location. When the SiteName value is used, the DynamicSiteName value is disregarded.

How DNS is used for AD replication

Replication topologies are configured both automatically and manually, and the information is stored in AD. These records assist replication partners in locating each other and in mutual authentication. However, the actual location requires more than a simple DNS lookup.

The DC finds its partner's GUID in AD. (A listing of GUIDs for each DC is at CN=NTDS Settings, CN=Sites, CN=Configuration, DC=domain_name, DC=domain_name_extension.) The DC queries DNS looking for an associated CNAME record. The CNAME record is of the form *guid.msdcs.forest.root*, as shown in Figure 7-16.

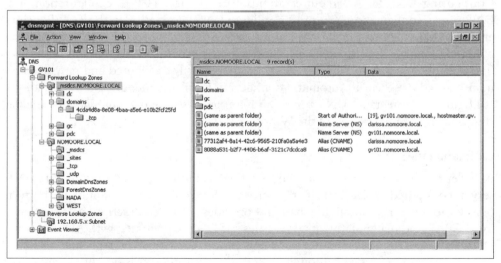

Figure 7-16. DC GUIDs are recorded in DNS to assist the location of replication partners

If the query is successful, the name of the DC is returned. A second DNS query is used to obtain the host record. The IP address from the host record is used to request a connection to the replication partner. If CNAME or host record is missing from DNS, a connection cannot be made and replication will not occur.

Configuring DNS for AD

For many AD environments, Windows DNS is the DNS of choice. Even if an alternative DNS service exists in the enterprise, a Windows DNS server may be used to manage the Windows systems. This discussion details configuring Windows DNS to support AD and includes configuring AD Integrated Zones, configuring Dynamic DNS, and using AD Application Partitions for DNS Zone information.

For a new AD domain to be created, DNS must be available. (A server can be promoted to DC even if it cannot locate a DNS server. However, its domain SRV and host record must be recorded in DNS, and the DC must be able to locate its DNS server, or it will not be able to function as a domain controller.) DNS requirements include the following:

- If the DC will be the first DC in the root domain of the forest and the root domain is the first-level domain (that is, it has no parent domain), then the DNS server can be created at the same time as the domain is created, or a preexisting DNS server can be used.

- If the DC is not the first DC in the root domain of the forest, or if the root domain is a child domain of an existing domain, then DNS must be available.

Configuring DNS for AD requires attention to the DC TCP/IP configuration and DNS server configuration You must configure DNS information in the TCP/IP properties of each Windows DC (or Windows server that is to become a DC), be able to configure domain records in DNS (these records should be created automatically, but you must be able to confirm that they are correctly configured and may need to manually adjust them if automatic configuration fails), configure DNS delegation, configure AD integrated DNS zones, and configure secure dynamic DNS. The first step is correct configuration of the Windows server.

Configuring the server

In order for dynamic registration to occur, the DC must have the location of its DNS server configured in its TCP/IP properties. This configuration should be correct before the server is promoted. (Chapter 4 provides a detailed description of configuring TCP/IP and manipulating its properties.) If DNS is integrated with AD, only one DNS server's IP address is necessary. Registration records will be replicated to other AD integrated DNS servers automatically. If the domain records do not or cannot be properly registered, you may need to do so manually. To do so you will need to know what records for each DC should be in DNS. The next section will address these issues.

Correctly Configure Windows 2000 DC TCP/IP to Avoid DC Islands

When servers are promoted using the dcpromo tool, the IP address of a relevant DNS server must be configured in the server's TCP/IP records. The new DC's information can then be recorded in DNS dynamically and can be replicated to other DNS servers. When DNS is integrated with AD, zone information is replicated using AD. However, when multiple DCs exist in the domain, unless they are properly configured, it is possible for the phenomena of a *DC island* to exist. That is, the DC is properly registering its DNS information in DNS, but that information is not replicated to other DNS servers. This can occur when

- Windows 2000 DCs are part of the DC (in a 100% Windows Server 2003 DC domain this problem cannot occur).
- Multiple DCs in the forest root domain have the DNS service installed.
- The DC DNS server is a primary for the *_msdcs.ForestDnsName* domain.
- The DC DNS server is pointed to itself as the preferred or alternate DNS server.

When these circumstances occur, the DNS zone information on a DC may not have a CNAME record for *dsaGUID._msdcs.ForestDnsDomain*. This record is required for replication. For example, let's say that two DCs exist for the forest root domain *nomoore.local*: DC1 and DC2. Let's also assume that each has the DNS service installed, and each one points to itself as the DNS source. On each server, the DNS records only include the *dsaGUID._msdcs.nomoore.local* for itself. When there is an attempt to replicate from DC1 to DC2, DC1 will not find the dsaGUID record for DC2, and will not be able to replicate.

To resolve the issue, a single DNS server in the domain should be designated as the primary DNS server. All DCs should point to this server as the source for DNS. In this example, if DC1 is designated as the primary, DC2 should have the IP address of DC1 as its source for DNS and DC1 should point to itself. If additional DCs are added to the domain, they should point to DC1 as the source of DNS. The DCs can be configured with a secondary DNS server.

Another solution is to configure the primary DNS services of a server before it is promoted to be a DC to point to a DNS server that contains the domain controller locator CNAME record for *dsaGuid._msdcs.ForestName*. Then, install the DNS service on the new DC and enable integrated AD DNS. After replication has occurred, change the new DC to point to itself as the primary or secondary DNS server. However, if there are IP address changes to DCs in the root forest domain, you may need to point all DCs to a single DNS server until these changes have replicated before returning to this configuration.

Configuring domain records

When a DNS server that supports dynamic registration is used to support AD, Windows Server 2003 and Windows 2000 DCs can automatically register all necessary host and SRV records with DNS. It is not recommended that you manually configure DNS records for DCs. However, if you must, you can locate the requirements by viewing a properly registered domain, or by referring to the server documentation. You should be aware that records for Windows Server 2003 DCs are organized slightly differently than those for Windows Server 2000.

Dynamic registration occurs during the dcpromo process, and again each time the DC reboots. However, you can also request registration by using the `ipconfig` command `ipconfig /registerDNS`. During dcpromo, a pop up indicates a successful attempt, and advises you to refer to the logs where any problems will be recorded.

To view the newly created records, open and expand the DNS zone records using the DNS console. Two zones are created during the creation of a forest: the zone for the new domain (*DNSDomainName*) and the zone for the child domain (*_msdcs.DNS-DomainName*). There are multiple containers in each zone. The pane on the left side of Figure 7-16 displays the expanded DNS structure for the forward lookup zones of the forest root domain *nomoore.local*. (No reverse lookup zones are created by default. If you create appropriate reverse lookup zones, PTR records can also be dynamically registered.) The pane on the right side of Figure 7-17 shows the delegated zone record for the *msdcs* zone and displays its contents (the name of the name server that is authoritative for the delegated subdomain).

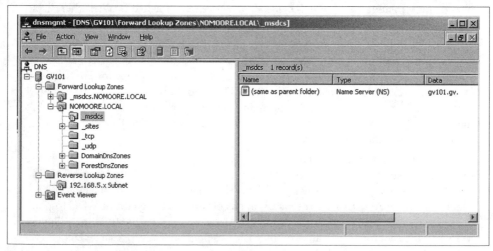

Figure 7-17. The Forward Lookup zones for the domain nomoore.local

Refer to this figure as you explore Tables 7-2 and 7-3. The tables will also help you understand your own AD DNS structure and the Windows Server 2003 uses of DNS explained in the section "How AD Uses DNS" earlier in this chapter. Table 7-1 lists and describes the types of SRV records that are created. Tables 7-2 and 7-3 list and describe the DNS records that are created during this process. In a production environment, additional sites may exist and, therefore, one or more site-specific folders (in addition to the *Default-First-Site-Name* folder) will also exist. The contents of their folders will be similar to that described for the default site. The number of SRV records of the same type in any one folder will depend on the number of DCs in the domain or site. Also described in the table are the *ForestDnsZones* and *DomainDnsZones* containers. These containers provide host records for non-SRV-aware LDAP clients.

Table 7-2. Windows Server 2003 forward lookup zone DNS records (DNSDomainName)

Folder	Record	Description
N/A	N/A	Contains all record types for this domain.
_msdcs.DNSDomainName	N/A	A Delegation record delegating authority for the _msdcs child domain to the zone_msdcs.domain.extension.
_sites.DNSDomainName	N/A	Contains site records for all sites.
Default-First-Site-Name._sites.DNSDomainName	N/A	Contains site records for this default site. A similar container exists for each site.
_tcp.Default-First-Site-Name._sites.DNSDomainName	N/A	Contains TCP records for services offered in this site.
_tcp.Default-First-Site-Name._sites.DNSDomainName	_kerberos	Used by a client to locate a server running KDC services for domain *DnsDomainName* in the site *Default-First-Site-Name*.
_tcp.Default-First-Site-Name._sites.DNSDomainName	_ldap	Used by clients to locate a server running LDAP service in the domain *DNSDomainName* in the site *Default-First-Site-Name*.
_tcp.Default-First-Site-Name._sites.DNSForestName	_gc	Used by clients to locate a GC server for this domain. Only servers running LDAP and that are a GC for the forest *DnsForestName* will register here.
_tcp.DNSDomainName	N/A	Contains SRV records for each service in the domain that can be accessed via TCP.
_tcp.DNSForestName	_gc	Enables a client to locate a GC in *DNSForestName*.
_tcp.DNSDomainName	_kerberos	Used by clients to locate KDC in *DNSDomainName*.
_tcp.DNSDomainName	_kpasswd	Used by clients to locate the Kerberos Password Change server for the domain. (All Widows Server 2003 DCs offer this service.)

Table 7-2. Windows Server 2003 forward lookup zone DNS records (DNSDomainName) (continued)

Folder	Record	Description
_tcp.DNSDomainName	_ldap	Used by clients to locate a LDAP server in the domain *DNSDomainName*.
_udp.DNSDomainName.	N/A	Contains SRV records for each service in the domain that can be accessed via UDP.
_udp.DNSDomainName.	_kerberos	Used by clients to locate KDC in *DNSDomainName* using UDP.
_udp.DNSDomainName.	_kpasswd	Used by clients to locate the Kerberos Password Change server for the domain using UDP.
DomainDNSZones	N/A	Contains information servers that store DNS records for this domain.
N/A	Host(A)	Provides a way for non-SRV-aware LDAP clients to find an LDAP server.
_sites.DomainDNSZones	N/A	Contains the folders for each site.
Default-First-Site-Name._sites.DomainDNSZones	N/A	Contains TCP folder for the *Default-First-Site-Name*.
_tcp. Default-First-Site-Name._sites.DomainDNSZones	N/A	Contains TCP records for this site (one for each DC).
_tcp. Default-First-Site-Name._sites.DomainDNSZones	_ldap.	Used by clients to locate an LDAP server in site *Default-First-Site-Name* in *DomainDNSZones*.
_tcp.DomainDNSZones	N/A	Contains the TCP records for this site.
_tcp.DomainDNSZones	_ldap	Used by clients to locate LDAP server in *DomainDNSZones*.
ForestDnsZones	N/A	Contains information on each server that hosts forest records.
N/A	Host(A)	Provides a way for non-SRV aware LDAP clients to find an LDAP server.
Default-First-Site-Name._sites. ForestDnsZones	N/A	Contains TCP folder for the *Default-First-Site-Name*.
_tcp.Default-First-Site-Name._sites. ForestDnsZones	N/A	Contains TCP records for this site (one for each DC).
_tcp.Default-First-Site-Name._sites. ForestDnsZones	_ldap	Used by clients to locate an LDAP server in site *Default-First-Site-Name* in *ForestDnsZones*.
_tcp.ForestDnsZones	N/A	Contains the TCP records for this site.
_tcp.ForestDnsZones	_ldap	Used by clients to locate an LDAP server in *ForestDnsZones*.
N/A	Start of Authority (SOA)	The FQDN of the authoritative server for this domain.

Table 7-2. Windows Server 2003 forward lookup zone DNS records (DNSDomainName) (continued)

Folder	Record	Description
N/A	Name Server (NS)	The FQDN of every name server that hosts the zone records.
N/A	Host (A)	The computer and IP address for each computer in the domain.

Table 7-3. Windows Server 2003 forward lookup zone DNS records (_msdcs.DNSDomanName)

Folder	Record	Description
N/A	N/A	Only exists in for the root.
dc._msdcs.DNSDomainName	N/A	Contains site and TCP information for each site.
sites.dc.msdcs.DNSDomainName	N/A	Contains site information for all sites. By default, the first site (*Default-First-Site-Name*) records are included. These are defined below. A similar record structure is defined for each site.
Default-First-Site-Name.sites.dc.msdcs.DNSDomainName	N/A	Contains a _tcp subfolder.
_tcp.Default-First-Site-Name.sites.dc.msdcs.DNSDomainName	N/A	TCP-related site records
_tcp.Default-First-Site-Name.sites.dc.msdcs.DNSDomainName	_kerberos	Used by a client to locate a DC running the Windows Server 2003 KDC service for domain *DNSDomainName* in the site *Default-First-Site-Name*.
_tcp.Default-First-Site-Name.sites.dc.msdcs.DNSDomainName	_ldap	Used by a client to locate a server running LDAP in the *Default-First-Site-Name* site of the *DNSDomainName*.
_tcp.dc.msdcs.DNSDomainName	N/A	Contains TCP records for services provided by this forest.
_tcp.dc.msdcs.DNSDomainName	_kerberos	Used by a client to locate a DC running KDC service for domain *DNSDomainName*.
_tcp.dc.msdcs.DNSDomainName	_ldap	Used by a client to locate a DC running LDAP service for domain *DNSDomainName*.
Domains._msdcs.DNSDomainName	N/A	Contains folders for each DC GUID.
dcGUID.domains._msdcs.DNSDomainName	N/A	Contains protocol folders for this domain.
_tcp.domainGUID.domains._msdcs.DNSDomainName	N/A	Contains TCP SRV records for this domain.
_tcp.doaminGUID.domains._msdcs.DNSDomainName	_ldap.	Used by a client to locate a DC in the domain *DNSDomainName* on the basis of its GUID. (Usually only used when the domain name has been changed.)

*Table 7-3. Windows Server 2003 forward lookup zone DNS records
(_msdcs.DNSDomanName) (continued)*

Folder	Record	Description
gc._msdcs.DNSDomainName	N/A	Contains global catalog (GC) server information for all GCs in the forest.
sites.gc.msdcs.DNSDomainName	N/A	Contains site information for all sites. By default, the first site (*Default-First-Site-Name*) records are included. These are defined below. A similar record structure is defined for each site.
Default-First-Site-Name. sites.gc.msdcs.DNSDomainName	N/A	Contains a *_tcp* subfolder.
_tcp.Default-First-Site-Name. sites.gc.msdcs.DNSDomainName	N/A	TCP-related site records for GCs.
_tcp.Default-First-Site-Name. sites.gc.msdcs.DNSForestName	_ldap	Enables a client to locate a GC server for this forest located in this site. Only DCs acting as GCs for the forest names in *DnsForestName* register here.
_tcp.gc.msdcs.DNSDomainName	N/A	Contains TCP records for GC services provided by this forest.
_tcp.gc.msdcs.DNSDomainName	_ldap	Used by a client to locate a GC server for this forest. Only DCs acting as GCs for the forest names in DnsForestName register here.
_pdc.msdcs.DNSDomainName	N/A	Contains records for PDC emulators for the forest.
_tcp.pdc.msdcs.DNSDomainName	N/A	Contains TCP records for services provided by PDCs in this forest.
_tcp.pdc.msdcs.DNSDomainName	_ldap	Used by a client to locate the DC acting as the PDC emulator in the mixed-mode domain *DNSDomainName*. Only the PDC emulator of the domain registers this record at this location.
N/A	Name Server (NS)	The fully qualified domain name (FQDN) of every name server that hosts the zone records.
N/A	Alias (CNAME)	The GUID and FQDN for DCs in the domain.

Note that the records are used to help locate services and the domain controllers they reside on. Sites may include member computers in this domain or users with accounts in this domain, but may not include DCs for this domain. When this is the case, an SRV record for the closest DC in the domain will be registered in DNS for the site. The closest DC in the domain to a specific site is determined by an examination of the *replication cost matrix*. The replication cost matrix is just a way of comparing sites based on the speed of the connection and the replication latency based on the replication topology. You will recall that replication between sites is based on the configuration of a site link, an object defined by administrators to represent a path between two sites. One of the properties of the site link is a cost that represents the speed of the connection between the sites. The closest site to any domain is the one whose access can be done at the least cost.

You should notice in Table 7-3 that many SRV records have the same purpose: the location of specific services. Their duplication of records (located in different folders) enables the lookup of services by different processes. For example, during logon the NetLogon service attempts to find the KDC server in the nearest site and appends site information to its query. Other processes may attempt to use UDP instead of TCP. More information on the algorithms clients use to select SRV resource records can be found in *RFC 2782: A DNS RR for specifying the location of services (DNS SRV)*.

These SRV records are created for each domain in the DNS zone that is authoritative for the domain. When your AD infrastructure supports multiple domains, you must configure DNS to support each of them. An organization's DNS infrastructure may consist of multiple zones and multiple DNS servers, each of which support different zones and different domains. You may need to configure DNS domain delegation in order to support a multiple domain forest infrastructure.

Configuring DNS delegation

If the parent zone will host the AD domain, the records will reside there and there is no need for delegation. However, if a unique zone is created to host the AD domain, then the DNS domain must be delegated.

If the DNS domain is delegated, the DNS infrastructure must have the DNS delega tions necessary to enable name resolution during domain controller location. A DNS delegation entry must exist in the DNS zone that is the parent of the zone that will support AD. These records are added by whoever administers the DNS server hosting the parent zone.

To continue with our example, the domain *nomoore.local* is the root domain in the forest. During its creation (that is, during promotion using dcpromo for the first DC), DNS services were added to the server and the zone information created for the zone. Figure 7-18 shows the zone information in the DNS console.

Let's create a new child domain that we'll call *west.nomoore.local*. The DNS domain records could be added to the *chicago.local* zone, or a second zone can be created. If the DNS records are added to the *nomoore.local* zone, a DNS domain name record is created prior to running dcpromo. If a second zone is desired, then a delegation record must be created in the *GV101* zone.

To create a delegation record, begin by opening the DNS console. Right-click on the domain where the delegation record should reside, in this case the *nomoore.local* domain. Select New Delegation and then click Next. Enter a name for the new domain,

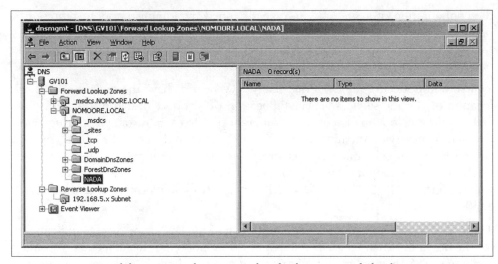

Figure 7-18. A new subdomain record appears within the domain records for the zone

as shown in Figure 7-19. Note that the FQDN of the domain is built in the uneditable text box when the domain name is entered. In other words, you enter only the domain name, not the FQDN of the new domain. Click Next.

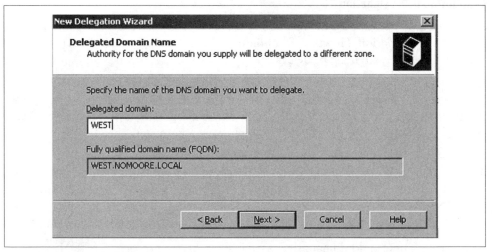

Figure 7-19. Create a delegation record

Click the Add button and add a name server to host the delegated zone and then click OK. If you use the browse feature, when the server name is selected from the list provided, its IP address is automatically added to the record. Repeat as necessary to add additional name servers; when completed, click Next. Click Finish and examine the entry in DNS as shown in Figure 7-20. Note that the record created in the new delegated domain is of Name Server type and includes the name of the server that will host DNS for this zone. You can distinguish delegated domain records from domain by the little certificate embedded in the domain folder.

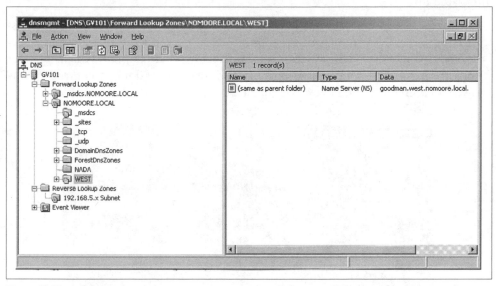

Figure 7-20. A delegated zone hosts a name server record that specifies where domain records can be found

Configuring AD-integrated DNS zones

Windows DNS servers can be configured to operate in the traditional manner, requiring both primary and secondary DNS servers whose zone file information is stored on the DNS server. The Windows DNS server supports both SRV records and dynamic update. However, when used in this manner, they do not support secure dynamic updating.

Windows DNS can also store its data in the AD database. Each zone is stored in the AD container class dnsZone, which contains a DNS node object for every unique name in the zone. In this scenario, DNS data is replicated to all domain controllers in the domain, unless AD application partitions have been configured for DNS Zone information. Regardless, every domain controller that has DNS zone information replicated to it has the potential to become a DNS server. Traditional secondary DNS servers may be implemented and configured to obtain zone information from the AD-integrated DNS server; however, in many environments this is unnecessary. Traditionally, secondary DNS servers are implemented to provide backup, redundancy, and load balancing for zones. When DNS is AD integrated, multiple copies of the zone information already exist, so separate standalone secondary DNS servers are unnecessary. However, where multiple domains exist, or when local DNS support is desired for sites that do not include DCs, traditional secondary DNS servers may be implemented.

A Windows DNS server may be installed as an AD-integrated DNS server, or modified after installation. The DNS server service must be running on a DC to become integrated into AD.

To change the DNS server's status to AD-integrated, begin by opening the Administrative Tools → DNS Management console. Right-click on the domain and select Properties. Click the Change button next to the Type: description. Click to select "Store the zone in AD (available only if DNS server is a domain controller)," as shown in Figure 7-21, then click OK. Finally, click OK to close the Properties pages.

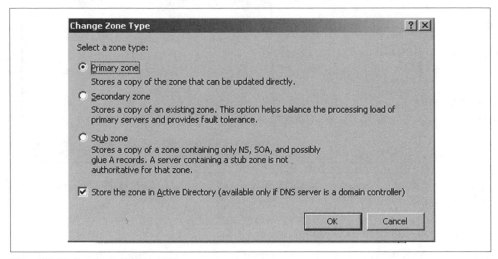

Figure 7-21. Integrate DNS in AD

Configuring and using secure dynamic DNS

Windows 2000, Windows Server 2003, and Windows XP computers can register an IP address in a DNS server that supports dynamic registration. This solves the problem created by DHCP whereby a computer's IP address may change, thus requiring a change to DNS. When DNS host records are manually configured, it may be difficult to keep up with dynamically changing IP address. However, dynamic registration of IP addresses creates another problem.

If rogue computers are assigned the same address as an authorized computer, the rogue computer may register its information in DNS, overwriting the name of the previous computer. Or, if a rogue computer on the network is named the same as a legitimate computer, it may register its name and IP address, thus effectively changing the IP address for the registered computer and redirecting traffic intended for the authorized computer to itself. If a rogue computer can do this, it is a serious security issue because it creates the potential for at least a denial-of-service attack, and at worst a situation where sensitive data can be intercepted.

This problem can be mitigated if DNS is integrated with AD, by ensuring that only a *secure* dynamic update is allowed. When a secure dynamic update is used, only the registered host can change its registration information. To configure secure dynamic updates, you must consider client DHCP configuration, DHCP server configuration, and DC configuration.

Client configuration depends on the client's operating system version. Only Windows XP Professional, Windows 2000, and Windows Server 2003 can perform dynamic update. (By default, they are configured to do so.) Earlier versions of Windows such as Windows NT 4.0 and Windows 98 use WINS for name resolution and cannot be configured to dynamically update DNS. However, if these systems receive their IP addresses from a Windows DHCP server, the DHCP server can be configured to update DNS A (host) and PTR (pointer) records for them and secure dynamic updates can occur.

To configure DHCP to register addresses for clients, begin by clicking Start → Administrative Tools → DHCP to open the DHCP console. Right-click the DHCP server to configure and select Properties. Select the DNS tab. Select "Enable DNS dynamic updates according to the settings below." Select "Always dynamically update DNS A and PTR records," as shown in Figure 7-22. Click OK to close the Properties pages.

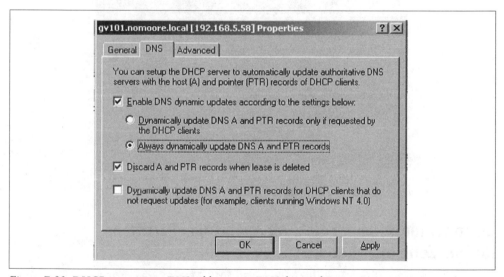

Figure 7-22. DHCP can register DNS addresses in DNS for its clients

If multiple DHCP servers are used, you can run into problems if the client obtains an address from a different DHCP server. When the client first obtains and IP address, the DHCP server registers the client information in DNS. Because it made the first registration, this DHCP sever becomes the only one that can update the client record. If a different DHCP server assigns the client an address and attempts to update DNS, it fails. To allow all DHCP servers to modify the client's address in DNS, make all DHCP servers members of the DNSUpdateProxy Windows group.

To change Windows dynamic DNS to secure dynamic DNS requires a single domain property change. Begin by clicking Start and then click Administrative Tools. Click DNS to open the DNS console. Right-click on the zone and select Properties. Select the General tab. From the "Dynamic updates" drop-down list, select "Secure only," as shown in Figure 7-23. Click OK to close the Properties pages.

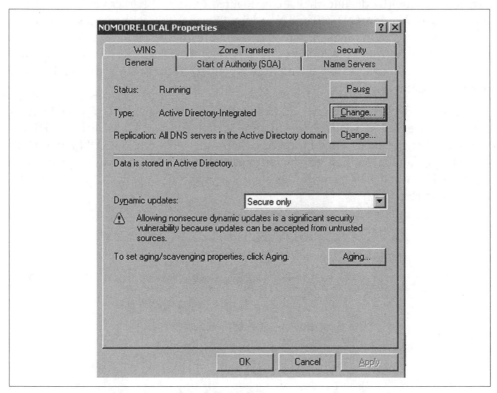

Figure 7-23. Secure dynamic DNS name registration

Using Windows Server 2003 AD Application Partitions for DNS Zone Information

AD application partitions are a new feature of Windows Server 2003. Data added to the AD is replicated by default to all domain controllers in the domain. However, this is not always a good idea and can create a performance issue because of excessive replication. If application data is not required on all domain controllers, consider the use of application partitions.

Using application partitions

DNS data is one type of data that may be constrained to application partitions. When DNS is integrated with AD, all zone information is stored in the AD and replicated by default to all DCs. Each DC does not, however, automatically become a DNS server, nor is this required. Therefore, it may not be necessary to replicate DNS data to every DC.

Two application partitions for DNS data (a domain-wide DNS application partition, and a forest-wide DNS application directory partition) are automatically created when the DNS server service is created during the dcpromo process on the first Windows Server 2003 DC in the forest. For all other domains, the domain-wide application partition is created when the DNS service is installed on the first Windows Server 2003 DC in the domain. The domain-wide application partition is unique for each domain and is replicated to all DCs in that domain that are running the DNS service.

The forest-wide application partition is replicated to all DCs in all domains that are running the DNS service. It is also possible to create a custom DNS application directory partition. A custom application directory partition for DNS will replicate its data to those DCs that enlist in the partition. These various partitions, along with the domain partitions, are referred to as *DNS replication scopes*.

By default, the Locator DNS resource records for the domain are stored in *_msdcs.DnsDomainName* subdomain for the domain. This subdomain is automatically created when the DNS root domain of a new AD forest is created on a Windows Server 2003 DC and is stored in the forest-wide DNS application directory partition.

 The domain partition is the only DNS replication scope available to Windows 2000 DCs. Windows 2000 DCs cannot access data in Windows Server 2003 application directory partitions. If Windows 2000 AD-integrated DNS servers must coexist with Windows Server 2003 AD-integrated DNS servers, you must change the DNS replication scope of the Windows Server 2003 DNS server to "To all domain controllers in the AD domain domain_name."

Migrating from Windows 2000 to Windows Server 2003

When migrating from Windows 2000 AD to Windows Server 2003 AD, you can reduce replication traffic and reduce the amount of material stored in the global catalog by changing the replication scope of the DNS zone information to the DNS application directory partitions.

To change DNS replication scope, first upgrade all Windows 2000 DCs to Windows Server 2003. Ensure that the domain naming master is hosted on a Windows Server 2003 DC. If there is an existing *_msdcs.forestroot_domain* zone on DNS, move it to the forest-wide DNS application directory partition. Open the DNS console on a DC that hosts a DNS server in a domain. Right-click on the DNS zone that uses the

FQDN of the AD domain and select Properties. Click the Change button for "Replication: All domain controllers in the AD domain." Click "To all DNS servers in the AD domain domain_name." Click OK. Repeat the DNS console steps for each domain.

DNS isn't the only network service that can impact the operation of AD. Much of AD's operation assumes synchronized time between member computers. The windows time service can ensure that time is synchronized.

Configuring the Windows Time Service

Many operations in an AD environment depend on synchronized time. For example, Kerberos requires that time be synchronized between server and client. (By default, if the time on the client is off by more than five minutes from that of the server, Kerberos logon will fail.) Other computer-to-computer operations will not succeed if the time on both ends of the connection is not close. Additionally, the date stamp on log files should be accurate to assist in troubleshooting and for incident investigation.

Windows Server 2003 includes the W32Time services, which is an implementation of the Network Time Protocol (NTP). A standalone server can be directed to synchronize with an Internet-available timeserver, or with a local hardware clock. In an AD domain, synchronization follows a hierarchical structure that incorporates the following:

- Windows client computers and member servers typically use their authenticating domain controller as their *inbound time partner* (the computer with which they synchronize their time).
- DCs in a domain typically use the PDC emulator for the domain as their inbound time partner.
- PDC emulators select their inbound time partner as the PDC emulator in their parent domain.
- The PDC emulator for the forest root-domain is the authoritative timeserver for the forest and should be configured to synchronize time with an Internet-available timeserver, or with a local hardware clock.
- The maximum positive and negative time changes that will be made during synchronization can be configured in the registry. This capability is meant to allow for reasonable automatic changes caused by imperfect clocks and time latency across networks. Keeping these values small will prevent the introduction of large time changes that could seriously impact operations and produce time gaps (as well as wildly divergent time stamped log data).
- If a time change is necessary, the event is logged.

Time services available on the Internet are not authenticated. It is possible to spoof such services and, therefore, provide misinformation. In a Windows forest, this means all computers would eventually adopt an incorrect time. To secure time operations, use a hardware clock such as a GPS receiver with time outputs.

Synchronizing with an external time source

To synchronize the PDC emulator of the domain with an Internet-based time source (or some other network-locatable time source), you should complete the following registry entries:

- Change the server type to NTP by changing the Type value to NTP at *HKEY_LOCAL_MACHINE\SYSTEM\CurrentControlSet\Services\W32Time\Config\Parameters*.

- Set the AnnounceFlags value to 5. This value is located at *HKEY_LOCAL_MACHINE\SYSTEM\CurrentControlSet\Services\W32Time\Config*.

- Enable the NTPServer by changing the Enabled value to 1 at *HKEY_LOCAL_MACHINE\SYSTEM\CurrentControlSet\Services\W32Time\TimeProviders\NtpServer*.

- Specify a time source by modifying the NtpServer value at *HKEY_LOCAL_MACHINE\SYSTEM\CurrentControlSet\Services\W32Time\Parameters*. Change the value from time.windows.com,0x1 to a list of URLs that indicate the external timeservers. Append 0x1 to each DNS name.

- Select a poll interval by editing the SpecialPollInterval value at *HKEY_LOCAL_MACHINE\SYSTEM\CurrentControlSet\Services\W32Time\TimeProviders\NtpClient*. Change the value to a number that represent the time in seconds.

- Configure time correction by changing the value MaxPosPhaseCorrection at *HKEY_LOCAL_MACHINE\SYSTEM\CurrentControlSet\Services\W32Time\Config*. Change the value to the time in seconds. The MaxPosPhaseCorrection is the largest possible positive time correction in seconds that the service makes. A reasonable value might be 3600 (1 hour) or less, depending on the poll interval, network conditions, and external time source.

- Complete the configuration of time correction by changing the value MaxNegPhaseCorrection at *HKEY_LOCAL_MACHINE\SYSTEM\CurrentControlSet\Services\W32Time\Config*. Change the value to the time in seconds. The MaxNegPhaseCorrection is the largest possible positive time correction in seconds that the service makes. A reasonable value might be 3600 (1 hour) or less, depending on the poll interval, network conditions, and external time source.

- At the command prompt, stop and start the Windows Time service by using the command net stop w32time && net start w32time.

Many of the entries mentioned here can be set using Group Policy. However, the PDC emulator for the domain is a single computer, and Group Policy is usually used to establish settings for multiple computers.

Synchronize with a hardware clock

To use the internal hardware clock of the server, you should use the following:

- Change the value of AnnounceFlags to A at *HKEY_LOCAL_MACHINE\SYSTEM\ CurrentControlSet\Services\W32Time\Config*.
- At the command prompt, stop and start the Windows Time service by using the command net stop w32time && net start w32time.

To synchronize with a separate hardware clock follow the instructions provided with the hardware.

As we've seen, time synchronization is automated by default within the AD forest. Automated time synchronization cannot occur, however, if member computers cannot connect to their domain, and that will not be possible if IP addressing is incorrect. DHCP is used in many networks to automate IP addressing. DHCP can also be integrated with AD.

Integrating DHCP with AD

If you will be using Windows 2000 or Windows Server 2003 DHCP servers in your AD environment, you should be aware that these Windows DHCP servers must be authorized in AD or they will not be able to start. This requirement can help prevent rogue Windows DHCP servers on the network. A rogue DHCP server can cause problems by issuing invalid IP addresses to clients, thus creating a denial of service. DHCP servers must either be DCs or member servers to be authorized. DHCP services on standalone Windows servers cannot be authorized in the domain. However, if they are on a subnet that does not have an authorized DHCP server, they will function. However, this configuration is not recommended. If the standalone DHCP server detects another DHCP server, it will stop leasing IP addresses to DHCP clients.

Non-Windows DHCP servers and Windows NT 4.0 DHCP servers will not be hampered and can initialize and service clients even if they are not authorized Windows DHCP servers on the network.

Detection of an unauthorized DHCP server is accomplished via the use of the DHCP information message (DHCPINFORM) and Microsoft-specific options types that are used to communicate information about the forest root domain. When DHCP member servers start, they query AD for the list of authorized DHCP server IP addresses. If the name is on the list, then the DHCP server starts servicing clients. If the name is not on the list, it does not provide service to DHCP clients.

In a multiple forest environment, member servers seek authorization information from their own forest only. This means that clients may obtain an IP address via a DHCP server in another forest, even though no DHCP server is available from their own forest. Member DHCP servers repeat the detection process every 60 minutes.

When a standalone DHCP server starts, it sends a DHCPINFORM message seeking other DHCP servers on the network and querying for other DHCP servers on the network. If there are DHCP member servers on the network, they reply with DHCP acknowledgment messages (DHCPACK) that include information about the forest root domain. If there are no member server DHCP servers on the network (the standalone DHCP server receives no reply), the standalone DHCP server begins servicing DHCP clients. If the standalone server receives a reply from an authorized DHCP server, the standalone server does not provide DHCP services to clients. The standalone DHCP server repeats its query every 10 minutes.

To authorize DHCP servers and benefit from this approach:

- The first DHCP server must be a member server in an AD domain.
- To authorize the DHCP server using its FQDN, the FQDN of the DHCP server cannot exceed 64 characters. (The IP address of the DHCP server can be used to authorize the server.)
- To authorize a Windows 2000 DHCP server in a Windows Server 2003 forest, the Windows 2000 DHCP server must be at service pack 2 or above.
- You must be a member of the Enterprise Admins group (or have been delegated the right to authorize DHCP) to authorize a DHCP server.

You can authorize DHCP servers in one of two ways. To authorize DHCP Servers using the DHCP Management Console, open the console and right-click DHCP. Select Authorize.

You could also authorize DHCP server using the `netsh` command. To use this method, enter the following at the command line:

```
netsh dhcp add server servername serverIP
```

For example, you could use the following command:

```
netsh dhcp add grnvalley.nomoore.local 192.168.5.40
```

To delete an authorized server using the `netsh` command, enter the following from the command line:

```
netsh dhcp delete server servername serverIP
```

To list the authorized servers in AD using the `netsh` command, enter the following from the command line:

```
netsh dhcp show server
```

NetBIOS and WINS in an AD Domain

As you can tell, AD serves as the backbone for many network services and is intimately related to others. These other services (such as DNS, DHCP and Windows time service) play crucial roles in an AD network. DNS is critical for AD's existence. Administration of an AD network is much easier because of its support of and use of DHCP and the Windows time service. Windows Internet Name Service (or WINS, a legacy Windows network service) can also play a role in the AD network.

All AD domains have both DNS names and NetBIOS names. DNS services are required for the operation of AD. All Windows XP Professional, Windows 2000, and Windows Server 2003 computers can use DNS to locate computers on the network. Some applications (and legacy Windows clients such as Windows 98) rely on the ability to locate computers on the network using NetBIOS. To assist these computers, the Windows Internet Name Service (WINS) can be implemented in an AD environment.

Integrating WINS in a DNS environment

WINS integration in a Windows DNS environment is configured to allow lookup of DNS names that cannot be resolved by querying the DNS namespace. Two DNS resource record types are used:

WINS resource record
> This integrates WINS lookup in forward lookup zones. When a WINS resource record is present in DNS, the WINS database can be used for forward queries for hostnames or names that are not found in the zone database. This service can even assist computers that are not WINS-aware (such as Unix).

WINS-R resource record
> This integrates a node adapter status request for reverse lookup zones.

A WINS lookup via a DNS query follows these steps, as shown in Figure 7-24:

1. The client queries its preferred DNS server for a client in a DNS zone that is integrated with WINS.

2. The normal DNS recursion process proceeds and locates the DNS server authoritative for the desired DNS zone.

3. The DNS server looks for a matching host (A) record matching the requested computer and doesn't find one.

4. Since the DNS server is enabled to do WINS lookup, the server separates the host part of the computer name from the FQDN in the DNS query.

5. The DNS server sends a NetBIOS name request for the host to the WINS server.

6. If the WINS server can resolve the name it returns the IP address to the DNS server. The DNS server creates a host (A) resource record using the resolved IP

address from the WINS server. This address is returned to the original, preferred DNS server.

7. The preferred DNS server passes the address to the requesting client.

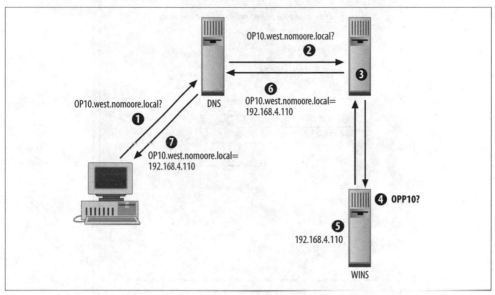

Figure 7-24. A Windows Server 2003 DNS server can take advantage of WINS lookup

A WINS reverse lookup via a DNS query follows these steps:

1. The WINS database is not indexed by an IP address and, therefore, the DNS service cannot simply send a reverse name lookup to WINS to get the name of the computer if the IP address is known. However, the DNS service can send a node adapter status request to the IP address in the DNS reverse query.

2. The computer responds to the node adapter status request with the computer name.

3. The DNS services appends the computer name to the DNS domain name and forwards the result to the requesting client.

 WINS and WINS-R resource records are only available in and used by Windows DNS servers. If zone transfers are approved between Windows DNS servers and other DNS servers, prevent these records from being included in zone transfers.

To enable WINS lookup in DNS, begin by opening the DNS console. Right-click the forward lookup zone for which you wish to enable WINS. Select the WINS tab and select the "Use WINS forward lookup" checkbox, as shown in Figure 7-25.

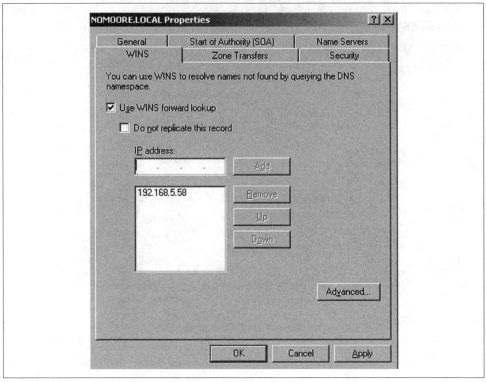

Figure 7-25. Enter the IP address of the WINS server in the DNS server properties

Enter the IP address of the WINS server to be used for WINS lookup and then click Add. Click OK.

To enable a reverse lookup, begin by opening the DNS console. Right-click the reverse lookup zone for which you wish to enable WINS. Select the WINS-R tab and select the Use WINS-R lookup checkbox. Enter the domain name to use in the "Domain to append to returned name" box, as shown in Figure 7-26.

In some networks, you may wish to restrict direct access to WINS records. You might do this to obscure the address of internal hosts while listing public addresses such as web servers. While the address can be found for a specific computer by doing a WINS lookup, if the addresses are accessible to a zone transfer, no previous knowledge of a computer NetBIOS name is necessary. While zone transfers should only be allowed to trusted DNS servers, the extra step of preventing the exposure of WINS records may be judged by your organization as an added security step.

To prevent WINS records from being included in zone transfers, begin by opening the DNS console. Right-click the zone to be configured not to include WINS resource records in a zone transfer. Select the "Do not replicate this record" checkbox.

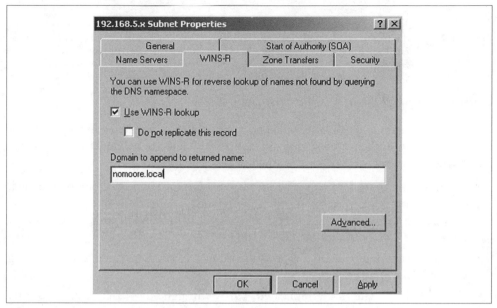

Figure 7-26. Provide the domain name to be used with the WINS provided IP address

In addition to using TCP/IP effectively with AD, you should also be aware of the benefits of using Group Policy. Group Policy can be used to provide security settings and other management options for computers joined in a Windows 2000 or Windows Server 2003 domain. While Group Policy for security management is discussed in Chapter 13, it is important to take a look at Group Policy when discussing how to manage network protocols.

Using Group Policy to Manage Network Protocols

Some network configuration settings for domain member computers and users with domain accounts can be set in Group Policy. When they are set here, they can automatically update multiple domain member computers.

These Group Policy settings reside in nodes under the Computer Configuration node and affect computers with accounts in the organizational unit (OU), domain, or site object to which the Group Policy Object (GPO) is defined. Organizational units are subdivisions of domains and can contain user and computer accounts and records for shares and printers. More information on OUs is provided in Chapter 3. Those settings in nodes under the User Configuration node affect users whose accounts reside in the OU, domain, or site object to which the GPO is linked. Computers and users are also affected by GPOs linked to the parent objects of the object their account resides in.

The settings discussed in this chapter are primarily applicable to only the Windows Server 2003 and Windows XP Professional computers. Group Policy cannot operate if either DNS or AD is not working correctly.

Dependency of Group Policy on DNS

Group Policy settings are downloaded and applied during computer startup and user logon from the authenticating domain controller. The following DNS issues can affect whether the correct GPOs are downloaded and applied:

- If a domain controller cannot be located, no Group Policy can be downloaded. While Group Policy cached from a previous connection can be used, any changes to Group Policy will not be available. Domain controller connectivity requires a DNS lookup of the DC IP address.

- If site information is incorrectly configured in DNS, it is possible that the wrong Group Policy may be applied.

- Group Policy changes are replicated, partly through AD Replication and partly through the File Replication Service (FRS). Both services are dependent on locating designated DCs. If DNS is not functioning correctly, then replication cannot occur or will not be synchronized. (Elements replicated by AD and by FRS must match.)

As you can imagine, Group Policy is a powerful administrative tool. While it can and should be used for multiple administrative functions, it cannot be used for all of them. It does not have the capability to provide extensive help for all TCP/IP or AD functions. There are, however, several TCP/IP, DNS, Windows Time Service, and SNMP configuration settings that can be made using Group Policy.

Managing TCP/IP Configuration Using Group Policy

Management of TCP/IP settings is primarily accomplished using DHCP to provide dynamic addressing, including information on the preferred DNS server. However, some configuration can be done using Group Policy for both users and computers. These settings are in the Network Connection nodes. Table 7-4 lists and explains settings for computer, while Table 7-5 lists and explains those for users. The first column lists the setting, while the second column explains it. The Computer Configuration, Administrative Templates, Network, Network Connection node contains settings useful in managing TCP/IP configuration that are not available via DHCP. Settings are described in Table 7-4. Three of the settings (those that impact Internet Connection Sharing, Internet Connection Firewall, and the network bridge) are location-aware (that is, the setting has no meaning if the computer is connected to a different DNS domain network than the one it was connected to when the setting was applied).

Table 7-4. Computer-based TCP/IP configuration via Group Policy

Group policy TCP/IP setting	Explanation
Prohibit use of Internet Connection Sharing on your DNS domain network	If disabled, an administrator can enable and configure the Internet Connection Sharing (ICS) feature of an Internet connection (if the ICS service can run on the computer). ICS lets a Windows computer act as an Internet gateway for a small network and provides network services such as DHCP to the private network. Enabling this setting prohibits the configuration of ICS and also removes the Advanced page of the Properties pages of a LAN or remote access connection. The Internet Connection Sharing page is removed from the New Connection wizard and the Network Setup wizard is disabled.
Prohibit use of Internet Connection Firewall on your DNS domain network	If enabled, prevents the use of the Internet Connection Firewall on the DNS domain network. Enabling this setting also removes the Advanced page of the Properties pages of a LAN or remote access connection. The Internet Connection Firewall page is removed from the New Connection wizard and the Network Setup wizard is disabled. If disabled, ICF is disabled when a LAN connection or VPN connection is created, but users can use the Advanced tab in the connection properties to enable it.
Prohibit installation and configuration of Network Bridge on your DNS domain network	If enabled, the user cannot install or configure a network bridge on a computer with two or more networks. A *network bridge* is a layer 2 MAC bridge that allows the connection of two or more network segments. If the setting is disabled (or not configured), users can create and modify a network bridge. If a network bridge is created before this setting is enabled, the existing network bridge is not affected. (Creating a network bridge is disabled by default and requires administrator privileges to create or configure.)
IEEE 802.1x Certificate Authority for Machine Authentication	802.1x authentication can be configured to require client (machine) certificates. If this is the case, a certificate must be acquired and installed on each client that will use the service. This setting enables the distribution of information on the Certification Authority that is used to sign the certificates issued to clients.

Table 7-5. User TCP/IP Group Policy settings

Group policy TCP/IP setting	Explanation
Ability to rename LAN connections or remote access connections available to all users	If enabled, all users can rename connections. If disabled (and the policy Enable Network Connection settings for Administrators is also enabled), users and Administrators cannot rename connections.
Prohibit access to properties of components of a LAN connection	If enabled (and the policy Enable Network Connection settings for Administrators is also enabled), then the network Properties button is disabled for administrators. (By default, it is disabled for users.)
Prohibit TCP/IP advanced configuration	If enabled (and the policy Enable Network Connection settings for Administrators is also enabled), then users cannot open the Advanced TCP/IP Settings Property pages and modify IP settings such as DNS and WINS server information.
Prohibit access to the Advanced Settings item on the Advanced menu	If enabled (and the policy Enable Network Connection settings for Administrators is enabled), then Administrators cannot access this menu to configure and view bindings and the order in which computers access connections, network providers, and print providers. (Users cannot access this page by default.)

Table 7-5. User TCP/IP Group Policy settings (continued)

Group policy TCP/IP setting	Explanation
Prohibit adding and removing component for a LAN or remote access connection	If enabled (and the policy Enable Network Connection settings for Administrators is enabled), then Administrators cannot install or uninstall network components. (Users cannot access this page by default.)
Prohibit access to properties of a LAN connection	If enabled (and the policy Enable Network Connection settings for Administrators is enabled), then Administrators and users cannot access LAN connection properties.
Prohibit Enabling/Disabling components of a LAN connection	If enabled (and the policy Enable Network Connection settings for Administrators is enabled), then Administrators cannot enable or disable LAN connection components. (Users cannot access this page by default.)
Ability to Enable/Disable a LAN connection	If enabled, then users can enable/disable LAN connections.
Prohibit access to the New Connection wizard	If enabled, the Make New Connection icon does not appear in the Start menu. If the policy Enable Network Connection settings for Administrators has also been enabled, users and administrators cannot start the New Connection wizard.
Ability to rename LAN connections	If enabled, nonadministrators can rename a LAN connection.
Prohibit viewing of status for an active connection	If enabled, the connection status taskbar icon and Status dialog box are not available to users, including administrators. (If you disable the setting Enable Network Connection settings for Administrators, this setting does not apply to administrators.)
Enable Windows 2000 Network Connection setting for Administrators	Windows 2000 included a number of settings that prevented administrators from performing some actions. Windows XP, while it lists these settings, does not honor them unless this setting is enabled. For an example, see the previous setting.

Table 7-5 lists and describes TCP/IP configuration-related settings in the User Configuration → Administrative Templates → Network → Network Connections node.

In addition to TCP/IP configuration, Group Policy also contains useful settings that can impact the client DNS service.

Managing DNS Client Configuration Using Group Policy

The Computer Configuration → Administrative Templates → Network → DNS Client node contains settings you can use to manage the DNS client service. Settings are described in Table 7-6. Note that settings applying to dynamic DNS registration do not apply if the client is not configured for dynamic registration.

Table 7-6. DNS client settings

Group policy DNS setting	Explanation
Primary DNS Suffix	Specifies the primary DNS suffix. If configured, this setting prevents users and administrators from changing the setting on client computers covered by the GPO. By default, computers use the local primary DNS suffix, usually the DNS name of AD domain in which is a member. However, administrators can change this. If this Group Policy setting is configured, any local setting is ignored.
Dynamic Update	Enables or disables the dynamic update of DNS information. If enabled, settings for specific network connections can be configured individually. If disabled, computers cannot dynamically register DNS settings.
DNS Suffix Search List	Settings here will determine any DNS suffixes that should be attached to an unqualified, single-label name before submitting a DNS query. Multiple DNS suffixes can be entered here. The DNS client will attempt a query using the first suffix in the list. If that fails, the DNS client will attempt a new query using the next suffix on the list, and so on, until it obtains a successful response or until it runs out of suffixes to try. If this setting is not configured, the primary DNS suffix configured for the client will be attached to any unqualified single-label names before submitting a DNS query.
Primary DNS Suffix Devolution	Single-label DNS names are names that do not include suffixes such as *.com*, *.org*, or *.net*. If DNS queries for a single-label name using the primary DNS suffix configured for the client do not work, the DNS client tries any configured connection-specific DNS suffix. If this fails, the client devolves (or removes the left-most label of the Primary DNS suffix), attaches this to the single-label name, and tries a new query. The process continues as long as there are labels that can be removed and still create a valid DNS suffix. If this setting is enabled, devolution can be used. If this setting is disabled, devolution cannot be used. If not configured, computers use their local settings.
Register PTR Records	If set to "Do not register," computers will never attempt PTR resource records registration. If set to Register, computers attempt PTR resource record registration even if the registration of an A record fails. (By default, PTR registration is only attempted if A record registration is successful.) If set to "Register only if A record registration succeeds," then PTR registration will only be attempted if A record registration succeeds.
Registration Refresh interval	Periodic reregistration is attempted by Windows XP and Windows 2000 computers configured to perform dynamic registration. If this setting is enabled, the refresh interval can be set for all affected computers.
Replace address in conflicts	If enabled, DNS clients attempt to replace conflicting A resource records (that is, overwrite existing records or records containing conflicting IP addresses) during dynamic update. This setting is useful in DNS zones that do not support secure dynamic updates. It can prevent a rogue computer from overwriting a legitimate IP address.
DNS Servers	Defines the DNS servers used by the DNS client for name queries. This list will supersede any locally configured or DHCP-configured DNS servers.
Connection Specific DNS Suffix	Defines the connection-specific DNS suffix. This setting will supersede any locally configured or DHCP-configured DNS servers.

Table 7-6. DNS client settings (continued)

Group policy DNS setting	Explanation
Register DNS records with connection specific DNS suffix	If enabled, the client can register its A and PTR records with a concatenation of its name and a connection-specific DNS suffix, as well as a concatenation of its name and is primary DNS suffix. If the setting is not configured (or not disabled), the client only registers its A and PTR records with a concatenation of its name and its Primary DNS suffix.
TTL Set in the A and PTR Records	The value for the Time-to-Live field in dynamically registered A and PTR resource records.
Update security level	If "Unsecure followed by secure" is set, clients will attempt secure dynamic updates only if nonsecure updates are refused. If Only Unsecure is set, clients send only nonsecure dynamic updates.
	If Only Secure is set, clients only send secure dynamic updates.
Update Top Level Domain Zones	If enabled, computers send dynamic updates to any zone that is authoritative for the resource record, except the root zone. If disabled, computers do not send dynamic updates to any zone that is not authoritative for its resource records.

Managing the Windows Time Service Using Group Policy

Earlier in this chapter, in the section, Configuring the Windows Time Service, you learned about registry settings applicable for configuring the timeserver on the PDC emulator. Settings for time service clients can be set in the Computer Configuration → Administrative Templates → Network, Windows Time Service node. Settings are described in Table 7-7.

Table 7-7. Windows time service Group Policy settings

Group policy time service setting	Explanation
Global Configuration Settings	A number of configuration settings such as update interval and polling intervals that can be used to tweak the operation of the Time Service client.
Enable Windows NTP Client	If disabled, the Windows NTP client will not be used. Disable this setting if you choose to use another time service. If enabled or not configured, the Windows NTP client is used for time synchronization.
Configure Windows NTP Client	Determines whether the client uses an external timeserver or the Windows domain hierarchy. If enabled, the NTP server must be entered, as well as various settings that control the NTP client's operation (and even logging).
Enable Windows NTP Server	Enabling this setting allows the computer to respond to NTP requests.

Managing SNMP Using Group Policy

SNMP is not integrated with AD nor required for the operation of AD, and is therefore not discussed in this chapter. Nevertheless, your organization may implement SNMP on the network and utilize it in the management of Windows computers that belong to an AD domain. Therefore, for completeness, the Group Policy settings that impact SNMP are listed here. The Computer Configuration → Administrative

Templates → Network → SNMP node contains settings useful in managing SNMP. Settings are described in Table 7-8.

Table 7-8. SNMP Group Policy settings

Group policy SNMP setting	Explanation
Communities	A list of communities defined to SNMP service. If enabled, SNMP only accepts request from management systems for these communities.
Permitted Managers	A list of permitted hosts that can submit a query to SNMP agent.
Traps for public community	A list of hosts that receive trap messages for the community sent by the SNMP service.

You've seen how Group Policy settings can be used to manage DNS, TCP/IP, the Windows Time Service, and SNMP, but what about other network services? There are no Group Policy-based configuration policies for network infrastructure servers such as WINS servers, Routing and Remote Access Service (RRAS) servers, or Internet Authentication Service (IAS) servers. However, there are important Group Policy-based settings that impact these network services

Managing WINS, RRAS, and IAS Servers Using Group Policy

WINS (discussed in Chapter 3 and briefly earlier in this chapter), Routing and Remote Access (RRAS) service (discussed in Chapter 8), and Internet Authentication service (IAS) (discussed in Chapter 10) are important Windows services. While there are no Administrative Templates settings for them, the System Services node of Computer Configuration, Windows Settings, Security Settings allows basic configuration of the services themselves. This node also allows service configuration for other services as well.

Two types of settings are available: startup and security. *Startup settings* determine whether the service is disabled or enabled. If enabled, these settings determine if it automatically starts at boot or must be manually started. *Security settings* can determine who can change the startup settings.

These settings can be used in two ways:

- Enabling and starting a service that is not necessary is counterproductive for security and performance reasons. The converse is also true. If the service is disabled in Group Policy, affected computers that may be designated as network infrastructure servers will not be able to start these services and fulfill their network role. In an AD domain, care should always be taken to ensure that Group Policy is correctly configured to enable or disable appropriate services. Disabling unnecessary services can also prevent their use, should they be installed where they are not authorized. Rogue infrastructure servers can be prevented from running even if installed.

- Using security settings can help to reduce and manage the number of administrators who can change the service startup settings. It is always a good practice to limit this authority to avoid accidental denials of service and wasted resources. This also helps to limit the risk of a successful attack based on some vulnerability in the service. If the service shouldn't be started and fewer people can start it, then there is less chance of it being incorrectly or accidentally started and thus less risk that any vulnerability can be exploited.

Summary

Windows Server 2003 does not have to be joined to an AD domain. However, if it is, administration of Windows computers and users can be centralized and simplified. Unfortunately, AD (the infrastructure that supports centralized administration) is complex. There are many terms to learn, as well as many operations to understand.

This chapter provides a firm grounding in the interrelationship and dependencies of AD, WINS, DHCP, and DNS. It also describes how to configure them for optimum operation and explains how to create and configure forests, domains, sites, site links, and bridgehead servers using AD administration tools. The use of Group Policy for network service management is also explored.

The benefits of spending the time necessary to fully understand and configure AD are immense. System configuration (including security configuration) can be rapidly deployed, and operations that are too complex to implement or not possible at all in workgroup networks become simple and mundane. Examples of such operations are single-sign-on across large numbers of computers and applications, public key infrastructure implementation, centralized remote access policy, granular delegation of administrative authority, and simplified authorization processes across large numbers of resources hosted on multiple computers.

In addition to forest-wide configuration of network services, an AD environment supports the centralization of remote access services. While Windows Routing and Remote Access Services (RRAS) can be implemented in a workgroup, in a domain RRAS can take advantage of the centralized database provided by AD. Chapter 8 explains the service and provides the details of its configuration and administration.

Controlling Remote Communications with Microsoft Routing and Remote Access Service

Secure remote access to information systems is no longer an option. Organizations must share and collate data, communicate information, and provide alternative work locations for employees. Branch office locations, partner projects, telecommuters, and traveling employees all require access from outside the perimeters of the network. You can use Windows Routing and Remote Access services (RRAS) and/or its earlier incarnation, Remote Access Services (RAS), to provide this access. RRAS on Windows Server 2003 and Windows 2000 provides the following capabilities:

- Basic routing services
- Dial-up access
- Virtual Private Network (VPN) services
- Network Address Translation (NAT)
- Protocol Filtering (basic firewall services)
- Remote access policies

 The desktop version of Windows offers a limited version of RAS in which a single remote access connection can be configured for any given computer running the OS. Employees can connect from home or on the road, directly to their desktops at work if a modem and the proper phone connection are available. Most security experts agree, however, that allowing this type of connection is not a sound practice. Their reasoning is that these machines act as unmanaged (and very possibly unprotected) back doors into the network. One of the cardinal rules of network security is to provide as few external connections as possible, so that these chokepoints can be monitored and secured. Therefore, this chapter will not provide step-by-step instructions on how to set up a desktop Windows system to provide remote access services.

In Windows Server 2003 and Windows 2000, RRAS is installed by default, but must be configured and enabled before it can be used.

This chapter begins with an examination of the basic routing services provided by RRAS, including IP multicast support, the Dynamic Host Configuration Protocol (DHCP) Relay Agent, Routing Information Protocol (RIP), Open Shortest Path First (OSPF) protocol, and Network Address Translation (NAT). The discussion then reviews basic firewall services, which include protocol filtering. To properly use RRAS in your network, you must plan the deployment of this service. An overview of this requirement includes a look at hardware provisioning, authentication choices, reversible encryption, data encryption, the VPN protocol, and more. This chapter also looks at configuring access modes for RRAS, including dial-up and VPN access. We'll discuss how to use a shared key for L2TP/IPSec VPNs, as well as how to configure clients to use RRAS. The chapter concludes with a discussion on how to configure logging and auditing for RRAS.

It's important to realize that RRAS provides basic routing services in addition to remote access. To begin your study of RRAS, start with an examination of routing services.

Routing Services

Configuring Windows routing services does not convert a Windows server into a replacement for your hardware-based router. Hardware-based devices have the advantage of speed and the fact that they are designed for that purpose. That is, while a Windows server can use multiple interfaces, and use routing protocols to route packets from one network to another, it will never be able to compete with a hardware device when placed under a load. Additionally, the Windows server comes equipped with much more in the way of services and software than a router needs. It is usually easier to harden a device that is dedicated to a single purpose, than to take a multipurpose computer and harden it to use a single service.

However, some of the several scenarios in which Windows routing services can (and should) be used follow:

In which some simple routing between networks is required and a server is available, but providing a hardware-based router is not an option
>   For example, a home-based or other small business may consist of a few machines, including a file and print server. If the computers have IP addresses in different subnets because of ISP assignments, routing services between the machines on the LAN may be required. The expense of purchasing a separate hardware-based router can be avoided by using RRAS.

In which routing is required to manage traffic received as a result of remote access services
>   Your internal network may be composed of multiple subnets. When incoming communications reach your network through the RRAS server, you may want to offer routing to some or all of these subnets. This routing service may include *unicast* (from one computer to another computer), *broadcast* (from one computer to

all computers), or *multicast* (from one computer to many computers) routing. RRAS routing services can be used.

In which port filtering is required to set up basic firewall services between two networks on a LAN

Typically, router Access Control Lists (ACLs) can be configured on the Windows machine. The border between internal and external networks is not the only place a firewall can be useful. You may want to use RRAS to filter communications between a sensitive area of your LAN (such as the financial network) and the rest of your organization's network.

When DHCP Relay services are needed

DHCP services for multiple subnets can be provided on a single DHCP server. However, DHCP packets may not be routed. A DHCP relay server in subnets without their own DHCP server can relay the packets from that network to the one where the DHCP server resides.

When NAT is required to forward packets between non-Internet routable private addresses on the internal network and the Internet

If your internal network uses private addressing and you want users to be able to use services on the Internet, you must provide support for address translation so that communications can be returned to the internal clients.

 The existence of routing services as part of remote access may seem strange. However, many remote access services require some routing to successfully pass packets from remote clients to internal network locations.

Each of these routing services is further explained in the sections that follow. We'll start with IP Multicast support.

IP Multicast Support

As indicated, routing support of all types may be required as a result of the remote access services that are provided, or when routing on a network is required but a separate routing device is not available. RRAS can be configured to use the Internet Group Management Protocol (IGMP) to support multicast routing. Once configured, the IGMP router forwards multicast traffic to listening devices on other networks, but it will not forward multicast traffic to networks where no multicast devices are listening. Use multicast forwarding only while routing with RRAS IGMP when you want to forward multicast traffic on a single-router network, or when you wish to forward multicast traffic between a single-router network and the Internet.

There are three versions of IGMP: Version 1 (as described in RFC 1112, *Host Extensions for IP Multicasting*), Version 2 (as described in RFC 2236, *Internet Group Management Protocol, Version 2*), and Version 3 (as described in RFC 3376, *Internet Group Management Protocol version 3*). In addition to the basic operations of Versions 1 and 2, Version 3 provides support for setting multicast boundaries to limit the receipt of multicast messages. More information on multicast boundaries is presented in the section "Configuring multicast boundaries" later in this chapter. Windows Server 2003 supports Version 3.

Understanding multicast components

Obviously, multicast support consists of two components: forwarding and routing.

The *forwarding component* provides the following services:

- The RRAS server configured for IGMP listens for multicast traffic. When multicast traffic is received, TCP/IP uses a multicast forwarding table to determine which (if any) of the network interfaces it should transfer the packet to. Traffic is either forwarded to another process running on the router, or to network segments that contain multicast group members (or downstream routers with interfaces that contain multicast group members).

- Locally attached networks send IGMP Host Membership Report messages. The information from these reports is added to a list of information. The list tracks the receiver network (that is, the IP network ID of a network segment on which there are listening multicast nodes) and the multicast group (that is, the multicast address registered by a listening node) pairs.

- The IGMP router queries each network for current multicast device information, and receives IGMP Host Membership Report messages. The TCP/IP multicast forwarding table is updated.

The *routing component* is responsible for the propagation of the multicast group listening information. Multicast routing protocols such as Distance Vector Multicast Routing Protocol (DVMRP) are not provided by RRAS. However, you can configure RRAS IGMP in routing mode and proxy mode to provide multicast forwarding between networks on a single-router network, or between a single-router intranet and the Internet.

On a single-router-intranet, all RRAS interfaces should be configured in IGMP routing mode. Multicast forwarding support will be provided for all multicast sources and listening hosts on any network.

To provide multicast support between Internet hosts and hosts on the single-router network, the intranet-facing interface of the RRAS router must be connected to a multicast-capable router on the Internet, which is a member of the Internet multicast backbone (a series of routers designated to route multicast traffic on the Internet:

Mbone). The RRAS Internet interface must then be configured in proxy mode, while all other interfaces are in router mode. In router mode, IGMP listens for IGMP Host Membership Report packets and tracks group membership. In proxy mode, IGMP sends IGMP Host Membership Report messages received on all other interfaces running in IGMP router mode to the upstream router. The upstream router adds these report messages to its multicast tables and, therefore, knows where to route multicast messages it may receive for hosts listening on networks behind the IGMP proxy mode router.

Figure 8-1 shows this arrangement. In the figure, note that the IGMP proxy mode router interface is connected to the Mbone router. When RRAS is used in this manner, it provides for the sharing of multicast traffic between a local intranet and hosts on the Internet.

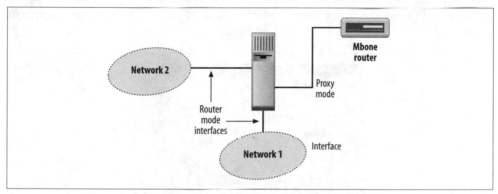

Figure 8-1. IGMP proxy mode and router mode interfaces combined to route LAN multicast listeners to an upstream router

Table 8-1 shows the services provided by the RRAS IGMP routing protocol component. The first column shows multicast services. The second column indicates whether the service is part of the forwarding or routing component. The third column identifies the Windows Server 2003 component that can provide this service.

Table 8-1. Multicast services

Multicast service	Forwarding or routing	Provided by
Listen for and forward multicast traffic	Forwarding	TCP/IP protocol
Listen for IGMP Host Membership Report and update TCP/IP multicast forwarding table	Forwarding	Network interface on which IGMP routing protocol is configured in router mode
Propagate multicast group listening information to other multicast-capable routers	Routing	Network interface on which IGMP is configured in proxy mode

Adding the IGMP services to RRAS

Adding an IGMP router and/or proxy mode services to RRAS is a three-step process. IGMP must be added, the RRAS server interfaces must be enabled for either router or proxy mode, and then any additional routing configuration is added.

To add IGMP to RRAS, begin by clicking Start, then Administrative Tools, and then clicking Routing and Remote Access to open the console. Right-click the General node and then select New Routing Protocol. Click IGMP Router and Proxy and then click OK.

To configure IGMP in router or proxy mode, begin by opening Routing and Remote Access. Right-click IGMP and then select New Interface. In the Details pane, click the interface on which IGMP should be enabled and click OK. Click the General tab, and note that the Enable IGMP checkbox is selected. Enable either router or proxy mode by clicking the appropriate radio button in the Mode box, as shown in Figure 8-2.

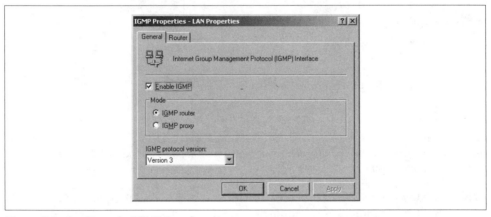

Figure 8-2. Configure the IGMP interface as router or proxy

To configure IGMP router properties, begin by opening Routing and Remote Access. Select the IGMP node. In the Details pane, right-click the interface and select Properties. Select the Router tab, as shown in Figure 8-3, and make any necessary changes.

Is it really appropriate to share all multicast traffic between the Internet and your intranet? Do you want to forward multicast traffic to all subnets on your LAN? These are questions you should answer after examining the requirements you have for forwarding multicast traffic on your network and after examining the risk of doing so. Let's take a look at how you can impose some controls on multicasting.

Configuring multicast boundaries

As previously mentioned, the Windows Server 2003 implementation of IGMP (which supports IGMP Version 3) can be configured to honor *multicast boundaries*,

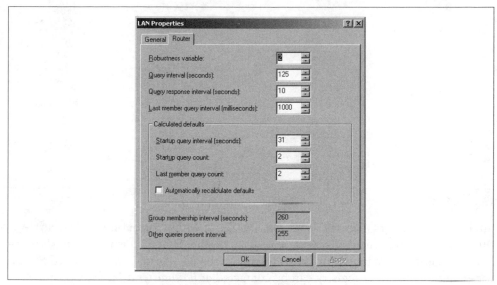

Figure 8-3. Adjust Router properties

which are barriers to multicast forwarding. In cases in which you have unrestrained multicast forwarding, all appropriate multicast traffic (that is, only traffic destined for listening hosts located on a network) is forwarded to that network. Multicast boundaries reduce the amount of multicast traffic by specifying either a range of IP addresses (known as a *multicast scope*) or a Time-to-Live (TTL). Setting the TTL limits the amount of time multicast traffic from a specific address

The multicast scope prevents the forwarding of multicast packets based on a multicast group or a range of IP addresses. Multiple scopes can be defined, and multiple scopes can then be assigned to the interface over which you want to set the boundary. The TTL boundary prevents the passing of multicast packets with a TTL less than the specified value. Only one TTL boundary can be set per interface.

To define a multicast scope, begin by opening the Routing and Remote Access node. Right-click the General node and click Properties. Select the Multicast Scopes tab, as shown in Figure 8-4. Click the Add button to add a scope. Use the Add Scoped Boundary dialog box to add a scope name, the base address of the IP range, and the mask of the range.

The range of appropriate addresses for multicast addressing will depend on whether they are used on your internal intranet (called *Administrative scoping*) or on the Internet (called *Global scoping*). Administrative scoping uses the 239.132.0.0 range of class D addressing with a mask of 255.253.0.0. More information on IP addressing is included in Chapter 1 of this book and in RFC 2365, *Administratively Scoped IP Multicast*. Global scoping addresses use the 233.0.0.0 range of the multicast address space. This is composed of a combination of the first 8 bits (the 233) as specified by

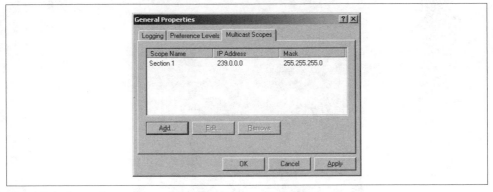

Figure 8-4. Create Scopes for use in setting multicast boundaries

an Internet network registry (such as IANA), a 16-bit Autonomous System (AS) number, and 8 bits chosen by you. The mask of 255.255.255.0 is used. An AS number is obtained from the appropriate Internet network registry. In the United States, for example, the ARIN registry can be contacted at *hostmaster.arin.net*. Consult RFC 1930, *Guidelines for creation, selection, and registration of an Autonomous System (AS)*, for more information.

If you need to define other scopes, click the Add button and use the Add Scoped Boundary dialog box. If you are finished adding scopes, Click OK to close the dialog box.

To configure a multicast boundary using the multicast scope, begin by opening the Routing and Remote Access node. Select the General node and right-click the interface on which you want to set the boundary. Select Properties and then select the Multicast Boundaries tab, as shown in Figure 8-5. Use the drop-down Scope list to select a scope.

As you can see in the lower half of Figure 8-5, you can also set the boundary by using the TTL. When you set the TTL you are limiting the number of links through which a packet can travel. This prevents multicast traffic that must be routed across a number of routers while it allows traffic that travels a more direct route. To set the TTL, select the "Activate TTL boundary" checkbox. You can then set a TTL value by entering a number in the "TTL value" field. Setting a rate limit can prevent the router from being overwhelmed by a lot of multicast traffic sent over a short period of time. To set a rate limit, enter the maximum number of kilobytes per second that are to be allowed in the "Rate limit (KBps)" field. If the Rate limit is set to 0, the amount of kilobytes per second is not restricted. Both "TTL value" and "Rate limit (KBps)" can be used together to restrict multicast traffic.

When you have finished setting the multicast boundary, click OK to accept your changes and close the Properties page.

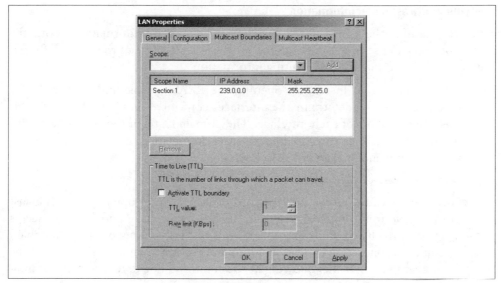

Figure 8-5. Add the scope to the Multicast Boundaries page

Configuring multicast heartbeats

You can configure RRAS to listen for the regular multicast notifications (or *heartbeats*) to a group address. These notifications verify that IP multicast connectivity is available. Heartbeats can be monitored on a specific network interface (for example, the Internet-facing network card or intranet-facing network card). When heartbeats are monitored and RRAS does not receive this notification, it flags the associated interface and sets multicast status on that interface to inactive. A network monitoring tool or a programmed notification event can then be used to alert an administrator that a problem has occurred. For example, if you have implemented an SNMP monitoring tool on the network, you might write a script that sends an SNMP trap to the SNMP management station if the status is inactive. Consult your SNMP monitoring tool documentation for instructions on how to do so.

To configure heartbeat support on a specific interface, begin by opening the Routing and Remote Access node. Select the General node. Right-click the interface you want to configure and then select Properties. From the ensuing screen (see Figure 8-5), select the Multicast Heartbeat tab. Select the Enable Multicast Heartbeat Detection checkbox. Enter the IP address of the multicast heartbeat group in the Multicast heartbeat group field. Click the arrows in the Quiet Time Before Alerting (minutes) field to set the number of minutes after which a heartbeat is not detected before alerting. When you have finished configuring the heartbeat, click OK to close the Properties page.

Once you have set up RRAS services and configured boundaries and heartbeats, you can check on the status of the router by using a couple of Windows tools.

Querying multicast router information

You can examine the RRAS IGMP interface to determine information about the router, or you can use two command-line tools to obtain some of this same information, as well as additional IGMP routing information.

The first tool is mrinfo. Instead of opening the RRAS console and inspecting the interfaces, use mrinfo to determine the interfaces configured on the multicast router, as well as the neighbors of each interface. The domain name of the neighbor, multicast routing metric, TTL threshold, and other information is displayed. To run mrinfo at the command line, enter the following:

    Mrinfo *IP-address-of-the-router*

You could display entries in the multicast forwarding table by opening the Multicast Forwarding Table from the RRAS console. (Open the Routing and Remote Access console, expand the IGMP node and select Multicast Forwarding to open the table.) Or, you could use one of several netsh commands to display information about the router. For example, enter the following at the command line to display a list of multicast forwarding entries (mfe):

    Netsh routing ip show mfe

To display packet statistics and interface information for entries in the table, you could open the RRAS Multicast Statistic table from the Routing and Remote Access node by right-clicking General, and then clicking Show Multicast Statistics. Or you could enter the following at the command line:

    Netsh routing ip show mfestats

And finally, to use the netsh command to view multicast groups locally joined on an interface, you would enter the following at the command line:

    Netsh interface ip show joins

IGMP routing is one service provided by RRAS. It allows you to route multicast packets between hosts on your intranet, or between hosts on your intranet and those on the Internet. Other data that may need to be routed between networks (but is not commonly done) are the DHCP messages used by hosts to request an IP address and DHCP servers to respond to that request. While DHCP messages are not commonly routed between networks, the RRAS DHCP Relay Agent is used to transfer DHCP messages between server and host across network boundaries.

Configuring the DHCP Relay Agent

As mentioned, RRAS provides the DHCP Relay Agent in order to relay DHCP messages between IP networks. This is necessary when DHCP clients are on a different IP network than the DHCP server from which they need to request an IP address. The DHCP Relay Agent must be enabled on each interface that lies between DHCP clients and their DHCP server. Figure 8-6 illustrates a single router network where

---

the DHCP server sits on one IP network, and DHCP clients are on three of the four IP networks.

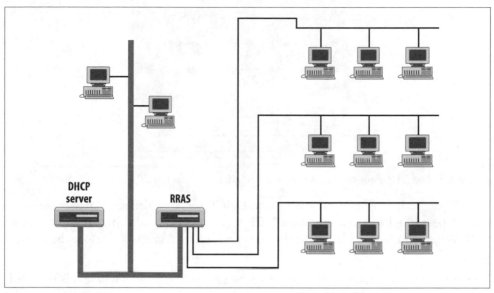

Figure 8-6. The RRAS server can serve as a DHCP proxy, enabling a single DHCP server to services multiple networks

 The DHCP Relay Agent is compliant with RFC 1542, *Clarifications and Extensions for the Bootstrap Protocol.*

To configure the DHCP Relay Agent, you must first add the DHCP Relay Agent to RRAS, configure its properties, and then enable DHCP on all appropriate interfaces.

First, add the DHCP Relay Agent to RRAS. Open the Routing and Remote Access console, expand the IP Routing node, right-click General, and then click New Routing Protocol. Click DHCP Relay Agent and then click OK. When the DHCP Relay Agent node appears, select the node, then right-click it and click Properties. On the General tab, add the IP address of the DHCP server to the "Server address" text box and click Add, as shown in Figure 8-7.

Best practices suggest that more than one DHCP server should be available on the network. While many DHCP servers might be used, the most common configuration is two. In this scenario, part of the available address range is configured on one DHCP server and the other part on the second. This provides redundancy. If one server is down, the other server can respond to requests for IP addresses. In some networks, multiple IP address ranges are used, one for each available network. If necessary, the DHCP relay service can be used to route messages to any or all DHCP

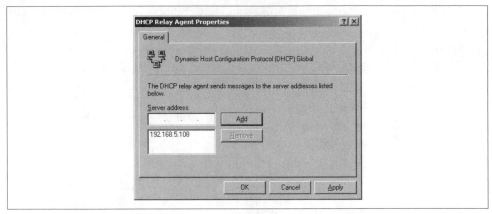

Figure 8-7. The DHCP proxy must be given the IP address of the DHCP server

servers as needed. After configuring one DHCP server address, if DHCP messages should be routed to an additional DHCP server, you can add their IP addresses as well. When you have added all of the server addresses, click OK to close the Properties page.

The next step is to enable DHCP to relay the network interfaces where it is required. To do so, right-click the DHCP Relay Agent node and click New Interface. Click the interface that you want to add and click OK. The General property page for DHCP Relay on the interface will be displayed. On the General page as shown in Figure 8-8, ensure that the "Relay DHCP packets" checkbox is selected. Modify the "Hop-count threshold" and "Boot threshold (seconds)" if required. Click OK to close the Properties pages.

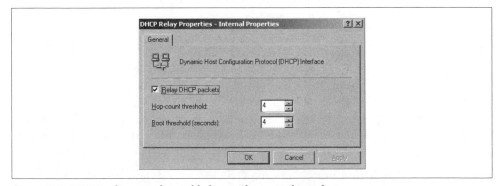

Figure 8-8. DHCP relay must be enabled on each required interface

 A DHCP Relay Agent cannot be installed and utilized on a Windows Server 2003 server configured to be a DHCP server, a NAT server, or Internet Connection Sharing (ICS) server.

RRAS provides the DHCP Relay server to transfer a specific type of packet (DHCP messages) from network to network. The Routing Information Protocol (RIP) is a more general routing protocol that can also be configured. Use RIP to allow network detection and automatic routing table configuration for RRAS servers.

Configuring RIP Version 2 for IP

Routing Information Protocol (RIP) for IP can be implemented to route and share routing information on a small to medium-sized network. RIP is easy to configure; however, its maximum hop count is 15, which limits its usefulness to networks with 15 or fewer routers. RIP announcements can also be a source of excessive traffic, and changes in routing are slow to propagate. RIP announcements communicate RIP routing table information to other RIP routers. Each RIP router updates its routing tables based on its local interface information, as well as the information received in announcements from other RIP routers.

RIP Version 2 announcements are made using multicast or broadcast, while RIP Version 1 routers use IP broadcast packets. RIP Version 2 provides other features not offered in RIP Version 1. For example, RIP Version 2 supports classless interdomain routing (CIDR) and variable length subnet masks (VLSM), two features often used in modern networks that are not supported by RIP Version 1. RIP Version 2 also offers an authentication feature. By default, RIP automatically updates its knowledge of the network based on messages from any RIP router. When authentication is used, a RIP router will only accept routing messages from those RIP routers that can provide the correct password. RIP Version 2 routing can be implemented using RRAS and is compatible with RIP Version 1 routers that may already be a part of your intranet. While periodic announcements keep RIP routers informed of accessible networks, changes in network topology can also trigger immediate RIP announcements.

The next section takes a look at the various options you have when configuring RIP interface properties.

Configuring general RIP properties

To implement RIP you must add the protocol, configure interfaces, and apply security for RIP. To add and configure RIP interfaces, begin by opening the Routing and Remote Access node. Select RIP. Right-click RIP and click New Interface. Select the interface on which you want to configure RIP and click OK.

You should now see the Properties page shown in Figure 8-9. Select the General tab.

The first drop-down list, "Operation mode," provides the following options:

Auto-static mode
> RIP routing information obtained from other RIP routers may be stored in memory and lost when the RIP router is stopped. To ensure retention of this information (which will speed up the process of returning to normal operation after a

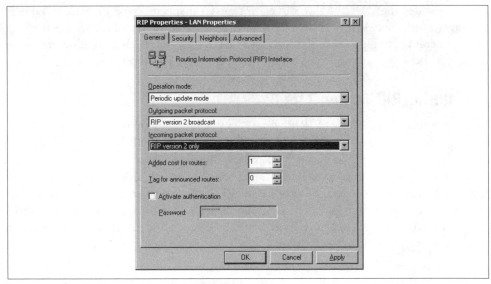

Figure 8-9. RIP can be configured to work only with other RIP Version 2 routers

restart), configure auto-static updates. When auto-static updates are configured, routing information received from other routers is automatically stored and is available after the RIP router is restarted. Auto-static mode is configured by selecting the auto-static update mode box on the General property page of each RIP interface.

Periodic update mode

This option allows you to tune a periodic update, as well as adjust the times for an announcement interval (how often an announcement is made), a route expiration time (when the route expires), and a route-removal time. To configure this mode, select "Periodic update mode," then enter the tuning information on the Advanced property page as described in the section "Configuring advanced RIP routing properties" later in this chapter.

The next field on the screen is the "Outgoing packet protocol" drop-down. Your choice here depends on the presence of RIP Version 1 routers on the same network as the interface and whether you want to use Silent RIP. (Silent RIP is explained in the following section, "Configuring Silent RIP mode.") If only RIP Version 1 routers are present, select "RIP version 1 broadcast." If RIP Version 1 routers are present, select "RIP version 2 broadcast." If there are no RIP Version 1 routers present, select "RIP version 2 multicast." If silent RIP is desired, select Silent RIP.

Toward the middle of the screen, click the "Incoming packet protocol" drop-down. Your selection here depends on whether RIP Version 1 routers are on the same network as the interface. If RIP Version 1 routers are present, select "RIP version 1 and 2." If RIP Version 1 routers are not present, select "RIP version 2 Only."

Hop count is the default method of comparison used when deciding the optimal route to take when routing a packet. The decision on the route to use when the packet is forwarded is based on the hop count, or the number of routers that will have to be traversed before reaching the packet's destination address network. Hop count by itself, however, is misleading because it does not take into account the speed of the network connection between routers. A router accessible across a slow link has a hop count equal to a router accessible across a high-speed link.

RIP Version 2 provides an alternative method for determining the route chosen: *cost*. This is a number that is based on the speed of the network connection and one that can be assigned to a route. Thus, because a high-speed connection is given a lower cost than a slow-speed connection, and because the lowest cost is preferred, the high-speed connection will be selected. Cost is configured in the "Added cost for routes" field.

The "Tag for announced routes" box is used to provide information for the "Route tag" field of the RIP message. This field is only used when specific routes are marked for administrative purposes. As defined in RFC 1723, *RIP Version 2, Carrying Additional Information*, it might be used to distinguish RIP routes from non-RIP routes. For more information see the RFC.

The last two items under the General tab are a checkbox for authentication and a field for a password. When authentication is configured, a RIP router must authenticate to another RIP router before router announcements will be processed. Announcements received from unauthenticated hosts are dropped. All RIP routers on the network must use matching passwords. RIP authentication is only possible for RIP Version 2 routers. If any RIP Version 1 routers are present and must share routing information with RIP Version 2 routers, do not configure authentication.

You can activate authentication by clicking in the "Activate authentication" checkbox. You must then enter a password in the Password field.

 RIP passwords are sent in clear text. A network sniffer can be used to capture the RIP packets and view the password. In a trusted network, RIP authentication can help prevent corruption of RIP routing table information. In a hostile environment, you must apply additional security. You could also encrypt RIP traffic using IPSec (see Chapter 1 for more information on IPSec).

Configuring Silent RIP mode

Silent RIP hosts receive RIP announcements and adjust their routing table but do not make their own RIP announcements. Silent RIP hosts are often used in Unix environments. To enable Silent RIP mode in RRAS, select Silent RIP from the "Outgoing packet protocol" box on the General properties page of the RRAS RIP interface shown in Figure 8-9. If unicast mode is configured, then you will need to identify the silent RIP hosts as RRAS RIP neighbors.

Configuring RIP security properties

Routing information is critical to the operation of your network. Securing access to this information is an important step toward ensuring that routing will operate correctly, and that internal routing information is not made available to untrusted RIP routers. To secure RIP routing, you must configure authentication, restrict router communications (by creating RIP peer lists and route filters), and restrict announcements to neighboring RIP routers. *Authentication* is the process by which a security principal (a user, device, or process) provides proof of identity. In this case, it is the router that must prove its identity to another router.

By default, each RIP interface accepts RIP messages from other RIP routers on its network and forwards its own routing table contents to other RIP routers. Blindly accepting routing information from untrusted sources is not a good security practice, nor is blindly sharing internal routing information with untrusted sources. A rogue (or improperly configured) RIP router could send incorrect information to your RIP router and either redirect communications to its own hosts, or it could simply prevent packets from getting to the correct hosts.

Your internal routing information might provide an attacker with the information needed to compromise internal systems. Configure the following items to further secure RIP announcements:

- To prevent a rogue RIP router from modifying the routing tables of the RIP router, configure a list of RIP peers (that is, RIP routers from which routing messages will be accepted).

- Configure route filters to limit internal routing information knowledge to trusted RIP routers and to limit the routers to which routing messages will be sent.

- To further restrict incoming and outgoing RIP announcements, configure route filters and limit outgoing route announcements.

To configure security for the RIP router begin by opening the Routing and Remote Access node. Select and then right-click the RIP node. Select Properties, and then select the Security tab. To configure RIP peers and limit the acceptance of router announcements to specific routers click the "Accept announcements from listed routers only" radio button and add trusted router IP addresses to the Router IP Address list by using the Add button, as shown in Figure 8-10.

To identify routers from which announcements should be ignored, click the "Ignore announcements from all listed routers" radio button and then add untrusted router IP addresses to the Router IP Address list by using the Add button.

Configuring route filters for specific RIP interfaces means going back to the familiar Properties page for the interface. Begin by opening the Routing and Remote Access

---

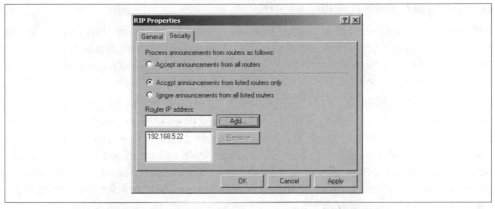

Figure 8-10. Limit the RIP routers from which this router will accept announcements

node. Select the RIP node then right-click the interface and select Properties. Select the Security tab. Select the "For incoming routes" option from the Action drop-down list box. To accept all incoming routes in a listed range, click the "Accept all routes in the ranges listed" radio button and add the routes to be accepted using the Add button, as shown in Figure 8-11.

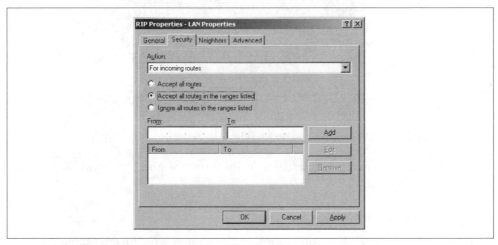

Figure 8-11. Define ranges for routes accepted by this router

To ignore specific incoming routes, click the "Ignore all routes in the ranges listed" radio button and add the routes to be ignored using the Add button.

We've now examined two of the tabs appearing on the RIP interface Properties page (General and Security). Let's take a look at the final two tabs, Neighbors and Advanced.

Configuring RIP neighbors routing properties

RIP announcements are broadcast or multicast and may be received by any node. To restrict RIP announcements, configure the RIP router to use unicast announcements. To do so, you must identify RIP neighbors, which is accomplished using the familiar Properties page.

To identify RIP neighbors and configure announcement mode, begin by expanding the Routing and Remote Access node. Select the RIP node then right-click the interface and select Properties. Select the Neighbors tab, as shown in Figure 8-12. To disable the use of neighbors, click "Use broadcast or multicast only." To use neighboring routers in addition to broadcast or multicast, click "Use neighbors in addition to broadcast or multicast." To use unicast only, click "User neighbors instead of broadcast or multicast."

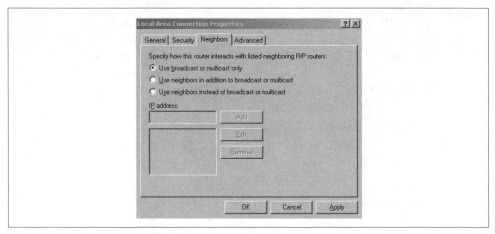

Figure 8-12. Configure RIP neighbors on the neighbor property page

To add neighbors, enter the IP address of the neighbor and click Add. Repeat this step for each neighbor.

Configuring advanced RIP routing properties

Routing problems such as routing loops (a situation in which router table information routes packets in a loop instead of to their destination) slow network recovery when topology changes occur, and excessive RIP broadcasts can be avoided by configuring advanced RIP routing properties on the Advanced property page. To do so, begin by expanding the Routing and Remote Access node. Select the RIP node, then right-click the interface. Select Properties and then click on the Advanced tab, as shown in Figure 8-13.

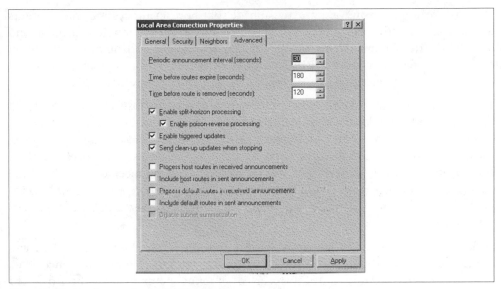

Figure 8-13. Configure advanced RIP properties

To configure the properties, enter the appropriate number, or check the box as described here. To configure routing properties for periodic update processing mode, configure the settings for the following:

Periodic announcement interval
   The amount of time in seconds between announcements

Time before routes expire
   The seconds after which a route will expire

Time before route is removed
   The seconds after which a route is removed from the routing list

Split-horizon processing is used to prevent unnecessary RIP announcements (which may be announcements of routing changes being announced back to the RIP router from which they came, or when both triggered and periodic announcements are made). When split-horizon processing is enabled, an announced change will not be made on the link from which the change was received. However, in a multiple RIP router network (where many links between routers exist), it is possible that a change might propagate back to the original RIP router by some other route. This can cause instability and inefficiencies in routing. Split-horizon processing improves efficiency when both announcement modes (periodic and triggered) are used. In this situation, it is possible that one or the other might not make any adjustment to the routing tables of the RIP router. If split-horizon processing detects that a change has already been announced, the duplicate announcement is not made.

To enable or disable split-horizon processing, check or un-check the "Enable split horizon processing" checkbox on the Advanced tab of the interface Properties pages.

Poison-reverse processing is an extension of split-horizon processing that prevents announcements from being sent to the router that originally announced them, and sets the metric to infinity. This corrects the gap left by split-horizon processing when multiple routers and links exist. To enable poison-reverse processing, check the "Enable poison-reverse processing" box on the Advanced properties page.

Host routes are routes used to route information to specific hosts on an intranet and are not included by default in outgoing messages, or processed by default if received in incoming messages. You can, however, have RIP include host routes in outgoing messages and process them if received in incoming messages. To process received host routes click the "Process host routes in received announcements" box on the Advanced properties page. To include host routes in outgoing RIP announcements click the "Process host routes in sent announcements" box on the Advanced properties page.

A default route is a route that can be used if no route is found for a network. These are not processed by default. To process default routes in received announcements click the Process default routes in received announcements box on the Advanced properties page. To include default routes in outgoing RIP announcements click the Include default routes in sent announcements box on the Advanced properties page.

Subnet summarization is a property of RIP Version 2. It is only available when classless routing (subnet mask or prefix-length information is included with IP address) is used. When this is the case, RIP Version 2 does not include every subnet available on a network, but lists instead only the network address. This reduces the amount of information that must be communicated in RIP messages, as well as the size of the routing table for routers. In flat routing schemes, every subnet must be included, even if the same gateway address to multiple subnets is used. This feature is enabled by default if RIP 2 multicast is configured. To disable this feature check the "Disable subnet summarization" box on the Advanced property page. This option is grayed out when RIP is configured for RIP Version 1 networks or mixed RIP Version 1 and Version 2 networks.

When you are finished configuring RIP click the OK button to close Properties pages.

RIP is not the only generic routing protocol supported by RRAS. A more efficient routing protocol, Open Shortest Path First (OSPF), is also available.

Configuring Open Shortest Path First (OSPF)

OSPF is a better routing protocol than RIP for exchanging routing information in a large network. It is more efficient than RIP, but more complex to configure and administer. OSPF uses the shortest path first algorithm to compute routes. This algorithm computes the least-cost path between the router and all other routers. It will not include any route loops.

Whereas RIP routers exchange route information via announcements, OSPF routers maintain a map (the *link state database*) of the network topology and update it after changes have been made. Link state database information is updated via synchronization carried out by OSPF neighbors configured in an adjacency, which is a logical relationship between routers created for this purpose. When changes are received, OSPF routers recalculate their routing tables.

In a large OSPF network, link state database information is segmented into *areas* (or collections of contiguous networks). Each OSPF router only keeps the database for those areas that it is connected to. When the router needs to route packets outside of these areas, it forwards packets to area border routers (ABRs) for forwarding. Figure 8-14 illustrates multiple OSPF areas linked via ABRs.

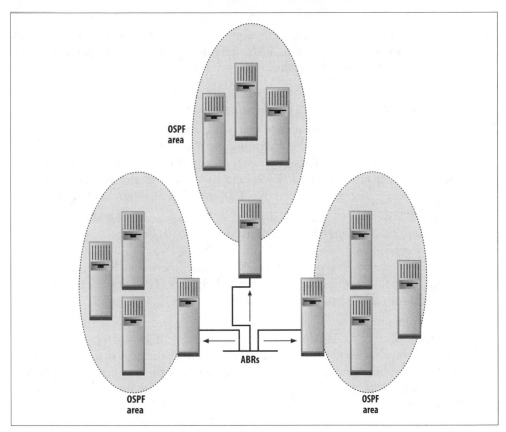

Figure 8-14. OSPF areas can be linked by area border routers

OSPF can be implemented in a small network by adding OSPF interfaces to the OSPF node in RRAS. The default settings of OSPF are designed to support a single-area OSPF network and the advanced planning necessary for a multiple-area OSPF network is not necessary. More planning steps should be considered when deploying an OSPF routed network.

While the design of an OSPF network is beyond the scope of this book, knowledge of these components (as well as the network information) is important when configuring OSPF routers implemented in RRAS. You should consult with network administrators responsible for OSPF routing administration to obtain these settings.

 Since OSPF is designed to be a more efficient routing protocol, many of its advantages can be gained with little extra configuration in a small network by accepting the default configurations. These defaults are defined in the RRAS help files under the topic *Deploying a Single-Area OSPF Internetwork*.

You should, however, be knowledgeable about the requirements for more complex OSPF networks in order to determine if the default settings are appropriate for your network. In a large network, this includes the following:

Subdividing the network into OSPF areas and assigning area IDs
   OSPF areas are simply a group of contiguous networks.

Identifying autonomous system boundary routers (ASBRs)
   In OSPF, routers that serve the areas of your network only advertise and maintain internal routes. When data must be routed outside of your network, a boundary router must be used. Each area router knows the addresses of these routers. These routers are called ASBRs, and they maintain external routing information.

Determining and configuring the network types used, such as broadcast, point-to-point, or Non-Broadcast Multiple Access (NBMA)
   NBMA networks are a type of Frame Relay-based network. For more information on network types, see the RRAS OSPF help files. The network type must be configured for each interface that will participate in OSPF routing.

Identifying virtual links
   A virtual link must be created when a physical link does not exist between an area and boundary routers. The *virtual link* identifies the area that does not have a physical link and one that does. The area without the physical connection to the ABR will route its link state database messages across the area to the physical connection.

Determining the backbone areas and identifying the ABRs
   Backbone areas are connections between ABRs that will enable communication between OSPF areas.

Identifying stub areas
   Routing information for most areas includes all of the possible routable networks within the area. In contrast, a *stub area* lists a single entrance point, or

network that is advertised. All hosts within the area can be reached by routing to this point. The use of stub areas, where possible, limits the amount of routing information that floods the network.

Once you have identified this information, you can add OSPF through the RRAS console and configure the OSPF interface.

Subdividing the network into OSPF areas

To add OSPF in the RRAS Console, begin by expanding the Routing and Remote Access node. Click the General node. Right-click General and select New Routing Protocol. Select Open Shortest Path First (OSPF) and click OK.

If your network will have multiple OSPF areas, you must configure the OSPF areas. Right-click the OSPF node and click Properties. Select the Areas tab and click Add.

On the General tab shown in Figure 8-15, enter the dotted decimal number that identifies the area in the Area ID box. Select the "Enable plaintext password" box. To mark the area as a stub, select the "Stub area" checkbox. Set the "Stub metric" and select the "Import summary advertisements" checkbox to import routes of other areas into the stub area.

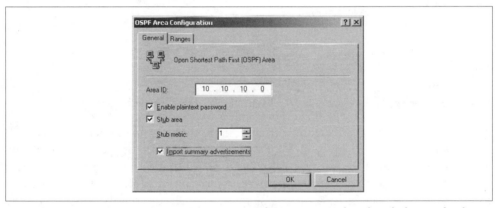

Figure 8-15. Create OSPF Areas to manage groups of OSPF routers that share link state database information

 While configuring your own password can help prevent other routers from corrupting routing data (by adding routes from unauthorized routers on the network), the use of a plain text password means that it can be discovered by using a sniffer to capture and analyze the router messages. To protect the password, and other communications between routers, the data can be encrypted by setting up an IPSec policy between the routers.

Select the Ranges tab and enter the destination network ID and network mask. Then click Add. Repeat the process for each range.

Identifying ASBRs

In a multiple-area OSPF network, you must enable ASBR and filter route sources. Begin by opening the Routing and Remote Access node. Right-click the OSPF node and select Properties. On the General tab, click "Enable autonomous system boundary router." Select the External Routing tab, as shown in Figure 8-16. Select either "Accept routes from all route sources except those selected" or "Ignore route sources except those selected." Select or clear the appropriate boxes below "Route sources."

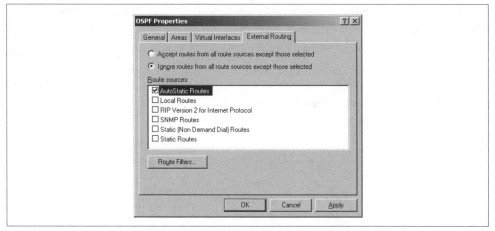

Figure 8-16. Restrict the acceptance of routes by configuring route sources

ABSRs receive routing information from routers that are not under your control. *Route filters* are used to prevent the use of or allow the use of specific routes. The external routing information that is received may include routes that you do not choose to use because of their congestion or the control of the routers used along those routes. You can exclude the use of specific routes, or identify only the specific routes that should be used by setting route filters.

To add route filters, begin by opening the Routing and Remote Access node, then right-click the OSPF node and select Properties. Select the External Routing tab and click the Route Filters button. Select either "Ignore listed routes" or "Accept listed routes," as shown in Figure 8-17. Be sure you understand the difference between these two choices and select the appropriate one. "Ignore listed routes" allows you to specify those routes that will be filters. All others will be accepted. On the other hand, "Accept listed routes" allows you to specify the only routes that will be accepted; all others will be ignored., Add the Destination network address and Network mask for the networks to filter Click OK to close the page, then click OK to close the OSPF Properties pages.

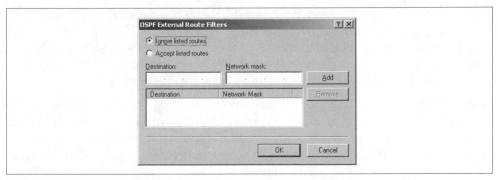

Figure 8-17. Add route filters

Configuring network type

To add and configure an OSPF interface, begin by expanding the Routing and Remote Access node. Select the OSPF node, right-click the node and select New Interface. Select the interface on which OSPF routing should be configured and then click OK. The General property page will be displayed, as shown in Figure 8-18.

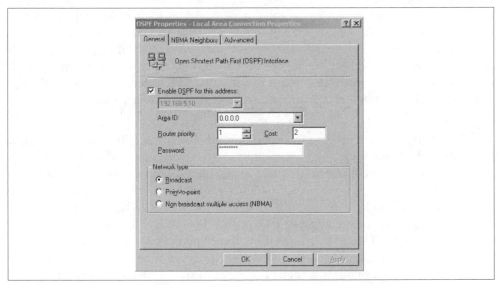

Figure 8-18. Configure the OSPF interface for each RRAS interface where it will be used

The "Enable OSPF for this address" box is preselected. If more than one IP address is available for this interface, use the drop-down box below it to select the address that OSPF will use. Use the Area ID drop-down list to select the Area ID. If more than one router will be used for this area, use the "Router priority" box to enter the priority for router use. Use lower priority numbers to indicate less busy routers. A lower number means the router will be selected before a router given a higher number. Use the Cost box to indicate a relative cost for the router. Cost is used to indicate possible speed, potential delays, or reliability issues. The idea is to identify the router that may get data to its destination faster. A low-cost router is faster and less likely to have issues that may slow communications. Enter a password in the Password box. The password is used by the router to authenticate to other routers.

Select a Network type: Broadcast, Point-to-point, or NBMA for this interface. If the interface is a single-adapter Frame Relay, X.25, or Asynchronous Transfer Mode (ATM) interface, select "Non-broadcast multiple access (NBMA)" and configure the Non-broadcast Multiple Access (NBMA) neighbors. NBMA neighbors are the routers with which this interface will communicate.

To configure NBMA neighbors, select the NBMA Neighbors tab. Enter the "Neighboring IP Address and router priority" and click the Add button. You will need to enter the IP address and router priority for each NBMA neighbor.

Identifying virtual links and backbone areas

In a multiple area OSPF network, areas are connected via physical links to area backbone routers. However, when a physical link is not possible, a virtual link can be configured. A virtual interface is another area that does have a physical connection with an ABR. The area without the physical connection to the ABR will route its link state database messages across the area to the physical connection. Figure 8-19 shows such a configuration. Here, area A has no physical connection, while area B does. Area A will use area B to connect to the ABR. The dotted line indicates the virtual connection between area A and the ABR. A virtual interface can only be configured if a nonstub area or nonbackbone area is configured.

To add a virtual interface, begin by expanding the Routing and Remote Access node. Right-click the OSPF node and then click Properties. Select the Virtual Interfaces tab then click Add. In the "Transit area ID" area, use the drop-down box to select the transit area ID (an OSPF area, over which you will connect the virtual link). The areas configured for this router will be listed for your selection. In the "Virtual Neighbor router ID" box, enter the OSPF router ID of the routers at the opposite virtual link endpoint. The OSPF router ID is the IP address of the router that will be used for the virtual link endpoint. A *virtual link endpoint* is a router that has a physical connection to a boundary router. A number of transit parameters are set to reasonable defaults and should not be changed until you evaluate how well routing is functioning. These parameters are as follows:

Transit delay
> The estimated time in seconds that it will take for the OSPF packets to reach a linked router.

Retransmit interval
> The time in seconds before another attempt is made if a communication is not received. This number should be larger than the round trip transit delay.

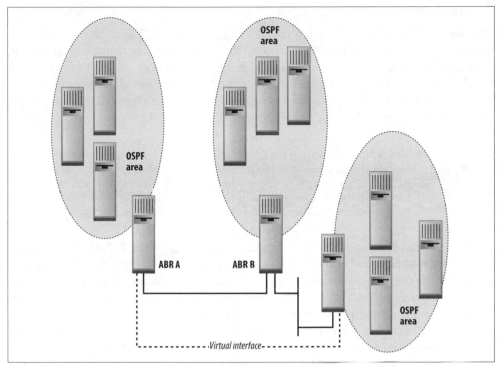

Figure 8-19. A virtual interface is created by linking two physical interfaces to provide access between two OSPF areas that do not share a physical connection

Hello interval

> The frequency at which a Hello message is sent. The default is 10 seconds.

Dead interval

> The amount of time during which no Hello message from an adjacent router is received. After this time the adjacent router is considered to be down. The default is 40 seconds. (An IETF draft recommendation suggests four times the Hello interval.)

If the backbone area is configured to have a password enter the password in the "Plaintext password" box. A password is often set by the administrator of the backbone area to prevent its unauthorized use. If you are not the backbone area administrator, you must obtain the password from the administrator.

To verify that a RRAS server is receiving OSPF announcements from all adjacent OSPF routers:

- View the routes available on the OSPF neighbors for the router by viewing their configuration information.

- Verify that all routes available on OSPF neighbors are included in the OSPF routing table.

Configuring security for OSPF

Like RIP, security for OSPF is improved by authentication. There are no configuration options for establishing route filters on individual interfaces since a dynamic link state database is automatically updated with information from all OSPF routers in an OSPF area. A rogue OSPF router cannot corrupt the link state database unless both its area ID and password match. To prevent corruption from external non-OSPF routers outside the OSPF area, establish route filters on ABRs.

 The default password for RRAS OSPF routers is 12345678 and should be changed. In addition, this password is sent in clear text and could be captured and read by using a sniffer. Additional security will be required to prevent corruption of the link state database information by rogue OSPF routers.

Both OSPF (the routing protocol discussed in this section) and RIP (the routing protocol discussed previously) provide a way to automatically update the routing tables of routers on the network so that it is possible to deliver data from any host on a network to any other host an any other network. However, it is sometimes advantageous (or even necessary) to translate the address of a host on one network to another address before routing data across networks. This is a common requirement when private network addressing is used on an internal network, and those hosts with private IP addresses need to communicate on the Internet. Network address translation (NAT) is a solution to this problem.

Network Address Translation (NAT)

When internal network addressing uses Internet Assigned Numbers Authority (IANA) private IP network IDs (as listed in Table 8-2), internal hosts cannot directly access other hosts on the Internet. Network Address Translation (NAT) can be used to provide Internet access for these local hosts. (See Chapter 2 for more information about IANA and NAT.) NAT works by replacing the outbound packet's source address with an Internet-routable address, and replacing an inbound packet's destination address with an internal private IP address. A table of communications is kept by NAT and, in normal operations only those inbound communications that are responses to outbound requests are translated and routed to the internal network.

Table 8-2. IANA private IP network IDS

Network ID	Subnet mast
10.0.0.0	255.0.0.0
172.16.0.0	255.240.0.0
192.168.0.0	255.255.255.0

If you are using addressing for your internal hosts that has not been assigned by IANA, or is not within the networks defined in Table 8-2, then you are using illegal or overlapping IP addresses. This means that you will not be able to reach hosts on the Internet to whom the IP addresses have been assigned. You should use only your assigned IP addresses or those from the IANA private IP network ID ranges.

To use NAT, you must perform the following steps:

1. Enable the service and configure it. This is the first step and is easily accomplished from the RRAS console.

2. Within the NAT node, create and configure network interfaces that will use NAT. A RRAS server has multiple network interfaces. Only configure the interfaces that should be used for NAT.

3. If required, create demand dial interfaces for dial-up connections. Demand dial interfaces allow data addressed to external networks to automatically initiate a connection.

4. Add a default static route and enable routing on the ports. A default static route is a route used when no other route is identified. A RRAS server is capable of managing multiple connections or ports. Routing must be enabled on those ports.

5. Secure the NAT server and allow inbound connections. Because the NAT server represents a connection between two networks, and in most cases this is a connection between a trusted and an untrusted network, the NAT server should be hardened to resist attacks.

Enabling and configuring NAT

You can enable and configure NAT by using the RRAS console. Begin by opening the Routing and Remote Access node. Right-click the IP Routing\General node and select New Routing Protocol. Select NAT/Basic Firewall and click OK. Right-click the NAT/Basic Firewall and select Properties. Select the Address Assignment tab.

By default, addresses are not assigned to hosts on the private network. To configure address assignment, click to select the box "Automatically assign IP addresses by using the DHCP allocator," then enter the network ID (IP address) and subnet mask (Mask) of the IP address range to assign, as shown in Figure 8-20.

You can exclude IP addresses in this range if the DHCP allocator is enabled. Click the Exclude button. Click Add to enter the IP address to exclude and then click OK. Repeat this process to add additional addresses. Click OK to close the Exclude Reserved Address dialog. You should exclude IP addresses if these addresses within the range assigned to the DHCP allocator are already statically assigned to devices on your network.

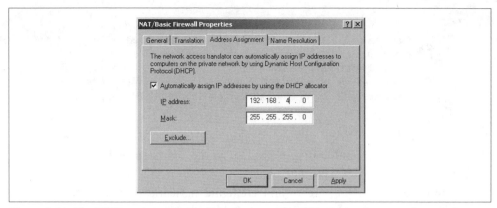

Figure 8-20. The NAT server can be configured to provide addresses for the internal network clients

To enable name resolution, first ensure that you are back at the NAT/Basic Firewall Properties screen. Select the Name Resolution tab and click Clients using Domain Name System (DNS). If an external DNS server should be used, click "Connect to the public network when a name needs to be resolved." If a demand dial-interface is used to reach the DNS server, select the demand-dial interface from the "Demand-dial interface" drop-down list. In most cases, you will want to enable name resolution so hosts on the internal network and the programs for which they might need to use NAT do not need to do their own name resolution. For example, most people enter Internet addresses in the form of a URL consisting of a web server domain name rather than an IP address. Without name resolution, the request will never be delivered to the correct server.

Creating and configuring NAT interfaces

You must configure two interfaces to configure NAT. One interface is on the internal network and the other is on the public interface. Begin by opening the Routing and Remote Access node. Right-click the IP Routing\NAT\Basic Firewall node and select New Interface. Select the internal interface on which to configure NAT then click OK. Select the interface type, "Private interface connected to private network," then click OK.

To configure the second interface, right-click the IP Routing\NAT\Basic Firewall node and select New Interface. Select the external interface on which to configure NAT then click OK. Select the "Public interface connected to the Internet" interface type. Select "Enable NAT on this interface" and then click OK.

Creating a Demand Dial interface for dial-up connections

If you are connecting to the Internet through a dial-up interface, configure a Demand Dial interface for the connection to the Internet. Demand Dial interfaces are configured from the Demand Dial Routing node.

Begin by opening the Routing and Remote Access node. In the RRAS console, right-click on the server and select Properties. Select "LAN and demand dial-routing," then click OK to close the server properties window. When prompted to allow the RRAS service to restart, click OK. Then, from the RRAS console, right-click Network Interfaces and click New Demand Dial Interface. Click Next on the Demand Dial Interface Wizard. Enter a name for the interface and click Next. Enter the IP address of the ISP and click Next. Check "Route IP packets on this interface" and click Next. Enter the username, domain, and password used to connect to your ISP and click Next. Then click Finish.

> Configuring Demand Dial interfaces for NAT over a dial-up connection is different from configuring Demand Dial interfaces for router-to-router VPN connections, but the principle will be the same—to automatically generate a connection to a remote router when the destination for traffic should be routed through that router. Information on Demand Dial interface configuration for VPNs is located in the section "Configuring and Using RRAS Demand-Dial VPN" later in this chapter.

Adding a default static route

A default static route must be added to provide the route to be used when no other route exists. To add a default static route for the NAT interface, begin by expanding the Routing and Remote Access node. Right-click Static Routes and click New Static Route. Click the "Interface to use for the default route." Use 0.0.0.0 for the Destination and use 0.0.0.0 for the Network mask. If the interface is a Demand Dial interface, select "Use this route to initiate demand-dial connections" checkbox. If the interface is for a LAN connection, enter a gateway address. Use the IP address of the router interface that is on the same network segment as the LAN interface. Figure 8-21 shows a completed static route.

Enabling routing on ports

You must enable routing on ports if you are using a dial-up connection. However, you do not need to enable routing on ports in the following situations:

- If the connection is a LAN interface (such as Frame Relay, permanent ISDN, xDSL, or cable modem)
- If the NAT server connects to another router before connecting to the Internet, and the LAN interface is configured with an IP address, subnet mask and default gateway

Figure 8-21. Add a static route

To enable routing on ports, begin by expanding the Routing and Remote Access node and then select Ports. Right-click Ports and click Properties. Select the Devices tab as shown in Figure 8-22. Click the device to configure and then click Configure. If the device is a modem used for demand dial connection to an ISP, select the checkbox "Demand-dial routing connections (outbound only)." Enter the phone number for the phone to be dialed in the "Phone number" box. If desired, limit the number of ports to be used by setting a number in the "Maximum ports box." Typically, the number of ports is limited to conserve limited resources. Click OK to close the page and apply the change.

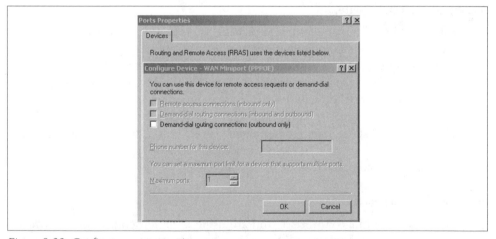

Figure 8-22. Configure port properties

Securing a NAT server

In addition to applying hardening for the NAT server, you can specify basic firewall settings by selecting "Enable a basic firewall on this interface" checkbox underneath the "Public interface connected to the Internet." The basic firewall configuration only accepts inbound packets that are in response to requests from the internal network. Hardening is defined as the process of applying all possible security configurations at the operating system level. A listing of hardening steps is beyond the scope of this book. A good reference is the book *Hardening Windows Systems* (Osborne-McGraw Hill). In addition, you should consult the security policy of your organization and keep up with current recommendations for securing Windows computers.

Allowing inbound connections

It is possible to allow inbound connections through a NAT server even if an outbound request has not been made. This then allows access to services such as a web server or mail server that sits behind a NAT server. Such connections should not be allowed without considering security. A NAT server is not a firewall, and though basic firewall ACLs can be configured on the RRAS server, a stronger defense via a dedicated firewall should be considered.

To configure NAT to allow a specific inbound connection, you must do the following:

- Assign the resource server a static IP address, and network mask from those assigned by the NAT server.
- Assign the private IP address of the NAT server as the resource server default gateway.
- Assign the private IP address of the NAT server as the resource server DNS server.
- Exclude the IP address assigned to the resource server from the range assigned by the NAT server.
- Configure a special port, or mapping of a public address assigned to the external interface of the NAT server and a port to the private address and port number of the resource server. This mapping is used to map an inbound request from an Internet user to a specific address on the internal network.

The first three steps we have discussed thus far represent TCP/IP configuration that is documented earlier in this book. The fourth step addresses the RRAS NAT configuration and is documented in the section "Enabling and configuring NAT" later in this chapter. The final step, configuring a special port on the NAT server, is detailed here.

To configure a special port on the NAT server, begin by opening the Routing and Remote Access node. Select the IP Routing\NAT\Basic Firewall node. Right-click the interface on which NAT is configured. In this case, we have renamed the network connection used for Internet connectivity as "Internet" and thus the properties page reflects this. Select the Services and Ports tab. On the page shown in Figure 8-23, select the service that exists on the private network and that you wish to grant external access. The Edit Service window will open.

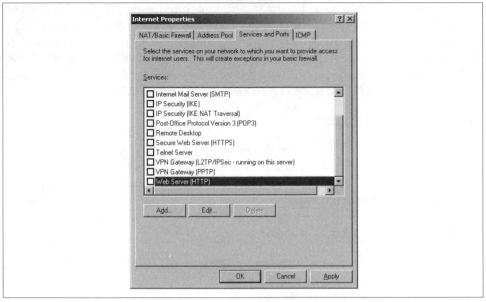

Figure 8-23. Configuring a special port on the NAT server

On the Edit Service window (shown in Figure 8-24) for this service, add or make the changes that are required. For example, when the web server service is selected, the only modification that can be made is to add the private IP address of the web server. Note the port information that is already configured. Add the address and click OK.

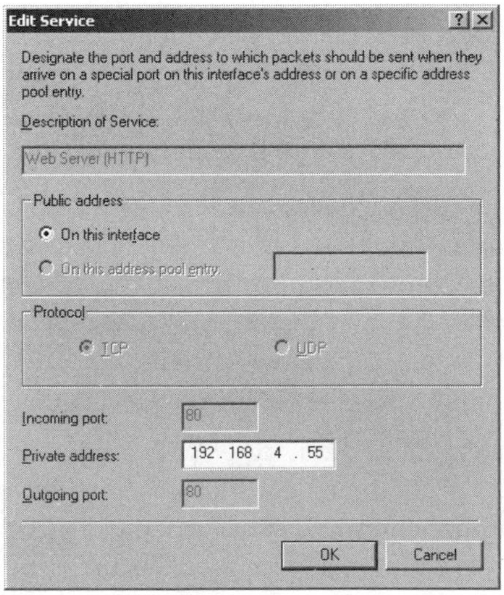

Figure 8-24. Configure the service

If the service is not listed, or if you must use custom ports, click the Add button on the screen shown when the Services and Ports tab has been selected (Figure 8-23). Complete the Edit Service page shown in Figure 8-24. The information required for this page is the information assigned for the service coupled with the private address of the server where the service is located. To configure the service, enter a description of the service in the Description of Service box. The "Public address" selection "On this interface" will be selected if the internal or public network interface has a static address. Select the protocol (either UDP or TCP) used by the service. Enter the incoming port (the port on which messages will be received by the server) in the "Incoming port" box. Enter the IP address of the server on the internal network that offers the service in the "Private address" box. Enter the outgoing port (the port on the server of the internal network that will offer the service) in the "Outgoing port" box. Click OK to add the service.

Internet Connection Sharing Versus NAT

In a small office or home office scenario, Internet Connection Sharing (ICS) can be used on the Windows Server 2003 server instead of NAT. Instead of configuring RRAS and NAT, configure the connection for the server to the Internet, and then configure ICS on the network interface. Address translation and name resolution services are provided for the internal LAN hosts. A single IP address can be configured for the Internet-facing connection and little configuration is necessary (or allowed). You can, however, configure access from the Internet for services on the internal network. ICS is configured on the Advanced tab of the network connection Properties page. Selecting the Settings button allows you to add services that can be accessed from the Internet on an ICS-enabled network interface.

If you need additional configuration choices, or need to support a larger number of external users, then configure NAT.

NAT is a way to provide Internet access for a host on an internal network that uses private dressing. To use it, you will have to understand how it works and how your network is configured, then spend a little time configuring the service. Like all routing services, RRAS NAT is a solid implementation of the service. Nevertheless, much can go wrong with any data communications. To monitor routing and to ensure information is available for troubleshooting and /or possible intrusion detection or forensics, configure RRAS logging.

Logging RRAS Routing Events

Routing events are logged in the Windows System Event log. These events indicate problems with routing so that you can troubleshoot the problems. In most environments, the default logging mode (Log errors and warnings) provides enough information during normal operation. When it is necessary to troubleshoot routing problems, adjust the logging level only for the routing component you need to examine. When the problem is resolved, return the logging level to the default. Remember, the more logging information you collect, the more system resources will be used. By adjusting logging levels only at the time there are problems, and only adjusting it for the node with the problem, you can gather information when you need it without wasting resources.

The following four logging levels are available:

- Log errors only
- Log errors and warnings
- Log the maximum amount of information
- Disable event logging

Table 8-3 lists the RRAS routing components for which logging may be adjusted, and indicates where this is done.

Table 8-3. Locations for adjusting RRAS routing logging

RRAS routing element	Where to adjust logging level
General	Properties pages for the IP Routing General node, Logging tab
IGMP	General tab on Properties page for the IGMP node
IP Routing\Network Address Translation (NAT)	General tab on Properties page for the NAT\Basic Firewall node
OSPF	General page of the OSPF node
RIP Version 2	General page of the RIP node

Now that you have configured basic routing and ensured that log information will be available, consider the use of additional RRAS services. The first one we'll look at is protocol filtering. Protocol filtering can provide a basic firewall service for your network. You should never consider protocol filtering as a firewall solution equal in scope to a dedicated firewall, since a dedicated firewall offers better protection. However, in emergencies, when no other firewall exists and one cannot be immediately put into place, or when RRAS is used on an internal network and only simple protocol filtering is desired, configure this RRAS service.

Protocol Filtering (Basic Firewall Services)

The basic firewall services provided by RRAS are just that: basic. You can add incoming and outgoing static packet filters based on a combination of source and destination IP address and port—that's all. That is significant, however, if no other firewall is being used, or if you just want to add some specific protection for the

RRAS server. To configure the firewall you create the NAT/Basic Firewall node, add an interface, enable the basic firewall, and create packet filters.

 To secure your Internet connection, consider a dedicated firewall. Both hardware- and software-based firewalls exist that can provide more than the basic firewall services. In addition to static packet filters, full-featured firewalls provide stateful packet filtering and application layer filtering. Also, a dedicated firewall can be tuned for the best performance and hardened to a greater degree because it is not also trying to support other services.

To add the NAT/Basic Firewall node, begin by opening the Routing and Remote Access node. Right-click IP Routing and select the General tab. Select New Routing Protocol. Select NAT/Basic Firewall and click OK.

To add an interface, right-click the NAT/Basic Firewall node and select New interface. Select the interface on which the firewall should be installed and click OK. On the NAT/Basic Firewall Properties page, select "Basic Firewall only."

Inbound packet filters determine which packets will be allowed onto the network and which packets will be dropped. To configure inbound filters, click the Inbound Filters button on the NAT/Basic Firewall tab to add inbound filters, or click the "Outbound filters" button to add outbound filters. On the inbound or outbound Filters page (the inbound page is displayed in Figure 8-25), select the filter action. Best practices for firewalls indicate that all packets should be blocked unless they are explicitly configured to pass. The filter action "Drop all packets except those that meet the criteria below" is used in conjunction with setting filters that identify the named exceptions that should be allowed to pass. To name the exceptions, click the Add button and enter the Source Address, Source Network Mask, Destination Address, and Destination Mask.

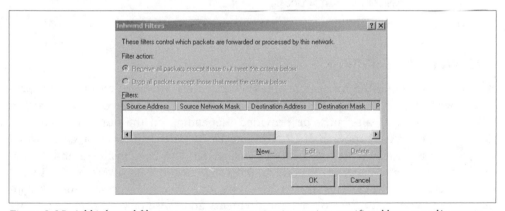

Figure 8-25. Add inbound filters to prevent communications using specific addresses and/or ports

To do so, select the "Drop all packets except those that meet the criteria below." Click the New button to add an allowed inbound packet. On the Add filter page, enter the source and destination network IP address and subnet masks. In the Protocol box, use the drop-down list to add the protocol type. Enter any additional information (for example, selecting TCP, provides a space to enter the source and destination ports). Click OK to close the page. To add additional filters, click the New button and follow the same procedure.

When you have finished, click OK to close the filter page. Repeat the process to configure packet filters for inbound or outbound packets. When you have finished, click OK to close the interface Properties page.

Remote Access Planning and Deployment

When dial-up services or VPN services are configured and used from remote locations, users can be provided the same access to data and information services that they would have if located on the local network. You must take great care to properly and securely implement dial-up and/or VPN remote access solutions.

This entails gathering information (common to both dial-up services and VPN services) in the following areas:

- Hardware provisioning
- Authentication choices
- Encryption
- Choosing a VPN protocol and Point-to-Point Protocol (PPP) extensions
- IP addressing and DHCP integration
- Domain functional level issues
- Remote access connection process
- Dial-in properties and remote access policies

Hardware Provisioning

Before configuring RRAS for remote access connections, you must ensure that appropriate hardware and software connectivity is in place. If dial-up access is the goal, a modem or modem bank must be provided (depending on the number of connections that you must support). If LAN connectivity via the Internet or other wired connection is required, then you should ensure that you have installed and configured the appropriate network interface and other external hardware and software prior to enabling RRAS. The type of hardware and software necessary for the connection will vary according to your requirements and those of your provider. However, you must ensure that any communications hardware and software to be installed in the Windows Server 2003 computer is compatible, and you must test connectivity before enabling and configuring RRAS.

Check hardware compatibility with Windows Server 2003. The hardware compatibility list can be searched at *http://www.microsoft.com/whdc/hcl/search.mspx*.

 Determine the load that will be placed on the hardware and software, then select and provision equipment and communications capabilities accordingly. Be aware of constraints. For example, each RRAS server can manage 255 simultaneous dial-up connections. If you require more than that, you must install and configure multiple RRAS servers.

Authentication Choices

Authentication is the process by which a security principal (a user, device, or process) provides proof of identity. Remote access connections may incorporate two types of authentication. Users may be required to provide a password, and client and server computers may also be required to prove that they are who they say they are. By requiring *user authentication*, RRAS attempts to ensure that only authorized individuals can connect to and access resources on your network. Requiring *computer authentication* ensures that only authorized systems are being used.

When RRAS server authentication to the client is required, the possibility that a rogue computer is masquerading as the server can be almost eliminated. When the RRAS client is required to authenticate to the server, the ability of an intruder to insert a computer into the middle of a communication session is reduced. If intruders can redirect remote access connections to a server of their choice, they may be able to obtain confidential information (or, at the very least, data that might enable successful attacks on your systems). If intruders can position their computers in between the RRAS server and client after the connection is made, they may be able to obtain confidential information and/or interfere with your ability to maintain the connection. The best authentication for remote access clients is one that requires both user authentication and mutual computer authentication. *Mutual authentication* is the process whereby the server must authenticate to the client and the client to the server.

Many authentication protocol choices are available for remote access clients. This makes it easy to accommodate multiple types of clients. However, not all authentication protocols are equally secure. Some do not require mutual authentication, and some protocols are weak. At a minimum, authentication choices should be restricted to only those protocols that are required according to the client computers that must have remote access. Best practices, however, require the elimination of clients that cannot use the more secure remote access authentication protocols.

The server controls the choice of authentication method used for remote access. While some clients can be configured with authentication protocol choices, clients can use only those authentication protocols enabled in the server configuration. If a client is not capable of using one of the enabled protocols, the client cannot connect. To ensure the use of the most secure authentication protocols where multiple clients are used, configure the server to only allow those protocols that are necessary to service all clients, and configure all clients to use only the most secure protocols.

Authentication methods available for Windows Server 2003 include the following:

Unauthenticated access
No authentication is required.

Password Authentication Protocol (PAP)
A clear text password is sent by the client and matched to the database entry stored for the client.

Shiva PAP (SPAP)
This is a proprietary extension of PAP used by Shiva products. A reversibly encrypted password is sent to the server from the client for comparison with the database stored.

Challenge Handshake Authentication Protocol (CHAP)
The server issues a challenge to the client in the form of a session number and random number. The client responds by using the user's password as the key in a hash of the challenge. The server makes its own hash of the challenge using its copy of the user's password. Both results are compared. A match authenticates the user. The MD5 hashing algorithm is used. The user ID is transmitted in clear text. The server must store a copy of the password in reversible encryption. This protocol may be required by UNIX clients.

Microsoft CHAP (MS-CHAP)
This is a proprietary version of CHAP in which a hash of the password is used as the key in a hash of the response to the server. This technology was introduced in Windows 3.1 and is required by Windows 95 clients. It is not selected by default in Windows Server 2003. An MD4 hash is used. MS-CHAP provides more sophisticated error messages than CHAP. One such message is an expired password error code. Software can use this message to give the user the ability to change his password during the authentication phase of the connection. An encryption key is created independently by the client and server based on the user's password. Microsoft CHAPv2 (MS-CHAPv2) adds mutual authentication of client and server and uses a longer challenge. Because encryption is based on the user's password, data security is only as good as the password.

Extensible Authentication Protocol (EAP)
EAP is an extension of the Point-to-Point (PPP) protocol that provides a modular base into which authentication modules (called EAP types) can be added. The EAP type used is dynamically negotiated during the authentication phase of

PPP. The EAP types available will depend on the implementation of EAP and can be changed as required. Windows Server 2003 EAP types include the following:

EAP-TLS with certificates or smart cards
EAP-TLS requires mutual authentication between client and server, and certificates must be used. Certificates may be produced by a Windows Certification Authority (CA) or by a third-party CA if certificate requirements are met. (See the Microsoft Knowledgebase article 814394 for a list of minimum certificate requirements.)

EAP-MD5 Challenge
EAP-MD5 Challenge uses MSCHAPv2 algorithms. The RRAS server must have a server certificate, but this is not required of clients. While EAP-TLS is more secure, using EAP-MD5 challenge is more secure than using MSCHAPv2.

Protected EAP (PEAP)
PEAP is a new algorithm associated with wireless network authentication scenarios and will be discussed in Chapter 10.

In addition to selecting authentication methods, you must also choose an authentication provider. You can use either Windows authentication or Remote Authentication Dial-in User Service (RADIUS) authentication. When Windows authentication is selected, the local account database (for standalone RRAS servers) or the Active Directory (for RRAS servers joined in a domain) is used. When RADIUS is selected, further configuration is needed to establish the RRAS server as a client of the RADIUS server. If the Microsoft Internet Authentication Server is designated as the RADIUS server, the IAS server's local account database (on standalone IAS servers) or the Active Directory (for IAS servers joined in a domain) will be used. More information on using IAS to manage remote access connections is included in Chapter 10.

You configure server-side authentication on the Properties page of the RRAS server. Begin by opening the Routing and Remote Access node. Right-click the server and select Properties. Select the Security tab. Note that the default authentication provider is Windows Authentication. Click the Authentication Methods box. Note that older (less secure) protocols (such as CHAP, PAP, and Shiva PAP) are not enabled, nor, as shown in Figure 8-26, is unauthenticated access allowed. If one of these methods is required, you will have to select it.

If none of the remaining authentication methods is required, click the checkbox to deselect it. It is always a good practice to enable only those authentication methods that are required.

If EAP is a requirement, click the EAP Methods box. By default, all three EAP Methods are enabled. Further configuration options are available by configuring remote access policies. The section "Remote Access Policies" later in this chapter provides the details. Click OK twice to close Properties pages.

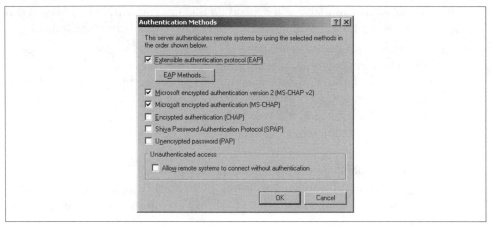

Figure 8-26. Older authentication protocols are not selected by default

Reversible Encryption

Windows passwords are not stored in clear text in the account databases. Instead, a cryptographic hashing algorithm is used. A *cryptographic hash* is a one-way encryption algorithm (that is, you cannot reverse the encryption process). Password validation is accomplished by creating a separate hash of the presented password using the same algorithm, and then comparing the results to the stored hash. Windows applications incorporate this algorithm. However, some third-party or legacy products and clients do not. For example, to use a Unix client to connect remotely to an RRAS server, you may need to store the passwords of some users using reversible encryption. *Reversible encryption* uses secret-key or symmetric encryption (that is, the stored, encrypted password can be decrypted). This is true if the CHAP protocol is used for remote access.

To store a copy of the password in reversible encryption is simple. The change can be made for the entire account database (not recommended) or only for those accounts that require it.

To make the change for the entire database, click Start → Administrative Tools → Domain Security Policy. Expand the Account Policies → Password Policy node. In the Details pane, double-click "Store passwords using reversible encryption." Click the Enabled radio button, as shown in Figure 8-27. Click OK to close the policy setting.

To make the change on a user account, click Start → Administrative Tools → Active Directory Users and Computers. Select the OU within which the user account is located. In the Details page, double-click the user account to open its Properties page. Select the Account tab. In the "Account options:" box, select "Store password using reversible encryption."

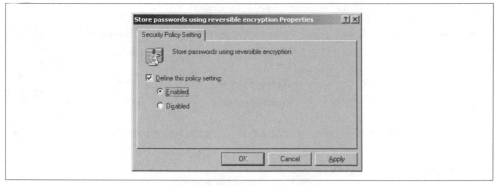

Figure 8-27. Reversible encryption can be enabled for the entire domain

In both cases (the entire database or individual user accounts), users will have to change their passwords before the passwords will be stored in reversibly encrypted form.

Data Encryption

Data encryption choices are available for both basic dial-up and VPN remote access connections. Encryption may be selected when using basic dial-up connections. The choice of encryption algorithms is determined by the type of VPN connection established. When basic dial-up connections are used, you must configure both the client and the server. The server, however, can require encryption. If it does, and the client cannot be (or is not) configured to use data encryption, the connection may be established, but it will be dropped.

Encryption types

Three types of data encryption may be used: third-party products, Microsoft Point-to-Point Encryption, or IPSec. You must select the connection method to select the encryption method. If a dial-up connection specifies encryption, or a Point-to-Point Tunneling Protocol (PPTP) VPN is established, MPPE will be used for encryption. If a Layer-2 Tunneling Protocol (L2TP) VPN is used, IPSec will be used for encryption. Table 8-4 lists the choices.

Table 8-4. Remote access data encryption choices

Remote access connection method	Authentication method	Data encryption
Dial-up	PAP CHAP	None
	Shiva-PAP	Proprietary
	MS-CHAP MS-CHAPv2	MPPE

Table 8-4. Remote access data encryption choices (continued)

Remote access connection method	Authentication method	Data encryption
	EAP-TLS EAP-MD5	MPPE
PPTP	All allowed methods	MPPE
L2TP	All allowed methods	IPSec

While MS-CHAP, MS-CHAPv2 and EAP authentication methods for dial-up all use MPPE for data encryption, there are additional encryption benefits to using MS-CHAPv2 and EAP:

- EAP and MS-CHAPv2 generate stronger encryption keys than those used by MS-CHAP. MS-CHAPv2 uses a unique session identifier and user credentials to generate encryption keys. EAP over a dial-up connection uses a server (or a client and server) certificate for authentication, and the Transport Level Security (TLS) algorithm is used to generate the encryption keys. TLS keys are unique to each TLS session. MS-CHAP, on the other hand, uses user credentials alone to generate encryption keys. This means that the encryption key might not change for further remote access connections.

- When EAP is used, different keys are used for sending and receiving data. An intruder would have to break both keys to interpret both sides of the conversation.

Choosing MPPE or IPSec encryption

Dial-up connections cannot specify the type of encryption used, but VPN connections can. By specifying the type of VPN (PPTP or L2TP/IPSec), you specify the type of data encryption used. PPTP VPNs use MPPE while L2TP/IPSec VPNs use IPSec. However, two factors must be considered when choosing between MPPE or IPSec encryption. First, because the type of VPN connection determines the encryption type, you must verify that either type of VPN can be used. There are many things that will prevent you from using L2TP (including its more complex configuration, and the difficulty of using IPSec from behind a NAT server). If either VPN type can be selected, then, second, you must consider the encryption protocols themselves. IPSec is considered the more secure encryption algorithm for the following reasons:

- IPSec can provide end-to-end encryption versus the link encryption provided by MPPE. *End-to-end encryption* occurs between the sending and receiving nodes. *Link encryption* encrypts data between the calling and answering routers.

- IPSec is an IETF standard. MPPE is a Microsoft proprietary algorithm. While MPPE is a proprietary encryption algorithm, it uses the Rivest-Shamir-Adleman (RSA) RC4 stream cipher.

- Standard encryption algorithms are considered more secure since more people, in general, have examined and tested the algorithm looking for flaws.

- IPSec provides stronger encryption. Encryption choices for IPSec are modular. Future implementations of IPSec may use newer, more secure algorithm standards.

- IPSec provides additional protection, including stronger integrity, data authentication, and replay protection. For more information, see Chapter 11.

Encryption strength selection for VPNs

Encryption strength for remote access connections is configured in remote access policies by selecting basic, strong, or strongest. Like authentication, the key strength for data can be restricted by the server. Key strength is negotiated during connection establishment. If the client cannot meet the requirements set by the server, the connection is rejected. Table 8-5 maps these choices to MPPE and IPSec implementations.

Table 8-5. Encryption strength

Encryption choice	L2TP/IPSec	PPTP
Basic	56-bit DES	40-bit MPPE
Strong	56-bit MPPE	56-bit DES
Strongest	128-bit MPPE	3DES

Now that we have a basic understanding of authentication and encryption, let's examine some considerations when choosing a VPN protocol.

Choosing a VPN Protocol

As the previous sections indicate, the selection of a VPN protocol can determine the choices available for authentication and data encryption. The two protocols available on a Windows RRAS server are PPTP and L2TP/IPSec. Two other items should influence your choice of VPN protocol:

- Configuration complexity
- Interoperability with NAT

On the surface, neither PPTP nor L2TP/IPSec present any real configuration problems. The complexity of IPSec is hidden behind the defaults selected by Microsoft for the VPN implementation. However, to use L2TP/IPSec in its default configuration, computers must be configured with computer certificates. A Windows Certification Authority (CA) or a third-party CA may supply the computer certificates if the third-party certificates meet the conditions set by Microsoft. You may substitute a shared key for the certificate when creating a demand-dial VPN. However, this weakens the VPN security. An alternative to the L2TP/IPSec VPN is to create a VPN using IPSec in Tunnel mode. This configuration does not require the establishment of a RRAS VPN, but relies on the configuration of IPSec policies instead.

As originally defined, Microsoft's implementation of L2TP/IPSec does not work from behind a NAT server. Window Server 2003 can work from behind a NAT-T server. NAT-T is a modified NAT server and is explained in the section Using L2TP/IPSec VPNs with NAT and NAT-T below. Updates for Windows 2000 allow it to access a Windows Server 2003 L2TP/IPSec VPN server from behind a NAT server.

In addition to PPTP and L2TP/IPSec, IPSec can be used in tunnel mode, thus eliminating the need for using L2TP. To determine which protocol is best for your situation you must consider each of these three possibilities (PPTP, L2TP/IPSec, and IPSec in tunnel mode), as described in the following sections.

PPTP considerations

PPTP was developed by Microsoft, but is an IETF standard. It can tunnel and encrypt multiprotocol traffic across an IP network. Keep the following points in mind:

- The PPTP tunnel negotiates authentication, compression, and encryption.
- The initial encryption key is generated during user authentication and is refreshed periodically.
- PPTP only encrypts the data payload. Figure 8-28 shows the PPTP packet and identifies the encrypted area.
- PPTP and L2TP/IPSec support dynamic assignment of client addresses.

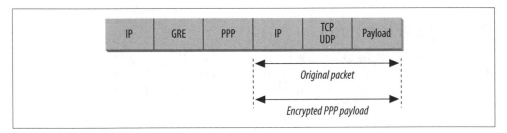

Figure 8-28. The PPP packet encrypts only a portion of the packet

L2TP/IPSec considerations

L2TP is a combination of Cisco Layer 2 Forwarding Protocol (L2F) and Microsoft PPTP. Keep the following in mind:

- L2TP can tunnel data across any network that transports PPP traffic such as IP, Frame Relay and Asynchronous Transfer Mode (ATM) networks.
- L2TP uses User Data Protocol (UDP) over IP messages for tunnel management.
- L2TP sends encapsulated PPP packets over UDP and payloads can be encrypted and compressed.

- IPSec Encapsulating Security Payload (ESP) is used to encrypt L2TP VPNs by using an automatically generated IPSec policy that uses IPSec in transport mode.
- IPSec ESP encryption encrypts more than the data payload portion of the packet. Figure 8-29 illustrates the packet and identifies the encrypted portion.
- L2TP/IPSec VPNs require user and mutual computer authentication. Computer authentication for VPNs requires computer certificates.
- L2TP/IPSec is generally considered more secure and does offer additional security beyond what PPTP offers.
- L2TP/IPSec may not work behind a Network Address Translation (NAT) server.

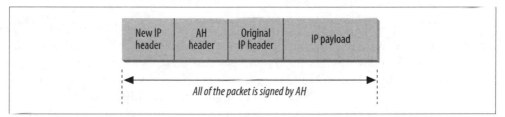

Figure 8-29. A larger portion of the L2TP/Ipsec packet is encrypted

IPSec in tunnel mode considerations

IPSec in tunnel mode has limited use as a VPN on a Windows Server 2003 network. Keep the following in mind:

- IPSec in tunnel mode is generally used to connect a Windows Server VPN server with a device such as a router than does not use L2TP.
- In IPSec tunnel mode, IP packets are encrypted using IPSec and tunneled across an IP network.
- IPSec in tunnel mode can be used for a demand-dial or client/server VPN. It does not support user remote access VPN, however.
- The use of IPSec filters to allow or block communications using specific protocols or ports is not supported in IPSec tunnel mode.

PPP Extensions

The PPP is used for remote access connectivity. In addition to authentication methods, RRAS can be configured to support Multilink and Dynamic bandwidth control (BAP), additional Link Control (LCP) extensions, and software compression.

PPP configuration is set on the PPP Properties page of the RRAS console server properties, as shown in Figure 8-30. To open this page, right-click on the server node in the console and select Properties, then select the PPP tab.

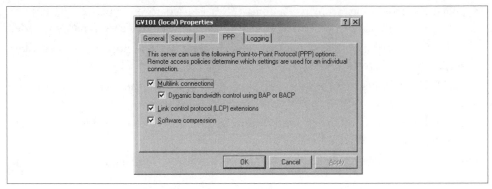

Figure 8-30. Software compression and other LCP extensions

The first option you see is "Multilink connection." If you can provide multiple physical links to the Windows Server 2003 remote access server, you can aggregate these links using Multilink. When Multilink is used, multiple physical links appear as a single logical link over which data can be sent and received. Multilink must be supported at both ends of the connection. Dynamic management of the changing bandwidth conditions (as links are added when needed or terminated when not needed) is not provided by Multilink. The Bandwidth Allocation Protocol (BAP) provides this support. When BAP is configured, the BAP enabled remote access client uses a BAP request to request an additional link if the physical link it is using reaches a configured level. If the remote access server can provide the requested link, it will return the information the client will need to use it. For example, if the client requests an additional analog phone line and one is available, the server will return the phone number of the available port on the remote access server.

The next checkbox is "Link control protocol (LCP) extensions." PPP uses LCP to establish and configure link and framing selections such as maximum frame size. These characteristics are negotiated during the connection process. Framing considerations are important because they specify how the data is encapsulated before transmission, and because each side of the connection must match the other. If LCP extensions are not enabled, it may be difficult for some types of PPP connections to be established.

The final checkbox is "Software compression." Many modems offer hardware-based compression, but software compression may offer performance enhancements over the provided hardware-based compression. Compression is used to reduce the amount of data that must be transported and the amount of time necessary for the data to be transferred.

IP Addressing and DHCP Integration

RRAS can be configured to use its local network DHCP server to provide remote access clients with network configuration information, or an address pool can be allocated on the RRAS server for use by remote access clients.

When the local network DHCP server is chosen, the RRAS server obtains ten DHCP addresses from the DHCP server when the first remote access client connects. The first DHCP address is used by the RRAS server and the remaining addresses are allocated to remote access clients as they connect. When all ten are allocated, another ten are obtained from the DHCP server. If the RRAS service is stopped, all IP addresses obtained through DHCP are released.

If no DHCP server is available and IP addresses cannot be obtained, then Automatic Private IP Addressing (APIPA) will be used. APIPA is that part of the post Windows 2000 modern Windows TCP/IP implementation that allows a computer to configure an address when a DHCP server or manual configuration is not available. The address range from 169.254.0.1 to 169.254.255.254 is used with a subnet mask of 255.255.0.0. IP address selection is random and the Address Resolution Protocol (ARP) is used to check the local network for address conflict. If an address conflict is found, APIPA will randomly select another address from the range until it finds one that is not in use. If the internal network is configured to use another address range, then the APIPA address will be unusable.

When an address pool is assigned on the RRAS server, be careful to exclude the range assigned by RRAS from the IP address scope allocated on the internal network DHCP servers, as well as those statically assigned on the internal network.

In addition to DHCP or address pool selection, you should enable (if required on your network) or disable (if not required) broadcast name resolution and select the adapter from which DHCP, DHS, and WINS addresses are obtained for dial-up clients.

To configure IP addressing, begin by opening the Routing and Remote Access node. Right-click on the server node and select Properties. Select the IP tab. Then, choose from the following:

- To use a local DHCP server, check the box Dynamic Host Configuration Protocol (DHCP). (The IP address of the DHCP server is configured elsewhere.)

- To set up a pool of addresses, check the box Static Address Pool and use the Add button to add IP address range(s) for use by remote access clients.

Click to select or deselect "Enable broadcast name resolution." Use the Adapter drop-down list to select how clients will obtain the address for DHCP, DNS, and WINS servers. You can allow RRAS to select the adapter or specify one of the existing network interfaces. In a typical installation, the network interface on the internal network is configured with this information and is the best choice. Click OK to close the Properties page.

If necessary, set up static routes (for instance, if IP address pools represent addresses in a different subnet than the internal adapter of the internal network interface of the RRAS server).

Domain Functional Level Issues

When the RRAS server is joined in a Windows Server 2003 domain or Windows 2000 domain, then the domain mode (Windows 2000) or functional level (Windows Server 2003) may impact the remote access capabilities of the RRAS server. When the first Windows 2000 or Windows Server 2003 domain controller in a new forest is created, the domain mode or functional level is set to mixed (that is, domain controllers that are Windows NT 4.0, Windows 2000, or Windows Server 2003 may coexist in the domain). This allows a smooth migration from earlier domain models, but it does not allow all of the features of later domain models to be utilized. When all older domain controllers are upgraded or decommissioned, the domain mode or functional level can be changed, and additional features can be used. More information on these issues is provided in Chapter 7.

The major advantage of advancing the domain mode or functional level is to be able to use RRAS remote access policies. To do so, Windows 2000 domains must be in Native Mode, and Windows Server 2003 domains must be at Windows 2000 functional level.

The Remote Access Connection Process

In addition to server-side settings that are applied to all remote access clients, many settings are configurable to further granularize the connection process according to user, device, and connection type. These settings are configured on the dial-in property page of the user account and in remote access policies. All settings (RRAS settings, dial-in settings, and remote access policies) are considered during the connection process. Dial-in settings and remote access policy settings are detailed later in this chapter. It is important to understand the interaction of these settings during connection. This knowledge will assist you in designing and implementing RRAS and in troubleshooting connection issues.

Before you can understand the process, you must be aware that the use of remote access policies is determined by both domain functional level and by selection in the user account property pages. If the functional level is mixed, the dial-in property page Remote Access Permission (Dial-in or VPN) is configured to "Deny access." Access can be changed to "Allow access" on a user-by user basis. If the domain functional level is Windows 2000 Native, then the default will be "Control access through Remote Access Policy." The default remote access policy denies access. You can select (on a user-by-user basis) to change to "Deny access" or "Allow access."

If no remote access policies are configured, RRAS and Internet Authentication Service (IAS) evaluate connection requests using the user dial-in property pages and RRAS settings. The RRAS and IAS default connection process follows these steps:

1. The connection attempt is evaluated against the first remote access policy conditions. A default remote access policy denies remote access connection. If no remote access policy exists, and accounts are configured to use remote access policies, then access is denied. Otherwise, the following process continues:

    a. RRAS checks the user's account dial-in property page Remote Access Permission.

    b. If the account setting is Allow, then the process continues. RRAS checks and applies the remote access policy conditions and applies remote access policy profile constraints if they affect authorization to connect. If all conditions are met, the connection is accepted. If they are not, then any remaining remote access policies are checked until the connection is accepted or denied.

    c. If the account setting is Deny, then the connection attempt is rejected.

    d. If the user account setting is "Control access through Remote Access Policy," then the remote access permissions setting of the policy is checked. If it is Deny, the connection is rejected. If it is Allow, then processing will continue.

    e. RRAS evaluates the account dial-in property page constraints and the remote access policy profile constraints.

    f. If all connection settings in the policy and the user dial-in page are met, then the connection is accepted.

    g. If a connection setting is not met, then the connection is rejected.

2. If all of the conditions of the remote access policy are met, the value of the Ignore-User-Dial in-Properties attribute (configured in the remote access policy profile) is checked. If it is set to true, any dial-in page constraints are ignored. This is an important consideration for wireless connections and device connections. For example, if callback is set on the dial-in property page, a wireless connection will not understand the requirement.

3. If all of the conditions of the remote access policy are not met, then the next remote access policy is evaluated. This is a critical point. When multiple remote access policies are in place, the connection attempt is evaluated against the list of remote access policies one at a time. If all the conditions of a remote access policy are met, then it is used to allow or deny the connection and no other remote access policies are considered. If the connection attempt does not match the policy being evaluated, the next remote access policy is evaluated. If the connection

attempt matches no policy (and the account access is managed by remote access policies) then the connection attempt is denied.

4. If no remote access policy matches the connection attempt, the connection attempt is rejected.

5. If the connection is allowed, it is constrained by the profile settings of the remote access policy.

This processing algorithm will be easier to understand as you learn more about remote access policies. However, it is important to understand the process before you design remote access policies. This conundrum (the need to understand part A of a process before you can understand part B, and yet understanding part B is dependent on understanding part A) is part of the challenge of many complex processes. Full understanding is often accomplished by lightly studying both parts of the process and then returning to study each in more depth.

Dial-in User Constraints

User account dial-in constraints are configured on the Dial-in user account property page, as shown in Figure 8-31.

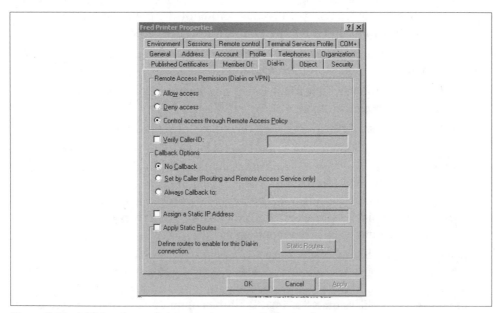

Figure 8-31. Additional user dial-properties are set in the user's account

The following setting choices are available:

Remote Access Permission (Dial-in or VPN)
Remote access is denied by default on a Windows 2003 server. For remote access on a user-by-user basis (the Windows NT 4.0–style remote access), change this to "Allow access." However, you will have to configure each user's account separately. In an Active Directory domain, this permission is set to Control Access by Remote Access Policy. This is the preferred option because it allows you to control access via policies using Windows groups and other options—a much more efficient and manageable process.

Verify Caller-ID
The Caller ID can be checked against a number entered on the page. If the user calls from another number, she will be denied access. Before implementing this feature, verify that all parts of the phone system provide Caller-ID services. Parts of the phone system include the caller, the phone system between the caller and the call answering equipment, and the phone system between the call answering equipment and the RRAS server. The call answering equipment must be able to provide the remote access server with the number called from.

No Callback
RRAS will not disconnect a connection and attempt to dial the user's computer.

Set by Caller (Routing and Remote Access Service only)
Callback choices are set in remote access policy.

Always Callback to
RRAS disconnects the authorized connection and dials the user at the phone number listed on the dial-in page. If the authorized user attempts a call from a different location, the user will not be able to gain remote access.

Assign a Static IP Address
The address entered here will be used remotely. The user's actions on the remote network can be tracked by the IP address assigned. If an address is statically assigned, a static route may need to be configured.

Apply Static Routes
Use the Static Routes button to enter static routes required when this user is remotely connected.

Remote Access Policies

Remote access policies both make management of remote access simpler and also provide additional access restrictions based on Windows groups, the type of connection, and time of day. Remote access policies also include profile constraints that can be applied to the authorized connection. Remote access policies configured on the local RRAS server are used when Windows is the RRAS authentication provider. However, when the authentication provider for RRAS is RADIUS and a Windows

IAS server is designated as the RADIUS server, then remote access policies on the IAS server manage the connection.

Remote access policy restrictions

Remote access policy restrictions define when a connection can be made, who can make it, and how a connection is made. When connections are managed by remote access policy, the caller characteristics are matched with those defined in remote access policies. If a match is found, the call is allowed or denied, and possibly managed by the rest of the information in the remote access policy. If there is no match, access must be managed by remote access policies and the connection will be denied. Table 8-6 lists the items that can be configured via remote access policies for Windows and IAS. Table 8-7 shows only the remote access policy constraints that are available if IAS is the authentication provider.

Table 8-6. Remote access policy eestrictions

Attribute	Choices
Authentication Type	All authentication choices.
Called Station ID	The phone number of the network access server or RRAS server. The equipment must support passing the caller ID to the RRAS server.
Calling Station ID	The phone number from which the call is placed.
Day and Time Restrictions	The day of the week and the time of the day for which a connection will either be allowed or denied. Use this restriction to reduce connections during nonbusiness hours. A common configuration is to allow connection during normal business hours for most users, while allowing full-time connectivity for some groups.
Tunnel type	Tunnel type requested by the client, either L2TP or PPTP.
Windows Groups	Group membership for the calling user.

Table 8-7. Additional remote access policy restrictions used by IAS

Attribute	Description
Client Friendly Name (IAS only)	Name of the RADIUS client requesting authentication. The RRAS server becomes the RADIUS client when IAS manages remote access. The Client Friendly name is configured in the setting tab properties of the RADIUS client in IAS.
Client IP address	The IP address of the RADIUS client or the RADIUS proxy.
Client Vendor	The vendor of the network access server requesting authentication
Framed Protocol	The incoming packet frame type (PPP, SLIP, Frame Relay, or X.25).
NAS Identifier	The name of the Network Attached Storage (NAS).
NAS IP Address	The IP address of the NAS or RADIUS client.
NAS Port Type	The type of media used by the access client. For example, you could use analog phone line (async), ISDN, tunnels, VPNs (virtual), IEEE 802.11 wireless, and Ethernet switches.
Service Type	Type of service requested. For example, you could use framed (such as PPP connection) or logon (such as a Telnet connection).

Profile constraints

If the connection request meets the conditions set by an RRAS or IAS remote access policy, RRAS or IAS evaluates the Allow or Deny authorization property of the remote access policy or the dial-in property page. Remote access policies include profiles, and they are also evaluated if the remote access policy authorization setting is Allow. Policy profile properties can further constrain or deny the connection. The constraints configured in the profile will only affect connections that meet the conditions set by the remote access policy. Table 8-8 lists and describes these properties.

Table 8-8. Remote access profile properties

Property	Description
Dial-in constraints	Sets idle time, connection limit, days and times, number of connections, and specific media that can be used (async, ISDN, virtual, or 802.11).
IP	The client IP address assignment. IP packet filters can be defined. Choices for IP address assignments are: • The access server must supply the address • The client can request an address • The address assignment is specified by the access server • The profile lists a static IP address
Multilink	Sets the number of ports a multilink connection can use and the BAP policies. (Multilink and BAP must be enabled on the RRAS server.)
Authentication	Authentication types allowed by the client. Settings in the remote access policy will override settings in the RRAS server property pages. You can also set whether or not the user can reset a password when using MS-CHAP.
Encryption	Defines encryption choices. Client and server negotiate the encryption strength that will be used. The specification here indicates the choices the server will accept. Choices are no encryption, basic, strong, and strongest.
Advanced	RADIUS attributes can be defined here. IAS uses these attributes to constrain an authorized connection between the RADIUS server (IAS) and the RADIUS client (RRAS). The Ignore user dial-in properties attribute is configured here.

Configuring remote access policies

To configure a simple remote access policy for RRAS, begin by opening the Routing and Remote Access node. Right-click the Remote Access policy node, select New Remote Access Policy, and then click Next. Select "Use the wizard to set up a typical policy for a common scenario." Enter a name for the policy and click Next. Select the Access method, as shown in Figure 8-32, then click Next. (Access methods are VPN, Dial-up, Wireless, or Ethernet.)

Select User or Group Access, as shown in Figure 8-33. When User is selected, the user access permissions are taken from the user account properties. When Group is selected, group permissions are used unless user permissions are different. In this case, user permissions override group permissions. Use the Add button to specify groups if required, then click Next.

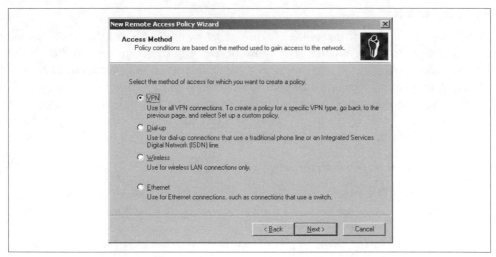

Figure 8-32. Select an Access method

Figure 8-33. Select groups

Select the allowed authentication methods. If EAP or smart cards is selected, use the Configure button to select the server certificate. (The certificate must already be in the server's certificate store.) If PEAP is selected, select the EAP type, then click Next. Select the encryption levels allowed, then click Next and then click Finish.

To configure a custom policy and edit the profile, begin by opening the Routing and Remote Access node. Right-click the Remote Access Policy node and select New Remote Access Policy. Click Next. Select "Set up a custom policy," enter a name for the policy, and click Next. Use the Add button to specify policy conditions that connection requests must match to be granted or denied access. (Policy conditions are items such as authentication type, called station ID, calling station-ID, and so forth.) After you have selected a policy condition, click the Add button (as shown in Figure 8-34) to complete the selection then click OK.

Figure 8-34. Policy conditions are configured by selecting attributes

Use the Add button to specify any additional policy conditions that connection requests must match to be granted or denied access. Then click Next. Select "Grant remote access permission" or "Deny remote access permissions," then click Next. Click the "Edit profile" button to add further constraints, as shown in Figure 8-35. (See Table 8-8 for constraint information.)

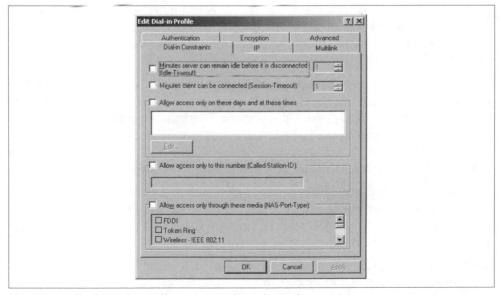

Figure 8-35. Configure the profile to manage the authorized connection

When you have finished adding constraints to the profile, click OK then click Next, then Finish.

 Chapter 10 illustrates the use of profile constraints when describing how to prepare a remote access policy to manage wireless connections.

Remote access policies are important to the control and management of remote access connections whether they are simple dial-up connections, VPN server connections, or demand-dial connections. If you understand how remote access policies do this, you are ready to install and configure remote access connections, as explained in the next section.

Configuring Dial-up or VPN Access

Many of the steps required to configure a RRAS server for dial-up access have been described in general in the previous sections. Many of these same procedures apply to both dial-up and VPN connections. You could use this information as a checklist to enable and configure remote access on the RRAS server.

This section presents a complete outline of the process using the wizard, which is accessible when you first enable RRAS. You may need to use the previous sections in this chapter to fill in the details of some of the configuration steps.

Let's take a look at the procedure to configure RRAS for dial-up access or VPN services on a Windows Server 2003 server. If the server is a Windows 2000 or Windows Server 2003 domain member, add the server computer account to the RAS and IAS Server security group in Active Directory. (If you are a domain administrator, this step may not be necessary, because the account should be automatically added when RRAS is enabled.)

If RRAS has not been enabled, right-click on the server icon in the Routing and Remote Access Service console and select Configure and Enable Routing and Remote Access. (If RRAS is already enabled, open the Properties page of the server (right-click on the server icon in the console and select Properties. Start with the General page and select "Remote access services," then configure the properties as described here. The Properties page tab name required is listed in the steps that follow.)

Click Next on the Welcome page. Select Remote Access (Dial up and VPN) and then click Next. Select both the Dial-up and VPN checkboxes (or select just one of them), and then click Next. Select the network interface to be used by the dial-up connection, and then click Next.

Select IP addressing (the IP page), either automatically (using a DHCP server on the LAN) or from a range of addresses. Click Next. If you selected a range of addresses, use the New button to add a range of addresses to be used and then click Next.

Select whether or not to use a RADIUS server (the Security tab). If Windows should be used as the authentication provider, select "No, use Routing and Remote Access to authenticate connection requests," as shown in Figure 8-36.

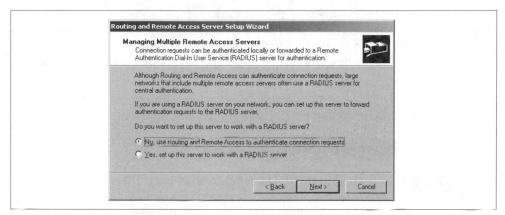

Figure 8-36. Windows authentication is selected by checking the RRAS button

Click Next, then click Finish.

Click OK in the warning box about configuring the DHCP relay agent with the IP address of the DHCP server. (Refer to the section "Configuring the DHCP Relay Agent" earlier in this chapter for information on configuring the DHCP Relay Agent.)

Open the server Properties page. Verify that the RRAS server is configured as a remote access server. using the General tab on the Properties page. Set an appropriate logging level. Change IP and/or PPP settings. Modify authentication methods as required.

Use the RRAS console to configure DHCP Relay as described in the section "Configuring the DHCP Relay Agent," earlier in this chapter. Use the Ports Properties page to configure additional or fewer L2TP and/or IPSec ports (128 of each are configured by default), and to limit ports to inbound-only connections if demand dial-up connections will not be needed. Use the IP Routing → Static Routes node of the RRAS console to configure any required static routes. Use the Active Directory Users and Computers console (in a domain) or the Computer Management console to configure user dial-in properties. Use the RRAS console to create remote access policies. Use the Properties page of the network interface to configure packet filters. Finally, create basic packet filters for the RRAS server.

These instructions have provided the basics of configuring remote access using the RRAS server. There are, however, other tasks and options that can provide just the feature or operation you may need, such as using L2TP /IPSec VPNs with NAT and NAT-T (defined below), or configuring a demand dial VPN.

Advanced Virtual Private Network (VPN) Process and Configuration

The basic settings put into place by the RRAS dial-up and VPN wizard establish the RRAS server as a VPN server. Both VPN protocols (L2TP and PPTP) are enabled and clients can connect directly to the VPN server. You may require additional options such as using the L2TP/IPSec VPN for use with NAT and NAT-T, configuring a demand dial VPN, configuring demand dial dial-in properties, using a shared key for a L2TP/IPSec VPN, configuration setting for firewalls that sit between the VPN and the external network, or configuring logging and accounting for the VPN.

Using L2TP/IPSec VPNs with NAT and NAT-T

IPSec encryption as defined in the IETF standard is incompatible with NAT. This is because the IPSec standard requires that the encryption of a large part of the IPSec-protected packet include a checksum that is calculated over much of the packet information, including the original source address. When a NAT server routes a packet, NAT replaces the original IP source address with an Internet-routable address assigned to it for this purpose. If NAT could decrypt the packet, calculate a new checksum, and then encrypt the packet, there would not be a problem. However, NAT cannot do this. When the IPSec packet is received, a new checksum is calculated over the new source address and compared to the decrypted checksum. Because a different source IP address is part of the new calculation, no match occurs. IPSec thinks the packet is corrupt, and, therefore, drops it.

If IPSec is implemented to match the standard (as it was in Windows 2000), then IPSec or L2TP/IPSec VPNs cannot operate behind a NAT server. This problem is solved by Windows Server 2003. Windows Server 2003 implements a new IETF standard track draft, *NAT-Traversal*, or *NAT-T*.

NAT-T uses UDP encapsulation of the IPSec packet. When the packet passes through NAT, NAT modifies the UDP header source address (not the IP header source address) and can route the packet to its destination. The source address in the IP header remains the source address used in the original calculation. Therefore, when IPSec calculates a new checksum, it matches the one sent with the IPSec encrypted packet.

A Windows Server 2003 VPN server can operate behind a NAT server, if the NAT server implements NAT-T. Internet Key Exchange (IKE), a component of the IPSec implementation, can detect NAT-T and then use UDP-ESP encapsulation. Windows clients must also be NAT-T compliant. The following updates and clients are available:

- Windows XP and the L2TP/IPSec update
- Windows 2000 and the L2TP/IPSec update

- Windows NT 4.0 and the L2TP/IPSec VPN client
- Windows 98 and the L2TP/IPsec VPN client

 A Windows 2000 server can be a NAT-T client, but cannot (as a VPN server) offer NAT-T capabilities to its clients.

Configuring and Using RRAS Demand-Dial VPN

By default, a Windows RRAS VPN configuration supports VPN clients. RRAS can be configured to support a demand-dial or router-to-router VPN. Figures 8-37 and 8 38 illustrate the difference. In Figure 8-37, multiple clients have created connections to the VPN server and can access resources on the main headquarters LAN. Each client must have VPN services configured.

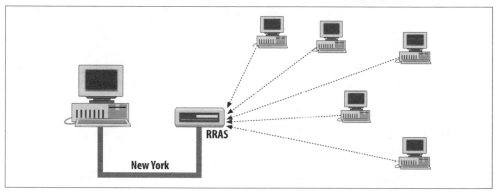

Figure 8-37. With a traditional VPN, multiple clients individually make a connection with the VPN server

In Figure 8-38, two Windows Server 2003 VPN servers (one at the New York head-quarters and one at the London branch office) create a demand-dial VPN. Clients at the branch office do not have to have VPN client software configured. They do not have to initiate a VPN connection with the VPN server. When traffic on the branch office network is destined for resources located on the headquarters LAN (New York), it is routed to the VPN server on the branch office network perimeter (London). At the VPN server, the traffic is routed to headquarters (New York) across the demand-dial VPN. The traffic is protected according to the specification of the VPN.

It is not difficult to configure a demand dial-VPN, but it can be confusing. Several pieces of information must be configured that must match their counterparts on the other server. Two key pieces of information must be understood.

First, the name of the interface becomes the name of the user account necessary to access that interface. The account will be created for you, if the option is selected during the configuration process. This account becomes the dial-in account name

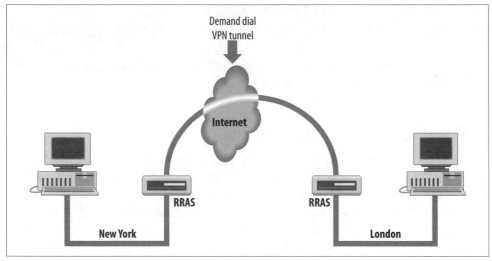

Figure 8-38. A demand-dial VPN automatically tunnels data between two VPN servers

referenced in the setup wizard. Secondly, the user account (the dial-out account requested in the setup wizard, which will be used to make a connection to the opposite VPN server) is the dial-in account name of the opposite VPN server.

 Do not let the name "demand-dial" confuse you. Though a demand dial connection can be made over a public phone network using a modem, it can also be made over the Internet or other WAN connection. It can be created so that a communication that requires the connection establishes the connection on demand, so that the connection is always kept alive.

To configure a demand-dial VPN that operates over the Internet between two offices, follow these steps. First, create a table and enter the configuration parameters for both servers. Table 8-9 provides an example of such a table. The parameters in the table will be used in this procedure, but you should replace them with your own requirements. Since you may be dependent on a VPN server administrator at a remote location for the configuration of the other side of the connection, share the table with the other VPN server administrator(s).

Table 8-9. Demand Dial VPN configuration table example

Parameter	Network one: New York	Network two: London
Router Name	VPNOne	VPNTwo
VPN protocol	PPTP	PPTP
IP Address of the other router's external interface	207.209.68.50	208.147.66.50
Interface name	DD_NewYork	DD_London

Table 8-9. Demand Dial VPN configuration table example (continued)

Parameter	Network one: New York	Network two: London
User account in the dial-out interface	DD_London	DD_NewYork
IP network address of the internal network	192.168.5.0	192.168.10.0
IP subnet mask of the internal network	255.255.255.0	255.255.255.0

You must then configure the VPNOne Router:

1. Begin by opening the Routing and Remote Access node.

2. Right-click the Network Interface node and select New Demand-Dial Interface. This starts the demand-dial interface wizard. Click Next. Enter the interface name from the table (**DD_NewYork**) and then click Next.

3. Select "Connect using virtual private networking (VPN)" and then click Next.

4. Select "Point-to-Point Tunneling Protocol (PPTP)" and then click Next. (PPTP is selected to simplify configuration. If you want to create a L2TP/IPSec demand dial-connection, you should first get the connection working using PPTP, and then modify it to use L2TP/IPSec. In this manner, you will know about any problem that may be caused by making the connection when using L2TP/IPSec, not by your other configuration elements.)

5. If L2TP is selected, IPSec certificates are used for VPN computer authentication in addition to the user account. However, each computer must be able to validate the certificate presented by the other. If different CAs issue the certificates for the computers, then a copy of the root CA certificate must be placed in the computer certificate store. Alternatively, you can configure the demand-dial connection to use a shared password, but this is not recommended.

6. Enter the IP address of the VPN router at the other location (in this case, the IP address for VPNTwo in the Table 8-9), then click Next.

7. Select "Add a user account so a remote router can dial-in" and then click Next. The user account will be created in the local account database, or in Active Directory if the RRAS server is a domain member. The account will be used by the other RRAS server to authenticate the connection to this VPN Server.

8. Use the Add button to add static routes for the local VPN Server. You will need to enter the IP address of the remote server's network and its network mask from Table 8-9.

9. Repeat the process to add additional routes, and then click Next.

 Note that, as shown in Figure 8-39, the interface name DD_NewYork is also the user account name. This is the account the other VPN server will use. The password entered here must be communicated to the administrator configuring the other side of the demand dial-VPN.

10. Complete the Dial-in credentials by entering a strong password and confirming the password. Click Next.

11. Enter the dial-out credentials. This is the account name, domain, and password configured on the other RRAS VPN demand-dial interface. Use the account name in Table 8-9, **DD_London**, and the password agreed upon with the VPN administrator of the other site. Click Next, followed by Finish to complete the wizard.

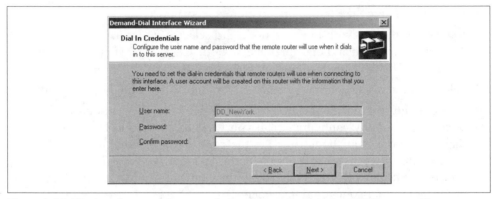

Figure 8-39. The interface name becomes the user name that the other VPN router will use to authenticate to this VPN router

The administrator for VPNTwo should follow these same steps to configure VPNTwo, except that the administrator should use the information in Table 8-9 for VPNTwo and the user account password you entered for the DD_NewYork user account. When both administrators have completed the configuration, test the connection by right-clicking the demand dial interface and selecting Connect.

Configuring Dial-in Properties

The demand-dial interface wizard described in the previous section establishes a basic demand-dial VPN. To modify its configuration, use the Properties pages of the network interface created in the Network Interface node of the RRAS server. Open the Properties pages by right-clicking on the interface and selecting Properties. The following properties can be modified:

IP address of the remote VPN demand-dial router
Change the address on the page shown by selecting the General tab.

Make the demand-dial connection persistent
Click the Options tab, and then click the "Persistent connection" radio button.

Change the idle-time before hang-up for the demand-dial connection
Click the Options tab use the "Idle time before hanging up" drop-down box.

Set dialing policy

Change the number of redial attempts in the "Redial attempts" drop-down box and/or change the average redial intervals setting in its drop-down box.

Remove data encryption requirement

Select the Security tab, and click to deselect the "Require data encryption (disconnect if none)" checkbox.

Modify data encryption requirement

Select the Security tab, and click the Advanced button. Then, on the Advanced Security settings page, select either "No encryption allowed (server will disconnect if it requires encryption)" or "Maximum strength encryption (disconnect if server declines)."

Modify authentication methods

On the Advanced Security page, select the protocols that are allowed.

Change the VPN protocol

Select the Networking tab, and then change the type of VPN or use the Setting button to change the VPN protocol configuration.

Change network connection settings

Select the Networking tab and modify the TCP/IP settings for the connection, or add and/or modify other connection settings.

Use a pre-shared key for a L2TP/IPSec connection

Select the Security tab and click the IPSec Settings button. Then click "Use pre-shared key for authentication." Enter the key in the Key text box, as shown in Figure 8-40. This setting will also have to be added to the other VPN server that needs to authenticate to this VPN server. No connection can take place until the other VPN server is configured.

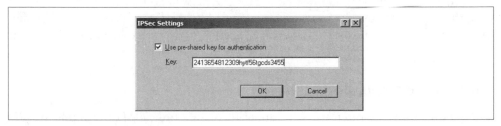

Figure 8-40. Use a long pre-shared key

Configuring a demand-dial VPN is not the only advanced technique that is worth knowing about. L2TP/IPSec VPNs require the use of digital-certificates for their operation. Each router must obtain a compatible certificate either from a public CA such as Verisign, or from a third-part CA established on their network. Alternatively, you can set up certificate services on a Windows server to produce the certificate. These options may not be suitable for you at this time. There is an option, albeit a less secure one. You may opt to use a shared key, as discussed next.

Using a Shared Key for a L2TP/IPSec VPN

A normal client-to-server VPN connection using L2TP/IPSec can also be configured to use a shared key. A *shared key* is simply a combination of letters and numbers that is created by an administrator and entered in the Properties pages of the VPN or other service for which shared keys are valid. Each VPN endpoint (router and client) will need to configure the shared key. This is not a good security solution, especially in a large network, because soon the key is so well known that unauthorized individuals may learn of it and use it to break into the network. When you allow the use of a shared key, you weaken security. This is because the shared key must be distributed to anyone who has to configure a connection to the VPN. The more people that know the shared key, the more likely a rogue, unauthorized system can create a connection to the VPN server. While user authentication is also required, by removing the need for a unique computer authentication, you have reduced the level of security. There is also no key management built in. If you want to change the key periodically, the process is manual and no connection can be made until the keys are replaced on all clients. Imagine the problems inherent in distributing a new shared key for thousands of VPN clients! In the real world, this will rarely (if ever) be done.

To use a shared key for a L2TP/IPSec VPN server, begin by opening the Routing and Remote Access node. Right-click on the server and select Properties. Select the Security tab. Select "Allow custom IPSec policy for L2TP connection." Enter a key to be used in the "Pre-shared key" text box. The key can be any non-null number of 8 to 256 characters in length. A longer key may improve security, as it will be less easy to guess. However, if the key is distributed with the service profile created for VPN clients, key length will not matter if the service profile is easy to obtain.

While shared keys weaken security, firewalls between the VPN and the external network improve security. You must configure the firewall so that the VPN traffic can pass through it. Follow the instructions provided by the firewall company to configure the firewall. The ports and other data needed to do so are included in the next section.

Configuring Firewalls for VPN

VPN connections are often used to tunnel through a firewall. For example, a VPN server may be located behind a firewall that sits between the VPN server and the Internet. Clients on the Internet can use their VPN connection to access data on the internal LAN. In order for Windows Server 2003 VPN connections to do so, the firewall must allow inbound data on the appropriate ports. Tables 8-10 and 8-11 list the ports used by the VPN protocols and the information required for input and output filters on the firewall.

Table 8-10. PPTP input and output filters

Interface IP	Subnet mask	Destination port for input filters, source port for output filters	Used for
Internet interface of the VPN router	255.255.255.255	TCP 1723	PPTP tunnel maintenance
Internet interface of the VPN routers	255.255.255.255	Protocol ID 47	PPTP tunneled data
Internet interface of the VPN routers	255.255.255.255	TCP source port 1723	Required for the calling router

Table 8-11. L2TP/IPSec input and output filters

Interface IP	Subnet mask	Destination port for input filters, source port for output filters	Used for
Internet interface of the VPN router	255l.255.255.255	UDP 500	Internet Key Exchange (IKE)
Internet interface of the VPN router	255.255.255.255	UDP 4500 input/UDP 5500 output	IPSec NAT-T
Internet interface of the VPN router	255.255.255.255	UDP 1701	L2TP traffic

Even if you have no need for the advanced configuration techniques described in this section, you need to configure clients to use remote access unless a demand-dial VPN is used.

Configuring Clients to Use Remote Access

Clients can be individually configured to use remote access connections. However, managing many clients is then difficult to do. To assist in managing clients, use the Connection Manager Administration Kit (CMAK) to create client profiles. The Connection Manager (CM) Profile is a self-executing file that installs a preconfigured dialer and any provided scripts on the client computer. Creating profiles ensures consistency in the configuration for each Windows OS.

In addition to a dialer, a phone book can be created that will provide traveling users with a listing of the telephone numbers for every location. The phone book can be updated on-line from an FTP server configured as a phonebook server.

 The CMAK is provided on the Windows Server 2003 installation CD-ROM, but not installed by default. You can install this tool by running the *adminpak.msi* program from the I386 folder on the installation CD-ROM. To create a profile, run the Connection Manager Administration Kit program from Start → Administrative Tools. A tutorial on setting up a Connection Manager profile can be downloaded from *http://www.microsoft.com/downloads/details.aspx?FamilyID=93fd20e7-e73a-43f6-96ec-7bcc7527709b&DisplayLang=en*.

Even if you make no mistakes in setting up firewalls, RRAS servers, and clients, you may still encounter problems as well as malicious attacks. You learned earlier how to set up simple logging for RRAS. The next section elaborates on the theme of logging and includes information on RRAS auditing.

Configuring Logging and Accounting (Auditing) for Remote Access

Logging for both RRAS and IAS consists of entries in the Windows event logs, as well as specific logs for RRAS and IAS. By default, connection requests are not logged, and only service start and stop events are recorded in the event logs. You should configure additional logging record information for troubleshooting and security events. The information on logging connection attempts and successes is useful not only for troubleshooting, but also for tracing remote access (as well as attempted and successful attacks). The service specific logs, if configured, include information about each connection request. Logging can also be redirected to a Microsoft SQL Server or to a named pipe. A *named pipe* is a pipe (a connection end-point represented by an address in memory) that has been given a name. *Pipes* are a form of *interprocess communication* (sharing of information between processes). Pipes are a one-way or duplex connection point to a running process and they might be used to send information to another computer.

Configure additional event log logging on the Logging page of the RRAS server Properties page. (Right-click on the server in the Routing and Remote Access console, and select Properties. Then click the Logging tab, as shown in Figure 8-41.

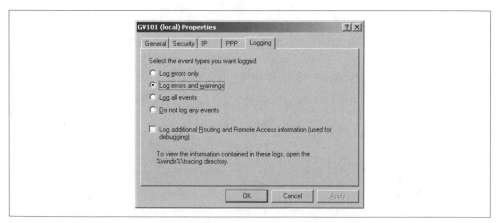

Figure 8-41. Configure event logging on the Logging tab of the Properties page

To configure request logging, select the Remote Access Logging folder in the Routing and Remote Access console (as shown in Figure 8-42) and double-click on the log file type in the detail pane on the right side of the screen.

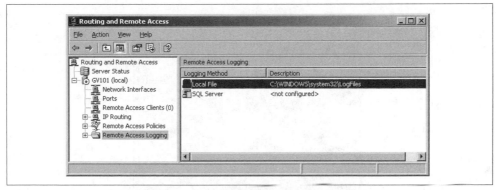

Figure 8-42. Configure request logging from the Remote Access Logging node

For logging to a file, select from the options displayed on the Settings tab, as shown in Figure 8-43. The Log File tab shown in Figure 8-44, can be used to change the location for the log file, the log file format, or the frequency of new log file creation.

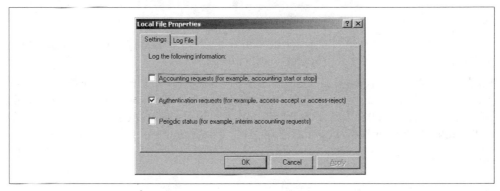

Figure 8-43. Setup request logging

Summary

As we have seen, routing remote access services entails more than providing dial-up connections for telecommuting employees. Remote access includes routing services for IGMP, DHCP relay, NAT, OSPF, and RIP. While no one expects the RRAS server to replace the need for dedicated routers on the network, routing services are often required on very small networks, or to support other remote access services such as dial-up remote access and VPNs. This chapter discussed all of the routing services provided by RRAS and how to configure them.

Also included was a complete discussion of how to use the server to provide traditional dial-up access, VPNs, and demand-dial VPNs. Remote access policies provide very granular control over remote access. Therefore, they were also explained along

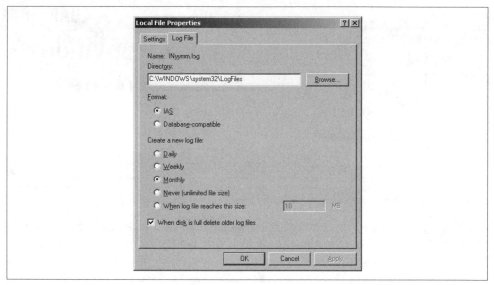

Figure 8-44. Configure the request log file

with configuration steps. Finally, critical information necessary for configuring firewalls so they can pass VPN protocols was included.

You must follow the firewall manufacturer's instructions for configuring the firewall, so it is fitting that the next chapter discusses the Windows host-based firewall. Windows Server 2003, like the Windows XP client computer that preceded the server release, has its own host-based firewall. Configuration of these firewalls is also covered.

## CHAPTER 9

Protecting Hosts with Windows Host Firewalls

It is no longer enough to provide firewall services at an organization's network perimeter. Each server and desktop computer that resides inside network boundaries requires its own security protection. In addition, when corporate laptops are plugged into the Internet from employee homes or hotel rooms, they become part of the perimeter of the corporate network. One way to protect hosts is by implementing a firewall on each individual host.

Firewall services are native to Windows XP and Windows Server 2003. While this book focuses on Windows Server 2003, it is important to have Windows XP information so that you can manage Windows XP clients in a Windows Server 2003 forest. This chapter examines Windows Server 2003 firewall services, including a personal firewall, TCP/IP protocol filters, a basic firewall as part of Routing and Remote Access Services (RRAS), and additional port filtering capabilities as part of the configuration of RRAS and its remote access policies. IP Security (IPSec) policies, also included in Windows Server 2003 firewall services, are discussed in Chapter 11.

Service Pack 2 (SP2) for Windows XP and Service Pack 1 (SP1) for Windows Server 2003 improve native firewall services by renaming and adding additional capability to the host-based Windows Firewall and by enabling it by default on Windows XP SP2 computers.

To begin our discussion of Internet connection firewalls, let's review some firewall basics.

Firewall Basics

Firewalls were originally implemented at the perimeters of networks to protect hosts on a trusted network against hosts on an untrusted network. The firewall was implemented on a device with multiple interfaces. One interface connected to the Internet or public (untrusted) network, and the other connected to the organization's trusted or private network. These early firewalls often allowed all outbound packets to pass from the private network to the public and blocked *all* inbound communications.

If a web server, DNS server, FTP server, or other host offered services that should be accessible from the public network, the host sat outside the firewall. Later, a second firewall was added to protect these public-facing hosts, and still later the single-perimeter firewall model added filters that allowed inbound packets to specific services available on the private network. The firewall inspected, rejected, or passed on all traffic attempting to pass through it, based on rules configured on the firewall.

Perimeter firewalls are still the most common example of firewalls today. However, a growing number of organizations are implementing firewalls on internal network segments, and organizations and individuals are implementing host-level firewalls. In some cases, the host firewall may be the only perimeter protection the host receives. These implementations recognize that there is risk on every network, even one placed behind a perimeter firewall.

Windows Server 2003 and Windows XP provide a native host firewall, as well as several ways to create rudimentary firewall services on the host. To implement Windows host firewalls correctly, and to determine if they are the best firewalls for the job, you must consider their capabilities.

The first firewalls were little more than *packet-filtering routers*. The firewall filtered all traffic bound from one network to the other and blocked or permitted packets based on internal rules that designated the ports and IP addresses that were unacceptable. Modern firewalls also provide *stateful filtering* and possibly *application layer filtering*. Stateful filtering only permits inbound packets that are responses to requests from hosts on the private network. The firewall maintains a table of current outbound connections, including source and destination IP addresses and ports. When an inbound packet arrives, its information is compared to entries on the list. If a match is found, the packet is allowed; if not, it is dropped. An application layer firewall blocks and permits based on packet content, not just header information. Traffic bound for port 80 on an internal web server must meet additional conditions beyond IP address and port information.

Some host firewalls offer all these services and some do not. Another difference between perimeter firewalls and host-level firewalls is that some host-level firewalls only offer ingress (or inbound) traffic filtering, while others offer both ingress and egress (or outbound) filtering.

Figure 9-1 illustrates a packet-filtering router/firewall. In the figure, a short rule list indicates the traffic that is allowed to pass. This firewall's job is to block all port 80 traffic, except traffic bound to the web server at IP address 192.168.5.60. Note that the log sample included shows that access to port 80 on 192.168.5.60 is allowed, but access to port 80 on 192.168.5.10 is blocked.

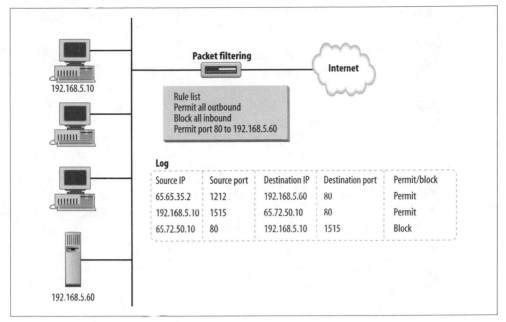

Figure 9-1. A simple packet-filtering router

Figure 9-2 shows a firewall with stateful inspection. Traffic may be passed to hosts on the internal network in response to their requests. In the figure, workstation 192.168.5.10 requests a web page from the Internet-based server and a response is returned.

Figure 9-3 shows an example of an application layer firewall. Packets are inspected not just by port and IP address, but also by content. Note that access to the web server, while permitted, is blocked after examination of the packet. The description in the log, of course, will be determined by the programming of the application layer firewalls.

Ingress and *egress* filtering is an important part of network protection. While ingress filtering seeks to protect hosts on the internal network from the actions of hosts on the external network, egress filtering seeks to protect hosts on all networks from hosts on the internal network. Recent malicious software (or malware) may require connection to external hosts to complete the infection, may provide remote control to external attackers, or may infect additional hosts. By provided egress filtering, you are not only being a good "Internet citizen" but also containing your losses by preventing the completion of the infection.

Each of these capabilities forms an important part of firewall protection and should be a part of your decisions on which type of firewall, perimeter firewall, or a host firewall, to select. It may appear to be a simple decision (that is, select the firewall that offers all of these services). However, other factors to consider including ease of

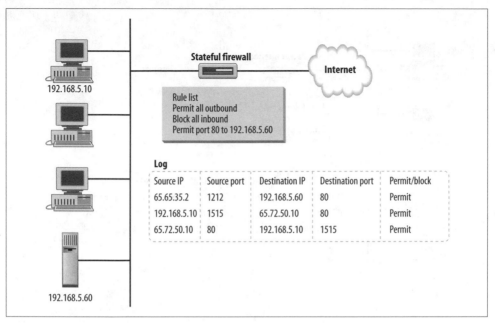

Figure 9-2. Stateful firewalls allow incoming responses to the requests of internal computers

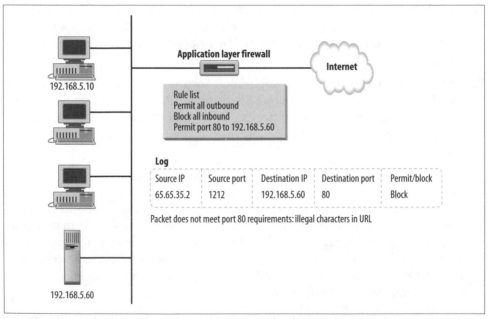

Figure 9-3. The application layer firewall uses the content of the packet for filtering decisions

management, protection during startup, cost, and support make that decision more complicated. In addition, some factors such as ease of management more important to host-level protection. The "Which Firewall Services Should You Use?" section later in this chapter addresses these issues. Meanwhile, you should study Windows firewalls and understand their capabilities.

A good starting point is an examination of Internet Connection Sharing.

Internet Connection Sharing

Internet Connection Sharing (ICS) is not a part of firewall services on Windows systems. However, if ICS is implemented, a firewall should also be used. ICS allows a Windows computer to act as a router between other hosts on an internal network and an external network such as the Internet. It provides network address translation (NAT), DHCP, and name resolution (DNS Proxy) services for other computers on the local network. Users can access the Internet and use the Outlook Express application as if their computers were directly connected to the Internet. It can also be configured to allow Internet access to computers on the local network such as web servers. ICS is most often used in small business and home or home office networks. Using ICS in a larger organization is not recommended, because the ICS-enabled computer will respond to DHCP client requests. Enabling ICS is, therefore, enabling a rogue DHCP server and can interfere with communications on the local network. (Hosts may obtain ICS network addresses instead of those required to communicate with servers and clients on the local network.)

 The Internet Connection Firewall (ICF) and the Network Bridge feature are available on Windows Server 2003 Standard Edition and the 32-bit version of Windows Server 2003. They are not available with Windows Server 2003 Web Edition, Datacenter Edition, or the 64-bit versions of Windows Server 2003. The ICF is discussed later in this chapter in the section "Windows Firewall."

When used, the ICS computer is rarely a dedicated router. Instead, the computer running ICS is used for daily work and pleasure if it is a workstation, and for other services (such as file and print) if it is a Windows server. You should understand its function so that you can disable its use in your Windows domain when necessary, or to ensure that it is securely deployed if you decide to implement it.

To fully understand the capabilities of ICS, you should have an understanding of the following:

- Enabling ICS
- Enabling Internet access to local services
- Using a network bridge with ICS

- Securing ICS
- Managing ICS via Group Policy

Enabling ICS

In the typical small network, all computers are connected to the same network and ICS is implemented to provide all computers access to the Internet. To set up ICS, select and configure one computer as the ICS computer. The ICS computer must have two network connections: an Ethernet connection to the local network and a connection to the Internet (via modem, ISDN, DSL, or cable modem). If these network connections are in place, and you have successfully tested the Internet connection, enable ICS as follows.

Click Start and select the Control Panel. Double-click Network Connections. Right-click the network connection to be shared and select Properties. Select the Advanced tab and click "Allow other network users to connect through this computer's Internet connection," as shown in Figure 9-4. In the figure, the network connection has been renamed to Internet.

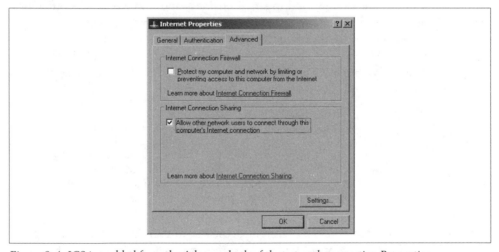

Figure 9-4. ICS is enabled from the Advanced tab of the network connection Properties

Click OK. Configure clients on the network to dynamically obtain an IP address.

When ICS is enabled, the following changes are made:

- The local network connection is assigned the IP address 192.168.0.1. Consequently, any connections to other computers on the network will be lost. In addition, any Internet connections must also be refreshed.
- The ICS service is started.

- A DHCP allocator is available to assign addresses with a default range of 192.168.0.0 with a subnet mask of 255.255.255.0. The ICS host address is reserved, and clients are assigned addresses in the range of 192.168.0.2 to 192.168.0.254.

- A local DNS proxy is enabled.

- Autodial is enabled.

You cannot disable the DHCP allocator or change the default range of addresses.

> ICS can be used to enable all computers on a network to access a VPN connection. The VPN connected must be ICS-enabled. For other computers to share the connection, the VPN connection must first be created on the ICS computer.

Enabling Internet Access to Local Services

ICS uses NAT to provide computers on the internal network access to the Internet. While NAT is not meant to provide security for internal hosts, external hosts do not know the actual IP address of internal hosts. Therefore, if you want to provide access to services such as web services, FTP services, or SMTP services, you must explicitly configure access. Begin by clicking Start and selecting the Control Panel. Double-click Network Connections. Right-click the ICS network connection and select Properties. Select the Advanced tab and click the Settings button to display a list of services, as shown in Figure 9-5.

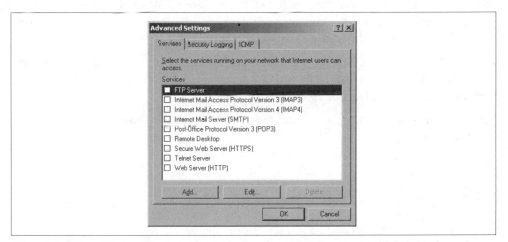

Figure 9-5. When ICS is enabled, access to services running on the private network can be configured

Click to select the service you wish to provide access to. On the Service Settings page enter the name of the host that offers this service, as shown in Figure 9-6, then click OK.

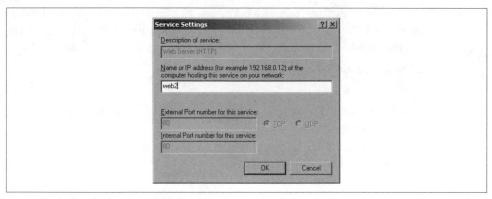

Figure 9-6. Identify the server that hosts the service to which you allow access

Click OK twice to exit the network settings Properties pages.

Using a Network Bridge with ICS

In a more complex small network, the ICS computer may have more than one private network connection. To enable ICS when the host computer is connected to multiple LAN segments, you must bridge the private networks before enabling ICS.

Begin by clicking Start and selecting the Control Panel. Double-click Network Connections. Select and hold down the Shift key and then click each of the adapters for the connections that should be included in the bridge. Wireless network connections, Ethernet, IEEE-1394 adapters, and telephone line connections can be included in a bridge. Do not include the network connection to the Internet.

Release the Shift key. Click on the Advanced menu and select Bridge Connections. The bridge is added to the Network Connections page and identifies the network connections that are bridged, as shown in Figure 9-7.

Select the Internet network connection and enable ICS, as explained in the earlier section "Enabling ICS."

 Do not bridge connections to the Internet. If you do so, you expose hosts on the internal network to the Internet. Some types of Internet connections (such as DSL, modem, and cable modem connections) cannot be added to a network bridge. Other connections (such as an Ethernet connection to a router that is connected to the Internet) can be bridged, but it should not be.

Securing ICS

ICS does not add security to the Internet connection. It does, however, provide NAT services that hide the IP address of the hosts on the internal network. Even so, it is

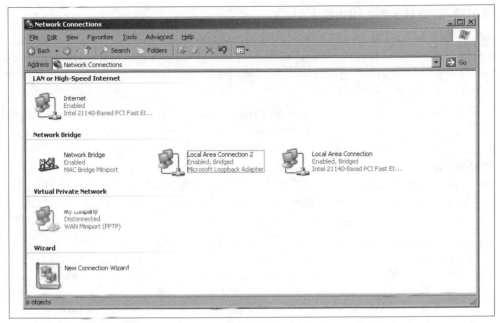

Figure 9-7. Private network connections can be bridged to allow access from all private network connections to the Internet over a shared public network connection

still possible for an Internet-based attack to be successful. It is also possible to misconfigure ICS and expose the ICS host and computers on the private network to the risk of compromise. Take the following steps to secure ICS services:

- Implement a firewall. A separate firewall can be placed between the ICS host and the Internet, the Windows built-in firewall can be enabled, or some other personal firewall can be installed. Be sure not to set up ICS without turning on the Windows Firewall. If no other firewall sits between the ICS host and the Internet, then the Windows Firewall (or some other firewall) should be used.

- When configuring ICS, ensure that ICS is enabled on the Internet connection, not on the connection to the private network. If ICS is configured on the private network connection, hosts on the internal network are subject to attack from the Internet if the ICS host is connected to the Internet.

- If a network bridge is created, ensure that the Internet connection is not part of the bridge.

- Avoid providing access to private network services. If they must be allowed, configure them via the Settings page for ICS, and only configure those services that are necessary.

- Harden the ICS host computer and, if at all possible, dedicate it to this task.

Managing ICS via Group Policy

By default, management of ICS is not restricted via Group Policy. A local administrator can enable the ICS, on a member computer. A good practice is to disable this service using Group Policy. The following two location-aware Administrative template policies can be configured to do so:

Prohibit use of Internet Connection Sharing on your DNS domain network. When enabled, administrators cannot enable ICS on the local computer. When disabled or not configured, administrators can enable ICS on the local computer.

Prohibit installation and configuration of Network bridge on your DNS domain network. When enabled, administrators cannot create a network bridge on the local computer. When disabled or not configured, administrators can create a network bridge on the local computer.

Location-aware policies operate only when a computer is connected to the same DNS domain network as the one it was connected to when the policy was refreshed. This means that administrators of laptop computers will not be able to enable ICS when the laptop is connected to its domain, but they will be able to enable ICS when the laptop is connected to a different network (such as a hotel or conference network).

Windows Firewall

The built-in Windows Firewall, first known as the Internet Connection Firewall (ICF), is part of Windows XP and Windows Server 2003. Service Pack 2 (SP2) for Windows XP and Service Pack 1 (SP1) for Windows Server 2003 improved the firewall and renamed it the Windows Firewall. This book will use the term *Windows Firewall,* but will identify the new features provided by the service packs. The firewall provides packet filtering, stateful inspection, and protection during system boot. Unsolicited inbound packets are silently dropped. It provides ingress filtering only—all outbound traffic is allowed.

 Do not confuse the built-in Windows Firewall with Microsoft Internet Security and Acceleration (ISA) Server. ISA is a software-based firewall that can be installed on Windows Server 2003 or Windows 2000 Server. Microsoft sells it separately. Unlike the host-based Windows Firewall, ISA server is a full-featured firewall that provides stateful filtering, application layer filtering, egress as well as ingress filtering, and many other enterprise-level features. It can also be used as a web proxy. Third-party add-ins are available to expand the services it offers.

Internet Connection Firewall (ICF)

The Windows Server 2003 built-in firewall is not enabled by default. Installation of SP1 will not change this. The firewall can be enabled and configured to provide rudimentary protection for the server. When enabled, logging is not turned on.

To enable and configure the ICF, begin by clicking Start and selecting the Control Panel. Double-click Network Connections. Right-click the network connection to be shared and select Properties. Select the Advanced tab and click "Protect my computer and network by limiting or preventing access to this computer from the Internet," as shown in Figure 9-8.

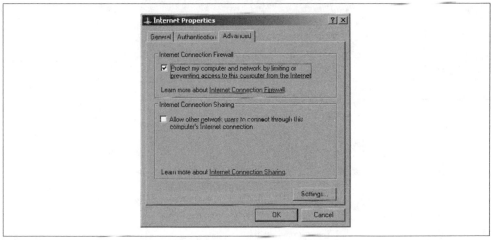

Figure 9-8. Enable the Internet Connection Firewall from the network connection using the Advanced tab on the Properties page

Click the Settings button. If you must provide access to services on the private network or on this host, select the service and enter the IP address of the server where the service resides. Click OK. Click the Security Logging tab and select "Log dropped packets" and/or "Log successful connections." If required, change log file options, as shown in Figure 9-9. "Log file options" include the Name options (the name of the firewall log file and the path to its location) and a "Size limit" in kilobytes. If the log file reaches the limit set in the "Size limit" box, a new firewall log file is created. Click OK.

Select the ICMP tab. Click to select ICMP options from those shown in Figure 9-10 if ICMP communications are permitted. Click OK twice to close network settings.

If you need to provide a service connection that is not listed by default on the Advance Settings Services page, as shown in Figure 9-11, you can configure a custom service definition.

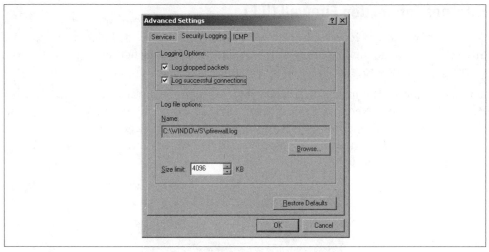

Figure 9-9. Logging is not configured by default and should be enabled

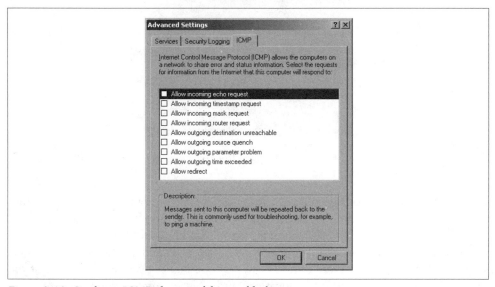

Figure 9-10. Configure ICMP if required for troubleshooting

To do so, select the Services page. Click the Add button and enter a description of the service. In the Service Settings page shown in Figure 9-12, enter the computer name or IP address of the computer on which the service will run.

Enter a value in the "External port number for this service" field and click TCP or UDP. Enter a value in the "Internal port number for this service" field. When you have finished, click OK.

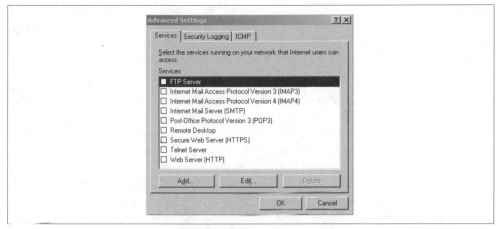

Figure 9-11. Some services are already configured as exceptions and can simply be selected

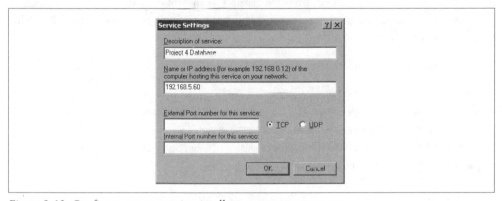

Figure 9-12. Configure custom services to allow access to programs

Now that you have enabled ICF and customized some of the service settings, it is time to examine some of the modifications that have been introduced with the service packs.

Service Pack Firewall Modifications

The security operations changed in Windows XP SP2 represent a radical departure from earlier versions of Windows. SP2 does this by making security configuration changes that interfere with the functional operation of Windows applications. Both Microsoft and third-party programs must be adjusted to enable them to continue to run after the application of SP2. This is a departure from traditional Windows updates, since earlier updates usually attempted to add features and correct bugs while seeking to maintain compatibility.

SP 2 changes are of interest to those who administer Windows Server 2003 networks because the changes provide additional centralized management features, change the default behavior of clients on the network, and are representative of changes in SP1 for Windows Server 2003. All service packs introduce change into a network and should be carefully reviewed before installation. However, SP2 for Windows XP makes radical changes that can interfere with the management of network clients.

Because the Windows XP SP2 firewall is enabled by default, and its default behavior is to block all unsolicited incoming traffic, network management and local computer services will be disrupted. Table 9-1 lists specific tools, applications, and services that are impacted. This should be referred to as an example of the type of issues that will occur, not as the definitive list of problems that must happen. The remote use of common Microsoft Management Console (MMC) based administration tools will be blocked. If the local computer offers network services (for example, web services), access to these services may be blocked as well. When SP2 is installed, the firewall is enabled by default. Administrators should review the impact this will have in their organizations and modify (as necessary) the Firewall INF file before installing SP2. In a domain, the firewall can be controlled using Group Policy. Information on modifying this file is included in the section "Modifying firewall behavior using the Windows Firewall INF file and unattend.txt" later in this chapter.

Table 9-1. Examples of tools and services blocked by default

Item	Specifics
Management Tools	SNMP, WMI, remote use of netsh or mmc snap-ins, Remote Assistance, Remote Desktop
Network Services	File and print sharing, message queuing, web services
Listening Services	Universal Plug-and-Play (UPnP), Routing Information Protocol (RIP)
Applications	Instant messaging, peer-to-peer network programs

 SP1 for Windows Server 2003 will not enable the firewall by default.

Modifications

The Windows XP firewall is turned on by default after the installation of SP2. The following are a few key changes to the firewall and its administration (more modifications are listed later in this chapter in the section "More modifications"):

Security Center
  A new service, the Security Center, is added to help end user security management.

Startup security
  This offers protection during system boot before firewall service is operational.

Firewall INF File
  This allows you to use the INF file to configure Windows Firewall behavior.

Control Panel Firewall Applet

This allows you to configure the firewall from a new Control Panel applet.

Windows registry control of alerting and notification

Three registry settings are available to control the alerting and notification feature.

New Group Policy settings

These enable better central management of firewall behavior.

Netsh commands

This set firewall configuration using the `netsh` commands.

A couple of these changes (the Security Center and startup security) deem some extra attention.

Security Center. A new service, the Security Center, is added. The Security Center monitors security services such as a host firewall, Windows updates, and local antivirus protection. It also provides a central location for changing security settings. It may be able to also determine if the antivirus protection is up to date. The Security Center uses a red icon in the notification area of the user's taskbar and provides an alert message at logon with links to the interface. This feature is turned on by default for XP computers in a workgroup, but turned off by default for computers joined in a domain. Figure 9-13 shows the Security Center on a computer where no virus protection is provided. (Note the Alert.)

The Security Center is not turned on for clients joined to a domain. However, if you wish to do so, a Group Policy setting can be used to turn it on. This Group Policy setting is "Turn on SecurityCenter (computers in Windows domains only)" and is located in Administrative Templates → Windows Components → Security Center. By default, this is not configured, as shown in Figure 9-14.

Startup Security. A new startup Windows Firewall Policy performs stateful packet filtering at boot after the network service is started and until the firewall service is successfully started. This means that startup tasks for services such as DHCP and DNS can operate, but unsolicited traffic will be dropped. After the firewall service has loaded, the startup policy is dropped.

Modifying firewall behavior using the Windows Firewall INF file and unattend.txt

If the service is installed without modification, then the firewall is installed as enabled, and all unsolicited traffic will be blocked. Administrators should configure the service pack installation so that the firewall is installed with appropriate settings for their networks. Use the Windows Firewall INF file (*netfw.inf*) when performing an interactive installation. Use the *unattend.txt* file, to configure settings for unattended installations of the service pack.

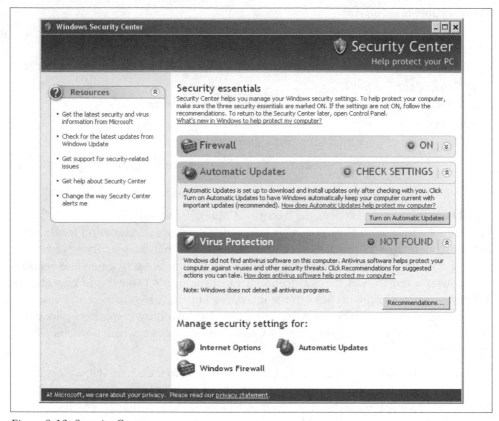

Figure 9-13. Security Center

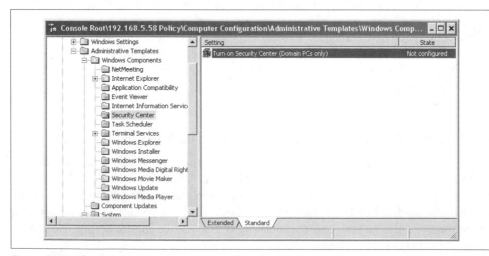

Figure 9-14. The Security Center can be turned on for domain member computers by using Group Policy

The Windows Firewall INF file (*netfw.inf*) is a configuration file that can be used by administrators to modify the behavior of the Windows Firewall. Use Notepad or another text editor to modify *netfw.inf* and use the new version during installation of the service pack to configure the firewall during installation. Modify the local *netfw.inf* after installation to modify firewall behavior. The *netfw.inf* file is located on a Windows XP CD-ROM in the I386 directory. There are several reasons why changes to the default behavior are necessary, including the following:

- A third-party vendor firewall is your default.
- Installed programs require filters configured for the Windows Firewall to enable traffic.
- Network services such as remote management are used in your network and, therefore, specific ports must be open.

To modify behavior, modify the *ICF.AddReg.DomainProfile* and/or *ICF.AddReg.StandardProfile* sections of the file. These profiles determine how the firewall is configured when the computer is connected to a domain or not, respectively. If the Windows computer is not a member of a domain, the *ICF.AddReg.StandardProfile* will always be enforced.

To reconfigure the *netfw.inf* file on an existing Windows XP SP 2 system, use Notepad or another text editor to open the *%windir%\Inf\netfw.inf* file, as shown in Figure 9-15.

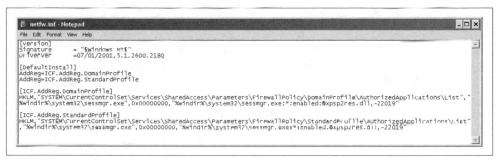

Figure 9-15. Use the netfw.inf file to modify firewall behavior

Make changes and save the file. Run the command `netsh firewall reset` from a command prompt. Firewall behavior is determined by registry settings included in the file. To make changes, add or adjust values located at the paths:

HKEY_LOCAL_MACHINE\SYSTEM\CurrentControlSet\Services\SharedAccess\ Parameters\FirewallPolicy\StandardProfile

or:

HKEY_LOCAL_MACHINE\SYSTEM\CurrentControlSet\Services\SharedAccess\ Parameters\FirewallPolicy\DomainProfile.

Table 9-2 lists and describes the values that may be changed in the *netfw.inf* file.

Table 9-2. Firewall INF settings

Value	Setting	Description
EnableFirewall	0x00010001,1	The firewall is enabled.
DoNotAllowExceptions	0x00010001,1	If the firewall is enabled and this setting is configured, the firewall blocks all unsolicited traffic, including that identified in an exception list.
DisableNotifications	0x00010001,1	Turns off notification when a program not already included in the exceptions list attempts to add itself or its traffic to an exceptions list.
DisableUnicastResponsesToMulticastBroadcast	0x00010001,1	Prevents incoming unicast response packets. By default, the firewall allows these packets in responses to outgoing multicast or broadcast packets.
RemoteAdminSettings: Enabled	0x00010001,1	Enables remote administration by statically opening ports TCP 135 and TCP 445 to unsolicited incoming traffic. Communication via named pipes is also permitted. These ports are required for Remote Procedure Call (RPC) and Distributed Component Object Model (DCOM) communications. They are blocked by default. When this setting is enabled, additional ports required by RPC are dynamically opened.
RemoteAdminSettings RemoteAddresses	0,00000000,"*scope*"	When RemoteAdminSettings is enabled, you may specify a scope of addresses from which this traffic is allowed.

Table 9-2. Firewall INF settings (continued)

Value	Setting	Description
IcmpSettings	*"ICMP MessageType",0x0001 0001,1*	Allows ICMP message types as specified.
GlobalyOpenPorts\List	*"Port number: protocol", 0x00000000, "port number:protocol: scope:mode:port's friendly name"*	Statically opens this list of ports. (See the following discussion.)

When opening TCP 135 and TCP 445 for remote administration, you should carefully limit the scope of addresses from which traffic may be accepted. By default all IP addresses are accepted, and this increases risk unacceptably. A large number of attacks are based on using these Windows ports. Narrow the scope of acceptable addresses to those used by administrators. While you can use the term LocalSubnet in the Firewall INF file to restrict incoming traffic to the local subnet, a better option is to create a custom scope by including a dotted decimal subnet mask or a prefix length. A list of IP addresses delimited by commas is also acceptable. Examples of scopes are 192.168.0.0/255.255.255.0 and 192.168.5.6, 192.168.5.10, 192.168.5.12.

 When configuring scope by creating a list of IP addresses, do not leave spaces between the IP addresses in the list, or else the list will be ignored and traffic from all IP addresses will be accepted.

Scope may also be limited when defining statically opened ports. When defining the entry for GlobalyOpenPorts\List, you should consider the scope option as well as add information to help identify the port in the Windows Firewall GUI. It is also possible to list ports that should not be statically opened. In the parameters for the option, use the following:

Port number
    This is the number assigned to the port.

Protocol
    This is either TCP or UDP.

Scope
    This is an IP address range.

Mode
    This is either "enabled" or "disabled." Use disabled to explicitly require the port not to be statically opened.

Port's friendly name
    This is a description you provide to help identify the statically opened port in the GUI (for example, "web server TCP 80").

An unattended installation of the service pack can reduce the need to provide feedback during service pack installation. Options for creating different types of service pack installations (including an unattended one) are fully discussed in the documentation accompanying SP2. To read and use the documentation prior to installation, unzip the *deploy.cab* file located on the service pack CD-ROM. This file is located in the *Support\Tools* folder. Extract the *deploy.chm* file and double-click on it to open. Specific information on *unattend.txt* can be found by extracting and consulting the *ref.chm* help file.

If you are installing from a command line or simple script, develop an *unattened.txt* file and use it during installation by entering **xpsp2.exe unattend:unattend.txt**. While there are many options that can be configured, those important to Windows Firewall installation are listed here. Modifications to the *unattend.txt* file that affect the Windows Firewall operation are in the sections.

[WindowsFirewall]
: This references the other sections.

[WindowsFirewall.Domain]
: These are settings that affect the computer when it is connected to the domain.

[WindowsFirewall.Standard]
: These are settings that affect the computer when it is not connected to the domain.

[WindowsFirewall.*program_name*]
: This adds a program by the name of program_name to the exceptions list.

[WindowsFirewall.*service_name*]
: This adds a predefined service such as File and Print to the exceptions list.

[WindowsFirewall.*portopening_name*]
: This adds a port to the exceptions list.

[WindowsFirewall.*icmpsetting_name*]
: This adds ICMP message types to the exception list.

Example 9-1 is a sample firewall section from the *unattend.txt* file as described in *ref.chm*. In the file, the number 1 is used to indicate that the feature is enabled.

Example 9-1. Sample firewall section from unattend.txt

```
[WindowsFirewall]
Profiles = WindowsFirewall.Domain, WindowsFirewall.Standard
LogFile = %WINDIR%\Pfirewall.log
LogSize = 4096
LogDroppedPackets = 1
LogConnections = 1
[WindowsFirewall.Standard]
```

Example 9-1. Sample firewall section from unattend.txt (continued)

```
Type = 3
Mode = 1
Exceptions = 1
Notifications = 1
MulticastBroadcastResponse = 1
AllowedPrograms = WindowsFirewall.RemoteAssistance
Services = WindowsFirewall.RemoteDesktop
PortOpenings = WindowsFirewall.WebService
IcmpSettings = WindowsFirewall.EchoRequest
[WindowsFirewall.Domain]
Type = 3
Mode = 0

[WindowsFirewall.RemoteAssistance]
Program = "%WINDIR%\System32\Sessmgr.exe"
Name = "Remote Assistance"
Mode = 1
Scope = 2
Addresses = "192.168.0.5,LocalSubnet"

[WindowsFirewall.RemoteDesktop]
Type = 2
Mode = 1
Scope = 2
Addresses = "192.168.0.5,LocalSubnet"

[WindowsFirewall.WebService]
Protocol= 6
Port = 80
Name = "Web Server (TCP 80)"
Mode = 1
Scope = 2
Addresses = "192.168.0.5,LocalSubnet"

[WindowsFirewall.EchoRequest]
Type = 8
Mode = 1
```

Modifying firewall settings using the Control Panel. After service pack installation, the "Protect my computer and network by limiting or preventing access to this computer from the Internet" checkbox is removed from the Advanced tab of a network connection Properties pages. While the Setting button remains, it launches the new Firewall applet in the Control Panel. Members of the local Administrators group can configure general settings and exceptions by using this applet. Figure 9-16 show the page from the Advanced tab, while Table 9-3 lists and describes the settings available on this page.

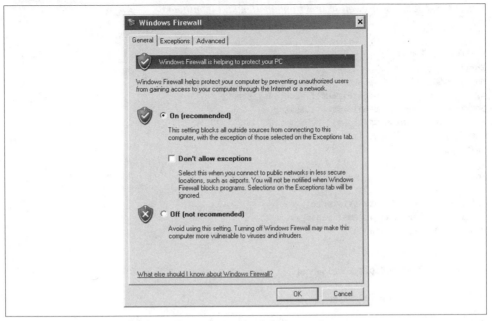

Figure 9-16. The Windows Firewall is turned on by default

Table 9-3. General firewall settings

Setting	Description
On	The default. Enables the firewall.
Don't allow exceptions	When selected, all traffic (even that configured via exceptions) is not allowed. Use this checkbox to temporarily disable exceptions when using the computer in a more risky situation (for example, in a hotel room or at a public setting such as a conference or wireless hotspot).
Off (not recommended)	Disables the firewall.

Click the Exceptions tab, as shown in Figure 9-17, to select or add programs that external clients are allowed to access. Selecting the program in the interface (or by using the Add Program button) asks the Windows Firewall to determine which ports should be opened.

 By default, both File and Printer Sharing and Remote Assistance programs are enabled. Both of these programs may be necessary to allow remote administration. However, if they are not used for remote administration, disable them here by unchecking the box.

Selecting the Add Program button allows browsing to any executable on the local hard drive, as shown in Figure 9-18. The "Change scope..." button is used to restrict the computers that can access these local programs, as shown in Figure 9-19. You

Figure 9-17. The Windows Firewall can open the ports required by a program—you do not have to know which ports are required

can also simply add a port filter using the "Add port" button, as shown in Figure 9-20.

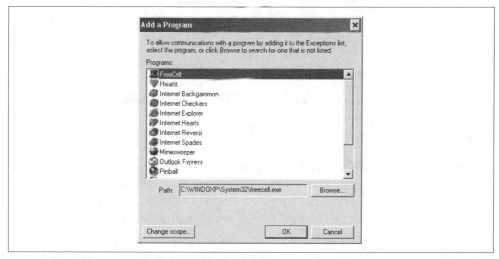

Figure 9-18. Add programs by browsing the local drive

Settings configured by using the Windows Firewall applet are set for all network connections by default. Use the Advanced tab shown in Figure 9-21 to configure settings for individual network connections, to configure logging, ICMP, or to restore the default settings.

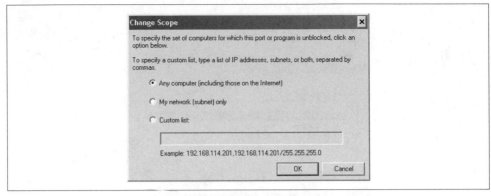

Figure 9-19. Restrict computers using the Change scope... button

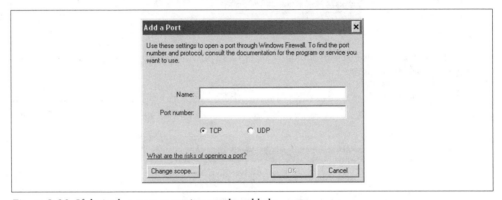

Figure 9-20. If desired, a port exception can be added

Selecting an interface, clicking the Settings button, and choosing the Advanced tab provides you with options for configuring different services and ICMP settings for unique network interfaces, as shown in Figure 9-22.

Modifying alerting and notification using the registry. Three registry settings values can be used to control the alerting and notification feature. Each one represents one of the security tools. Add the DWORD values to *HKEY_LOCALMACHINE\SOFTWARE\ Microsoft\Security Center* and change the value to 1 in order to suppress the alert and notification. The values are as follows:

- `AntiVirusDisableNotify`
- `FirewallDisableNotify`
- `UpdatesDisableNotify`

Modifying firewall behavior using Group Policy. In an Active Directory domain, new Group Policy options can be used to manage the behavior of the Windows Firewall. Windows Server 2003 or Windows 2000 domain controllers can be configured to

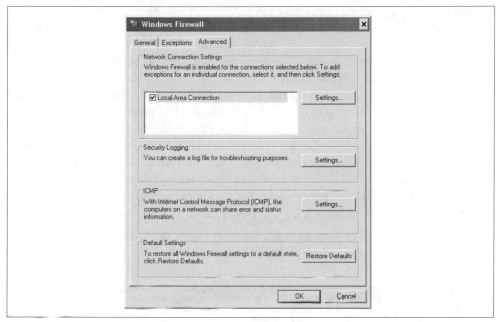

Figure 9-21. Use the Advanced page to complete firewall configuration

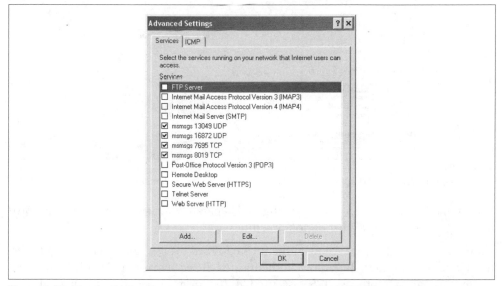

Figure 9-22. Use the Settings button to configure settings on a per network interface basis

support the deployment of these options for Group Policy Objects (GPOs) linked to organizational units (OUs) that include computer accounts for updated Windows Server 2003 SP1 and/or Windows XP SP2 computers.

To use the settings, install the service pack on a client computer joined to a test network domain. The service pack includes an updated *system.adm* file. After the post service pack installation reboot, log on as an administrator on the updated system and either add the Group Policy Object Editor snap-in to an MMC console, or open Group Policy Management Console. Select a GPO on a DC in the test network domain of which the client computer is a member. Expand the console tree and browse to Computer Configuration → AdministrativeTemplates → Network → NetworkConnections → WindowsFirewall. The updated *system.adm* file on the client can be used to configure the Group Policy. However, to use the new settings, you must use an updated system.adm file to replace the *system.adm* file on all domain controllers. You should test the use of these new settings in a test network before deploying on your production network. When satisfied, update all production GPOs that support updated clients.

Configure the policy. The first setting, shown in Figure 9-23, determines if authenticated IPSec traffic is excluded from the firewall's rule sets.

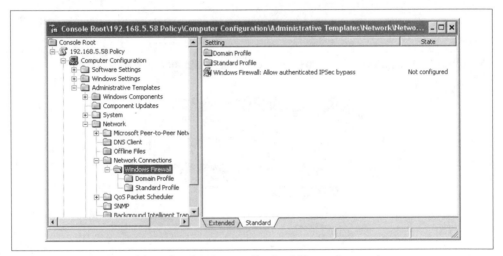

Figure 9-23. Determine if the policy for IPSec traffic should be implemented

Additional policy settings can be configured separately for standard or domain profiles. Figure 9-24 shows a list of policy settings.

Configure the setting for "Allow authenticated IPSec bypass" and then configure settings for both profiles. If "Allow authenticated IPSec bypass" is enabled, then the computer will not process IPSec-secured traffic from specified computers. IPSec-secured traffic is allowed by default. To enable this setting you must also add a Security Descriptor Definition Language (SDDL) string for the group accounts for the computers the policy should apply to. The string is added to the policy definition in the Group Policy properties. An SDDL string is of the form O:DAG:DAD(A;;RCGW;;;*sid*)

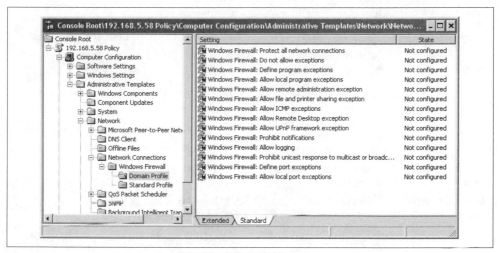

Figure 9-24. Establish a policy for domain and standard profiles

where *sid* represents the Security Identifier (SID) of a group account. To obtain the SID, use the Windows Resource Kit tool *Getsid.exe*. Because Getsid is usually used to compare SIDs, you must enter the DC and group name twice. A sample command line that can be used to specify the DC DC1 group REDTeam is as follows:

```
Getsid \\DC1 REDTeam \\DC1 REDTeam
```

Remember to establish settings for the appropriate profile (domain or standard). Profile settings are located underneath the Standard profile and Domain profile path. The domain profile is used when the computer is connected to the domain, and the standard profile is used when it is not. If neither of the profiles is configured, their defaults are used. The preservice pack upgrade setting "Prohibit use of Internet Connection Firewall on your DNS domain network" is still available for use in networks where some computers exist that have not been updated. Each profile includes the settings described in Table 9-4.

Table 9-4. Windows Firewall Group Policy settings

Setting	Description	Ports opened	Microsoft recommendation
Protect all network connections	All connections will have the firewall enabled.	None	Enabled
Do not allow exceptions	All unsolicited traffic is dropped, even if exceptions are configured. If the setting "Protect all network connections" is not set, a local administrator can bypass the firewall entirely by disabling it.	None	Not configured

Table 9-4. Windows Firewall Group Policy settings (continued)

Setting	Description	Ports opened	Microsoft recommendation
Define program exceptions	Defines allowed unsolicited traffic. The full path for the program must be identified. Variables such as %Program Files% can be used in the path statement. Windows Firewall only opens ports for these programs when they are running and listening for traffic.	Those defined	Configured for those applications allowed by policy
Allow local program exceptions	Enables local configuration of exceptions.	Those defined	Enabled
Allow remote administration exception	Enables remote administration using tools such as MMC consoles and Windows Management Instrumentation (WMI). If this setting is disabled, *SVCHOST.EXE* and *LSASS.EXE* are added to the programs exception list with a status of disabled.	TCP 135 and 445, as well as dynamically required RPC ports and incoming ICMP Echo Request messages	Disabled
Allow file and print sharing exception	Enables file and print traffic.	UDP 137, UDP 138, TCP 139, TCP 445, and incoming ICMP Echo messages	Enabled only if computers are file and print servers
Allow ICMP exceptions	Specifies ICMP traffic types that are allowed.	ICMP	Enabled for diagnostic or management purposes
Allow Remote Desktop exception	Opens ports for a Remote Desktop connection.	TCP 3389	Enabled if remote desktop management is used
Allow UPnP framework exception	Enables unsolicited UPnP message traffic.	UDP 1900, TCP 2869	Enabled if UPnP devices are used on the network
Prohibit notifications	Disables notification. When an application starts to listen on a port, the Windows Firewall adds the program to the exceptions list with a status of disabled and then notifies the user with a request to allow or disallow traffic to this port.	Those required by the program if this setting is not configured or disabled	Disabled
Allow logging	Configures the log file and enables logging of dropped traffic and successful connections. If enabled, the path to the log file must be selected or added and a maximum size must be specified.	N/A	Not configured

Table 9-4. Windows Firewall Group Policy settings (continued)

Setting	Description	Ports opened	Microsoft recommendation
Prohibit unicast response to multicast or broadcast requests	If enabled, discard unicast packets received in response to multicast or broadcast request messages. By default (if disabled or not configured), these packets are allowed for three seconds following a multicast or broadcast message. Unicast messages that are a response to a DHCP broadcast message are not dropped if this setting is enabled. It can interfere with NetBIOS name conflict detection. NetBIOS name conflict detection can prevent the use of duplicate computer names on the network.	None	Disabled
Define port exceptions	Specifies exceptions using ports. The port number, type (TCP or UDP), status (Enabled or Disabled) must be entered. Scope is optional.	Those defined	Enabled as required
Allow local port exceptions	Local configuration of port exceptions is allowed.	Those defined	Enabled if required

If ports are explicitly opened to allow unsolicited traffic, setting an exception to explicitly disable them via program name will not prevent the program from running or block them from receiving traffic.

When configuring exceptions, take advantage of the scope setting. The scope setting allows you to specify computers from which this type of traffic is allowed. Always keep in mind that the firewall protects the computer from attacks that use specific ports. These same ports may be used by legitimate traffic. If you open these ports for legitimate traffic, you also open it for malicious traffic. You can limit the risk of compromise by specifying the computers from which traffic is accepted. This is not a foolproof solution, but it does limit your risk.

If you specify programs more than once and use conflicting scopes or status, then any system specified by any entry can send messages.

Modifying firewall behavior using Netsh. Netsh is a network configuration utility that can be used at the command line or in scripts. Syntax is defined in the whitepaper *Deploying Windows Firewall Settings for Microsoft Windows XP with Service Pack 2.*

Netsh commands are available to configure the Windows Firewall and include the following:

Add allowedprogram
  This adds program exceptions.

Set allowedprogram
  This modifies the settings of an existing program exception.

Delete allowedprogram
  This deletes a configured program exception.

Set icmpsetting
  This specifies ICMP-accepted traffic.

Set multicastbroadcastresponse
  This specifies a unicast response to a muiltcast or broadcast request.

Set notifications
  This enables or disables notifications.

Set logging
  This configures logging options.

Set opmode
  This sets the mode to Enable, Disable, or "Do not allow exceptions."

Add portopening
  This creates a port-based exception.

Set portopening
  This modifies the settings of an existing port-based exception.

Delete portopening
  This deletes a configured port-based exception.

Set service
  This enables or disables predefined file and printer sharing, remote administration, remote desktop, and UPnP exceptions.

Reset
  This resets the configuration to the default.

Show
  This is used to display the current configuration.

More modifications. Following are a few other changes to the firewall and its administration:

Don't allow exceptions operating mode
  In addition to Enabled or Disabled, there is a new operating mode that prevents the addition of exceptions. If this mode is established, all incoming traffic is dropped, even if exceptions are configured.

Incoming traffic scoping
  Ports may be statically opened for use from specific IP addresses only.

Using an Administration Tool with the Firewall Implemented

If the firewall is enabled, by default you will not be able to use the Resultant Set of Policy (RSoP) snap-in to determine the Group Policy status on a remote Windows XP client. If you wish to retain the ability to use RSoP remotely while keeping the Windows Firewall enabled, make the following changes to Group Policy:

On the local computer, enable the Windows Firewall Allow remote Administration exception Group Policy settings. This setting is located at Computer Configuration → Administrative Templates → Network → Network connections → Windows Firewall → [Domain | Standard] Profile\.

To use the Group Policy Management Console (GPMC) on the administrative computers with the firewall enabled, upgrade to GPMC SP1. GPMC uses a callback on the administrative computer. The firewall blocks the callback mechanism of GPMC. To keep the firewall enabled on the administrative computer, upgrade to GPMC SP1 on a computer that does not use the callback mechanism.

To use RSoP, make these changes to the administrative computer: Enable the Windows Firewall: Define the program exceptions option and enter the full path to *unsecapp.exe*. (By default, *unsecapp.exe* is located in the *C:\Windows\System32\Wbem* folder.) Enable the Windows Firewall. Define the port exception policy to open port 135 *or* enable the Windows Firewall. Allow a remote administration exception in the Group Policy setting on the administrative computer.

Excepted traffic specified by program name
> This allows traffic from programs determined by program name, such as File and Print Sharing or Remote Assistance. (Program exceptions can also be specified by port numbers.)

Support for Ipv6
> This offers built-in support for Ipv6 traffic.

Global configuration settings
> Firewall settings will apply to all network connections. You do not have to reconfigure settings when multiple network connections are available on the same computer. (Settings can be configured for individual settings using scope settings.

New application programming interfaces (APIs)
> New APIs provide for more granular programmatic control. For information on these APIs and how to use them, study the *Windows Firewall* section of the *Windows Software Development Kit.*

IPSec Policy Aware
> If IPSec policies are configured, the Windows Firewall opens UDP ports 500 and 4500 to allow Internet Key Exchange (IKE) traffic. IKE traffic is used during the processing of IPSec connections. IPSec, a protocol used to encrypt and otherwise

protect network communications between two computers, is fully described in Chapter 11.

Windows Server 2003 SP1

The Windows Server 2003 firewall will be updated by SP1 and will work in a similar fashion to the Windows Firewall post-Windows XP SP2, with the exception that the Windows Firewall is disabled by default on Windows Server 2003. Since the firewall is not enabled by default, if you wish to use the firewall, you must enable it and configure exceptions. If you do so, the server should be restarted to enable the operating system to automatically add entries to the exceptions list for ports opened by programs that are already installed.

Host-based firewalls can provide excellent protection for servers and workstations. They will do so only if they are enabled and configured. Major changes to the Windows Firewall for XP were made in Service Pack 2, and similar changes are expected for Windows Server Service Pack 1. These changes include increased configuration control, including new Group Policy and registry settings, scope configuration for settings, and, for Windows XP, the firewall is enabled by default. In addition to host-based firewalls, perimeter firewalls should be in place between trusted and untrusted networks. The RRAS firewall can provide rudimentary firewall services for this purpose. The RRAS firewall may not be appropriate in all situations. You should always consider your firewall requirements before selecting a firewall.

Routing and Remote Access Basic Firewall

One of the options in RRAS is the Basic Firewall. The Basic Firewall is a stateful firewall that can be enabled for any public interface, including an interface used to provide NAT. The Basic Firewall cannot be configured for the private interface of an RRAS server. Static packet filters can be configured.

To configure the Basic Firewall, you must enable RRAS and select the Basic Firewall service, configure firewall properties, and then configure inbound and outbound filters. The following instructions for configuring the firewall assume that RRAS has already been enabled.

To enable RRAS and select the Basic Firewall service, begin by opening the Routing and Remote Access console. Right-click the server and select Enable Routing and Remote Access. Click Next. Select "Custom configuration" and click Next. Click NAT and Basic Firewall, then click Next, followed by Finish.

When prompted, click Yes to start the service. In the console, expand the IP Routing node. Right-click NAT/Basic Firewall and select New Interface. Select a public (external interface) and click OK to open the Network Address Translation Properties page. Select the NAT/Basic Firewall tab and select "Public interface connected to the Internet." Select the "Enable a basic firewall on this interface" checkbox, as shown in Figure 9-25.

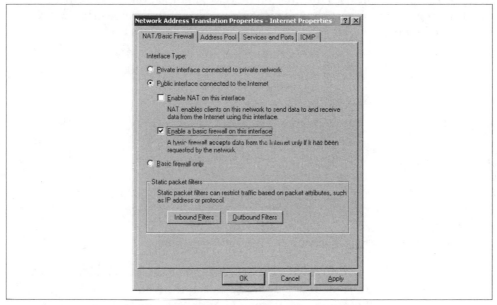

Figure 9-25. Configure the basic firewall on a network interface in RRAS

Click "Basic firewall only." Configure the firewall properties and any static filters. Then click OK when you have finished; this will return you to the RRAS console.

To configure firewall properties, right-click on the NAT/Basic Firewall node and select Properties. Select the General tab, and then configure event logging by selecting among the choices shown in Figure 9-26.

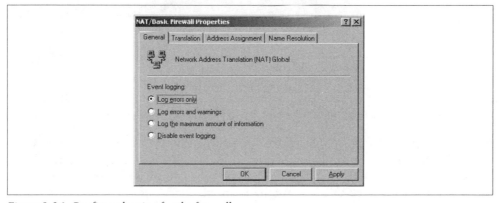

Figure 9-26. Configure logging for the firewall

Click the Translation tab as shown in Figure 9-27 and adjust the mapping after minutes. Mapping after minutes indicate the duration of any TCP and/or UDP mapping. When outbound traffic uses the firewall interface, information is added to a table so that the firewall can accept inbound responses to this traffic. These mappings should be removed if not active.

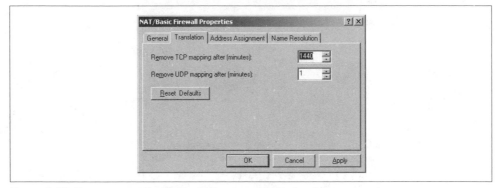

Figure 9-27. Ensure mapped responses are removed after they become inactive

If NAT is also configured on the page displayed from the General tab and a DHCP server will not be used to allocated addresses, click the Address Assignment tab as shown in Figure 9-28 to configure a range of addresses for the DHCP allocator to use.

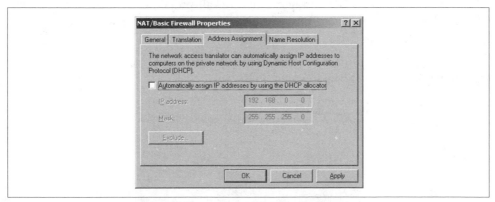

Figure 9-28. Configure a range of addresses for the DHCP allocator to use

If services on the local, private network are accessible from the private network, select the Name Resolution tab as shown in Figure 9-29 and make the selection to allow clients to use DNS for name resolution. When you have finished configuring the firewall service, click OK to close the Properties pages of the firewall and return to the RRAS console.

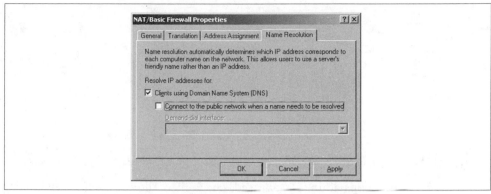

Figure 9-29. Configure DNS if required

Next, configure the firewall interface. Select the NAT/Basic Firewall node. In the details pane of the console, right-click the interface and select Properties. Select the Address Pool tab as shown in Figure 9-30. This address pool is used if your ISP assigns multiple addresses. Each address can be used by any connection, or it can be reserved for use by a particular service.

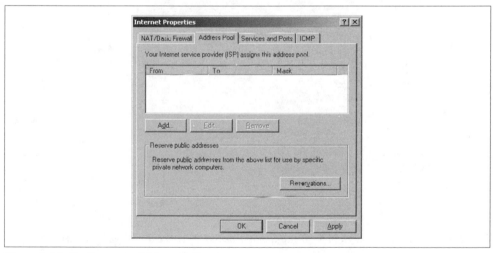

Figure 9-30. Configure the Address Pool

Click the Add button to add IP addresses assigned to the interface. These addresses are usually assigned by your ISP. Add the start address, mask, and end address, then click OK. Click the Reservations button to add addresses from this range for a specific computer on the private network. The reservation matches a public IP address with a private internal address. Click the Add button. In the Add Reservations box shown in Figure 9-31, enter the public IP address and the corresponding IP address of the computer that the reservation should be used for.

Figure 9-31. Reserve an ISP assigned address for a specific service available on the private network

If incoming traffic to this address is allowed, check the "Allow incoming sessions to this address" box and then click OK. Click OK twice to return to the Properties page. Select the Services and Ports tab as shown in Figure 9-32.

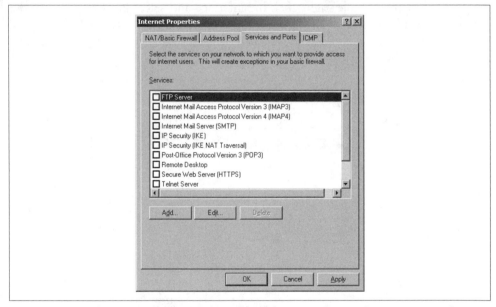

Figure 9-32. Use the services and ports tab to allow access to services on the private network

Select a service that is provided on the private network that is accessible to the public network. Click the Edit button. In the Edit Service page shown in Figure 9-33, select either "On this interface," or "On this address pool entry." If the address pool entry selection is made, enter the IP address.

Enter the "Private address." If additional services are required and are present in the list, click on the Services and Ports tab to repeat the process.

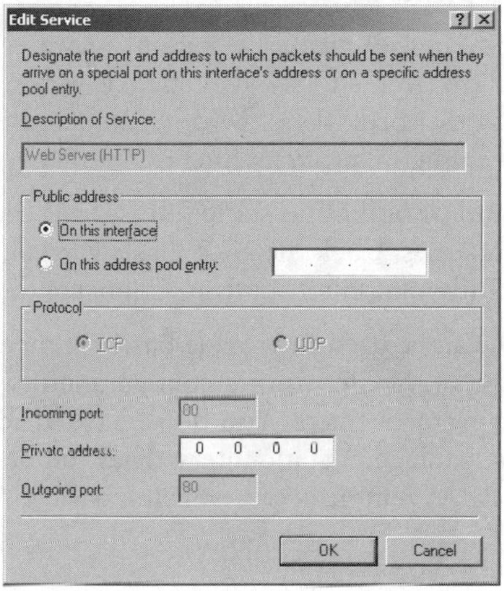

Figure 9-33. A specific address can also be allocated to a local service

If the service you need is not present, you can define it by clicking the Add button and using the Add Service page to add the incoming and outgoing ports and the private address.

Select the ICMP tab, as shown in Figure 9-34. Select any additional ICMP messages that are allowed. The four messages that are selected in Figure 9-34 are the defaults.

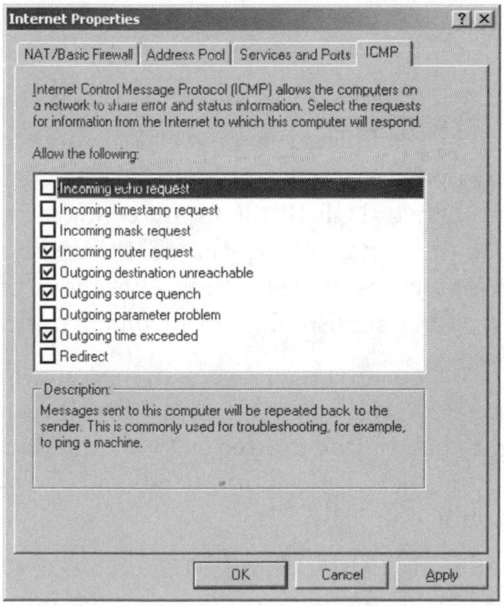

Figure 9-34. Configure ICMP for the firewall

Click OK to close the Properties page.

Starting the RRAS Basic Firewall creates a stateful firewall. The firewall blocks all unsolicited traffic. To allow access to services such as web servers, use the interface Properties pages as just described. To allow other inbound traffic, or to block outbound traffic, you must configure protocol filters.

To configure inbound and/or outbound static filters, right-click the NAT/Basic Firewall node and select Properties. Click the NAT/Basic Firewall tab, and then click the Inbound Filters or the Outbound Filters button. Configure the required static filters.

The RRAS basic firewall can be used to provide basic perimeter firewall services. It is simple to configure. One of the steps in its configuration is the setting of inbound and/or outbound static protocol filters. You don't have to configure the RRAS firewall, however, to take advantage of static filters. They can be set directly on the network connection using RRAS remote access policies, IPSec filters, and TCP/IP.

Protocol Filters

The Windows Firewall and the RRAS Basic Firewall are not the only options available for restricting incoming traffic. Several options exist that can be used to permit and/or block traffic by setting protocol filters. TCP/IP Filters can be set directly on the network connection. Routing and Remote Access Policies provide an option to set remote access protocol filters. IPSec policies can be established that block or permit access to specific ports. Unlike the Windows Firewall, the RRAS Basic Firewall protocol filters are not stateful. Protocol filters can be set for incoming and outgoing traffic.

TCP/IP Filters

Basic protocol filters can be established on any TCP/IP interface. These packet filters are static filters and only operate to filter inbound TCP/IP communications based on port or protocol IP number. If TCP/IP filters are configured, all traffic is dropped except for what is sent to the ports and/or protocol IP numbers specified in the interface. In this way, filtering occurs by exception; either it is not used at all, or only those ports defined in the filter are listening for incoming traffic.

To create packet filters on an interface, begin by opening the interface Properties page. Click Start, then select and open Control Panel. Select and open "Network connections," then right-click on the desired network interface and click Properties. Click the Advanced button. Select the Options tab and click the Properties button. You will see the screen shown in Figure 9-35.

Select Enable TCP/IP Filtering (All Adapters). For each box (TCP Ports, UDP Ports, and IP Protocols), leave the default Permit All or select Permit Only. If Permit Only is

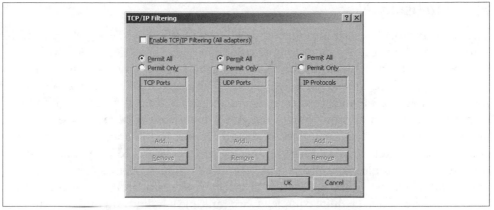

Figure 9-35. Simple protocol filters can be configured within the TCP/IP properties pages

selected, click the Add button and enter a port to allow and then click OK. Repeat the process until all required ports have been selected and appear in the boxes.

 By default, TCP/IP filters will block all communications with the exception of those protocols you configure. Before enabling filtering, ensure that you understand what ports are required.

Routing and Remote Access Protocol Filters

In addition to providing a basic firewall service, protocol filters can be added to an RRAS routing interface, or to an RRAS remote access policy. To set remote access protocol filters, create a remote access policy or configure filters for an existing policy. The policy should establish parameters for connectivity. Adding inbound and outbound filters is an additional configuration item. Packet filters can be configured for inbound and outbound traffic, and can be set to pass all traffic except packets defined in filters, or to discard all traffic except packets allowed by filters.

To configure protocol filters on a routing interface, begin by opening the RRAS console and selecting the General node. In the detail pane, right-click the interface on which to add a filter and click Properties. Click the General tab and then click either Inbound Filters or Outbound Filters. Select the filter action. Click New to add a port to filter. On the "Add IP filter" page, select either Source Network or Destination Network. Enter the IP address and subnet mask. Use the drop-down Protocol box to select TCP, UDP, ICMP, Any, or Other. Enter the required source and destination port. Click OK twice to return to the General page. Repeat the process to add additional filters.

Filtering Using IPSec

The IPSec protocol is built into the network stack of Windows Server 2003. In addition to providing security for communications between hosts on a LAN, IPSec can also be configured to block or permit inbound and/or outbound communications. An IPSec policy is composed of one or more rules, each of which can contain multiple filters. Each IPSec filter defines a source and destination IP address, and source and destination port or protocol ID. Therefore, in addition to filtering based on port alone, IPSec can block communications based on port and IP address combinations. A filter action determines whether the specific packet is blocked or permitted. IPSec policies can be simple (such as one that "blocks all traffic to port 23"), be a combination of filters (such as "block all traffic except port 80 traffic from this specific range of IP addresses"), and be quite complex (with multiple inbound and outbound filters).

All IPSec filters are static filters. IPSec policies can be implemented locally, or applied via a Group Policy if the computer is joined in a domain. All of these implementation options are discussed and instructions provided for implementation in Chapter 11.

Which Firewall Services Should You Use?

With so many options for creating host-based firewall services, which option should be used? Like most security decisions, the answer is, "It depends." Many factors are likely to influence this decision, but the most important deciding factors are your specific business and security requirements. Use Table 9-5 to select a firewall service that meets all of your requirements. If multiple services do so, in most cases the one that is simplest to implement will be the best choice.

Table 9-5. Firewall services decision points

Attribute	TCP/IP protocol filtering	Windows Firewall	IPSec	RRAS basic firewall	RRAS protocol filters
Implementation difficulty	Simplest	Simple	Complex	Simple to complex	Simple to complex
Direction of traffic that can be filtered	Inbound	Inbound	Inbound and outbound	Inbound and outbound	Inbound and outbound
Filters can be based on the IP address of the source	No	Yes (called *exception scope*)	Yes	Yes	Yes
Provides a DHCP allocator	No	The Windows Firewall used with ICS	No	Yes	Yes
DHCP range is configurable	N/A	No	N/A	Yes	Yes

Table 9-5. Firewall services decision points (continued)

Attribute	TCP/IP protocol filtering	Windows Firewall	IPSec	RRAS basic firewall	RRAS protocol filters
Designed to be combined with NAT on the same system	No	The Windows Firewall used with ICS	No	Basic firewall plus NAT	No
Can be managed via Group Policy	No	Yes	Yes	No	No
Provides options for central management	No	Via Group Policy	Group Policy	IAS and remote access policies	IAS and remote access policies
Provides static filtering	Yes	Yes	Yes	Yes	Yes
Provides stateful filtering	No	Yes	No	Yes	No
Provides application layer filtering	No	No	No	No	No

Summary

Windows Server 2003 offers a number of options that can be used to configure a host firewall. When using protocol filters and/or the basic firewall service of RRAS or when using Internet Connection Sharing with the Windows Firewall, the host firewall can also double as a perimeter firewall. If Active Directory is implemented, the Windows Firewall and IPSec can be centrally managed via Group Policy. A combination of these services might be the best approach when implementing firewall services for hosts on a network.

Another service that can be used to protect the network yet allow access to the internal network by authorized individuals is the Internet Authentication Service (IAS). Chapter 10 describes this service in detail.

Centralizing Authentication and Authorization with Internet Authentication Server

Internet Authentication Server (IAS) is the Microsoft implementation of *Remote Authentication Dial-in User Service* (RADIUS), which provides centralized authentication, authorization, and accounting for dial-up, VPN, and wireless network access. It is also often used as a centralized *Authentication, Authorization, and Accounting* (AAA) server for network devices such as routers and switches, or as a proxy to forward authentication requests to another RADIUS server. In a Windows environment, IAS is also used as follows:

- As an extension of RRAS to provide centralized AAA services, including central management of Remote Access Policies

- As the central component in Microsoft's Network Access Quarantine Control, a process that protects the network from viral and worm infections by quarantining VPN clients until they meet certain security requirements

- As the heart of Network Access Protection, a new process that, combined with anti-viral or other security gateways, will restrict a LAN client until the client complies with an organizations security policy

IAS is a critical security tool whose purpose is to provide centralized authentication, authorization, and accounting functions. After introducing you to the RADIUS protocol, this chapter will provide the necessary information for installing and configuring IAS to provide secure remote access, to use IAS as a RADIUS proxy, to secure wireless access, and to secure IAS operations.

The RADIUS Protocol

Microsoft's *Internet Authentication Service* (IAS) supports the RADIUS protocol as defined in RFC 2865, *Remote Authentication Dial-in User Service (RADIUS)*, and RFC 2866, *RADIUS Accounting*. IAS can interoperate with other RADIUS servers. However, any Microsoft-specific functionality (for example, using the IAS server as a central authority for Remote Access policies) is available only with Microsoft's ISA

Server. Knowledge of the RADIUS protocol is necessary to correctly configure and use RADIUS. There are two areas to consider:

- What RADIUS does (the authentication, authorization, and accounting processes)
- How RADIUS communicates (RADIUS messages)

Authentication, Authorization, and Accounting RADIUS Processes

The RADIUS protocol is the de facto standard for remote user authentication and has been used since the early days of dial-up remote access. The protocol was originally written to provide authentication, authorization, and accounting services for dial-up communications, but it has been adapted to provide these services for use with VPN servers, wireless access points, authenticating Ethernet switches, DSL, and other network access methods. Let's examine the authentication, authorization, and accounting services provided by RADIUS.

Authentication

Authentication is the process of validating identity. In the RADIUS RFC (RFC 2865, *Remote Authentication Dial-in User Service*), the authentication process is described as two parts. In the first step, an end user's computer or access client uses the *Point-to-Point protocol* (PPP) over a dial-up connection to a *Network Access Server* (NAS). The NAS is often referred to simply as the *access server*. The NAS does not authenticate the client; instead the NAS acts as a *RADIUS client* and connects to the RADIUS server. In this second step, a RADIUS *authentication request* is sent by the NAS to the RADIUS server. The RADIUS server uses a user database to check the user credentials. The user database is traditionally resident on the RADIUS server but does not have to be. A separate device can store the user database and this is the case when IAS is integrated with Active Directory (AD). (IAS uses AD instead of its own local database.) If the client can be authenticated, the RADIUS server returns *authorizations*, which includes configuration information to the NAS server that authorizes network service for the user. Once network service is approved, the RADIUS server is no longer part of the user's network connection. The *authentication request*, authorizations, and other RADIUS messages are defined in the RADIUS protocol and use UDP port 1645 for authentication messages and UDP port 1813 for accounting messages. (Older RADIUS ports, 1645 and 1646, may be used by older RADIUS servers.) Figure 10-1 illustrates a successful RADIUS authentication. In the figure, communication is forwarded by the NAS to the RADIUS server, but once authentication has occurred, client communications do not use the RADIUS server.

 Don't get confused between the *access client* (which is the computer used to request a connection to the intranet) and the *access server* (which can be a RRAS server, a wireless access point, or some other NAS).

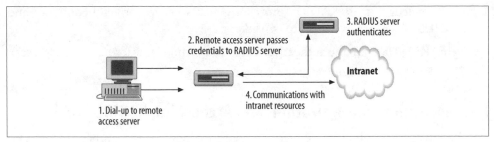

Figure 10-1. When RADIUS is used for authentication, the NAS acts as an intermediary

It is also possible to use a *RADIUS proxy* to further centralize authentication. In this scenario, the NAS contacts a RADIUS proxy that, in turn, becomes the RADIUS client of another RADIUS server. The final RADIUS server is used for authentication. This is particularly useful when a service provider is used at many remote locations to allow an organization's employees to connect locally, but when the authentication should be done at the organization's central location. Figure 10-2 illustrates this variation. In the figure, a service provider's RADIUS proxy accepts connection requests from users. The proxy forwards these requests to the RADIUS server located at the organization's headquarters in Atlanta. The Atlanta RADIUS server authenticates the user requests and provides them access to the organization's LAN.

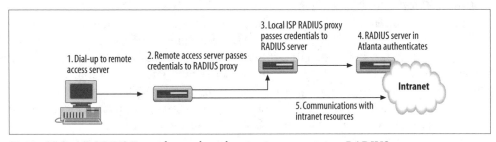

Figure 10-2. A RADIUS Proxy forwards authentication requests to a RADIUS server

In the Microsoft implementation, an RRAS server becomes the RADIUS client (or NAS) and the IAS server user database (or AD) can be used to store user credentials. A Windows Server 2003 server can also become a RADIUS proxy.

A number of authentication protocols can be specified for remote access authentication to the IAS server. The IAS server, RRAS server, and the computer used by the end user requesting a connection must be configured to use the same protocol(s). Configure the RRAS server to use the approved protocols and configure it to use the RADIUS server as its authentication provider. When a connection request is received, the strongest available authentication selection will be made among those available on the RRAS server. All authentication choices for IAS, with the exception of PEAP, are defined in the section "Authentication Choices" in Chapter 8. PEAP is detailed in the section "Securing Wireless Access with IAS" in this chapter.

When EAP is used, the RRAS server does not process the EAP messages, but merely passes them to the RADIUS server for processing. However, the RRAS server must support negotiation of EAP types and the passing of the messages to the RADIUS server.

Authorization

Authorization specifies what the authenticated user may do. The RADIUS server also evaluates authorization information. Authorization information is stored in a policy that defines criteria that must be met before access is allowed. The criteria can be time of day, phone number used, and so on. As a result of this evaluation, even if a user can successfully be authenticated, he or she may be denied network access, or provided limited access based on other criteria such as the phone number his connection originated from, the type of remote connection (for example, dial-up, VPN, or wireless), and so on. Because RADIUS can evaluate these criteria, it can help administrators use technical controls to enforce security policy. For example, remote employees may be authorized to work from home. To prevent an attacker who obtains an account ID and password from connecting to the network, remote access can be restricted for that account. Only if the connection originates with the correct phone number will the access be authorized. Authorization criteria are entered in the user's profile and in RRAS Remote Access policies as discussed in Chapter 8. When RADIUS is used, additional, RADIUS-only criteria (or properties) are also available. The IAS server becomes the centralized RRAS Remote Access policy server for its RRAS clients. You can find additional information on IAS remote access policies in the section "Remote Access Policies" in Chapter 8.

Accounting

Accounting records the activities of systems and users. RADIUS collects information on remote access communications with clients, so you can generate reports on network activity for accounting purposes. The RADIUS client uses *accounting request* messages to provide user logon and logoff as well as other usage information to the RADIUS server (which it stores either in its own local database, or if configured to do so, in a centralized database). These messages, as well as other messages passed by the RADIUS protocol, are described in the following section.

RADIUS Messages

To accomplish authentication, authorization, and accounting processes, messages are exchanged between the RADIUS client and the RADIUS server. Table 10-1 defines these messages.

Table 10-1. RADIUS messages

Message	Sent by	In response to	Definition
Access-Request	RADIUS client	User request for network access	Requests authentication and authorization for network access
Access-Accept	RADIUS server	Access-Request	Informs the client that the connection is authenticated and authorized
Access-Reject	RADIUS server	Access-Request	Informs the client that the connection is rejected either because of authentication or authorization failure
Access-Challenge	RADIUS server	Access-Request	Requests information from the client such as user credentials or other details about the connection
Accounting-Request	RADIUS client	N/A	Provides accounting information for an accepted connection
Accounting-Response	RADIUS server	Accounting-Request	Acknowledges receipt and processes an Accounting-Request message

Each RADIUS message includes a RADIUS header and RADIUS attributes. The RADIUS attributes in the Access-Request messages specify information about the connection attempt such as IP address of the NAS server, the connection protocol, or user information that may be used during the authorization process. The RRAS Remote Access policies define attributes on which authorization is based. Access-Accept messages use the RADIUS attributes that define the type of connection that can be made, as well as any connection constraints and vendor-specific attributes. This information can also be part of the RRAS Remote Access policy.

Dozens of RADIUS attributes are defined in multiple RFCs and Internet drafts. Information on some of these attributes is included in Table 10-2 presented in the section "Configuring a Connection Request Policy" later in this chapter.

When a client attempts a connection attempt via RADIUS, the following steps take place:

1. The client requests a connection to the NAS.
2. The NAS attempts to negotiate a connection with the client using the most secure protocol first, then the next secure, and so on. For example, if all authentication protocols are approved, the NAS will try them in the following order: EAP, MS-Chap v2, MS-CHAP, CHAP, and PAP.
3. The authentication request is forwarded by the NAS to the RADIUS server in a RADIUS Access-Request message.
4. The IAS server sends a RADIUS Access-Challenge message requesting information from the client, and the request is passed to the client by the NAS.
5. The client returns information to the NAS, and it is forwarded to the IAS server.

6. The IAS server validates the message. The message is discarded and the connection attempt fails in the following cases:

    a. The digital signatures are enabled and verification fails.

    b. The connection times out.

    c. The IAS server cannot reach its domain controller and, therefore, cannot validate the user's credentials.

7. If digital signatures are enabled and verification succeeds, the IAS server contacts AD to validate the user's logon credentials.

8. If the user logon credentials are validated, the connection request is evaluated against the remote access policies and the dial-in properties of the user's account.

9. If the request matches at least one Remote Access policy and the dial-in properties, the Remote Access properties and profile properties of that policy are evaluated.

10. If the evaluation authorizes the user, a RADIUS Access-Accept message is returned to the NAS, and the client is authorized to access the remote network.

11. If the evaluation does not authorize the request, other Remote Access policies will be evaluated in order. If none of them authorizes the connection, the IAS server returns a RADIUS Access-Reject message to the NAS, which disconnects the client.

Now that we understand how the RADIUS protocol operates, let's take a look at how to install and configure IAS.

Installing and Configuring IAS

IAS is a free network service available with Windows Server 2003 that doesn't come installed by default. An IAS server does not have to be a member of an AD domain, but if it is, it can be used in more RADIUS deployment scenarios. If IAS is not a domain member, the local user database is used for authenticating users. If IAS is a domain member, AD is used.

In the following example, we will install IAS on a domain member computer. After installation, the server is registered in AD. If the server is not registered, it will not be able to access user information in AD and, therefore, not be able to authenticate users. As this is the reason that IAS is installed, the registration process is essential to the operation of IAS. If you want to use the IAS server to authenticate users from multiple domains, the server must be given permission to access user information in each domain. To do so, register IAS in each domain. The registration process is detailed in the "Registering IAS in AD" sidebar later in this chapter.

Installing IAS

To install and register an IAS server, begin by opening the Add or Remove Programs applet in Control Panel and click Add/Remove Windows Components. In the components list, scroll down and select Networking Services. Click the Details button. Select Internet Authentication Service, click OK, and click Finish. If prompted, insert the Windows Server 2003 installation CD-ROM, or browse to the location for installation files. When the process is complete, click Finish and then close the Add/Remove applet.

Open the Internet Authentication Service console from the Administrative Tools folder. Right-click the Internet Authentication Service (see Figure 10-3) and then click Register Server in Active Directory.

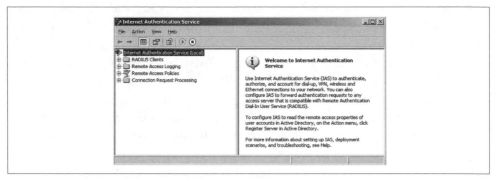

Figure 10-3. The Internet Authentication Service console

In the Register Internet Authentication Server in Active Directory dialog box (Figure 10-4), click OK to indicate you want to authorize this computer to read the user's dial-in properties.

Figure 10-4. You must register IAS server in AD in order to use RADIUS authentication

In the Register Internet Authentication Server in Active Directory dialog box, click OK.

Configuring IAS for Remote Access

After you install IAS, you must configure it before you can use it. This consists of configuring a connection request policy, configuring access servers (network access servers sometimes referred to as NAS, or as the RADIUS clients), configuring logging, and configuring Remote Access policies. Optional configuration options

Registering IAS in AD

An IAS server should be registered in AD during IAS installation. If not, then it must be registered after installation by one of the methods given below. Moreover, if users from domains other than the one that IAS is installed in will be using the IAS server, then it must be registered in those domains as well. Several methods may be used to register IAS in AD. To check to see which IAS servers are registered, open the Properties page of the RAS and IAS Servers group and select the Member tab. To register IAS you must be a member of the Domain Admins group in the domain within which the IAS server is a member.

To register IAS using the IAS console, right-click on the IAS server and select Register Server in Active Directory. When the Register Internet Authentication Service in Active Directory pop up appears, click OK.

You can also register IAS using the netsh command. Open a command prompt and type the following:

```
netsh RAS add registeredserver
```

You can also add a registered server from another domain by extending the command and adding the DNS domain name and IAS server name as follows:

```
netsh RAS add registeredserver DNSdomainNAME IASServerNAME
```

To register IAS using the Active Directory Users and Computers console, select the Users folder. In the details pane, right-click the RAS and IAS Servers group and click Properties. Select the Member tab, and then add the IAS server.

An IAS member server can be registered in any domain in the forest.

---

include configuring different or additional RADIUS ports, and configuring *account lockout*. Additional configuration may be necessary to support authentication switches, VLANs, and wireless clients. The process is not complete until the access servers (RADIUS clients) are configured and any additional access client account or client software is configured. Access clients are the end-user computers used to request connections to the remote network.

Configuring a connection request policy

Connection request policies are rules that define whether authentication will take place locally or remotely. Therefore, they help define whether the IAS server will become a RADIUS server or a RADIUS proxy. They consist of *conditions* and a *profile*, and are similar to Remote Access policies.

Conditions are RADIUS attributes that are compared to the RADIUS attributes of an incoming connection request. If multiple conditions exist in the policy, the attributes of the policy must be matched by all of the incoming connection request attributes. The conditions and attributes for connection request policies can also be set in

Remote Access policies on the RADIUS server. They may also be used when configuring RRAS servers as RADIUS clients. Table 10-2 defines condition attributes that can be set in IAS.

Table 10-2. Attributes that can be defined in a connection request policy

Attribute	Definition
Called Station ID	Phone number of NAS.
Calling Station ID	Phone number of caller.
Client Friendly Name	Name of the RADIUS client computer requesting authentication. A *friendly name* is a name assigned by an administrator during installation. The use of a friendly name makes it easier to identify which RADIUS client is attempting a connection and to trace activity in the RADIUS server logs.
Client IP address	IP address of the RADIUS client.
Client-Vendor	The NAS vendor.
Day and Time Restrictions	Day of week and time of day of connection request.
Framed Protocol	Type of frame for incoming packets (such as FTP, SLIP, Frame Relay).
NAS Identifier	Name of NAS.
NAS IP Address	IP address of NAS server.
NAS Port type	Media used such as asynch (phone), tunnels, virtual (VPN), Ethernet (switches), and wireless.
Remote RADIUS to Windows User Mapping	Authentication can occur for users of a remote RADIUS server. In other words, partners authenticate to their own RADIUS and can use one of your user accounts to access LAN resources.
Service Type	Service requested such as framed (PPP) and login (Telnet).
Tunnel Type	Tunnel type such as PPTP and L2TP.
User Name	Username used by access client in RADIUS message Typically this is a realm (domain) name and user account name.

Profiles are sets of properties that are applied to the incoming connection request and used by IAS to determine if the client requesting access is authorized to do so. They include information on Authentication, Auditing, Attribute Manipulation, and some advanced processes as explained in Table 10-3. Profile properties and processes are often collectively referred to as *profile elements*. Table 10-3 defines profile choices for IAS as a RADIUS server. Profile choices relevant to the use of IAS as a RADIUS proxy is provided in the section "Configuring IAS as a RADIUS Proxy" later in this chapter.

Table 10-3. RADIUS connection request profile elements

Type	Elements	Definition
Authentication	Authenticate Requests on this Server	Use the Local user database.
Authentication	Forward the request to another RADIUS server in a remote RADIUS server group	This IAS server is acting as a RADIUS proxy.

Table 10-3. RADIUS connection request profile elements (continued)

Type	Elements	Definition
Authentication	Accept the connection attempt without performing authentication or authorization	Used for some mandatory tunnels. Cannot be selected if MS-CHAP v2 or EAP/TLS are used for authentication because these authentication protocols implement mutual authentication. A choice to not require IAS to authenticate should not prevent the client from requiring it. Therefore, this option is not available when mutual authentication is required.
Accounting	Forward accounting information in a specific remote RADIUS server group	Pass accounting information from this RADIUS proxy to a RADIUS server. (Connection request records will always be logged to the RADIUS proxy where received.)
Attribute Manipulation	User-ID	Find and replace this attribute before subjecting the request to authentication and authorization. User-ID manipulation is changing the realm (domain name) from the default.
Attribute Manipulation	Called Station ID	This option applies to the Called Station ID, which identifies the RADIUS side of the connection. Find and replace this attribute before subjecting the request to authentication and authorization.
Attribute Manipulation	Calling Station ID	This option applies to the Calling Station ID, which identifies the client side of the connection. Find and replace this attribute before subjecting the request to authentication and authorization.
Advanced	Various RADIUS attributes	Add attribute value to the RADIUS response message of a RADIUS authentication or accounting server, or a RADIUS authentication or accounting proxy server. The value will replace any present in the request message.

The default connection request policy is set to configure IAS as a RADIUS server, but must be completed with the specifics of the network on which it operates.

Configuring RADIUS clients for the IAS server

RADIUS clients are the access servers to whom the access clients connect. A RADIUS client can be a RRAS server, a wireless access point or an authenticating switch. A maximum of 50 RADIUS clients and 2 remote RADIUS server groups can be configured on an IAS server installed on Windows Server 2003 Standard Edition. If IAS is installed on Windows Server 2003 Enterprise Edition or Windows Server 2003 Datacenter Edition, an unlimited number of RADIUS clients and RADIUS server groups can be configured.

An important part of the RRAS and RADIUS server configuration is the use of a *shared secret*. The shared secret becomes the key that is used during the encryption of the RADIUS messages used in communications between them. Information on how to make this process more secure is included in the section "Shared Secret" later in this chapter.

Refer to Table 10-2 for explanations of many of the required parameters when adding an RRAS server as a RADIUS client. To add an RRAS server as a RADIUS client, begin by opening the Start → Administrative Tools → Internet Authentication Service console. Right-click the RADIUS client's node and click New RADIUS Client. Enter a friendly name (a name that will help an administrator identify the server) for the RRAS server in the "Friendly name" box of the Name and Address page. Enter the clients IP address or DNS name in the "Client address (IP or DNS)" field, as shown in Figure 10-5.

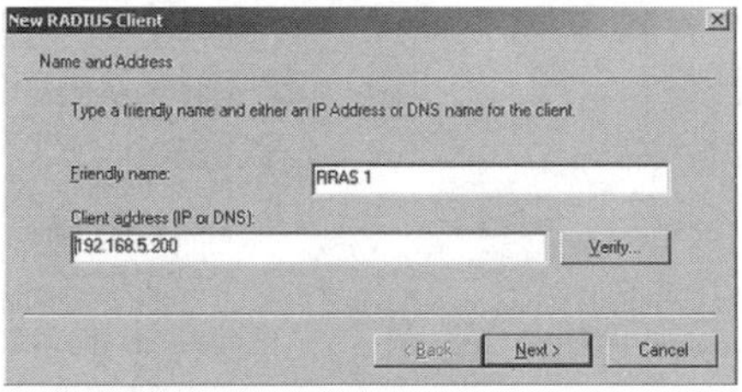

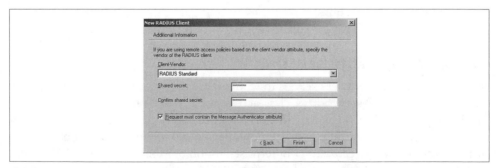

Figure 10-5. Identify the RADIUS client by a friendly name

Click the Verify button to verify that the server is present on the network. Click Next. If necessary, use the Client-Vendor drop-down list to select the manufacturer of the client. In this case, the default is fine because we are using Windows RRAS servers as clients. Enter a shared secret and then enter it again to confirm. The shared secret must match the one entered in the configuration of the RRAS server. Check the box "Request must contain the Message Authenticator attribute," as shown in Figure 10-6. Then click Finish.

Figure 10-6. Adding the use of the Message Authenticator improved the security offered by using a shared secret

Configuring RRAS servers as RADIUS clients

Before IAS server can be used to authenticate remote access requests, RRAS servers (or other access servers) must be configured to use RADIUS for authentication and accounting.

To configure a Windows Server 2003 server to be a RADIUS client, begin by opening Routing and Remote Access. Right-click the server and select Properties. Select the Security tab. Change the "Authentication provider" to RADIUS Authentication by using the drop-down list. Change the "Accounting provider" to RADIUS Accounting by using the drop-down list, as shown in Figure 10-7.

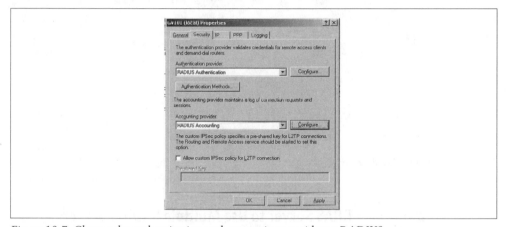

Figure 10-7. Change the authentication and accounting provider to RADIUS

Click the Configure button next to the "Authentication provider" drop-down list. Click the Add button to add information on the RADIUS server. Enter the server name of the RADIUS server and select the "Always use message authenticator," as shown in Figure 10-8, and then click OK. The Time-out (seconds) and Initial score entries should be left to defaults until the operation of the server as a RADIUS client is tested. If connections time out, then this value may be increased. More information on these settings is provided in the sidebar "Configuring a RRAS Server to Use Multiple RADIUS Servers" later in this chapter.

Click the Configure button next to the "Accounting provider" field in the Security tab of the Properties window (see Figure 10-7). Click the Add button to add information on the RADIUS server. Enter the server name of the RADIUS server, then select the "Send RADIUS Accounting On and Accounting Off messages," as shown in Figure 10-9. Click OK twice to return to the Properties page.

If you need to allow a shared secret IPSec policy for communications between RADIUS and RRAS servers, select "Allow custom IPSec Policy for L2TP connection" (see Figure 10-7). Click OK to exit the Properties page.

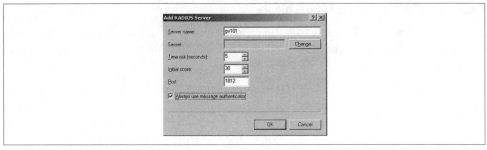

Figure 10-8. Add a RADIUS server

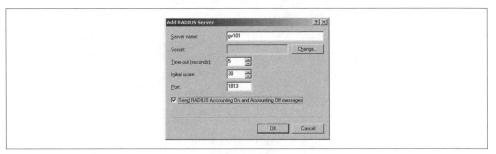

Figure 10-9. Configure the RADIUS server for accounting

Configuring a RRAS Server to Use Multiple RADIUS Servers

Multiple RADIUS servers are often implemented for redundancy. Rather than allowing a single RADIUS server to become a single point of failure, two RADIUS servers are provided, and each RRAS server is configured with information on both of them. The initial score parameter of the Add RADIUS Server configuration window identifies which RADIUS server is the primary server. The RRAS server will attempt a connection with the primary RADIUS server (the one configured with the lower "Initial score"). If a connection attempt times out, the RADIUS server will attempt a connection with the RADIUS server with the next-lowest "Initial score." This is why the "Time-out (seconds)" parameter should be carefully considered before it is changed. If set too low, connections may needlessly time out, forcing the RRAS server to attempt to connect to the secondary RADIUS server. If the time-out is set too high and the RADIUS server becomes unavailable, unnecessary time is wasted before the RRAS server attempts to connect to the secondary server.

Configuring auditing and logging

By default, minimal IAS data is logged in IAS log format to a log file at *%windir%\System32\Log Files*. Only authentication information is recorded, and a new log is started monthly (as shown in Figure 10-10). As a best practice, you should put log files on a different drive than the system drive. Log file data can also be forwarded to a remote server by using a UNC format log file path.

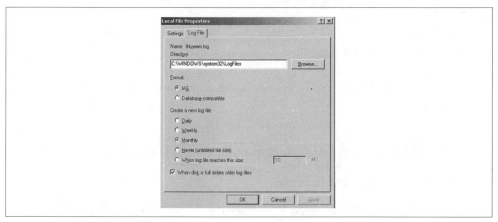

Figure 10-10. The log files should be configured to reflect the needs of your organization

It is imperative that logging be configured so that information on each connection attempt (whether successful or denied) is recorded. The purpose of IAS is to protect information assets by only allowing authenticated and authorized access to the network. To ensure that it's doing its job, IAS must be configured to log connection information. That information must be reviewed on a regular basis. Reviewing the logs can uncover attacks (both successful and unsuccessful). Finding this information may help to thwart an in-progress attack, identify sources of attacks, and provide evidence useful in closing security holes or in prosecuting attackers. The frequency of log review will depend on the sensitivity of the information IAS protects and the resources available for the reviewing.

The following list shows other reasons for collecting and analyzing IAS log information:

Troubleshooting
Both connection and session state information are logged.

Billing
When IAS is used to manage customer access to the network, or where departmental use of resources must be accounted for, IAS data provides the records necessary to determine usage.

Auditing
Knowing who has connected and when they connected can be an important part of usage reporting as well as key information in a security investigation.

Log format and creation. Log data is not consistent. That is, the data recorded depends on the data collected by the type of access server or NAS acting as the RADIUS client, rather than some strict IAS-determined list of characteristics. Log data for IAS is recorded in one of the following:

- IAS format
- Database-compatible format
- Microsoft SQL Server logging

Logging to SQL Server is a new feature in Windows Server 2003.

Table 10-4 provides information on log file formats and their locations.

Table 10-4. IAS log location and file format

	IAS format	Database-compatible	SQL server logging	Event log
Location of file	Local	Local	SQL server computer	Local Application Event Log
File format	Text	Text	Records sent to SQL Server XML compliant database	Windows Event Log

Before configuring SQL logging, the SQL Server database, stored procedures and related applications must be installed and configured.

To configure local text file logging for IAS, begin by opening the IAS console. Select the Remote Access Logging node. In the details pane, right-click Local File and then click Properties. Select the Log File tab, as shown in Figure 10-10. In the Directory box, enter the filename and path for storing the local log file.

To change the file format from the IAS log default, select "Database-compatible" in the Format box. In the "Create a new log file" section, schedule the opening of new log files by clicking Daily, Weekly, or Monthly. To keep all data in one log file, click "Never (unlimited file size)." To limit log file size, click "When log file reaches this size" and then enter a file size in the field next to the option. To delete old log files automatically, click "When disk is full delete old log files." If the file is the current file, it will not be deleted.

To provide adequate log file storage and to prevent disk-full issues that might interfere with system operation, place the log file on a separate disk. Select the Settings tab, as shown in Figure 10-11. Table 10-5 provides information on these settings.

Figure 10-11. To log additional items, modify the Settings page

Table 10-5. RADIUS log file property settings

Log request	Definition
Accounting requests	Accounting requests and responses
Authentication requests	Access-Accept and Access-Reject messages
Periodic status	Status updates such as interim accounting packets

In addition to IAS-specific log files, information is recorded in the Windows Application Event log. To maximize the information recorded to the event log, begin by opening the IAS console. Right-click on the service and select Properties. Select the General tab, as shown in Figure 10-12.

Figure 10-12. Maximize event log information on authentication.

Enter a "Server description" that will aid you in identifying the server in the log entries. In this case, there is only one IAS server so we are simply identifying it as IAS. If multiple IAS servers are active, then a more descriptive entry should be used. Select "Rejected authentication requests" and "Successful authentication requests." Click OK.

Log contents. The log files contain extensive data about connections. Table 10-6 identifies logged items.

Table 10-6. IAS log data

Data	Sent by	Definition
Accounting-on request	Access server	The access server is online and ready to accept connections.
Accounting-off request	Access server	The access server is going offline.
Accounting-start request	Access server	An authenticated user session is starting.
Accounting-stop request	Access server	The user session has ended.
Accounting Interim requests	Some access servers	Sent during a user session when the Acct-Interim Interval RADIUS attribute is configured on the IAS server. If an access server supports this feature, it will send data for logging; if not, no data is sent. (See the section "RADIUS Messages" for a discussion on RADIUS attributes.)
Authentication requests	Access server	Sent on behalf of the user attempting to connect to the network.
Authentication accepts (Access-Accept message)	IAS	The connection is accepted.
Authentication rejects (Access Reject)	IAS	The connection is denied.

SQL server logging. Ordinary IAS text logs can be used for analysis and reporting. Logging to SQL Server provides the advantages of maintaining data on a non-IAS computer, using a relational database, and the capability of providing customized applications for log analysis. Logging to a modern relational database provides the following:

- Large amounts of data can be stored; terabytes of data can be efficiently managed and used.

- Relationships between data tables enable flexible creation of dynamic data views.

- Data backup can be written in parallel to multiple backup devices. You can also use differential backups, which are backups that only record the data changed after the last backup. Both features allow fast backup, which is especially important for large databases.

- Multiple IAS servers can log to the same database for centralized management and reporting, as well as a more comprehensive view.

- SQL Server logging can provide failover and redundancy.

SQL Server logging can be configured to log to the Microsoft SQL Server Desktop Engine (MSDE 2000) or to SQL Server 2000. Data is passed to the database in XML format to a *stored procedure* (a collection of stored *Transact SQL* statements compiled into a single executable program). The stored procedure is developed by your SQL Server staff and must be called *report_event*.

To determine the data fields that must be created in the database tables, you must understand both the nature of the data collected by the different devices that you use as RADIUS clients and also the minimum requirements of IAS server logging. A Microsoft document, *Deploying SQL Server Logging with Windows Server 2003 Internet Authentication Service (IAS)*, is available from *http://www.microsoft.com/downloads/details. aspx?familyid=6e4357f7-4070-4902-95f1-3ad411d963b2&displaylang=en*. This is a good place to prepare for development efforts. Setting up the SQL Server logging process requires configuration of IAS, development of a SQL Server database, creation of the *report_event* stored procedure, and creation of applications that can be used to query the database and create reports, trouble tickets, and so forth. Only an experienced SQL database programmer or administrator should attempt setting up SQL Server logging for IAS.

Configuring Remote Access policies

Remote Access policies can be configured on RRAS servers or IAS servers to control remote access authorization and communication configuration. When an IAS server is used for centralization of authentication, authorization, and accounting, any Remote Access policies configured on the RRAS servers identified as the IAS server's RADIUS clients will not be used. In addition, new remote access conditions and profile options are available for configuration. These elements, as well as those defined for both RRAS and RADIUS Remote Access policies, are passed as RADIUS attributes in the RADIUS messages between RADIUS servers and clients.

Many of the elements provide support for the use of additional RADIUS clients (such as authenticating switches and wireless access points). Their use is discussed in the sections "Configuring IAS for Use with VLANs" and "Securing Wireless Access with IAS," which describe IAS in those environments later in this chapter. Chapter 8 describes elements that are configurable for both RRAS and IAS remote access policies. Generic RADIUS-specific elements are described in Tables 10-2 and 10-3. Other elements are described where they are needed to configure some aspect of RADIUS.

For a complete listing of RADIUS specific attributes, see the Microsoft document *RADIUS Attributes* at *http://www.microsoft.com/resources/ documentation/WindowsServ/2003/standard/proddocs/en-us/Default. asp?url=/resources/doncumentation/windowsserv/2003/standard/prod-docs/en-us/sag_rass_radius_attrib.asp*.

Two RFCs are also excellent resources for more in-depth information: RFC 2865, *Remote Authentication Dial In User Service (RADIUS)* and RFC 2548, *Microsoft Vendor-specific RADIUS Attributes*.

Configuring additional ports

By default, IAS uses ports 1812 and 1645 for authentication, and ports 1813 and 1646 for accounting. To configure additional ports, begin by opening the IAS console.

Right-click on the service and select Properties. Select the Ports tab, as shown in Figure 10-13. Add, and/or remove ports and then click OK.

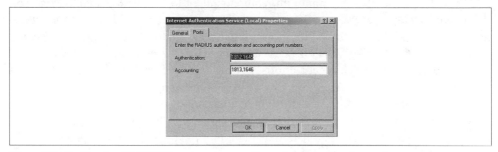

Figure 10-13. Standard RADIUS ports are preconfigured, but can be changed

Configuring account lockout

You can lock a user account after a number of failed attempts by using *account lockout* for IAS client connections. This is not the same as account lockout as specified for user accounts in the domain GPO. Account lockout for remote access connections must be configured in the registry of the IAS server, (If RRAS is not configured as a RADIUS client, you configure account lockout in the registry of the RRAS server.) Values are configured under the following key:

HKEY_LOCAL_MACHINE\System\CurrentControlSet\Services\RemoteAccess\ Parameters\AccountLockout

By default, the MaxDenials value is set to 0, meaning account lockout is disabled. To enable account lockout, set the value to 1 (or greater) to indicate the maximum number of failed attempts before an account is locked out. The "ResetTime (mins)" value should be set to the number of minutes before the account will automatically be reenabled.

If a user account is locked out, the account name will be added as a subkey to the AccountLockout key in the format *domainname:username*. If the account is automatically reset, the subkey will be deleted. To manually reset the user account, delete the subkey.

Now that you are familiar with the RADIUS protocol, how to install IAS, and how to configure IAS, let's take a look at how to configure IAS as a RADIUS proxy.

Configuring IAS as a RADIUS Proxy

RADIUS servers can themselves act as RADIUS clients and forward authentication and/or authorization request to another RADIUS server. For example, an ISP may use a RADIUS server to protect access to its network. If its customers are using the ISP to obtain access to their organization's remote access services, the organization may want to use its own database for authentication. Alternatively, an organization may want remote RADIUS servers at its own remote offices to forward requests to a central location. When IAS is used to forward requests to another RADIUS server, IAS is acting as a RADIUS proxy.

Setting up IAS to act as a RADIUS proxy entails a few general steps. First, you must configure a *remote RADIUS server group* (that is, a list of one or more RADIUS servers to which connection requests are forwarded by the proxy). If one of the servers is unreachable, the proxy will attempt a connection with another member of the group. You must also create a *connection request policy* that forwards authentication requests to the remote RADIUS server group. Finally, you must either delete the default connection request policy or change the processing order so that the new policy is evaluated first.

Configuring a RADIUS Server Group

The servers in the RADIUS server group may be administered by another person, or even by another organization. It is critical that administrators of the RADIUS servers in the RADIUS server group and the RADIUS proxy administrator have the correct information on the other's servers. Before configuring a RADIUS server group, collect the information required and test connectivity to these servers. Then, from the console of the RADIUS proxy, configure the RADIUS server group.

To configure a RADIUS server group with two servers, begin by clicking Start → Administrative Tools → Internet Authentication Service. Select and expand the Connection Request Policies node. Right-click Remote RADIUS Server Groups and the select New Remote RADIUS Server Group. Then click Next. Select "Typical (one primary server and one backup server)." Enter a group name, as shown in Figure 10-14, and then click Next.

Figure 10-14. Name the RADIUS remote server group

In the next screen shown in Figure 10-15, enter the server name or IP address of the primary server in the "Primary server" field and the backup server in the "Backup server" field. Click the Verify button next to the field for each server to verify the servers can be reached from the RADIUS proxy server. Enter the shared secret that will be used by the RRAS servers to connect to the proxy in the "Shared secret" field and retype the shared secret in the "Confirm shared secret" field. Click Next followed by Finish.

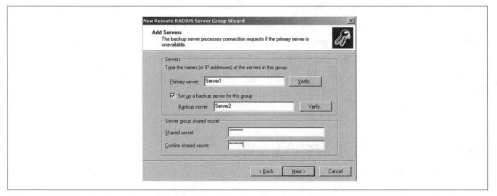

Figure 10-15. The shared secret added for the group must be added to each RRAS server in the group

To edit the default properties for each server, double-click on the server group in the IAS console, then double-click on the server. Select the Authentication/Accounting tab. Use this page to modify ports used for authentication and accounting and modify shared secrets, as shown in Figure 10-16. If the same shared secret is used for authentication and accounting, check the box "Use the same shared secret for authentication and accounting." The same shared secret might not be used if you have configured authentication and accounting to be managed by different IAS servers. If such is the case, and each IAS server uses its own shared secret, then make sure this box is unchecked and enter the correct shared secret for each server.

Select the Load Balancing tab, as shown in Figure 10-17, and modify information on the server priority. An entry of 1 indicates that this server is the primary server. (A connection to the primary server will be attempted first.) Enter larger numbers to indicate the order in which connection requests should be attempted. Connections to servers will be attempted in sequence, starting with the lowest number. In Figure 10-17, this server is given a priority of 2, which means that it will be used if the primary server cannot be contacted. If multiple servers are assigned the same priority, then use the Weight box to indicate how often connection requests should be sent to this particular server. In the Figure 10-17, the number 50 in entered to indicate that 50% of the requests should be sent to this server. Adjust timing information in the fields under "Advanced settings" as necessary to accommodate any network latency.

Click OK to close and implement the changes.

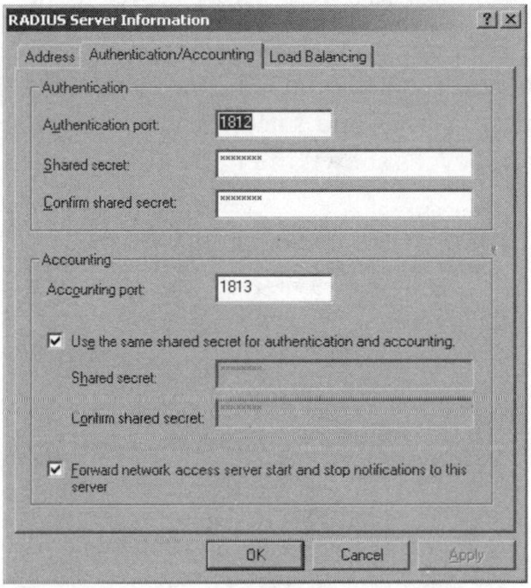

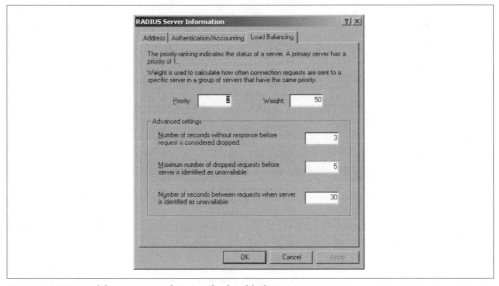

Figure 10-16. Modify ports and shared secrets as necessary

Figure 10-17. Modify priority and timing for load balancing

Configuring a Connection Request Policy

An IAS RADIUS server is, by default, configured to act as a RADIUS server and uses the default connection request policy: use Windows authentication for all users. Connection request policies specify how incoming connection requests are handled by IAS. To configure IAS as a RADIUS proxy server, configure a new connection request policy.

To create a new connection request policy, begin by opening the IAS console. Right-click Connection Request Policies and select New Connection Request Policy. Enter a name for the request policy, as shown in Figure 10-18, and then click Next.

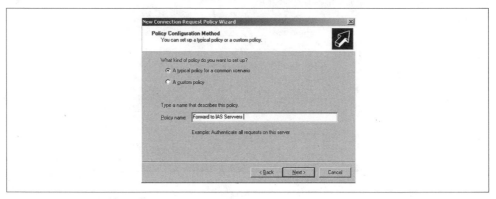

Figure 10-18. Name the policy

Click to select "Forward connection requests to a remote RADIUS server for authentication," as shown in Figure 10-19, and then click Next.

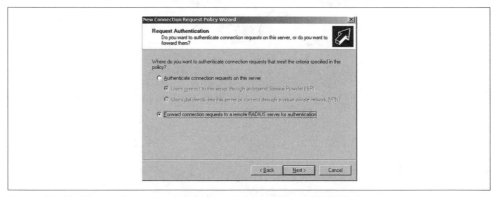

Figure 10-19. Change the connection request to forward to a RADIUS server

Enter the "Realm name" (which is the server name of the RADIUS server). Select the "Server group" from the drop-down list, as shown in Figure 10-20. Then click Next followed by Finish. A new server group can be created at this time by clicking the New Group button and following the wizard. The connection request policy can be edited. Double-click the policy and edit much as you would a Remote Access policy.

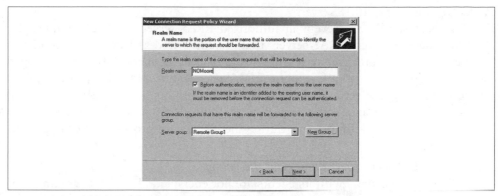

Figure 10-20. Add the Realm name and identify the Server group

If the username does not include the domain name, the default domain name is used. This name is the name of the domain of which the IAS server is a member. You can specify the default domain by editing the DefaultDomain value at *HKEY_LOCAL_MACHINE\System\CurrentControlSet\Services\RasMan\PPP\ControlProtocols\BuiltIn*.

Whether the IAS server is used as a RADIUS server or as a RADIUS proxy, security is extremely important. The IAS server should be secured and communications between RRAS and IAS should also be hardened, For example, if these communications can be intercepted and read, sensitive information such as passwords might be attacked and later used to compromise networks. If a rogue RRAS server can successfully connect to the IAS server, it might also be possible to fraudulently obtain remote access to your network.

Securing Communications Between RRAS and IAS

You can secure communications between RRAS and IAS by taking advantage of the *chokepoint security principle*. This principle requires that channels passing into a trusted network be narrowed. The theory here is that a narrow channel is easier to protect. (You can think of this as the same principle behind the use of a moat and drawbridge in the design of ancient castles.)

The chokepoints used to protect IAS to RRAS communications are as follows:

Limit information on the RRAS server(s)
When using IAS, the first chokepoint is the RRAS server. Access to the RRAS server can be limited by knowledge of its existence. Only authorized individuals should have its access phone numbers or network location address. While this, like many security-through-obscurity techniques, is not very effective, it does help some but it is only the beginning.

Protect against rogue RRAS servers

The next step is to prevent unauthorized RRAS servers from communicating with the IAS server. RRAS servers that are authorized as IAS clients are identified in the IAS property pages by listing their server names. To prevent rogue RRAS servers from spoofing authorized client identities, IAS clients are required to use a shared secret and an optional Message-Authenticator Attribute. (If EAP is used, the Message-Authenticator Attribute is always used.) The shared secret is created by the administrator during the installation process and can be up to 128 characters.

Secure IAS/RRAS communications using encryption

IAS communications with its clients are not encrypted. To protect communications as they traverse the wire, use IPSec between the RRAS server and the RADIUS server.

When all three techniques are properly implemented, they can protect IAS from spoofing attacks. Let's take a closer look at protecting against rogue RRAS servers and securing communications by using encryption.

Shared Secret

The RRAS and IAS shared secret is used for mutual authentication. However, the authentication process does not use traditional authentication mechanisms. Instead, it relies on comparing hashes made of the RADIUS message. Authentication must occur before other communications are permitted between the servers. Using shared secrets for authentication, however, is not the best mechanism. It is difficult to keep a shared secret a secret for the following reasons:

* It is readily available to RRAS and IAS administrators.
* It is difficult to create a strong shared secret in some implementations.
* The possibility that RADIUS messages might be captured can help to enable successful offline dictionary or brute force attacks.

The use of a shared secret can be hardened and successfully used to prevent a rogue server from impersonating either the RRAS server or the IAS server. The first step is to use good shared secret management techniques. These include the following:

* Make the shared secret long (at least 22 characters) and composed of a random sequence of letters, numbers, and punctuation. (The shared secret can be up to 128 characters.) Use a computer program to generate the random sequence.
* Change the shared secret often. (You will have to do so manually.)
* Use a different shared secret for each RADIUS server and RRAS client pair.
* Use a different shared secret for each RADIUS proxy and RADIUS server pair.

If you specify RRAS servers by IP address range, each RRAS server will have to use the same shared secret.

Message-Authenticator Attribute

Next, use the Message-Authenticator Attribute to protect IAS from spoofed communications. The Message-Authenticator Attribute creates an MD5 hash of the entire RADIUS Access-Request message using the shared secret as the key. The hash accompanies the message. The recipient of the message uses its own copy of the shared secret and creates its own hash of the message. The two hashes are compared. If the hashes match, then the communication has not been altered, and the message must have come from an authorized server. If the Message-Authenticator Attribute is required and is not present, or if the hashes do not match, the request is dropped. Windows 2000 and Windows Server 2003 IAS servers and RRAS servers support this attribute. If another NAS must be used, then Remote Access Account Access should be used. Of course, if the shared secret has been compromised, an attack might still be successful.

IPSec

Finally, to protect communications and require further authentication beyond the shared secret approach, an IPSec policy can be created that secures all communications between IAS and its RRAS clients, and/or the IAS RADIUS proxy and additional RADIUS servers. Two possible ways to do so would be to create a policy that secures traffic between IAS and its clients, and/or RADIUS proxy and its RADIUS peer(s) based on the IP address of the authorized servers or based on the use of the RADIUS ports. If certificates are used for IPSec authentication, even an attacker who knows the shared secret and can spoof a legitimate RRAS server IP address will be prevented from making a connection unless he can obtain a valid certificate. Certificate distribution can be controlled to ensure that only authorized servers can obtain a certificate. The use of IPSec to secure RADIUS communications is detailed in RFC 3162, *RADIUS and IPv6*. For information on configuring IPSec in Windows Server 2003, see Chapter 11.

Now that you have learned the basic configuration of RADIUS server and RADIUS proxies using IAS and how to protect the communications between RADIUS client and servers, you may be interested to know that there is more to IAS than remote access. The same secure authentication communications capabilities that make IAS the perfect arbitrator of remote access connections make it a great added security device for VLANs and wireless networks. We'll cover each of these options in their own sections, starting with instructions on how to configure IAS for use with VLANs.

Configuring IAS for Use with VLANs

Virtual Local Area Networks (VLANs) allow logical groupings of network resources that may exist in different physical locations or on different physical subnets. To the user, it looks as if all resources are on the same subnet. VLANs can also be used to segregate a network between different groups of users (for example, by user role, position, or access level). If these groups are created in AD, a Windows Server 2003 IAS server can be used to create a Remote Access policy for each group and define the VLAN to which the group is assigned. When the user makes a connection request to the network the Remote Access policy determines which VLAN the user can use. Such policies might be used to allow visitors and contractors access to the Internet but refuse them access to the rest of your network, or allow members of the accounting department access to accounting resources on the accounting VLAN while keeping other employees out.

VLANs are created using a combination of VLAN-aware network hardware (routers, switches, wireless access points, and access controllers). To use IAS to control access to the VLANs, you must configure the network hardware as RADIUS clients for the IAS server. Use the manufacturer's instructions on how to do this. To configure the IAS server, configure the IP address of the VLAN hardware devices as RADIUS clients in the IAS interface and configure Remote Access policies for each AD user group that will be permitted specific VLAN access. Table 10-7 lists the requirements for using IAS to segregate a network between different groups of users.

Table 10-7. Requirements for IAS segregated VLANs

Components	Requirements
Network hardware	Must be VLAN-aware and capable of being configured as RADIUS clients
User account database	Windows Server 2003 AD
Domain functional level	Windows Server 2003
RADIUS server	Windows Server 2003 IAS server

Use the following steps to configure the IAS Server. The details of steps 1, 3, and 4 are presented as tutorials earlier in this chapter, or in Chapter 8. Step 2 (creating AD groups) is a standard Windows Server 2003 administrative activity. To create a Remote Access policy for VLANs (step 5), use the instructions in the section "Creating a Remote Access Policy for VLANs."

1. Configure each VLAN hardware device as a RADIUS client in the IAS interface.

2. Ensure that appropriate AD groups have been created.

3. Ensure that the IAS server is registered in AD. This is necessary to permit the IAS server to read user account information in AD.

4. Configure the Remote Access Permission (Dial-in or VPN) property of user accounts to be determined through Remote Access policies. (This option is selected by default if a user is added to a Windows Server 2003 functional level domain.)

5. Create a remote access policy for VLANs based on authorization by group.

Creating a Remote Access Policy for VLANs

Once you have created a Remote Access policy, as detailed earlier in the section "Configuring Remote Access policies," based on authorization by group, and you have added the access methods (VPN, dial-up, and so on, as required), you are ready to configure the properties of the Remote Access policy.

Begin by opening the Properties page of the Remote Access policy. Under Policy conditions, click Add. In Attribute Types, select Day-and-Time-Restrictions and then click Add. In the "Time of day restraints" area, select Permitted and configure the days and times that you wish to permit this group to connect. Then click OK.

In the Properties page, click "Grant remote access permission." Click Edit Profile and then click the Advanced tab. To specify connection attributes for VLANs, click Add and then add the attributes according to the following:

- In Tunnel-Medium-Type, ensure that this matches your access type (for example, use 802 for wireless).
- In Tunnel-Pvt-Group-ID, use the integer for the VLAN number to which group members will be assigned.
- In Tunnel-Type, select Virtual LANs (VLAN).
- In *Tunnel-Tag*, use the value that comes from the network VLAN hardware device.

Configure any additional IAS connection request policies as required.

In addition to using IAS with a VLAN, you can also use IAS to secure wireless access to your network. This is the topic of our next discussion.

Securing Wireless Access with IAS

Wireless network access can be secured using *Wi-Fi Protected Access* (WPA) as defined in the IEEE 802.11i standard and/or using IEE 802.1x authentication. (WPA requires 802.1x authentication, but 802.1x can be used without WPA.) To implement WPA, wireless clients and wireless access points must support 802.1x authentication. If a RADIUS server is not used for authentication, 802.1x can be supported by a shared secret. However, a more secure solution is to use a RADIUS server. IAS server supports 802.1x authentication and its configuration is discussed here. Support for WPA and 802.1x is available for Windows clients.

Table 10-8 describes the support for 802.1x authentication and WPA in Microsoft products.

Table 10-8. 802.1x and WPA support in Microsoft Products

Product	Details for 802.1x	Details for WPA
Windows Server 2003	Group Policy can be used to configure client settings.	Obtain from Microsoft and install the WPA client. Obtain network card driver and firmware updates as necessary.
Windows XP	Group Policy can be used to configure client settings (SP1 and above). A wireless update download is available (see KB article 826942).	Windows XP SP1 or later; obtain and install the Windows WPA Client. Obtain network card driver and firmware updates as necessary.
Windows 2000	SP3 or later and the Microsoft 802.1x upgrade for Windows 2000 or SP4.	Obtain and install a new WPA-compliant configuration tool from the wireless network card adapter.
Pocket PC 2002	N/A	N/A
IAS Server	Windows Server 2000 with SP4 or later, and Windows Server 2003.	N/A
Windows 98, Millennium, and Windows NT 4.0 Workstation	802.1x client support available for Microsoft Premier and Alliance support customers only.	N/A

Authentication is a major component of secure access to wireless networks. While there are several choices that can be used for authentication, the use of *Extensible Authentication Protocol* (EAP) or *Protected EAP* (PEAP), and the 802.1x authentication process is the best solution. An understanding of the EAP, PEAP, and the 802.1x authentication process is necessary to correctly implement them. Many installations fail simply because of lack of knowledge about these protocols.

Understanding EAP and PEAP

The 802.1x IEEE standard for network port authentication defines how EAP can be used for authentication by IEEE 802 devices including wireless access points and Ethernet switches. The standard uses the IETF RFC 2284, *PPP Extensible Authentication Protocol* (PEAP). Only EAP authentication types are supported. To use 802.1x the following components must support 802.1x and PEAP:

- Wireless access points (APs)
- Wireless client
- RADIUS server

EAP is flexible and extensible, but does not encrypt the authentication channel. Therefore, it might be possible for a malicious user to capture and analyze successful authentication and possibly gain information that might assist in an attack. For example, if password protocols such as the *Challenge Handshake Access Protocol* (CHAP) that are susceptible to offline password cracking attacks are used, the attacker might be able to crack the password of a valid user. In addition, the attacker might be able to inject packets into the communication and interfere with communications. PPP authentication protocols select authentication methods during link establishment as part of the connection validation. EAP does not use the authentication mechanism during link establishment. Instead, authentication methods (or the choice of an EAP type) are chosen during the connection and authentication phase. However, when EAP is used for 802.1x, communications authentication takes place before packets are encrypted using the Wired Equivalency Privacy (WEP) protocol.

PEAP encrypts the entire communication (including the user authentication process). PEAP uses Transport Layer Security (TLS) to create a secure, encrypted channel. Messages are also checked for integrity. The channel is created before the client is authenticated. When PEAP is used, even those authentication protocols that are susceptible to attacks can be used because the communications channel is encrypted before user authentication takes place. Windows Server 2003, Windows XP SP1 or later, and Microsoft 802.1x Authentication clients support PEAP-MS-CHAP v2 and EAP-TLS as defined in RFC 2716, *PPP EAP TLS Authentication Protocol*. EAP-TLS is very similar to the protocol used in *Secure Sockets Layer* (SSL), the protocol used to authenticate and secure communications with e-commerce servers.

When PEAP-MS-CHAP v2 is used, wireless clients do not need certificates, but the IAS server does. If you have implemented a Windows *Certificate Authority (CA)* based *Public-Key Infrastructure* (PKI), issue a certificate for the IAS server. However, if you do not already have a PKI, you may use a third-party certificate for the server. The client must have a copy of the *root CA certificate* for the server's certificate to validate the digital signature of the IAS server certificate. The certificate is used to authenticate the client to server connection, and provide encryption keys for further communications (including the user's MS-CHAP v2 authentication). Chapter 13 provides more details on PKI and how certificates are used in a Windows network.

When EAP-TLS is used, both clients and servers need certificates. Certificates may be stored on the client computer or on smart cards.

 Other 802.1x authentication schemes are Cisco's LEAP (which requires the use of Cisco wireless access points) and EAP-MD5 (which is not recommended for wireless communications).

Third-party components can be used to provide the IAS server with support for PEAP authentication methods such as the use of *token cards* such as the RSA SecureID. (For more information, see the article *Enterprise Deployment of Wireless and Remote Access with RSA Secure ID and Microsoft Internet Authentication Service* at:

http://www.microsoft.com/downloads/details.aspx?familyid=2466f0e3-231b-46b5-ae1e-0e5d3c3cacad&displaylang=en.)

After authentication, 802.1x generates *dynamic encryption keys* that are used for WEP encryption. (The keys are frequently changed and distributed to clients.) The use of dynamic keying for WEP mitigates one of the major vulnerabilities of WEP. Because WEP keys can be cracked if enough WEP messages are captured, frequent rekeying can reduce the chance that this will occur.

EAP over RADIUS is not a defined EAP type, but is the method by which EAP messages can be passed by the NAS server to a RADIUS server for authentication. The EAP message is included as a RADIUS attribute part of the RADIUS message. The NAS server does not process the EAP message; the RADIUS server and the origination access client do. After the RADIUS server has processed the EAP message, it returns an EAP message encapsulated in the RADIUS message back to the NAS server. The NAS server returns the EAP message to the client that requested the connection.

Understanding the 802.1x Authentication Process

The 802.1x authentication process is also referred to as *port authentication*. This is because a two-port configuration is used. One port, the *uncontrolled port*, is used for communications between the wireless access point and the RADIUS server. Client communications are forwarded over this port. No direct communications between the client and the RADIUS server (or any other intranet resource) can use this port. The second port, the *controlled port*, is available only to authenticated and authorized clients and is used for communications between the client and the intranet over the wireless access point. Communications required to perform client authentication to the RADIUS server are proxied by the access point. The access point is the RADIUS client.

There are three new 802.1x specific definitions:

Port Access Entity (PAE) or LAN port
   This supports the 802.1x protocol that is associated with a logical or physical port. The PAE can be either an authenticator or supplicant (or both).

Supplicant
   This is a LAN port used to request access to services through the authenticator. In a wireless network, the supplicant is the LAN port on the wireless LAN network adapter.

Authenticator

This is the LAN port on the access point or NAS server that is used for communications with the RADIUS server. In a wireless network the authenticator is the LAN port on the wireless access point. The authenticator does not authenticate the supplicant's request; instead it forwards the supplicant's request to an authentication server (the RADIUS server).

The authenticator has both an uncontrolled port and a controlled port. The uncontrolled port is used for uncontrolled communications between the wireless AP and other devices on the wired network (for example, RADIUS messages). A wireless network client's frames are never forwarded through the uncontrolled port. The controlled port does forward an authenticated wireless client's frames between the client and the wired network. Think of the controlled port as if it was an electrical switch. Until the client has authenticated, the switch is open (no connection exists, electricity cannot flow) and no client communications can be forwarded. After the client has been authenticated, the switch is closed and data can flow between the client and the wired network.

Figure 10-21 illustrates the controlled and uncontrolled ports on the AP. In the figure, the uncontrolled port is communicating with the RADIUS server to forward the connection request from client 1. The controlled port logical switch is open. Another part of the controlled port is closed to support communications for client 2. Client 2 has already been authenticated.

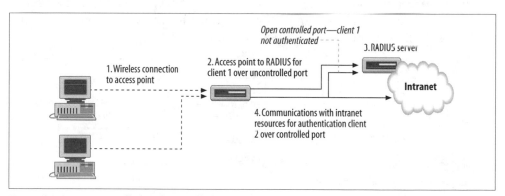

Figure 10-21. Uncontrolled and controlled ports

The *authentication server* is a server that checks the credentials of the supplicator on behalf of the authenticator and returns the results (authenticated or denied) to the authenticator. The authentication server can be a component of the AP, in which case the AP must be configured with the user credentials. In a wireless network, the authentication server is usually a RADIUS server and the wireless AP uses the RADIUS protocol to send and receive connection requests and results with the RADIUS server.

The authentication process follows these steps as illustrated in Figure 10-22:

1. The access client uses its wireless network card and sends a connection request to the wireless access point. The connection request includes the user identity.

2. The wireless access point acts as a RADIUS client and uses the uncontrolled port to forward an Access-Request message, including the user identity to the RADIUS server.

3. The RADIUS server sends an Access-Request back to the wireless access point requesting the user's credentials (user ID and password).

4. The wireless access point requests this information from the access client.

5. The access client provides this information to the wireless access point, which then forwards it to the RADIUS server.

6. The RADIUS server performs an authentication check against either its local database or AD, depending on how the RADIUS server is configured.

7. If the user credentials are valid, an Access-Accept message is returned to the wireless access point.

8. If the user credentials are not valid, the RADIUS server returns an Access-Reject message to the wireless access point.

9. If the user credentials cannot be verified (a domain controller cannot be located, for example), the connection request is dropped.

10. If the wireless access point receives an Access-Accept message, the user is allowed to communicate with the intranet using the controlled port of the wireless access point; otherwise, this port remains closed.

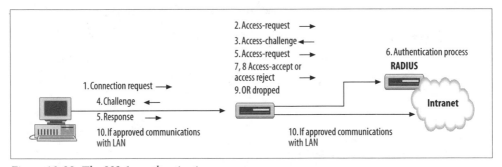

Figure 10-22. The 802.1x authentication process

Implementing 802.1x Authentication

To implement 802.1x authentication, three components must be configured:

- The 802.1x capable wireless access point
- The IAS server
- The Windows client

It is also beneficial to create a Windows custom security group whose members are those users who are authorized for wireless access.

To configure the wireless access point, use the manufacturer's instructions.

Configuring IAS to support 802.1x authentication for wireless clients

To configure IAS to support 802.1X authentication, the wireless access point is added to the RADIUS server as a RADIUS client and a Remote Access policy is created to manage wireless connections. If the RADIUS server does not already have a certificate, one must be obtained and installed before the Remote Access policy can be configured. Information on obtaining and installing the certificate appears later in this chapter.

Configuring a Remote Access policy for wireless. The Remote Access policy should have the following configuration characteristics:

EAP authentication
> The authentication method must be defined for the policy. For wireless access, the first choice made is between PEAP or smart cards. The use of smart cards for wireless access requires the use of an EAP protocol. For wireless access remote access policies, you will always identify a type of EAP authentication.

Ignore dial-up properties attribute
> When Remote Access policies are evaluated, the dial-up properties of the user account are considered. If call-back is configured, the wireless access point cannot respond. Therefore, the dial-up properties must be ignored for wireless connections

Framed MTU attribute
> This is used with EAP authentication. This informs the RADIUS server of the *maximum transmission unit* (MTU) negotiated with the client. (The MTU specifies the largest IP datagram that can be transmitted.) This prevents the RADIUS server from sending EAP messages too large for the client to accept.

Tunnel-Pvt-Group-ID attribute
> If a VLAN is used to manage wireless clients, this attribute allows specification of the VLAN ID.

To create the policy, create a new Remote Access policy and then edit the policies profile. Finally, remove the default Remote Access policy, or move it down so the wireless access policy is evaluated first.

To create the policy, begin by opening the IAS console. Right-click Remote Access Policies and then click New Remote Access Policy. Then click Next. Enter a name for the policy (for example, Wireless Access), then click Next. Select Wireless and then click Next. Use the Add button and add the Windows group representing users who are authorized to connect to the wireless network. Then click Next.

In the Authentication Methods window, use the Type drop-down list to select a method. (You can choose between PEAP or smart cards. The instructions that follow are for the PEAP option.) Select Protected EAP (PEAP), as shown in Figure 10-23.

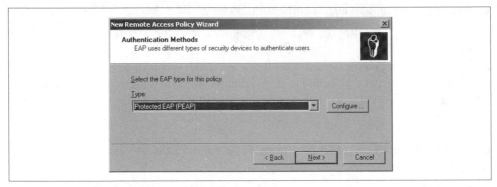

Figure 10-23. Select the authentication method

Click the Configure button next to the drop-down list box. Configure Protected EAP Properties, as shown in Figure 10-24. The server certificate must already be present on the server. If desired, check the Enable Fast Reconnect box. This box allows the server and client to reconnect quickly when a connection is dropped. However, it avoids some security checks and therefore might allow an attacker to successfully hijack a connection between a valid client and the server. For this reason, it is left blank in our example.

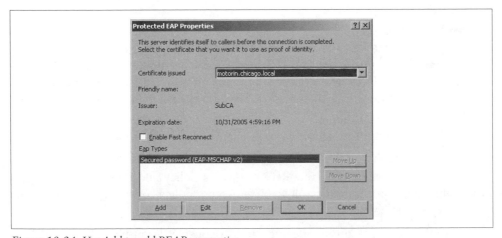

Figure 10-24. Use Add to add PEAP properties

Use the Add button to identify the EAP Type allowed for this connection. Then click OK, followed by Next, and then Finish.

To edit the profile, expand the Remote Access Policies node and double-click on the wireless policy in the detail pane. On the Settings page, click the Edit Profile button to edit the profile. Review the configuration settings and compare them against network requirements (for example, modifying acceptable encryption requirements or adjusting dial-in constraints). Select the Advanced tab, as shown in Figure 10-25, and click the Add button to add an Attribute.

Figure 10-25. Edit the profile

Scroll down and select Ignore-User-Dial-In-Properties and then click Add. This property is necessary to prevent the IAS server from processing user properties that the wireless access point won't understand. The primary user property that can cause problems is the Call-Back phone number listed in a user account Dial-In properties page in Active Directory Users and Computers. Click True and then click OK. Repeat this process for other required attributes.

Examples of attributes that may be required are those required for VLANs. If a VLAN is used to manage wireless clients, add the attributes Tunnel Type (select Virtual LAN (VLAN)) and Tunnel-Pvt-Group-ID (add the value of the VLAN ID that contains the certificate server for the wireless clients).

Click Close to return to the Settings page. Click OK twice to close the policy.

Understanding and fulfilling certificate requirements for EAP and PEAP

Client and server certificates for EAP and PEAP must meet specific requirements. This is true whether the certificate is produced by a Microsoft Windows CA or a third-party CA. Chapter 13 provides information on Windows CA's, certificates, and definitions for the items referred to here, along with simple PKI implementation information for Windows. The requirements are listed here for reference when planning your IAS/wireless deployment.

Specific certificate requirements for EAP and PEAP are as follows:

- The client certificate must be issued by a Windows Enterprise CA or be mapped to a user account or computer account in the AD. (An Enterprise CA is integrated with AD and automatically maps its issued certificates to AD accounts.)

- The user or computer certificate *chains* to a trusted root CA. (It is issued by the root CA or by a CA in the root CA's hierarchy.)

- The user or computer certificate on the client includes the Client Authentication purpose.

- The user or computer certificate does not fail one of the checks performed by CryptoAPI certificate store and passes requirements in the Remote Access policy.

- The 802.1x client does not use registry-based (stored in the registry) certificates that are smart-card certificates, or that are protected with a password. (Smart-card certificates stored on a smart card can be used.)

- The Subject Alternative Name extension in the client certificate contains the *user principal name* (UPN) of the user.

- When clients use PEAP with EAP-TLS and EAP-TLS authentication, a list of all installed certificates valid for EAP-TLS are display in the Certificates snap-in.

- The IAS or VPN server certificate must also be configured with the "Server authentication" purpose (a certificates purpose designates how it can be used. The server authentication purpose means the certificate can be used to prove the server is who it claims to be). The object identifier (an number which is used to classify an object) for server authentication is 1.3.6.1.5.5.7.3.1.

- The IAS or VPN server certificate must have the name in the "Subject line" of the certificate that matches the name configured on the client for the connection.

- For use with wireless clients, the IAS or VPN server certificate must be configured with the Subject Alternative Name extension containing the name of the IAS or VPN server.

Using a Windows CA server certificate

If a server certificate is required and a Windows Enterprise CA is present to provide certificates for the domain, the Windows Enterprise CA may already have issued a server certificate to the domain member IAS server. Use the Certificates console to verify if this is so. If the CA is not configured to automatically provide server certificates, a certificate can be requested using the Certificates console. Third-party certificates can also be used. (See the beginning of the section "Implementing 802.1x Authentication" earlier in this chapter.)

To verify if a computer certificate from an enterprise CA is available, first create a Certificates console for the local computer by adding the Certificates snap-in to an MMC console on the IAS server. When the Certificates snap-in is selected, a prompt for user or computer certificates is offered. Select the "Local computer account (the computer this console is running on)" option, as shown in Figure 10-26.

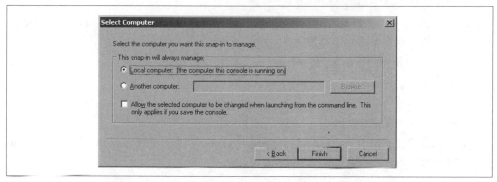

Figure 10-26. Identify the computer whose certificates are to be checked

Check for the existence of a server certificate for this computer. The certificate, if present, is located in the Certificates (Local Computer) → Personal → Certificates node of the Certificates console, as shown in Figure 10-27.

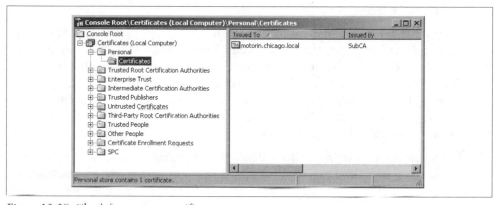

Figure 10-27. Check for a server certificate

If a certificate is not present, you must request a computer certificate. To request a certificate, begin by right-clicking the Personal folder of the Certificates console for the IAS server and then click All Tasks. Select Request New Certificate and then click Next. The available certificate types are listed. Select Computer for the Certificate types and then click Next twice. Then click Finish.

Click OK in response to the prompt that the certificate request was successful.

Using a third-party certificate

By default, Windows wireless clients already store a copy of the root CA certificates of many third-party CAs. Purchase a certificate for the IAS server from one of these

CAs, and you will not need to configure the clients to trust the IAS certificate. You may use another third-party CA, but then you must install a copy of the CA's root certificate on every wireless client.

To configure the server by obtaining and installing an IAS/PEAP server certificate from Verisign, follow these steps:

1. Obtain a certificate from Verisign.

2. Install the certificate.

3. If the certificate is automatically installed by the download routine, verify that the certificate is installed.

4. If a proxy server is used, add the proxy server information using the local security context.

Obtaining and installing a Verisign certificate. This procedure obtains and installs a certificate from Verisign, but an Internet connection is needed from the IAS server (including the ability to run scripts). This additional risk can be avoided by obtaining the certificate using an *administrative station* (a computer dedicated for this type of administrative task) and then manually moving the certificate from the administrative station to the IAS server.

Log in to the IAS server. Alternatively (and to improve security), you can log on to an administrative machine. Open Internet Explorer. Browse to the *http://www.verisign.com/ products/wlan/ Wireless LAN Server Certificates* web page. Click the Buy button to open the WLAN Server Enrollment for Microsoft IAS Server page. Choose a validity period of 1 or 2 years. Enter the information requested and be sure to enter your email in the Enter Your Technical Contact Information text box on the page. Read the subscriber agreement. If you agree to the terms, click Accept.

Check your email for a message from Verisign that includes a URL and PIN. If you completed the steps in the previous paragraph from an administrative machine, log on to that machine. If you completed those steps from the IAS server, log on to the IAS server using a local Administrator account. (This account is used by the certificate installation program.)

Open Internet Explorer. Browse to the URL listed in the email message. Enter the PIN from the email message. Click Install. (The certificate is automatically installed if the page is accessed from the IAS server.) If an administrative machine is used, you must install the certificate manually on the IAS server (as detailed in the following section).

Click the Yes button when warned about a potential scripting violation. Use the Certificates console to verify that the certificate is installed.

Manually installing the WLAN certificate. If the IAS certificate is obtained using an administrative station, you must copy the certificate from this computer to the IAS computer and then install it.

Click the Start button, click Run, enter **mmc**, and then click OK. From the File menu, click Add/Remove Snap-in and click Add. Double-click the Certificates snap in. Select the Local Computer Account and then click Finish. Click Close. Use "File Save as" to name and save the console as Certificates.

In the console, expand the Certificates (Local Computer) node, expand Personal, and click Certificates. Select the certificate that is issued to the name you entered in the certificate enrollment process. From the Action menu, select All Tasks and then click Export.

Click Yes, export the private key, and then click Next. Click "Include all certificates in the certification path if possible" and then click Next. Enter a password to be used to import the certificate on the IAS server. Enter a filename and then click Finish.

Log on with local administrative privileges at the IAS server. Copy the file to the IAS server. Create a certificates console as described at the beginning of this section. In the console, expand the Certificates (Local Computer) node, expand Personal. From the Action menu, select All Tasks, click Import, and then click Next. Enter the name of certificate file (or browse to its location and select it). Enter the password you created earlier and then click Next. Ensure that "Place all certificates in the following store" points to the Personal store, and then click Next, followed by Finished.

Verifying the certificate is installed. If the certificate is obtained from the IAS server, it is automatically installed. Use the Certificates snap-in to verify the certificate is installed. Click the Start button, click Run, enter **mmc**, and then click OK. From the File menu, click Open. Double-click the Certificates console you saved previously. In the console, expand the Certificates (Local Computer) node, expand Personal, and click Certificates. In the details pane, search for the Versign WLAN server certificate.

Configuring proxy settings. The Verisign certificate revocation list (CRL) source will point to a Verisign server on the Internet. The CRL is necessary to check the certificate validity. If you use a proxy server between clients and the Internet, then you must configure IAS to use the proxy server. To configure proxy settings, use the Internet Explorer Connections page LAN Setting page.

Configuring the Windows XP wireless client to use 802.1x authentication

Windows XP enables IEEE 802.1x authentication using EAP-TLS authentication by default for LAN-based network adapters. The first step in configuring the XP wireless client is to configure the wireless network adapter. Select Control Panel → Settings → Network Connections → Wireless Network Connection. Click the Advanced button. Click the Add button to add a network. Select the Association tab, and enter the network SSID, as shown in Figure 10-28.

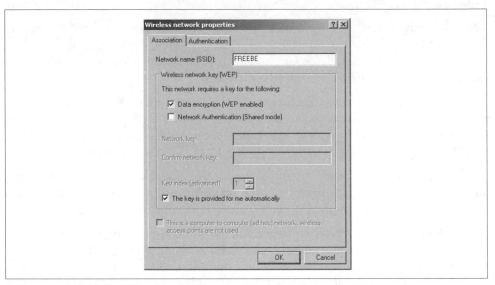

Figure 10-28. Add the SSID

Ensure that the "Data encryption (WEP enabled)" checkbox is checked. Select the Authentication tab and ensure that the "Enable IEEE 802.1x authentication for this network" checkbox is selected. Use the "EAP type" drop-down list to select Protected EAP (PEAP) or "Smart Card or other certificate," as shown in Figure 10-29.

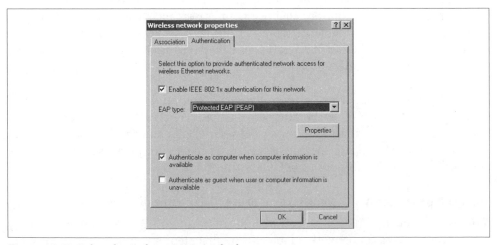

Figure 10-29. Select the Authentication method

Click the Properties button. If a "Smart Card or other certificate" will be used for client authentication, first ensure that the "Validate server certificate" checkbox is checked. If multiple RADIUS servers are used, enter the portion of the RADIUS server DNS name that is common for all servers in the "Connect only if server name ends with:" box. Select the trusted root certificate in the Trusted root certificate authority drop-down list. The list of available certificates corresponds to the certificates stored in the computer's certificate store. If the username required for authentication is different than the one listed on the client certificate, then select "Use a different user name" for the connection checkbox. When prompted, select the client certificate from those presented.

If PEAP is selected, first ensure that the "Validate server certificate" checkbox is checked. Click the "Connect to these servers" box and enter the name of the RADIUS server. Select the "Trusted root certificate" in the "Trusted root certificate authority" list. The list of available certificates corresponds to the certificates stored in the computer certificate store. Use the Select an Authentication Method dropdown list to select Secured password (EAP MS-CHAPv2), as shown in Figure 10-30.

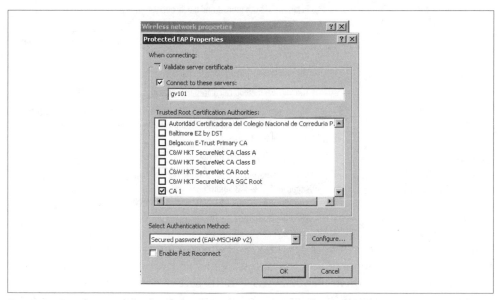

Figure 10-30. If PEAP is used and client certificates are not, select MS-CHAPv2

Click the Configure button to open the EAP MS-CHAPv2 Properties window. Uncheck "Automatically use my Windows logon name and password (and domain if any)." This will require the user to manually enter credentials before connecting using the wireless access. Furthermore, it will prevent connections by unauthorized personnel if the client computer is left unattended while the user is logged on. Click OK as many times as necessary to close the Network Connections property pages.

After a user connects to a wireless network using PEAP, his or her user credentials are stored in the registry and used to reauthenticate to the wireless network even after a reboot. To remove these credentials, use the registry editor and delete the following key (of course, using normal registry editing precautions): *HKEY_CURRENT_USER\Software\Microsoft\Eapol\UserEapInfo*.

Understanding and Using WPA

Wi-Fi Protected Access (WPA) is specified in the IEEE 802.11i wireless networking standard. Table 10-9 shows WPA specifics.

Table 10-9. WPA security specifics

Item	Requirements
Authentication	802.1x.
Key management	Rekeying of both unicast and global encryption keys.
Unicast encryption key	*Temporal Key Integrity Protocol* (TKIP) is used to change the unicast encryption key for every frame and synchronizes changes between the wireless client and the WAP. TKIP replaces WEP.
Global encryption key	The wireless AP advertises the changed key to the connected wireless clients.
Integrity	The *Michael method* calculates an 8-byte *message integrity code* (MIC).
Replay protection	A new frame counter in the 802.11 frame is used by MIC to help prevent replay attacks. (If a frame, identified by this counter has already been received, the frame will be dropped.)
Encryption	WPA specifies support for the *Advanced Encryption Standard* (AES) is optional.
Support for mixed WEP and WPA clients	During migration to WPA, a mixed client base of WPA and WEP clients can be supported. The WAP identifies which protocol the client is using. The global encryption key cannot be dynamic because WEP clients cannot support it. Other benefits are maintained (including integrity).

Wireless access points, network adapters, and client programs must support WPA. It may be possible to upgrade wireless access points and network cards via firmware updates provided by their manufacturers. Both access points and network cards must support the new WPA information element. They should be configured for WPA to support WPA two-phase authentication (EAP or RADIUS with 802.1x), TKIP, and Michael. Support for AES is optional.

Windows clients will require an updated network card driver that supports WPA. Windows XP and Windows Server 2003 clients require the driver to be capable of passing the adapter's WPA capabilities and security configuration to the *Wireless Zero Configuration Service*. In many cases, the updated driver (when installed on the client) will update both firmware and the network card driver.

Windows client software must be updated to permit configuration of WPA authentication, as well as shared key and WPA encryption algorithms (TKIP and optional AES).

Securing wireless access to your networks is a critical step in securing your networks. This section has detailed how to do so using IAS. By now, you can see how complex and detailed IAS configuration can be. No matter how you use IAS, it is extremely important to back up the configuration information so that you can more easily restore remote access operations in the case of server failure or other disaster. The next section applies to all uses of IAS.

Using Backup and Restore (Importing IAS Configuration)

To ensure the availability of remote access connections, you should deploy IAS servers in pairs. Both servers can be managed from a single IAS console. Be sure to synchronize changes to the servers: when a large number of changes must be made, use netsh commands to export settings to a script, and then run the script to duplicate settings on the second IAS server.

Having at least two IAS servers can ensure remote access connectivity if one of the servers crashes. Still, you'll want to restore the crashed IAS server ASAP. To ensure the ability to restore a failed IAS server, back up its configuration information in a script that can be used to restore the settings to a newly installed IAS server.

The netsh aaaa dump command can be used to store the Windows Server 2003 IAS configuration information in a script that can be used with the IAS aaaa exec command to restore IAS configuration on the IAS server or to import duplicate settings to a new IAS server. The dump command saves the IAS database and the IAS registry keys. Use the dump command and store a copy of this script as backup. It can be used to quickly restore or to configure a new IAS server. This can save a lot of time and maintain consistency if a duplicate IAS server is required, or if you must quickly configure a new IAS server to replace one that has suffered hardware failure.

The netsh aaaa show config > *path\filename* command can be used to export the IAS server configuration into a script.

Figure 10-31 displays part of the file created.

The netsh exec command can be used with the script to import IAS server settings into another server, as shown here:

```
Netsh exec > path\filename
```

Figure 10-31. *The script file created with netsh can be used to restore an IAS server configuration, or to create a secondary IAS server*

 Additional netsh commands that are useful when managing IAS are documented in the *Tools and Settings* section of the *IAS Server Technical Reference* at:

> *http://www.microsoft.com/resources/documentation/WindowsServ/*
> *2003/all/techref/en-us/Default.asp?url=/resources/documentation/*
> *windowsServ/2003/all/techref/en-us/W2K3TR_ias_intro.asp*

IAS can also provide other services to your network, including load balancing and protection from malicious computers.

Providing Load Balancing for Multiple RAS Servers

When multiple RAS servers are required, load balancing can ensure the best use of resources and reduce connection failures. One way to do so is to install IAS as a RADIUS server on a domain controller and use IAS as a proxy server. When the IAS proxy servers are configured, the RADIUS servers are added as members of a remote RADIUS server group. The load balancing properties of each server are configured with a priority of 1 and a weight of 50. Since all RADIUS servers have the same load-balancing characteristic, they are each as likely to receive a forwarded connection request from the proxy. If multiple domains are used, configure a different connection request policy for each domain.

Figure 10-32 illustrates the load-balancing scenario where multiple IAS servers are required. In the figure, two IAS RADIUS proxies provide fault tolerance and load balancing for multiple IAS servers.

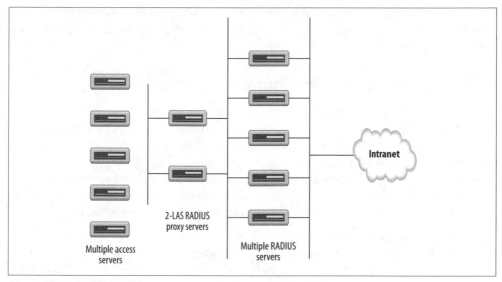

Figure 10-32. IAS RADIUS proxy servers can be used to load balance connection requests across multiple RADIUS servers

Using IAS to Protect the Network from Bad Computers

It's not enough anymore to set protective devices at the perimeters of the network. Traditional firewalls and secured remote access servers cannot protect network resources from all types of attacks. Two additional mechanisms that should be in place are *host-hardening techniques* and a *review of clients before granting network access.*

Host-hardening techniques for LAN computers can prevent (or at least mitigate the results of) a malicious attack that evades or compromises perimeter protections. Comprehensive and exhaustive host-hardening techniques are beyond the scope of this chapter (and this book). However, IAS server does offer unique functions that can assist you in the new security techniques of client network access policy compliance evaluation.

Two techniques are recommended: *network access quarantine control* and *network access protection* (NAP). Network access quarantine control is the process of isolating untrusted computers that request remote access until they can prove that they meet a defined network access policy. NAP is the process of providing a similar security review for clients connecting to the LAN. To use either requires extensive research, scripting, and network provisioning to meet the needs of the organization's security policy. In addition, it should be realized that neither are defenses that can protect the network from a determined attacker. Instead, they are defenses that protect the network from bad computers. *Bad computers* are those that do not use any hardening techniques (such as a personal firewall, antivirus products, and keeping patching up to date). These computers are more likely to be infected or compromised and, thus, more likely to spread infection or serve as a platform for an attack if connected to the LAN.

Network Access Quarantine Control

The normal remote access process validates the credentials of the requesting user. Requiring computer authentication can ensure that only authorized computers (as well as authorized users) obtain remote network access. However, nothing about the process or the connection can prevent an authorized connection from providing a path for attacks, whether malicious or unintentional (as in the spread of malware such as viruses and worms). If the remote client is compromised, remote access does nothing to prevent the client computer from being used to compromise the LAN.

Network Access Quarantine Control can prevent (or mitigate the impact of) compromised or infected computers that are used for remote access by users with valid credentials. It does this by requiring that the remote computer be inspected for adherence to a network access policy. The policy is designed by the organization and implemented in the form of a script that runs on the remote client. The script attempts to determine if the computer meets the security policy requirements. The script might be designed, therefore, to answer the following questions:

- Does the client have a personal firewall enabled?
- Does the client have antivirus protection enabled using a specific (or perhaps one of many acceptable) antivirus product?
- Is the antivirus product engine up to date?
- Are the antivirus product signatures up to date?
- Does the client have the most recent service pack installed?
- Is routing disabled?
- Is a password-protected screensaver with an adequate wait-time active?
- Is the client up to date with patches?

Understanding network access quarantine control

Network access quarantine control works by providing a quarantine network for untested clients and those not in compliance with the network access policy; the client cannot access any other portion of the LAN until the security policy is met. The quarantine can be a network subnet that provides resources the client can use to update security products and find information on required policy restrictions, or it may merely provide information on how clients can meet conditions and prevent clients from connecting until they do.

Two types of restrictions, *quarantine restrictions* and *time restrictions*, are generally used, though there is no requirement to use either. Quarantine restrictions are a minimum of a set of packet filters that restrict traffic that can be sent to and from a quarantined remote access client. Time restrictions add a quarantine session timer that restricts the amount of time the client can be connected. Providing time restrictions can cause problems for legitimate clients attempting to update their systems using the quarantine network resources, but also limits the amount of time attackers might use to attempt to find ways around the quarantine.

The following components are used to implement network access quarantine control:

Quarantine compatible remote access clients
These are computers that support *Connection Manager* (CM) *profiles* created by the Windows Server 2003 Connection Manager Administration Kit (CMAK). This includes Windows Server 2003, Windows XP Professional and Home Edition, Windows 2000, Windows Millennium Edition, and Windows 98 Second Edition.

CM profiles
These include a *post-connect action* that runs the network access policy script, a copy of the network access policy requirements script, and a notifier component to inform the remote access server that a script was run successfully. The Windows Server 2003 Resource Kit provides the *rqc.exe* notifier. (Third-party dialer programs may be used if they can be configured to run a post-connection action to install the script, run it, and notify the remote access server.)

Quarantine compatible remote access server
This is a Windows Server 2003 RRAS server configured to support the listener components such as the Resource Kit *rqs.exe* software and the MS-Quarantine-IPFilter and MS-Quarantine-Session_Timeout RADIUS vendor-specific attributes. These are used to enforce quarantine settings. The listener component listens for notification from the notifier component in the CM profile that announces the remote client meets the security policy.

Quarantaine compatible RADIUS server (optional)
The RRAS server can be configured to use Windows authentication and, therefore, a RADIUS server is optional. If an RRAS server is used, Windows authentication is selected and the vendor-specific attributes must be configured in the RRAS Remote Access policy. When RADIUS is used, the vendor-specific attributes must be configured in an IAS server Remote Access policy.

Quarantine resources
Connecting remote clients must have access to appropriate resources before they are approved for network access. These resources should reside on the quarantine network and are name resolution servers such as DNS, access to the latest CM profile (remote, anonymous access), or access instructions and components required to make the client meet the network policy (such as web servers with anonymous access allowed). Anonymous access is required even though the client uses authorized credentials to access the remote access server, since the client

might not be using the domain credentials required for domain member web resources. The location of these resources can be on a special quarantine network, or on the intranet. If resources are on the intranet, special packet filters must be configured to allow access to them, though this access may pose a security concern because it allows access to the LAN.

Accounts database

This is either AD or Windows NT 4.0 domain user database.

Notifier component

This consists of a *notifier (rqc.exe)* and a *listener (rqs.exe)*, which are two programs available from Microsoft.

Quarantine remote access policy

The remote access policy includes the MS-Quarantine-IPFilter and MS-Quarantine-Session_Timeout RADIUS vendor-specific attributes. The MS-Quarantine-IPFilter attribute contains the input and output packet filters that allow traffic generated by the notifier component. This traffic includes specific notifier messages on port 7250, DHCP messages, and any traffic to access quarantine resources.

> The security policy script can be an executable or a simple batch file, and is the single most difficult part of the implementation. This is because an organization may have many clients and may be using third-party firewall, antivirus, or other security products. Providing code to test a large variety of unique parameters is always time-consuming and may be particularly so when the products are complex.

Figure 10-33 shows these components and provides a numbered flowchart for the process. In this scenario, a RADIUS server is used.

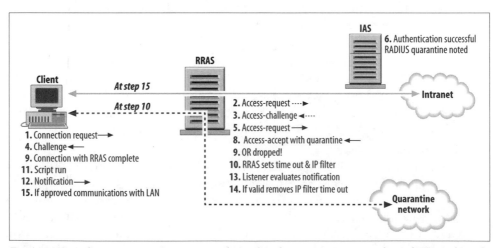

Figure 10-33. Client access to the intranet is limited to the quarantine network until it is evaluated against a network access policy

Following are the steps shown in Figure 10-33:

1. The CM profile on the remote access client is used to connect with the RRAS server.
2. The RRAS server sends a RADIUS access-request message to the IAS server.
3. The IAS Server sends a RADIUS access-challenge to the RRAS server sending the RADIUS access-request message.
4. The remote access client passes its authentication credentials to the RRAS server.
5. The RRAS server sends a RADIUS access-request message to the IAS server.
6. The IAS server validates the authentication credentials. If the credentials are valid, IAS checks remote access policies and finds the quarantine policy is matched.
7. The connection is accepted with quarantine restrictions.
8. A RADIUS access-accept message containing the MS-Quarantine-IPFilter and MS-Quarantine-Session_Timeout attributes (as well as any other policy attributes) is sent to the RRAS server.
9. The connection between the client and the RRAS server is completed, including providing the client with an IP address.
10. The RRAS server configures the IPFilter and Timeout settings on the connection. The remote access client can only operate within these restrictions.
11. The CM profile runs the quarantine script as the postconnect action.
12. Assuming the script verifies that the client complies with policy by running *rqc.exe*, *rqc.exe* sends a notification to the remote access server indicating successful script running.
13. The listener component (*rqs.exe*) receives the notification. It evaluates the script version string in the messages and returns a message that indicates the script version is valid or invalid.
14. If the version is valid, the listener component calls a function that causes removal of the IPFilter and Timeout settings from the connection, and normal connection constraints are configured.
15. Normal access to the intranet for the client is now possible.

Implementing network access quarantine control

Instructions on implementing network access quarantine are beyond the scope of this chapter because:

- Many third-party applications may be part of an organization's remote client setup.
- A custom notifier, listener or other scripts may be used.
- The security policy for network access will vary.

However, the following are generic instructions. First, create quarantine resources. Create a script or program that validates client configuration. Install *rqs.exe* or another listener component on the RRAS servers. Create a quarantine CM profile with the Windows Server 2003 CMAK. The profile must include the *rqc.exe* or other notifier and the script. Distribute the CM profile for installation on remote access client computers. Configure a quarantine Remote Access policy.

To create the Remote Access policy, create a Remote Access policy whose conditions either affect all remote access connection attempts, or create a mixture of Remote Access policies with at least one that includes the remote access attributes IPFilter and Timeout. Although it may seem silly to allow remote access connections where the security policy is not evaluated on the remote access client, it is difficult to establish a script that will provide perfect results on all clients, especially when first implementing the new remote access policy. If at least one Remote Access policy does not require quarantine controls, it will be possible to provide access to clients that fail the script, at least until it can be determined why they failed (even though every attempt was made to make them compliant), and the script adjusted.

While evaluating every client and denying those that don't meet the specs will reduce the chance of infection via a compromised remote client, allowing critical access to network resources may be judged of higher importance Some manual method should be used to qualify remote access clients before they are added to the quarantine-free remote access policy. Access can be granted by adding them to a Windows groups identified by the policy as a condition of policy use.

Creating a remote access policy for quarantine is not difficult because it consists of creating a policy via the normal method. Follow the instructions provided earlier in this chapter, but instead of adding attributes specific to those implementations, add the quarantine attributes listed here. Specifics of the policy should include

- Conditions such as membership in a Windows group (time-of-day and such)
- Access method of VPN
- Addition of any normal constraints
- Addition and configuration of the MS-Quarantine-Session-Timeout attribute and the MS-Quarantine-IPFilter and Timeout attributes.

To configure the MS-Quarantine-IPFilter and MS-Quarantine-Session-Timeout attributes, begin by opening the Remote Access policy. Click the Edit Profile button. On the Advanced Profile page, click the Add button. Select the MS-Quarantine-IPFilter attribute and click Add. In the IP Filter Attribute Information box, click Input Filters. In the Inbound Filters dialog box, click New to add a filter. Select TCP or UDP in the protocol drop-down list. Enter the source or destination port as defined in Table 10-10. Click OK. Repeat for each required port. Click "Permit only the packets listed below as shown." Click OK to save the filter list. On the Advanced Profile page, click the Add button. Select the MS-Quarantine-Session-Timeout attribute and click Add. In the Attribute Information box, enter the quarantine session time in the Attribute value box in seconds. Then click OK. Click OK to save the profile settings. Click OK to save the changes to the Remote Access policy.

Table 10-10. Port requirements for IPFilters

Service	Source or destination	Port number
rqc.exe	Destination	TCP 7250
DHCP	Source	UDP 68
DHCP	Destination	UDP 67
DNS	Destination	UDP 53
WINS	Destination	UDP 137
HTTP	Destination	TCP 80
NetBIOS over TCP/IP for file sharing	Destination	TCP 139
Direct Hosting for file sharing	Destination	TCP 445

To configure the packet filters for the IPFilter attribute, use the standard ports as defined in Table 10-10, or create services running on alternative ports and configure packet filters that allow those ports.

For more information on implementing network access quarantine control including a sample script, obtain the KB document *Microsoft Windows Server 2003 Network Access Quarantine Control*, at *http://www.microsoft.com/windowsserver2003/techinfo/ overview/quarantine.mspx*.

Network Access Protection

When network access quarantine control was first announced, many people asked if it could be used for restricting access to the LAN by inspecting each new connection attempt. They reasoned that laptops returning to the local LAN from use on other untrusted networks are just as likely to spread infection as untested remote access clients. Sadly, this is not now possible. Network access quarantine control is implemented using RRAS and RADIUS, and the IAS server can be used to manage access via wireless networks and authenticating switches. However, network access quarantine control cannot be used for wireless networks or with authenticating switches because it requires the use of a RRAS service and the ability to run a post-connect script on the wireless client or switch client. However, alternative methods for doing security compliance testing are possible. Two methods are:

- Providing a network policy compliance script that is run as part of the computer's startup and domain logon sequence (wireless clients and switch clients do require a domain account)
- Using Network Access Protection (NAP)

NAP is currently scheduled to be released with the next release of Windows (code-named Longhorn).

Summary

IAS is Microsoft's implementation of the RADIUS protocol and provides centralized authentication, authorization, auditing for remote access, and a RADIUS proxy service. This chapter documents both the details of the IETF RADIUS protocol and instructions on how to implement IAS for multiple types of remote access control. Included in the chapter are discussions on and instructions for using centralized Remote Access policies, management of wireless access, the use of RADIUS to manage authenticating switches, RADIUS proxy services, and the use of Network Access Quarantine control to prevent network access by unsecured computers.

Whether you want to block specific communications from occurring, are performing simple file sharing, or are using complex IAS client-server communications (or something in-between), the IP Security (IPSec) protocol can be used. Chapter 11 describes this protocol in detail, documents how it is implemented in Windows Server 2003, and provides instructions on how to configure it.

## CHAPTER 11

Protecting Network Communications with Internet Protocol Security

It is not uncommon for communications across untrusted networks to be protected using VPNs, SSL, and S/MIME to provide confidentiality (keeping information secret), integrity (making sure the information sent is the information received), and authentication (ensuring that communications are coming from who and where they claim to come from). Firewalls act as the demarcation points between public and private networks. Many organizations ignore security in their private networks. As an IT professional, you may have been taught to regard internal communications as "trusted" (that is, free from malicious attack or unauthorized capture and monitoring). However, today, you cannot afford to do so. Self-propagating malware, disgruntled and clueless employees, and attacks that pierce perimeter defenses (or navigate around them), all provide ample motivation for protecting internal communications. In a modern Windows network, you can protect communications using *Internet Protocol Security* (IPSec).

IPSec, an Internet standard protocol, is built into the TCP/IP stack of Windows 2000, Windows XP, and Windows Server 2003. It can be used to do the following:

Prevent an individual computer from receiving external communications
> IPSec can be used to block all communications from specific computers, some types of communication from specific computers, or some types of communications from all computers. For example, using IPSec, you might block all traffic to port 23 from any computer.

Prevent an individual computer from communicating with other computers using unauthorized services or prevent the computer from accessing unauthorized systems
> Likewise, in addition to blocking incoming communications, IPSec can be used to block outgoing communications from a computer to all computers, from a computer to some computers, or to block specific types of communications. For example, you might prevent a computer from any communication with a financial database, or prevent a computer from using port 80 to access web sites.

Protect communications between computers

IPSec can do this in many ways. It can be used to authenticate both sides of a communication and guarantee the integrity of a communication. It can also provide confidentiality via encryption and, provide resistance to replay (the capture and reuse of a communication). Finally, IPSec can provide data authentication (the practice of verifying the identity of the sender during the session, not just during the connection).

To use IPSec to prevent communications (or to protect communications) is not difficult, but it requires some study of the IPSec protocol and the Windows IPSec implementation, practice with the IPSec graphical and command-line tools, an understanding of where IPSec should be applied and exactly which IPSec features should be used.

IPSec Basics

Before you jump right in and start using IPSec, it's important that you learn about the protocol itself, both what it is capable of and how it works. Since it is possible to shut down all communications on a network by using IPSec improperly, taking the time up front to learn the basics can save you many hours of troubleshooting and embarrassment. It can also ensure that you are aware of the many features of IPSec and are able to fully utilize the many advantages of this complex protocol.

Security Advantages of IPSec

IPSec was originally developed for IPv6, and then back-ported to IPv4. IPSec has many advantages, including the following:

- It can be used to block, permit, and secure communications.
- It provides in-depth defense by layering multiple security technologies (such as authentication, confidentiality, and integrity).
- It can be used to tunnel communications across networks or to secure them on the LAN.
- It provides flexibility by offering a variety of security algorithms to choose from.

Blocking, permitting, and securing communications

You implement IPSec by writing *IPSec Policies*, a collection of elements that define how IPSec is used on a specific computer. Information on the components in the policy and how they are configured is located in the section "Configuring a Windows IPSec Policy" later in this chapter. To secure communications using IPSec, a policy must be present on both *IPSec peers* (the two computers involved in the communication) and each policy must be compatible with the other. When a communication attempt that meets the requirements set in the filter (a definition of the protected

IPSec or Personal Firewall?

Since IPSec and a personal firewall (either Microsoft's built in firewall or any other product) can be used to permit or prevent communications between a computer and another device on the network, when should you use one or the other? While the answer is not always clear, here are some guidelines:

- First, and most obvious, a personal firewall is not equipped to provide secure communications between computers. The purpose of a personal firewall is to block or allow communications between the computer it's installed on and any other device. For example, a personal firewall cannot encrypt communications between the computer it is installed on and any other computer. (A full-featured firewall may provide secure remote communications using VPN services.) When you need to secure communications between computers on a LAN, IPSec should be your methodology of choice.

- Second, IPSec was not designed to act as a personal firewall. It can only permit or block communications based on protocol type (selection and port number) or device identification (IP address). These operations can provide rudimentary firewall protection similar to that of *access control lists* (ACLs) on a router. Modern firewalls provide stateful filtering and application layer filtering, neither of which can be done by IPSec. IPSec, however, is a very effective blocking mechanism and may often be your choice when you want to establish simple block/permit scenarios, when a personal firewall is not available, or when it's necessary to create complex protection for communications of a specific type.

- Third, IPSec can be scripted for ease of implementation. In a Windows Server 2003 or Windows 2000 domain, IPSec policies can be configured in Group Policy and rapidly deployed to thousands of computers. This makes it ideal when simple permitting and blocking must be quickly deployed and centrally managed without purchasing third-party products. While configuration of some personal firewalls can also be centrally managed, to provide centralized management in a mixed Windows environment (Windows 2000, Windows XP, and Windows Server 2003) would require additional expense. IPSec also can block ingress (incoming) and egress (outgoing) communications, while some firewalls (including the free Microsoft firewall) only block incoming communications.

- Finally, IPSec can be scripted and applied to systems during startup to protect communications before all services are initialized. Many personal firewalls do not do this. (Boot protection via IPSec is enabled by default when the Windows Firewall installed by Windows XP SP2 is installed.)

type of communication) begins, the connection is negotiated using the information contained in the policy. Figure 11-1 illustrates the location of policies when you want to secure a communication.

IPSec RFCs and Drafts

The IPSec protocol is defined in many Internet Engineering Task Force (IETF) Requests for Comments (RFCs) and drafts. You should examine this information. You can read it at *http://www.ietf.org/rfc.html*. Following are a few of the important RFCs:

- RFC 2409, *The Internet Key Exchange (IKE)*
- RFC 2402, *IP Authentication Header*
- RFC 2406, *IP Encapsulating Security Payload (ESP)*
- RFC 2401, *Security Architecture for the Internet Protocol*
- RFC 3948, *UDP Encapsulation of IPSec ESP Packets*
- RFC 3947, *Negotiation of NAT-Traversal in the IKE*

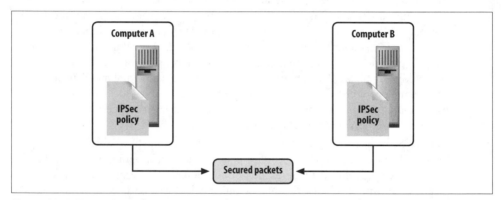

Figure 11-1. Two IPSec policies are required to secure communications between computers

In addition to securing communications between computers, you can block or permit communications to and from a single computer. A properly crafted IPSec policy can mimic a port filtering router. Just as you might use the router's ACLs to block port 21 traffic from computer A while permitting port 80 traffic, or permit port 1434 traffic from a specific host on network B to a specific host on network A, you can block and permit traffic at the host level using IPSec. Figures 11-2 and 11-3 illustrate this point. Figure 11-2 shows a simple scenario in which a router controls communications between network A and network B. Figure 11-3 mimics this setup using an IPSec policy on a single computer.

Defense in depth

To many people, encryption is synonymous with communications protection, and IPSec can be used to encrypt the data being passed between two computers. However, encryption only provides *confidentiality*. Captured, encrypted data is protected

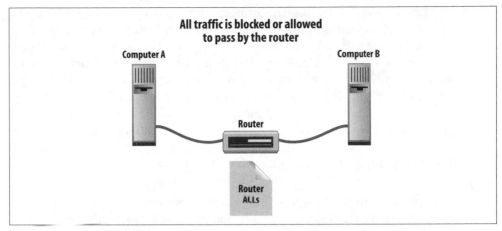

Figure 11-2. Using a port filtering router

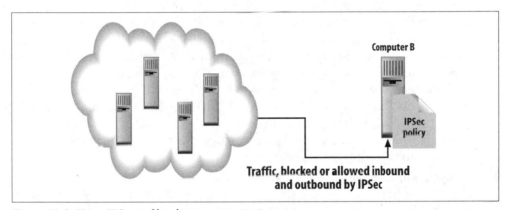

Figure 11-3. Using IPSec to filter host communications

from those who do not have the ability to decrypt it. There are, however, other requirements for protecting communications, and IPSec can also provide them. The following will help you understand how IPSec provides confidentiality and some of these other requirements:

Confidentiality

IPSec uses secret key encryption to protect data. Knowledge of the secret key is only shared between IPSec peers. Since an attacker does not have the key, the attacker cannot decrypt the message. While encryption provides strong protection, its success requires that the secret key is itself kept secret, that the encryption algorithm and its implementation be exemplary so that no weakness in its design or implementation allow an attack to beat it, and that the key size be large enough to prevent brute-force attacks. *Brute-force attacks* are those that attempt to use every possible key combination. If the key size is small, it may be possible to deduce the key in this manner. IPSec provides the implementer with the ability to select from among the most current encryption algorithms. The Windows implementation provides choices between Data Encryption Standard (DES) and Triple DES (3DES). DES is the former United States government encryption standard for data. Triple DES is a more secure version of that standard. In general, you should always choose the more secure encryption algorithm. However, you must also consider the issues of speed and compatibility. Triple DES will increase processing time, albeit slightly on today's systems. Processing time will probably not be a factor in encryption strength selection. However, compatibility may be. Both systems must be able to use the same algorithm and some IPSec-capable devices may not provide the option.

Integrity

Communications might be intercepted and different, encrypted data substituted for the original data payload, or the original encrypted data might be tampered with. IPSec provides integrity by requiring an *Integrity Check Value* (ICV), a cryptographic *hash-based message authentication code* (HMAC), of the data in each packet. A *hash* is a one-way, mathematical summary of some piece of data. A *cryptographic hash* uses a secret key in its calculation. When the IPSec peer receives a communication, it can verify that the data received has not been tampered with. It does so by creating its own ICV and matching it with the one received with the communication. Windows IPSec can be configured to use either HMAC Message Digest algorithm 5 (MD5) or HMAC Secure Hash Algorithm-1 (SHA-1) for integrity. SHA-1 is considered to be a more secure algorithm. However, while processing speed should not be a factor here, you will also want to consider compatibility.

Data origin authentication

If a normal hash algorithm were used, it could verify the integrity of the message, but it could not validate who sent the message. However, because a cryptographic hash is used, and only the IPSec peer shares the knowledge of the secret key, the origin of the data can be authenticated. Attackers cannot calculate a correct ICV because they do not have the key and, therefore, can't get at the data.

Authentication

An attacker might attempt to replace one end of the communications stream by pretending to be one of the IPSec peer computers, or by inserting himself between both hosts to intercept and then pass along data—the classic "man-in-the-middle" attack. To combat this, IPSec requires mutual peer authentication. Windows IPSec policies can use Kerberos, certificates, or a shared secret for authentication.

Key management

Without sound key management, encryption keys may be exposed to attackers. Eventually, an encryption key can be broken, given enough time and computing resources. IPSec's secret keys (which are used to encrypt data) are never transported across the network. Instead, both peers calculate the keys using the

Internet Key Exchange (IKE) algorithm. IPSec uses a combination of a master key and session keys, and the policy can require that the keys change frequently.

Replay resistance

If IPSec traffic is captured by an attacker, can it be used at a later time in a replay attack? Several features of IPSec prevent this. First, each communication is assigned a *Security Association* (SA) and is given a timestamp and sequence number. SAs are a set of information that identify a secured communication and enable its session key lookup. Since many SAs may exist for any specific host, each SA is uniquely identified by a *Security Parameters Index* (SPI). The SA consists of the SPI, the session key, and the security protocol. Once a communication is started, the SA, the SA sequence number, and the timestamp can uniquely identify each packet. IPSec communications can be configured to establish new SAs periodically and to time out an SA if its lifetime is exceeded. If the attacker waits too long to attempt a replay attack, the attack will fail because the SA no longer exists. If the SPI of the SA of the replay packet matches a current SA SPI but its timestamp is out of sequence, the packet will be dropped. If the SPI, timestamp, and sequence number match a combination that has already been received, the packet will be dropped.

IPSec tunnels

IPSec is often used to protect communications between computers on the LAN. It can, however, also be used in tunnel mode to carry data from LAN to LAN across a wide area network. When an IPSec tunnel is used, data is encapsulated within a new header and routed between two endpoints. The tunnel creates a virtual network. One endpoint sits on one network (as an example, perhaps corporate headquarters), and the other sits on another (for example, a branch office network). The data may be routed across the Internet or any other network(s). The IPSec tunnel is similar to the VPN tunnel as described in Chapter 8. The tunnel does not make the data any more secure. IPSec tunnels are not often recommended because there are more effective tunneling protocols available. In fact, Windows VPNs that use IPSec use the layer 2 tunneling protocol instead of the IPSec tunnel.

Flexibility

IPSec is flexible because of the following characteristics:

- You can choose from a selection of authentication, encryption, and integrity algorithms to best suit your environment. For example, you can select algorithms that meet constraints supplied by a requirement to support IPsec between devices supporting different algorithms, or perhaps where communications must be protected and legal constraints do not allow some algorithms.

- You can select key management options such as the frequency of changing keys or the strength of the keys. This means, once again, that you may be able to use

IPSec between more types of devices. Selecting very frequent key change or longer keys may reduce performance. If this is a concern, the option to balance security against performance is available.

- You can choose between transport or tunnel mode. In *tunnel mode*, data is encapsulated and may be transported between two networks over a third. In *transport mode*, no tunnel is required, which is suitable for securing LAN communications.

- You can choose to use encryption with Encapsulating Security Payload (ESP), or to use superior integrity protection with an Authentication Header (AH). ESP and AH are the two IPSec sub-protocols. To select specific security features of IPSec (such as integrity or encryption), you must first select AH and/or ESP. Both protocols offer several of the same security benefits, but differ in how they do so. ESP offers an additional benefit—encryption. You should be aware of these differences in order to select the right protocol for your requirements. More information on how the protocols differ follows.

Differences Between AH and ESP

The major differences between AH and ESP are that ESP provides encryption and AH doesn't, and that AH provides better integrity protection than ESP. The packet structures of AH and ESP provide the key to understanding why AH provides better integrity protection than ESP. The packets contain typical IP fields (such as the payload) and typical IP structures (such as destination and source IP address and port). They also include fields specific to AH or ESP, the SPI, sequence number, and *authentication data*.

The authentication data area is the location of the ICV. Figure 11-4 illustrates AH transport mode. You should note that the ICV calculation is performed over most of the IP header (not identified in the figure), all of the AH header, and the payload. The parts of the IP header that are allowed to change in transport are not included. Instead the ICV calculation assumes they are set to 0.

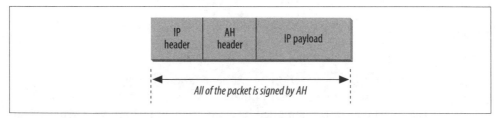

Figure 11-4. Transport mode AH

In tunnel mode, the original IP datagram is encapsulated. In this case, those fields in the outer IP header that may change during transport are not included in the ICV calculation. The original IP packet and the AH header are included. Compare Figure 11-4 with the AH tunnel mode packet illustrated in Figure 11-5.

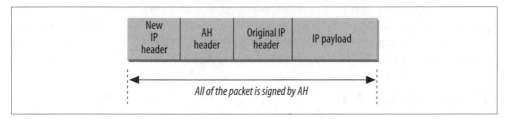

Figure 11-5. Tunnel mode AH

ESP does the ICV calculation differently. In Figure 11-6, you can see the portion of the packet that is encrypted. Compare the fields included in the ICV calculation with those used in AH. ESP transport mode is shown in Figure 11-6. Here the IP header is excluded from the ICV calculation. It is also excluded in ESP tunnel mode, as shown in Figure 11-7.

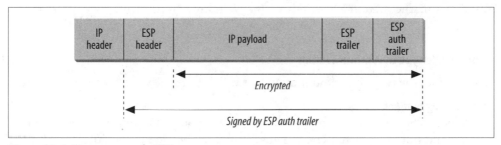

Figure 11-6. Transport mode ESP

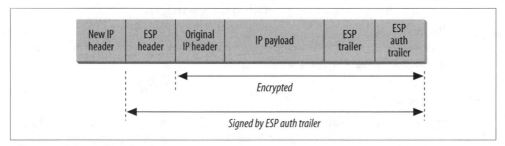

Figure 11-7. Tunnel mode ESP

To summarize, AH provides better authentication because more of the packet is included in the ICV calculation. Remember, the ICV allows the recipient of the packet to determine that the host identified as the source sent the data. If some information in the packet is not included in the ICV, an attacker might modify that data, and the modification might be undetected by the recipient. While the peer authentication required before a connection can be established, and other defenses provide some protection, a sophisticated attacker might be able to overcome this and other protection to complete a successful attack.

In some cases, both AH and ESP are used together to provide superior protection. ESP provides confidentiality through encryption, and AH provides superior authentication. In other cases, where only authentication is required or where encryption cannot be used because of legal restrictions, only AH is used.

Process and Procedure

An IPSec policy performs the following functions:

- Defines the type of communication that will trigger policy enforcement
- Determines whether the policy will block, permit, or secure the communication
- Defines how the communication will be secured (if required)

To implement IPSec, you must write the policy and then apply it (by assigning it) to a specific computer or computers. The specifics of that process are described for Windows in the section "Specifics of the Windows Implementation" later in this chapter. This section explains how IPSec works.

Defining the type of communication

IPSec defines the type of communication that will trigger policy enforcement as follows:

Step 1: triggering
When IPSec policies are assigned, each attempt at communication (both incoming and outgoing) is matched against a filter list defined in the policy. Each filter defines the IP address and protocol information for both source and destination. If a packet matches this information, the policy is triggered.

Step 2: filter action
A filter action defines what will happen when a packet triggers the policy. Filter actions are block, permit, and secure.

Blocking and permitting

A blocking filter action prevents the communication from occurring. If the source address of the packet is the local host, the packet does not leave the computer. If the source address is not that of the local host, the packet will be dropped. A permitting filter action allows the communication to occur.

 Blocking and permitting policies are only implemented on a single computer. A securing policy requires that two computers (the source and the destination) have policies configured.

It is possible, therefore, to block all communications and only permit specific types, or to simply block some specific communication while allowing all others. By default, the IPSec policy permits all communication.

 If a "block all" policy is assigned, be careful to write a "permit" rule that includes IKE and any authentication or other protocols required. "Block all" means to block all communications, unless the specific implementation exempts some protocols from this policy. The Windows implementation provides some defaults in this case. For more information see the section "Disable default exemptions" later in this chapter.

An example of one use for a blocking policy would be to block all TCP port 80 traffic from any computer to the local host. This means that any traffic inbound to TCP port 80 on the local host will be dropped. Another example would be to block the host from sending any Trivial File Transfer Protocol (TFTP) or File Transfer Protocol (FTP) traffic. Blocking incoming TCP port 80 traffic would prevent the computer from serving as a web server that accepts TCP port 80 traffic, even if a web server were installed on the machine. Conversely, blocking all traffic except port 80 traffic can harden a web server against malicious traffic that uses other ports. (You should note that other, desirable traffic such as remote management that uses any port other than port 80 will also be blocked.) Blocking outgoing traffic to FTP and TFTP might prevent a worm from downloading additional malicious code, prevent further infection of network computers, and/or prevent an attack from succeeding at uploading data from the host to the attacker's machine.

Another example that uses both blocking and permitting filter actions might be implemented to allow a specific host connection for a specific task. You might block all inbound NetBIOS traffic to Host A, while permitting inbound NetBIOS traffic from Host B. In this manner, you can permit the use of some remote administrative tools from a specific administrative workstation, while blocking possible malicious use of NetBIOS ports. This type of combination works because the most specific filter for a packet will be the one on which the filter action is based.

Securing or negotiating

To secure communications requires the connection to be negotiated between the two endpoints. When the filter is triggered, both computers must authenticate, and they must be able to agree upon the selections for encryption protocols and strength (or not to use encryption at all), and on integrity protocols. Both computers must generate master and session keys and must be configured with the same key management choices.

An example of a secured communication is AH in transport mode. AH in transport mode is often used to prevent rogue or unauthorized computers from accessing resources on the network. In this example, no encryption is required. Instead, it is important that only computers authorized to use network resources can do so. By requiring computers to authenticate, this goal can be met. For example, all authorized computers might be issued certificates and certificate authentication would be required. No unauthorized computer would have a certificate and, hence, be unable to authenticate. When AH in transport mode is required, both computers must authenticate to each other. If either fails to do so, no communication will occur. If each computer successfully authenticates to the other, and they are able to successfully negotiate the integrity algorithm that should be used, communications will occur. The data passed between the computers will also be authenticated, and its integrity is ensured, but encryption does not take place.

When encryption is required, the ESP protocol is used and many other IPSec factors must be negotiated. In all negotiation processes, the IPSec connection and establishment process proceeds in two phases:

- Phase I: IDE (or Main) mode
- Phase II: Quick mode

Phase I: IKE Mode, or Main Mode. Phase I is also known by the names IKE mode or main mode in various RFCs, articles, and help files. You will find that these names are used interchangeably. When you see them, just remember that they are talking about the same process. Their use will often depend on the author or the company producing the documentation. Microsoft uses all three. The names do help to identify the process. Phase I refers to the fact that the process occurs first. Internet Key Exchange (IKE) is used during the negotiation of the connection (hence its use as a name). Using the term "main mode" just expresses the fact that this process must occur successfully or the others will not.

Phase I includes peer authentication, the negotiation of which security attributes (security algorithms and key management choices) to be used, and the creation of the master key. The master key is created using a *Diffie-Hellman exchange* and is generated on each peer. A Diffie-Hellman exchange is a process that permits the transfer of some private data between computers that each will use in a complex mathematical equation to create the same key. In IPSec, this key is called the master key and is used to create the session keys. Session keys are used to encrypt the data. Figure 11-8 illustrates the process described in the following steps:

1. The offer. ComputerA sends a proposal that includes the acceptable security attributes (the ones configured in its policy). If ComputerA is configured to accept a variety of algorithms, all are included. This information is recorded in the key exchange security methods dialog box in the IP Security Policy.

2. The response. ComputerB responds by sending a proposal that includes the set of security attributes offered by ComputerA that are acceptable to ComputerB.

3. Diffie-Hellman number generation. The Diffie-Hellman algorithm consists of the generation of numbers, an exchange between peers, and an algorithm that calculates a key. ComputerA and ComputerB both generate their own set of numbers.

4. Authentication. The exact authentication process will vary depending on the type of authentication selected for the policy.

5. Diffie-Hellman Exchange. During the Diffie-Hellman Exchange, each computer will share some of its information with the other, while keeping some information private. ComputerA sends ComputerB its information while keeping the rest private. ComputerB sends ComputerA some of its information while keeping some private.

6. Diffie-Hellman calculation of the master key. Both computers use their own information and the information provided by their peer to calculate the master key. Even though all of the information is not the same (because of the nature of the data, and the algorithm used), the results will be the same and no other computer can generate the same key. Even if the Diffie-Hellman Exchange data were captured, the attacker would not be able to generate the key because the attacker would only have the information provided by each computer to the other, but would not have private information from either computer.

7. Creation of the IKE SA. The IKE SA identifies the secured communication channel created between the two IPSec Peers during Main Mode.

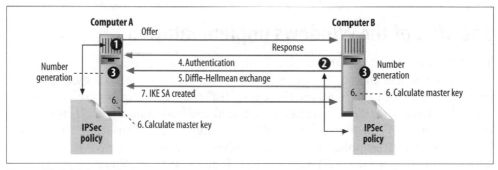

Figure 11-8. Main Mode

Phase II, or Quick Mode . Phase II (also known as Quick Mode) negotiation occurs after Phase I is complete, or when an existing SA expires. Quick Mode determines the type of traffic that will be secured and how it will be secured. The negotiation uses the IKE SA and creates two SAs (one inbound and one outbound) for each protocol secured. Figure 11-9 illustrates the process described in the following steps:

1. Begin negotiation of traffic to be secured. ComputerA sends information (IP addresses, ports, Protocol IDs, and so forth) about traffic that is to be secured and a list of the security algorithms to be used.

2. Completion of negotiation for a type of traffic to be secured. ComputerB, if its policy matches, returns the first set of information from ComputerA's list.

3. Completion of two SAs. These SAs are used for communications. Each one permits traffic in one direction. Two SAs are created for each secured traffic type.

4. New SA negotiation. If additional traffic must be secured, a new SA negotiation begins. (Each protocol secured gets its own inbound and outbound SA.)

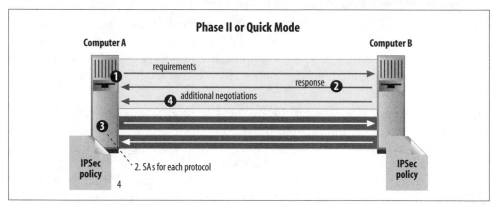

Figure 11-9. Quick Mode

As mentioned earlier, to implement IPSec, you must write the policy and then apply it (by assigning it) to a specific computer or computers. Let's take a look at the specifics of that process.

Specifics of the Windows Implementation

The Windows IPSec implementation is supported by an IPSec Policy Agent service (the IPSec Service) and an IPSec Driver. The IPSec Service is enabled by default and provides the IPSec driver with the IPSec filter list. During normal network operation, the IPSec driver uses the list to filter all inbound and outbound traffic. If an inbound or outbound packet matches the list, the driver applies the filter action (block, permit, or secure). IPSec policies can be written and assigned using a MMC snap-in or with scripts. If Windows XP Professional, Windows 2000, or Windows Server 2003 computers are joined in a Windows 2000 or Windows Server 2003 domain, IPSec policies can be implemented as part of Group Policy. When Group Policy is used, different policies can be quickly implemented and updated per Organizational Unit (OU).

The IPSec Policy Agent Service

The IPSec Policy Agent is implemented as a service. The service is responsible for obtaining the policy from the registry or from Group Policy, polling for changes in policy and passing the policy on to the IPSec Driver. The Policy Agent retrieves the policy from the registry (if the computer is a workgroup member), and from Group Policy (if the computer is a member of a domain and IPSec has been implemented via Group Policy for that member computer). The Group Policy-based IPSec policy (one enabled on the host computer) is cached in its registry and can be used if the computer is not able to connect to a domain controller (DC) or otherwise has problems receiving or implementing Group Policy. When the computer is next able to connect to a DC, any updated IPSec policy will be downloaded.

Retrieval occurs at startup, during the time specified in the policy and at the normal Group Policy polling. An administrator can manually update Group Policy by using the gpupdate command. During computer boot and operating system startup, there will be a short period of time after which the networking driver has started, but the IPSec Policy Agent service has not. Therefore, the policy is not working to protect communications. While the time is small, automated attacks (if they occur during this time) might compromise the system. It is possible, with Windows Server 2003 IPSec to create a persistent policy and other protections during this timeframe. The section "Extending IPSec Operations" later in this chapter provides information on how to implement this protection.

The IPSec Driver

If the traffic matches a filter in the IPSec policy, the action that the IPSec Driver takes depends on the filter action recorded in the policy for the filter.

If the filter action is "negotiate security," the IPSec main mode negotiation and quick mode negotiation are attempted. If they succeed, SAs are created. (If they fail, packets are discarded.) The driver stores the current quick mode SAs in a local database.

If an inbound packet is secured by IPSec, the Driver uses the SPI to match packets to the correct SA in its database. This matching allows the Driver to identify the encryption key required for encryption or decryption.

If an unsecured inbound packet is received, the Driver attempts to match it to its filter list. If a match is not made, the packet is delivered. If a match is made and the block or permit filter action is applied, the packet is blocked or permitted accordingly. If a match is made and the filter action is secure, the unsecured packet will be dropped.

New in Windows Server 2003

IPSec was fully implemented in Microsoft Windows 2000. While it was praised for its ease of use, administrators had three major issues with the first version:

- The existence of default exemptions (protocols that were not blocked by default when a "block all" policy was enabled)
- The inability to use IPSec across a NAT server
- The need for more comprehensive scripting and troubleshooting facilities

To answer these complaints and further enhance IPSec for Windows Server 2003, several changes were made, including the following:

Resultant Set of Policy (RSOP) support
RSOP can be used to help troubleshot Group Policy issues.

2048-bit Diffie-Hellman group 3
The largesize of the numbers used in the Diffie-Hellman algorithm means increased protection.

NAT traversal support
The ability to use IPSec across a NAT server.

Command-line support using netsh
Ipsecpol and ipseccmd tools are replaced by netsh ipsec commands.

Default exemptions are reduced
Only Internet Security Association and Key Management Protocol (ISAKMP) communications (the messages used in IPSec policy negotiation) are exempted from IPSec.

Persistent IPSec policies
These can be used to protect systems during startup.

Stateful filtering during boot
This provides additional protection during boot.

IPSec Security Monitor
This is a comprehensive monitoring and troubleshooting tool for IPSec.

Disable default exemptions

A "block-all" policy, by definition, blocks all traffic, or does it? Windows 2000 exempted the following communications—even if a block-all policy was configured:

- Kerberos (might be used for authentication)
- ISAKMP (used in IPSec negotiations)
- Broadcast traffic
- Multicast traffic
- RSVP Quality of Service traffic

Windows Server 2003 exempts only IKE (ISAKMP). While it might be argued that a "block all" policy should also block IKE, a negotiated policy requires IKE. Hence, if IKE were blocked, negotiations to determine whether communications should occur could not take place. Rather than create a "catch-22," Windows Server 2003 IPSec exempts IKE.

To modify the Windows 2000 exemptions, you must modify the registry. Begin this procedure by going to Start → Run, and enter **regedit** (to start the *regedit.exe* program). Navigate to the following registry key:

```
HKEY_LOCAL_MACHINE\SYSTEM\CurrentControlSet\Services\IPSec
```

Add a new value by right-clicking IPSec and selecting New → "DWORD value." Name the entry NoDefaultExempt. Assign the new value one of the following:

0   Kerberos, multicast, broadcast, RSVP, and ISAKMP traffic are exempt (the default for Windows 2000 and Windows XP).

1   Multicast, broadcast, and ISAKMP traffic are exempt.

2   Kerberos, ISAKMP, and RSVP traffic are exempt.

3   ISAKMP is exempt (the default for Windows Server 2003).

Close the registry editor.

Exemptions can be modified in Windows Server 2003 using the netsh command. To change the exemption on Windows Server 2003 to be like Windows 2000, open a command prompt and run the following command:

```
netsh ipsec dynamic set config ipsecexempt value=0
```

IPSec NAT traversal

IPSec hashes and signatures may include source IP address and port information. This information may also be encrypted. If this information is modified or must be modified during transport, then IPSec security mechanisms will reject the packets as being tampered with, or won't be able to process the packets. IPSec cannot differentiate between a malicious modification and one that might occur when Network Address Translation (NAT) is used. This means that, as originally implemented in Windows 2000, IPSec could not be used to protect communications that occur across a NAT box.

Windows Server 2003 supports IPSec NAT traversal (NAT-T), as defined in two RFC documents (RFC 3948, Proposed Standard, *UDP Encapsulation of IPSec Packets, version 2*; and RFC 3947, Proposed Standard, *Negotiation of NAT-Traversal in the IKE, version 2*). This means that a NAT-T compliant sender notifies of its NAT-T capability during main mode and sends a hash of the source and destination packets address and port number so that the receiving peer can tell if NAT changed the IP address or port. If the receiving peer discovers that the address or port has been changed, it assumes that NAT is being used and defines a new IKE header that uses UDP port 4500. Thus, the IPSec communications are encapsulated by UDP, IKE negotiations can complete, and IPSec traffic can traverse the NAT box.

Default IPSec Policies

Windows IPSec has three default policies that are available for you to examine and test. However, you should not use these polices, but rather create your own. Feel free to examine them to see how they are configured, but you should test them before attempting to implement a policy in your production environment. Figure 11-10 displays the IPSec policy node of Group Policy and the three default policies.

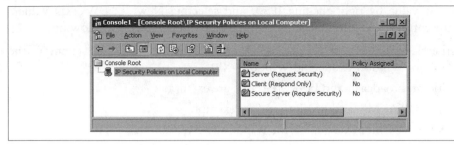

Figure 11-10. Windows IPSec default policies

The default policies include:

Client
> The recipient of an IPSec ISAKMP negotiation request will respond using its configured specifications.

Server (Request)
> The server will initiate an IPSec ISAKMP negotiation request. However, if the recipient is not configured to use IPSec, the server will drop back to unsecured communications.

Server (Security Required)
> The server initiates an IPSec ISAKMP negotiation request. However, if the recipient is not configured to use IPSec, the connection will be dropped.

You should now have a good understanding of how the IPSec protocol works and what new features have been introduced in Windows Server 2003. This is a good time to start examining how to configure Windows IPSec policy.

Configuring a Windows IPSec Policy

Configuring a Windows IPSec policy is not difficult—if you understand how IPSec works and take the time to learn where to enter the information the Policy Agent needs. The preceding sections provide information on how the protocol works. In this section, you'll learn how to use the Windows interface, write a policy, assign it, test it, and monitor it. *Do not implement your first policy on production computers.* Your first test policies should be deployed in a test environment. Start by using a local policy.

Following is an overview of the steps to configure IPSec:

1. Review configuration requirements such as the protocols to be blocked permitted or secured, and other parameters before beginning.

2. Run the IPSec Policy Wizard or create a script using netsh.

3. Assign the policy.

4. Monitor and/or test the policy.

---

5. If required, add additional filters and rules to the policy to complete its requirements. Test after the addition of each new item until the policy is working the way you want it.

6. If secure communications are part of the policy requirements, monitor communications during the test to ensure that communications are secured in the manner required.

7. If the policy will be used on multiple computers in a domain, use the IPSec Policy Wizard within a Group Policy Object (GPO) linked to a test OU to create a policy and assign it. Move at least two test computers to the test OU.

8. Monitor and test the policy.

9. When the policy is working the way it should, then implement it in the production network.

After successfully completing these steps, you should feel comfortable about having learned how to create and implement IPSec policies. Later in this chapter, by using this knowledge and your understanding of IPSec, you will be able to determine how you might use IPSec to protect communications on your network.

 It is possible to configure an IPSec policy in a GPO and destroy communications between all of the computers affected by the GPO. If the GPO is linked to the domain controller's OU, it is entirely possible to impact domain controller communications to such an extent that you cannot correct the situation. So, be very careful with this.

Reviewing Configuration Requirements

When developing a policy using the wizard or by creating a script, you will need to enter information to configure a number of elements. Table 11-1 lists these policy elements, along with a description. Several of the elements are optional (that is, they may not be necessary for blocking and permitting policies). The type of policy within which the element must be configured is included in the "Required" column.

Table 11-1. IPSec policy elements

Element	Description	Required for
Rule	Rules are composed of a filter list that may have one or more filters. Each policy includes one or more rules.	Securing, blocking, permitting
Filter List	A collection of filters.	Securing, blocking, permitting
Filter Action	Determines what action is taken when an inbound or outbound packet matches a filter.	Securing, blocking, permitting
Authentication type	Selects peer authentication mode. Choices are Kerberos, shared secret, or certificates.	Securing
Integrity algorithm	Selects MD5 or SHA1	Securing
Encryption algorithms	Selects DES or 3DES	Securing

Table 11-1. IPSec policy elements (continued)

Element	Description	Required for
Diffie-Hellman Group	The Diffie-Hellman group is used to determine the length of the base prime numbers used in key material. Group 1 uses 768 bits, group 2 uses 1,024 bits, and group 3 uses 2,048 bits. Group 3 is only available between Windows Server 2003 peers.	Securing
Perfect Forward Security (PFS)	Ensures that keying material and keys used to protect communications are not used to generate new keys. Master Key PFS requires reauthentication as well. Session PFS does not require reauthentication, but does require a new Diffie-Hellman (DH) exchange to generate new keying material.	Securing
Key lifetime	Determines when a new key is generated. Set key lifetime to force key regeneration after a specified interval. The SA will also be renegotiated.	Securing
Session key refresh limit	Session keys are generated using the Diffie-Hellman shared secret. A session key refresh limit can be imposed (that is, you can decide how many sessions can use the same session key). Setting this limit to 1 is the same as selecting Master key PFS.	Securing
Tunnel or not	Determines if tunnel or transport mode is used. If tunnel mode is used, a tunnel endpoint must be designated.	Securing
Network application	Determines which type of network communication is affected by the policy. Choices are LAN, remote, or both.	Securing

This table demonstrates that blocking and permitting policies require few settings and, therefore, might be a good place to start your tests. You can use the instructions in the following section to create and test a blocking policy and then a permitting policy before you attempt a securing policy.

In the example, instructions for following these steps are given assuming the use of a policy. In another section, a script writing example will be provided.

Using the IPSec Policy Wizard to Create a Policy

Before you can create a policy, you must define what you want it to do. In this example, the end result is that a single computer can be used to remotely administer a computer using Terminal Services. All other computers will be denied access via Terminal Services. We'll step you through a simple blocking policy (block all access to the computer via Terminal Services). We'll show you how to assign and test that policy, and then we'll show you how to add a rule that allows one specific computer to access the computer using Terminal Services.

The simplest way to learn to use IPSec to protect communications is to create a simple blocking policy. You might, for example, create a policy that blocks port 3389 from any IP address and, therefore, blocks remote access using Terminal Services (including the Remote Desktop connectivity).

Start the IPSec Monitor and observe its recordings. When you have tested the policy and found it to be working, add a rule that permits the use of remote access using Terminal Services from one specific IP address. When you test the policy again, you should find it only possible to use Terminal Services to get into the machine from that specific IP address. Finally, change the filter action on the permit rule to require security. You must create a similar policy on the computer whose IP address is indicated in the policy. Be sure to inspect the IP Security Monitor to prove that encryption is taking place. Create these policies locally at each computer, not locally through Group Policy.

For these exercises the computer names ComputerA and ComputerB will be used.

Creating an MMC console

Domain-based IPSec policies can be created in Group Policy, but you should always start tests using a local policy. The first step is to load the IP Security Policy Management snap-in in a Microsoft Management Console (MMC).

Open an MMC on ComputerA by clicking Start → Run, and then entering **mmc**. Click the OK button. Select the File menu and select Add/Remove Snap-in. Then click Add. Under the Add Standalone Snap-ins option, select IP Security Policy Management, and then click Add. From the Select Computer or Domain dialog, accept the default "Local computer" selection and click Finish, then Close, and then click OK, as shown in Figure 11-11.

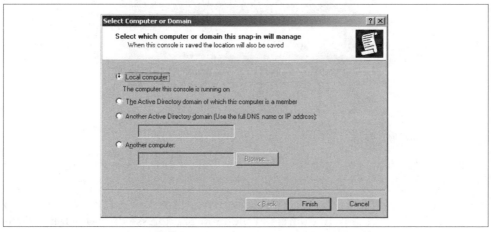

Figure 11-11. Use the Local Computer IPSec policy

Select the File menu, click Save As, and enter the name **IPSecurityPolicy1**. Click Save. Leave the console open for the next exercise.

Create a blocking rule

The simplest type of policy is a blocking rule, which blocks some unwanted communication. Configuration is straightforward.

On ComputerA, in the IPSecurityPolicy1 console created earlier, right-click on the IP Security Policies on the Local Computer container and select Create an IP Security Policy. Click Next on the wizard welcome page. Name the policy Block TS, enter a brief description, and then click Next. Click to deselect the default response rule.

 The default response rule allows negotiation of unencrypted communication and should not be used in most cases in which IPSec negotiation is required. If it is left checked, and your rules are not properly implemented, you may inadvertently allow unsecured communications. The policy you are configuring first is a blocking policy, and unchecking the default policy will have no affect. However, you will be building on the policy and it's better to take this step now so it will not be forgotten later.

Click Next, and then click Finish. In the Block TS Properties Rules page shown in Figure 11-12, uncheck the Use Add Wizard box and click Add.

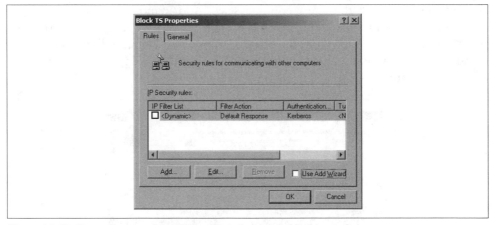

Figure 11-12. Forgo the use of the Wizard here for simple blocking policies

Select the IP Filter List tab on the New Rule Properties page, as shown in Figure 11-13. Click Add to create the filter list.

Name the filter list Block TS Filter. Uncheck the Use Add Wizard box and click Add to add a filter. Select Any IP Address in the "Source address" drop-down list. (This will apply the filter to traffic from any host.) Select My IP Address in the "Destination address" drop-down list, as shown in Figure 11-14, and then click the Protocol tab.

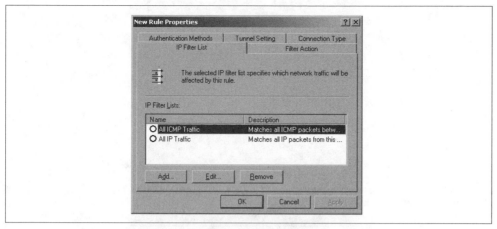

Figure 11-13. You'll need to add a filter list to build the rule

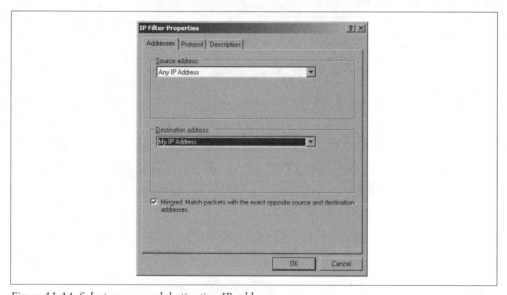

Figure 11-14. Select source and destination IP address

Select TCP in the Select a Protocol Type box. In the "Set the IP protocol port" area shown in Figure 11-15, select To This Port and enter **3389**. Click OK.

Click OK to close the IP Filter Properties page. In the IP Filter Lists box, select the Block TS Filter and then click the Filter Action tab. Click to deselect the Use Add Wizard button and click Add to add a Filter Action. On the Security Methods page shown in Figure 11-16, click Block.

Select the General tab and enter Block TS Action as the Filter Action Name, and then click OK. On the Filter Action page, click the Block TS Action button, and then click Close. On the Block TS Properties page, click OK.

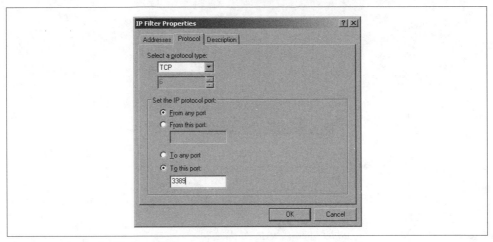

Figure 11-15. Set the IP protocol port

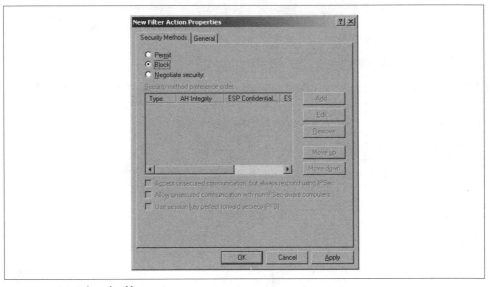

Figure 11-16. Select the filter action

Assigning the Policy

Before assigning the policy, you must test your ability to connect remotely using Ter-minal Services. If you are not able to connect, then you should test communications before you assign the policy; otherwise, you will not know if you have written a suc-cessful policy or if communications are failing for other reasons.

To test Terminal Services, follow these steps:

1. On ComputerA, open the Start → Control Panel → Systems applet and select the Remote page.

2. Ensure that the Allow Users To Log On checkbox is selected and click OK.

3. On ComputerB, select Start → All Programs → Accessories → Communication, Remote Desktop Connection.

4. Enter the IP address of ComputerA and click Options.

5. Enter your password and the domain name.

6. Enter your user ID if it is different on ComputerB.

7. Click the Experience page and select the connection speed: "LAN (10 Mbps or higher)."

8. Click Connect.

9. The TS Remote Desktop window will appear and display the desktop of ComputerA. If it does not, troubleshoot this process and resolve it before you proceed.

10. Log off and close the connection by clicking Start → Shutdown, and then choosing Log Off, and clicking OK.

11. From the Remote Desktop Connections window General page, click the Save As button and save the file with a name of ComputerA.

12. Now, let's assign the policy. On ComputerA, in the IPSecurityPolicy1 console, right-click the Block TS policy and click Assign.

Testing the Policy

On ComputerB, open the Remote Desktop Connection. If the IP address of ComputerA is not in the Computer window, use the drop-down arrow to select it, or use the Options button and then the Open button to open the ComputerA connection information saved earlier. Click the Connect button. The connection will fail. Click the OK button to close the warning window.

Testing a blocking policy is simple. If your policy is more complex (for example, if it includes encryption requirements or other secure communications), setting up the testing will also be more complex. In the next section, we'll continue with the creation of our policy and then provide information on how to monitor and test this more complex setup.

Creating Additional Rules

The ultimate goal of this policy is to allow one particular computer and only that computer to connect using Terminal Services. To do so you must add another rule.

Create a permit rule

If all traffic to the Terminal Services port is blocked, you can specify a computer or computers from which to permit TS traffic. Because the IPSec Policy Agent service will attempt to match packets against the more specific rules first, packets from the allowed computers will be accepted because it matches the "permit" rule, while packets from all other computers won't match that rule, but will match the generic "block" rule.

To create a permit rule, follow these steps:

1. Open the IPSecuirtyPolicy1 console created earlier on ComputerA.
2. Right-click the Block TS policy and select Un-assign. Double-click the policy to open it.
3. Click Add on the Block TS policy properties page to add a rule. (You must add a new rule because an IPSec rule can only have one filter action.)
4. On the IP Filter List page, click Add to add a filter list.
5. Name the filter list **Permit ComputerB** and provide the description **Permits ComputerB to TS to ComputerA**.
6. Click Add to add a filter. In the "Source address" drop-down list, select "A specific IP Address."
7. Enter the IP address of ComputerB. In the "Destination address" drop-down list.
8. Select My IP Address, as shown in Figure 11-17.

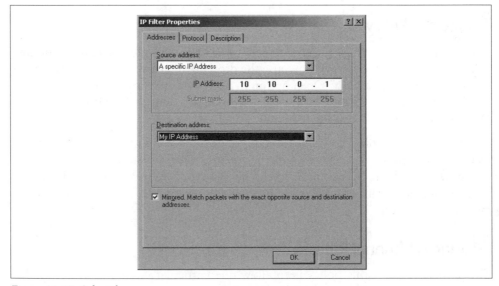

Figure 11-17. Select the source

9. Select the Protocol tab. In the Select a protocol type box, select TCP.

10. In "Set the IP protocol port," select To This Port and enter **3389**, then click OK. Click OK to close the IP Filter list page.

11. In the "IP Filter lists" box, select Permit ComputerB, and then click the Filter Action tab.

12. In the Filter Actions: list, select Permit then click Close.

13. On the Rules page, two rules should be selected, as shown in Figure 11-18. Click OK.

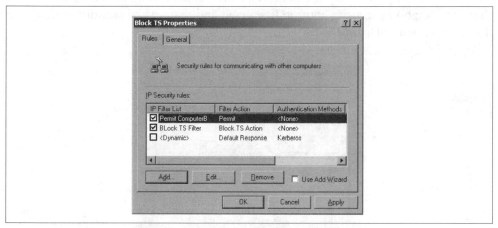

Figure 11-18. The Rules page will show two rules are selected

Now let's test the policy. In the IPSecurityPolicy1 console created earlier on ComputerA, right-click the Block TS policy and select Assign. On ComputerB, open the Remote Desktop Connection. If the IP address of ComputerA is not in the Computer window, use the drop-down arrow to select it, or use the Options button and then the Open button to open the ComputerA connection information saved earlier. Click the Connect button. You should get the ComputerA desktop. This proves that the exception, ComputerB, is able to use Terminal Services to ComputerA.

To test that all other computers are blocked, log off the current connection. Change the IP address of ComputerB. On ComputerB, open the Remote Desktop Connection. If the IP address of ComputerA is not in the Computer window, use the drop-down arrow to select it, or use the Options button and then the Open button to open the ComputerA connection information saved earlier. Click the Connect button. The connection should fail.

Change the IP address of ComputerB back to its original address and test the connection again. When you are able to connect using the Remote Desktop Connection, log off, and close the connection.

Changing the permit rule to secure

Now that you've established a channel that only the approved computer, ComputerB, can use, practice securing the content of the communication and adding the additional security that authentication will provide. The easiest way to do this is to change the Permit rule to Secure.

To change the rule, open the IPSecurityPolicy1 console created earlier on ComputerA. Right-click the Block TS policy and select Un-assign. Double-click the policy to open it. On the Rules page, select the Permit ComputerB rule and click Edit. Select the Filter Action page. Select the Require Security action. Click the Edit button. Note that the "Negotiate security" button is selected and that several security methods are listed, as shown in Figure 11-19.

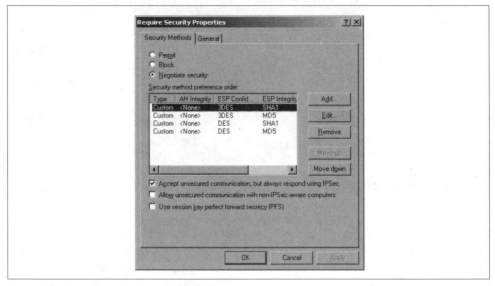

Figure 11-19. Review the Security Methods page

Click OK to close. Select the Authentication Methods page. Note that Kerberos is selected as the default security method. If both of these computers are in a domain, this is a good choice. If they are not, then for your tests you must change the method or the connection will fail.

Click the Add button. In the New Authentication Method Properties page shown in Figure 11-20, click the "Use this string [preshared key]" button and enter the word **secret** in the text box. Using a preshared key is OK in a test; in a production environment, you should use Kerberos or certificates.

Click OK. Select the Kerberos method and click Remove. Click the Tunnel Setting page and ensure that the "This rule does not specify an IPSec tunnel" button is selected. Click the Connection Type page and ensure the "All network connections"

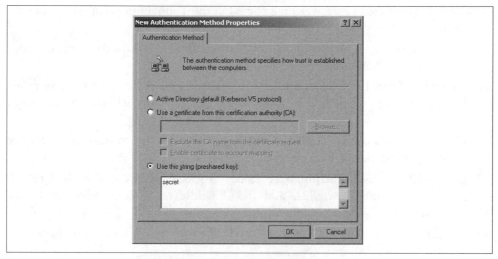

Figure 11-20. Use a preshared key for the tests

button is selected. Click Close, and then click OK. On the IPSecurityPolicy1 console, select the Block TS policy and select Assign.

Creating an IPSec policy on ComputerB

Before you can test the policy, you must create a negotiate security policy for ComputerB. Remember, blocking and permitting policies do not require IPSec peers, but securing policies do. The connection security is negotiated between two computers.

Here are the steps to follow:

1. Open an MMC on ComputerB by clicking Start → Run, and enter **mmc**. Click the OK button.

2. Select the File menu, and select Add/Remove Snap-in, and then click Add.

3. On the Add Standalone Snap-ins page, select IP Security Policy Management, then and click Add. From the Select Computer or Domain dialog, accept the default "Local computer" selection, and click Finish. Then click Close, and click OK.

4. On ComputerA, in the IPSecurityPolicy1 console created earlier, right-click on the IP Security Policies on Local Computer container and select Create an IP Security Policy.

5. Click Next on the wizard welcome page. Name the policy Secure TS, enter a brief description, and then click Next. Click to deselect the default response rule.

6. Click Next, then click Finish.

7. In the Secure TS Properties Rules page, click Add. This time you will use the wizard to add a rule.

8. Click Next at the wizard welcome page. On the Tunnel Endpoint page, note the default is not to specify a tunnel and click Next.

9. On the Network Type page, note that the default is to use the "All network connections" selection and click Next.

10. On the IP Filter List page, click Add to create the filter list. Name the filter list Secure TS Filter. Click Add to add a filter. This time you will use the wizard to add a filter.

11. Click Next. On the IP Traffic Source page, leave My IP Address in the Source drop-down list, then and click Next.

12. On the IP Traffic Destination page, select "A specific IP address" in the Destination address drop-down list, add the IP address for ComputerA, and then click Next.

13. On the "IP Protocol type" page, select TCP in the Select a Protocol Type box, and then click Next.

14. On the "IP Protocol port" page, select To This Port and enter **3389**, then click Next. Click Finish. Click OK to close the IP Filter List page.

15. In the "IP Filter lists" box, select Secure TS Filter and then click Next.

16. On the Filter Actions page, select Filter Action Require Security and then click Next. Click to deselect the Use Add Wizard button and click Add to add a Filter Action.

17. On the Authentication Method page, select "Use this string to protect the key exchange [preshared key]" and type the word **secret** in the text box. Click Next followed by Finish. Click OK twice.

18. In the IP Security Policies1 console, right-click on the Secure TS policy and select Assign.

Setting Up the IPSec Monitor and Testing the Policy

You could test the policy as you have previously, but you should use the IP Security Monitor tool to monitor IPSec activity. This tool can help you understand your policies, troubleshoot policy problems, and verify that encryption is taking place. To use the tool, create a new MMC on ComputerA. In this example, you'll monitor both computers from one console. However, you can create a console on each computer if you wish.

Open an MMC console on ComputerA and add the IPSec Monitor snap-in. ComputerA will be monitored automatically. Right-click on The IP Security Monitor and select "Add computer." Enter the IP address for ComputerB and click OK. Expand both computers and select the Active Policy node for one of the computers, as shown in Figure 11-21. The Active Policy node provides information on the active policy.

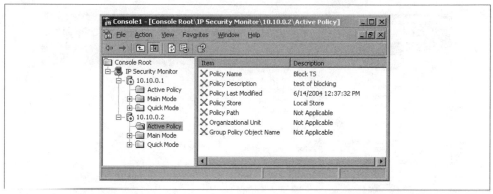

Figure 11-21. Display the active policy

On ComputerB, repeat the process so that you can monitor both computers from either computer. On ComputerA, in the IPSecurityPolicy1 console, right-click the Block TS policy and click Assign. On ComputerB, open the Remote Desktop Connection. If the IP address of ComputerA is not in the Computer window, use the drop-down arrow to select it, or use the Options button and then the Open button to open the ComputerA connection information saved earlier. Click the Connect button. The connection should succeed.

On ComputerA (or by opening the IP Security Monitor console on ComputerB's remote desktop of ComputerA), select the Quick Mode → Statistics node, as shown in Figure 11-22. You should see some numbers in the Confidential Bytes Sent and Authenticated Bytes Sent categories. Not shown in the figure, but available if Main Mode statistics are displayed is the Soft Associations category. You should not see any numbers except 0 in the Soft Associations category. Soft Associations are unsecured bytes, and this policy requires encryption.

Click the Security Associations node which includes a section for each SA. Double-click on a specific SA to display the information shown in Figure 11-23. This will provide you with information on which protocols are being used to secure the communication.

Spend some more time viewing the parts of the IP Security Monitor. Familiarity with this tool when things are normal and correct will help you whenever you need to troubleshoot your IPSec policies.

If the connection does not succeed, you may be able to use the IP Security Monitor feedback to troubleshoot the problem. For example, if there is no information in the Quick Mode → Statistics node, then the failure occurred during Main Mode. If the Main Mode → Statistics node shows authentication failures, check to ensure that the same authentication method is chosen. Check the spelling of the shared secret. If negotiation failures occur, then check the protocols that are being used, the ports that

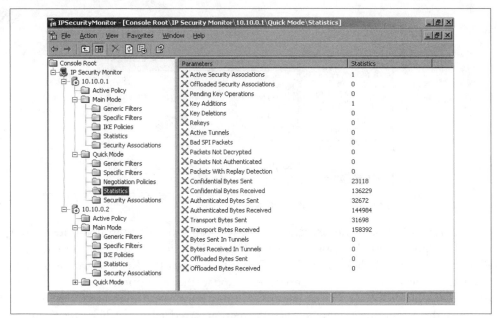

Figure 11-22. The presence of Confidential Bytes indicates that encryption is taking place

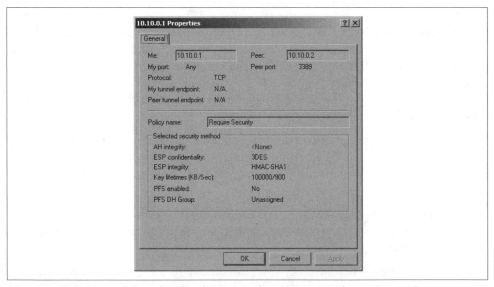

Figure 11-23. View confidential and authentication bytes sent to verify security

should trigger the response and so forth. More information on the IPSec Monitor is included in the section "Monitoring and Troubleshooting IPSec" later in this chapter.

Once you have learned how to create and assign policies using the wizard, you should also explore how to create a policy using a script. The netsh command is used to do so. Not only is this a useful technique, but knowing how to use netsh is a good idea. You can only create persistent policies by using netsh, and netsh has some useful monitoring commands as well. The following section describes how to write a policy to do the same task described earlier by using the wizard.

Writing Policies Using netsh

You can use netsh at the command line to create IPSec policies for the local computer. If you use the netsh commands in a script, you can run it on as many computers as you wish. You will, however, have to adjust any computer-specific information in the script. The netsh command is a complex command that offers much more functionality than that used to create and assign IPSec policies.

 A complete list of netsh IPSec commands is provided in the Windows Server 2003 Help and Support Center. You can locate them in the *%system root%\Help\ntcmds.chm::/netsh_ipsec.htm* file.

IPSec netsh commands can be executed as either *static* or *dynamic*. Static mode is used to create policies for assignment later. Nothing you do actually changes the use or non-use of IPSec on the computer unless you include the assign command in the script, or execute it later at the command line. Otherwise, the IPSec Policy Agent is not aware of them. On the other hand, dynamic mode IPSec netsh allows you to make immediate changes to IPSec policy. If the Policy Agent service is stopped, however, the dynamic changes are discarded. Dynamic IPSec should be used only if you must make immediate changes to IPSec processing. There will be no warning and no opportunity to discover a mistake in your command. If you create a valid command that does not do what you want, it will still run.

Before creating IPSec policies or changing them, enter the IPSec context by entering **netsh ipsec** at the command line, then enter the word **static** or **dynamic** to select the mode. Alternatively, you can enter all three words at the same time (for example, **netsh ipsec static**).

To create and assign the policy, you'll follow steps similar to those outlined for the GUI interface of the wizard as described earlier. You add the information for IKE configuration and add rules that are composed of filter lists, filter actions, and other configuration parameters. You can create blocking, permitting, and security negotiation rules, and do other things such as monitor IPSec and create special types of IPSec policies that cannot be created with the GUI.

 A guide to the netsh commands can be found at *Netsh commands for Internet Protocol Security* at *http://www.microsoft.com/technet/treeview/ default.asp?url=/technet/prodtechnol/windowsserver2003/proddocs/standard/netsh_ipsec.asp*.

The following steps will create an IPSec policy that blocks Terminal Services (access to a Remote Desktop session, and/or access to a terminal server using either Remote Administration mode or Application mode) from all computers except from ComputerB. To test your script, be sure to unassign any polices assigned on ComputerA and ComputerB.

The easiest way to work is to add the lines to a text file and save it as a batch file using the extension *.bat*. You can then run the batch file by entering its name at the command line. You will also be able to use it on another computer with slight adjustments. You can also enter each line at the command line, and when you press the Enter key, it will be executed. If your syntax is correct, a new command prompt will be made available. If you make mistakes, or need to remove the policy, you do so by using the delete policy command. An example, using the Block TS policy name is shown here:

```
Delete policy name="SecureTSBlock TS"
```

To create policies, first, create a policy for ComputerA that will block all Terminal Services, but negotiate security for Terminal Services from ComputerB. In this example, the IP address of computers on a test network is used so that you can see the complete syntax of the command. When you create your test, substitute the actual IP address of the computer used in the test.

Enter IPSec static mode:

```
netsh ipsec static
```

Create the policy on ComputerA. The parameters in the following statement below are fairly easy to interpret, except the mmsecmethods parameter. The mmsecmethods parameter is the main mode security methods information.

```
add policy name="SecureTS" description="block all terminal services except
connections from ComputerB" activatedefaultrule=no mmsecmethods="3DES-MD5-3"
```

To block all terminal services except that from ComputerB, two rules must be written. Each rule needs a filter added to the rule's filter list, so create that first. Here is a filter to identify ComputerB. It adds the IP address of ComputerB in the policy written on ComputerA. Src and dst stand for source and destination, respectively (for example, srcaddr stands for source address, and dstaddr stands for destination address).

```
Add filter filterlist="TS computerB" srcaddr=10.10.0.2 dstaddr=Me
description="computerB terminal services to computerA" protocol=TCP mirrored=yes
srcmask=24 dstmask=32 srcport=0 dstport=3389
```

Next, add a negotiate filter action. The qmsecmethods parameter identifies the quick mode security method. The qmpfs=no parameter indicates perfect forward security is not used. Inpass=no indicates that insecure communication is not allowed.

```
Add filteraction name="negotiate TS" qmpfs=no inpass=no soft=no action=negotiate
qmsecmethods="ESP 3=DES-MD5"
```

Add the rule for negotiation:

```
Add rule name="SecureTS Rule" policy="SecureTS" filterlist "TS computerB"
filteraction="negotiate TS" psk="secret" description="this rule negotiates a terminal
services connection if the source address belongs to computerB"
```

> Note how the filteraction is identified by name, as is the policy and the filterlist. The rule statement ties these important parts together.

Create the second rule, the blocking rule. First, create a filter:

```
Add filter filterlist="blockTS Filter" srcaddr=Any dstaddr=Me description="block all
terminal services to ComptuerA" protocol=TCP mirrored=yes srcmask=24 dstmask=24
srcport=ANY dstport=23
```

Add the filter action:

```
Add filteraction name="Block TS Action" inpass=yes action=block
```

Add the rule:

```
Add rule name="BlockTS" policy="SecureTS" filterlist "blockTS filter"
filteraction="Block TS Action" psk="secret" description="this rule blocks all
terminal services"
```

> The shared secret is entered in clear text in the Add rule statement using the psk parameter. It is, therefore, visible to anyone who can obtain access to the script. In a production environment, always use alternative authentication methods to improve security. If you must use a shared secret, protect the secret. *Do not leave scripts and notes lying around in hard copy, and do not store the script file where it can be opened and read.* If a script is used to add a policy, remove the script file afterward.

Next, create a policy on ComputerB. This policy only needs a single rule, the negotiate rule. The easiest way is to copy the policy created for ComputerA, and delete the blocking rule. Then, if necessary, you can adjust the statements. A copy of the policy written previously is listed here with the adjustment made to the filter. The change is necessary to switch the source and destination addresses.

Enter IPSec static mode:

```
netsh ipsec static
```

Create the policy on ComputerA. The mmsecmethods parameter is the main mode security methods information:

```
add policy name="SecureTS" description="block all terminal services except
connections from ComputerB" activatedefaultrule=no mmsecmethods="3DES-MD5-3"
```

Add a filter to identify ComputerB:

```
Add filter filterlist="TS computerB" srcaddr=10.10.0.1 dstaaddr=10.10.0.2
description="computerB terminal services to computerA" protocol=TCP mirrored=yes
srcmask=24 dstmask=32 srcport=0 dstport=3389
```

Next, add a negotiate filter action. The qmsecmethods parameter identifies the quick mode security method. The qmpfs=no parameter indicates perfect forward security is not used. Inpass=no indicates that insecure communication is not allowed.

```
Add filteraction name="negotiate TS" qmpfs=no inpass=no soft=no action=negotiate
qmsecmethods="ESP 3=DES-MD5"
```

Add the rule for negotiation:

```
Add rule name="SecureTS Rule" policy="SecureTS" filterlist "TS computerB"
filteraction="negotiate TS" psk="secret" description="this rule negotiates a terminal
services connection if the source address belongs to computerB"
```

The final step is to assign the policy. Remember to add this line to each batch file:

```
Set policy name=SecureTS assign=yes
```

Using Group Policy to Implement IPSec

IPSec policies can also be created as part of a Group Policy Object (GPO) and will be distributed to the computers whose accounts are targeted by the GPO. These policies can be created by right-clicking on the IP Security Policies on Active Directory node of the GPO, selecting Create IP Security Policy, and following the wizard. Or, you can import a saved policy into the IP Security node of the GPO. Keep the following in mind when creating IPSec Group Policy–based policies:

- Create and test the policy in a test network between two computers.
- Assign the policy to an OU in a test forest. The OU should contain computer accounts from representative computers (for example, Windows 2000, Windows XP, and Windows Server 2003, if all of these operating systems will be assigned the policy in the production network).
- When the policy is working as expected, add the policy to the production domain, but assign it (at first) to a small test OU.
- After testing, assign the policy to larger groups of computers in the production domain.

To create an IPSec policy directly in a GPO, begin by opening the GPO for editing. Expand the GPO and drill down to the Windows Settings → Security Settings → IP Security Policies on the Active Directory node, as shown in Figure 11-24.

Right-click on the node and select Create IP Security Policy. Follow the wizard to implement the desired policy. The wizard works the same way as it does for the local IP Security Policy described earlier.

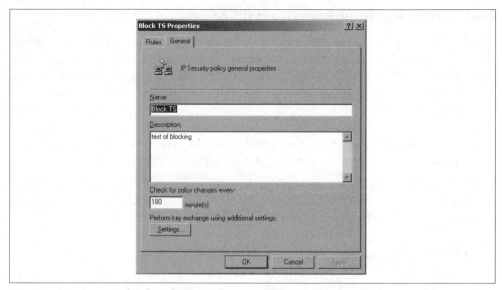

Figure 11-24. Group Policy based IPSec Policies can be created by running the wizard from with in a GPO

To import a saved IP Security Policy into a GPO, begin by opening the GPO for editing. Expand the GPO and drill down to the Windows Settings → Security Settings → IP Security Policies on Active Directory node. Right-click on the node and select All Tasks, then select Import Policies, as shown in Figure 11-25.

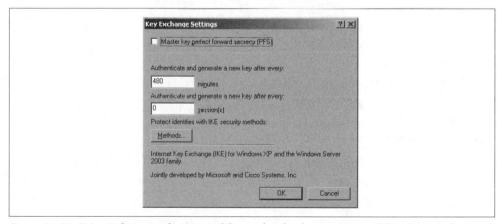

Figure 11-25. IPSec Policies can be exported from a local policy or GPO and then imported into a GPO

Browse to and select a saved IPSec policy and click Open.

Monitoring and Troubleshooting IPSec

When an IPSec policy does not work, it is often a simple configuration error. Many of these errors can be easily discovered by reviewing the policy configuration. Common errors are IP addresses that are entered incorrectly, mismatched encryption or integrity algorithms, and wrong port numbers. However, because there are a large number of things to be configured, knowing how to use monitoring and diagnostic tools is important. In addition, it is easy to configure a policy that does not work, but that you may think is working because the systems are communicating. If you monitoring IPSec, you can confirm that encryption is taking place.

Two Windows Server 2003 tools that can be used to monitor and troubleshoot IPSec on Windows Server 2003 are the `netsh ipsec` show command and the IP Security Monitor snap-in.

Using netsh to monitor IPSec

The `netsh show` command can be used to obtain policy information on the current IPSec session and to obtain diagnostics and logging information. If you can obtain the information using the graphical IP Security Monitor, you can obtain it using `netsh`.

To display the current IPSec policy, use the `netsh ipsec static show all` command. This will list all the information on the current policy. To narrow down the range of information displayed, you can use variations such as the following:

- Show the filter list:

      show filter list name=filterlist

- Show a specific rule:

      show rule name

- Display a specific policy:

      show policy name=policy name

To find diagnostic information use the `netsh ipsec dynamic set config` commands, such as the following:

- Set diagnostic logging from level 0, or disabled, to level 7 for all logging:

      ipsecdiagnostic value=7

- Turn on or off IKE (Oakley) logging:

      Ikelogging value=

- Disable Certificate Revocation List (CRL) checking (0), fail certificate validation if the certificate is revoked (1), or fail if any CRL check error occurs (2):

      strongcrlcheck value=

Several show commands provide useful troubleshooting information, including the following:

- Resolve DNS or NetBIOS computer names associated with an IP address (helpful in determining if the policy impacts the correct computers):

  ```
  show all resolvedns=yes
  ```

- Display information on the IPSec main mode SA:

  ```
  show mmsas
  ```

- Display quick mode SAs:

  ```
  show qmsas
  ```

- Display IKE main mode and/or IPSec quick mode statistics:

  ```
  show stats
  ```

 netdiag is a command-line tool for Windows 2000 and Windows Server 2003. It can be used to display IPSec information, as well as test and view network configuration for Windows 2000 computers. The command can be used to test and view network configuration of Windows Server 2003 computers, but the netdiag /test:ipsec option is not available. The netsh command can be used to provide this information.

Using the IP Security Monitor to monitor IPSec

In the section "Setting Up the IPSec Monitor and Testing the Policy," the IP Security Monitor was used to monitor the test of the security negotiation policy. The tool is also available as an MMC snap-in for Windows XP. It cannot be used to monitor Windows 2000 IPSec. Use the tool to monitor the active Windows Server 2003 and/or Windows XP IPSec policy. Policy configuration information, quick mode and main mode statistics, as well as information on active SAs can be obtained.

Much of the information the tool presents is straightforward. However, some of the information on IPSec main mode and quick mode statistics is not. Some of this data only makes sense when it is collected and monitored over time, and when it is considered in context. For example, whether the number of pending requests or messages queued represents a problem (perhaps few are being serviced) may depend on the amount of processing normally done on this computer. Other policy statistics are easy to interpret. For example, if there are a large number of authentication failures and failed connections, it probably means that authentication is misconfigured, or it could mean an attempt is being made from an unauthorized computer. Table 11-2 provides an explanation of main mode statistics, and Table 11-3 provides an explanation of Quick Mode statistics.

Table 11-2. Main Mode statistics in the IP Security Monitor

Statistic	Explanation
Active Acquire	The number of pending requests for IKE negotiation between IPSec peers.
Active Receive	The number of IKE messages queued for processing.
Acquire Failures	The number of established outbound SA requests that have failed since the IPSec service started.
Receive Failures	The number of errors in received IKE messages since the IPSec service started.
Send Failures	The number of errors during IKE negotiation.
Acquire Heap Size	The number of successive outbound requests required to establish SAs.
Receive Heap Size	The number of IKE messages in IKE receive buffers.
Authentication failures	The number of failed authentication failures since the start of the IPSec service. When connections are failing, check to see if authentication failures increase during connection attempts. If this is the case, authentication is most likely the problem. Look for common errors depending on the type of authentication used. If shared secrets are used, check to see if they match. If the method is Kerberos, are IPSec peers members of the domain? When the method is certificates, make sure that are they available and correct.
Negotiation failures	The number of main mode and quick mode negotiation failures. If connections are failing and negotiation failures increase during connection attempts, check to see if security methods (or possibly authentication) are mismatched. .
Invalid cookies received	Cookies are values in received IKE messages and are used to help identify the corresponding main mode SA. (SPIs are used to identify quick mode SAs.) If invalid cookies are received, then the failure is with IKE negotiation.
Total acquire	The number of requests submitted to IKE. (Including those resulting from soft SAs).
Total get SPI	Requests to driver for the SPI.
Key addition	The number of outbound quick mode SA additions.
Key updates	The number of inbound quick mode SAs added by IKE.
Get SPI failures	The number of failed requests for a unique SPI.
Key addition failures	The number of failed outbound quick mode SA addition requests submitted by IKE.
Key update failures	A failed inbound quick mode SA addition request.
ISADB List Size	The number of main mode state entries. This includes successful main modes, main modes in negotiation, and those that have failed or expired, but have not been deleted.
Connection list size	The number of quick mode negotiations in process.
IKE Main Mode	The number of successful SAs in main mode.
IKE quick mode	The total SAs in quick mode.
Soft associations	SAs that are not the result of an encrypted, main mode negotiation.
Invalid packets received	The number of invalid IKE messages. This can be the result of invalid header fields, payload lengths, and incorrect values. The preshared key may be mismatched. It may also be the result of retransmitted IKE messages.

Table 11-3. Quick Mode statistics

Statistic	Explanation
ActiveSecurity Association	Number of quick mode SAs. (Though two SAs are used during quick mode, only one of them will be shown here.)
Offloaded Security Associations	Number of quick mode SAs offloaded to hardware.
Pending Key Operations	Number of key exchange operations.
Key Additions	Number of keys added for quick mode SAs since the computer started.
Key Deletions	Number of keys quick mode SAs that have been successfully deleted since computer started.
Rekeys	Number of successful rekey operations for quick mode.
Active Tunnels	Number of active tunnels.
Bad SPI Packets	Number of packets with incorrect SPI. This may mean that the SPI expired and an old packet just arrived. If rekeying is frequent and/or there are a large number of SAs, this number may be higher than normal without being indicative of anything wrong. It might also indicate a spoofing attack.
Packets Not Decrypted	Number of packets not decrypted. Packets are not decrypted if they fail a validation check.
Packets not authenticated	Might indicate IPSec packet spoofing or modification attack or corruption by network devices.
Packets with Replay detection	Number of packets that contain an invalid sequence number. Watch for increase because they might indicate a network problem or replay attack.
Confidential bytes sent	Number of encrypted bytes (those sent using ESP protocol).
Authenticated bytes sent	Number of bytes authenticated using AH or ESP.
Transport bytes sent	Number of received bytes using IPSec transport mode.
Bytes sent in Tunnels	Bytes sent using IPSec tunnel mode.
Bytes received in tunnels	Bytes received.
Offloaded bytes sent	Number of bytes sent that use the hardware offload.
Offloaded bytes received	Number of bytes received using hardware offload.

To learn the basics of configuring, testing and monitoring IPSec, you must perform extensive preparation and practice. Once you have successfully written a few policies with the wizard, monitored them using the IPSec Monitor, and rewritten them using netsh, you are ready to write and use all but the most complex IPSec policies. While those policies may require more intensive study and testing, they are built on the information you've learned. A few of these extended operations are covered in the following discussion.

Extending IPSec Operations

Even IPSec protected systems are vulnerable to attack during times when the IPSec policy is not in effect. Following are two times when this may occur:

- During startup (after the IPSec driver starts, but before the IPSec Policy Agent service starts).
- When Group Policy fails and the IPSec Policy is newly implemented or modified through Group Policy. (Group Policy IPSec policies are cached in the local computer registry and can be used when a domain controller is not available at computer boot. However, no changes to Group Policy, and, therefore, to IPSec policy, will be downloaded if there is a Group Policy failure.)

To ensure protection against these potential gaps in coverage, you should use persistent policies and configure the IPSec driver mode.

Use Persistent Policies

You can only assign one IPSec policy per computer. However, you can establish a persistent IPSec policy using the netsh command that will work in concert with that IPSec-assigned policy. Use persistent policies to do the following:

- Extend IPSec for individual computers that receive an IPSec policy via Group Policy. (The Group Policy based IPSec policy may have to be general to work for a large number of computers. The persistent policy can be applied to a single computer and the restrictions it requires may be added.)
- Temporarily extend or override local IPSec policy.
- Provide additional protection during computer startup.
- Provide protection when Group Policy based IPSec policies fail to be applied.

To make a policy persistent, first create the policy using netsh. It is not possible to create a persistent policy using the GUI. For example, assume a simple policy called Block80 is created to block all port 80 traffic to the local computer. To make the policy persistent, assign the policy using netsh, as follows:

    set policy name=Block80 assign=yes

Make the policy persistent by using the netsh as follows:

    set store location=persistent

Configure IPSec Driver Modes

The section "Specifics of the Windows Implementation" earlier in this chapter defined the driver as the Windows component that filters communications to determine if they meet the requirements specified in an active IPSec policy. In Windows Server 2003, the IPSec driver operates in one of several modes. You can configure driver modes to improve security. IPSec driver modes are established during computer startup and are adjusted using `netsh`. IPSec Driver modes are as follows:

Startup

The IPSec driver is loaded into this mode during Windows Server 2003 operating system boot. There are three communication options within this mode.

Operational

When the IPSec Policy Agent starts, it changes the IPSec Driver mode to operational mode.

Diagnostic

Can be set by using the `netsh` command.

Startup mode

The IPSec Computer Startup communication options during startup mode are as follows:

Permit

This is the default startup mode if an IPSec policy has never been assigned and if the IPSec Policy Agent is set to Disabled or Manual startup mode. No IP packets are processed by IPSec.

Block

All inbound and outbound IP packets are dropped unless they match filters created for use during block mode, or they are DHCP traffic (so that a computer can obtain an IP address). To configure block mode use the `netsh ipsec dynamic set config bootexemptions` command. For example, to set the computer to block mode and apply a filter that will allow the use of the Remote Desktop connection during startup, issue the command `netsh ipsec dynamic set config bootexemptions value=tcp:0:3389:inbound`.

Stateful

All outbound traffic is allowed and inbound permit filters are created in response to outbound traffic. All other inbound traffic is dropped including unicast, broadcast and multicast. If an IPSec policy is assigned to a computer and the IPSec Policy Agent service is set to automatic startup, then the computer startup mode of the IPSec driver will be stateful mode.

The computer startup mode can be modified by using the `netsh ipsec static set config bootmode value={stateful | block | permit}` command, or by modifying the registry. To modify the registry, add and set the DWORD value OperationMode under the key *HKEY_LOCAL_MACHINE\SYSTEM\CurrentControlSet\Services\IPSEC*.

Use a value of 0 to set Permit mode, 1 for Block mode, and 3 for Stateful mode.

Operational mode

After the IPSec Services service starts, the IPSec Policy Agent sets the IPSec driver to operational mode. If computer startup mode filters are in place, they are discarded. The operational mode cannot be changed by using commands or registry settings. Instead configure IPSec policies and IPSec persistent policies to ensure the protection that you desire. Operational modes are as follows:

Secure

> All IPSec policy filters are enforced. If a persistent policy is configured the persistent policy is applied, the IPSec Policy Agent sets the IPSec driver into secure mode and applies the Active Directory IPSec policy or local policy if one is assigned. If no persistent policy is configured, secure mode cannot protect the computer until the Active Directory or local policy can be applied.

Permit

> No IPSec protection is provided, so no IP packets are processed by IPSec. The Permit operational mode is active when the IPSec service is manually stopped.

Block

> All inbound and all outbound traffic is dropped. If filters are configured for computer startup mode, they are not applied here. Block mode is active if a persistent policy is configured but cannot be applied.

Diagnostic mode

Diagnostic mode is disabled by default. Diagnostic mode can be used to record all inbound and all outbound dropped packets and other packet processing errors to the System Event log. To enable diagnostic mode, use the `netsh ipsec dynamic set config ipsecdiagnostics value={0-9}`. Larger numbers mean that more information is collected. A value of `0` disables diagnostic mode.

Designing IPSec Policies to Meet Secure Communications Needs

It's not enough to know how to create an IPSec policy. You must also know when to create one. While it is important to consider security for communications on the LAN, it is not a good idea to attempt to protect all communications on the LAN with IPSec. So, when should IPSec be used?

There is no single answer to that question. In the example earlier in the chapter, remote access via the Remote Desktop connection was restricted to secured communication from a single computer. Likewise, other administrative access scenarios are good candidates for IPSec. In addition, the following list shows a number of scenarios where IPSec might be used:

- Protect communications between a web application and a Microsoft SQL Server.
- Protect Active Directory replication across a firewall.
- Prevent rogue computers from accessing domain resources. (Requires certificate authentication.)
- Block access during startup by creating persistent policies.
- Block access to well-known ports utilized by Trojans (for example, TFTP inbound and outbound, and SMTP inbound on the desktop).
- Block access to other ports on computers where these services should be disabled, such as telnet and web server. (Services should be disabled but might be enabled anyway; blocking the port provides defense in depth.)
- Restrict access to ports or IP addresses to specific computers.
- Protect communications between sensitive servers and authorized users, such as financial databases and authorized financial department staff computers.

Hardening IPSecurity Policies

Once you have become familiar with the process of setting up IPSec policies, you should review the choices you can make to further increase their security. You can, for example, change the frequency with which the master and session keys are created. Changing keys more frequently increases security. Other possibilities are to use stronger authentication and to harden security methods by ensuring that the most secure security protocols are used.

Hardening Authentication

As you know, a shared secret is best used only for testing. It does make the test easier, and is also quite useful in troubleshooting. By using a shared secret, you eliminate the possibility that Kerberos or certificate authentication is the problem. When both computers are joined in the same domain, or if a trust relationship exists between the domains they are members of, Kerberos is a good choice as well. However, when computers are not joined in a domain, certificates may be used. Using certificates is more complex. Each computer will require its own certificate and, if the certificates are not issued by the same Certification Authority (CA), then a copy of the root certificate for the issuing CA will need to be available in the computer certificate store of the other computer. (Chapter 8 provides more information on using certificates with IPSec.)

Hardening Security Methods

As implemented in Windows, IPSec provides several possible choices of integrity, encryption, and Diffie-Hellman settings. If the default settings are used, it is possible that the actual security settings used may not be the most secure. When multiple choices exist, the settings are negotiated at connection, and the first option that can be used will be selected.

To ensure that the most secure settings are selected, you should limit choices and make sure the list of choices is in the order of most to least secure. You should be aware of the computers on your network that will need to make a connection using IPSec and may have to adjust your choices accordingly. For example, Windows Server 2003 is the only Windows operating system that can use the Diffie-Hellman group 3 setting. If you can (or need to) ensure that only Windows Server 2003 computers are allowed to make the connection, then you can ensure that it is selected. However, don't block Windows 2000 and/or Windows XP machines from making a connection, if you require and permit them to do so.

Table 11-1 lists the IPSec Policy Elements and where they are used. Several of these elements provide security configuration choices. You should modify the defaults to provide the best security for your situation. To change the defaults, make selections during the creation of the IPSec policy or use the following procedure. This procedure modifies the settings to ensure that only 3DES, SHA1, and Diffie-Hellman high(3) security methods are used. The following procedures show how to do that using the example policy created earlier in this chapter.

On ComputerA, open the IPSecurityPolicy1 console and double-click on the Block TS policy to open it. Select the General tab and then click the Settings button, as shown on Figure 11-26.

Figure 11-26. Use the Setting button to expose the key settings and Security Methods

On the Key Exchange Settings page, click the Methods button, as shown in Figure 11-27.

Figure 11-27. Click the Methods button to modify Security Methods

Select the 3DES, SHA1, Medium (2) security method and click Edit. Use the drop-down box for the Diffie-Hellman group and select High (2048), as shown in Figure 11-28. Then click OK.

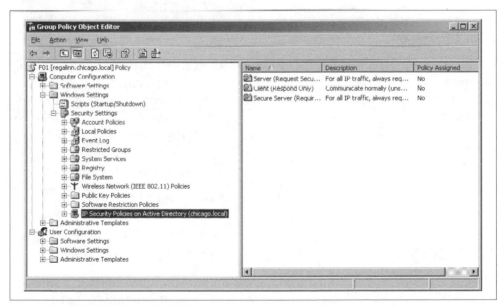

Figure 11-28. Modify the Diffie-Hellman group

Select the 3DES, MD5 security method and click Remove. Select each of the two DES security methods and remove them. Ensure that the page looks like Figure 11-29 and then click OK.

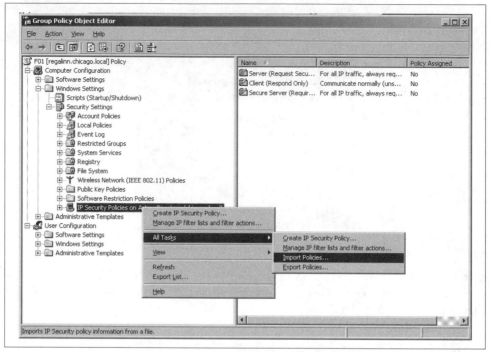

Figure 11-29. Verify your Security Methods settings

Click OK twice more to close the policy. On ComputerB, repeat the process, only this time, edit the Secure TS policy. Test the policy by opening a Remote Desktop connection from ComputerB to ComputerA. Verify the security method settings by double-clicking on the Security Associations node and double-click to open the SA. (The SA settings will not indicate the Diffie-Hellman group used.)

If IPSec policies are not working as you expected after you have made changes, it may be because the policy has not refreshed. You can force a policy refresh by stopping and restarting the IPSec Services. This action will quickly clear any policy information.

Summary

IPSec is a complex protocol that can be used to provide a high level of security for data in flight, as well as preventing unauthorized communications between computers. The Windows Server 2003 implementation simplifies the configuration process by providing GUI-based IPSec policy configuration and the ability to use Group Policy to configure multiple computers automatically without visiting them. The IPSec neophyte should be aware, however, that the ease with which IPSec can be configured means that it is very easy to use it to halt critical communications on a network.

It can also confuse communications to such an extent, that the only solution is to reinstall multiple systems. The wise administrator will spend the required time to become thoroughly informed and use due diligence in testing proposed policies before implementation.

IPSec is used to secure communications. Which communications are secured is based on the IP address of the sending and receiving computer and the ports and protocols used during the communication. It is not necessary to make any change to the application that produces the communication in order to provide security using IPSec.

Chapter 12 addresses a different issue: how to configure intranet and Internet web services using Internet Information Server (IIS). Configuring web services, in this context, is used generically to describe the administration of IIS, not writing code to provide specific applications that operate across multiple web servers. In Chapter 12, you will learn how IIS operates, and how to perform a basic installation and configuration.

CHAPTER 12

Configuring Internet and Intranet Web Services with IIS

Microsoft Internet Information Services (IIS) 6.0 (the version of IIS that is native to Windows Server 2003) marks a radical change in philosophy, design, and configuration from previous versions. Unlike Windows 2000 IIS, IIS 6.0 does not install by default. If IIS services are required, they must be selected during server installation or added at a later time. This is the first version of IIS that, when installed, becomes a static web server. The administrator must select, install, and configure the additional features to use them. In addition, IIS has a substantially different architecture, including the following:

- An XML *metabase* (the configuration database for IIS)
- Support for automatic metabase versioning and history
- Improved performance because of kernel mode caching
- Worker process isolation mode installed as the default

 A *worker process* is user-level code that is used to process requests. *Worker process isolation mode* refers to how the code is isolated from other user-level code running on the server.

Before installing IIS, you must determine the reason for its installation. This may be the need for a static web site, a web-based application, or even an IIS-based service such as the need for Simple Mail Transfer Protocol (SMTP) services for Active Directory replication. The configuration of IIS depends on knowledge of its use. Once that has been decided, IIS administration requires knowledge of the following:

- IIS installation (including the configuration of web servers and sites)
- Key IIS services (such as mail services)
- The running IIS applications

A special version of Windows Server 2003, the Web Server Edition, is a single function, economical, dedicated server. It supports 2 GB of RAM and 10 inbound server message block (SMB) connections for content publishing. Use of the server for non-web serving applications is prohibited. Unlike other versions of Windows Server 2003, the Web Server Edition cannot be a domain controller or support other Windows Server 2003 functions. Most of the information on IIS 6.0 in this chapter is applicable to the Web Server Edition, but other information about Windows Server 2003 in this chapter and throughout the book may not be. Before selecting the Web Server Edition for a specific application or purpose, review that purpose with an authorized dealer for the product.

This chapter provides information on these basic IIS administrative duties. It does not provide detailed information on the administration of Network News Transport Protocol (NNTP), SMTP, or POP3 services, nor information on the many IIS extensions and alternative components. Chapter 13 provides some information on using WebDAV for the transport of files encrypted with the Encrypting File System (EFS) and using IIS's SMTP service for SMTP-based Active Directory replication.

Server Preparation and IIS Installation

Before installing IIS, you must prepare Windows Server 2003. The steps to take are dictated by your intended use of IIS. For example, if IIS will support Internet-facing web sites, it will need a higher level of security hardening and a location in the network infrastructure where it can be protected from external attacks and isolated from the internal network. It should also be installed as a dedicated web server. When IIS is used as an intranet web server, security is still important, but may be less dramatically applied.

In all cases, only the necessary server and IIS components should be enabled. Prior to installation, determine what components are required based on how the server will be used. If the uses of IIS cannot be clearly defined, then IIS should not be installed. The following instructions assume that the IIS server will be a dedicated web server. The following sections provide basic administration instructions, including how to customize the basic server for web sites and their application. In the following sections, you will learn how to install and prepare Windows Server 2003, as well as how to install IIS.

Install and Prepare Windows Server 2003

The foundation on which IIS will rest is very important. The major steps required are:

- Determine the proper location and network support for the server. Provide a secure network infrastructure. Plan to locate the web server behind such perimeter protection as firewalls, malware gateways, and application filters. The server should not be installed in this location. The web server should not be built and tested here.

- Prepare the physical server. Ensure that it has appropriate processor(s), memory, networking hardware, and drives for its intended use. Best practices indicate that a dedicated disk volume should be provided for web site content. This can not only be more secure (because of the potential for compromise of the system volume), but it will be easier to back up content.

- Install Windows Server 2003 as a stand-alone server with no connections to a production network or to the Internet. Use only the Windows NT File System (NTFS) filesystem. Do not install networking components inappropriate for its intended use. For example, do not install DHCP server services. They are not necessary for IIS. Install only essential server services and options.

- If current service packs and security patches are not slipstreamed into the installation, update the server so that it is current with all packs and patches.

- Set permissions on the root of the disk volume intended for web content. Grant the local Administrators group Full Control privileges and remove all other groups.

- Disable services that are not required by a dedicated web server. Windows Server 2003 services that may be disabled on a dedicated web server are listed in the section "Hardening of dedicated web server services" later in this chapter.

- Configure server auditing to monitor logons and policy changes. Turn on object auditing so that web server file access can be monitored.

- Apply *security hardening* steps for the server. *Hardening* means to follow known best practices for securing the server. Consult security references, including security pages at *http://www.microsoft.com/technet/security* for specifics. Information on security for IIS is embedded within the administration instructions in this chapter.

- Test the server's network operation on an isolated test network.

- If the server will be a member of a Windows domain, add it to the domain after all tests and configuration. If the web application is dependent on domain membership, the web application should be tested on a test network in which IIS is installed in a test domain prior to being hosted on a live web server.

Documenting the server configuration

Prior to installing IIS, document the server configuration. Modify the documentation after installing IIS and after installing web server applications. Two purposes are served here. First, if the server must be duplicated, solid information on its requirements and a working configuration is available. Second, if the server must be replaced or restored, the files are available and the process will be much easier.

Hardening of dedicated web server services

Windows Server 2003 installs many services by default. The startup status of these services can be disabled, manual (can be started by an administrator or by a process) or automatic (enabled and running at computer boot). For performance and security reasons, no service should be running if it is not required to support the web server function. The fewer services that are running, the more computer resources there will be available for the web server. The fewer services that are running, the fewer opportunities there will be for malfunction or for vulnerability to attack. Before installing IIS, review the status of server services and disable those services that are not required for the server or for the operation of IIS. You should also document the status of installed services so that the status can be maintained.

The following server services are disabled by default and should remain disabled on the web server:

- Alerter
- Clipbook
- Human Interface Device Access
- IMAPI CD-Burning COM Service
- Internet Connection Firewall(ICF)/Internet Connection Sharing (ICS)
- Intersite Messaging
- Kerberos Key Distribution Center
- License Logging Service
- Messenger
- Network DDE
- Network DDE DSDM
- Routing and Remote Access
- Themes
- Terminal Services Session Directory
- Web Client
- Windows Audio
- Windows Image Acquisition (WIA)

After disabling services, test the function of the server both before and after installing IIS. The instructions here are generic; your specific purpose and server requirements should also be considered.

In addition to these services, Microsoft recommends disabling many other services on a dedicated web server. Table 12-1 lists and describes these services.

Table 12-1. Microsoft recommended modifications to server service startup

Service	Function	Change
Application Management	Provides software installation services for applications deployed using Control Panel → Add or Remove Programs.	After web server setup and configuration, disable this service to prevent unauthorized installation of software. Disabling this service will not prevent installation of software that does not require the use of Add or Remove Programs.
Automatic Updates	Downloads and installs Windows updates such as security patches.	If manual updates will be performed, disable this service.
Background Intelligent Transfer Service	Manages background file transfer and queues. Used by Automatic updates.	If automatic updates are disabled, disable this service as well.
Distributed File System	Manages logical volumes distributed across a LAN or WAN.	Disable.
Distributed Link Tracking Client	Maintains links between NTFS filesystem files and other servers in a domain.	Disable.
Distributed Link Tracking Server	Tracks information about files moved between NTFS volumes throughout a domain.	Disable.
Error Reporting Service	Collects, stores, and reports application crashes to Microsoft.	Disable.
Fax Service	Provides the capability to send and receive faxes.	Disable.
Indexing Service	Indexes content and file properties to enable rapid access.	Disable unless web server applications leverage the use of this service for searching site content.
NetMeeting Remote Desktop Sharing	Allows remote administration through NetMeeting.	Disable.
Print Spooler	Manages local and network print queues and controls all print jobs.	Disable unless printing from the web server is required.
Remote Access Auto Connection Manager	Detects unsuccessful attempts to connect to a remote network or computer and attempts to try alternative configurations if available.	Disable unless dial-up or VPN connections are initiated from the web server.
Remote Access Connection Manager	Manages VPN and dial-up connections from web server to Internet or other networks.	Disable unless dial-up or VPN connections are initiated from the web server.

Table 12-1. Microsoft recommended modifications to server service startup (continued)

Service	Function	Change
Remote Desktop Help Sessions Manager	Manages and controls remote assistance.	Disable. (Use Terminal Services for administration.)
Remote Procedure Call (RPC) Locater	This is required by RPC clients using the RpcNs* family of application programming interfaces (APIs) to use local RPC servers and to manage the RPC name service database. (This is called the RpcNs* family because all RPC name service APIs begin the "RpcNs.")	Disable if no applications use the RpcNs* APIs.
Special Administration Console Helper	Enables remote administration via Emergency Management Services	Disable if Emergency Management Services will not be required for the web server.
Removable storage	Manages and catalogs removable media and automated removable media devices (such as tape auto loaders).	Disable if all removable media devices are directly connected to web server. Required to access some tape devices.
Telephony	Provides Telephony API (TAPI) support for client programs that control telephony devices.	Disable if applications do not require TAPI.
Telnet	Enables the use of a telnet connection. Enables command-line applications on the web server through this connection.	Disable.
Terminal services	Allows multiple remote users to connect and run desktops and applications.	Disable unless used for remote administration.
Upload Manages	Manages file transfers between clients and servers on the network. Can supply help to users in locating required drivers.	Disable.
Volume Shadow Copy	Manages volume shadow copies. These can be used for backup.	If volume shadow copies will not be used on the web server, disable this service. (*Volume shadow copies* are snapshots of the filesystem and may be used in the backup and restore process.)
WinHTTP Web Proxy Auto-Discovery Service	Implements the Web Proxy AutoDiscovery (WPAD) protocol and enables an HTTP client to discover a proxy configuration.	Disable.
Wireless Configuration	Enables configuration for IEEE 802.11 adapters.	Disable.
WMI Performance adapter	Provides performance library information from Windows Management Instrumentation (WMI) providers to clients.	Disable.

In addition, the following services may be candidates to be disabled. Review their purposes closely before disabling because they may be used in your organization and, therefore, it may not be wise to disable them.

File Replication Service
Used to automatically copy and maintain files simultaneously on multiple servers.

Help and Support
Runs the Help and Support Center on the web server

Portable Media Serial Number Service
Retrieves the serial number of a portable media player connected to the server.

Remote Registry Service
Remote users use this service to remotely modify the registry. By default, only Administrators and Backup Operators group members have the required permissions to do so. If remote administration is not required, disable this service.

Smart Card
Provides management and control access to a smart card used in a smart card reader attached to the web server. If smart cards are not used, disable the service.

Uninterruptible Power Supply
Manages an uninterruptible power supply (UPS) connected to the web server via a serial port. Disable if this type of UPS system connection is not used.

To disable a service, begin by opening Start → Administrative Tools → Services. Scroll to and double-click the service to open its Properties page. Use the "Startup type" drop-down list to select Disabled. If the service is started, click Stop. Click OK.

Now that you have installed and prepared Windows 2003, you can begin the process of installing IIS.

Installing IIS

Before starting the installation process, review the default installation options and determine if this installation requires additional services and options. Services and options can be added during or after installation. Optional items include services, administration tools, and subcomponents. Table 12-2 lists and describes the IIS services that may be installed.

Table 12-2. IIS 6.0 services

Service	Description	Installed/ enabled by default?
FTP	These services provide file-transfer services through the file transfer protocol (FTP) and the ability to manage the service.	No
IIS Admin	This service provides administrative services through the IIS Management console.	Yes
Indexing	You can use this service to create catalogs of file information that can then be searched. Once installed and started, the administrator uses the built in Microsoft Management Console (MMC) snap-in for the Indexing service or the Indexing service node in Computer management to administer the service. The service works in the background to extract information from files and build catalogs. Space for catalogs may be from 15 to 40% of the size of the original files and, therefore, care must be taken to ensure adequate disk space is available. Catalogs are associated with web sites, NNTP sites, or external file directories. Use the Indexing service for web sites built to leverage the use of this service. Developer information is located at *http:// whidbey.msdn.microsoft.com/library/default.asp?url=/library/ en-us/indexsrv/html/indexingservicestartpage_6td1.asp.*	No
NNTP	This service supports the management of NNTP virtual servers for the purpose of supporting NNTP news groups and services. Links to articles on NNTP administration is located at *http:// www.microsoft.com/resources/documentation/WindowsServ/ 2003/standard/proddocs/en-us/Default.asp?url=/resources/doc- umentation/WindowsServ/2003/standard/proddocs/en-us/ nntp administration.asp.*	No
SMTP	Many web site applications require the ability to send and receive email. Both SMTP (for sending) and POP3 (for receiving) services are available for IIS 6.0. Both are installed as virtual servers and configurable via IIS Manager. By default, SMTP is config- ured to send and receive locally generated messages and to restrict the sending of messages generated by remote users, as well as restrict those generated by named users on the local computer. Mail relay through the SMTP server is also disabled by default.	No
POP3	POP3 is available as separate service from IIS and is configurable from its own MMC snap-in.	No
World Wide Web Publishing Service	This provides services for administering the web server and for transferring files using HTTP.	Yes

Installation of IIS is hidden beneath the more generic Application Server, which is a collection of components. If the Application Server is selected for installation and no changes are made during the process, the following subcomponents of the Application Server are installed:

Application Server Console
> The MMC snap-in is used for administration of Web Application Server components.

Network COM+ Access
> Web servers can host COM+ components for distributed applications.

Internet Information Services
> Basic web and FTP services are installed, but FTP is not enabled by default.

The following subcomponents of IIS are enabled:

Common Files
> These are files required by IIS for it to run.

Internet Information Services Manager
> This is an administrative interface for IIS. It can be disabled if the web server will not be administered locally.

SMTP Service
> This supports the transfer of electronic mail. It can be disabled if email is not managed or required by the web server.

World Wide Web Service
> This supports static and (if configured) dynamic content. Only the World Wide Web Service subcomponent of this service is enabled by default. (Other subcomponents are Active Server Pages, BITS, Internet Data Connector, Remote Administration via HTML, Remote Desktop Web Connection, Service Side includes, and WebDAV.)

To install IIS, begin by opening the Control Panel → Add or Remove Programs → Add/Remove Widows Components. Select the Application Server, as shown in Figure 12-1.

Click the Details button and continue to expand components and select those required for a specific installation. Only install essential components. Components can be installed later if necessary. Click OK until returned to the Windows Components page of the wizard. Click Next. If prompted, provide the installation CD-ROM. Click Finish when installation is complete.

After installation, inspect changes to the server. Note, for example, that the World Wide Web Service is installed and started, as are other services if you selected them during the installation. Note the creation in the filesystem of a *webroot* folder and *Administrative*

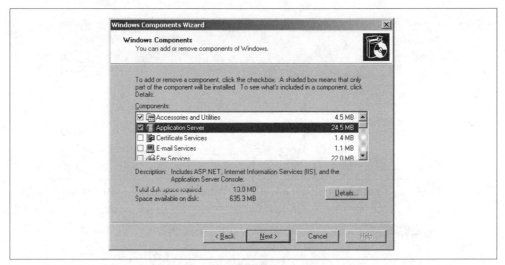

Figure 12-1. To install IIS, select the Application Server

scripts folder underneath the *inetpub* folder. This is the default location for the default web site, as well as any other default virtual servers. If installed, an *ftproot* and *mailroot* exist as well. The *Administrative Scripts* folder contains two files: *adsutil.vbs* (which uses VBScript with Active Directory Service Interfaces, or ADSI, to manipulate the metabase) and *synciwam.vbs* (used to synchronize the identity of the IWAM account, the identity for out-of-process applications). These are useful learning administrative tools, but the scripts should be removed from the web server. Furthermore, they are unsupported scripts. Supported scripts are installed in the *%systemroot%\system32* folder. A list of supported scripts can be viewed at *http://www.microsoft.com/resources/documentation/IIS/6/all/techref/en-us/iisRG_TAS_37.mspx*.

To inspect changes to the server, click Start → Administrative Tools, and open the Internet Information Server (IIS) Manager console. Expand and select the Default Web Site. Note the location of a default *.htm* file, as shown in Figure 12-2.

Browse to the file location *C:\inetpub\wwwroot* and double-click on the *iisstart.htm* file to open in Internet Explorer. This file is shown in Figure 12-3 and is the page seen by any user who is able to access the default web site at this time. It is simply a placeholder page that tells everyone that the site is "Under construction" This allows you to test connectivity to the web site. The default web site is mapped to the default AD domain. To use other domains, create new web sites. Creating new web sites is described in the section "Creating a Web Site" later in this chapter.

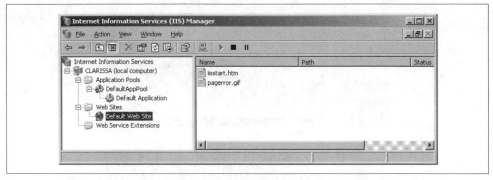

Figure 12-2. Files in the home directory folder are displayed in the IIS Manager console

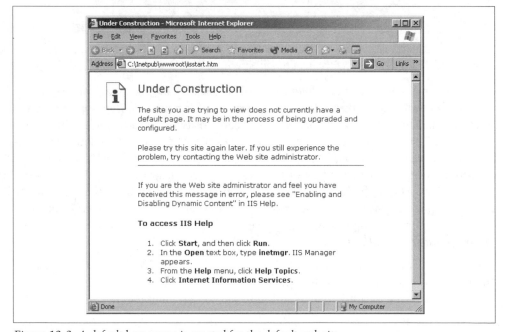

Figure 12-3. A default home page is created for the default web site

Installing and Configuring Web Servers and Sites

Configuring web servers and web sites includes preparing disk locations and filesystem permissions, creating virtual web servers and web sites, and then configuring them. The applications that will run on these sites and servers dictate how they are set up. To administer IIS, you should be able to perform a number of tasks. Creating a web site is just the first step. You must be able to configure it in order to secure it and to enable it to provide specific services. In addition, services other than web services are available, and you should be familiar with them. The following are the minimal operations you should know:

Creating a web site

A default web site is created when IIS is installed. However, you may want to create your own unique web site to fulfill some specific purpose, or you may want to have multiple web sites on the IIS server.

Managing IIS permissions

IIS permission settings determine how data and code on the IIS server can be used. These permissions are different than server filesystem permissions or user rights. They include the capability to run scripts and programs and to read and/or write files.

Configuring user authentication

Much web access is done anonymously. However, web applications may require authentication when sensitive operations or access to sensitive data is enabled. There are a number of options here and authentication must be carefully configured to match requirements and maintain security.

Configuring web site properties

In addition to permissions and authentication, a web site's properties include its IP address; restricting access from designated computers, domains and networks; NTFS permissions; and components, services, and extensions.

Reviewing web server security

Knowledge of web server configuration by itself is not enough. You must know which options provide better security and how to maximize security for each web server use.

Editing the metabase

IIS configuration information is stored in a special file, the metabase. It is important to know how to configure IIS using this file, because it may be easier to configure certain items using the metabase rather than the GUI, and some items can *only* be configured this way.

Using IIS backup and recovery

Configuration and operations of a web server is not complete without a regular backup program that is periodically tested. Performing backups is a simple task and can make the process of restoring a damaged or inoperable web server much easier.

Configuring SSL

E-commerce site communications (as well as that of web sites that provide access to sensitive data) must be protected. The use of SSL is one way to do so. It must, however be correctly implemented or it offers no protection at all.

Configuring FTP

While the file transfer protocol (FTP) is not used as frequently to upload and download files across the WAN, its services are available with IIS. You should learn how to securely implement FTP services.

Creating a Web Site

Each web site must have a *home directory*, which is the central location of published web pages (including a home page or index file to serve as a portal to other pages). The home directory includes subfolders that contain application code or content. The home directory is mapped to domain name of web site or name of the web server. Web sites can also store web content in a *virtual directory*. Web site content can be located in folders underneath the home directory, or in folders elsewhere. When folders outside of the home directory path are used, they are called virtual directories.

> Creating a home directory on a disk volume other than the system volume reduces the risk that a compromised web site can be used to compromise the entire server.

To create a web site, begin by creating a folder in the NTFS filesystem on a disk volume other than the system volume. Open the Internet Information Services (IIS) Manager. Right-click the *Web sites* folder, select New, and then "Create a web site." Enter a description for the site and click Next. Select the IP address and port number to be used for the site, and then click Next. (Each web site hosted on a single server must have either a unique IP address, a unique port or a unique host header. Host headers let you identify multiple domains on a single web server.) Enter or browse to the file folder location that will be used for the web site and click Next. If anonymous access to the site will not be allowed, clear the "Allow anonymous access" checkbox. Click Next. Modify the default "Web permissions" for the site. Table 12-3 explains the permissions shown in Figure 12-4. Click Next, followed by Finish.

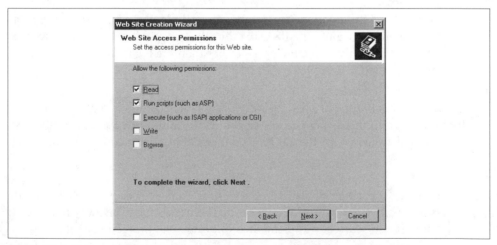

Figure 12-4. Set permissions during install; they can be modified later as well

Table 12-3. IIS permissions set through the Wizard

Permissions	Description
Read	Read the data.
Run scripts (such as ASP)	Run scripts.
Execute (such as ISAPI applications or CGI)	Run applications.
Write	Write data to the web server.
Browse	View directories and files.

 An excellent article on host headers and how to use them can be found at *http://www.windowsitpro.com/Article/ArticleID/7176/7176.html?Ad–1*. An interesting use of host headers for security is at *http://www.microsoft.com/technet/technetmag/issues/2005/01/hackerbasher/default.aspx*.

A virtual directory is a folder that is not a subfolder of the home directory, but is configured so that it can be addressed using a folder name. The virtual directory can be a physical directory on the web server, or in a Uniform Naming Convention (UNC) addressable location. Figure 12-5 provides an example of a virtual directory. In the figure, the home directory of the peaceweaver.com web site is the file folder *peaceweaver* on drive F of the server. Another folder on the same server, the p-catalog folder, represents a virtual directory. When created, it was given an alias of products. Its content can be accessed using the *http://peaceweaver.com/products* address. You should use an *alias* (or assigned name) for the virtual directory because it hides the directory name and because it may make it easier to use. Ease of use might mean an alias that better fits the content, or an alias that is shorter than the directory name. In this case, virtual folders containing other catalogs for other web sites can be created and might use an abbreviated first-letter hyphenated catalog name. In addition to the *http://peaceweaver.com/products* address, another alias and its server address might be *http://somewebsitename.com/products*. You can use the same alias name for multiple virtual directories if they are located on different web sites. In this case, the alias for each can be *products*, since the complete address for each will include a different web site.

To create a virtual directory, you should first create the folder in the NTFS filesystem on a disk volume other than the system volume. This improves security and performance.

To create a virtual directory using IIS Manager, begin by opening the IIS Manager console. Expand the *Web sites* folder and expand the web site to which a virtual folder will be added. Right-click the web site or folder. Select New, then click Virtual Directory, and then click Next. Enter a name for the virtual directory in the Alias box, as shown in Figure 12-6, and then click Next.

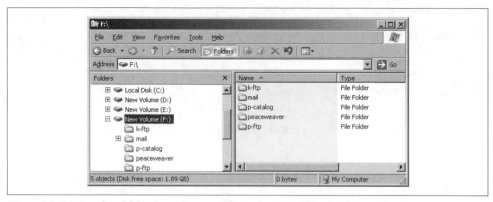

Figure 12-5. Note that folders must be created prior to virtual directory creation

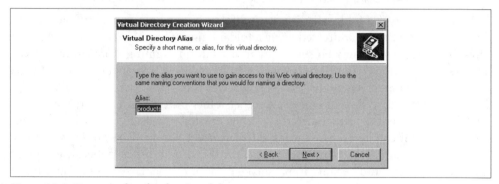

Figure 12-6. Enter an alias for the virtual directory

Enter (or Browse to) the path of the physical directory to be used and then click Next. Select the checkboxes for the access permission to assign for users and then click Next followed by Finish. (The permissions mentioned here and in the next paragraph are the web permissions explained in the next section, "Managing IIS Permissions.")

To create a virtual directory using Windows Explorer, begin by opening Windows Explorer. Right-click the folder to be used by the virtual directory and click Properties. Click the Web Sharing tab. Click "Share this folder." In the Edit Alias box, enter the name for the virtual directory. Select the checkboxes under Access Permissions for the types of access to grant. Click OK twice.

Managing IIS Permissions

Permissions should be set both at the file level, using NTFS and at the web server level using IIS *web permissions*. Don't confuse web permissions with NTFS file permissions. One controls access through web connections, and the other provides control through filesystem access. Both permission sets do impact web access, but only file permissions affect local access. If NTFS permissions and IIS permissions conflict, the more restrictive permission applies. To set web permissions for a web site, right-click on the web site in Internet Information Services Manager and select Properties. Then select the Home Directory tab. The Home Directory tab also provides information on data location and application configuration, things that are not related to setting web permissions. To set permissions directly in the filesystem for a virtual directory, use the Web Sharing tab in Explorer, as described in the previous section. Figure 12-7 displays the Home Directory property page for a web site. Table 12-4 lists and describes IIS permissions. Note that during web site creation, it is possible to configure the web site to allow scripts to run. The "Scripts only" permission must be selected from the "Execute permissions" drop-down list in order to provide the appropriate permissions.

Figure 12-7. Configure permissions on the Home Directory page of the web site properties

Table 12-4. IIS 6.0 permissions

Permission	Description
Script Source Access	Users can access source files. Combined with the read permission, users can read files. Combined with the write permission, users can modify source files.
Read	View content and properties of directories and files. Required for static content. Can be removed for scripted content such as ASP content.
Write	Users can change content and properties of directories and files.
Directory browsing	Users can view file lists.
Log visits	A log entry for each visit is created.

Table 12-4. IIS 6.0 permissions (continued)

Permission	Description
Index this resource	The indexing services will be used to index the content.
Execute permissions	The three choices are None (no scripts or executables can run), Scripts only (only scripts can run), or Scripts and Executable (both can run).

Web permissions can also be set on virtual directories and on files in the same manner. If file properties are examined in IIS, the File tab is used (Figure 12-8) instead of the Home Directory tab shown in Figure 12-7. The File tab is located on the properties pages for each file. To configure these permissions, right-click the file in the details pane of the Internet Information Server Manager and select Properties. Since you are configuring permissions for a file and not a web site, the directory browsing permission is not present. Script or program execution and indexing a web site are also possible directory level permissions.

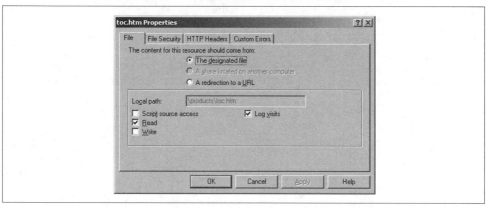

Figure 12-8. Configure file web permissions

Configuring User Authentication

There are several possible user authentication methods that are configurable for web sites and applications. These methods should be selected and configured based on the requirements of the applications that are supported. Authentication methods can be anonymous or require the use of individual user accounts. They can also require that user credentials be encrypted and thus protected from possible capture and reuse by unauthorized persons or software. Authentication choices may also be dependent upon the web browser used by the clients. To select and configure the right authentication method for a web site and application, all of these things must be considered. Table 12-5 lists and describes authentication methods that do provide some protection for user credentials.

Table 12-5. Authentication methods

Authentication method	Protection for credentials in transit	Requires as client	Protection for credentials stored on the server	Additional exceptions
Digest	Encrypts	Microsoft Internet Explorer 5.0 or later.	User passwords stored unencrypted in password store. Associated Application Pool identity must be LocalSystem.	Requires Active Directory on Windows 2000 or later. (No local accounts can be used.)
Advanced Digest	Encrypts	Microsoft Internet Explorer 5.0 or later.	No.	Requires Active Directory on Windows Server 2003. (No local accounts can be used.)
Integrated Windows	Encrypts	Microsoft Internet Explorer 2.0 or later; requires Microsoft clients.	No.	No.
Client Certificates	Entire session including credentials exchange can be encrypted	Client must support use of certificates.	No.	Requires public key infrastructure (PKI). Client certificates can be mapped to Active Directory accounts (Windows 2000 or later).
Microsoft .NET Passport	Encrypts	Microsoft Internet Explorer 4.0 or later, Netscape Navigator 4.0 or later.	No.	If account mapping is used, requires Active Directory. The .NET Passport authentication service must be licensed by the organization.

 An *application pool* is a structure that consists of URLs serviced by a common worker process(s). In IIS 6.0, each application pool is isolated from every other application pool.

In addition to these authentication methods, another authentication method that requires the use of user credentials is the *Basic authentication* method. Requiring *Secure Socket Layer* (SSL) connection can protect this method, which otherwise passes user credentials in the clear. When SSL is used, the entire session is encrypted including the credentials exchange. Using the combination of Basic authentication and SSL is often the best solution since it does not require a specific client, does not require Active Directory, and only requires that the server have an appropriate certificate and associated private key. Unlike client certificates, it is practical to implement SSL without a PKI as only one certificate is required.

> ## Digest Authentication in Windows 2000 Domains
>
> When an IIS 6.0 web server is joined in a Windows 2000 domain and digest authentication must be configured, subauthentication may need to be installed. Subauthentication is a component required for digest authentication in Windows 2000 domains, but not by Windows Server 2003 domains. It is not installed by default with IIS 6.0. To install subauthentication for IIS 6.0, enter the following command at the command prompt and then press Enter:
>
> ```
> rundll32 %systemroot%\system32\iissuba.dall, RegisterIISSUBA
> ```
>
> If application pools use Digest authentication, set the application pool identity to Local System.
>
> To unregister the subauthentication component, use the following command:
>
> ```
> rundll32 systemroot\syste32\iissuba.dll,UnregisterIISSUBA
> ```

To configure authentication, obtain any certificates and perform any server-side configuration for the authentication types that will be selected in IIS. Open the IIS Manager console. Right-click the site, directory or file to configure authentication for, and then click Properties. Click the Directory Security tab (click the File Security tab if you are configuring a file). Click Edit in the "Authentication and access control" section. To enable or disable anonymous authentication, click to select or deselect the "Enable anonymous access" checkbox. If anonymous authentication is enabled, enter or browse to the valid user account for anonymous access. To configure other authentication choices, click the checkbox in the "Authenticated access" box, as shown in Figure 12-9.

Configuring Web Site Properties

Web site configuration consists of adjusting a number of properties by using the IIS Manager, directly editing the metabase, or using scripts. While scripting may be a more efficient way to manage multiple web sites, using the IIS Manager is more efficient and less prone to error when managing a single site or when only occasional administration is required. The IIS Manager is opened from Start → Administrative Tools → Internet Information Server. The following administrative tasks are common ones that you should be familiar with:

- Configuring the IP address used for the server
- Configuring access by computer IP address, domain name, or subnet range for web sites, applications, or files
- Setting *Multipurpose Internet Mail Extensions* (MIME)
- Configuring NTFS permissions
- Configuring logging

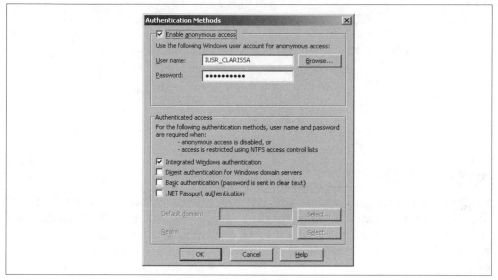

Figure 12-9. Configuring authentication

- Adding IIS components and services
- Enabling and configuring extensions

Configuring the IP address used for the server

To configure the IP address used for the server, open the IIS Manager console. Expand the local computer and right-click the web site to configure, and then select Properties. To configure the IP address assigned to a web site, click the Web Site tab and use the IP Address drop-down list box to select the IP address. Click OK.

Configuring access

To configure access by computer IP address, domain name, or subnet range for web sites, applications, or files, begin by opening the IIS Manager console. To configure IP address and domain name restrictions, click the Directory Security or File Security tab. Click the IP address and domain name section Edit button to display choices shown in Figure 12-10.

Select "Granted access" to explicitly deny an IP address subnet or domain access by using the "Except the following:" box. Select "Denied access" to explicitly grant an IP address subnet or domain access by using the "Except the following:" box.

To add a single computer as an exception, click Add and then click "Single computer." Click "DNS lookup" to search for computers or domains by name rather than by IP address. Enter the DNS name for the computer. To add a subnet of computers to the exception list, use the "Group of computers" selection instead of the "Single computer" selection, and then add the Network ID and "Subnet mask" box

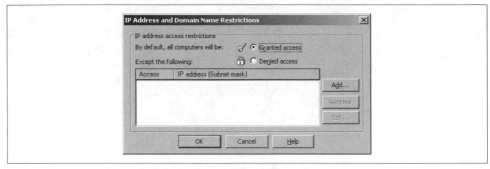

Figure 12-10. Configure IP address/domain name restrictions

to specify a subnet. To grant or deny access to a domain, use the "Domain name" box. Note that if exceptions are managed by IP address, changing the IP address of a computer will mean that the exception no longer applies.

Setting MIME

Setting MIME is important because IIS will only recognize those file types that you've defined. Remove those MIME types not used to avoid possible exploits coded using them. Add new types as necessary to accommodate application requirements. MIME types can also be edited to create a better description or to correct the extension.

To change MIME types, begin by opening the IIS Manager console. Right-click on the local computer and select Properties. Click the "MIME types" button to display the current list, as shown in Figure 12-11.

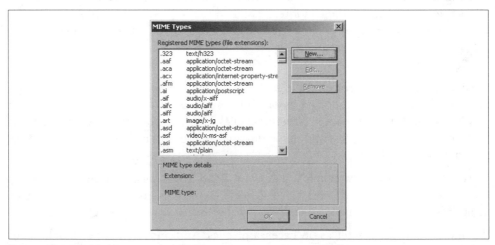

Figure 12-11. Add, delete, or edit MIME types

To add a MIME type, click New and then enter a file extension and description. Then click OK. To remove a MIME type, select a MIME type from the "Registered

MIME types (file extensions)" list and then click Remove. Click OK three times to exit.

Configuring NTFS permissions

NTFS permissions can be configured on the filesystem and directly on the web site or file. To configure NTFS permissions from IIS Manager, begin by opening the IIS Manager console. Right-click the web site or file, and then click Permissions. Use the object picker to add usernames or groups. Select the username or group and click the appropriate permission. To remove permissions, select the username or group and reconfigure.

NTFS permissions granted directly on an object override permissions granted via inheritance. For example, an explicit Allow assigned on a file in a *Web site* folder will override a Deny permission on the *Web site* folder.

Configuring logging

Logging at the web site level is enabled by default. To configure logging, begin by opening the IIS Manager console. Expand the local computer ikon, then expand the *Web Sites* or *FTP Sites* directory, and then right-click on the web or FTP site to enable logging. Click Properties. To enable logging for a virtual directory, right-click the virtual directory and click Properties. Click the "Enable logging" checkbox. Select a log file format. Table 12-6 defines the log file formats.

Table 12-6. Log file formats

File format	Description
W3C Extended log file format	Text-based, and customizable for a single site (the default).
National Center for Supercomputing Application (NCSA) Common log file format	Text-based and fixed format for a single site.
IIS log file format	Text-based, and fixed format for a single site.
ODBC logging	Fixed format for a single site. Data can be stored in an ODBC-compliant database (such as SQL Server).
Centralized binary logging	Binary-based, unformatted data. Not customizable. Data can be collected in a central location and can combine data from multiple web sites. A special parser is required to read the logs.
HTTP.sys error logging	Fixed format for *HTTP.sys*-generated errors.
UTF-8 Format	To read text-based (W3C extended, IIS, and NCSA Common) log files in languages other than English, enable UTF-8. (UTF-8 is configured by checking the "Encode Web logs in UTF-8" checkbox in the local computer properties.)

Logs are stored by default at the *%systemroot%\system32\logfiles* folder. Click the Properties button to configure a different log location, or schedule the frequency of log creation, as shown in Figure 12-12.

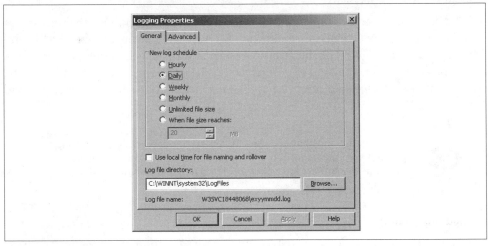

Figure 12-12. Configure log files

Use the Advanced tab shown in Figure 12-13 to modify the information that is collected in the log (if the format is W3C).

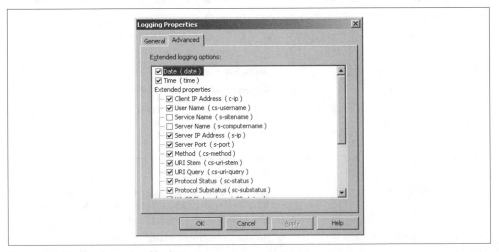

Figure 12-13. Configure log file data

Click OK twice.

When changing the log file location, configure NTFS security to match that of the default. The default file security is Administrators and SYSTEM Full Control. No user access is configured (nor is it required).

Adding IIS components and services

If new uses for the web server require additional IIS components, services, and extensions, they can be easily installed and configured. To add IIS components and services, select Control Panel → Add or Remote Programs → Add/Remove Windows Components. Click Application Server and then click Details. Click Internet Information Services (IIS) and then click Details. Enable or disable the IIS component and service by selecting the checkbox or clearing it to remove the component or service.

Enabling and configuring extensions

To enable extensions, open the IIS Manager console. Expand the local computer and click Web Service Extensions, as shown in Figure 12-14.

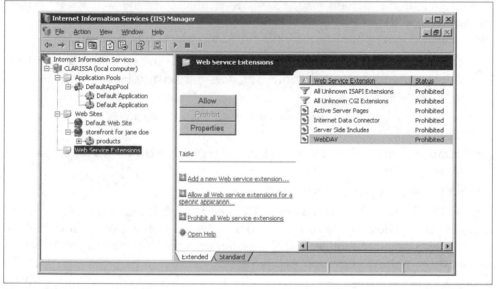

Figure 12-14. Allow or prohibit extensions

In the Details pane on the right of the screen, select a web service extension to disable or enable it. Click Allow to enable the extensions, or click Prohibit to disable the extension.

If an HTTP request handler (a programmed module created to respond to HTTP requests such as requests for URLs or URL extensions within an application) is not in the list of web service extensions, you must register it by adding the HTTP request handler to the list of web service extensions. To do so, open the IIS Manager console and select the desired web service extensions. In the details pane on the right of the screen, click "Add a new web service extension" and then click Add. Enter or browse to the extension's path. If desired, click the "Set extension status to Allowed" checkbox. Click OK.

To allow an application to call a web service extension, open the IIS Manager console. Expand the local computer and click Web Service Extensions. In the details pane on the right of the screen, click "Allow all web service extensions for a specific application." Select the name of the application from the Application list box.

To prohibit all web service extensions, open the IIS Manager console. Expand the local computer and click Web Service Extensions. Click "Prohibit all Web service extensions" and click Yes.

Reviewing Web Server Security

You should review web server security prior to placing a web server in production. Periodic review of a production web server should also be done. The security review should include the location for the web server, the server and web server security hardening, and the security policy (written rules) and posture (actual practice) of the organization. Security hardening for IIS should include the following:

- Enable only essential MIME types. Attacks often leverage a vulnerability related to a specific file type. If that file type does not need to be stored on the web server, disable it.

- Create root level directories for each web site and create subfolders for each application.

- Install web site applications in folders and set NTFS permissions for appropriate access.

- Set IIS web site permissions.

- Set IP address and domain name restrictions to explicitly grant or deny access to web sites where this makes sense (for example, granting only those internal domains or subnets allowed access to intranet sites). Restrictions can be set for an entire web site or per application.

- Configure web sites and application for *isolation*. Isolation is configured by assigning separate resources, anonymous accounts, and permissions to web sites, and by assigning applications to application pools. Configuring isolation can prevent a poorly behaving application from having an affect on other web sites and applications, and can make it more difficult for security incidents affecting one application or web site from spreading to others.

- Configure appropriate user authentication and secure user credentials during transport.

- Configure SSL to encrypt confidential data transported between web server and clients, and between web server and SQL servers (if a SQL Server database is part of a web application).

- Use IPSec or VPN for remote administration.

- Ensure that the server, web server, and applications are kept up-to-date and patched.
- Enable file access auditing for web site content.
- Configure IIS logging and logs.

Editing the Metabase

When the IIS Manager console is used to configure IIS, changes are written to the IIS metabase, an XML file that represents IIS configuration. In addition to IIS Manager–based changes, some configuration steps are only done by directly editing the metabase file. An IIS administrator should become familiar with the metabase file and comfortable enough to work with it as necessary. However, caution should be used, since improper changes to the file can make the web server, a web site, or an application inoperable.

> An excellent text for learning metabase properties and usage is the *Working with the Metabase* chapter of the *IIS 6.0 Technical Reference*, which is online at *http://www.microsoft.com/resources/documentation/ IIS/6/all/techref/en-us/iisRG_MET_29.mspx.*

In addition to the metabase file, *metabase.xml*, predefined information properties for the metabase are described in the *metabase schema file, MBSSchema.xml*. Both files are located at *%systemroot%\system32\inetserv* and can be edited by using a text editor. If necessary, the metabase can be edited while IIS is running by enabling the edit-while-running feature described next. After the edit is complete, and the file is saved, the properties will be replaced in the in-memory metabase. IIS maintains a history of changes made to the metabase file and saved to disk. Metabase history files are saved using the HistoryMajorVersionNumber property of the metabase file. Files are saved in the *systemroot\system32\inetsrv\history* folder.

To enable the edit-while-running option, begin by opening the IIS Manager console. Right-click the local computer and select Properties, as shown in Figure 12-15.

Select Enable Direct Metabase Edit checkbox. Click OK.

The metabase can be backed up by using the IIS Manager or the command-line script *issback.vbs*, which is located in the *%systemroot%\System32* directory. Two types of backup can be created: a *portable backup* that can be restored to another server, and a *nonportable backup* that can only be restored to the same server. The type of backup created depends on whether a password or the machine keys are used to encrypt secure metabase properties.

To create a backup, begin by opening the IIS Manager console. Right-click the local computer and select All Tasks, then select Backup/Restore Configuration. Click Create Backup. Enter a name for the backup file. To make the backup portable, select

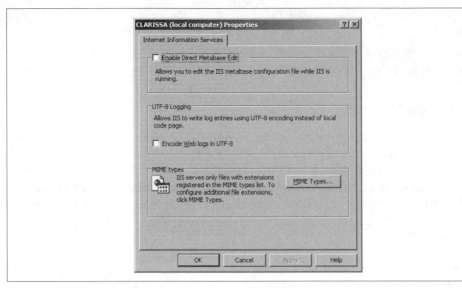

Figure 12-15. Configure direct metabase edit

the "Encrypt backup using password" checkbox and enter a password in both the Password box and the "Confirm password" box. Click OK and then click Close. A copy of the metabase is created in the *%systemroot%\System32\inetsrv\MetaBack* folder.

To restore the backup, begin by opening the IIS Manager console. Right-click the local computer and select All Tasks, then select Backup/Restore. Click the version of the Automatic Backup file to use in the restore and click Restore. If prompted for a password, enter the password used when creating the backup.

Using IIS Backup and Recovery

Although backing up the metabase is important, a complete backup of the web server should also be performed regularly. A complete backup includes the backup of all the web sites, applications, and data stored on the web server. It also includes a backup of the System State and of the boot and system volumes, as well as the metabase. In addition to a regular backup, a complete web server backup should be performed before migration, before allowing client access to a newly created web site or application, or before changing configuration settings on an existing web server. Backup files can be saved to hard disk, or other removable or nonremovable media. ntbackup.exe and third-party backup programs can be used.

To back up using *ntbackup.exe*, click Start → All Programs → Accessories → System Tools → Backup. Click Advanced Mode. Click the Backup tab. Select the System State checkbox on the left side of the screen, as shown in Figure 12-16, then select the boot and system volume.

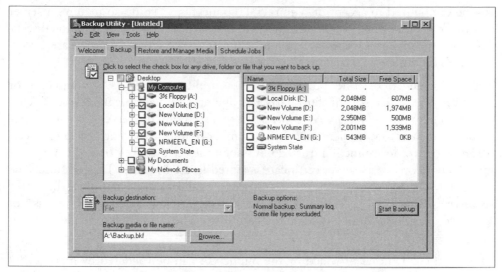

Figure 12-16. Backup the System State and other critical server and web server files

Select web server data, including the backup destination type and media or file-name. Select the file or tape location in the "Backup destination" drop-down box. Enter a file path or select the tape to use, respectively, in the "Backup media or file name" text box. Click Tools and then click Options and complete options such as backup type and log file type. Then click OK. Use the Advanced button to set such advanced backup options as data verification or hardware compression. Then click OK. When you have selected all the appropriate options, click Start Backup.

To restore using *ntbackup.exe*, click Start → All Programs → Accessories → System Tools → Backup. Click the Advanced Mode. Click Restore and Manage Media and then expand the media item that contains the backup. Select the System State box for that file. Select other data to restore. Click "Original location" if backups should be placed in the same folder or folders as they were when backed up. Or, click "Alternate location" and designate a folder. The folder structure of the backup will be preserved. Click the Tools menu and then click Options. Click the Restore tab and then select either "Do not replace the file on my computer to retain files remaining on the disk" (these files may be more recent versions) or "Replace the file on disk only if the file on disk is older," or check "Always replace the file on my computer." Click OK. Click Start Restore. Use the Advanced button for other options such as restoring security settings.

Configuring SSL

SSL is a method that can provide clients with a way to authenticate the server they are connected to. Authenticating the server means to verify that it is who it says it is; SSL provides encryption of the communications between client and server. Web sites can be configured to accept or require SSL connections. To do so requires a server certificate. The use of client certificates is optional, but can provide additional security since the clients are then able to authenticate to the server. In most cases, however, SSL is configured to require a *server certificate* only.

The certificate can be either purchased from a public *Certification Authority* (CA) or produced by a Microsoft or third-party CA operated by your organization. When a browser client is used for an SSL connection to a web site, the server presents its certificate and the browser client performs a number of tests, including checking its certificate store to determine if a trusted CA issued the certificate. A *trusted CA* is a CA for which a copy of its server certificate is stored in the browsers Trusted store. The public key stored in the certificate can be used to validate the signature of the issued server certificate signed by the associated CA private key. If the certificate is not available, the client cannot validate the certificate. The client then provides a warning to the user.

Because the certificate provided by the public CA can be validated by most (if not all) browser clients, it is better to obtain an SSL certificate from a public CA for e-commerce and for other sites that expect connections from the public. Privately produced SSL certificates may better serve private, or intranet sites. To facilitate their use, clients will need a copy of the CA certificate to be able to validate the server certificate.

To configure IIS 6.0 to use SSL, you generally must do the following:

- Request a certificate from a CA
- Install the certificate
- Configure the web site to require SSL
- Back up or restore a certificate

Requesting a certificate

To request a SSL certificate, begin by opening the IIS Manager console. Right-click on the web site the that certificate will be used in and select Properties. Select the Directory Security page and then click the Server Certificate button in the Secure Communications section and then click Next. Click Create a New Certificate (as shown in Figure 12-17) and then click Next.

Click "Prepare the request now," but send it later, as shown in Figure 12-18. Then click Next.

Enter a name for the certificate. Change the key strength, if required, by entering the information on this page and then click Next. *Key strength* (or length) is important because, in general, the longer the key, the more secure the communication. However, longer keys can mean slower communications, and more expense if certificates

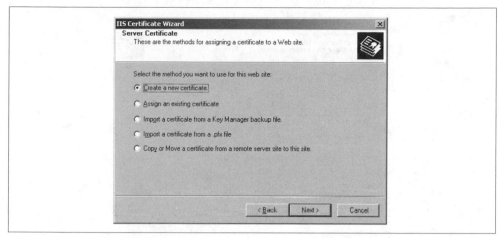

Figure 12-17. Create a certificate request

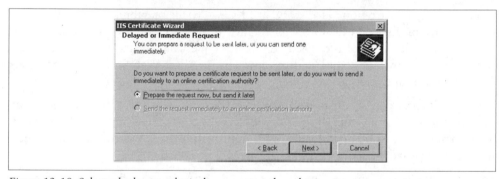

Figure 12-18. Select whether to submit the request or do so later

are purchased. Enter the organization name and department name ("Organizational unit"), as shown in Figure 12-19. Click Next.

Enter the common name and then click Next. This should be the fully qualified domain name (FQDN) for the web server domain if the server will be on the Internet, but can be the server NetBIOS name if the web server will be on the intranet. Enter city, state, and country information, and then click Next. Browse to a location to save the certificate file and click OK. The file is saved as a text file and given a *.cer* extension.

The certificate request must be submitted to a CA to receive a certificate. When using a public CA, follow the instructions provided by the CA. If you are using a non-Microsoft CA, follow the CA instructions. If you are using a Microsoft CA, copy the certificate text file produced in the previous steps to the CA, and use these instructions.

At the CA, browse to the CA's web site (for example, *http://localhost/crtsrv*). Click Request a Certificate. Click Advanced Certificate Request. Click "Submit a certificate

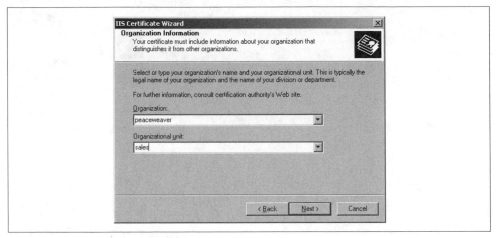

Figure 12-19. Add organization information

request using a base 64 Encoded CMC or PKCS # 10 file or submit a renewal request using a base 64 Encoded PCKS #7 file." Click Browse to look for a file to insert and browse to the location of the saved certificate request file created earlier in this section. Use the certificate template drop-down list to select Web Server and then click Submit to submit the request.

If the certificate request must be approved, a warning will appear, indicating that an administrator with appropriate permissions on the CA must approve the request. The certificate must be downloaded after approval. If the CA is configured to automatically approve the request, the certificate will be issued.

Select "Download certificate" and browse to a location to store the certificate file.

Installing the certificate

After the certificate file is obtained, you must return it to the web server for installation. Open the IIS Manager console. Right-click on "Web site" and select Properties. Select the Directory Security page and click Server Certificate. Click "Process the pending request and install the certificate," as shown in Figure 12-20, and then click Next.

Browse to the certificate file. Specify the SSL port to use or accept the default of 443 and then click Next followed by Finish.

Configuring the web site to require SSL

Once the certificate is installed, it can be used to create an HTTPS connection to the web server. However, HTTP connections will still be allowed unless the web server is configured to require an SSL connection. To require an SSL connection return to the

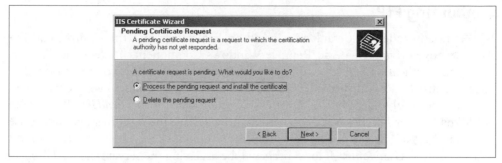

Figure 12-20. Install the certificate from a file

Directory Security property page (as explained previously), click Edit, and select Require Secure Channel (SSL).

Backing up and restoring certificates

SSL certificates should be backed up. This makes them available for a restore when the web server must be moved to another server. The backing up of certificates is referred to as *exporting* them. Likewise, they can be restored to a server via an *import* operation.

To back up the SSL certificate, begin by opening an empty MMC console. Select the File menu and then click Add/Remove Snapins. Click Add and then select the Certificates snap-in. When prompted, select Local Computer and then click OK to return to the MMC console. You should use the File → Save As menu function and save the console for later use. In the console, expand the stores and then select the Personal store. In the detail pane on the right side of the screen, right-click the certificate to export and click All Tasks and then click Export. Click "Export private key." Click Next. Do not select "Delete the private key if export is successful." Enter the filename. Click Finish.

When a certificate is purchased, or requested via a local CA, the certificate is often delivered via the network and installed directly to the certificate store via the IIS Manager. This also assigns the certificate for use in SSL. Alternatively, a certificate file can be used to install a certificate on the web server. If the certificate is damaged, or if it is accidentally deleted from the server, it can be replaced in the certificate store by using the import function as we'll discuss next.

To add a certificate to the certificate store, open the certificates snap-in in an MMC console. Right-click on the Personal store and select All Tasks and then select Import. Click Next. Enter the name of the file or browse to it. Enter the password for the file. Click Next. The certificate will be installed. Click OK if a pop-up window confirms this. Close the console.

Configuring FTP

FTP is not installed by default. To install an FTP server, use the Control Panel → Add/Remove Programs → Add/Remove Windows Components applet. The FTP service is an Application Server component. To configure the server, you must provide a root level file folder and subfolders for FTP content. If *user isolation* will be used, you must create a subfolder entitled *LocalUser*, a subfolder called *LocalUser\Public*, and subfolders under *LocalUser* for every user who will have the right to store and/or use files on the FTP server. The user subfolders should be of the form *<FTProot>\ <LocalUser>\<UserName>* if local users will be accessing the server, and *<FTProot>\ <DomainName>\<UserName>* if Active Directory user accounts will be used.

In our discussion on configuring FTP, we will look at the following tasks:

- Create FTP sites and select a user isolation mode (if required)
- Configure FTP authentication

Creating an FTP site

To create an FTP site, begin by opening the IIS Manager console. Right-click on the local computer and select New, then "Create an FTP site." Enter a name for the site and then click Next. Select an IP address and port number to be used, and then click Next. Every FTP site on the same server must have a unique IP address or port. Select FTP isolation mode required and then click Next. In Figure 12-21, the user isolation mode is selected. The default is no isolation. Table 12-7 describes the FTP user isolation modes.

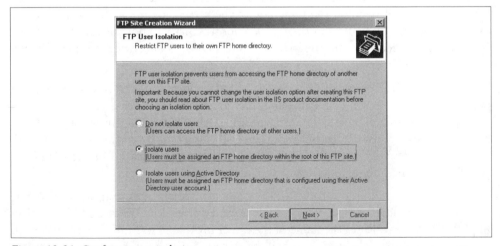

Figure 12-21. Configure user isolation

Table 12-7. User isolation modes

Isolation mode	Description
Do not isolate users	Users may gain access to the home directory of other users.
Isolate users	Each user has his or her own directory. To the users, it looks like the FTP root.
Isolate users using Active Directory	The FTP service is integrated with Active Directory to retrieve home directory information for users. The Active Directory user object is extended with properties to hold the FTP root (the FTP share) and FTP directory (the relative path to the user's home directory). A script (*%systemroot%\system32\iisftp.vbs*) can be used to get and set the properties.

Configure access permissions, as shown in Figure 12-22, and then click Next. Click Finish.

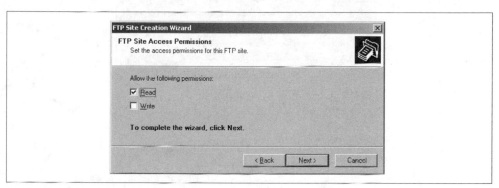

Figure 12-22. Configure access permissions

Configuring FTP authentication

You must configure authentication for FTP separately from authentication for HTTP. FTP authentication is either anonymous FTP or basic FTP. *Anonymous FTP authentication* requires no user credentials, while *basic FTP authentication* requires a username and password. Unfortunately, basic FTP authentication sends credentials in plain text.

To configure FTP authentication, open the IIS Manager console and select "FTP sites." In the detail pane on the right side of the screen as shown in Figure 12-23, right-click the FTP site, directory, virtual directory, or file to configure. Then select Properties.

Click the Security Accounts tab. To allow anonymous connections, select the "Allow anonymous connections" checkbox as shown in Figure 12-24. Enter the username and password for the anonymous logon username.

To enable basic FTP Authentication, clear the "Allow anonymous connections" checkbox. Click OK.

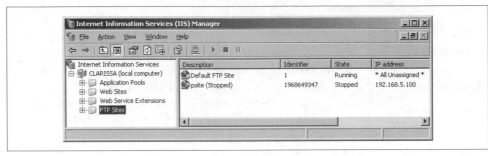

Figure 12-23. Locate the site

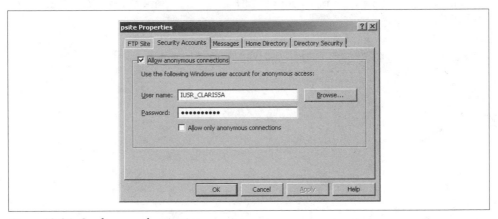

Figure 12-24. Configure authentication

Setting up an FTP site concludes the discussion on basic administration tasks for IIS. You should now feel comfortable creating web sites, configuring authentication and permissions, as well as configuring SSL and creating virtual directories. There are other operations that you may be required to perform. One of the lesser known is configuring IIS mail services. While this process can be quite complex, you should know a little bit about the IIS mail services that are available.

IIS Mail Services

Using and configuring mail services (SMTP, POP3, NNTP) is a complex task and is beyond the scope of this book. However, basic SMTP services may be required for many web-based applications and can be used by other Windows operations such as SMTP-based Active Directory replication (as described in Chapter 13). Some introductory information is, therefore, included here.

When SMTP is added to IIS, a filesystem location for the *mailroot* must be specified. The *mailroot* is the parent directory for all subfolders required by the email system. Each SMTP virtual server can have a different mailroot. Table 12-8 lists and describes the subfolders under *mailroot*.

Table 12-8. mailroot folders

Folder name	Description	Monitor
Badmail	This stores undeliverable messages that cannot be returned to sender.	Monitor the *Badmail* folder and use the error messages associated with bad mail to help diagnose the problem.
Drop	This stores all incoming messages addressed to recipients located on the server. If POP3 is configured, the message bypasses the *Drop* folder and is placed in the appropriate mailbox store.	Read messages here and forward as necessary, or delete.
Mailbox	This stores mailboxes for POP3 users. Each domain is configured as a separate folder. Email messages are stored in mailbox folders as flat files.	N/A
Pickup	Any mail placed here is picked up by the SMTP service and transferred to the *Queue* folder. An application or an administrator can place mail in this folder.	Messages should pass through this folder quickly. If they remain here, something is wrong. They may be corrupt, or there may be a problem with the SMTP service. If no mail is being processed, check the permission settings on the folder to ensure that the SMTP service can read its contents.
Queue	This holds messages ready for processing and delivery.	Monitor this folder to ensure that mail is flowing. Problems may be related to network connections.
Route	This is used when a route domain for an SMTP virtual server is configured.	Monitor to ensure that mail is flowing.
SortTemp	This is a temporary sorting area for messages.	Temp files are placed here and cleared when messages are sorted for delivery.

Mail messages are processed by SMTP if they are either received by the SMTP service, or placed in the *Pickup* folder. Messages are then placed in the *Queue* folder to await processing. If POP3 is not configured and the mail is for a local recipient (that is, a recipient with an email domain serviced locally by SMTP), the message is moved to the *Drop* folder. If POP 3 is configured, the message is moved to the appropriate mailbox store. If a message is for a remote recipient (that is, a recipient with an email domain that is not serviced locally), messages are sorted by domain so that SMTP can deliver the message to the recipients as a group. After sorting, the mail is queued for delivery. If messages cannot be delivered, they are marked as nondeliverable, a nondelivery report is generated, and an attempt is made to deliver this to the original message sender.

With this brief background, we can now look at three important tasks:

- Configuring email services
- Using a mail gateway with the SMTP virtual server
- Monitoring SMTP

Configuring Email Services

The SMTP service is not installed by default, but can be installed by using the Add Windows Components program. The SMTP service is an Application Server component. However, the POP3 service must be installed from the E-mail Services section of Windows Components. When SMTP is installed, a default SMTP virtual server is created. The default virtual server is set to monitor the default domain. To set additional virtual SMTP servers to monitor additional domains create a new virtual SMTP server:

If a new IP address will be used by the SMTP service, configure the IP address before creating the virtual server. Create a folder to hold SMTP folders and files. When the new SMTP virtual server is created, the folders identified in Table 12-8 will be created.

Open the IIS Manager console. Right-click the computer and select SMTP Virtual Server. Enter a name for the web site. Use the IP drop-down list to select an available IP address. Choose All Unasssigned to allow SMTP to respond on all unassigned IP addresses configured on the server. Each SMTP server must have a unique IP address or port. Click Next. Enter the path to the directory to be used for the mail root. Specify the default domain for the virtual server. Click Finish.

To stop, start, and pause SMTP, begin by opening the IIS Manager console. Select the local computer. Right-click the virtual server and click Stop to stop the server, or Pause to pause it. To restart a paused server, click Pause again. To start a stopped server, click Start.

 When SMTP is stopped, all SMTP virtual servers are stopped. When SMTP is paused, no new connections can be made, but existing connections are not dropped.

To stop and start POP3, select Start → All Programs → Administrative Tools. Click POP3. Right-click the computer icon and select Connect. On the resulting shortcuts menu, choose All Tasks and then choose to stop, start, or pause the service.

To configure an SMTP virtual server, begin by opening the IIS Manager console. Right-click on the SMTP virtual server and select Properties. To change the IP address used, use the "IP address" drop-down list. To change the port, click the Advanced button. Select the IP address to configure and click Edit. Enter a new port number and click OK. The Advanced tab can be used to add multiple IP addresses and multiple ports on which the SMTP server can listen.

Using a Mail Gateway with the SMTP Virtual Server

By default, the SMTP service is configured not to relay mail. This is important, since it prevents the SMTP server from being used to distribute spam. Unfortunately, it also prevents the SMTP service from forwarding mail to a mail gateway. You can configure the SMTP service to relay mail to and from a specific mail server used as a mail gateway. To do so, create a remote domain that represents the mail gateway, and configure the remote domain and the local SMTP virtual server to relay mail.

Begin by opening the IIS Manager console. Expand the virtual SMTP server entry and select Domain to see the default domain, as shown in Figure 12-25.

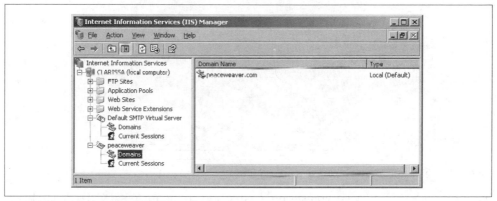

Figure 12-25. Domains can be local, as is the default domain here, or remote

Right-click a domain and click New. Then select Domain. Select Remote as the domain type and then click Next. Enter the domain address space (that is, the DNS domain name of the remote domain). Click Finish.

In the IIS Manager console, select the SMTP virtual server Domain node and right-click the remote domain entry. Select Properties. On the General page, set the properties for routing and securing message delivery. Click "Allow incoming mail to be relayed to this domain," as shown in Figure 12-26. Click OK.

Monitoring SMTP

Monitoring SMTP entails more than checking to see that the service is running. Logging should be configured, logs reviewed, and the mail folder should be monitored, as described in Table 12-6. User sessions can also be monitored and disconnected if necessary.

A user session starts when a user connects to a virtual server. User sessions are tracked separately and can be manually disconnected. To do so, begin by opening the IIS Manager console. Double-click the virtual SMTP server. Select the "Current sessions" node for the server. In the detail pane on the right of the screen, right-click the session and select Terminate. To disconnect all users, right-click in the detail pane and select "Terminate all."

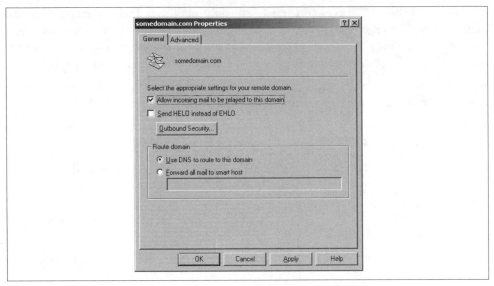

Figure 12-26. Configure mail relay to a mail gateway

To monitor SMTP activity, you should enable and configure logging. To do so, begin by opening the IIS Manager console. Right-click the virtual SMTP server and select Properties. To enable logging, check the "Enable logging" box. To change the logging file format, use the "Active log format" box.

This brief introduction to mail services in IIS is not meant to make you an SMTP expert, but rather to give you a glimpse into what's available should you want to provide such services for IIS applications. The main purpose of IIS is, of course, as a basis for web applications. Web applications should be written by those who understand not just web server administration, but how to translate application requirements into production quality applications that fulfill them. Application authors are responsible for detailing which IIS services and extensions are required. As an administrator, you should understand how to install and run IIS applications as described next.

Installing and Running IIS Applications

The methods used to deploy and run IIS-based applications will vary depending on the application. Some applications will include provisioning scripts or installation packages that install and configure virtual directories and enable components as necessary. Others will require a substantial amount of preparation and configuration.

Windows Server 2003 server and IIS may also need to be configured to accommodate the applications that will run on them. For example, if an *asp.net* application does not have an installation script, the following steps must be taken:

- If necessary, install and/or enable Windows Server 2003 services and components.
- If necessary, install, enable and/or configure IIS services, components, and attributes (such as the IIS process isolation mode).
- Create the web site and virtual directories for each *asp.net* application.
- If necessary, create and configure an application pool.
- Assign the application to an application pool.
- Copy the *asp.net* application content to the web server.
- If session state should be retained, configure IIS to use the *asp.net* application session state method.
- If out-of-process session state is retained, enable common storage for the *asp.net* session state. Out-of-process session state data can be managed by the *asp.net* state service or by the SQL server.
- If necessary, configure encryption and validation keys used to protect session state data. Session state data is only accessible from the web server that created the data. To accommodate the use of multiple web servers as used in a web farm, all web servers in the farm must be configured to use the same encryption and validation keys in order to share session state data. Keys are stored in the *<machine key>* section of the metabase.
- Configure *asp.net* to use session state.
- If necessary, configure impersonation, (the ability for an application to use the identity of a user.)
- Secure the *asp.net* session state connection string.
- Ensure security and availability of the application.
- Verify that the *asp.net* application was deployed successfully by examining the System log on the web server. IIS 6.0 creates events in the System log if a web site fails to start.
- Back up the web server.
- Enable client access to the *asp.net* application. This includes creating DNS entries for the *asp.net* application and placing the server on the network.
- Monitor client traffic to see that clients are accessing the application.
- Establish a monitoring period (perhaps a few hours a day) to check response times.

Now that you understand the general process involved with installing and running IIS applications, let's take a look at some key areas that deserve special attention:

- Determining session state requirements
- Using web site and application isolation
- Choosing a process isolation mode
- Managing application pools and worker processes

Determining Session State Requirements

Session state data is per-user and per-application data that can be retrieved across multiple requests. The data is typically cached by the application and is the total of the data generated by the user during one connection to the server. Session state data is independent of other sessions and does not survive the user session. Session state is also not part of the HTTP protocol, but rather is an abstraction layer built by the server-side environment (such as our *asp.net* example). The data is stored in components called *providers*. The example *asp.net* application can use three different providers: InProc (or in-process storage, which means the data is kept by the worker process assigned to the application; a *worker process* is user-level code that is used to process requests), StateServer (an out-of-process store that is kept by a separate worker process), and SQLServer (an out-of-process store in a SQL server table). If an in-process provider is used, and the application is recycled, all session state data is lost. If an out-of-process provider is used and the application is recycled, the session state data is maintained.

Using Web Site and Application Isolation

Many web servers host multiple web sites and applications. For example, an Internet Service Provider (ISP) may host hundreds of web sites and applications for hundreds of organizations. Some web sites will require a dedicated server, but many will be hosted together with others on the same server. Organizations may also host several of their own unique web sites and want to make use of a single server. When multiple sites and applications are hosted on a single server, you should provide some isolation to ensure availability, improve performance, and enhance security. Isolation is the process by which web sites and applications are kept separated and prevented from having an impact on each other. This can be accomplished in a number of ways, including providing them their own disk or subdirectories, their own worker processes, and their own security context.

Isolation by disk and/or subdirectory

When applications or web sites are hosted on separate disks, it is harder for failure or compromise on the part of one of them to impact the other. If an application fails, uses up available disk space, or the disk itself fails, web sites and applications running on other disks are less likely to be impacted (and may not be impacted at all). If an application is compromised, it will be harder for others on separate disks to be compromised because it is harder to gain access to different disks. Permission settings can also be modified to prevent access and are less likely to be incorrectly set when different disks are involved. If unique subdirectories off the root are assigned instead, there is less protection, but still more protection than if not. Restricting root drive access to the local Administrators group will also make this operation more secure.

Isolation via unique worker processes

When applications are assigned to unique application pools they can be assigned unique worker processes. Because the worker processes are unique to the application pool, a poorly behaving application (or one that fails) has no impact on those assigned to other application pools and processes. As has already been described, a number of application pool configurations can also improve performance and availability. (We'll examine this approach later in this chapter.)

Security context and impersonation

The *security context* of a web application is the identity under which the application operates. This can be either the identity of the user who is accessing the web site (or its application), or the application pool identity that is used by the web site (and its applications). If anonymous access is allowed, then the security context may be the IUSR_name_of_server account or other account assigned to the web site for anonymous access. (*Anonymous access* of web sites and applications is done by a web site user who has no authenticated credentials. The anonymous account assigned to the web site still authenticates, and must be provided permissions to access resources on the server.) If basic (or Windows Integrated) authentication is configured, then the security context can be any user who has a valid account and is authorized to use the application and its resources. When the application pool identity is used, by default, this is the built-in Network Service account.

When multiple applications and web sites are hosted on one server, using the *application pool identity* to run the application can provide isolation of the applications regardless of the individual user accessing the server. However, since all application pools default to the Network Service account, if this account is compromised, then there is a potential for compromise of all applications, and/or the data they have access to. This can be prevented if a unique service account is created and assigned for each application pool.

Impersonation is the ability of a worker process to run under security credentials other than its *base identity*. A worker processes base identity is established by the application pool identity (which is the account assigned to the application pool, such as the default Network Service account).

Ordinarily, the worker process runs under this identity. However when a client request is processed, the authenticated users *token* (that is, a token associated with the identity of the client) is used for the duration of the request. Impersonation, therefore, determines the access a web application user has to resources on the server. The authenticated users token may be the anonymous account assigned to the web site (if anonymous access is allowed), or that of a specific Windows user account (if some other form of authentication is configured). Before a client request is served, the user's token is verified against the access control list (ACL) assigned to the resources the request is attempting to use.

> Impersonation is disabled for *asp.net* applications by default. All resource access is verified against the process token of the application worker process, regardless of what authentication methods are configured or used. If an *asp.net* application requires the use of impersonation, this must be configured.

Choosing a Process Isolation Mode

IIS 6.0 can run in two different application isolation modes: the *IIS 5.0 isolation mode* and the *IIS 6.0 worker process isolation mode*. Running applications in isolation mode provides better security and availability because application code can be separated from the web server code and from other applications. IIS 6.0 worker process isolation mode is superior to IIS 5.0 isolation mode because it runs all application code in an isolated environment without a performance penalty. IIS 5.0 isolation mode is available for backward compatibility with those applications that depend on its behavior.

All new installations of IIS 6.0 will default to worker process isolation mode, while all upgrades of IIS 5.0 to IIS 6.0 will default to IIS 5.0 isolation mode. To change from one mode to another, open the IIS Manager console. Right-click on the Web Sites node and select Properties. Select the Service tab. Change the checkbox of the "Run WWW service in IIS 5.0 isolation mode," as shown in Figure 12-27. (Enabling this box with a check runs IIS 50; clearing the box runs worker process isolation mode.) Click OK.

> IIS 6.0 cannot run in both modes on the same server.

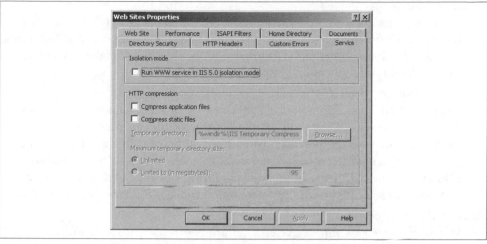

Figure 12-27. Change process isolation mode

Worker process isolation mode supports multiple application pools, each of which can have a different configuration. Worker process application mode provides the following improvements to performance, availability, and security:

Processor affinity
> Support for processor affinity (that is, when a process will always attempt to use the same processor). For worker processes it means that worker processes can take advantage of processor caching to improve performance. Instructions for setting processor affinity are in the article *Assigning Processor Affinity*, at *http.//www. microsoft.com/resources/documentation/IIS/6/all/techref/en-us/IISRG_WAS_35.mspx.*

Automatic shutdown of idle worker process and reclamation of unused resources
> Configures application pools to shut down idle processes. The processes will restart when requested. When idle processes are shut down, the resources they were using can be freed for use by other processes, thus making operation more efficient and improving the performance of heavily used processes. When a web site supports multiple applications or a web server supports multiple sites, this arrangement can mean improvements in scalability, or a reduction in the need for as many servers, or even the need for larger servers.

Web garden
> A *web garden* is an application pool with multiple worker processes available to service client connections. When multiple worker processes are used, more clients can be served with greater speed and efficiency.

Fault-tolerant request processing
> Assigning multiple worker processes to an application pool also means that, should one worker process fail, others are available to do the work.

Reduced restarts

Fewer restarts are required because many common operation tasks do not need the server or the web service to be restarted. Upgrading web sites and debugging web applications in one application pool probably will not make any impact on the availability of application or sites.

Health monitoring

Configure an application pool to monitor its health, including the health of worker processes servicing the application pool. IIS can determine when processes fail (or have the potential to fail) and automatically start a new process. Application requests can be queued until the new process is ready. Administrators can be notified of failures by configuring this tab. Old processes can be orphaned or separated from the pool for debugging, rather then simply ended.

Rapid-fail protection

If a web site enters into a cycle of failure and restart, it can consume system resources and cause availability problems for other sites and applications. Rapid-fail protection stops an application pool when too many of the worker processes assigned to an application pool are found unhealthy during a specific period of time.

Scheduled automatic restart

Applications with memory leaks, bad coding, or other problems must be rewritten. Meanwhile, keep them operational by scheduling automatic restarts.

Managing Application Pools and Worker Processes

When multiple applications and/or web sites will be hosted on a single server, the applications and web sites should be assigned to application pools and the applications pools should be configured. To do so requires thought as to the best assignment. It is not always the best choice to simply assign every application to its own application pool. Doing so may increase administration efforts and provide a diminishing return on performance and availability.

For best results, follow these steps:

1. Make a list of the web sites and applications that will be hosted on the server.
2. Group them by organization, if multiple organizations will be assigned to the server or business unit, or if all web sites and applications are the product of a single organization.
3. Split these groups by their need for the same user rights and resource access. These groups become candidates for unique application pools.
4. Remove from these groups any known problem applications (such as those that are poorly written, or those that have memory leaks). The problem applications may need their own application pool.

5. Isolate new applications temporarily into their own application pool until their behavior is known.

6. Create as many application pools as determined by Steps 3, 4, and 5.

7. Create a unique service account to be used for each application pool. This account is assigned as the application pool identity.

8. Add these accounts to the IIS_WPG group. This group has user rights and resource access required by most web sites and applications.

9. Assign additional rights and resource access to each new service account as appropriate. (Each application and web site may require access to specific resources. Do not assign these rights and accesses to all service accounts, but rather only to the one that will be used by the web site and application.)

10. Assign each service account to its specific application pool.

11. Assign web sites and applications to application pools.

Creating and configuring application pools

To create an application pool, begin by opening the IIS Manager console. Right-click "Application pools," select New, and then select Application Pool. Enter a name for the new application pool, as shown in Figure 12-28 and then click OK.

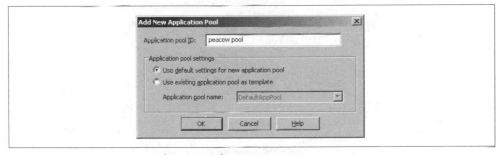

Figure 12-28. Create a new application pool

To assign a service account (that is, configure the identity) for an application pool, first expand the local computer in the Internet Information Services Manager and expand Application Pools. Right-click the application pool to configure and click Properties. Click the Identity tab, as shown in Figure 12-29. Click either Predefined (use a standard service account such as Network Service, Local Service, or Local System) or Configurable (use an account created).

Use the drop-down list box to select a Predefined account or use the "User name" and Password boxes in the Configurable section to enter the username and password of the account. Click OK.

To assign web sites and applications to an application pool, begin by opening the IIS Manager console. Right-click "Web site" and select Properties. Select the Home

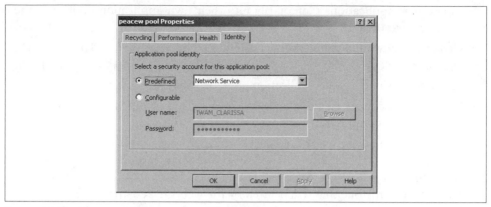

Figure 12-29. Assign an identity to the application pool

Directory tab. In the "Application pool" field, use the drop-down list to select the application pool, as shown in Figure 12-30.

Figure 12-30. Assign an application pool to a web site

Monitoring the health of application pools

There are many settings that can be used to detect Application Pool health, to keep applications running efficiently, and to improve performance.

IIS 6.0 supports application availability by detecting problems with worker processes and taking action based on the problem detected. The basic detection method is a ping, and the action taken is based on the worker process response. If the worker process doesn't respond, it is considered unavailable. The worker process may respond to the ping by requesting a recycle. Adjust the ping response time property (that is, the interval between pings to the worker process) to accommodate the specifics of applications and servers on the organization's network. The ping response time should not be set too short, as normally busy worker processes will take some time to respond; and a too short ping response time may cause a shutdown of a healthy worker process.

Worker process pinging is enabled by default. To manage worker process pinging, open the IIS manager console, right-click on the application pool, and select Properties. Click the Health tab. To modify worker process pinging, select the "Enable pinging" checkbox, as shown in Figure 12-31.

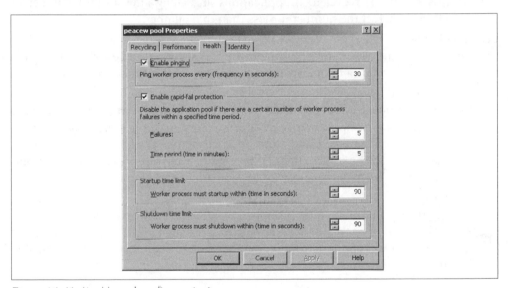

Figure 12-31. Enable and configure pinging

Enter the number of seconds before the worker process should be pinged. To configure rapid-fail protection, select "Enable rapid-fail protection" checkbox. *Rapid fail protection* disables the application pool if a selected number of failures occur within a selected number of minutes. This prevents a damaged application from continuing to needlessly consume resources. Enter the maximum number of failures allowed. Enter the "Time Period (in minutes)" during which the number of failures is counted. In the "Startup time limit" box, enter the time in seconds in which the Worker process must start up. In the "Shutdown time limit" field, enter the time (in seconds) to elapse before shutting down a failing worker process. Click OK.

Recycling worker processes

Misbehaving worker processes can be stopped and restarted. This process is often called *process recycling,* but is sometimes referred to as *application recycling.* Process recycling can be configured based on the following properties:

Elapsed time
> Specify the number of minutes after which the worker process should be recycled. If applications have problems running for long time periods, determine the maximum amount of time they can run and set the elapsed time for less than that time.

Number of requests
> Specify the number of HTTP requests that can be processed before the worker process should be recycled. If applications are failing after a given number of HTTP requests, set the number for less than that number.

Scheduled times
> Specify the time within a 24-hour period when a worker process should be recycled. This should be a frequency that prevents an application from failing.

Virtual memory
> Specify the amount of virtual memory the worker process can use before it must be recycled. When applications reserve memory multiple times, the memory heap becomes fragmented and there is a steady rise in the amount of virtual memory used. Start with less than 70 percent of available virtual memory, monitor the worker processes memory usage, and adjust this figure.

Used memory
> Specify the amount of memory used by the *W3wp.exe* process before the worker process should be recycled. If an application has memory leaks, the amount of memory used will continue to increase. Set to less than 60 percent of available memory.

On demand
> Specify that worker process recycling occurs via the use of the MMC console or a script that requests recycling of an application pool.

To immediately recycle the worker processes assigned to an application pool, expand the local computer node from the IIS Manager console and right-click the application pool. Then click Recycle. To configure a worker process to be recycled after a set elapsed time, right-click the application pool in the IIS Manager console and then click Properties. Select the Recycling tab, as shown in Figure 12-32.

Select the "Recycle worker processes (in minutes)" checkbox. Enter the number of minutes to elapse before the worker process is recycled. To configure the worker process to be recycled after a number of processing requests, select "Recycle worker process (number of requests)" and enter the number of requests to be processed before worker process recycling. To configure the worker process to be recycled at scheduled

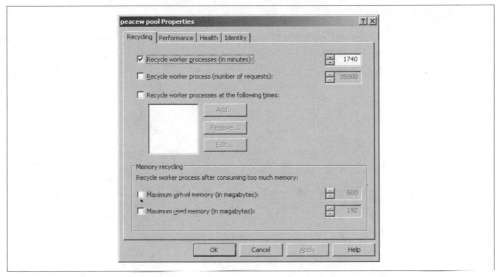

Figure 12-32. Configure recycling

times, select the "Recycle worker process at the following times" checkbox. Click Add to add a time to the list, Remove to delete a time, or Edit to change a time. To configure a worker process to be recycled after consuming a set amount of memory, select the "Maximum virtual memory (in megabytes)" checkbox. Enter the maximum amount of virtual memory allowed before the worker process is recycled. Memory consumption can also be limited by clicking the "Maximum used memory (in megabytes)" and entering the maximum amount of memory to be used before the process is recycled. Click OK to apply the changes.

Many of the application pool configurations will improve web server and application performance since they limit memory use, constrain or stop misbehaving applications and so on. Other performance settings are also available.

To configure application pool performance, begin by opening the IIS Manager console. Expand the local computer and right-click the application pool. Select the Performance tab, as shown in Figure 12-33.

In the Idle Timeout areas, select "Shutdown worker process after being idle for (time in minutes)" checkbox. Enter the number of minutes before the worker process will be recycled. To configure a request queue limit, select "Limit the kernel request queue (number of requests)" checkbox. Enter the maximum number of requests to allow in the request queue limit field. To configure CPU monitoring, select the "Enable CPU monitoring" checkbox. Enter the percent maximum CPU threshold in the "Maximum CPU use (percentage)" checkbox. Enter the number of minutes before the CPU usage numbers are refreshed in the "Refresh CPU usage numbers (in minutes)" field. Use the "Action performed when CPU usage exceeds maximum CPU use" drop-down box to select an action to take. To configure a web garden

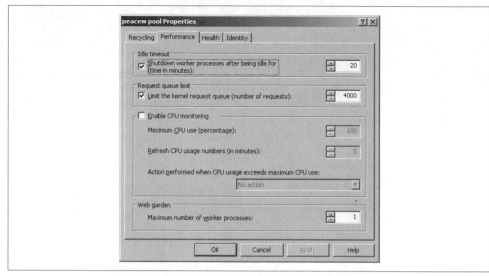

Figure 12-33. Configure performance

(that is, assign multiple worker processes), use the "Web garden maximum number of worker processes" text box and enter the number of worker processes to assign to the application pool. When you have finished configuring the performance, click OK.

Summary

IIS can be used as a simple static web server or a rich application server. The number of services and components that must be installed and configured will depend on the applications that it will host and the requirements that they have. IIS was designed to provide the web server administrator with flexible configuration capabilities and the ability to monitor server health and respond automatically to many conditions.

This chapter concludes the discussions of specific Windows Server 2003 networking services and how to administer them. However, there are several security components and properties of Windows Server 2003 on which these components rely. If you understand these security administration basics about Windows, it will go a long way toward empowering you to do the best administratively, no matter which network service you must administer. Chapter 13, therefore, describes basic Windows security philosophies, such as "the administrator is all powerful" and how permissions and rights are used. It also provides critical information on administrative delegation, certificate services, and EFS.

## CHAPTER 13

Network Security Administration

Security is an integral part of network administration. It's not something that should be bolted on afterward, but rather it needs to be built into any properly designed and managed network, much as we build in reliability, maintainability, and performance. To help in the fulfillment of this goal, this book weaves in the appropriate security information within all topics. However, it is also important that network administrators understand the overall *security framework* on which the continuity of the Windows network lies, and how that fits within the organization's information security management process. In addition, advanced networking configuration is often predicated by security needs.

This chapter explores the following areas:

- An organization's *security administration framework,* including the network administrator's role in establishing that framework.
- The underlying *Windows security posture,* including permissions and privileges, delegation of authority, role separation, centralized administration with Group Policy, and security templates.
- Configuring advanced network security features, including Encrypting File System (EFS) over Web Distributing, Authoring, and Versioning (WebDAV), Private Key Infrastructure (PKI), Server Message Block (SMB) integrity, Lightweight Directory Access Protocol (LDAP) security, and using SMTP for Active Directory (AD) replication.

Our discussion begins with a look at security administration framework.

Security Administration Framework

Security administration is separate and distinct from network administration. This does not mean that network administration has nothing to do with security, but rather that network administrators should not be setting *security policy.* Security administration concerns itself with the overall security of the organization, not just the security of information that happens to reside on (or be transported between) computers. An overall security policy forms the basis for what management determines should be done to provide a secure base for the organization's operations, its people, its products, and its information. This includes *physical security* and *information security*. In addition, information security is more than just securing computer and network systems. It concerns itself with information in any form, including phone conversations, printed documents, videos, handwritten notes, financial documents, meeting minutes, and so on. A security administration framework includes those people directly involved in security administration, the security policy, and associated documents, as well as the people who must implement and live by the security policy. The security policy is the document that specifies the organization's rules for security implementation. All employees must abide by the security policy.

The job of the network administrator is to fulfill that part of the security policy that concerns the networks and information systems he is responsible for. The network administrator may also influence security policy by being able to explain to management the potential threats to information (and information systems) and the mitigations that are possible.

For example, the security policy defines which communications should be protected and to what extent. If these communications take place over the network, the policy may or may not specify encryption, and may or may not specify the strength of that encryption. Policy experts believe that the policy should only specify the degree of protection and that another official document, the *standard,* should dictate technical controls (such as strength of encryption, firewalls, authentication, and so forth). This is because this splits the decision of what must be protected from the technical fulfillment. Technology usually changes much more rapidly than the sensitivity of data. By separating the two, the technical standard can be upgraded as encryption strength and algorithms improve without forcing a reexamination of security policy.

A third document, the *procedure*, details how to implement the technology standard. The procedure is even more flexible, changing as necessary to allow for the introduction of upgrades and replacements. This book (and, indeed, most technical books on security) concentrates on the how-to of procedures and the standards that are possible using the hardware and software described in the book. It may recommend some sound security practices and describe how to implement them, but it is not a security book. Network administrators should follow their organization's security policy, standards, and procedures. Still, if an administrator does not understand the "why" behind what he or she is doing, the administrator may easily (and inadvertently) weaken security to make something work, instead of attempting to make things work with security in place.

Examples of such mistakes can be found in most organizations. Users are designated as administrators because some application may not work if they are not. Often, some configuration changes will make the application work. Sometimes there is no solution, but one should still be sought. Users are designated as domain administrators when a local Administrators group would be sufficient. It is just done because of an ignorance of the difference in power between the two. Password policies are readjusted to allow blank passwords when high-ranking management complains that they can't remember their passwords. Keypad locks are placed on doors to server rooms, but then the combination is provided to all employees because it's quicker to get to a break room if they can pass through the server room. Even default security settings are removed because administrators don't know how to make functions work with them. (For an example, see the section "SMB Signing" later in this chapter. SMB signing is on by default in Windows Server 2003, but it is not on by default in earlier versions of Windows. Instead of turning it on for those systems, it gets turned off for Windows Server 2003.)

A security administration framework will vary depending on the organization, and may not even be formally recognized as such. It will still be the job of the network administrator to provide security for information systems. To do so with Windows operating systems, network administrators must understand the underlying security posture of such systems and the technologies that are available to them.

Windows Security Posture

A *security posture* defines the central basis for security design and practice within an organization or product. Those who know the security posture of an operating system can anticipate how the operating system will respond in a given circumstance. They can then use this information in designing their own systems and infrastructures, in securing information systems, and in troubleshooting problems. While you should always confirm your understanding by using documentation and practice, being able to apply security posture knowledge can save time and avoid unnecessary testing. The person who understands that Windows is designed to give administrators supreme power on the system will understand that a user with administrator rights can overcome every technical control placed on a system. Perhaps this knowledge will lead to not making users administrators, to the design of applications that do not require administrative rights to run, and to better security designs.

Keep the security posture of Windows in mind when designing, implementing, and troubleshooting Windows networking. It will make things easier, and of course more secure.

The security posture of Windows is what it is. This section is *not* a discussion on whether the security design of Windows is good or bad; it simply reports on what it is. Those who use, deploy, troubleshoot, and administer Windows can't change these things about Windows. They can, however, understand them and use them to get their jobs done, and to keep systems and data secure.

This section reviews the following areas of Windows security posture:

- Permissions and privileges
- Anonymous and Null sessions
- Roles of administrators
- Delegation of authority
- Role separation
- Centralized administration with Group Policy
- Security configuration with security templates
- Domains and security

Let's begin this discussion with a look at permissions and privileges, including the pecking order and function of specific types of each.

Permissions and Privileges

Authorization defines what a user can do on a system. It defines whether a user can connect to or authenticate to a computer, which resources they can access once connected, and what additional privileges they have on the system. Windows defines several categories of authorization:

Permissions

Access to resources such as files and folders, registry keys, printers, and Active Directory objects is controlled through permissions. Permissions are assigned using *access control entries* (ACEs) that define the user or group account, permission (such as read, write, or execute), and whether the permission is to be permitted or denied. Permissions are granular and are specific to a type of object. Many different users and groups can have permissions on an object. ACEs are added to an object's *discretionary access control list* (DACL).

Privileges

Privileges define what a user can do on the system. While privileges are defined explicitly by assignment in the security policy User Rights section, they are also sometimes implicit (such as the administrator's ability to take ownership of an object, or the right to install services and some types of applications). Privileges are often divided into *user rights* and *logon rights*.

Logon Rights

Those privileges that have to do with logon, such as the right to *log on locally* (authenticate at the console of a computer), or the right to *log on as a service* (authenticate and have access to computer resources as a service).

To view the rights explicitly assigned to users on a Windows Server 2003 domain, open Start → Administrative Tools → Domain Controller Security Policy, expand the Local Policies node and select User Rights Assignment, as shown in Figure 13-1.

Chapter 7 defines many of the Windows Server 2003 groups. A complete discussion of privileges assigned by membership in default Windows groups can be found at:

http://www.microsoft.com/resources/documentation/WindowsServ/2003/standard/proddocs/en-us/Default.asp?url=/resources/documentation/WindowsServ/2003/standard/proddocs/en-us/sag_adgroupscreatewhere.asp

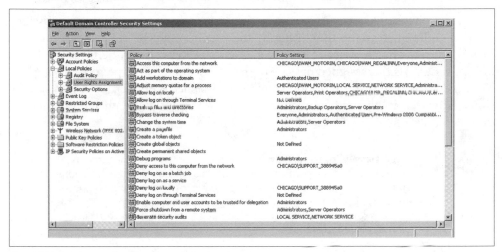

Figure 13-1. User Rights are set in Group Policy

Privileges and permissions not explicitly granted are denied

On a Windows computer, privileges and permissions must be explicitly granted. Users can be individually assigned a privilege, or given Allow permissions on an object. Users can also obtain privileges and permissions because they are members of a group that has been granted this permission. While privileges and permissions can be explicitly denied, if a privilege or permission is not granted, it is implicitly denied. This means that there is little need to assign Deny permissions.

An example of the use of implicit denial is the use of object permissions. Consider the following example. A folder named Accounting is created on the file server Server1. The permission Allow Full Control of this folder is granted to the Administrators group, Allow Modify is granted to members of the Accounting group. The user SamP is not a member of either group, but does have the privilege to log on locally at Server1. SamP can view the filesystem on Server1 using Windows Explorer, but, because he has no permissions at all on the Accounting folder, he cannot access files within that folder.

Deny permissions may or may not override allow

Permissions may be assigned directly on an object or inherited from parent objects. For example, the permissions on a folder may be inherited by files in the folder, and the files may have permissions assigned directly to them. Both sets of permissions may be a mixed batch of Allow and Deny permission settings, and both sets are used in determining the results of a file access request. Earlier Windows systems followed the rule, "Deny always overrides allow." If a single Deny permission was applicable, then access was denied. Windows 2000, Windows XP, and Windows Server 2003 do not follow this rule because of the different way inherited permissions are stored.

The access a user has to an object is determined by reviewing the permissions granted and denied to the user either by the user account, or because of his or her membership in any groups that have been granted Allow or Deny permissions on the object. If permissions assigned directly to the object are the only permissions applied to it, then it is true that any Deny permissions assigned will override Allow permissions. However, if inherited permissions must also be considered, then things may be different.

 Since Deny permissions always overrode Allow in earlier versions of Windows, the rule permeates many discussions of NTFS permissions and traps administrators into improperly assigning permissions or interpreting what they see. They may think they have properly protected resources, when they have actually left them open to access by unauthorized individuals.

Inherited permissions are those assigned to parent folders. For example, if folder A includes a subfolder A1, then permissions directly (sometimes called "locally") assigned to folder A are inherited by folder A1. The files in folder A1 inherit permissions from folder A1. Folder A1 may also have permissions directly assigned to it. What type of access a specific user has to folder A1 and the files within A1 depend on the interaction of both direct (local) and inherited permissions. Permissions are evaluated starting with the permissions assigned to the local object. Permission evaluation stops when the permissions requested are granted. If the user requests permission to read and write the file, and those permissions are allowed on the local object, permission evaluation stops and the user is allowed to read and write the file. Any inherited permissions are ignored. This means that an inherited Deny Read permission, even if explicitly given to the user, is not applied. Consider the following example.

SherryY is granted Allow Read permission directly on the *august14.doc* file, which is located in the *Accounting* folder. Sherry belongs to the Clerks group, which is given the Deny Read permission on the *Accounting* folder. Because local permissions are evaluated first, SherryY is allowed to read the *august14.doc* file. The Deny Read permission is never evaluated.

Inheritance can be blocked. The inheritance feature is controlled by a checkbox in the Properties pages of the object. To view or change this feature for a folder or file, right-click the object in Windows Explorer and select Properties, then click the

Advanced button. The Permissions page, as shown in Figure 13-2 is displayed. By default, the Advanced object property checkbox "Inherit from parent the permission entries that apply to child objects." "Include these with entries explicitly defined here" is checked. It has been unchecked in the figure. If the check is removed, only locally defined permissions are applied.

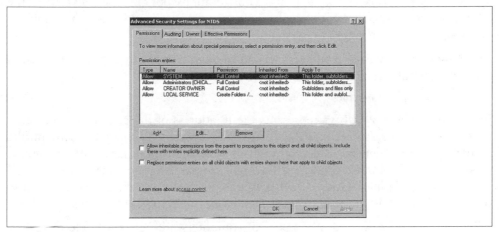

Figure 13-2. Permission inheritance can be prevented

When inheritance is blocked, only local permissions are evaluated. For example, if an Allow permission is set on a folder but not inherited by the files within the folder, the Allow permission has no affect. This also means that carefully established permissions in a subdirectory cannot be inadvertently modified just by setting new permissions on the directory root. The Windows subdirectory is configured this way just so that it will maintain its permissions settings, even if the permissions on the root of *C:* are modified.

Anonymous Access and Null Sessions Are Possible

Anonymous access is defined as access that can be gained by someone who is not authorized to access a system. The completion of a connection without a user account and password is called a *null session*. In today's security-conscious world, this seems like a terrible thing, but it is necessary in some circumstances. For example, the authorization to access resources on a computer can only be determined after a user has authenticated. A user must connect to the computer before that user can authenticate. How else can that connection be made unless it is made anonymously?

The main problem with anonymous access is that an unauthorized individual might obtain information that would allow an easy compromise of the system, or, because after connecting anonymously, an attacker might be able to access resources that were unprotected.

In earlier Windows systems, anonymous access via null sessions was designed to assist networking. For example, a null session was used to obtain a *browse list* of Windows computers from a Windows server on the network. Applications and services were also written that depended on the ability to access network shares and *named pipes* (that is, defined access points to applications) using null sessions. Most of these applications have been rewritten, and configurations options exist that allow the administrator to specify which applications may use an anonymous connection. By doing so, anonymous access opportunities are narrowed.

Anonymous access using a null session can be demonstrated by entering the following command at a command prompt.

```
net use \\ip_address\ipc$ "" "/user:"
```

In the command, *ip_address* represents the IP address of the computer. Once connected, access to resources and the ability to exercise privileges will depend on the access granted to anonymous users. In this context, anonymous represents an implicit group consisting of those connected via a null session. A programmatic use of a null session to obtain information about a Windows system is detailed by the security organization Foundstone at *http://www.foundstone.com/resources/proddesc/about.htm*.

Windows Server 2003 and Windows XP computers are not vulnerable to anonymous attacks by default. A null session connection can be made with the previous command, but access is limited. However, a malicious individual, malware, or even a well-meaning administrator may change default settings and make Windows Server 2003 vulnerable to such attacks. It may also be necessary to relax the default by providing anonymous access to specific shares or named pipes.

Anonymous access (that is, the granting of privileges and access permissions to anonymous users) should be curtailed. Windows Server 2003 provides the capability to do so in the following ways:

- By default, anonymous access is restricted because the implicit anonymous logon group is not a member of the group Everyone. This means that any access granted to the group Everyone (and there is a lot of it) is not available to anonymous unless the Security Option Let Everyone permissions apply to anonymous users is enabled.

- By default, the Security Option "Network access: Do not allow anonymous enumeration of SAM accounts" is enabled. (SAM stands for "Security Accounts Manager.") This prevents an anonymous connection from being used to list user accounts, which in turn makes a password-cracking attack more difficult.

- The Security Option "Network access: Do not allow anonymous enumeration of SAM accounts and shares" can be enabled to prevent unauthorized users from obtaining a list of shares and accounts.

- By default, the Security Option, Network Access: Restrict anonymous access to Named Pipes and Shares is enabled which means anonymous access to Shares and Named Pipes is restricted to those listed explicitly in the following two Security Options:

- The Security Option "Network Access: Shares that can be accessed anonymously" is available so that only those named shares can be anonymously accessed. By default, several shares are listed, but those that are not needed can be removed.

- The Security Option "Network Access: Named Pipes that can be accessed anonymously" is available so that only those named pipes that are specified in this policy can be anonymously accessed. By default, several named pipes are listed, but they can be removed if the applications that require them are not running on the server.

 If anonymous access must be granted to enable the use of network applications, do so by determining what access is required, and then granting only this access. For example, if a specific share must be anonymously accessed, add this share to the Security Option "Network Access: Shares that can be accessed anonymously" instead of disabling the Security Option "Network Access: Restrict anonymous access to Named Pipes and Shares." If access to resources is required, grant access to that resource only explicitly to the implicit ANONYMOUS LOGON group, instead of enabling the Security Option "Let Everyone permissions apply to anonymous users."

Administrators Are All-Powerful

Windows defines different administrative roles and the term "administrator" is often loosely applied to any user role that has some elevated privilege. In this section, the narrower use of the term is applied. There are only three administrative roles that are defined as having full administrative rights:

- Local Administrators
- Domain Admins
- Enterprise Admins

Although there are exceptions, members of these administrative groups are supremely powerful within the administrative scope assigned to them. Members of the local Administrators group are all-powerful on the computer; members of Domain Admins are all-powerful in the domain; and members of Enterprise Admins group are all-powerful in the forest.

Administrators of Windows systems have complete power over the operating system, as well as most data kept on the system. Administrators can load device drivers, install all types of applications, debug programs, add users, assign access permissions and user rights, and configure operating system components (including networking). Users also have default rights and permissions on the system, and while users can deny administrators access to resources that the user creates or otherwise gains ownership of, administrators can take ownership of these objects and assign themselves any permission they desire. Of course, it is possible for an administrator to perform some operation that kills the operating system. The operating system is built with the premise that the administrator knows what she is doing.

Exception Proves the Rule

The exception to "the administrator rules overall" concept is the use of the EFS on Windows XP Professional and Windows Server 2003 standalone systems. Files encrypted using EFS on these systems are only accessible to the individual who encrypted the files, and only this individual is authorized to access them. (Unless new EFS File Recovery agents are defined, EFS encrypted files on Windows 2000 standalone systems and on Windows XP Professional, Windows 2000, Windows XP Professional, and Windows Server 2003 can be read by anyone who can log on using the local Administrator account because that account is the File Recovery agent for EFS.)

While members of the local Administrators group have power on a single system, if their computers are joined in a domain, then members of the Domain Admins group also have authority on the local system. While local Administrators can make changes to settings made by Domain Admins (and Domain Admins can change them back), Domain Admins can preempt some of the authority of the local Administrators group by using Group Policy. When Group Policy is used, local settings are overridden. Likewise, members of the Enterprise Admins group have administrative privileges throughout the forest. They can do everything the Domain Admins and local Administrators can do, and more. For example, only an Enterprise Admin can change the functional mode of the forest. Table 13-1 summarizes these administrative rules.

Table 13-1. Administrative power rules

Rule	Administrators (local)	Domain Admins	Enterprise Admins
Can administer	Single computer	Domain.	Forest
Power extends to	N/A	All computers in the domain.	All domains in the forest
Can reset changes made by a more powerful administrator?	Can reset changes made, but cannot override Group Policy changes as long as Group Policy is applied	Can reset changes made by Enterprise Admins.	N/A
Can elevate privileges?	Only through attack	Have privileges in configuration container of Active Directory. Can programmatically gain access to other domains. This is considered an attack.	N/A

One aspect of this table that makes this delineation of power troubling is the ability of the Domain Admin to extend power outside of the domain. It interferes with an idealistic approach to the management of a large infrastructure. In a perfect world, there is the ideal that management and rule is hierarchical. Small-managed areas at each level are autonomous, but are, in turn, ruled by some more powerful group above. Each higher level has absolute control over that below. This model is simplistic, but is easy to describe.

In a large network infrastructure, power is neither absolute nor autonomous, but exists on a continuum. There are strong and well-protected rules in place, but you should be aware of what they are, where they are, and where they can be more easily broken, as well as the role that people play in maintaining security.

Delegation of Authority

In small systems, one group of administrators can manage all of the systems and perform all administrative roles. These individuals configure systems, install programs, train users, and keep things running. In a small business or organization that has implemented an Active Directory forest, the administrators may all be members of Enterprise Admins, Domain Admins, and local Administrators groups. In a larger shop, it is more efficient to provide specialized administrative roles. Its also makes information systems more secure. By specializing, administrators can concentrate on different areas of administration and become very good at them. When authority is delegated, less-experienced people can do the less-complicated chores, and do so with supervision. The cost of administration is reduced and a training ground provided. By spreading authority across multiple individuals, there is also less chance of undiscovered fraud. Delegation fits well-known security principles such as *least privilege* (give individuals the privileges and permissions they need to get their jobs done), *role separation* (divide critical and sensitive tasks up into distinct roles and never let the same individual perform both roles), and *defense in depth* (layer security so that any attacker who compromises a lesser administrative role can do less harm on the system).

Windows supports delegation of authority in three ways:

- Multiple administrative groups
- Granular permission and rights assignment
- Formal delegation of control process in Active Directory

Multiple administrative groups

Windows recognizes more than a supremely powerful group and general users. Multiple default groups are part of the Windows infrastructure. On the single system level, Windows Server 2003 includes several "operator" groups (each with a number of administrative privileges specific to its role, but lacking in overall administrative powers):

- Server Operators
- Account Operators
- Print Operators
- Backup Operators

Additional groups provide specialized privileges to members. These include the following:

- Remote Desktop Users
- Performance Log Users
- Performance Monitor Users

A built-in group that is used for network administration is the Network Configuration Operators group. Membership in this group provides the right to modify network configuration. If users must be able to modify network configuration (for example, on laptop computers), membership in this group is better than providing them full administrator rights for the same purpose.

Specialized groups also exist for the administration of domains and forest. For example, DNS Administrators can administer DNS servers, Schema Admins can modify the Schema, and Group Policy Creator Owners can administer Group Policy.

Local accounts are viewed and managed by opening the Computer Management console (Start → Administrative Tools → Computer Management → Local Users and Groups) and selecting the Users node, as shown in Figure 13-3

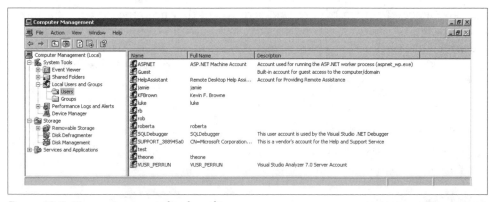

Figure 13-3. User accounts on a local machine

Domain and forest accounts can be viewed and managed in Active Directory Users and Computers. To do so open the console (Start → Administrative Tools → Active

Directory Users and Computers) and select the Built-in node, as shown in Figure 13-4, and the Users node, as shown in Figure 13-5.

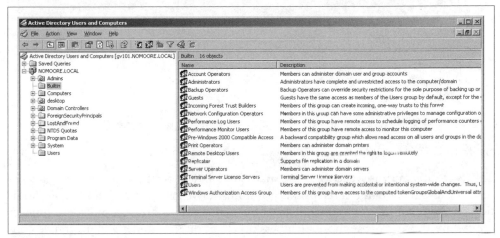

Figure 13-4. Built-in User accounts in the domain

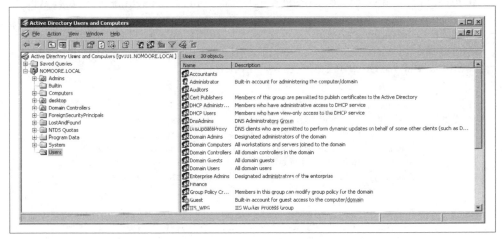

Figure 13-5. Users accounts in the domain

In a well-managed forest, user and group accounts are often moved to or created in *Organizational Units* (OU). To view these groups and accounts, select the OU as shown in Figure 13-6.

Windows Server 2003 also has default user accounts. The Administrator account is the built-in administrator of the system. The Guest account, as the lowest-level privilege built-in account, was originally meant to provide access to users who do not have an account on the system. It has few privileges but is recognized as a possible source of attack, and the account is disabled by default.

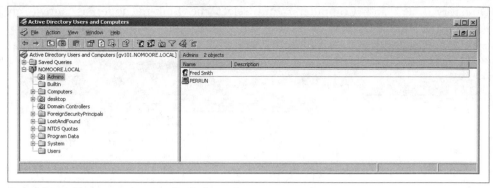

Figure 13-6. User accounts may also be located in OUs

These groups and user accounts are accessible and under the control and management of members of the three primary administrative groups (see Table 13-1). Additionally, implicit groups and specialized built-in accounts are also provided. *Implicit groups* are those groups whose membership is not directly under administrative control (that is, no administrator can grant group membership). Instead, membership in these groups is caused by something a user has done. For example, any user who is locally logged on is a member in the Interactive group, while every user connecting remotely to a Windows computer is in the Network group. The Everyone group is composed of all accounts that have authenticated to the system. An administrator can grant or deny access to resources for implicit groups.

 An exception to the rule that administrators can't add or remove accounts to implicit groups is that, in Windows Server 2003, administrators control whether or not those able to connect anonymously to the server are members of the Everyone group. By default, anonymous is not a member of Everyone. However, administrators can use the Security Option "Network Access: Let Everyone permissions apply to anonymous users."

Special, built-in user accounts exist by default on the system, but cannot be assigned passwords by administrators. They do not appear in any listing (local or domain or forest) of users. However, they do appear when resource assignments, user rights, and other privileges are being viewed or made. The Local System account (often shown as the System account in the GUI) represents the operating system. An administrator can remove or assign the System account from access control lists (ACLs). The Service account represents all system services.

Two new specialized user accounts are available in Windows Server 2003 and Windows XP. These accounts are Local Service and Network Service. Both have little more than the privileges of ordinary users on the local computer. The difference between the two is that the Local Service account can access network resources as a null session with no credentials, while the Network Service account can access network resources using the credentials of the computer account. These accounts are used as *service accounts*. A service account is used by a service to authenticate to the system and to grant a service access and rights on the system.

 Implicit accounts such as Local System, Local Service, and Network Service do not have passwords associated with them. An attacker cannot therefore "authenticate" to these accounts by using an ID and password. An attacker may gain the privilege to run these accounts, however, by compromising an application or service running in the security context of the account.

In the past, an administrator had the choice of using the LocalSystem account or creating an ordinary user account for this purpose, and then assigning it the rights and permissions it required for doing its job. Neither choice was really good. Using the LocalSystem account gives the service too many privileges; giving an ordinary user account the correct privileges can be difficult. There are also security issues with these choices. If a service can be compromised, an attacker can gain the privileges of the service account. If this account is the LocalSystem account, then the attacker has the entire power of the operating system to command. If the account is a privileged user account, its password may be weak and rarely changed, making it an easy target for attackers. Because the LocalService and NetworkService accounts have fewer privileges than the operating system but are managed by it, they pose less risk if the service is compromised and less risk that they will be compromised compared to a normal user account used as a service account.

Management of the two new implicit accounts is shared between the operating system and its administrators. The operating system manages the account, while administrators can make it the service account assigned to specific services, and can grant the accounts resource access. Figure 13-7 shows the Log On page of a service, indicating that its logon account is the NetworkService account.

Granular permissions and rights assignment

In addition to providing multiple privileged groups, Windows administrators can create *custom groups* and provide them with privileges and permissions. Therefore administrators can create custom administrative groups, or even simply create groups that reduce the attack surface by reducing the number of ways an attack might gain access to a system.

A custom administrative group might be one created to manage user accounts contained in an OU. The group can be given the capability to create, delete, and manage users in a specific OU only by granting the group permissions on a specific OU object in Active Directory. Another group might be given permission to manage resources (such as files and folders) that belong to a specific area within a company (such as Human Resources). An example of reducing privileges is the creation of a

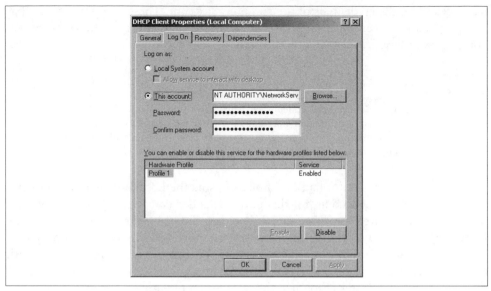

Figure 13-7. The Network Service account can be used for service authentication

local group on a server, giving it the user right "Access this computer from the network," and then removing this right from the Everyone group (or explicitly giving other groups that right). By reducing the number of accounts able to connect to the computer from the network, the administrator reduces the number of vectors for an attack on the computer and/or the computer's resources.

 Changing default assignments of user rights and permissions is not without risk. It is possible to remove access and privileges from critical system operations (for example, preventing the LocalSystem account from accessing some of its own resources, or preventing computer accounts from access to domain controllers). Any reduction in default privileges and permissions must be researched and tested thoroughly before introduction in a production network.

In Windows Server 2003, *computer accounts* are also service principals like users. This means that computer accounts can give privileges and access to resources. An example of a computer group is the domain RAS and IAS Server group, which consists of computers that are authorized with read access to domain user accounts and to operate as remote access servers in the domain.

Creation of (and memberships in) computer groups should be restricted because, in addition to any explicit privileges assigned to a group, there are implicit privileges that may result in security vulnerabilities. When a computer account is added to a group, the service accounts on the computer also get the access that is given to the group. Since this access can mean full access to all resources on the computer, on a domain controller this can mean full access to Active Directory, which, in turn, means access to domain-wide resources.

Delegation of control

Permissions on Active Directory objects are complex and can be used to create specialized administrative groups. (An example was given in the previous section.) In addition, the Delegation of Control wizard can be used to easily assign permissions within Active Directory containers. Understanding and using the wizard is easy. Using it to correctly assign permissions within Active Directory is a very complex undertaking. Still, some permissions assignments easily support mundane administrative tasks such as *password reset*, *account lockout reset,* and other Help Desk-type administrative tasks. In the past, many help desk personnel were given full administrator privileges when all they really required was the ability to perform a few administrative tasks. Now we can create custom groups with just the power they need. The help desk employee can do his job, but cannot do other administrative tasks. Using the wizard to permit custom administrative groups empowers users without giving them more power than they require. Some built-in roles are defined within the wizard, and the wizard can be used to create a custom role.

Figure 13-8 shows the wizard. In the figure, the Task to Delegate page shows the assignment of the password reset task. Note the Create a custom task to delegate radio button. If selected, additional options are available.

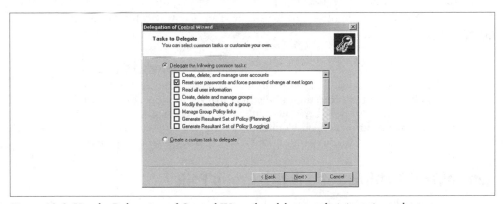

Figure 13-8. Use the Delegation of Control Wizard to delegate administrative tasks

Role Separation

Role separation is a security principle that says a sensitive operation must be split so that no one individual can perform the entire task. This is done to reduce fraudulent activity. An example of such an operation is the purchasing of goods and services. Two tasks within this role are issuing a purchase order (PO) and writing the check in payment of the order. If one individual can do both, that individual could easily issue a fraudulent PO and make payment for goods or services never received. By splitting the operation into purchasing and accounts payable tasks, the opportunity for fraud is reduced. At least two individuals would have to collaborate. This is less likely to happen and more difficult to keep covered up. To paraphrase Benjamin Franklin, "Two can keep a secret, if one of them is dead."

Information systems are not usually created with role separation in mind, and Windows is no exception. If purchasing and accounts payable employees are granted resource access via membership in custom Windows operating system groups, there is nothing to prevent a user account from having membership in both groups. For example, an accounts payable employee might be able to produce a PO by becoming a member of the purchasing group. A properly designed accounting system, with luck, provides more sophisticated controls within both its computer and manual operations to prevent this, but no control on the operation system level exists.

However, increasing attention to security and the requirements of some levels of *Common Criteria evaluation* are forcing all operating systems to look more closely at role separation and to provide more direct support for its implementation. An example of operating system–supported role separation would be the roles of Certificate Manager and CA Administrator and the ability to enforce role separation in the administration of *Certification Authorities* (CAs). The CA Administrator manages a CA, while the Certificate Manager manages the certificates issued by the CA. When role separation is enforced on a CA, no single user account can be a member in both groups.

 Common Criteria is an international standard for information system product security. Products are evaluated at a specific level against a documented protection profile or list of security operations. Window Server 2003 has been submitted for Common Criteria evaluation. More information on Common Criteria can be located through the Common Criteria portal at *http://www.commoncriteriaportal.org/*.

Centralized Administration with Group Policy

Chapter 7 introduced Group Policy and its function. It was designed to provide the administrator with the capability to centrally administer entire networks of computers, and yet do so in a granular manner by creating Group Policies specific to different groups of users and computers. Many parts of Group Policy assist in the control of network functions and are discussed in Chapter 7. Other parts of Group Policy help the administrator apply a wide range of security settings in an automated fashion across a domain of many computers. Security settings available through Group Policy are things like Account Policy (which includes Password Policy), Event Log settings, permissions on System Services, and so on.

Security Templates for Security Configuration

Security templates are predefined lists of security settings in specially crafted *.inf* files. These security settings include most of the ones found in the Group Policy Windows Configuration → Security Settings node that are specific to a single computer. New security templates can be produced and existing templates modified to match the security policy required for a computer, a domain, or an OU. The Security Templates snap-in can be used to display and modify settings in security templates.

Figure 13-9 shows the Security Templates snap-in in an MMC console. The snap-in is loaded in the same manner as any snap-in. First open an MMC console by clicking Start, then Run, and then typing **mmc**. Click OK. From the File menu, select Add/Remove Snap-in, click Add, and then select the Security Templates snap-in. Complete the procedure by clicking Add, then Close, followed by OK. In Figure 13-9, the hisecdc template (high security for domain controllers) is selected. Note that the nodes of the template (Account Policies, Local Policies, Event Log, Restricted Groups, System Services, Registry, and File System) are the same as many included in the Group Policy Security Settings node.

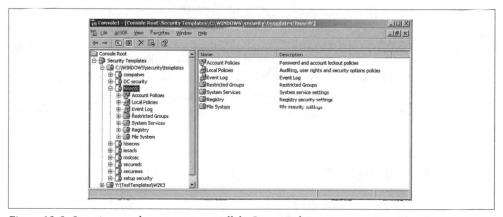

Figure 13-9. Security template structure parallels Group Policy security settings

The security templates can be applied to a single computer using the Security Configuration and Analysis Tool or the secedit command. If they are imported into a Group Policy object, they can be used to apply security to many computers. Security templates can also be used to analyze the security settings of a computer against a specific template. This is a good way to audit security settings against a security policy by using a template that is configured to meet a security policy and comparing it to the security settings on an existing computer. The Security Configuration and Analysis tool and the secedit command can also be used for this purpose. For a discussion on how to use these tools to apply security and audit security settings see the book *Hardening Windows Security* (Osborne-McGraw Hill). Figure 13-10 shows the results of such an analysis. Those items marked with an "X" within a circle show variances between the local computer security settings and those of the template.

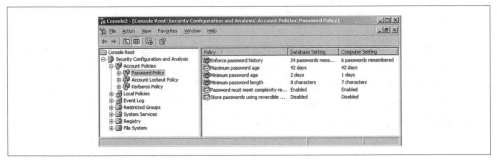

Figure 13-10. Security Configuration and Analysis can be used to audit security settings

Domains Are Not Security Boundaries

In the old Windows NT 4.0 world, domains are security boundaries. That is, an administrator or a user in one domain cannot be assigned privileges or permissions in another domain. A trust relationship can be created between two domains if access is desired, but the trust must be approved by Domain Admins from both domains. Windows 2000 and Windows Server 2003 domains are not security boundaries. In Active Directory, all domains in the forest trust each other. The trust does not have to be approved by administrators from domains in the same forest. The mutual trusts enable administrators to assign users from one domain access and privileges on their domains. This means that domains are autonomous. Domain Admins do exercise some control over which users and groups from other domains have access.

However, their autonomy is not the same as the isolation provided by Windows NT 4.0 domains. First, members of the Enterprise Admins group can also grant and remove access permissions, as well as the assignment of privileges. Second, because members of Domain Admins have access to the configuration partition in Active Directory, they may be able to use it to attack other domains and obtain access to the resources in other domains without approval or action by other Domain Admins. While this access is not a desirable feature, nor is it available in the GUI, it can be accomplished and administrators must be aware of this potential abuse of power. When complete isolation is required, create different forests instead of domains.

Configuring Advanced Network Security Features

This book provides information on administering networking for Windows Server 2003 servers and for forests with Windows Server 2003 domain controllers. It does not, however, completely define every possible Windows service or administrative tool that might impact networking. Some of these more advanced topics may not be used in many Windows Server 2003 networks. However, some of these topics may be part of your network, or the service that they offer is used but not fully understood because little configuration must take place. An understanding of these topics will help administrators do a better job of managing other networking elements that rely on them. An introduction into the more obscure topics will assist administrators when they are required to implement them or when faced with a problem they will know that a native solution exists.

This section examines the following topics:

- Storage and use of EFS-encrypted files on network servers using WebDAV
- Integration of certificate services into Windows networking
- SMB signing

Storage and Use of EFS-Encrypted Files on Network Servers Using WebDAV

The EFS is a feature of the NTFS filesystem. Users with an EFS certificate can encrypt and decrypt files. When EFS-encrypted files must be stored on network file servers, the file servers must be configured to store the files and the network transport of the files may need to be protected.

There are two ways of facilitating this:

- Using a share on a file server
- Using a web folder and WebDAV

File servers must be configured to allow storage of EFS-encrypted files. You can find information on how to do this in the article "Encrypting File Systems in Windows XP and Windows Server 2003" at *http://www.microsoft.com/technet/prodtechnol/winxppro/ deploy/cryptfs.mspx*. If file servers are configured to allow storage of EFS-encrypted files, then protection for the data being transported must be provided. This is because file servers and clients use the Server Message Block (SMB) transport, and SMB is not EFS-aware. The encrypted files must be decrypted, the data transported, and then the data must be encrypted on the server. If files are created on the server, the data must still be decrypted, because a client must view the file remotely. To protect the data, the following two possible solutions are available:

- Provide an IPSec policy that protects data during its transport to and from the file server
- Establish an SSL session for transport

Chapter 11 discusses IPSec policies. SSL will require implementation of IIS or another web server service on the file server. Chapter 12 discusses IIS and SSL.

Another way of transporting EFS-encrypted data without having to provide additional transport protection is to use WebDAV, which is the protocol that extends the HTTP 1.1 protocol to allow clients to remotely publish, lock, and manage files on a web server. It is available as an optional service of IIS 6.0 on Windows Server 2003.

 WebDAV is also available on IIS 5.0. It is enabled by default. However, IIS 5.0 and WebDAV cannot be used to facilitate server storage of EFS-encrypted files.

When WebDAV is enabled, transport between clients and the filesystem of a web server can be accomplished without the use of SMB or file shares. WebDAV works differently than SMB. The data in files is transported without the need to decrypt the file. The use of WebDAV for storing EFS-encrypted files is only available on Windows Server 2003 and is only accessible to Windows XP or Windows Server 2003 clients.

 Caution should be used when enabling WebDAV on IIS or any web server. Adding additional services to a web server provides another possible way to attack it. WebDAV provides the ability to store and retrieve files from a remote server. WebDAV shares are not SMB file shares and do not provide the capability to use strong ACLs like SMB file shares do. Any process that allows data transfer across the network will be a prime target for attackers attempting to compromise the system. If you want to use WebDAV for transporting EFS-encrypted files, do so on isolated servers dedicated to internal use, and do not allow access to them from the Internet. Harden the web server and train users and administrators on the proper use of this service.

To use WebDAV as a transport for EFS encrypted files, begin by installing IIS on a Windows Server 2003 computer. Enable the WebDAV extension in IIS. Create a web shared folder on the web server. (This is not the same as a share in the filesystem. There is no need to create a file share on the server to use WebDAV.) Check the status of the WebDAV client on Windows XP. The WebDAV client is implemented as part of the Web Client and is started automatically. Chapter 12 provides information on installing and configuring IIS.

To enable WebDAV on IIS, begin by opening the IIS Manger by selecting Start →
Administrative Tools → Internet Information Services (IIS) Manager. Select the Web
Services Extensions node. In the details pane on the right side of the screen, select
WebDAV and then click the Allow button, as shown in Figure 13-11. This will
change the Web Server Extension status for WebDAV to Allowed.

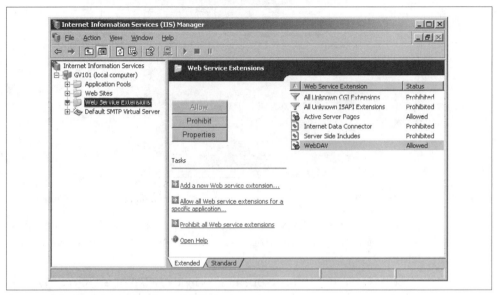

Figure 13-11. WebDAV must be enabled in IIS 6.0

Next, create a virtual directory. The filesystem folder assigned to the virtual directory must be on an NTFS partition. Give users Read and Write permissions on the
IIS virtual directory. These permissions are needed for users to publish and read files.
Give users the Directory Browsing permission so that they can list files and folders
on the site. Click OK.

To create a shared folder on the web server, right-click on the folder assigned to the
virtual directory and select Properties. Select the Web Sharing tab. Click the "Share
this folder" radio button, as shown in Figure 13-12. In the figure, the folder name in
the filesystem, *webefs*, is listed on the title of the Properties page. Note that the
"Share on" drop-down list indicates that this folder will be shared on the Default
web site. Use this drop-down list to select the correct web site from which it can be
accessed. Note that the alias for the folder, Finance, is listed in the Aliases text box.

Apply permissions for the folder by selecting the Security tab, selecting the user
groups to provide permissions to, and selecting the appropriate permissions as determined by their access needs. Permissions are Read, Read and Execute, List, Write,
and Modify. Read, Write, and Modify permissions are necessary if users are to use
the folder for storing EFS-encrypted files. Click OK to close the Properties folder.

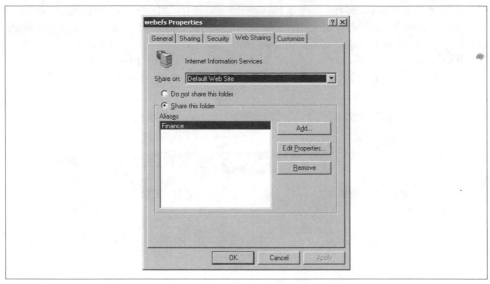

Figure 13-12. The virtual directory filesystem folder is web-shared and does not use file sharing

To test the use of EFS over WebDAV, you should set up a Network Place pointing to the web share, copy an encrypted file to the share, and then attempt to open it using a different identity.

To set up a Network Place, begin by opening Windows Explorer. Select My Network Places, double-click Add Network Place, and then click Next. Select "Choose another Network location" and then click Next. Enter the address of the virtual directory (such as **http://192.168.5.58/Finance**), as shown in Figure 13-13. Click Next.

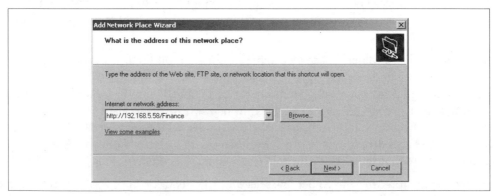

Figure 13-13. Create a network place to access WebDAV folders

Enter a name or select the default provided. Click Next followed by Finish. The network place will now be accessible from Windows Explorer, just as any local folder or network share.

You now have the ability to copy an EFS-encrypted file to the Finance folder on the web server. Only those who have encrypted the file will be able to decrypt the file. To test this, copy a file that you have encrypted using EFS from your desktop computer to the network place, then double-click on the file and note that you can read it. Log off your computer and log on using another user account. Create a Network Place for the same location for this user. (The user must have permissions set on the web server to access the folder.). Then double-click on the EFS-encrypted file. You will receive an Access Denied warning in a pop-up box and will not be able to read the file.

Integration of Certificate Services into Windows Networking

Certificate services are integrated into Windows Server 2003 operations by default. Some operations (such as encrypting files) require certificates, and these certificates are created by the operating system without any special activity. Certificates for other operations (such as for authentication in IPSec or the SMTP transport of replication of Active Directory) requires certificates that have been issued by a CA. These certificates can be obtained in one of three ways:

- By purchasing them from a public CA such as Verisign.
- By implementing third-party *Public-Key Infrastructure* (PKI), including third-party CAs. A PKI is the sum of the hardware and software required to support the use of certificates.
- By implementing native Windows PKI including Windows CAs.

Follow the instructions provided by Verisign to obtain certificates and by various Windows services for installing them. Follow the instructions provided by the third-party producers of any CAs purchased. Be aware that the certificates you purchase or produce using third-party CAs must meet the requirements of any Windows service or application that requires certificates. Interoperability may or may not be available.

Implementation of Windows PKI is beyond the scope of this book. Good documentation is provided on the Microsoft site and is also available the book *Windows Server 2003 Security: A Technical Reference* (Addison-Wesley). However, basic knowledge about Windows native CAs and their use is critical knowledge for network administration. This section provides an introduction.

A Windows CA can be installed on any Windows Server 2003 server or Windows 2000 server. Windows Server 2003 offers considerable improvements and additional features beyond those provided in Windows 2000 and should be used for any new CA implementation. Two types of CAs can be installed:

Enterprise CA
> The Enterprise CA is integrated with Active Directory and must be installed on a server that is a member in a Windows Sever 2003 or Windows 2000 domain.

Standalone CA
> Standalone CAs are not integrated with Active Directory, but they may be installed on both standalone servers and servers that are domain members. A standalone server does not provide many of the features and benefits offered by Enterprise CAs.

CAs can be used to provide authority for other CAs. Doing so creates a *CA hierarchy* that can provide effective management of certificate services, a more secure PKI, and a hierarchy of trust. To establish a hierarchy, a CA is implemented as a *root CA* and used to issue *CA certificates* for other *subordinate CAs*. The CA certificate is what makes a CA a CA. The private key associated with the certificate is used to digitally sign the certificates that the CA issues. The signature can be validated by using the associated public key stored in the certificate. The root CA creates its own certificate and associated private key; subordinate CAs do not. Issued CA certificates are digitally signed by the CA that issues them. Subordinate CAs can issue CA certificates for other subordinates (thus creating several tiers), or can be used to produce certificates for end use (such as EFS certificates, IPSec certificates, computer certificates, and so on).

A mixture of Standalone and Enterprise CAs can be part of a hierarchy. Figure 13-14 shows a typical CA hierarchy. In the figure, there are three tiers: the root CA, subordinate CAs (established for different geographic locations), and issuing CAs (often dedicated to issuing specific types of certificates). Note that the root CA is a standalone CA.

Security for the PKI infrastructure is added by hardening CA servers and establishing an *offline CA root*. The root CA is the most critical part of the CA hierarchy. If it is compromised, the entire PKI is compromised. An offline root CA can be more effectively protected since it never connected to the network. Additional physical security is usually provided by isolating the CA in a vault or other locked room and by using a *Hardware Security Module* (HSM) to manage the CA public and private encryption keys. A manual request at the root CA server console obtains the CA certificate and related private key for subordinate CAs. A root CA protected in this manner should be a standalone CA installed on a standalone server with no network connectivity. Its subordinate CAs can be Enterprise CAs. Requests for certificates from standalone (but network-interfaced CAs) and from enterprise CAs can be entered in web forms created during the CA installation process. Enterprise CAs can also be configured to automatically issue certificates. This eliminates the manual certificate requests that can thwart ease of implementation and make managing a PKI labor-intensive.

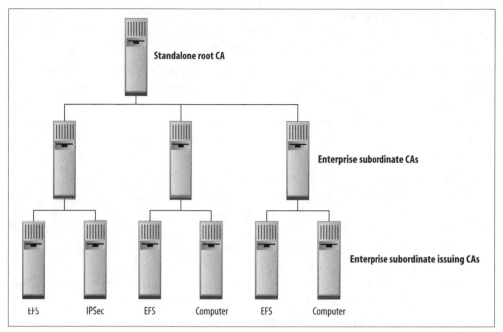

In addition to this basic knowledge of Windows PKI, the following important PKI terms should be familiar to network administrators:

Authority Information Access (AIA)
> This is the location where a copy of the CA certificate can be downloaded. The AIA can be stored at file shares, URLs, and in the Active Directory. Locations are configured on the CA and included in the certificates issues.

Certificate Revocation List (CRL)
> This is a list of certificates that have been revoked. All certificates are given an expiration date, and programs that use certificates should check this date before accepting the certificate. There are other reasons for rejecting a certificate such as the user it is assigned to having left the company, or the certificate having been compromised. These are reasons for a Certificate Manager to revoke a certificate. The CA lists the revoked certificate in the CRL and makes the list available so that applications can check it before proceeding.

CRL distribution point
> This is a location where the CRL can be downloaded. CRLs can be stored at file shares, URLs, and in the Active Directory. Locations are configured on the CA and included in the certificates issues.

Certificate templates
> Enterprise CAs use certificate templates to define the types of certificates that can be issued by the CA. Certificate template definitions can be managed by the

Certificate Manager. Permissions to obtain a CA certificate are set on the templates. If a user does not have this permission, she cannot obtain this type of certificate. An Enterprise CA can be limited to issuing specific types of certificates.

Setting up a PKI is not a trivial task and should not be undertaken without sufficient study, preparation, and the development of corporate policy that directs how certificate services will be implemented, used, and protected. However, there are several aspects of Windows PKI implementation that every Windows administrator should be aware of that are often sticking points in PKI or administration. Those aspects described include the following:

Configuring domains to use certificate services
When a CA is installed in a domain, Active Directory is usually automatically configured so that the domain members can use the certificates the CA issues. Still, you should know these requirements in case troubleshooting is required, and you need to be able to use the certificates in other domains in the forest.

Obtaining certificates for DCs and servers
Many networking techniques require that servers have their own certificate. There are several ways to obtain certificates for DCs and servers.

Configuring SMTP transport for AD replication
One of the network techniques that requires DC certificates is the use of SMTP transport for AD replication. Using this transport is often mentioned, but rarely explained.

Configuring domains to use certificate services

After an Enterprise CA is installed and configured, the computers and users in the domain in which the CA is installed can request certificates from the CA. If they are authorized to obtain the certificate, the CA will issue it to them and the certificate will be automatically installed on the computer. By default, Windows XP, Windows 2000, and Windows Server 2003 computers will automatically request and be issued a certificate when they are rebooted. This process is called *automatic enrollment*. Automatic enrollment for user certificates can be configured.

The domain in which the CA is installed is automatically configured to trust the CA. Child domains in the forest must be configured to use the CA. To do so, add the CA to the Cert Publishers group in the domain. Add a copy of the CA's certificate to the domain's Trusted Root Certification Authority store in Active Directory. The CA must be trusted by the domain before it can issue certificates to domain computers and users. Configure the templates for use by the child domains. The security permission Enroll must be granted to any computers or users authorized to obtain certificates.

Since exercises outlined later in this chapter require a DC certificate, these instructions are focused on obtaining one for a child domain. In the example, an Enterprise

Certification Authority has been installed in the *nomoore.local* root domain. The *west.nomoore.local* domain will be configured to obtain a DC certificate.

First, you must add the CA computer to the *west.nomoore.local* Cert Publishers group. Open the Start → Administrative Tools → Active Directory Users and Computers console for the *west.nomoore.local* domain. Select the Users node. In the detail pane on the right side of the screen, double-click on the Cert Publishers group. This group's members are authorized to issue certificates for domain users and computers. Select the Members tab, as shown in Figure 13-15.

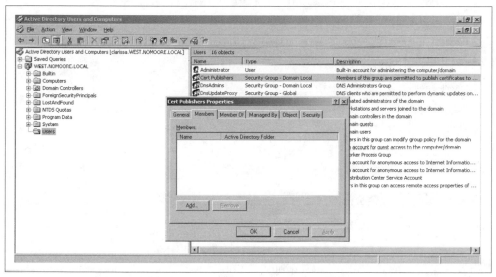

Figure 13-15. Members of the Cert Publishers group are trusted CAs for the domain

Click the Add button. Click the Object Types button and select Computers. Then click OK. Click the Locations button in the object picker and select the *nomoore. local* domain. Then click OK. Click Advanced followed by Find Now. Select the computer account where the Certification Authority is located (in this case, GV101), then click OK three times. The computer is added to the Cert Publishers group in the *west.nomoore.local* domain.

Next, you must add a copy of the CA's certificate to the *west.nomoore.local* domain's Trusted Root Certification Authority store.

Open Internet Explorer and enter **http://ip-address-of-GV101/certsrv**. This opens the Certification Authority web site. Select Download CA certificate, as shown in Figure 13-16.

Select Save and enter (or browse to) a place to store the certificate and then click Save. When the process is complete, click Close. Open the Start → Administrative Tools → Active Directory Users and Computers console. Right-click on the domain

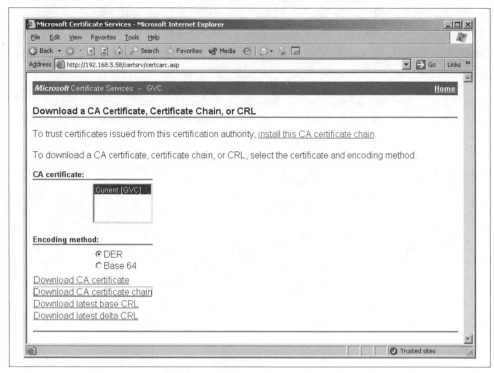

Figure 13-16. The web interface can be used to request certificates

and select Properties. Select Group Policy and click the Edit button. Expand the Windows Settings → Security Settings → Public Key Policies node. Right-click the Trusted Root Certification Authorities node and select Import, then click Next. Enter or browse to the file location and click Next twice. Click OK when told the import was successful. The certificate will appear in the Trusted Root Certification Authorities node detail pane, as shown in Figure 13-17.

Finally, you must configure Certificate templates. (An authorized CA administrator or Certificate Manager is required to perform this step.) On the CA, open the Start → Administrative Tools → Certification Authority console. Right-click the Certificate Templates node and select Manage. This opens the Certificate Templates console, as shown in Figure 13-18.

Double-click the Domain Controller template. Select the Security page. Click Add, then click Location. Select the *west.nomoore.local* domain and then click OK. Click Advanced then click Find Now. Double-click on the Domain Controllers entry and then click OK. Select the Allow/Enroll checkbox, as shown in Figure 13-19, and then click OK.

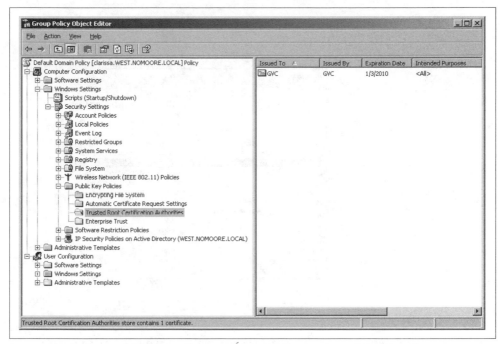

Figure 13-17. A copy of the CA certificate must be added to the Trusted Root Certification Authorities Public Key Policy

Obtaining certificates for DCs and servers

Many advanced networking features require that the servers involved have their own server certificates. If a server is a domain controller, a special DC certificate will automatically be issued to it. If a server is a member server, a server certificate will be automatically issued to it. As mentioned previously, this process is called *automatic enrollment*. If an Enterprise CA is installed in the forest root domain, the forest root domain is automatically configured for automatic enrollment. To obtain certificates for servers in child domains, configure child domains to trust the CA, and set the Enroll permission on the certificate template(s).

Computers will request and be issued certificates when they are next rebooted.

To obtain a computer certificate without rebooting, request a certificate using Internet Explorer or the Certificates template as detailed here.

Click Start → Run, and enter **mmc**. Then click OK. From the File menu, select Add/Remove Snap-in. Click Add. Select the Certificates snap-in and click Add. Select the "Computer account" radio button and then click Finish. Select "Local computer (the computer this console is running on)." While you can also select "Another computer" and enter its name or browse to it, you can only request certificates when opening the certificates console on the local computer. Click Finish, click Close, and

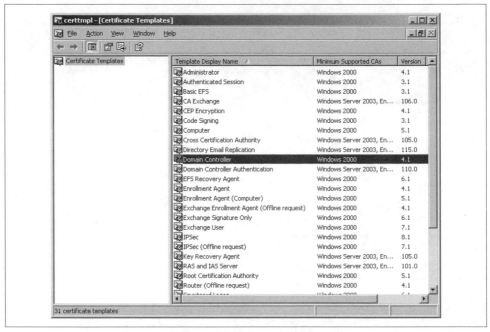

Figure 13-18. Certificate permissions must be configured in the Certificate Templates console

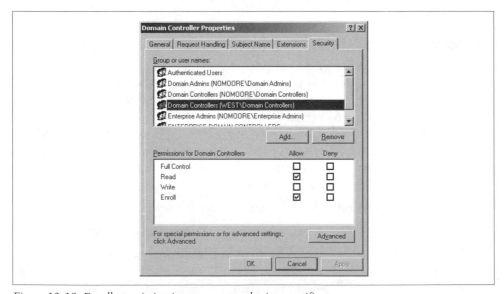

Figure 13-19. Enroll permission is necessary to obtain a certificate

then click OK. Expand the "Certificates (name-of-computer)" node. Right-click on the Personal node and select All Tasks. Select Request New Certificate. Click Next, select Domain Controller, and then click Next. Enter a friendly name (this will help you identify the certificate in the Certificates console) and click Next followed by Finish. Select the *Personal* folder to see the certificate in the folder.

To determine the type of certificate from the Certificates console, double-click on the certificate in the details pane, then click the Details tab, as shown in Figure 13-20. In the figure, note that the Certificate template is Domain Controller and that the "Enhanced key usage" shown includes server authentication.

Figure 13-20. Identify the certificate usage by viewing certificate details

Configuring SMTP transport for AD replication

Active Directory replication uses IP by default. SMTP may be used for replication between sites, but only for the replication of schema, configuration, and application partitions. The domain partition cannot be replicated using SMTP because the domain partition must be synchronized with the contents of the *SYSVOL* filesystem folder. *SYSVOL* is replicated using File Replication Service (FRS) and FRS cannot use SMTP for replication. Therefore, if domain controllers for the same domain exist in different sites, replication over SMTP cannot be used. If each site contains domain controllers from different domains, then replication over SMTP can be used. Using SMTP for replication may be useful when connectivity between sites is slow. In the following example, SMTP replication between the Default Site and the Boston site is configured and tested.

To configure SMTP transport for AD replication, first install a certificate for the DCs that are bridgehead servers in both sites. Each DC needs its own certificate. If a Microsoft Certification Authority server is installed, it can be configured to automatically provide DC certificates to all DCs. The certificate and its related private key are used in the encryption process of the SMTP messages and to authenticate the DC. To test this, you must have at least one child domain in addition to the root domain. To obtain certificates see the section "Obtaining certificates for DCs and servers" earlier in this chapter.

Install the SMTP service on both servers. SMTP is an optional service of IIS 6.0. Set up the SMTP intersite transport in Active Directory Sites and Services. Test replication using the *repadmin* tool. The *repadmin* tool is one of the Support Tools provided with Windows Server 2003.

The installation of certificates was detailed earlier in this chapter. Chapter 12 discusses how to set up the SMTP service.

To set up the SMTP intersite transport, begin by expanding the "Inter-sites transport" container. Right-click SMTP and select "New site link." Enter a name for the site link, as shown in Figure 13-21. The site link must have at least two sites. Add the sites to be used. In this example, there are only two sites and they are automatically added to the "Site in this site link" box.

Figure 13-21. A new site link must be configured for SMTP replication

Click OK. To set the cost for the site link, double-click on the site link in the detail pane to open its Properties pages. Change the cost in the Cost list box, as shown in Figure 13-22. *Cost* is an arbitrary number that you make up. For example you might set the cost of the IP site link at 200 and the cost of the SMTP link at 100. By setting the cost of the SMTP link at less than the cost assigned to the IP site link, the SMTP link will be given priority over the IP link. Traffic will be routed over the SMTP link. (If the SMTP link is unavailable, the IP link will be used.) Click OK to close the Properties box and return to the Active Directory Sites and Services console.

In Active Directory Sites and Services, right-click the NTDS Settings object and click Check Replication Topology. The Knowledge Consistency Checker (KCC), a built-in

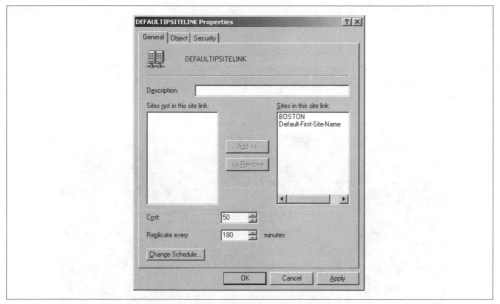

Figure 13-22. Setting a low cost on the site link makes it a preferred transport

process, evaluates the transports available, selects that with the lowest cost, and creates a connection object. Check the connection object's preferred transport by double-clicking the connection object to see the Properties pages, as shown in Figure 13-23. Note that the preferred transport, SMTP, is displayed in the Transport drop-down box.

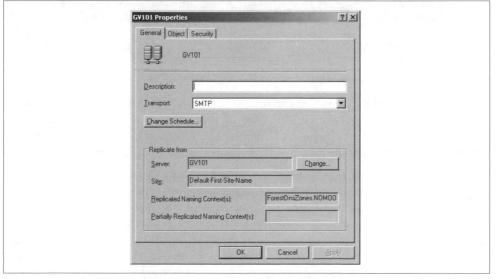

Figure 13-23. Check KCC preferred transport for connection objects

Repeat this procedure for the DC in the other site. Right-click the connection object and select Replicate Now to force replication and test the SMTP configuration. Repeat this for the other site.

To check replication using *repadmin*, open a command prompt by selecting Start → Run. Enter **repadmin /showreps** and click OK. View the results, looking for the "via SMTP" notes, as shown in Figure 13-24.

Figure 13-24. Check replication transport using repadmin

Securing LDAP communications

LDAP communications can be secured by using SSL. If the DC has a DC certificate and an LDAP client requests SSL, then the DC will support it. The Windows Server 2003 DC can also be set to require LDAP over SSL. If it is configured to do so, then it will reject communications from an LDAP client that is not configured to use LDAP.

To configure the DC to require LDAP over SSL, provide all DCs in the domain with DC certificates. (To obtain a DC certificate, see the section "Obtaining certificates for DCs and servers" earlier in this chapter.) Then, open the Start → Administrative Tools → Domain Controller Security Policy console. Expand the Local Policies node. Select Security Options and double-click on the security policy "Domain Controller: LDAP server signing requirements" to open it. Click "Define this policy setting" and use the drop-down list box to set the policy to "Require signing," as shown in Figure 13-25. Click OK.

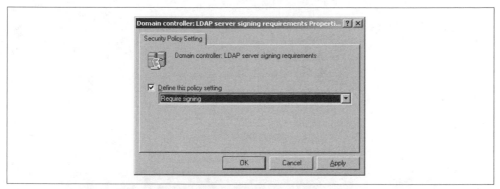

Figure 13-25. Require LDAP over SSL in Security Options

To configure DCs to support requests from clients to use SSL for LDAP, provide each DC with a Domain Controller certificate and configure the application using LDAP to use SSL. If either step is skipped, LDAP will not use SSL. LDAP signing can be required. A DC cannot be configured to require LDAP communications to use SSL. To obtain a DC certificate, see the section "Obtaining certificates for DCs and servers" earlier in this chapter. Each application that uses LDAP may need a different configuration to use SSL. In most cases, the primary configuration required is to set the port to the assigned LDAP SSL port (636).

To test the use of SSL for LDAP, you must configure the Active Directory search tool and create an SSL connection. Right-click the Start button and select Search. Click "Other search options." Click "Printers, computers or people." Click "People in your address book." In the Find People dialog box, use the drop down list to select Active Directory. Right-click Active Directory and select Properties. Select the General tab, and then enter a server name, as shown in Figure 13-26.

Select the Advanced tab and enter a search base (for example `CN=users,DC=west, DC=nomoore,DC=local`). Click "This server requires a secure connection (SSL)," as shown in Figure 13-27. Note that in the figure the port has been changed to 636.

Click OK. In the Find People box, enter the name of a user to locate and click Find Now. Use the Properties button to find information on this user.

There is one final advanced network security feature that you should be aware of and that is SMB Signing. SMB signing, explained in the following section, is turned on by default in Windows Server 2003 and may therefore cause you problems in network communications since earlier versions of Windows do not have it turned on by default.

SMB Signing

Systems Message Block (SMB) is the basis for file and print sharing in Windows computers. It is also used for other purposes such as disseminating Group Policy from

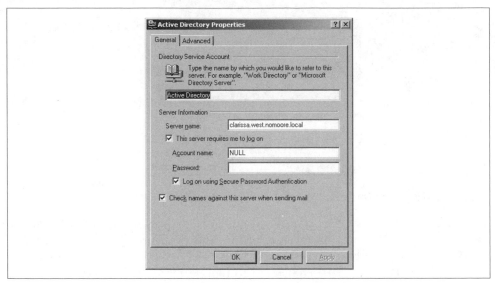

Figure 13-26. Set the server name for the DC to use

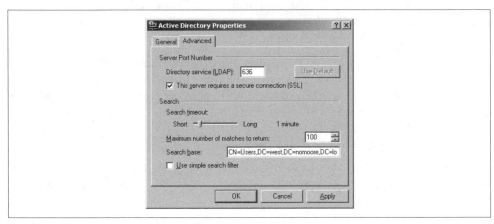

Figure 13-27. Requiring SSL changes the port

domain controllers to member computers during logon. SMB packets can be digitally signed, thus ensuring that the identity of the server from which they came. This protection can foil an attack in which a rogue computer is inserted between a client and server (called a *man-in-the-middle attack*) or in which a server is spoofed. These attacks might be used to either obtain sensitive data (*data hijacking*), or to modify data in transit. To protect data from the possibility of data hijacking or modification, use SMB Signing.

SMB Signing may significantly impact performance. Computers on which SMB signing is enabled may experience up to 15% degradation. This nontrivial impact can be offset by scaling the servers to ensure that they have the necessary power.

SMB signing has been available since Service Pack 3 for Windows NT 4.0 and is on by default in Windows Server 2003. Both client and server must be configured for SMB Signing or they will not be able to communicate. This means that administrators will have to configure SMB signing for earlier versions of Windows computers, or change the default settings on Windows Server 2003.

The SMB protocol supports both a client component and server component, and both Windows workstations and servers are capable of using both components. A Windows XP Professional computer on which a share has been configured will act as a server when another computer downloads a file from it. It will act as a client if it is attempting to download a file from any other Windows computer. Likewise, a Windows Server 2003 server can be either a client or a server. This is why settings for both client and server should be configured for SMB signing, and why settings on both computers must be evaluated if troubleshooting is required.

The following Windows Server 2003 settings that control SMB signing are set in Group Policy in Windows Settings → Security Settings → Local Policies → Security Options:

Microsoft network client: Digitally sign communications (always)
    If enabled, when the computer is a client, it will always sign SMB packets. It will not communicate with a server that does not have SMB signing enabled. (SMB packet signing is required.)

Microsoft network client: Digitally sign communications (if server agrees)
    If enabled, when the computer is a client, it will negotiate signing with the server. If the server cannot digitally sign communications, the client will still communicate.

Microsoft network server: Digitally sign communications (always)
    If enabled, the server will always sign SMB packets. It will not communicate with a client that does not have SMB signing enabled. (SMB packet signing is required.) This setting is enabled by default in the Domain Controller Security Policy and in the Local Security Policy of a standalone Windows Server 2003 server.

Microsoft network server: Digitally sign communications (if client agrees)
    If enabled, the server will sign packets if the client requires it. This setting is enabled by default in the Domain Controller Security Policy and in the Local Security Policy of a standalone Windows Server 2003 server.

To implement SMB signing in earlier versions of Windows, follow these instructions:

For Windows 2000
Use the Security Options as described earlier for Windows Server 2003.

For Windows NT 4.0 SP3 and above
Enable SMB signing for a server by adding the value Enable Security Signature and setting it to 1. To require SMB signing, add the value Require Security Signature to 1. Both REG_DWORD values should be added at *HKEY_LOCAL_MACHINESystem\CurrentControlSet\Services\LanManServer\Parameters*.

For Windows NT 4.0 SP3 and above
Enable SMB signing for a client by adding the value Enable Security Signature and setting it to 1. To require SMB signing, add the value Require Security Signature to 1. Both REG_DWORD values should be added at *HKEY_LOCAL_MACHINESystem\CurrentControlSet\Services\Rdr\Parameters*.

For Windows 98
Enable SMB signing for a client by adding the value Enable Security Signature and setting it to 1. This REG_DWORD value should be added at *HKEY_LOCAL_MACHINE System\CurrentControlSet\Services\VxD\Vnetsup*.

To remove the SMB signing requirement from Windows Server 2003, change the enabled settings to Disabled or Not configured.

 The removal of the SMB signing requirement is not recommended because this reduces security.

Summary

Security has always been an important part of network administration. It has not always been easy to accomplish without purchasing third-party programs, and even basic security has not always been possible to do at all. Windows Server 2003 provides native tools that can be used to make both the operating system and network communications more secure. To use them, the network administrator must understand the basic security posture of Windows, what tools and functions are available, and how they can be (and when they can be) used. Understanding the security posture can make securing Windows systems easier. Knowing what can be done (and how) empowers the network administrator by providing solutions to security problems.

Now that you have studied network operations and security, it is time to take a look at how to troubleshoot basic networking operations. Chapter 14 provides information on how to find the cause of and fix networking problems.

## CHAPTER 14

Troubleshooting TCP/IP

Network administration tasks fall into two very different categories: configuration and troubleshooting. Configuration tasks prepare the system for the expected network environment; they require detailed knowledge of system configuration but are usually simple and predictable. Once a system is properly configured, there is rarely any reason to change it. The configuration process is repeated each time a new release of Windows is installed, but usually with very few changes.

In contrast, network troubleshooting deals with the unexpected. Troubleshooting frequently requires knowledge that is conceptual rather than detailed. Network problems are apt to be unique and sometimes difficult to resolve. Troubleshooting is an important part of maintaining a stable, reliable network service.

This chapter discusses the tools you can use to ensure that the network is in good running condition. However, good tools are not enough. No troubleshooting tool is effective if applied haphazardly. Effective troubleshooting requires a methodical approach to the problem and a basic understanding of how the network works. So we'll start our discussion by looking at ways to approach a network problem.

Approaching a Problem

To approach a problem properly, you need a basic understanding of how networks operate. The first few chapters of this book discuss the basics of TCP/IP protocols, and provide enough background information to troubleshoot most network problems. Knowledge of how data is routed through the network, between individual hosts, and between the layers in the protocol stack is important for understanding a network problem, but detailed knowledge of each protocol usually isn't necessary. The fine details of the protocols are rarely needed in debugging. When they are used, they should be looked up in a definitive reference—not recalled from memory.

Not all TCP/IP problems are alike, and not all problems can be approached in the same manner. But the key to solving any problem is understanding what the problem is. This is not as easy as it may seem. The surface problem is sometimes misleading, and the real problem is frequently obscured by many layers of software. When the true nature of the problem is understood, the solution to the problem is often obvious.

First, gather detailed information about exactly what's happening. When the problem is reported, talk to the user. Find out which application failed. What are the remote host's name and IP address? What are the user's hostname and address? What error message was displayed? If possible, verify the problem by having the user run the application while you talk him through it. If possible, duplicate the problem on your own system.

Testing from the user's system and other systems helps you learn:

- Does the problem occur in other applications on the user's host, or is only one application having trouble? If only one application is involved, the application may be misconfigured or disabled on the remote host. Because of security concerns, many systems disable some services.

- Does the problem occur with only one remote host, all remote hosts, or only certain groups of remote hosts? If only one remote host is involved, the problem could easily be with that host. If all remote hosts are involved, the problem is probably with the user's system (particularly if no other hosts on your local network are experiencing the same problem). If only hosts on certain subnets or external networks are involved, the problem may be related to routing.

- Does the problem occur on other local systems? Make sure you check other systems on the same subnet. If the problem occurs only on the user's host, concentrate testing on that system. If the problem affects every system on a subnet, concentrate on the router for that subnet.

Once you know the symptoms of the problem, visualize each protocol and device that handles the data. Visualizing the problem will help you avoid oversimplification and will keep you from assuming that you know the cause even before you start testing. Using your network knowledge, narrow your attack to the most likely causes of the problem, but keep an open mind.

Troubleshooting Hints

There are several useful troubleshooting hints you should know. These are not a troubleshooting methodology, just good ideas to keep in mind. Here they are, listed in no particular order:

- Approach problems methodically. Allow the information gathered from each test to guide your testing. Don't jump into another test scenario, based on a hunch, without ensuring that you can pick up your original test scenario where you left off.

- Work carefully through the problem, dividing it into manageable pieces. Test each piece before moving on to the next. For example, when testing a network connection, test each part of the network until you find the problem.

- Change only one variable at a time and rerun the test for each variable changed.

- Keep good records of the tests you have completed and their results. Keep a historical record of the problem in case it reappears.

- Keep an open mind. Don't assume too much about the cause of the problem. Don't assume a problem seen at the application level is not caused by a problem at a lower level. Some people assume their network is always at fault, while others assume the remote end is always the problem. Some people are so sure they know the cause of a problem that they ignore the evidence of the tests. Don't fall into these traps. Test each possibility and base your actions on the evidence of the tests.

- Be aware of security barriers. Security firewalls sometimes block ping, tracert, and even ICMP error messages. If problems seem to cluster around a specific remote site, find out if it has a firewall.

- Pay attention to error messages. Error messages are often vague, but they frequently contain important hints for solving the problem.

- Listen carefully to the user's trouble report. Many users are quite knowledgeable and can provide useful help troubleshooting. Even a naïve user can provide insight because they have observed the problem and may have seen it several times.

- Duplicate the reported problem yourself. Don't rely too heavily on the user's problem report. The user may have seen this problem only from the application level. If necessary, obtain the user's data files to duplicate the problem. Even if you cannot duplicate the problem, log the details of the reported problem for your records.

- Most problems are caused by human error. You can prevent some of them by providing information and training on network configuration and usage.

- Keep your users informed. This not only reduces the number of duplicated trouble reports, but also prevents duplication of effort when several system administrators work on the same problem without knowing others are already working on it. If you're lucky, someone may have seen the problem before and have a helpful suggestion about how to resolve it.

- Don't speculate about the cause of the problem while talking to the user. Save your speculations for discussions with your networking colleagues. Your speculations may be accepted by the user as gospel and become rumors. These rumors can cause users to avoid using legitimate network services and may undermine confidence in your network. Users want solutions to their problems; they're not interested in speculative technobabble.

- Stick to a few simple troubleshooting tools. For most network software problems, the tools discussed in this chapter are sufficient. You could spend more time learning how to use a new tool than it would take to resolve the problem with an old familiar tool.

- Thoroughly test the problem at your end of the network before locating the owner of the remote system to coordinate testing with him. The greatest complication of network troubleshooting is that you do not always control the systems at both ends of the network. In many cases, you may not even know who controls the remote system. The more information you have about your end, the simpler the job will be when you have to contact the remote administrator.

- Don't neglect the obvious. A loose or damaged cable is always a possible problem. Check plugs, connectors, cables, and switches. Small things can cause big problems.

Diagnostic Tools

Because most problems have a simple cause, developing a clear idea of the problem often provides the solution. Unfortunately, this is not always true, so in this section we begin to discuss the tools that can help you attack the most intractable problems. Most of the tools discussed in this chapter are software tools, but you should also keep some hardware tools handy.

You need enough simple hand tools to maintain the network's equipment and wiring. A pair of needle-nose pliers and a few screwdrivers may be sufficient, but you may also need specialized tools to maintain your wiring. For example, attaching RJ45 connectors to Unshielded Twisted Pair (UTP) cable requires special crimping tools. If you buy a network maintenance toolkit from your cable vendor, it will probably contain everything you need.

A full-featured cable tester is also useful. Modern cable testers are small handheld units with a keypad and LCD display. Tests are selected from the keyboard and results are displayed on the LCD screen. It is not necessary to interpret the results, because the unit does that for you and displays the error condition in a simple text message. For example, a cable test might produce the message "Short at 74 feet." This tells you that the cable is shorted 74 feet away from the tester. What could be simpler? The proper test tools make it easier to locate, and therefore fix, cable problems.

A properly configured laptop computer is also a useful piece of test equipment. Take the laptop to the location where the user reports a network problem. Disconnect the Ethernet cable from the back of the user's system and attach it to the laptop. Configure the laptop as appropriate for the user's subnet and reboot it. Then run a series of tests from that location. If everything works, the fault is probably in the user's computer. The user trusts this test because it demonstrates something he does every day. Unlike an unidentifiable piece of test equipment displaying the message "No faults found," the user has confidence in the laptop. If the test fails, the fault is probably in the network equipment or wiring. That's the time to bring out the cable tester.

Another advantage of using a laptop as a piece of test equipment is its inherent versatility. It can run a wide variety of test, diagnostic, and management software. Install Windows on the laptop and run the software discussed in the rest of this chapter from your desktop or your laptop.

Many diagnostic tools are available, ranging from commercial systems with specialized hardware and software that may cost thousands of dollars, to free software that is available from the Internet. Many software tools are provided with your Windows system. This book emphasizes the software diagnostic tools that come with Windows Server 2003:

ipconfig
: Provides information about the basic configuration of the interface. It is useful for detecting bad IP addresses, incorrect subnet masks, and improper broadcast addresses.

arp
: Provides information about Ethernet/IP address translation. It can be used to detect systems on the local network that are configured with the wrong IP address. arp is covered in this chapter and is used in an example in Chapter 2.

netstat
: Provides a variety of information. It is used to display interface statistics, network sockets, and the network routing table.

ping
: Indicates whether or not a remote host can be reached. ping also displays information about packet loss and packet delivery time.

portqry
: Reports the status of a remote port, including whether or not the port is filtered by a firewall. Used like ping to troubleshoot connectivity problems.

nslookup
: Provides information about the DNS name service. nslookup is covered in detail in Chapter 6.

tracert
: Prints information about each routing hop that packets take going from your system to a remote system.

Network Monitor
: Analyzes the individual packets exchanged between hosts on a network. Network Monitor is a TCP/IP protocol analyzer provided with Windows Server 2003. It can examine the contents of packets and is useful for analyzing protocol problems.

Each of these tools, even those covered earlier in the text, is used in this chapter. We start with ping, which is used in more troubleshooting situations than any other diagnostic tool.

Testing Basic Connectivity

The ping command tests whether a remote host can be reached from your computer. This simple function is extremely useful for testing the network connection, independent of the application in which the original problem was detected. ping allows you to determine whether further testing should be directed toward the network connection (the lower protocol layers) or the application (the upper layers). When ping shows that packets can travel to the remote system and back, the user's problem is probably in the upper layers. When packets can't make the round-trip, lower protocol layers are probably at fault.

Frequently, a user reports a network problem by stating that he can't telnet (or FTP, or send email, or whatever) to some remote host. He then immediately qualifies this statement with the announcement that it worked before. In cases like this, where the ability to connect to the remote host is in question, ping is a very useful tool.

Using the hostname provided by the user, ping the remote host. If your ping is successful, have the user ping the host. If the user's ping is also successful, concentrate further analysis on the specific application that the user is having trouble with. Perhaps the user is attempting to telnet to a host that only provides web service. Perhaps the host was down when the user tried his application. Have the user try it again, while you watch or listen to every detail of what he or she is doing. If he is doing everything right and the application still fails, detailed analysis of the application with Network Monitor and coordination with the remote system administrator may be needed.

If your ping is successful and the user's ping fails, concentrate testing on the user's system configuration, and on those things that are different about the user's path to the remote host, when compared to your path to the remote host.

If your ping fails, or the user's ping fails, pay close attention to any error messages. The error messages displayed by ping are helpful guides for planning further testing. The details of the messages may vary, but there are only a few basic types of errors:

hostname not found
> The remote host's name cannot be resolved by name service into an IP address. The name servers could be at fault (either your local server or the remote system's server), the name could be incorrect, or something could be wrong with the network between your system and the remote server. If you know the remote host's IP address, try to ping that. If you can reach the host using its IP address, the problem is with name service. Use nslookup to test the local and remote servers, and to check the accuracy of the hostname the user gave you.

network unreachable

The local system does not have a route to the remote system. If the numeric IP address was used on the `ping` command line, reenter the `ping` command using the hostname. This eliminates the possibility that the IP address was entered incorrectly, or that you were given the wrong address. If a routing protocol is being used, make sure it is running and use `netstat` to check the routing table. If a static default route is being used, make sure the default route is in the routing table. If everything seems fine on the host, check its default gateway for routing problems.

no answer

The remote system did not respond. Most network utilities have some version of this message. Some print the message "100% packet loss"; others print the message "Connection timed out" or the error "cannot connect." All of these errors mean the same thing: the local system has a route to the remote system, but it receives no response from the remote system to any of the packets it sends. There are many possible causes of this problem. The remote host may be down. Either the local or the remote host may be configured incorrectly. A gateway or circuit between the local host and the remote host may be down. The remote host may have routing problems. Only additional testing can isolate the cause of the problem. Carefully check the local configuration using `ipconfig`. Check the route to the remote system with `tracert`. Contact the administrator of the remote system and report the problem.

All of the tools mentioned here will be discussed later in this chapter. However, before leaving `ping`, let's look more closely at the command.

The ping Command

The basic format of the `ping` command is `ping` *destination*, where *destination* is the hostname or IP address of the remote host being tested. Use the hostname or address provided by the user in the trouble report. For example, to check that 192.168.0.12 can be reached from the local host use the following command:

```
D:\>ping 192.168.0.12

Pinging 192.168.0.12 with 32 bytes of data:

Reply from 192.168.0.12: bytes=32 time=1ms TTL=64
Reply from 192.168.0.12: bytes=32 time=1ms TTL=64
Reply from 192.168.0.12: bytes=32 time=1ms TTL=64
Reply from 192.168.0.12: bytes=32 time<1ms TTL=64

Ping statistics for 192.168.0.12:
    Packets: Sent = 4, Received = 4, Lost = 0 (0% loss),
Approximate round trip times in milli-seconds:
    Minimum = 0ms, Maximum = 1ms, Average = 0ms
```

By default, the Windows `ping` command sends out four 32-byte test packets. The sample test shows a good high-speed local area network link with no packet loss and extremely fast response. The round-trip takes less than 1 millisecond. A small packet loss, and round-trip times that are two orders of magnitude higher, would not be abnormal for a connection made across a wide area network. The statistics displayed by the `ping` command can indicate low-level network problems. The key statistics are:

- The sequence in which the packets are arriving, as shown by the ICMP sequence number (`icmp_seq`) displayed for each packet.

- How long it takes a packet to make the round-trip, displayed in milliseconds after the string `time=`.

- The percentage of packets lost, displayed in a summary line near the end of the `ping` output.

If the packet loss is high or the response time is slow, there could be a network hardware problem. If you see these conditions when communicating great distances on a wide area network, there is nothing to worry about. TCP/IP was designed to deal with unreliable networks, and some wide area networks suffer a lot of packet loss. But if these problems are seen on a local area network, they indicate trouble.

On a local network cable segment the round-trip time should be near zero, there should be little or no packet loss, and the packets should arrive in order. If these things are not true, there is a problem with the network hardware. On an Ethernet the problem could be improper cable termination, a bad cable segment, or a bad piece of active hardware, such as a hub, switch, or transceiver. Check the cable with a cable tester as described earlier. Good hubs and switches often have built in diagnostic software that can be checked. Cheap hubs and transceivers may require the brute-force method of disconnecting individual pieces of hardware until the problem goes away.

The results of a simple `ping` test, even if the test is successful, can help you direct further testing toward the most likely causes of the problem. But other diagnostic tools are needed to examine the problem more closely and find the underlying cause.

Using portqry

`ping` uses the ICMP Echo message to test connectivity. This means that `ping` can test the network connection independent of the network application in which the problem was observed, which helps you focus testing on the application or on the underlying network. However, because `ping` works via ICMP, it cannot test the upper layers of the protocol stack directly or check the specific port associated with an application. `portqry` addresses these limitations by testing connectivity to a specified port and by understanding the upper-layer protocols necessary to communicate with the port.

portqry tests connectivity to a remote port and attempts to determine if the port is filtered. portqry reports its findings to the user using three status values:

LISTENING

> This status indicates that portqry received the expected response from the remote host.

NOT LISTENING

> This status indicates that portqry received an ICMP message from the remote host or an intermediate router indicating that either the port or the host is unreachable.

FILTERED

> This status indicates that portqry received no response from the remote host or any intermediate gateway. portqry makes three attempts to connect to the remote port before displaying this status.

portqry knows how to properly query a remote port and how to interpret the response from the port because it understands the upper-layer protocols used to communicate with the port. portqry supports a wide range of application protocols. Selecting Predefined Services from the Help menu in the Port Query window shows some of the protocols supported by portqry.

Selecting Predefined Queries from the Help menu displays a detailed list of the predefined queries in the Query result box at the bottom of the window. Notice the variety of protocols just in the section of the listing visible in Figure 14-1. RPC, LDAP, Kerberos, SMB, NetBIOS, WINS, ISAKMP, PPTP, DNS, and DHCP are all visible in this example, and there are several more supported protocols. Support for a wide range of protocols is one of the things that make portqry useful for testing and troubleshooting.

The predefined queries listed in Figure 14-1 are the same queries that can be run by selecting "Querying predefined service" and choosing the service to be queried from the "Service to query" drop-down list. This type of query can be used to test that a service is up and running and is often used to test the services that your server offers to others.

When troubleshooting a specific network problem, the focus is sometimes on an individual port associated with one troublesome application. In that case, you may want to enter the port manually. To do so, select "Manually input query" ports and enter the exact ports that you want to query in the "Ports to query" box. Figure 14-2 shows a manual query of DNS on a remote system.

The IP address or full hostname of the remote system that is being queried must be entered in the box near the top of the window. In Figure 14-2, 192.168.0.3 is the IP address of the remote host we are testing. We are querying port 53 because that is the standard port used for DNS. Notice the Protocol box in Figure 14-2. It contains the value BOTH, which means that both TCP port 53 and UDP port 53 will be queried.

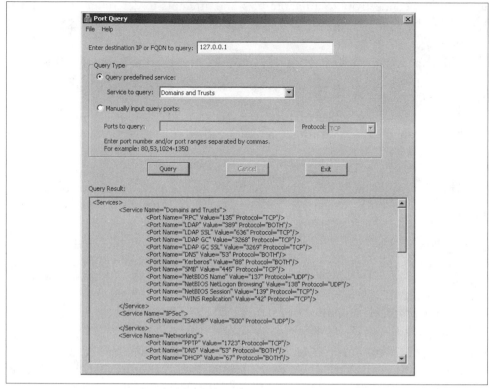

Figure 14-1. Predefined services in portqry

The other possible selections in the Protocol drop-down list are TCP and UDP, which limits the query to the selected transport protocol.

The result of the query is shown in the box at the bottom of the window. In Figure 14-2, portqry reports that the remote system is listening to both TCP port 53 and UDP port 53. This means that the remote system is running DNS and we can reach the DNS port of the remote system from our local system, which in turn means that we have end-to-end connectivity to that port.

In Figure 14-2, one port (53) was queried via multiple transport protocols (TCP and UDP). It is also possible to query multiple ports. As an example, assume you're dealing with a private web server and are not sure whether the server is listening on the standard HTTP port 80, or on port 8080, which is sometimes used for private web servers. You could run a query such as the one shown in Figure 14-3.

In Figure 14-3, two ports, 80 and 8080, are listed in the "Ports to query" box. portqry first tests port 80 and then it tests port 8080. In this example, the query result says that port 80 is not listening and that port 8080 is listening. The remote server, in this case, is running the web server on 8080 and not on the standard port 80.

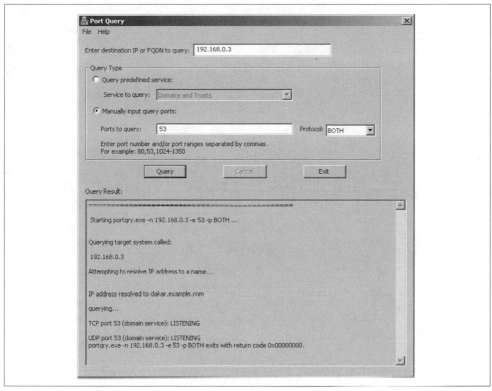

Figure 14-2. A portqry test of the DNS ports

All of the examples in this section have shown the graphic user interface for portqry, which is launched by running the command portqueryui. However, portqry itself can be run directly from the command line. The same query shown in Figure 14-3 could be run from the command line as follows:

```
C:\PortQryUI>portqry -n dakar.example.com -e 80,8080 -p TCP

Querying target system called:

 dakar.example.com

Attempting to resolve name to IP address...

Name resolved to 192.168.0.3

querying...

TCP port 80 (http service): NOT LISTENING

TCP port 8080 (unknown service): LISTENING
```

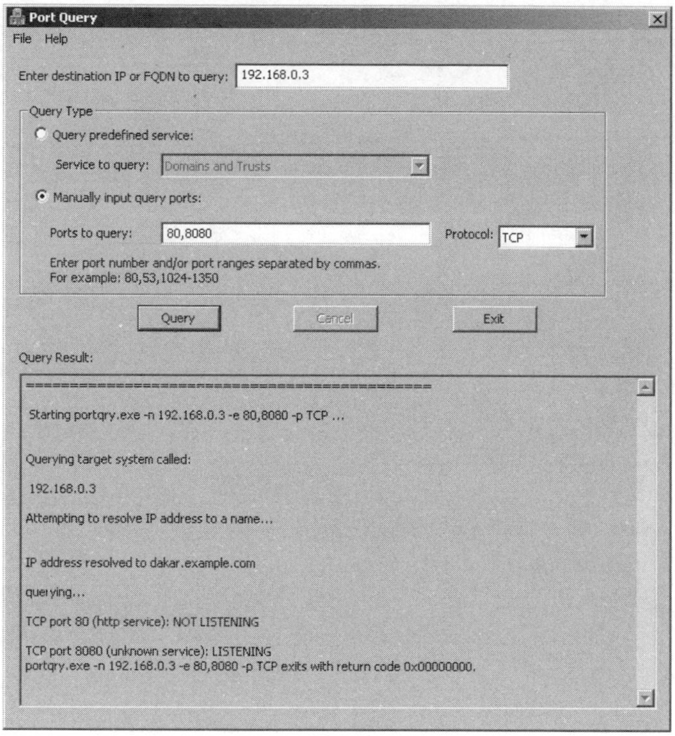

Figure 14-3. Querying multiple ports

In this example, the command-line options identify the remote system, the ports being queried, and the transport protocol being used. These are the most commonly used options; however, the portqry command has several others. The full portqry syntax is:

```
portqry -n remote_host [-p protocol] [-e | -r | -o port] [-q] [-l file] [-y] [-q] [-sp
source_port] [-sl] [-nr] [-cn community_name]
```

The command-line options are as follows:

-n *remote_host*

    The IP address or full hostname of the system to be queried.

-p *protocol*

    The transport layer protocol, which must be TCP, UDP, or BOTH.

-e *port*

    One or more ports to be queried. A range of port numbers can be specified by placing a hypen between the lower and upper values of the range, e.g., 80-96. A list of port values and port ranges can be specified by separating the individual values in the list with commas, e.g., 67,68,80-96.

-r *port_range*

The range of ports to be queried specified by separating the lower range value from the upper range value with a colon, e.g., 80:96. Note that port ranges can be specified with the –e option; the –r option is not required for port ranges; it is just another way of specifying them.

-o *list_of_ports*

A comma-separated list of the ports to be queried. Note that a list of ports can be specified with the –e option; the –o option is not required to define a list of ports; it is just another way to do it.

-l *file*

The filename of the log file where the output of the portqry command should be written.

-y

Tells portqry to overwrite an existing log file without prompting the user before doing so. By default, portqry will not overwrite an existing log file without explicit permission from the user.

-q

This option directs portqry to run in quiet mode. In this mode, no output is displayed or written to the log file. In quiet mode only the following return codes are used by the portqry command to indicate the query result:

0   The remote port is listening.

1   The remote port is not listening.

2   The remote port is filtered.

-sp *source_port*

Defines the port on the local host that portqry should use to issue the query. By default, portqry uses a dynamically assigned source port—the same as any other application.

-sl

This option is used to inform portqry that the query will travel on a slow link and that portqry should allow more generous timeouts to compensate for the slow network performance.

-nr

This option prevents portqry from doing a DNS lookup to convert the IP address provided by the –n argument into a hostname. By default, the IP address is resolved to a hostname for the portqry output.

-cn *community_name*

This option defines the SNMP community name needed to query an SNMP port. The community name must be enclosed in exclamation marks (!).

The Port Query graphic user interface is flexible enough for most troubleshooting situations. The command-line interface, however, is easily scripted, which makes it useful for complex testing. The interface you use is up to you. Both work well.

Version 2.0 is the current version of portqry at this writing. That is not the version that shipped with Windows XP or Windows Server 2003. Microsoft highly recommends that portqry users upgrade to Version 2.0, which can be downloaded from *http://www.microsoft.com*.

Troubleshooting Network Access

The "no answer" and "cannot connect" errors indicate a problem in the lower layers of the network protocols. If the preliminary tests point to this type of problem, concentrate your testing on routing and on the network interface. Use the ipconfig, netstat, and arp commands to test the Network Access Layer.

Troubleshooting with the ipconfig Command

ipconfig checks the network interface configuration. Use this command to verify the user's configuration if the user's system has been recently configured, or if the user's system cannot reach the remote host while other systems on the same network can.

When ipconfig is entered with the /all argument, it displays the current configuration values assigned to the interface. For example:

```
C:\>ipconfig /all

Windows IP Configuration

        Host Name . . . . . . . . . . . . : komodo
        Primary Dns Suffix  . . . . . . . : example.com
        Node Type . . . . . . . . . . . . : Unknown
        IP Routing Enabled. . . . . . . . : No
        WINS Proxy Enabled. . . . . . . . : No
        DNS Suffix Search List. . . . . . : example.com

Ethernet adapter D-Link Ethernet Adapter:

        Connection-specific DNS Suffix  . : example.com
        Description . . . . . . . . . . . : D-Link DFE-530TX+ PCI Adapter
        Physical Address. . . . . . . . . : 00-50-BA-3F-C2-5E
        DHCP Enabled. . . . . . . . . . . : No
        IP Address. . . . . . . . . . . . : 192.168.0.20
        Subnet Mask . . . . . . . . . . . : 255.255.255.0
        Default Gateway . . . . . . . . . : 192.168.0.1
                                            192.168.0.250
        DNS Servers . . . . . . . . . . . : 192.168.0.20
                                            192.168.0.1
```

The `ipconfig` command displays information about the TCP/IP configuration and information about the network interface. Check the information for configuration errors. The Windows Server 2003 `ipconfig` command clearly labels each piece of information it provides from *Host Name* to *DNS Servers*. You should know what values are correct for your network, and thus be able to quickly detect a configuration error if one has been made.

Two common interface configuration problems that occur when users are required to manually configure their own systems are (1) incorrect subnet masks and (2) incorrect IP addresses. A bad subnet mask is indicated when the host can reach other hosts on its local subnet and remote hosts on distant networks, but it cannot reach hosts on other local subnets. If a bad subnet mask is set, `ipconfig` quickly reveals it.

An incorrectly set IP address can be a subtle problem. If the network part of the address is incorrect, every ping will fail with the "no answer" error. In this case, using `ipconfig` will reveal the incorrect address. If the host part of the address is wrong, the problem can be more difficult to detect. A desktop system that only connects out to other systems and never accepts incoming connections can run for a long time with the wrong address without its user noticing the problem. Additionally, the system that suffers the ill effects may not be the one that is misconfigured. It is possible for someone to accidentally use your IP address on his system, and for the mistake to cause your system intermittent communications problems. An example of this problem is discussed later. This type of configuration error cannot be discovered by `ipconfig` because the error is on a remote host. The `arp` command is used for this type of problem.

Troubleshooting with the arp Command

The `arp` command is used to analyze problems with IP to Ethernet address translation. It has several options, three of which are particularly useful for troubleshooting:

-a
    Display all ARP entries in the table

-d *hostname*
    Delete an entry from the ARP table

-s *hostname ether-address*
    Add a new entry to the table

With these three options you can view the contents of the ARP table, delete a problem entry, and install a corrected entry. The ability to install a corrected entry is useful in buying time while you look for the permanent fix.

Use `arp` if you suspect that incorrect entries are getting into the address resolution table. One clear indication of problems with the ARP table is a report that the wrong host responded to some network command. Intermittent problems that affect only certain hosts can also indicate that the ARP table has been corrupted. ARP table problems are usually caused by two systems using the same IP address. The problems appear intermittent, because the entry that appears in the table is the address of the host that responded quickest to the last ARP request. Sometimes the correct host responds first, and sometimes the wrong host responds first.

If you suspect that two systems are using the same IP address, display the address resolution table with the arp -a command. Here's an example:

```
C:\>arp -a

Interface: 192.168.0.20 --- 0x10003
  Internet Address      Physical Address      Type
  192.168.0.2           00-e0-4c-9b-99-19     dynamic
  192.168.0.3           00-00-c0-9a-72-ca     dynamic
  192.168.0.12          00-10-a4-8b-8b-97     dynamic
```

It is easiest to verify that the IP and Ethernet address pairs are correct if you have a record of each host's correct Ethernet address. For this reason you should record the Ethernet and IP address of each host assigned a static address when it is added to your network. (We emphasize static addresses because addresses assigned by DHCP do not cause address conflicts, which is one more advantage to using DHCP.) If you have a record of Ethernet addresses, you'll quickly see if anything is wrong with the table.

If you don't have this type of record, the first three bytes of the Ethernet address can help you to detect a problem. The first three bytes of the address identify the equipment manufacturer. A list of these identifying prefixes is found at *http://www.iana.org/assignments/ethernet-numbers*.

From the vendor prefixes we see that one of the ARP entries displayed in our example is a system with an SMC board (00-00-c0), one uses a VIA Technologies adapter (00-e0-4c), and one entry is a system with a Xircom board (00-10-a4). If one of those addresses is really supposed to be assigned to a Cisco router, we know there is a mistakenly configured IP address because the Cisco prefix is 00-00-0c.

If neither checking a record of correct assignments nor checking the manufacturer prefix helps you identify the source of the errant ARP, try using Telnet to connect to the IP address shown in the ARP entry. If the device supports Telnet, the logon banner might help you identify the incorrectly configured host.

ARP problem case study

A user called in asking if the server was down, and reported the following problem. The user's desktop system (*yukon.example.com*) appeared to lock up for minutes at a time when certain programs were used, while other programs worked smoothly. The programs that depended on access to the file server all caused the lock-up problem, but some unrelated commands also caused the problem.

The commands that failed on the client were commands that either required the server's services or else were stored in a directory shared from the server. The commands that ran correctly were installed locally on the user's workstation. No one else reported a problem with the server, and we were able to ping the client and the server and get good responses.

We had the user check the Event Viewer for recent error messages, and she discovered a message indicating that the client detected another host on the Ethernet responding to its IP address. The imposter used the Ethernet address 00-00-c0-dd-d4-da in its ARP response. The correct Ethernet address for *yukon.example.com* is 08-00-20-0e-12-37.

We checked the server's ARP table and found that it had the incorrect ARP entry for *yukon.example.com*. We deleted the bad *yukon* entry with the arp -d command, and installed the correct entry with the -s option, as shown here:

```
C:\>arp -d yukon.example.com
C:\>arp -s yukon.example.com 08-00-20-0e-12-37
```

ARP entries received via the ARP protocol are temporary. The values are held in the table for a finite lifetime and are deleted when that lifetime expires. New values are then obtained via the ARP protocol. Therefore, if some remote interfaces change, the local table adjusts and communications continue. Usually this is a good idea, but if someone is using the wrong IP address, that bad address can keep reappearing in the ARP table even after deletion. Manually entered values are permanent, however; they stay in the table and can only be deleted manually. This allowed us to install a correct entry in the table, without worrying about it being immediately overwritten by a bad address.

This quick fix resolved *yukon*'s immediate problem, but we still needed to find the culprit. We checked the DHCP configuration to see if we had an entry for Ethernet address 00-00-c0-dd-d4-da, but we didn't. From the first three bytes of this address, 00-00-c0, we knew that the device was an SMC card. We guessed that the problem address was recently installed because the user had never had the problem before. We sent out an urgent announcement to all users asking if anyone had recently installed a new PC, reconfigured a PC, or configured TCP/IP software on a PC. We got one response. When we checked his system, we found out that he had entered the address 192.168.6.7 when he should have entered 192.168.6.17. The address was corrected and the problem did not recur.

Nothing fancy was needed to solve this problem. Once we checked the error messages, we knew what the problem was and how to solve it. Involving the entire network user community allowed us to quickly locate the problem system and to avoid a room-to-room search for the PC. Reluctance to involve users and make them part of the solution is one of the costliest, and most common, mistakes made by network administrators.

Checking the Interface with netstat

If the preliminary tests lead you to suspect that the connection to the local area network is unreliable, the `netstat -e` command can provide useful information. The example below shows the output from the `netstat -e` command:

```
C:\>netstat -e
Interface Statistics

                           Received            Sent

Bytes                     11379130        12969996
Unicast packets              31887           33913
Non-unicast packets          21367           11432
Discards                         0               0
Errors                           0               0
Unknown protocols                0
```

The command displays the total amount of traffic that this system has received from and sent to the Ethernet—in both bytes and packets. It also displays the number of packets in error. *Discards* are packets that were received from the network and then discarded by the local system because they contained errors or could not be processed. *Errors* are damaged packets, including packets sent from this system that were damaged in the local buffer. These errors should be close to zero. Regardless of how much traffic has passed through this interface, 100 errors in either of these fields is high. High output errors could indicate a saturated local network or a bad physical connection between the host and the network. High input errors could indicate that the network is saturated, that the local host is overloaded, or that there is a physical network problem. Tools, such as the Network Monitor or a cable tester, can help you determine if it is a physical network problem.

The problem may be an overloaded network. To reduce the network load, reduce the amount of traffic on the network segment. A simple way to do this is to create multiple segments out of the single segment. Each new segment has fewer hosts and, therefore, less traffic.

The most effective way to subdivide an Ethernet is to install an Ethernet switch. Each port on the switch is essentially a separate Ethernet. Therefore, a 16-port switch gives you 16 Ethernets to work with when balancing the load. On most switches the different ports can be used in a variety of different ways (see Figure 14-4). Lightly used systems can be attached to a hub that is then attached to one of the switch ports to allow the systems to share a single segment. Servers and demanding systems can be given dedicated ports so that they don't need to share a segment with anyone.

Fast Ethernet (100 Mbps) switches are the most commonly used for desktop networking. 10/100 switches with auto-sensing ports allow every port to be used at either 100 Mbps or at 10 Mbps, which gives you the maximum configuration flexibility. Higher speed technologies, such as Gigabit Ethernet, are also available. However, Gigabit

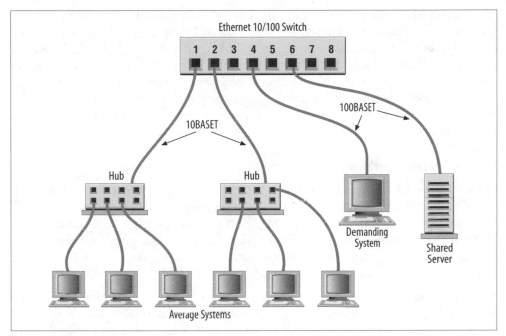

Figure 14-4. Subdividing an Ethernet with switches

Ethernet is mostly used to create backbones for networks or to interconnect high performance servers.

Figure 14-4 shows an 8-port 10/100 Ethernet switch. Ports 1 and 2 are wired to Ethernet hubs. A few systems are connected to each hub. When new systems are added they are distributed evenly among the hubs to prevent any one segment from becoming overloaded. Additional hubs can be added to the available switch ports for future expansion. Port 4 attaches a demanding system with its own private segment. Port 6 attaches a heavily used server. In a real network, of course, many switches and many hubs would be used.

Before allocating the ports on your switch evaluate what services are in demand and who talks to whom. Then develop a plan that reduces the amount of traffic flowing over any segment. For example, if the demanding system on Port 4 uses lots of bandwidth because it is constantly talking to one of the systems on Port 1, all of the systems on Port 1 will suffer because of this traffic. The computer that the demanding system communicates with should be moved to one of the vacant ports or to the same port (4) as the demanding system. Use your switch to greatest advantage by balancing the load.

Should you segment an old coaxial cable Ethernet by cutting the cable and joining it back together through a router or a bridge? No. If you have an old network that is finally reaching saturation, it is time to install a new network built on a more robust technology. A *shared media* network, which is a network where everyone is on the same cable, as with a coaxial cable Ethernet, is an accident waiting to happen. Design a network that a user cannot bring down by merely disconnecting his system, or even by accidentally cutting a wire in his office. Wire equipment located in the user's office to a hub securely stored in a wire closet. The network components in the user's office should be sufficiently isolated from the network so that damage to those components does not damage the entire network. The new network will solve your traffic load problem and reduce the amount of hardware troubleshooting you are called upon to do.

Network hardware problems

Some of the tests discussed in this section can show a network hardware problem. If a hardware problem is indicated, contact the people responsible for the hardware. If the problem appears to be in a leased telephone line, contact the telephone company. If the problem appears to be in a wide area network, contact the management of that network. Don't sit on a problem expecting it to go away. It could easily get worse.

If the problem is in your local area network, you will have to handle it yourself. Some tools, such as the cable tester described earlier, can help. But frequently the only way to approach a hardware problem is by brute force—disconnecting pieces of hardware until you find the one causing the problem. The switch or hub is a convenient point where this can be done. If you identify a device causing the problem, repair or replace it. Remember the problem can be the cable itself, rather than any particular device.

Checking Routing

The "network unreachable" error message indicates a possible routing problem. If the problem is in the local host's routing table, it is easy to detect and resolve. First, use either netstat -nr or route print (both commands produce the same output) to see whether or not a valid route to the destination is installed in the routing table.

For example, a user reports that the "network is down" because she cannot FTP to *ftp.microsoft.com*, and a ping test returns the following results:

```
C:\>ping ftp.microsoft.com

Pinging ftp.microsoft.com [207.46.133.140] with 32 bytes of data:

Destination host unreachable.
Destination host unreachable.
Destination host unreachable.
Destination host unreachable.

Ping statistics for 207.46.133.140:
    Packets: Sent = 4, Received = 0, Lost = 4 (100% loss),
```

Based on the "network unreachable" error message, check the user's routing table for a default route. The default route is displayed with a *Network Destination* address of 0.0.0.0. In general, the "network unreachable" error is not displayed when a default route exists because the system believes that all destinations are reachable through the default route. When the routing table contains a default route, the error displayed for an unreachable host is frequently "connection timed out" or "100% packet loss."

To look for a specific route to a destination, as opposed to a default route, you need the IP address of the destination. In the example, the IP address of *ftp.microsoft.com* is 207.46.133.140, which is a class C address. The destination for most routes is a network as opposed to a host, so we check for a route to network 207.46.133.0. (If a specific route is not found, don't forget to look for a default route as described in the preceding paragraph.) If netstat shows the correct specific route, or a valid default route, the problem is not in the routing table. In that case, use tracert, as described in the next section, to trace the route all the way to its destination.

If netstat doesn't return the expected route, it's a local routing problem. There are two ways to approach local routing problems, depending on whether the system uses static or dynamic routing. Most systems that use static routing rely on a default route, so the missing route could be the default route. Use the *General* tab of the *Internet Protocol (TCP/IP) Properties* window to define the default route as described in Chapter 4. If you use multiple static routes, use route -p add to define them, which is also covered in Chapter 4. If you're using dynamic routing, make sure that the routing program is running. Routing and Remote Access Service (RRAS) provides the various routing protocols for Windows Server 2003.

Tracing Routes

If the local routing table is correct, the problem may be occurring some distance away from the local host. Remote routing problems can cause the "no answer" error message, as well as the "network unreachable" error message. The "network unreachable" message does not always mean a routing problem. It can literally mean that the remote network cannot be reached because something is down between the local host and the remote destination. The program that can help you locate these problems is tracert.

tracert traces the route of UDP packets from the local host to a remote host. It prints the name (if it can be determined) and IP address of each gateway along the route to the remote host.

Two techniques are employed by tracert, small TTL (time-to-live) values and an invalid port number, to trace packets to their destination. tracert sends out UDP packets with small TTL values to detect the intermediate gateways. The TTL values start at one and increase in increments of one for each group of three UDP packets sent. When a gateway receives a packet, it decrements the TTL. If the TTL is then zero, the packet is not forwarded and an ICMP Time Exceeded message is returned to the source of the packet. tracert displays one line of output for each gateway from which it receives a Time Exceeded message.

When the destination host receives a packet from tracert, it returns an ICMP Unreachable Port message. This happens because tracert intentionally uses an invalid port number to force this error. When tracert receives the Unreachable Port message, it knows that it has reached the destination host, and it terminates the trace. In this way, tracert is able to develop a list of the gateways, starting at one hop away and increasing one hop at a time, until the remote host is reached. Figure 14-5 illustrates the flow of packets tracing the route to a host three hops away.

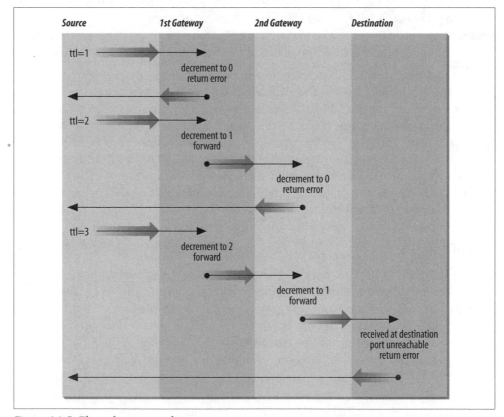

Figure 14-5. Flow of tracert packets

The following is an example of tracert output. tracert sends out three packets at each TTL value. If no response is received to a packet, tracert prints an asterisk (*).

If a response is received, tracert displays the packet's round-trip time in milliseconds and the address of the gateway that responded.

```
C:\>tracert potomac.example.net

Tracing route to potomac.example.net [192.168.13.23]
over a maximum of 30 hops:

  1      2 ms      1 ms      1 ms   192.168.0.1
  2     14 ms     11 ms     11 ms   10.17.200.1
  3     16 ms     17 ms     13 ms   vl7.aggr1.lnh.md.rcn.net [207.172.11.129]
  4     51 ms     66 ms     70 ms   ge3-0.core2.lnh.md.rcn.net [207.172.15.2]
  5     14 ms     12 ms     52 ms   ge4-0.core3.lnh.md.rcn.net [207.172.15.19]
  6     59 ms     21 ms     14 ms   ge1-1.border1.eqnx.va.rcn.net [207.172.19.64]
  7     14 ms     13 ms     31 ms   unknown.level3.net [63.210.25.209]
  8     13 ms     15 ms     15 ms   ae-25.bb2.dc1.level3.net [4.68.121.33]
  9     53 ms     17 ms     13 ms   so-0.edge1.dc1.level3.net [209.244.11.14]
 10     25 ms     14 ms     16 ms   uunet-level3-oc48.dc1.level3.net [209.244.219.158]
 11     19 ms     31 ms     22 ms   0.so-2-2-0.xl1.dca5.alter.net [152.63.43.182]
 12     31 ms     36 ms     18 ms   0.so-6-0-0.xl1.dca8.alter.net [152.63.42.186]
 13     22 ms     21 ms     17 ms   pos6-0.gw2.dca8.alter.net [152.63.39.173]
 14      *         *         *      Request timed out.
 15      *         *         *      Request timed out.
 16    130 ms    100 ms     90 ms   potomac.example.net [198.49.45.10]
Trace complete.
```

This trace shows that 15 intermediate gateways are involved, that packets are making the trip, and that round-trip travel time for packets from this host to *potomac.example.net* is about 107 ms.

Variations and bugs in the implementation of ICMP on different types of gateways, and the unpredictable nature of the path a datagram can take through a network can cause some odd displays. For this reason, you shouldn't examine the output of tracert too closely. The most important things in the tracert output are

- Did the packet get to its remote destination?
- If not, where did it stop?

When tracert fails to get packets through to the remote end-system, the trace trails off, displaying a series of three asterisks at each hop count until the count reaches 30. If this happens, contact the administrator of the remote host you're trying to reach, and the administrator of the last gateway displayed in the trace. Describe the problem to them; they may be able to help.

Checking Name Service

Name server problems are indicated when the "unknown host" error message is returned by the user's application. Name server problems can usually be diagnosed with `nslookup`. Three features of `nslookup` are particularly useful for troubleshooting remote name server problems. These features can:

- Locate the authoritative servers for the remote domain using the NS query
- Obtain all records about the remote host using the ANY query
- Browse all entries in the remote zone using the `nslookup ls` and `view` commands

When troubleshooting a remote server problem, directly query the authoritative servers returned by the NS query. Don't rely on information returned by nonauthoritative servers. If the problems that have been reported are intermittent, query all of the authoritative servers in turn and compare their answers. Remote servers returning different answers to the same query sometimes cause intermittent name server problems.

The ANY query returns all records about a host, thus giving the broadest range of troubleshooting information. Simply knowing what information is (and isn't) available can solve a lot of problems. For example, if the query returns an MX record but no A record, it is easy to understand why the user couldn't telnet to that host! Many hosts are accessible to mail that are not accessible by other network services. In this case, the user is confused and is trying to use the remote host in an inappropriate manner.

If you are unable to locate any information about the hostname that the user gave you, perhaps the hostname is incorrect. If you have the IP address, use the PTR query to do a reverse lookup. Without a valid hostname or address, looking for the correct name is like trying to find a needle in a haystack. However, `nslookup` can help. Use the `nslookup ls` command to dump the remote zone file, and redirect the listing to a file. Then use the `nslookup view` command to browse through the file, looking for names similar to the one the user supplied. Many problems are caused by a mistaken hostname.

The `nslookup` features and commands mentioned here are described in Chapter 6. Some examples using these commands to solve real name server problems are shown here. The two examples that follow use fictitious hostnames but are based on actual trouble reports.

Some Systems Work, Others Don't

A user reported that he could resolve a certain hostname from her desktop system, but could not resolve the same hostname when logged into the central mainframe system. However, the central system could resolve other hostnames. We ran several tests and found that we could resolve the hostname on some systems and not on others. There seemed to be no predictable pattern to the failure. So we used `nslookup` to check the remote name servers.

```
C:\>nslookup
Default Server: komodo.example.com
Address: 192.168.0.20
```

```
> set type=NS
> foo.edu.
Server: komodo.example.com
Address: 192.168.0.20

foo.edu nameserver = gerbil.foo.edu
foo.edu nameserver = red.example.net
foo.edu nameserver = shrew.foo.edu
gerbil.foo.edu inet address = 198.97.99.2
red.example.net inet address = 184.6.16.2
shrew.foo.edu inet address = 198.97.99.1
> set type=ANY
> server gerbil.foo.edu
Default Server: gerbil.foo.edu
Address: 198.97.99.2

> hamster.foo.edu
Server: gerbil.foo.edu
Address: 198.97.99.2

hamster.foo.edu inet address = 198.97.99.8
> server red.example.net
Default Server: red.example.net
Address: 184.6.16.2
> hamster.foo.edu
Server: red.example.net
Address: 184.6.16.2
```

```
*** red.example.net can't find hamster.foo.edu: Non existent domain
```

This sample nslookup session contains several steps. The first step is to locate the authoritative servers for the hostname in question (*hamster.foo.edu*). We set the query type to NS to get the name server records, and queried for the domain (*foo.edu*) in which the hostname is found. This returns three names of authoritative servers: *gerbil.foo.edu*, *red.example.net*, and *shrew.foo.edu*.

Next, we set the query type to ANY to look for any records related to the hostname in question. Then we set the server to the first server in the list, *gerbil.foo.edu*, and queried for *hamster.foo.edu*. This returns an address record. So server *gerbil.foo.edu* works fine. We repeated the test using *red.example.net* as the server, and it fails. No records are returned.

The next step is to get SOA records from each server and see if they are the same:

```
> set type=SOA
> foo.edu.
Server: red.example.net
Address: 184.6.16.2

foo.edu origin = gerbil.foo.edu
    mail addr = amanda.gerbil.foo.edu
    serial=10164, refresh=43200, retry=3600, expire=3600000,
    min=2592000
```

```
> server gerbil.foo.edu
Default Server: gerbil.foo.edu
Address: 198.97.99.2

> foo.edu.
Server: gerbil.foo.edu
Address: 198.97.99.2

foo.edu origin = gerbil.foo.edu
    mail addr = amanda.gerbil.foo.edu
        serial=10164, refresh=43200, retry=3600, expire=3600000,
        min=2592000

> exit
```

If the SOA records have different serial numbers, perhaps the zone file, and therefore the hostname, has not yet been downloaded by the slave server. If the serial numbers are the same and the data is different, as in this case, there is definitely a problem. Contact the remote domain administrator and notify her of the problem. The administrator's mailing address is shown in the `mail addr` field displayed for the SOA record. In our example, we would send mail to *amanda@gerbil.foo.edu* reporting the problem.

The data is here and the server can't find it

The administrator of a slave name server reported this problem. The administrator reported that his server could not resolve a certain hostname in a domain for which his server was a slave server. The master server was, however, able to resolve the name.

The problem was replicated on several other slave servers. The master server would resolve the name; the slave servers wouldn't. All servers had the same SOA serial number, so why wouldn't they resolve the hostname to an address?

Visualizing the difference between the way master and slave servers load their data made us suspicious of the zone file transfer. Master servers load the data directly from local disk files. Slave servers transfer the data from the master server via a zone file transfer. Perhaps the zone files were getting corrupted. We displayed the zone file on one of the slave servers, and it showed the following data:

```
C:\Windows\System32\Dns>type sales.example.com.dns
PCpma       IN    A    192.168.64.159
            IN    HINFO"pc" "n3/800salesexamplecom"
PCrkc       IN    A    192.168.64.155
            IN    HINFO"pc" "n3/800salesexamplecom"
PCafc       IN    A    192.168.64.189
            IN    HINFO"pc" "n3/800salesexamplecom"
accu        IN    A    192.168.65.27
cmgds1      IN    A    192.168.130.40
cmg         IN    A    192.168.130.30
PCgns       IN    A    192.168.64.167
```

```
             IN    HINFO"pc" "(3/800salesexamplecom"
gw           IN    A    192.168.65.254
zephyr       IN    A    192.168.64.188
             IN    HINFO"Sun" "sparcstation"
ejw          IN    A    192.168.65.17
PCecp        IN    A    192.168.64.193
             IN    HINFO"pc" "n^Lsparcstationstcom"
```

Notice the odd display in the last field of the HINFO record for each PC. This data might have been corrupted in the transfer or it might be bad on the master server. We used nslookup to check.

```
C:\>nslookup
Default Server: komodo.example.com
Address: 192.168.0.20

> server mandy.sales.example.com
Default Server: mandy.sales.example.com
Address: 192.168.6.1

> set query=HINFO
> PCwlg.sales.example.com
Server: mandy.sales.example.com
Address: 192.168.6.1

PCwlg.sales.example.com CPU=pc OS=ov
packet size error (0xf7fff590 != 0xf7fff528)
> exit
```

This nslookup example sets the server to *mandy.sales.example.com*, which is the primary server for *sales.example.com*. Next we query for the HINFO record for one of the hosts that appeared to have a corrupted record. The "packet size error" message clearly indicates that nslookup had trouble retrieving the HINFO record directly from the master server. We contacted the administrator of the master server and told her about the problem, pointing out the records that appeared to be in error. She discovered that she had forgotten to put an operating system entry on some of the HINFO records. She corrected this, and it fixed the problem.

Analyzing Protocol Problems

Problems caused by bad TCP/IP configurations are much more common than problems caused by bad TCP/IP protocol implementations. Most of the problems you encounter will succumb to analysis using the simple tools we have already discussed. But on occasion, you may need to analyze the protocol interaction between two systems. In the worst case, you may need to analyze the packets in the data stream bit by bit. Protocol analyzers help you do this.

Network Monitor is the tool we'll use. It is provided with Windows Server 2003. Although we use Network Monitor in our examples, the concepts introduced in this section should be applicable to any analyzer, because most protocol analyzers function in basically the same way. Protocol analyzers display network statistics and allow you to select packets and to examine those packets byte by byte. We'll discuss all of these functions.

Network Monitor

Network Monitor comes with Windows Server 2003, but it is not installed by default. To install the monitor, go to the Control Panel and start Add or Remove Programs. In the Add or Remove Programs window click the Add/Remove Windows Components button to launch the Windows Components Wizard. Network Monitor is part of the Management and Monitoring Tools component. Install that component to install the monitor. Once the monitor is installed, it is run from the Administrative Tools menu.

When Network Monitor first starts, it asks you to select which network attached to the server is to be monitored, and it opens the "Select a network" dialog so that you can do just that. The "Select a network" dialog is shown in Figure 14-6. Select the network by highlighting the interface attached to the network and clicking OK.

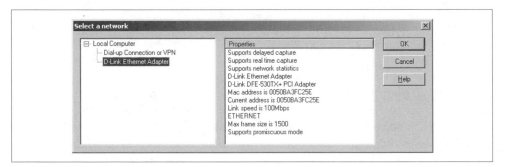

Figure 14-6. Selecting a network to monitor

To see any interesting statistics or data, you must select Start from the Network Monitor's Capture menu. Figure 14-7 shows the Network Monitor window while a capture is running. The window displays a graph of the network load. It displays a scroll pane that contains network statistics, statistics about the capture buffer, Ethernet card statistics, and errors. At the bottom of the window, it displays a scroll pane that shows every network address detected, the number of frames and bytes transferred by that address, and whether the frames were unicast, multicast, or broadcast. Clearly, Network Monitor provides much more statistical information than a simple netstat command.

Select Stop and View from the Capture menu to view more details of the packets that have been captured. This stops the packet capture and opens the Capture (Summary) pane, which lists summary information about every packet received during the

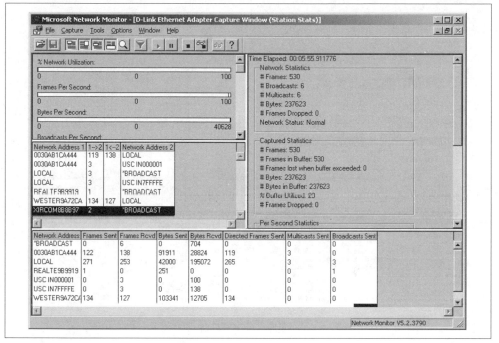

Figure 14-7. Gathering statistics with Network Monitor

capture. The Network Monitor displays a single line of summary information for each packet received. Each line in the display is sequentially numbered, and displays:

- The time the packet was received
- The source and destination Ethernet addresses
- The protocol carried in the packet
- The source and destination IP addresses.

This summary information is sufficient to gain insight into how packets flow between two hosts and into potential problems. Frequently, this is enough to solve the problem. However, troubleshooting protocol problems sometimes requires more detailed information about each packet.

To display the data contained in a packet, double-click on the summary line of the packet in the Capture (Summary) window. Figure 14-8 shows the Capture (Detail) window that Network Monitor uses to display the details of a packet.

The Capture (Detail) window that displays an individual packet is divided into three separate scroll frames. The top scroll frame is the same summary information mentioned above. The middle scroll area is a break out of the individual fields in the frame header. Clicking the plus sign (+) next to any item in this scroll area provides more detail about the item. (Look at the description of the various header fields in Chapter 1 for a better understanding of what is displayed in this frame.) The scroll

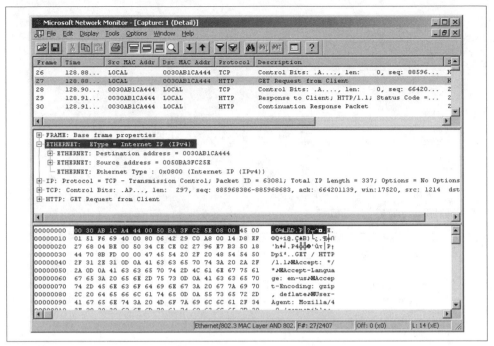

Figure 14-8. Detail packet information

section at the bottom of the pane displays the packet data in hex and ASCII. In most cases, you don't need to see the entire packet. Usually, the headers are sufficient to troubleshoot a protocol problem. But the data is there when you need it.

By default, Network Monitor captures all of the packets to or from the local host. This can create lots of information, much of which may be of no interest. Filters are used to select a subset of these packets. Filters can be defined to capture packets from, or to, specific hosts or protocols, packets that contain specific data, or combinations of all these.

The Network Monitor supports two types of filters. You can create a *capture filter* before you start to capture data so that only the data you want is collected in the capture buffer. The advantage of a capture filter is that it saves buffer space. The other type of filter is a *display filter*. It filters the packets that are already in the buffer so that only those you want are displayed.

To define a *capture filter*, select Filter from the Capture menu before you start to capture data. The Capture Filter window shown in Figure 14-9 appears. The filter shown in Figure 14-9 is the default filter that Network Monitor uses to capture all data into and out of the system. Because it captures everything, it filters nothing out.

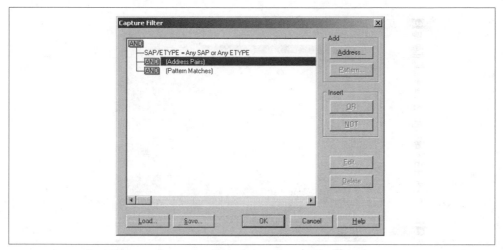

Figure 14-9. Defining a network monitor filter

Capture filters can select packets using three types of information:

- The physical network frame type (SAP/ETYPE). The default filter captures any SAP or ETYPE.

- The source or destination address of the packet, defined as either an Ethernet address or an IP address.

- The data contained in the packet, defined in either hexadecimal or ASCII format.

To add an address to the filter, highlight Address Pairs and click Address. The dialog that appears allows you to select an address from a scroll box or to define your own address by clicking Edit Addresses. The dialog also allows you to specify whether only packets sent to the address should be captured, only packets coming from the address should be captured, or all packets going to and coming from the address should be captured.

Add pattern matching to the filter by highlighting Pattern Match and clicking Pattern. In the dialog that appears, enter the pattern as hexadecimal numbers or as an ASCII string, and define the pattern's position in the packet by defining an offset from the start of the frame or the start of the data field.

To change an existing value in a filter, highlight it and select Edit. In Figure 14-9, the only value set in the filter is the value set for SAP/ETYPE. To change it, highlight the SAP/ETYPE line, click Edit, and select the setting you want from the scroll box that appears.

The display filter is defined in a similar way. The biggest difference is that the filter is defined after the capture. First capture data. Then select Stop and View from the Capture menu. The Capture (Summary) window is displayed. Select Filter from the Display menu. This opens the window shown in Figure 14-10.

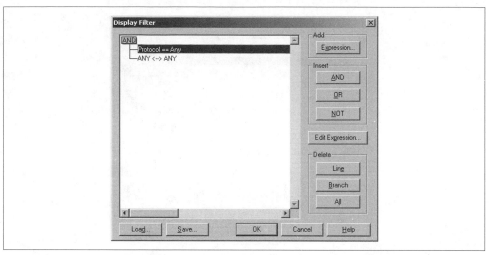

Figure 14-10. Network Monitor's default display filter

Modifying values in this filter controls which frames are displayed in the Capture (Summary) pane. The display filter can filter on protocol type and addresses. In Figure 14-10 the filter displays packets from or to any address (ANY <--> ANY). To change this, highlight the ANY <--> ANY line and click Edit Expression. The Address tab of the Expression dialog appears. Select the address you want from the scroll boxes in the dialog.

The protocols selected by the filter shown in Figure 14-10 are defined by the Protocol == Any line, which tells us the filter will display packets from any protocol. Change the protocols affected by the filter by highlighting the Protocol == Any line and clicking the Edit Expression button to open the Protocol tab of the Expression dialog shown in Figure 14-11.

To change from Protocol == Any, first select Disable All, then select the individual protocols that you wish to display and click Enable to add each protocol to the list. Combining selected protocols and addresses, build exactly the filter you need.

Use the capture file to capture the information you want, and then use the display filter to display exactly the packet you're interested in when researching a specific network problem. In the following section we look at how a protocol analyzer was used to troubleshoot a network problem.

Protocol Case Study

This example is an actual case that was solved by protocol analysis. The problem was reported as an occasional FTP failure with the error message:

```
netout: Option not supported by protocol
421 Service not available, remote server has closed connection
```

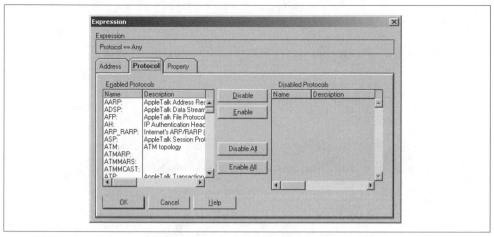

Figure 14-11. Editing the protocol expression in the display filter

Only one user reported the problem, and it occurred only when transferring large files from a workstation to the central computervia our fiber optic backbone network.

Using the user's data file we were able to duplicate the problem from other workstations, but only when we transferred the file to the same central system via the backbone network. Figure 14-12 graphically summarizes the tests we ran to duplicate the problem.

We notified all users of the problem. In response, we received reports that others had also experienced it, but again only when transferring to the central system and only when transferring via the backbone. They had not reported it because they rarely saw it. But the additional reports gave us some evidence that the problem did not relate to any recent network changes.

Because the problem had been replicated on other systems, it probably was not a configuration problem on the user's system. The FTP failure could also be avoided if the backbone routers and the central system did not interact. So we concentrated our attention on those systems. We checked the routing tables and ARP tables, and ran ping tests on the central system and the routers. No problems were observed.

Based on this preliminary analysis, the FTP failure appeared to be a possible protocol interaction problem between a certain brand of routers and a central computer. We made that assessment because the transfer routinely failed when these two brands of systems were involved, but never failed in any other circumstance. If the router or the central system were misconfigured, they should fail when transferring data to other hosts. If the problem was an intermittent physical problem, it should occur randomly regardless of the hosts involved. Instead, this problem occurred predictably, and only between two specific brands of computers. Perhaps there was something incompatible in the way these two systems implemented TCP/IP.

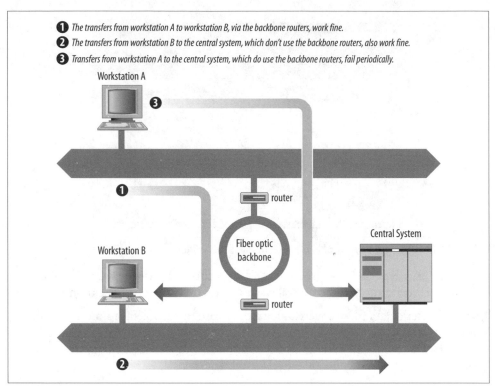

① *The transfers from workstation A to workstation B, via the backbone routers, work fine.*

② *The transfers from workstation B to the central system, which don't use the backbone routers, also work fine.*

③ *Transfers from workstation A to the central system, which do use the backbone routers, fail periodically.*

Workstation A

router

Fiber optic
backbone

Central System

Workstation B

router

Figure 14-12. FTP test summary

Therefore, we used a protocol analyzer to capture the TCP/IP headers during several FTP test runs. Reviewing the analyzer output showed that all transfers that failed with the error message had an ICMP Parameter Error packet near the end of the session, usually about 50 packets before the final close. No successful transfer had this ICMP packet. Note that the error did *not* occur in the last packet in the data stream, as you might expect. It is common for an error to be detected, and for the data stream to continue for some time before the connection is actually shut down. Don't assume that an error will always be at the end of a data stream.

Detailed analysis of the packets involved in the error showed that the router issued an IP Header Checksum of 0xffff, and that the central system objected to this checksum. We know that the central system objected to the checksum because it returned an ICMP Parameter Error with a Pointer of 10. The Parameter Error indicates that there is something wrong with the data the system has just received, and the Pointer identifies the specific byte that the system thinks is in error. The tenth byte of the router's IP header is the IP Header Checksum. The data field of the ICMP error message returns the header that it believes is in error. When we displayed that data we noticed that when the central system returned the header, the checksum field was corrected to 0000. Clearly the central system disagreed with the router's checksum calculation.

Occasional checksum errors will occur. They can be caused by transmission problems, and are intended to detect these types of problems. Every protocol suite has a mechanism for recovering from checksum errors. So how should they be handled in TCP/IP?

To determine the correct protocol action in this situation, we turned to the authoritative sources—the RFCs. RFC 791, *Internet Protocol*, provided information about the checksum calculation, but the best source for this particular problem was RFC 1122, *Requirements for Internet Hosts—Communication Layers*, by R. Braden. This RFC provided two specific references that define the action to be taken, as described on page 29:

> In the following, the action specified in certain cases is to "silently discard" a received datagram. This means that the datagram will be discarded without further processing and that the host will not send any ICMP error message (see Section 3.2.2) as a result… A host MUST verify the IP header checksum on every received datagram and silently discard every datagram that has a bad checksum.

Therefore, when a system receives a packet with a bad checksum, it is not supposed to do anything with it. The packet should be discarded, and the system should wait for the next packet to arrive. The system should not respond with an error message. A system cannot respond to a bad IP header checksum, because it cannot really know where the packet came from. If the header checksum is in doubt, how do you know if the addresses in the header are correct? And if you don't know for sure where the packet came from, how can you respond to it?

IP relies on the upper layer protocols to recover from these problems. If TCP is used (as it was in this case), the sending TCP eventually notices that the recipient has never acknowledged the segment, and it sends the segment again. If UDP is used, the sending application is responsible for recovering from the error. In neither case does recovery rely on an error message returned from the recipient.

Therefore, for an incorrect checksum, the central system should have simply discarded the bad packet. The vendor was informed of this problem and, much to their credit, they sent us a fix for the software within two weeks. Not only that, the fix worked perfectly!

Not all problems are resolved so cleanly. But the technique of analysis is the same no matter what the problem.

Summary

Inevitably a network breaks. This chapter discusses the tools and techniques that are used to recover from network problems, and the planning and monitoring that can help avoid them. The solution to a problem is sometimes obvious if you can just gain enough information to know exactly what the problem is. Windows Server 2003 provides several built-in software tools that can help you gather information about system configuration, addressing, routing, name service, and other vital network components. Gather your tools and learn how to use them before a problem occurs.

DHCP Options

The TCP/IP configuration values exchanged by a DHCP server and a client are called DHCP *options*. There are great many DHCP configuration options. While Table A-1 covers a large number of these, it does not cover them all. It does, however, cover all of the DHCP options that are listed under Available Options in the Scope Options window. In fact, it covers more than the options listed there. The additional options covered in the table are:

- Those options discussed in Chapter 5 that the client sends to the server to identify itself as a member of a user or vendor class
- Some additional options described in RFC 2132, *DHCP Options and BOOTP Vendor Extensions*
- The Classless Static Routes option defined in RFC 3442, *Classless Static Route Option for DHCPv4*
- The LCI option defined in RFC 3825, *Dynamic Host Configuration Protocol Option for Coordinate-based Location Configuration Information*, which was used as an example in the text

Table A-1. DHCP options

Code	Name	Description/value
1	Subnet mask	A signed 32-bit integer that specifies the address mask of the client subnet. Defined in the New Scope Wizard or the Scope Properties dialog. Cannot be set in the Scope Options or Server Options dialogs.
2	Time offset	A signed 32-bit integer that specifies the client's offset from Universal Coordinated Time (UCT) in seconds.
3	Router	A preference-ordered list of IP addresses for routers on the client's subnet.
4	Time server	A preference-ordered list of IP addresses of the RFC 868 time servers available to the client.
5	Name servers	A preference-ordered list of IP addresses of the IEN 116 name servers available to the client.

Code	Name	Description/value
6	DNS servers	A preference-ordered list of IP addresses for the DNS name servers available to the client. Multihomed computers can have only one list per computer, not one per adapter card.
7	Log servers	A preference-ordered list of IP addresses for the MIT_LCS User Datagram Protocol (UDP) log servers available to the client.
8	Cookie servers	A preference-ordered list of IP addresses for the RFC 865 cookie servers available to the client.
9	LPR servers	A preference-ordered list of IP addresses for the RFC 1179 line-printer servers available to the client.
10	Impress servers	A preference-ordered list of IP addresses for Imagen Impress servers available to the client.
11	Resource location servers	A preference-ordered list of the RFC 887 Resource Location servers available to the client.
12	Host name	The client hostname, which may be up to 63 characters and must be formatted as defined in RFC 1035. The name may or may not be qualified with the local DNS domain name, but including the domain name is not equivalent to providing DHCP option 15.
13	Boot file size	An unsigned 16-bit integer defining the size, in 512-byte blocks, of the client's default boot image file.
14	Merit dump file	The ASCII pathname of the file to which the core image of a client should be dumped if the client crashes.
15	Domain name	The DNS domain name the client should use as the default domain name for DNS queries.
16	Swap server	The IP address of the client's swap server.
17	Root path	The ASCII pathname for the client's root disk.
18	Extensions path	A file retrievable via TFTP that contains information to be processed as if it were a BOOTP vendor-extension field.
19	IP layer forwarding	A value of 1 directs the client to enable IP layer packet forwarding. A value of 0 disables packet forwarding. Enabling packet forwarding causes the client to act as if it were a router.
20	Nonlocal source routing	A value of 1 directs the client to route datagrams from nonlocal sources. A value 0 directs the client to route datagrams only if they are from local sources. Routing must first be enabled with option 19.
21	Policy filter masks	A list of IP addresses and masks pairs that are the only acceptable next-hop addresses for nonlocal source routes. Any source-routed datagram with a next-hop address that does not match one of the filters is discarded by the client.
22	Max datagram reassembly size	An unsigned 16-bit integer that specifies the largest datagram that the client can reassemble. The minimum value is 576.
23	Default IP time-to-live	A single octet value that specifies the default time-to-live (TTL) that the client uses on outgoing datagrams.
24	Path MTU aging timeout	An unsigned 32-bit integer that specifies the timeout for Path MTU (Maximum Transmission Unit) values discovered by the mechanism defined in RFC 1191.

Code	Name	Description/value
25	Path MTU plateau table	Defines a table of MTU sizes the client should use when performing Path MTU Discovery as defined in RFC 1191. The table is formatted as a list of unsigned 16-bit integers, and is ordered from smallest to largest. The minimum MTU value is 68.
26	MTU option	An unsigned 16-bit integer that specifies the maximum transmission unit the client should use on this interface. The minimum MTU value is 68.
27	All subnets are local	Specifies whether or not the client may assume that all subnets of the IP network to which the client is connected use the same MTU as the subnet of that network to which the client is directly connected. A value of 1 indicates that all subnets share the same MTU. A value of 0 means that the client should assume that some subnets of the directly connected network may have smaller MTUs.
28	Broadcast address	A four-octet value that specifies the broadcast IP address in use on the client's subnet.
29	Perform mask discovery	A value of 1 directs the client to use ICMP subnet mask discovery. A value of 0 tells the client not to perform ICMP address mask discovery.
30	Mask supplier	Specifies whether or not the client should respond to ICMP subnet mask discovery requests. A value of 1 means that the client should respond. A value of 0 means it should not respond.
31	Perform router discovery	A value of 1 means that the client should perform ICMP router discovery, as defined in RFC 1256. A value of 0 indicates that the client should not perform ICMP router discovery.
32	Router solicitation address	Specifies the IP address to which the client should send ICMP router discovery requests.
33	Static route	A list of static routes that the client should install in its routing cache formatted as destination address and router address pairs. Each static route is eight octets long. If multiple routes to the same destination are specified, they are listed in descending order of priority. The default route (0.0.0.0) is an illegal destination for this option.
34	Trailer encapsulation	A value of 1 means that the client should attempt to negotiate the use of RFC 893 trailers when using the ARP protocol. A value of 0 indicates that the client should not attempt to use trailers.
35	ARP cache timeout	An unsigned 32-bit integer that specifies the timeout in seconds for ARP cache entries.
36	Ethernet encapsulation	A value of 0 tells the client to use Ethernet Version 2 (RFC 894) encapsulation on it Ethernet interface. A value of 1 tells the client to use IEEE 802.3 (RFC 1042) encapsulation on its Ethernet interface.
37	Default time-to-live	A single-octet value that specifies the default TTL that the client should use when sending TCP segments.
38	Keepalive interval	An unsigned 32-bit integer that specifies the number of seconds that the client should wait between sending keepalive messages on a TCP connection. A value of 0 tells the client not to send keepalive messages, unless specifically requested to do so by an application.
39	Keepalive garbage	A value of 1 tells the client to send TCP keepalive messages with an octet of garbage for compatibility with older implementations. A value of 0 means that a garbage octet should not be sent.

Table A-1. DHCP options (continued)

Code	Name	Description/value
40	NIS domain name	The name of the client's Network Information Service (NIS) domain.
41	NIS servers	A preference-ordered list of IP addresses of the NIS servers available to the client.
42	NTP servers	A preference-ordered list of IP addresses of the Network Time Protocol (NTP) servers available to the client.
43	Vendor specific	Clients and servers use this option to exchange vendor-specific information. The information that follows this tag is interpreted by vendor-specific code on the clients and servers.
44	WINS/NBNS servers	A preference-ordered list of IP addresses of the NetBIOS name servers (NBNS) available to the client.
45	NetBIOS over TCP/IP NBDD	A preference-ordered list of IP addresses of the RFC 1001/1002 NetBIOS datagram distribution servers (NBDD) available to the client.
46	WINS/NBT node type	A single octet value that tells the client what type of node it should configure itself to be for NetBIOS over TCP/IP name registration and name resolution. The acceptable octet values are 0x1=B-node, 0x2=P-node, 0x4=M-node, and 0x8=H-node. On multihomed computers, the node type is assigned to the entire computer, not to individual adapter cards.
47	NetBIOS scope ID	A string that defines the NetBIOS over TCP/IP Scope ID for the client, as specified in RFC 1001/1002. On multihomed computers, the scope ID is assigned to the entire computer, not to individual adapter cards.
48	X Window system font	A preference-ordered list of IP addresses for X Window System font servers available to the client.
49	X Window system display	A preference-ordered list of IP addresses for X Window System Display Manager servers available to the client.
50	Requested IP Address	A four-octet value defining the IP address that the client is requesting from the server. This value is sent by the client to the server in the client's DHCP request.
51	Lease time	A four-octet value that specifies the time in seconds from address assignment until the client's lease on the address expires. In a client's DHCP request, this option requests a lease time. In a server reply, this option specifies the lease time the server is willing to offer. For the Default User Class, lease time is specified in the New Scope Wizard or in the Scope Properties dialog box.
60	Vendor class identifier	A variable-length string that defines the vendor class to which the client belongs. This option is sent from the client to the server in the client's DHCP request. If the server has vendor-specific options for the specified vendor class, the server uses option 43 to provide those vendor-specific options to the client.
61	Client identifier	A unique identifier associated with an individual client. Usually this is the client's MAC address. This value is sent from the client to the server in the client's DHCP request.
64	NIS+ domain name	An ASCII string defining the name of the client's Network Information Service+ (NIS+) domain.
65	NIS + servers	A preference-ordered list of IP addresses of the RFC 2132 NIS+ servers available to the client.

Code	Name	Description/value
66	TFTP server name	An ASCII character string used to identify the TFTP server when the server name (sname) field in the DHCP header is used for DHCP options. Microsoft refers to this option as Boot Server Host Name.
67	Bootfile name	An ASCII string that identifies the bootfile when the file field in the DHCP header is used for DHCP options.
68	Mobile IP home agents	A preference-ordered list of IP addresses of the RFC 3344 mobile IP home agents that are available to the client.
69	SMTP servers	A preference-ordered list of IP addresses of the Simple Mail Transport Protocol (SMTP) servers available to the client.
70	POP3 servers	A preference-ordered list of IP addresses of the Post Office Protocol (POP3) servers available to the client.
71	NNTP servers	A preference-ordered list of IP addresses of the Network News Transport Protocol (NNTP) servers available to the client.
72	Web servers	A preference-ordered list of IP addresses of the default web servers available to the client.
73	Finger servers	A preference-ordered list of IP addresses of the default Finger servers available to the client.
74	IRC servers	A preference-ordered list of IP addresses of the Internet Relay Chat (IRC) servers available to the client.
75	StreetTalk servers	A preference-ordered list of IP addresses of the StreetTalk servers available to the client.
76	STDA servers	A preference-ordered list of IP addresses of the StreetTalk Directory Assistance (STDA) servers available to the client.
77	User class	Variable-length data that defines the user classes to which the client belongs. This option is sent from the client to the server in the client's DHCP request. If the server has configuration options for the specified user class, the server uses those options when constructing its DHCP reply for the client.
121	Classless static routes	A list of destination descriptor and router pairs that define static routes for the client. The destination descriptor contains one octet for the address mask prefix length followed by the significant octets of the destination address. The router part of the destination/router pair is the router's 32-bit IP address. This is the standard classless static route format defined in RFC 3442.
249	Classless static routes	A list of destinations, address masks, and routers that define static routes for the client. This is the classless static route format available by default in the DHCP console.

Despite the large number of available options, very few are used by Microsoft clients. Normally, the basic options used by Microsoft clients are 1, 3, 6, 15, 44, 45, 46, 47, and, if accompanied by the Microsoft vendor-specific options, option 43. The remainder of the options are supported by the Microsoft DHCP server software in case you need them to support third-party client software or non-Microsoft clients.

In addition to the standard DHCP options shown in Table A-1, there are a few Microsoft vendor-specific options. These are listed in Table A-2.

Table A-2. Vendor-specific options

Code	Name	Description/value
001	Microsoft Disable NetBios	This option is an unsigned 32-bit integer that tells the client to enable or disable NetBIOS over TCP/IP (NetBT). A value of 1 tells the client to enable NetBT, and a value of 2 directs the client to disable NetBT. By default, Windows clients enable NetBT on all network connections that use TCP/IP.
002	Microsoft Release DHCP Lease on Shutdown	A value of 1 in this option tells the client to send a DHCP release message when the client shuts down. (The DHCP release message ends the client's lease on its address.) A value of 0 in this option tells the client not to send a DHCP release message when it shuts down. Not sending a release message at shutdown is the default behavior. This option is four octets in length.
003	Microsoft Default Router Metric Base	This option is a 32-bit integer that defines the router metric that the client should use for all default routes. If this option is not provided, the client will use the cost metric associated with its network interface, or a default cost of 1.

DHCP Audit Log Identifiers

DHCP audit logging provides a wide variety of informative messages about the state of the DHCP server, the protocol interactions, the address pool, DNS interactions, authorization, and more. The audit log is a text file that contains audit entries one per line. Each audit entry has a two-digit numeric identifier that indicates the type of message being logged. (See Chapter 5 for a description of the structure of audit log entries.)

Table B-1 lists all of the log identifiers in numeric order and provides a short description of the purpose of each type of log entry.

Table B-1. Audit log identifiers

Identifier	Description
00	Logging started at the specified date and time.
01	Logging stopped at the specified date and time.
02	The DHCP server suspended logging because available disk space is less than the value set in the `DhcpLogMinSpaceOnDisk` registry key or because the current log file is larger than 1/7 of the value set in the `DhcpLogFilesMaxSize` registry key.
10	The specified IP address was leased to the client.
11	The client renewed the lease on the specified address.
12	The client released the lease on the specified address.
13	The specified IP address conflict was detected.
14	All addresses in the scope's address pool have been exhausted.
15	The specified lease request was denied.
16	The specified address lease was deleted.
17	The specified address lease has expired.
20	The specified BOOTP address was leased to the client.
21	The specified dynamic BOOTP address was leased to the client.
22	All addresses in the scope's address pool for BOOTP have been exhausted.
23	The specified BOOTP IP address was deleted after checking to see it was not in use.

Table B-1. Audit log identifiers (continued)

Identifier	Description
24	DHCP database cleanup began at the indicated date and time.
25	Database cleanup statistics.
30	A dynamic DNS update request was sent to the specified DNS server.
31	The dynamic DNS update failed.
32	The dynamic DNS update succeeded.
50	The DHCP server was unable to reach the domain required for its Active Directory configuration.
51	The DHCP server was successfully authorized.
52	The DHCP server upgraded to Windows Server 2003.
53	The DHCP server is using a cached authorization because it was unable to contact an Active Directory server.
54	The DHCP server's attempt to authorize failed.
55	The DHCP service is starting as a result of successful authorization.
56	The DHCP service is shutting down because the server is not authorized.
57	Another DHCP server exists and is authorized for service in the same domain.
58	The DHCP server could not locate the specified domain.
59	A network failure prevented the server from checking its authorization.
60	The DHCP server was unable to locate a domain controller.
61	Another DHCP server that belongs to the Active Directory domain was found on the network.
62	Another DHCP server was found on the network.
63	The DHCP server is retrying the authorization process.
64	The DHCP server was unable to bind to any network interface.

DNS Resource Records

This appendix provides detailed information about the DNS standard resource records (RR) used to construct domain database files. This is primarily a reference to use in conjunction with the tutorial information in Chapter 6. This appendix is divided into three sections.

The first section covers the most commonly used resource records. It shows the DNS console dialog used to enter each commonly used record and the syntax of each standard resource record as it appears in the zone file.

The second section of the appendix covers the resource records that, while available in the DNS console, are less commonly used. In fact, a few of the records covered in this section should not be used because they are obsolete or potential security problems. Where that is the case, we note it. The zone file syntax of the less commonly used records is discussed.

The final section of the appendix covers the syntax of the optional boot file. This file can be used when transitioning a server from a Unix system running BIND 4 to a Windows Server 2003 system. The boot file has nothing to do with DNS resource records. However, it needs to be covered somewhere, so it has been added to this appendix.

Basic Resource Records

Standard resource records define the domain data contained in the zone file. The format of standard resource records, sometimes called RRs, is defined in RFC 1033, the *Domain Administrators Operations Guide*. The format is:

    [name] [ttl] IN type data

The individual fields in the standard resource record are:

name
> This is the name of the object affected by this resource record. The named object can be as specific as an individual host, or as general as an entire domain. The

string entered for *name* is relative to the current domain unless a fully qualified domain name is used.* Certain *name* values have special meaning:

A blank name field denotes the current named object. The current name stays in force until a new name value is encountered in the name field. This permits multiple RRs to be applied to a single object without having to repeat the object's name for each record.

.. Two dots in the name field refer to the root domain. However, a single dot (the actual name of the root) also refers to the root domain, and is more commonly used.

@ A single at sign (@) in the name field refers to the current origin. The origin is the domain name associated with the current zone.

* An asterisk in the name field is a wildcard character. It stands for a name composed of any string. It can be combined with a domain name or used alone. Used alone, an asterisk in the named field means that the resource record applies to objects with names composed of any string of characters plus the name of the current domain. Used with a domain name, the asterisk is relative to that domain. For example, `*.example.com.` in the name field means any string plus the string .example.com.

ttl

Time-to-live defines the length of time in seconds that the information in this resource record should be kept in the cache. The time is specified as a numeric value up to eight characters in length. If no value is set for *ttl*, it defaults to the value defined for the entire zone file in the default TTL field of the SOA record.

IN

This field is the address class of the resource record. The Internet address class is IN, which is the only address class supported by Windows Server 2003. Thus, all resource records used in this book have an address class of IN.

type

This field indicates the type of data the record provides. For example, the A type RR provides the address of the host identified in the name field. All resource record types available in the DNS console are discussed in this appendix.

data

This field contains the information specific to the resource record. The format and content of the data field vary according to the resource record type. The data field is the meat of the RR. For example, in an A record, the data field contains the IP address.

---

* The FQDN must be specified all the way to the root; in other words, it must end with a dot.

In addition to the special characters that have meaning in the name field, zone file records use these other special characters:

;

> The semicolon is the comment character. Use the semicolon to indicate that the remaining data on the line is a comment.

( )

> Parentheses are the continuation characters. Use parentheses to continue data beyond a single line. After an opening parenthesis, all data on subsequent lines is considered part of the current line until a closing parenthesis.

\x

> The backslash is an escape character. A nonnumeric character following a back-slash (\) is taken literally and any special meaning that the character may ordinarily have is ignored. For example, \; means a semicolon—not a comment.

\ddd

> The backslash can also be followed by three decimal numbers. When the escape character is used in this manner the decimal numbers are interpreted as an absolute byte value. For example, \255 means the byte value 11111111.

The same general resource record format is used for all of the resource records in a zone file. Windows can read and process the same zone files as any other DNS server.

Most Windows administrators do not edit the zone files directly. Instead they use the DNS console to create resource records. We recommend that you do the same and that you never directly edit the zone files. Using the console is simpler, more intuitive, and less prone to error. Chapter 6 explains how to use the DNS console. The following sections examine the syntax for each of several key resource record types, and where appropriate, show the DNS console dialog boxes used to create those records.

Start of Authority Record

The Start of Authority (SOA) record marks the beginning of a zone, and it is usually the first record in a zone file. Each zone has only one SOA record. All of the records that follow are part of the zone declared by the SOA. The SOA record defines parameters for the entire zone.

Unlike the other resource records, the SOA record cannot be created through the New Resource Record dialog. The New Zone Wizard creates the SOA record when a new primary zone is created. However, the values in the SOA record can be modified later through the Start of Authority (SOA) tab of the zone properties dialog, as described in Chapter 6.

The format of the SOA record is:

```
zone [ttl] IN SOA origin contact (
 serial
 refresh
 retry
 expire
 minimum
 )
```

The components of the SOA record in the zone file are:

zone

> This is the name of the zone. Usually the SOA name field contains an at sign (@). When used in an SOA record, the at sign refers back to the domain name declared in the New Zone Wizard when the zone was created.

ttl

> This is the time-to-live for the SOA record itself. This field is left blank on the SOA record unless the default value in the "TTL for this record" box of the Start of Authority (SOA) tab is changed, as described in Chapter 6.

IN

> The address class is IN for all resource records on a Windows DNS server.

SOA

> SOA is the resource record type. All the information that follows this is part of the data field and is specific to the SOA record.

origin

> This is the hostname of the master server for this domain. It is normally written as a fully qualified domain name. For example, *komodo* is the master server for *example.com*, so this field contains komodo.example.com. in the SOA record for *example.com*. For this field, the New Zone Wizard uses the hostname defined on the Computer Name tab of the System Properties window of the system on which the zone file was created.

contact

> The email address of the person responsible for this domain is entered in this field. The address is modified slightly. The at sign (@) that usually appears in an Internet email address is replaced by a dot. Therefore, if *Administrator@.example.com* is the mailing address of the administrator of the *example.com* domain, the *example.com* SOA record contains Administrator.example.com. in the contact field.

serial

> This is the version number of the zone file. It is an eight-digit numeric field usually entered as a simple number—for example, 9. Slave servers use the serial number to determine if the zone file has been updated. To make this determination, a slave server requests the SOA record from the master server and compares the serial number of the data the slave has stored to the serial number

received from the master server. If the serial number has increased, the slave server requests a full zone transfer. Otherwise, it assumes that it has the most current zone data. The serial number must increase each time the zone data is updated for the new data to be disseminated in this manner. The DNS server automatically increases the serial number each time the zone data changes.

refresh

This specifies the length of time that the slave server waits before checking with the master server to see if the zone has been updated. Every *refresh* seconds the slave server checks the SOA serial number to see if the zone file needs to be reloaded. On their own, slave servers only check the serial numbers of their zones when they restart. The *refresh* interval provides a predictable cycle for reloading the zone that is controlled by the domain administrator. The process of retrieving the SOA record, evaluating the serial number and, if necessary, downloading the zone file is called a *zone refresh*. Thus the name "refresh" is used for this value. The value used in *refresh* is a number, up to eight digits long, that is the maximum number of seconds that the masters' and slave servers' databases can be out of synch.

A low *refresh* value keeps the data on the servers closely synchronized, but a very low *refresh* value is not required. The master server alerts the slave whenever a zone update is made using a Notify message. DNS Notify keeps the servers tightly synchronized. The refresh timer is simply a "fail safe" mechanisms used to backup the DNS Notify mechanism. A value set lower than needed places an unnecessary burden on the network and the slave servers. The value used in *refresh* should reflect the reality of how long you can stand to have the servers out of synch. Most sites' domain databases are very stable. Systems that must be accessed by name are added periodically, but not generally on an hourly basis. When you are adding a new system that must be accessed by name, you can assign the hostname and address of that system before the system is operational. You can then install this information in the name server database before it is actually needed, ensuring that it is disseminated to the secondary servers long before it has to be used. If extensive changes are planned, the *refresh* time can be temporarily reduced while the changes are underway. Therefore, you can normally set *refresh* time high, reducing load on the network and servers.

retry

This defines how long slave servers should wait before trying again if the master server fails to respond to a request for a zone refresh. *retry* is specified in seconds and can be up to eight digits long. Do not set the *retry* value too low. If a master server fails to respond, the server or the network could be down. Quickly retrying a down system gains nothing and costs network resources. A slave server that backs up a large number of zones can have problems when *retry* values are short. If the slave server cannot reach the primary servers for several of its zones, it can become stuck in a retry loop. The New Zone Wizard uses 10 minutes (600) as a default. Don't set *retry* any lower than this.

expire

This defines how long the zone's data should be retained by the slave servers without receiving a zone refresh. The value is specified in seconds and is up to eight digits long. If after *expire* seconds the slave server has been unable to refresh this zone, it should discard all of the data. *expire* is often a very large value. 3,600,000 seconds (about 42 days) is sometimes used. This says that if there has been no answer from the master server to refresh requests repeated every *retry* seconds for the last 42 days, discard the data. Forty-two days is long, but commonly used. A week (604800) is adequate. However, one day (86400), which is the default provided by the New Zone Wizard, is much too short.

minimum

Microsoft uses this value as the default TTL for any resource record that does not have an explicit TTL value. The value set for *minimum* is also used by remote servers as the TTL value for negative cache information.

A sample SOA record for the *example.com* domain is:

```
@    IN    SOA      mandy.example.com. Administrator.example.com. (
                    9                  ; serial
                    43200              ; refresh twice a day
                    1800               ; retry every half hour
                    604800             ; expire after one week
                    1800               ; default ttl half an hour )
```

This SOA record says that *mandy* is the master server for this zone and that the person responsible for this zone can be reached at the email address *Administrator@ example.com*. The SOA serial number indicates the cached zone has been updated fewer than 10 times. The SOA tells the slave servers to check the zone for changes twice a day and to retry every half hour if they don't get an answer. If they retry for a week and never get an answer, they should discard the data for this zone. Finally, if an RR in this zone does not have an explicit TTL, the TTL of the RR will default to 30 minutes.

Name Server Record

Name Server (NS) resource records identify the authoritative servers for a zone. These records are the pointers that link the domain hierarchy together. NS records in the top-level domains point to the servers for the second-level domains, which in turn contain NS records that point to the servers for their subdomains. Name server records pointing to the servers for subordinate domains are required for those domains to be accessible. Without NS records, the servers for a domain would be unknown. NS records are so important that they are created by the New Zone Wizard whenever a primary zone is created. However, the list of NS records associated with the zone can be modified through the Name Servers tab of the zone properties dialog, as described in Chapter 6. The syntax of the NS RR, as it appears in a zone file, is *domain* [*ttl*] IN NS *server*, where:

domain

Is the name of the domain for which the host specified in the *server* field is an authoritative name server. Any one of the valid *name* field formats described at the beginning of this appendix can be used in this field.

ttl

Is the explicit time-to-live for this record. Time-to-live is usually blank.

IN

The address class is always IN on Microsoft servers.

NS

The Name Server resource record type is NS.

server

Is the hostname of a computer that provides authoritative name service for this domain. Usually domains have at least one server that is located outside the local domain. That server name cannot be specified relative to the local domain; it must be specified as a fully qualified domain name.

Address Record

The majority of the resource records in a forward lookup zone file are address records. Address records are used to convert hostnames to IP addresses, which is the most common use of the DNS database. Figure C-1 shows the address record dialog box used to create A records via the DNS console.

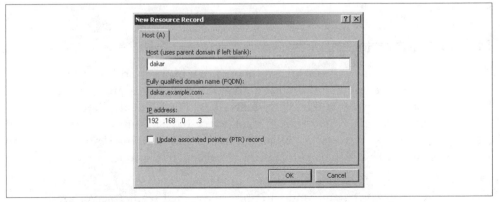

Figure C-1. The address record dialog box

Enter the hostname and the IP address in the dialog box to add an address record to the zone. The A record added to the zone file contains the following fields (*host* [*ttl*] IN A *address*):

host

> The name of the host whose address is provided in the data field of this record. If the host is a member of the current zone, the hostname can be written relative to the current domain. If the host is external to the current zone, the name must be a fully qualified domain name.

ttl

> The explicit time-to-live field is usually blank. The dialog box used to create this record does not provide a means to input an explicit TTL.

IN

> The address class is always IN.

A

> The Address resource record type is A.

address

> The IP address of the host is written here in dotted decimal form, for example, 192.168.0.3.

A *glue record* is a special type of address record. Most address records refer to hosts within the zone, but sometimes an address record needs to refer to a host in a subordinate zone. Recall that the NS record for a subdomain server identifies the server by name. An address is needed to communicate with that server, so an A record must also be provided when a subdomain is delegated its own zone. The address record and the name server record combine to link the domains together—thus the term glue record. Chapter 6 describes glue records in the discussion of how to delegate a subdomain.

Mail Exchanger Record

The mail exchanger (MX) record redirects mail to a mail server. It can redirect mail for an individual computer or an entire domain. MX records are extremely useful because most domains contain many systems that don't run mail server software and many systems that are offline for part of every day. MX records redirect mail addressed to those systems to reliable servers that run mail server software. Figure C-2 shows the dialog used to add an MX record to the zone.

Use the dialog box to define the name, preference, and server fields of the MX record. The mail server name and the priority assigned to that server are filled in Figure C-2, but the name field, which is taken from the "Host or child domain" box, is left blank. A blank name field means that this MX record is being defined for the

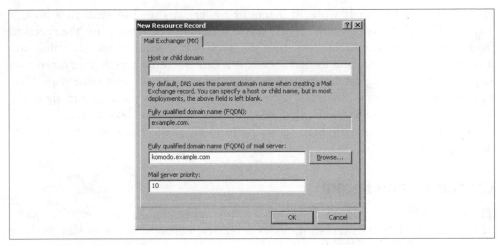

Figure C-2. The MX dialog box

current zone. In effect, this defines a mail server for the entire domain. The format of the MX RR in the zone file is [*name*] [*ttl*] IN MX *preference server*:

name

> The name of a host or domain to which the mail is addressed, which is taken from the "Host or child domain box" of the dialog shown in Figure C-2. Think of this as the value that occurs after the @ in a mailing address. Mail addressed to this name is sent to the mail server specified by the MX record's *server* field.

ttl

> Time-to-live is usually blank.

IN

> The address class is always IN.

MX

> The Mail Exchanger resource record type is MX.

preference

> A host or domain may have more than one MX record associated with it. The *preference* field specifies the order in which the mail servers are tried. The server with the lowest *preference* number is tried first. Preference values are usually assigned in increments of 5 or 10, so that new servers can be inserted between existing servers without editing the old MX records. The preference value is defined using the "Mail server priority" box of the dialog shown in Figure C-2.

server

> The name of the mail server to which mail is delivered when it is addressed to the host or domain identified in the *name* field. The name of the server is defined in the "Fully qualified domain name (FQDN) of mail server" box in the dialogue.

Here is how MX records work. If a remote system has mail to send to a host, it requests the host's MX records. DNS returns all of the MX records for the specified host. The remote server chooses the MX with the lowest preference value and attempts to deliver the mail to that server. If it cannot connect to that server, it tries each of the remaining servers in preference order until it can deliver the mail. If no MX records are returned by DNS, the remote server delivers the mail directly to the host to which the mail is addressed. MX records only define how to redirect mail. The remote system and the mail server perform all of the processing that actually delivers the mail.

Canonical Name Record

The Canonical Name (CNAME) resource record defines an alias for the official name of a host. The CNAME record provides a facility similar to nicknames in the host table. The facility provides alternate hostnames for the convenience of users, such as *www* for web servers, *ns* for name servers, and *smtp* for email servers. Figure C-3 shows the dialog box used to add CNAME records to the zone file.

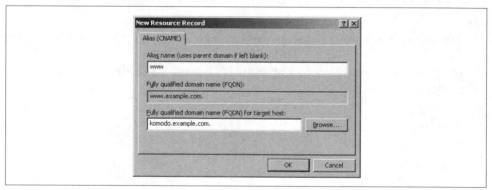

Figure C-3. The CNAME dialog box

Use the dialog box to enter the alias of the host as well as the canonical name of the host. The format of the CNAME record that the dialog inserts into the zone file is *alias* [*ttl*] IN CNAME *hostname*:

alias
> This hostname is an alias for the official hostname that is defined in the *hostname* field.

ttl
> Time-to-live is usually blank, and it cannot be explicitly set using the dialog box.

IN
> The address class is IN.

CNAME

The Canonical Name resource record type is CNAME.

hostname

The Canonical Name of the host is provided here. The *hostname* must be the official hostname; it cannot be an alias.

One important thing to remember about the CNAME record is that all other resource records must be associated with the official hostname, and not with the alias. This means that the alias cannot appear in the name field of any other resource record. For example:

```
www      IN   MX      5 jamis.example.com.
```

Assume that *www* is an alias assign, as shown in Figure C-3. In that case, the MX record in this example is illegal because it contains an alias in the name field. The DNS console will not let you make this mistake. Trying to create the MX record shown above using the DNS console generates the error shown in Figure C-4.

Figure C-4. MX record creation error

Domain Name Pointer Record

The Domain Name Pointer (PTR) resource record is used to convert a numeric IP address to a hostname. This is the opposite of what is done by the address record, which converts a hostname to an address. PTR records are used to construct the *in-addr.arpa* reverse domain files.

Don't ignore the reverse domain even if name service appears to run fine without it. Programs use the reverse domain to map IP addresses to hostnames when displaying information messages that include IP addresses. Some service providers use reverse domains to track who is using their service, and if they cannot map an IP address back to a hostname, they reject the connection.

The DNS console lets you keep the reverse domain updated automatically. Notice the "Update associated pointer (PTR) record" checkbox on the address dialog shown in Figure C-1. When that box is checked, the DNS console adds a PTR record to the reverse lookup zone when the A record is added to the forward lookup file. PTR records can also be added to the reverse lookup zone using the Pointer (PTR) dialog shown in Figure C-5.

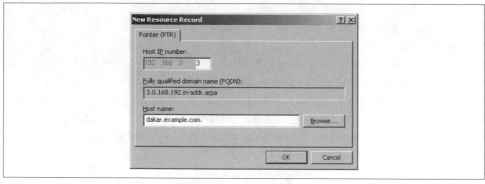

Figure C-5. The Pointer (PTR) dialog box

Use the dialog box to define the IP address that appears in the name field of the PTR record and the hostname that appears in the data field. The format of the PTR record in the zone file is *name [ttl]* IN PTR *hostname*:

name

> The *name* specified here is actually a number. The number is defined relative to the current *in-addr.arpa* domain. Names in an *in-addr.arpa* domain are IP addresses specified in reverse order. If the current domain is *0.168.192.in-addr.arpa*, then the *name* field for *dakar.example.com* (192.168.0.3) is 3. The digit 3 is added to the current domain *0.168.192.in-addr.arpa* to make the name *3.0.168.192.in-addr.arpa*.

ttl

> Time-to-live is left blank to use the zone default. While not explicitly shown in Figure C-3, turning on Advanced in the DNS management console will display the TTL for each record.

IN

> The address class is IN.

PTR

> The Domain Name Pointer resource record type is PTR.

hostname

> This is the fully qualified domain name of the computer whose address is specified in the *name* field. The host must be specified as a fully qualified name because the name cannot be relative to the current *in-addr.arpa* domain.

Service Location (SRV)

The Service Location record, which is defined in RFC 2052, provides a standardized way to locate network servers. Generic names such as *www.example.org* and *ftp.example.org* are widely used to locate network servers, but these names are not really a standard. The SRV record provides a standard convention for creating generic server names and it adds features for server selection and load balancing. SRV records are used extensively in AD integrated DNS, which is covered in Chapter 7. The format of the SRV record is:

```
_service._protocol.name [ttl] IN SRV priority weight port server
```

The name field of the SRV record has a unique _service._protocol.name format. Dots are used to separate the components in the name field just as there are in any domain name. The underscore characters (_) are used to prevent the service name and the protocol name from colliding with real domain names. *service* is the name of the offered service as listed in the *%SystemRoot%\system32\etc\services* file. *protocol* is either _tcp or _udp depending on which transport protocol is associated with the specified service. *name* is a standard host or domain name that would be found in any name field. Using these criteria, the name that could be used to find the FTP servers for the *example.org* domain would be *_ftp._tcp.example.org*. A correctly formatted name is built by selecting a service from the Service drop-down list and a protocol from the Protocol drop-down list in the Service Location (SRV) dialog box.

The data field of the SRV record contains four values:

priority
> A number used to select the most preferred server when multiple SRV records exist for the same service. The servers are sorted by preference number, so the server with the lowest number is the most preferred. All traffic is sent to the most preferred servers; servers with a higher preference number are only used if the preferred server is not available.

weight
> Used to balance the load among servers with the same preference number. *weight* is a number that defines the share of traffic sent to a server, with 1 being the base number. If server A has a weight of 1 and server B has a weight of 2, B gets twice as much traffic as A.

port
> The port number used for the service. The standard port number for the service selected from the Service drop-down list appears automatically in the "Port number" box. But it is possible to enter a nonstandard port number in the box if the services has been configured to use a nonstandard number.

server
> The canonical hostname of the computer running the requested service.

Figure C-6 shows the dialog box used to add a SRV record to the zone.

The SRV *service* and *protocol* values are selected from drop-down lists. When a service value is selected, the correct *port* value for that service appears in the "Port number" box. In this example, a *priority* of 10 was selected to simplify adding other FTP servers in the future. (10 allows for future servers to be easily added with lower or higher priority numbers.) A base *weight* value of 1 was used even though there are

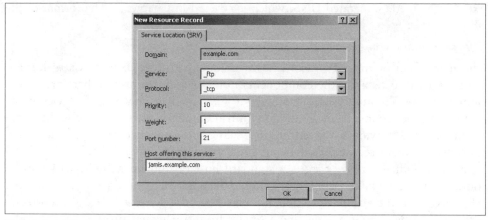

Figure C-6. The Service Location (SRV) dialog box

no other FTP servers defined at this time. These values can be easily changed in the future if necessary.

The dialog shown in Figure C-6 creates the following zone file entry:

```
_ftp._tcp              SRV     10 1 21 jamis.example.com.
```

It is easy to see how the values in the dialog box map to the finished resource record.

This concludes our short tour of the basic resource records. There are several more resource records that can be defined in the DNS console than those already covered. Those other RRs are described in the next section However, the few resource records described in this section make up the bulk of most zone files.

Less Commonly Used Resource Records

The basic resource records covered in the previous section are all either created by the New Zone Wizard or through their own entries in the DNS console Action menu. To create the less commonly used resource records described in this section, select the Other New Records item from the Action menu to open the Resource Record Type dialog shown in Figure C-7.

Highlighting a record type in the "Select a resource record type" list box and then clicking Create Record opens a dialog specific to the type of record selected, where you can then enter the data required by the record type. The records available through this dialog box that have not already been covered in this appendix are described here in the order they appear in the list box. The purpose of each record and the type of data the record requires are covered.

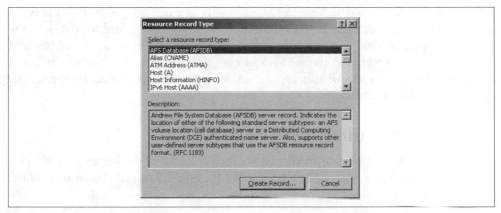

Figure C-7. Creating less commonly used resource records

AFS Database (AFSDB)

The experimental AFSDB record points to the server for an AFS or DCE cell. AFS, originally called the Andrew File System, is a distributed filesystem that is optimized for use over wide area networks (WANs). DCE, the Distributed Computing Environment, is just that, a standard that describes the interactions between computers in a distributed computing environment. AFS and DCE systems use DNS to point to their servers. They do this by using cell names that are compatible with DNS domain names. The AFSDB record maps the cell name to the correct server. The format of an AFSDB record is:

```
cell_name [ttl] IN AFSDB type server
```

The *cell_name* looks just like a domain name and, in fact, is often the name of the current domain. The Microsoft DNS server defaults to using the current domain name unless a specific name is entered in the *AFS Database (AFSDB)* dialog. The *type* field, which is correctly set in the dialog by simply clicking a button, contains a 1 if the server is an AFS server or a 2 if it is a DCE server. The *server* field contains the DNS domain name of the AFS or DCE server. The AFSDB record is defined in RFC 1183.

ATM Address (ATMA)

The ATMA record maps a hostname to an Asynchronous Transfer Mode (ATM) address. ATM is a high-speed fiber optic network technology. It transmits small chunks of information that are only 53 bytes long to make it easier to optimize support for real-time traffic such as voice or video. The ATMA record was not standardized in an RFC. Instead, it is standardized by the ATM Forum in *ATM Name System Specification Version 1.0*. The format of the ATMA record is:

```
name [ttl] IN ATMA atm_address
```

name is the hostname to which the ATM address is assigned; *atm_address* is the ATM address written in either the E.164 international telephone standard format or in the ISO NSAP (network service access point) standard format. When the hostname and ATM address are entered in the ATM Address (ATMA) dialog box, either the E.164 address button or the NSAP address button must be selected to indicate the format you used to enter the address.

Host Information (HINFO)

The Host Information record provides a short description of the hardware and operating system used by a host. RFC 1035 defines the HINFO record. The format of the HINFO record is:

    host [ttl] IN HINFO hardware software

Originally, the hardware and software items in the data field were supposed to come from an official list of hardware and software registered in RFC 1700, *Assigned Numbers*. That might have worked in the days of mainframes when computer models changed slowly, but it wouldn't work today. Administrators who use this record simply make up descriptive entries for the hardware and software and enter those in the "CPU type" box and the "Operating system" box of the Host Information (HINFO) dialog.

Adding this record to the zone file is generally discouraged because it can provide information to network intruders and has no particular use.

IPV6 Host (AAAA)

The AAAA record maps a domain name to an Internet Protocol Version 6 (IPv6) address. The AAAA record is defined in RFC 3596, *DNS Extensions to Support IP Version 6*. The format of the AAAA record is:

    name [ttl] IN AAAA ipv6_address

The format is the same as an A record except that the address provided in the data field is a 128-bit IPv6 address instead of a 32-bit IPv4 address. Instead of the dotted decimal notation used to write an IPv4 address, an IPv6 address is written as eight, 16-bit hexadecimal numbers separated by colons, as follows:

    big6 IN AAAA 1234:a:b:c:d:e:f:9876

The traditional PTR record is used to map IPv6 addresses back to domain names. A new top-level reverse-mapping domain was created called *ip6.int*. When IPv6 addresses are converted to names in the reverse-mapping domain, they are reversed and written out as 32, four-bit nibbles separated by dots. Thus, the IPv6 address 1234:a:b:c:d:e:f:9876 becomes:

    6.7.8.9.f.0.0.0.e.0.0.0.d.0.0.0.c.0.0.0.b.0.0.0.a.0.0.0.4.3.2.1.ip6.int.

Only systems that use IPv6 are assigned IPv6 addresses, and only systems that run the IPv6 protocol stack need to lookup AAAA records. Unless you run IPv6 on your network you won't use this record.

ISDN

The experimental ISDN record maps a domain name to an ISDN address. Integrated Services Digital Network (ISDN) is a digital telephone service that can carry voice and data. Poor price/performance has limited the number of ISDN users in the United States, but it is popular in many other countries. The format of the ISDN record is:

```
name [ttl] IN ISDN ISDN_address subaddress
```

The ISDN record is rarely used because most IP-to-ISDN bridges have internal mechanisms to map from IP addresses to ISDN addresses. The ISDN record is defined in RFC 1183.

Mail Group (MG)

The obsolete Mail Group record defines mail delivery instructions for mailing lists using a scheme in which the list name and the mailboxes of the individual recipients in the list are defined in DNS. In actuality, mailing lists are processed by mail servers and are defined in the configuration of those servers, not in DNS. This record is no longer used. It is, however, documented in RFC 1035 and thus listed in the Resource Record Type dialog.

Mailbox (MB)

The obsolete Mailbox record defines mail delivery information for an individual user. As originally envisioned, every user in the domain would be given a unique MB record. This record has been obsolete for many years. The mail server, not DNS, handles mail delivery to individuals. The MB record is documented in RFC 1035 and is therefore listed in the Resource Record Type dialog. However, you should not use this record.

Mailbox Information (MINFO)

The obsolete Mailbox Information record defines control information for MG mailing lists by defining both the email address of the email administrator and an email address where error messages should be sent. This record is directly related to the obsolete Mail Group record. Mailing lists and the administrative information about mailing lists are defined in the mail server configuration, not in DNS. The MINFO record is documented in RFC 1035 and is therefore listed in the Resource Record Type dialog. However, this record is no longer used.

Next Domain (NXT)

The Next Domain record provides a way to formally document and authenticate nonexistent domain information. The SIG record, described later, is used to authenticate domain database records. However, a digital signature can only be calculated against an existing record. By its very nature, the information involved in negative caching has no database record to be authenticated. If the information returned by the authoritative name server states that no MX record exists for a given domain name, how is that information authenticated before being added to the cache? The NXT record is the solution. The format of the NXT record is:

```
name [ttl] IN NXT next_name type_list
```

The *type_list* is a list of the types of resource records that do not exist for the object identified by *name*. Thus, if no MX record existed for the domain name *parrot.example.org*, you might have the following NXT record:

```
parrot.example.org. IN NXT puffin.example.org. MX
```

The function of the *next_name* field is a little more obscure. This field contains the next domain name in canonical order as defined by RFC 2535. A simple way to think of canonical ordering is as if each label in the names were sorted without regard to case. The *next_name* field is used to provide evidence that a name does not exist.

The NXT record is only needed when strong authentication is used. By default, all data from an authoritative server is cached, whether it is a positive response that provides the requested resource records or a negative response that indicates that the requested information does not exist. In the default situation, there is no need to document nonexisting data with the NXT record.

Public Key (KEY)

The Public Key record provides the public key for a given domain name. The KEY record is defined in RFC 2535. The format of the KEY record is:

```
name [ttl] IN KEY flags protocol algorithm public_key
```

The *public_key* is an encryption key, written in base 64 encoding, that is to be used for public key cryptography when communicating with the object identified by *name*. The value for the *public_key* field is entered in the "Key (base 64)" box of the Key (KEY) dialog box when the Key record is created.

The value of the *algorithm* field can be 1 for RSA/MD5, 2 for Diffie-Hellman or for DSA, 4 for Elliptic Curve, or 252 for indirect key. Set the *algorithm* value by making a selection from the Algorithm drop-down list of the Key (KEY) dialog box.

The *protocol* field defines the protocol that will use the public key. The key is limited specifically to DNS security by RFC 3445. When the record was originally designed, however, it was to be accessible to other protocols that might want to use the key. Therefore, multiple protocol values were defined, and are supported by the DNS console. Select DNSSEC from the Protocol drop-down list to set the correct value. The full list of *protocol* field values is:

1
> TLS is no longer valid and is now officially referred to as "reserved."

2
> Email is no longer valid and is now officially referred to as "reserved."

3
> DNSSEC is the only valid setting for *protocol*.

4
> IPSEC is no longer valid and is now officially referred to as "reserved."

255
> All is no longer valid and is now officially referred to as "reserved."

The *flags* field is a binary bit mask that contains several different subfields. The "Bit field representation" box of the Key (KEY) dialog shows the changing bit values as you configure the KEY record. Figure C-8 shows how each bit in the flags field is defined by RFC 2535.

Figure C-8. The KEY record flags bit mask

Every bit marked with a Z in Figure C-8 is reserved for future use and must be set to 0. That leaves four active subfields:

A/C
> These two bits define whether the key is used for authentication or for confidentiality. If the first bit is 1 (10), the key cannot be used for authentication. If the second bit is 1 (01), the key cannot be used for confidentiality. Thus, 00 means the key can be used for either task, and 11 means that the zone is not secured. To set these bits make a selection from the "Key type" drop-down list.

XT
> This bit is reserved for the future when more than one flags field may be required. If set to 1, it means that the flags are extended to a second 16-bit word. Currently, the value must be 0 because there are no valid extensions.

NAMTYP
> These two bits identify what type of domain name is found in the name field. (Use the "Name type" drop-down list to set this field.) Bits 00 means that the name is a username such as would be found on an RP or SOA record. Bits 01

means that the name is the domain name of the zone. Bits 10 means that the name is the name of an object, such as a host or subdomain, contained within the zone. Bits 11 is reserved for future use.

SIG

These four bits indicate whether or not the key can be used to sign updates for dynamic DNS. If the field is nonzero, the key can be used to sign dynamic DNS updates. (The "Signatory field" checkboxes set values in this field.) If the field is 0, the key can still be used to sign a dynamic DNS update, but only if the name type is "zone" and the update is for the specified zone, i.e., the NAMTYP field contains 01 and the dynamic update is for the zone identified in the *name* field.

Rename Mailbox (MR)

The obsolete Mail Rename record defines a mail alias. A mail alias is a nickname for a user that permits mail addressed to the nickname to be delivered to the real user. For example, *postmaster@example.org* might be an alias for *david@example.org*. In that case, mail addressed to *postmaster* would really be delivered to *david*. The mail server handles aliases; this function is not handled by DNS. The MR record is documented in RFC 1035 and is therefore listed in the Resource Record Type dialog. However, this record is no longer used.

Responsible Person (RP)

The Responsible Person record, which is defined in RFC 1183, identifies the point of contact for a host or domain. The format of the RP record is:

```
name [ttl] IN RP mail_address text_pointer
```

The *mail_address* is the email address of the responsible person. The @ usually included in an email address is replaced with a dot. Thus, *craig@example.org* becomes *craig.example.org*. The *text_pointer* is the domain name of a TXT record that contains additional information about the responsible person. Here's an example of how an RP record is used with a TXT record:

```
ibis.example.org.    IN RP  craig.example.org. ibisRP
ibisRP.example.org. IN TXT "Craig Hunt (301)555-1234 X237"
```

The RP record states that the person responsible for *ibis.example.org* can be reached via email at *craig@example.org* and that additional information about the person can be obtained in the TXT records for *ibisRP.example.org*. The TXT record in this example provides the contact person's name and phone number, but it could provide any information you wish.

RP records could make it easier for system administrators to contact each other when things go wrong. However, most domains don't use RP records because these records can expose internal email addresses to the outside world.

Route Through (RT)

The experimental Route Through record points to a gateway that can be used to route packets to networks that are not part of the Internet. The X.25 and ISDN networks mentioned in the description of other resource record are good examples of such networks. The RT record is defined in RFC 1183. The format of the RT record is:

```
name [ttl] IN RT preference gateway
```

The *preference* value in the RT record is similar to the preference value of an MX record. It is a numeric value and the lower the number, the more preferred the gateway. *preference* permits DNS to define multiple gateways to the remote host allowing applications that use the RT records to select the best route. When a server returns an RT record as the response to a query, it also includes all A, X25, and ISDN records that define addresses for the gateway. This allows applications on various types of networks to find addressing and routing information from DNS.

The RT record is rarely used. There are no widely available applications designed to use it. Routing protocols handle the distribution of routing information. RT was primarily of interest as a possible technique for integrating dissimilar networks.

Signature (SIG)

The Signature record provides a digital signature to authenticate a set of resource records. The format of the SIG records is:

```
name [ttl] IN SIG type_list (
algorithm
labels
original_ttl
signature_expiration
signature_ inception
key_tag
signer_name
signature )
```

The fields for the SIG record are as follows:

type_list
    A list of the resource record types for the specified domain name that are digitally signed by this SIG record. Set the value for this field using the "Type covered" drop-down list in the Signature (SIG) dialog box.

algorithm

The encryption algorithm used to produce the digital signature. There are five algorithm values available from the Algorithm drop-down list of the dialog box. They are:

1

For the RSA/MD5 algorithm defined in RFC 2537

2

For the Diffie-Hellman algorithm defined in RFC 2539

3

For the DSA algorithm defined in RFC 2536

4

For the Elliptic Curve algorithm described in RFC 3278

252

For indirect key

labels

Specifies the number of parts in the domain name. For example, *example.org* has two parts, *example* and *org*, so it has a *labels* value of 2. *terns.example.org* has three parts and thus a *labels* value of 3. Use the Labels box to set the *labels* value.

orginal_ttl

The TTL value from the original resource record that was used when the digital signature was calculated. Because the TTL is decremented by servers that hold records in their caches, the *orginal_ttl* is needed to recalculate the signature when verifying the record. The "Original time to live" box sets this value.

signature_expiration

Defines the date that the signature becomes invalid. The date is defined as the number of seconds from January 1, 1970. The DNS console correctly calculates this value based on the date you enter in the "Signature expiration (GMT)" box.

signature_inception

Defines the date on which the signature was created. The date is defined as the number of seconds from January 1, 1970. The DNS console correctly calculates this value based on the date you enter in the "Signature inception (GMT)" box.

key_tag

When used with the RSA/MD5 algorithm, is a 16-bit piece of the key that is used to select the correct key when multiple possible keys are involved. For all other algorithms, the *key_tag* field holds a checksum of the SIG resource record. Only use the "Key tag" box to enter this value when using RSA/MD5 with multiple keys.

signer_name
> The domain name of the entity that created the digital signature. It is usually the domain name of the zone that contains the signed records, and it is entered in the "Signer's name" box.

signature
> The digital signature that authenticates the resource records. This value is entered in the "Signature (base 64)" box as a base-64 encoded string.

RFC 2535 defines the SIG record.

Text (TXT)

The Text record is used to define free-form information about the named object. RFC 1035 defines the TXT record. The format is simple:

> *name* [*ttl*] IN TXT *string*

The TXT record can be used to provide information useful for supporting a host. The following example illustrates this use:

> buzzard IN TXT "Accounting Department server in room B152"

Because of its free-form nature, the TXT record has been used over time for special purposes, such as providing input to locally developed programs that collect domain information. As noted previously, the TXT record is also used with the RP record.

Well Known Services (WKS)

A Well Known Services record advertises the network services offered by a host. The format of the WKS record is:

> *host* [*ttl*] IN WKS *address protocol services*

The data field of the WKS record contains three fields:

address
> The IP address of the host advertising the services. The address must be one of the addresses that are valid for the computer identified by the *host* field.

protocol
> Either UDP or TCP. To advertise services for both transport protocols, use one WKS record for UDP and one for TCP for each host.

services
> The list of advertised services. The services should be identified using the names found in the *%SystemRoot%\system32\etc\services* file.

These two WKS records are an example of advertising UDP and TCP services for the host *crow*:

```
crow IN WKS 172.20.5.5 TCP ftp telnet
crow IN WKS 172.20.5.5 UDP domain smtp
```

The WKS record is rarely used. There are no widely distributed programs that take advantage of WKS record, and there is the threat that network intruders will use the information in the WKS record to exploit the advertised system.

X.25

The experimental X25 record maps a domain name to an X.25 address, called an X. 121 address. X.25 is an international standard for public packet-switched networks. X.25 networks have not been widely used in the United States for many years. The advent of personal computers and the Internet made them largely obsolete, though some countries still use X.25. The X25 record is defined in RFC 1183. The format of the X25 records is:

```
name [ttl] IN X25 X.121_address
```

The X25 record is rarely used because most X.25 networks provide their own mapping to IP addresses. The scale of the Internet makes it impossible for X.25 networks, or any other network for that matter, to ignore IP. In fact, implementations of IP that run directly over X.25 have long been available.

The Boot File

There is one DNS configuration file that is not built of standard resource records. The boot file defines the name server configuration and tells the name server where to obtain database information. If the server is configured using the DNS console, the boot file is not used. However, the Microsoft DNS server can use a boot file for compatibility with BIND 4 servers and to simplify the transition from a BIND 4 server to a Windows Server 2003 DNS server. Windows Server 2003 supports the following types of boot file records:

primary *domain-name file-name*
> The primary command declares the local name server as the master server for the domain specified by *domain-name*. As a master server, the system loads the name server database from the local disk file specified by name in the *file-name* field.

secondary *domain-name server-address-list file-name*
> The secondary command makes the local server a slave server for the domain identified by *domain-name*. The *server-address-list* contains the IP address of at least one other authoritative server for this domain. Multiple addresses can be provided in the list, but at least the master server's address should be provided. The local server will try each server in the list until it successfully loads the name

server database. The local server transfers the entire zone file and stores all of the data it receives in a local file identified by *file-name*. After completing the transfer, the local server answers all queries for information about the domain with complete authority.

cache . *file-name*

The cache command points to the file used to initialize the name server cache with a list of root servers. This command starts with the keyword cache, followed by the name of the root domain (.), and ends with the name of the file that contains the root server list. This file is usually named *cache.dns* on systems running the Microsoft DNS server software.

BindSecondaries | NoBindSecondaries

This command provides zone transfer compatibility with Unix BIND 4 DNS servers. If any of the secondary servers for the Microsoft DNS Server are BIND 4 servers, use the BindSecondaries command for compatibility. If none of the secondary servers are BIND 4 servers, use NoBindSecondaries for more efficient zone transfers.

A sample boot file is located in the *%SystemRoot%\system32\dns\samples* directory. That file, named BOOT, explains the syntax of the boot file commands as if you might build your own boot file. While that is possible, it is unlikely. The primary reason to use a boot file is to rapidly migrate an old BIND 4 Unix server to Windows Server 2003. In that case, you would start with an existing BIND 4 boot file such as the following one:

```
;
;          BIND 4 boot file
;
directory                                /etc/named
primary     example.com                  example.com.hosts
primary     0.168.192.IN-ADDR.ARPA       192.168.0.rev
secondary   example.net      172.16.12.6  example.net.hosts
secondary   16.172.IN-ADDR.ARPA  172.16.12.6  172.16.rev
secondary   example.org      172.22.1.3   example.org.hosts
secondary   22.172.IN-ADDR.ARPA  172.22.1.3   172.22.rev
primary     0.0.127.IN-ADDR.ARPA         named.local
cache       .                            named.ca
```

Lines that begin with a semicolon are comments. Use a semicolon to "comment out" unneeded lines and unsupported commands, such as the directory command in this sample file. (On a Windows DNS system the zone files are always located in the *%SystemRoot%\system32\dns* directory. Therefore, the directory command is not needed or supported.) On the other hand, the BIND 4 file will not contain the BindSecondaries or NoBindSecondaries command. If you need one of those commands, you must manually add it to the file.

Most of the primary command lines in the BIND 4 files can be used as is. Simply copy the zone files from the old Unix server to the *%SystemRoot%\system32\dns* directory and ensure that the filename specified on each primary command is the name used for the corresponding file copy. One exception to this is the `primary` command for the 0.0.127.IN-ADDR.ARPA reverse zone, which is found in many BIND 4 boot files. That `primary` command is not needed for Windows Server 2003 and should be commented out. The second to last line in the sample file shows an example of this unneeded `primary` command.

BIND 4 secondary command lines also require very little editing. Check that the address of the master server specified in each secondary command is still valid. Often, more than one server is migrated from Unix to Windows at approximately the same time. Therefore, all server addresses should be double-checked. If addresses have not changed, the secondary commands can often be used as is.

Finally, edit the cache command to change the filename field to *cache.dns*. When the boot file is to your liking, copy it to the *%SystemRoot%\system32\dns* directory and give it the filename *boot*.

These instructions assume that you are migrating from an existing BIND 4 server to a new Windows server and that you have decided to use the boot file. Generally, the boot file is not used and the configuration is built directly through the DNS console.

Index

Symbols

\ddd, resource records, 637
\x escape character, resource records, 637
802.1x authentication, 428
    implementation, 430–439

A

AAA (Authentication, Authorization, and
        Accounting) server, 398
AAAA (IPV6 Host) resource record, 650
activating servers, DHCP, 169
Active Directory (see AD)
active routes, routing table, 47
AD (Active Directory)
    application partitions, 271
    authentication, 101
        latency, 243
    authorization, 101
    backups, system state, 251
    databases, 99
    dcpromo tool, 235
    DCs, 100
    dependencies, 254
    DHCP integration, 274
    DNS and, 255–258
    DNS configuration, 258–270
    GC servers, 98
    Group Policies, 104
    IAS server registration, 405
    migrating 2000 to 2003, 271
    NetBIOS and, 276–279
    OUs, 96

replication, 98
    bridgehead servers, 247
    DNS and, 257
    granular replication control, 243
    SMTP and, 551, 583
    sites, configuration, 242–247
    time service, 272–274
    trusts, 101
    WINS and, 276–279
AD Sites and and Services administration
        tool, 243
Adapter Properties window, 110
Adapter Status window, 109
adapters, configuration, 111–114
address bit masks, 30
address records, 641
Address Resolution Protocol (ARP), 50
addresses
    ARP, 50
    broadcast addresses, 29
    class-structured design, 36
    Destination Address, 14
    DNS servers, 122
    dynamic, DHCP, 136
    link-local, 40
    loopback addresses, 30, 40
    MAC, 41
    multicast, 29, 176
    NAT, 38, 314
    site-local, 40
    unicast, 29
    (see also IP addresses)
addressing, 28

We'd like to hear your suggestions for improving our indexes. Send email to *index@oreilly.com*.

About the Authors

Craig Hunt has almost 30 years of computing experience, first as a programmer, then a systems programmer, network architect, manager of network operations, and head of network research. Craig is now an independent computer consultant. He is currently working on the Microsoft antitrust settlement, with a particular focus on the Microsoft Communications Protocol Program (MCPP). Craig is the author of nine computer books, including *TCP/IP Network Administration*, and is the editor of five others. Find out more about Craig's professional activities at his web site at *http://www.wrotethebook.com*.

Craig lives with his wife, Kathy, in Gaithersburg, Maryland. Their home is two blocks from the trailhead where Craig indulges his passion for mountain biking.

Roberta Bragg's computing life started in 1975. She has been employed as an operator, programmer, systems administrator, network administrator, security consultant, trainer, teacher, editor, and author. Her many publications include five programming and administration instruction curriculum guides, six certification guides, four technical reference books, and hundreds of freelance IT-oriented articles. For seven years, she was a columnist writing about Windows security. Currently, she consults and writes on information security.

Roberta lives in downtown Kansas City, Missouri, 12 blocks from the Kansas City Arts Incubator where she produces and sells glass-fused and slumped objects, and stained-glass mosaics.

Colophon

Our look is the result of reader comments, our own experimentation, and feedback from distribution channels. Distinctive covers complement our distinctive approach to technical topics, breathing personality and life into potentially dry subjects.

The animal on the cover of *Windows Server 2003 Network Administration* is an avocet. The American variety (*Recuvirostra americana*) can be found in western North America in spring, summer, and autumn, and in Texas, Florida, Louisiana, and as far south as Guatamala in the winter. They inhabit ponds, marshes, mudflats, and wetlands. Occasionally, they can also be spied around tidal flats, rocky seashores, and coastal islands.

These graceful waders have blue legs and an upcurved black bill, which is more pronounced in females; the male's bill is straighter and longer. Avocets have distinctive black and white features on their wings and backside, which helps to distinguish them from black-necked stilts (*Himantopus mexicanus*), which are members of the same family.

American avocets drag their open bills across shallow water to feed on aquatic insects. They also enjoy crustaceans, aquatic vegetation, seeds, and invertebrates.

Breeding takes place between April and June. Avocets are monogamous and colonial. Once pairs form, complicated courtship displays commence. These involve bowing, crouching, swaying, and dancing with wings outspread. Nests are often no more than shallow holes dug in the ground and lined with mud or dry grass. During the rest of the year, avocets travel in dense flocks.

When their nests are threatened, avocets have been known to dive-bomb intruders and make a deafening ruckus that consists of piercing "kleeeep" and "pleeet" sounds. When not threatened, they are quiet and docile, and can communicate using complex body movements. Primary nonhuman predators include skunks and foxes.

Matt Hutchinson was the production editor for *Windows Server 2003 Network Administration*. GEX, Inc. provided production services. Darren Kelly, Lydia Onofrei, and Mary Anne Mayo provided quality control.

Ellie Volckhausen designed the cover of this book. The cover image is from the Dover Pictorial Archive. Karen Montgomery produced the cover layout with Adobe InDesign CS using Adobe's ITC Garamond font.

David Futato designed the interior layout. This book was converted by Keith Fahlgren to FrameMaker 5.5.6 with a format conversion tool created by Erik Ray, Jason McIntosh, Neil Walls, and Mike Sierra that uses Perl and XML technologies. The text font is Linotype Birka; the heading font is Adobe Myriad Condensed; and the code font is LucasFont's TheSans Mono Condensed. The illustrations that appear in the book were produced by Robert Romano, Jessamyn Read, and Lesley Borash using Macromedia FreeHand MX and Adobe Photoshop CS. The tip and warning icons were drawn by Christopher Bing. This colophon was written by Matt Hutchinson.

Better than e-books

Buy *Windows Server 2003 Network Administration* and
access the digital edition FREE on Safari for 45 days.

Go to www.oreilly.com/go/safarienabled
and type in coupon code 9TQJ-RCTP-HH5K-47PX-3H9X

Search
thousands of
top tech books

Download
whole chapters

Cut and Paste
code examples

Find
answers fast

Search Safari! The premier electronic reference
library for programmers and IT professionals.

Related Titles from O'Reilly

Windows Administration

Active Directory Cookbook

Active Directory, *2nd Edition*

DNS on Windows Server 2003

Essential SharePoint

Exchange Server Cookbook

Learning Windows Server 2003

Securing Windows Server 2003

SharePoint Office Pocket Guide

SharePoint User's Guide

Windows Server 2003 in a Nutshell

Windows Server 2003 Network Administration

Windows Server Cookbook

Windows Server Hacks

Windows XP Cookbook

O'REILLY®

Our books are available at most retail and online bookstores.
To order direct: 1-800-998-9938 • *order@oreilly.com* • *www.oreilly.com*
Online editions of most O'Reilly titles are available by subscription at *safari.oreilly.com*

Keep in touch with O'Reilly

Download examples from our books

To find example files from a book, go to:
www.oreilly.com/catalog select the book,
and follow the "Examples" link.

Register your O'Reilly books

Register your book at *register.oreilly.com*
Why register your books? Once you've
registered your O'Reilly books you can:

- Win O'Reilly books, T-shirts or discount
  coupons in our monthly drawing.
- Get special offers available only to
  registered O'Reilly customers.
- Get catalogs announcing new books
  (US and UK only).
- Get email notification of new editions
  of the O'Reilly books you own.

Join our email lists

Sign up to get topic-specific email announcements of new books and conferences,
special offers, and O'Reilly Network
technology newsletters at:

elists.oreilly.com

It's easy to customize your free elists subscription so you'll get exactly the O'Reilly news
you want.

Get the latest news, tips, and tools

www.oreilly.com

- "Top 100 Sites on the Web"—PC Magazine
- CIO Magazine's Web Business 50 Awards

Our web site contains a library of comprehensive product information (including book
excerpts and tables of contents), downloadable
software, background articles, interviews with
technology leaders, links to relevant sites, book
cover art, and more.

Work for O'Reilly

Check out our web site for current
employment opportunities:

jobs.oreilly.com

Contact us

O'Reilly Media, Inc.
1005 Gravenstein Hwy North
Sebastopol, CA 95472 USA
Tel: 707-827-7000 or 800-998-9938
 (6am to 5pm PST)
Fax: 707-829-0104

Contact us by email

For answers to problems regarding
your order or our products:
order@oreilly.com

To request a copy of our latest catalog:
catalog@oreilly.com

For book content technical questions
or corrections: **booktech@oreilly.com**

For educational, library, government,
and corporate sales: **corporate@oreilly.com**

To submit new book proposals to our
editors and product managers:
proposals@oreilly.com

For information about our international
distributors or translation queries:
international@oreilly.com

For information about academic
use of O'Reilly books:
adoption@oreilly.com
or visit:
academic.oreilly.com

For a list of our distributors outside
of North America check out:
international.oreilly.com/distributors.html

Order a book online

www.oreilly.com/order_new

 **O'REILLY**®

Our books are available at most retail and online bookstores.
To order direct: 1-800-998-9938 • *order@oreilly.com* • *www.oreilly.com*
Online editions of most O'Reilly titles are available by subscription at *safari.oreilly.com*